THE FUTURE OF RELIGION

Studies in Critical Social Sciences Book Series

The Studies in Critical Social Sciences book series, through the publication of original manuscripts and edited volumes, offers insights into the current reality by exploring the content and consequence of power relationships under capitalism, by considering the spaces of opposition and resistance to these changes, and by articulating capitalism with other systems of power and domination—for example race, gender, culture—that have been defining our new age.

Haymarket Books is pleased to be working with Brill Academic Publishers (http://www.brill.nl) to republish the Studies in Critical Social Sciences book series in paperback editions. Titles in this series include:

THE FUTURE OF RELIGION
TOWARD A RECONCILED SOCIETY

EDITED BY MICHAEL R. OTT

Haymarket Books
Chicago, Illinois

First published in 2007 by Brill Academic Publishers, The Netherlands
© 2007 Koninklijke Brill NV, Leiden, The Netherlands

Published in paperback in 2009 by
Haymarket Books
P.O. Box 180165
Chicago, IL 60618
773-583-7884
www.haymarketbooks.org

ISBN: 978-1-608460-38-0

Trade distribution:
In the U.S., Consortium Book Sales, www.cbsd.com
In the UK, Turnaround Publisher Services, www.turnaround-psl.com
In Australia, Palgrave Macmillan, www.palgravemacmillan.com.au
In all other countries, Publishers Group Worldwide, www.pgw.com

Cover design by Ragina Johnson.

This book was published with the generous support of the Wallace Global Fund.

Printed in the United States on recycled paper containing 100 percent post-consumer
waste, in accordance with the guidelines of the Green Press Initiative,
www.greenpressinitiative.org.

10 9 8 7 6 5 4 3 2 1

Library of Congress Cataloging-in-Publication Data is available.

This work is dedicated to Rudolf J. Siebert, my teacher, friend, colleague and brother in the struggle for a more reconciled future society: In Love, Hope, Solidarity, and Shalom!

Contents

Conceptions of the Future of Society

Acknowledgements

This book is an expression of the work from various academic disciplines and life experiences of international scholars who have wrestled with the question concerning the future of religion in the transitional, socio-historical context of the globalization of Modern society. I thank them for their excellent contributions and work to make this book a reality.

However, this book and the work it expresses would not be possible at all without the critical mind, the extraordinary loving spirit, and relentless commitment in both theory and praxis toward a more reconciled future society and world of Professor Dr. Rudolf J. Siebert, the creator and dynamic *"spiritus rector"* of the Future of Religion course, in which the contributions that make up this book were given. Our beloved "Rudi" created this international course in 1976, and has led the annual discourses on the various sub-topics of our major theme over these past 31 years. I thank him not only for this Course and his leadership of it, but even more so for his continuing the ancient yet ever-living spirit of the prophetic, Messianic, and eschatological struggle for a more humane, good, loving, just, rational, and shalom-filled future world in the form of a new critical theory of religion and a critical, political theology.

I would like to thank the administration and staff of the Inter-University Centre in Dubrovnik, Croatia for all their assistance and support of our Future of Religion course for the past 31 years in the beautiful and stimulating location of Dubrovnik.

I also want to thank my family – my wife, Mary Louise, our sons John and Michael and his wife, Elizabeth, and my father, Robert Ott – for their love and support of me while I worked on this book.

Finally, I want to thank Brill and the series editor, David Fasenfest, for their assistance in the publication of this book.

Preface

The Future of Religion:
Toward a Reconciled Society

Michael R. Ott, Editor

This book is comprised of 20 chapters, authored by 18 scholars from 8 countries, that has been developed from edited papers that were presented during
the international course on *The Future of Religion* from 2001–2006. This course
has been held annually for the past 30 years at the Inter-University Center
in Dubrovnik, Croatia.

Since its inception in 1976, one of the guiding themes of this Course – and
thus, of this book – has been the analysis of the increasingly antagonistic
divide in Modernity between the sacred and the profane, religion and secularity, faith and reason as well as the theoretical and practical struggle for
its reconciliation in the construction of a more reconciled future society in
terms of a new critical theory of religion. In this work, the modern antipathy
between religion and secularity has been particularly addressed in the form
of the theodicy question. How can religion's notion of God – particularly,
of the prophetic, Abrahamic religions – be justified in the face of what
G. W. F. Hegel called the "slaughterbench" (1956:21) or "Golgotha" (1967a:808)
of history, wherein the "non-identical" (Adorno 1973: Part II) – the poor,
oppressed, exploited, disenfranchised, voiceless, suffering, dying and even
the dead – get trampled under and forgotten by a globalizing, identity-
producing social system that serves the ever-increasing profit and domination
interests of the world's elite. Is religion any longer relevant or meaningful
in the globalizing development of modern subjectivity, inter-subjectivity,
family, civil society, state and history? If so, how is it relevant, for whom is
it relevant and to what end is it relevant?

A dialectical corollary to the problem of theodicy is the sociodicy question
of how modern civil society and its promised existential and socio-political
norms of freedom, equality and fraternity in the name of democracy can
be justified in the face of the antithesis of these norms being systematically
realized through the ever increasing systemic antagonisms between the classes, races, genders, nation states, "civilizations," etc., resulting in the further

catastrophes of wars, massive ecological destruction and increased human suffering and death. It is precisely this developing catastrophe – that affects all nations but particularly the Third World or "periphery" nations and the world's billions of working and poor people – that is the very concrete result of the dominant trans-national, neo-liberal/neo-conservative system and movement of "globalization." It is thus due not only to the critical theoretical analysis of this Western system of capitalist globalization but also the concrete experience of its structurally and systematically produced negative consequences that this movement increasingly has been called a new form of imperialism.

In the midst of this dominant, highly secular and contentious globalization movement, the question of the meaning and relevancy of religion has entered directly into the contemporary discourse on and struggle for the future of humanity. This can be clearly seen in the socio-political rise of the so-called religious/Christian Right in the United States and in Western Europe, as well as the neo-conservative prognosis of the future becoming a "clash of civilizations," meaning that between the so-called Christian, or more correctly stated, the modern capitalist civil society of the West versus non-Western, particularly, Islamic societies. As an expression of human longing for meaning, transcendence, personal autonomy in collective solidarity, happiness and redemption, can the world religions be a theoretical and/or practical force for social change toward a more reconciled future global society? Or, is religion now only a functionalized component of Modern civil society that has the responsibility of producing and maintaining the status quo equilibrium of society's multifaceted and globalizing antagonisms?

Or, is religion to be relegated to the reactionary, counter-revolutionary role of legitimizing the existing antagonisms and horror of modern society, defined by Thomas Hobbes (1968:185) as the *"bellum omnium contra omnes* [the war of all against all]?"* Can human society move from the threatening "clash of civilizations" toward a more reconciled, just, humane, good, equitable and peaceful future where both personal autonomy and universal solidarity prevail? Can civil society be critically transformed into a civilizing society with a cosmopolitan constitution, and what is religion's dynamic role in this struggle? International scholars from the expert cultures of Anthropology, Comparative Religion, History, Philosophy, Physics, Political Science, Sociology, Theology, and Social Work have researched, reflected on and addressed these and other similar questions in the chapters of this book.

This book begins with an Introduction by the Course's creator and director, Rudolf J. Siebert. Siebert gives an historical overview of the Course's inception and critical, contextual development from 1975–2007. This introduction sets the stage for the work addressed in this book.

The first part of this book critically analyzes and grounds the contemporary discourse on the future of religion in the past relationship of religion and society under the heading of *Historical Foundations*. In chapter one, James Reimer looks at the fourth century as the period that gave birth to Christendom and was determinative in the shaping of Western law and present day church-state relations. Reimer focuses on the struggle within the Christianity begun in the fourth century and which continues today: between the Constantinian State church and the minority monastic, so-called heretical and Free Church movements that implicitly if not explicitly protested the Constantinian synthesis of Christ and culture. With the collapse of Christendom in the development of Modernity, Reimer states that the traditional designation of "state church" has now become anachronistic. However, the notion of the "Constantinian Church" and the consequent homogenization of church and state are still relevant in contemporary society, particularly on issues of war and peace. Reimer critically investigates the historical development of this "Constantinian shift" of the church to support and legitimize the policies, laws and actions of the "state," especially in terms of its use of violence, warfare, and the subsequent development of the Just War theory.

In the second chapter, Denis Janz explores the experience of the "heaviness of the [historical] past" in terms of a collective or national sense of guilt. If there is such a thing as national guilt, is there also the corollary of national redemption? Janz locates the source of the notion of national guilt, national repentance and redemption in the West in the Hebrew Scriptures and the teachings of Jesus of Nazareth; notions that have been essentially lost in Christian tradition until more recently in terms of critical, political theologies and liberation theologies. However, in the twentieth century, the notion of national guilt came to the fore in a number of nations as they reflectively confronted their history. As examples of this national struggle with guilt, Janz focuses on Germany's wrestling with its Nazi past, Russia's memory of the Bolshevik Revolution's purges and Stalin's systematic horror in the name of a utopian dream, South Africa and apartheid, and the United States' history of slavery and racism. Acknowledging the problematic dialectic of guilt, Janz also states that the struggle with national, collective guilt can be legitimate, liberating, transformative and healthy. The chapter ends with a brief re-thinking of the traditional doctrine of original sin and baptism as the entrance into an alternative society, *i.e.* the church, which anticipates and works towards the reconciled society of the future.

The third chapter, by Hans K. Weitensteiner, gives a critical historical comparison and analysis of the contradictory documentation dealing with Pope Pius XII's actions and/or "silence" in the face of the rise to power of Hitler, the resulting horror of World War II and particularly that of the Holocaust. Beginning with the recent, very contentious debates about the possibility of the beatification of Eugenio Pagelli/Pope Pius XII, Weitensteiner tells the story of Pagelli's priestly career to his election as Pope on March 2, 1939 and the rapidly ensuing world developments that led to World War II and its aftermath. The reputation of Pope Pius XII remained untarnished after the war until the appearance of Rolf Hochhuth's drama "The Deputy" in 1963, wherein he assumed that Pius XII had been quiet about the Third Reich at a point in time when a public declaration from the Pope would have put an end to the National Socialistic murder of Jews. In 1964, Pope Paul VI made available 5,000 documents contained in 11 volumes entitled *"Actes et Documents du Saint Siège relatifs à la Seconde Guerre Mondiale"* that address the factual activity of Pope Pius XII. Since then the debate about the "silence of the Pope" has increasingly been discussed. In a non-partisan manner, Weitensteiner gives historical expression to both sides of the debate, showing the tortuous struggle for that which is Right in the concrete socio-historical context of the church – state relationship.

Perhaps some of the best examples of the migration of the sacred from pre-modern religions into the new religions of modernity can be found in the rituals of nationalism as they developed in the early modern period. In the fourth chapter, Brian Wilson investigates the origins and processes that led to the development of nationalist pilgrimages by comparing four pilgrimages that arose in the colonial periods of Mexico and the United States. As Wilson explains, the transformation of a pilgrimage into a stable nationalist ritual was not a simple or straightforward process, and many elements had to mesh precisely for such a transformation to occur successfully. Of the four colonial pilgrimages discussed, only three became the object of nationalist sentiment and of the three, only two have survived as nationalist pilgrimages to the present day. The author explains some of the chief reasons why the migration of the sacred was successful in some cases, but not in others. The chapter concludes with a discussion of some of the key similarities and differences between nationalist pilgrimages in Mexico and the U.S.

The subject matter addressed in the fifth chapter, by Anja Finger, is the apparent contradictory views on religion held by the early British socialist Robert Owen (1771–1858): condemning all of religion while yet proposing a new religion at the same time. If this ambivalent attitude was not only the product of a troubled mind, there would have to be a substantial social reason for and background to the statements of this religious revolutionary. The author addresses these issues by analyzing how Owen's views on religion could be grasped in theoretical terms. The author focuses on the idea of a constitutive ambivalence of religious phenomena derived from a re-contextualization and re-interpretation of Marx's opium metaphor. The chapter begins with some remarks on Robert Owen's life, which also indicate the religious surroundings of his time. Because Owen does not neatly fit into any of the dominant categories of the Sociology of Religion, the author lays the groundwork for a new theoretical alternative in the chapter's second section. In the third section, Lenin's version of the opium metaphor and its context is presented in comparison with Marx. In section four, the author illustrates how this metaphorical concept can be applied to Owen, including an excursus on the "sigh" as a crystallization of ambivalence. This then leads to a more general exploratory reading of what the metaphor could look like and what it might give to the Sociology of Religion. Finally, the author addresses the question of the ambivalence of the opium metaphor in speaking to the contemporary religious situation.

Given the analysis of various historical issues in the development of religion and society, the second part of this book addresses various *Conceptions of the Future of Religion*. Michael Ott begins this section with the explanation of Max Horkheimer's notion of the totally Other in terms of the materialistic sublimation or inversion of this religious and theological concept into his critical theory of society and religion. Unlike other appraisals that Horkheimer returned to religion at the end of his life due to the failure of the critical theory and other forms of revolutionary theory and praxis, Ott demonstrates that Horkheimer's critical theory of religion was a fundamental and dynamic part of his entire critical theory from the very beginning. Horkheimer's critical theory of religion, poignantly expressed in the materialistic notion of the totally Other, is an expression of and a catalyst for resistance to the continuing barbarization of modern society in its development toward a globalized, totally administered society. For Horkheimer, religion was not merely a pre-modern, mythological expression of the antediluvian childhood of humanity, which thereby needed to be forgotten. Neither was religion only understood to be an ideological conservative force of control and legitimization of the existing social systems of class exploitation and domination. Religion, particularly the prophetic and Messianic Abrahamic religions, also gives expression to the radical and revolutionary critique of such social systems that produce the horror, suffering and death of innumerable generations of innocent victims. It is this inherent social critique of religion in its narrative form of revolutionary longing for that which is other than the status quo of "what is the case" – both in terms of a more reconciled future society and even the totally "Other" than this world – that is negatively appropriated into Horkheimer's critical theory of religion and society.

In chapter seven, Gottfried Küenzlen analyzes the limits and dangers of the functional view of religion. According to the author, sociology, which functions in the service for the enlightenment of Western societies, has become a hermeneutic authority, whose concepts and images concerning human existence and the world govern the modern understanding of the external and internal factors of human life. However, lurking behind these endeavors of sociology can be found a hypostatic view of society that determines – as a metaphysical variable – the rank and destiny of the people living in it. An expression of this modern world-view can be found in the functional theory begun by Emile Durkheim and its tradition. In such a functional theory, religion is reduced to a formality – to a "social fact," that is characterized by its effective use and service in the context of the existing status quo. The author focuses on the fact that such a functional conception of religion has, to a large extent, entered into and even casts its spell on theological thinking and ecclesiastical practice itself. Küenzlen seeks to expose some of the limits and potential dangers of the theological and ecclesiastical internalization of the functional view of religion.

In chapter eight, Helmut Fritzsche analyzes the practice of religion as a motivation to free oneself and others from internal and external barriers that hide the truth that life is worth living and is capable of actions that are worthy to be undertaken. Due to the many connotations of the word religion, the author does not pretend to provide a timeless and comprehensive notion of religion.

Rather, his thesis focuses on some contemporary issues due to the revival of traditional religions in many regions in the world today. Thus, related to this are the issues of the rapidly growing loss of religious education in Europe, and the world-wide threats to the physical, socio-political and mental conditions of life and a growing loss of awe of life. Fritzsche uses William James' pragmatic understanding of religion as a variety of mystical experiences of the value of life as his starting point. In order to discuss the importance of religion for practicing a life worth living within the circumstances of our life today, he takes up the metaphor "space of reasons" as a symbol for the truth that a life worth living is surrounded with "motivational reasons" in the form of desires stimulated by value experiences on the one hand, and with "normative reasons" providing critical and self critical standards for life worth living on the other. The importance of religion for a life worth living and actions worthy to be undertaken are demonstrated in the context of some contemporary schemes of the philosophy of religion, as well as in the framework of a philosophy of personality and, finally, in view of public debates about some issues of justice and morality.

Within in the modern socio-historical context of what is termed 'globalization,' where the inter-relatedness between civilizations, nations, and other collectivities is increasing, Reimon Bachika's chapter nine investigates what universal aspects of culture already exist or could be developed to affect a more balanced relationship between these globalizing collectivities. The essential question the author seeks to address is whether a universal *telos* can be found in the development of the various world cultures. To this end, Bachika discusses the notion of a universal spiritual culture; one which contains a holistic meaning of life that transcends the limiting material, socio-cultural conditions and problems of human life, expressed in terms of ignorance, suffering and evil. The author finds the possibility of such a universal spiritual culture in the notions of symbolization and valuation.

Gottfried Küenzlen's second article in which he addresses the future of religion in terms of the question of the future of Europe ends the second part of this book. In light of the "clash of civilization" debates that are unfolding both theoretically and politically into new forms of global confrontation, Küenzlen addresses the issue of Europe's – and specifically Germany's – identity and future in terms of the identity and future of Christianity. According to the author, after the end of secular ideologies, the 21st century is being characterized by the great world religions returning as powerful guides of individual, cultural and political life. Only those civilizations that know who they are and have not lost faith in themselves will survive the course of time. Western European Christianity, however, has lost much of its cultural power and influence due to the development of secularity. Few of the cultural intelligentsia are concerned about this erosion of Christianity's influence in Europe. Therefore, this chapter wrestles with the questions of: What future does European civilization have? Where is it heading since its original religion, which formerly shaped it, has let itself become culturally marginalized? The importance of such questions arises from the fact that, according to the author, almost all of the Western world's ideas and concepts of humanity have originated in the context of Christianity. Any kind of civilization must have an answer to the question concerning what it means to be and to become a human being. However, for Western civilization, this answer still needs to be found.

The third section of this work on the *Conceptions of the Future of Society* addresses the notion of the future of religion in the contemporary socio-historical context of what is called "globalization" and its consequences. In chapter eleven, utilizing Walter Benjamin's (1969:257) notion that the working class in modern civil society lives perpetually in a "state of emergency," Michael Ott critically addresses the question of why modern, so-called enlightened Western society, with all the technological and scientific capabilities of overcoming the vast majority of social antagonisms that cause such horrific suffering and death to billions of people in the world, has collapsed into a new form of barbarity? In an effort to make a contribution to the contemporary struggle in both theory and praxis toward answering this extremely relevant "emergency" question, this chapter is divided into two parts. The first part focuses on Horkheimer's and Adorno's research on the above question concerning the collapse of bourgeois society into ever new forms of barbarity. The second part gives expression to Horkheimer's critical theory of religion and the longing for the totally Other as a way by which humanity can free itself from the reifying mythical spell of the enlightenment in the form of positivistic science and the increasingly cybernetic production and consumption process of capitalism.

In chapter twelve, Kjartan Selnes addresses the contemporary issue of culture and multiculturalism in the context of globalization. Of particular importance is the struggle of the various world cultures to preserve their unique values and identity in the midst of this global movement. Selnes addresses this very complex and contentious issue through a brief analysis of a number of concerns. First, although the dominant manifestation of the current globalization movement has taken an economic form, which brings with it a leveling, homogenizing mass culture, Selnes asks whether or not globalization hasn't also created a stronger consciousness about the value and importance of diversity. Cultural imperialism and the creation of an artificial uniformity for the purpose of increasing profit can also produce its opposite – a cultural relativism, which taken to its extreme can also become untenable. The goal advocated by the author is for an intellectual universality in diversity: the universality of well argued knowledge and the universality of well argued values. The hope to succeed in reaching a cross-cultural consensus about the fundamentals of life is a regulative idea that is needed if we want a betterment of the global human condition.

In chapter thirteen, Mislav Kukoč critiques the Hegelian-Marxian revolutionary concept of *"Aufhebung"* in light of his analysis of the Croatian praxis theorists attempt to abolish morality, ethics, religion, philosophy – the entire 'ideological superstructure' – as well as the base structures of work, the family, state, and other institutions of the existing world. Incorporating the work of Milan Kangrga and Gajo Petrovic in his analysis of the concept of *"Aufhebung"* and the complex issue of human morality in the work of Kant, Hegel, and Marx, Kukoč focuses specifically on the Croatian praxis philosophy's attempt and, according to the author, ultimate failure to abolish ethics and morality in terms of replacing moral behavior with historical, revolutionary practice. In terms of the Kantian unresolved antinomy between *Sein und Sollen*, – being and becoming, the real and ideal – the dialectical determinate negation of the moral law into concrete historical praxis opens the possibility for the justification of any and all actions, even the most barbaric. In the midst of this theoretical and practical human condition, according to the author, the purpose of religion as the carrier and guarantor of the eternal moral paradigm of humanity is found.

In the globalizing, historical development toward a post-modern world, Hans-Herbert Kögler, while acknowledging the often times self-contradictory position of postmodernism's critique of modernity's "meta-narratives" of truth, morality, and so-called "grand narratives," offers a re-conceptualization of the issue of normativity. The author outlines the possibility of a normative commitment built into our interpretive practices, based on its dialogical reconstruction and the recognition of the other's beliefs and assumptions. By means of a comparison between modern and postmodern conceptions of social science, Kögler presents an interpretation of the relevance of the post-modern challenge with regard to modern social theory. Based on this, he then sketches a fourfold discursive field of positions addressing the justification of normative perspectives, which serve as a backdrop against which the concept of a hermeneutic competence of dialogical perspective-taking can emerge as a plausible candidate for grounding normative intuitions.

In the fifteenth chapter, Werner Krieglstein addresses the question of how science can solve the contemporary spiritual crisis. Krieglstein contends that the creation of vital communities is the single most important factor in achieving the kind of global society that can produce healthy individuals and inspire human life on earth to be creative and fulfilling. It is just these vital communities that have been and continue to be undermined over the past few centuries. According to the author, societies must help each person, not just the privileged few, to be the best he or she can be, and each person must in turn help society to be the best it can be. This is the only way that the syste-matically created deadness of a totally administered society can be avoided and that the vision of a more reconciled future society furthered historically. According to Krieglstein, such an idea of community can only come from a re-evaluation of our current philosophies of nature and the development of a naturalistic approach to the necessity of community as a prerequisite for human happiness. To this end, Krieglstein explores how a new scientific understanding of the processes within the natural world – a synergistic force – could reshape our understanding and need for community and promote a spiritual stance. Since the traditional, religious notions of community have failed, the author looks to a scientific methodology with its emphasis on openness, empirical testing and trust in falsification to help in developing and promoting a concept of community, free of ideological force.

The focus of the book takes on a more analytical approach in chapter sixteen as Dunja Potočnik analyzes the socializing influence and the development of youth between 15–29 years of age in transitional countries, particular in Croatia. Potočnik gives a short review of youth problems in Croatia, as well as the ways in which youth NGOs and youth church organizations deal with these problems. The specific group that the author focuses on are the young Catholics in Croatia where they encompass more than 90% of the population.

In chapter seventeen, Alexandra Basa analyzes the historical relationship of the church – state relationship in Serbia, regarding the contemporary demands of modernity on both. According to the author, religion has always colored life in Serbia and the relationship of faith and the nation is an inherited tradition that is unlikely to change. That which is religious and that which is national are easily interchangeable. However, today, this relationship is fraught with many problems. Serbian society has passed through huge changes: World War II and the civil war that followed it; 50 years of socialism with the communistic ideology of self-management; explosion of mass communications; roads, cars, phones; urbanization, migrations and the drastic change of population. Many of these problems the Serbian society did not solve until recently in generally accepted and satisfactory ways. The Church, however, has not managed to handle these changes well. The author addresses the question of whether the Orthodox people, who resisted pagans, Muslims, and communists for centuries, will resist the harsh demands of a globalizing Modernity.

Chapter eighteen is a narrative of the work of Aurelia Margaretic to educate female and male students of the sixth grade in the framework of a project orientated "education toward humanity." In this attempt, the author begins from the demand of Theodor W. Adorno (1981:88) "…that Auschwitz may not happen again." This chapter therefore constitutes a coming to terms with the past and the "burden" of being a German. The author combines her own moving experiences in narrative form with the theoretical tradition that reaches from the Socratic demand for truth and justice over F. D. Schliermacher to Herman Nohls claims on education. Margaretic connects the theoretical demand to be the "advocate of the child" with the modern demand for orientation according to the "key problems" of our society, e.g., the revival of nationalism, the wars originating from it [the Yugoslav civil wars] and as consequence of these wars, the question of refugees. To confront these problems, Margaretic tells the stories of refugee children for the purpose of educating children against the coldness of the "social monad" toward empathy and warmth in the relationships among human beings. It is the author's humanistic pedagogical contention that children who have an idea of what a refugee child has lost will be able to encounter him or her with humanity and warmth and they will facilitate and make his or her integration easier.

Chapter nineteen is a short analysis by Jan Fennema of the future possibility of humanity [homo-sapiens] evolving or being socially constructed
into what is being called "homo techno-sapiens." Fennema reflects on this
evolutionary possibility of humanity from the dual notions of the "cosmos"
and morality. According to the author, the notion of homo techno-sapiens
is a reductionist perspective derived from the idea of a cosmic evolution as
a process of nature (encompassing culture), that is founded in biology and
even sociobiology. Assuming this scientistic, evolutionary scenario to prevail, Fennema addresses such questions as: what kind of human being may
we expect to be most likely in those coming times? Will that human being,
as homo techno-sapiens, be a conscientious being; physically and mentally
free because of mastering all there is to be mastered? Or will this being have
internalized the laws, the logics of whatever things he masters, to such an
extent that he will virtually have become their robot-like appendage? Will
such homo techno-sapiens still be considered to be truly human beings?
The author addresses these questions from the moral categories of human
autonomy, responsibility, hope and "ecosophy."

In the midst of this dominant, highly secular and contentious globalization
movement, the question of the meaning and relevancy of religion enters
directly into the contemporary discourse on and struggle for the future of
humanity. In the final chapter of this book, Rudolf J. Siebert addresses this
issue through his analysis of the antithetical theologies of revolution and
counter-revolution. As Siebert expresses, over the past 30 years the Dubrovnik
Circle of scholars and students learned of the theology of revolution through
the work of Thomas Müntzer, Ernst Bloch, Johann Baptist Metz, Jürgen
Moltmann, Harvey Cox, and the Central and South American theologies of
liberation. This theology of revolution was and is understood as a form of
resistance and contradiction to the traditional fascist theology of counter-revolution of Carl Schmitt, the jurist and political theologian of Adolf Hitler, and
his contemporary neo-conservative followers. As Siebert explains, the very
core of both theologies is the theodicy: the justification of God in the face
of the suffering, terror and death of innocent victims in society and nature.
The radical difference between the theology of revolution and the theology
of counter-revolution is grounded in their answer to the theodicy. In terms of
his analysis of Thomas Müntzer's theology of revolution, which was expressive of Müntzer and the farmers' class struggle against the feudal lords in the

16th century, Siebert explains the contemporary need of the revolutionary prophetic, Messianic, eschatological purpose of the Abrahamic religions to migrate into the secular critical theory of society and religion's struggle for Future Alternative III – a more reconciled future society and world.

Introduction

The Development of the Critical Theory
of Religion in Dubrovnik from 1975 to 2007

Rudolf J. Siebert

In 1977, my late wife Margaret and I initiated the international course on "The Future of Religion" in the Inter-University Center for Post Graduate Studies (IUC) in Dubrovnik, Yugoslavia, on invitation by professors of the University of Zagreb, Zagreb, in 1975. Since then an international group of about 30–40 scholars – psychologists, sociologists, philosophers, comparative religiologists, theologians, etc. – have been meeting in the IUC during the communist and post-communist period, in order to explore the modern antagonism in civil and socialist society between the religious and the secular consciousness, language and action, and its resolution in the form of possible, probable and desirable futures of religion and secular enlightenment in the 20th and 21st centuries.

I. The Critical Theory of Society and Religion

The critical theory of subject, society, culture and history of the Frankfurt School, which has been of central interest in the Dubrovnik group, had originated in the experience of the horror of World

War I. Max Horkheimer, Walter Benjamin, Theodor W. Adorno, Friedrich
Pollock, Erich Fromm, Herbert Marcuse, Alfred Sohn-Rethel, Leo Löwen-
thal and other critical theorists tried to make sense out of the senseless war
experience in Frankfurt a.M., Berlin, Stuttgart, or elsewhere, by exploring
the writings of Plato, Aristotle, Machiavelli, Gottfried W. Leibniz, Baruch
Spinoza, Immanuel Kant, Michel Montaigne, Gotthold E. Lessing, Voltaire,
Friedrich W. J. Schelling, Georg W. F. Hegel, Wolfgang von Goethe, Arthur
Schopenhauer, Ludwig Feuerbach, Karl Marx, Auguste Comte, Friedrich
Nietzsche, Sigmund Freud, Emile Durkheim, Max Weber, V. I. Lenin, Vilfredo
Pareto, Edmund Husserl, Max Scheler, Martin Heidegger, Bertolt Brecht, Karl
Kraus, Carl G. Jung, Thomas Mann, Paul Tillich, Karl-Otto Apel and other
outstanding thinkers of Antiquity, the Middle Ages and particularly Modernity. While the critical theorists were usually well read in the philosophical,
scientific and even theological literature of Antiquity and Modernity, they
were somewhat weak concerning the Middle Ages. Here Karl Heinz Haag,
a theologian, philosopher and critical theorists of the second generation and
well versed not only in Hebrew and Greek but particularly also in Latin, had
to be of some help in Horkheimer's and Adorno's philosophical seminars at
the University of Frankfurt a.M. in the 1950's and 1960's.

Historical Causes and Consequences

With the support of those thinkers, the critical theorists hoped to discover
the social-psychological, economic, political and cultural, shortly, the historical causes and consequences of World War I, and later on of the different
forms of capitalism, nationalism, fascism, anti-Semitism and other forms of
racism, and of anti-socialism, and of World War II, and of the following Cold
War, of the unending restoration period, and of the false return to religion,
its pragmatism and its conformism and its alliance with positivism understood as the metaphysics of what is the case. The critical theorists thought
that if – with the help of great thinkers of the past – they would be able to
understand theoretically the causes and consequences of those events and
phenomena, they could then maybe prevent practically something similar
from happening once more in the future. In this hope, Horkheimer began the
formal and systematic development of the critical theory in the Institute for
Social Research at the Johann Wolfgang von Goethe Universität in Frankfurt

a.M. from 1930 to 1933: the year in which Adolf Hitler came into power and drove the critical theorists, whom the fascists called "negativists", out of their Institute, which the fascists named "Cafe Marx" and which they confiscated, into Swiss, French, British and American exile which lasted from 1933 to the end of World War II.

Praxis Philosophy, Neo-Conservativism, Postmodernism

The critical theory was developed first in Germany and then in America in a continual encounter with the classical social theory of Marx, Nietzsche, Freud, William James, George H. Mead, Charles S. Peirce, Durkheim, Weber, and Georg Simmel. It was also formed in continual discourse with representatives of functionalism and neo-functionalism, conflict theory and symbolic interactionism, phenomenology and ethnomethodology, exchange theory and rational choice theory, feminist theory and neo-conservativism, pragmatism and cognitivism, post-modernism and poststructuralism as well as with thinkers like Norbert Elias, Pierre Bourdieu, Anthony Giddens and Steven Seidman. While the critical theory was rooted in the praxis philosophy – derived from Western Marxism, American pragmatism and French existentialism – it was at the same time critically opposed to neo-conservativism – connected with Weber's time diagnosis and determined in America by liberal traditions and in Germany by Arnold Gehlen's pessimistic anthropology and by Joachim Ritter's and E. Forsthoff's Right-Hegelian compensation theory, as well as to the philosophy of departure from modernity: which in the succession of Nietzsche was inspired through the fundamental experiences of the aesthetical avant-garde from Heidegger and Georges Bataille to J. Derrida and M. Foucault. While the neo-conservatives performed their identification with social modernity – i.e. monopoly and oligopoly capitalism – for the price of the rejected cultural modernity – i.e., bourgeois, Marxian and Freudian enlightenment movements – and while the post-modernists deconstructed that system of fundamental notions in which modernity had explicated itself since the bourgeois enlightenment of the 18th century, the praxis philosophers – including the critical theorists – held on to the rational claim of occidental rationalism and to a – however skeptically broken – continuation of the project of modernity: to be sure, in a most dialectical way.

Globalization

After World War II, there took place an intensive and extensive Europeaniza-
tion, Americanization and globalization of the critical-theoretical discourse.
The Frankfurt School developed in a very complex way. While Horkheimer
and Adorno returned to Germany in 1949, Marcuse and the other members
of the group of critical theorists in New York and Los Angeles remained in
the United States. The split resulted in the Americanization of the critical
theory of society on one hand, and the formation of a new, second generation of critical theorists in Germany on the other. During the 1950's and early
1960's the two strands more or less followed their own path. After the
immediate post-war critical-theoretical discourse a linguistic paradigm shift
took place in the writings of Habermas, the leading member of the second
generation of critical theorists. It had a major impact not only on the German,
but also on the American critical-theoretical discourse. The impact made
itself felt primarily in the social philosophy and in the political theory. In
the humanities – i.e. aesthetical theory, literature and music – the critical-
theoretical model of the first generation of critical theorists – i.e. that of
Adorno and Benjamin – remained central for the American critical-theoretical
discourse of the 1970's. However, during the 1980's the American understanding of crucial aesthetical and cultural issues – i.e. modern art and mass
culture – began to move away from the position of the Frankfurt School. This
happened in the context of the rising neo-conservativism and deconstructionism. Adorno's and Benjamin's critical theory was appropriated by younger
American theorists: among them Frederick Jameson, Susan Buck-Morris and
Martin Jay. They differed in more than one way from the German reception
of the critical theory. Habermas's theory of communicative action made an
impact on American theorists such as Sheila Benhabib, Thomas McCarthy
and Nancy Frazer. In the German experience, after the death of Adorno in
1969, a reformation of cultural and aesthetical critical theory took place under
the influence of the Habermasian model by theorists such as Peter Berger
and Albrecht Wellmann and their reception in the United States. Finally, the
third generation of critical theorists on both sides of the Atlantic – among
them Axel Honneth and Christopher Menke – tried to come to terms with
the poststructuralist theory. The globalization of the critical theory came to
its peak during the 1990's.

Dubrovnik Discourse

Our Dubrovnik discourse about the "Future of Religion" in the IUC from 1977 to 2007 was based mainly on Horkheimer's and Adorno's critical theory of society and on their Frankfurt School. We identified the dialectical theory of religion and the political theology as theodicy intrinsic to it, and developed at the same time our own new critical theory of religion with a particular emphasize on the theodicy problem. We did this in the context of the over all internationalization of the Frankfurt School and its critical theory of society after World War II. While in our Dubrovnik discourse we concentrated always on one dichotomy in modern civil society, that between the sacred and the profane, we did this nevertheless in the context of the other antagonisms: that between the genders, that between the individual and the collective, that been the races and most of all that between the social classes. We were always aware of the interconnection among these un-reconciled antagonisms in late capitalist society. We could not deny the fact that it makes a great difference if one looks at the contradiction between the religious and the secular from a male or female, individualistic or collectivistic, African, Asian, Semitic or Aryan, bourgeois or proletarian perspective.

Oppositional Schools

In the past 31 years, the Dubrovnik group has developed out of the critical theory of society of the Frankfurt School a critical theory of religion in continual discourse not only with the three generations of critical theorists, but also in contact with other, more or less oppositional schools of social theory: e.g. social Darwinism, pragmatism, realism, naturalism, pre- and post-Roosevelt liberalism, structural-functionalism, neo-functionalism, conflict theory, neo-Maxism, existentialism, symbolical interactionism, ethno-methodology, exchange-network, rational choice theories, post-modernism, feminism, structuralism, post-structuralism, neo-fascism, and theories rooted in minority experiences and cognitivism. We encountered a variety of particularly American theorists: e.g. C. S. Peirce, John Dewey, Morris Cohen, Richard Rorty, W. V. O. Quine, Susan Haak, Cornell West, Carol Gilligan, John Rawls, Robert Nozick and others. We dealt especially with outstanding theorists of religion like Marx, Freud, E. B. Tylor, J. Frazer, Durkheim, Weber, Mircea Eliade, E. E. Evans-Pritchard, Clifford Geertz and Talcott Parsons.

Structural Functionalism

In Dubrovnik, we sharply differentiated our critical theory of religion from the great Parsonian structural-functionlist system theory. This happened because we found already in structural-functionalism's scientistic or positivistic demand of a sociological knowledge without any break, fracture, rupture, breach, leap, or discontinuity something of a harmonistic and thus, ideological or even mythological tendency. We discovered that the absence of any break in the structural-functional form of representation and in the systematization of the social phenomena had in itself already the tendency – unconsciously, of course, as effect of what Hegel had called the objective spirit – to explain away the constitutive, fundamental contradictions of civil society: the antagonisms between the sacred and the profane, between the genders, between the individual and the collective, between the classes, and between the races. Our critical theory of religion has been essentially ideology- and mythology-critique. Precisely as such, it has been devoted to not hiding and not merely affirming but rather working and fighting through and resolving of the fundamental modern dichotomy between the religious and the secular, monotheism and radical enlightenment, in order precisely thereby to contribute indirectly to the resolution of the other basic contradictions of civil society as well: in direction of its identity change and of the arrival of global alternative Future 3 – the reconciled society.

Rescue through Inversion

Our main thesis and argument in our Dubrovnik circle was and continues to be that if the demythologization and secularization process that had dominated the whole 20th century would continue to prevail into the 21st century, one would have to try to rescue through inversion the religious semantic potentials, motives and motivations from the depth of the mythos for secular modern society. If these religious semantic potential, motives and motivations ever had contributed to the humanization of man, then they need to be rescued by inversion into a secular form in order to help stop the further regression of the Euro-American life form into re-mythologization, re-enchantment, neo-paganism and most of all into further re-barbarization. This re-barbarization could easily be noticed throughout the Euro-American civilization: e.g. all the shootings at home: in families, schools, churches, offices, factories etc.; and abroad: in one local war, or civil war after the other since the end of World War II, the re-awakened nationalisms since 1989 and the accompanying Right-wing extremism, often steered by the myth of origin in one form or the other to an always increasing extent, the anti-Semitism and other forms of racism and the connected hate crimes, the anti-Marxism and anti-democratism, and the revolutionary, state, or nihilistic terrorism at home and abroad.

Antagonistic Totality

Nietzsche (1967:80) stated "only that which has no history is definable." The critical theory of society, out of which we in Dubrovnik developed our critical theory of religion, has a history and therefore cannot be defined. However, in terms of a working definition we can say that the critical theory is the insight into society: into the essential of society. The critical theory is the insight into what is the case in society but that in such a sense that this insight is critical. This insight is critical in the sense that it measures what is the case in society by what the latter itself claims to be in order to discover in this contradiction the potentials or the possibilities of a change of the identity of the total social constitution. The dialectical theory is a social theory that understands modern civil society as an antagonistic totality of non-equivalent exchange processes. The critical theorists do not join those liberals, who consider the open society to be entirely harmoniously pluralistic. It also differs from the neo-conservatives i.e. disgusted liberals, who see the contradictory character of civil society but consider its competitiveness as a vehicle for progress, ignoring the immense human suffering involved: selfishness, greed, avarice are right! To the contrary, the critical theorists are deeply impressed by the great human pain connected with the antagonistic character of modern society. Therefore, the critical theorists try to fight through the painful antagonism of civil society toward alternative Future 3, i.e. a society which will no longer reproduce itself through the *bellum omnium contra omnes*, a war of everybody against everybody, nationally or internationally. The new society was rather to reproduce itself in terms of universal, i.e. mimetic, present, and proleptic solidarity. In the new society, universal solidarity and personal autonomy and sovereignty are to be reconciled. In the new society also those human actions are to be considered valuable that do not carry a price tag on them and have not been commodified. Egoism, greed and avarice and the consequent exploitation are no longer to be considered right. The few would no longer be allowed to live through the labor and money of the many.

Religion in the Antagonistic Social Totality

From its very start, the critical theory of society contained in itself more or less latently a dialectical theory of religion. Its prototype was Hegel's (1984, 1985, 1987) philosophy of religion dealing with the beginning of the history of religion in terms of magic and fetishism, with the Chinese religion of measure, with Hinduism as the religion of imagination, with Buddhism as the religion of inwardness, with Zoroastrianism as the religion of light and darkness, or good and evil, with the Syrian religion of pain, with the Egyptian religion of riddle, with the Jewish religion of sublimity, with the Greek religion of beauty and fate, with the Roman religion of utility, with the Christian religion of freedom, and with Islam as the religion of law. The critical theory of religion, which is potentially contained in the critical theory of society, and which we in Dubrovnik developed further, can be defined in terms of a working definition as the insight into the essential of religion. It is the insight into that what is the case in the history of religions, but that in such a way that the latter is critical. The insight is critical in the sense that it measures what is religiously the case by that what the religion itself claims to be in order to recognize in this contradiction at the same time the potentials or the possibilities of a change in the identity of the totality of the religious constitution. The critical theory of religion explores the position of religion in the antagonistic social totality. It tries to discover to what extent religion is ideology – understood not only affirmatively as the mere combination of ideas and motivating values, but rather critically as the masking of national and class interests or simply as the untruth. It tries to discover to what extent religion legitimates the interests of the ruling classes and nations, or to what extent religion identifies with the oppressed and exploited poor classes and masses. The critical theory of religion is not only interested in the notion of happiness but also in that of redemption as it occurs in different world religions. The two notions are different and even contradictory, but they can also support each other. The critical theorist of religion sees the friendly and happy living together of free human beings, characterized by communication without domination, as the very location from which arises the longing for redemption: the hope for the totally Other as the radical but nevertheless still determinate negation of what on earth is called injustice, human abandonment and alienation. The critical theory of religion differentiates sharply between the bad religion of domination, which guilds the unjust world, on one hand, and the good religion of emancipation, which states, that it has to become different – i.e. right.

II. Judaism and Other World-Religions

In Dubrovnik, we discovered that the first generation of critical theorists had been of Jewish origin and that the critical theory of society contained in itself a theory of religion the very core of which was a comparative theory of Judaism as well as of anti-Semitism and anti-feminism and that its very center was a critical political theology as theodicy. According to Horkheimer's and Adorno's (1972:23) common work, *Dialectic of Enlightenment* of 1944, in the Jewish religion, which Hegel (1987:152–160, 423–454, 669–687) had called in his *Philosophy of Religion* the religion of sublimity, the idea of the patriarchate culminated in the destruction of the mythos. In the already highly demythologized Jewish religion the bond between name and being, was nevertheless still recognized in the third commandment of the Mosaic *Decalogue*: in the ban on pronouncing the name of God.

Disenchanted World

According to Horkheimer and Adorno, the already widely demythologized and disenchanted world of Judaism conciliated magic and fetishism by negating them in the idea of God. The Jewish religion no longer allowed any word that would alleviate the despair of all that is finite and mortal. The Jewish religion associated hope only with the third commandment of the Mosaic Law in the Torah, in the book *Exodus*: the prohibition against calling what is false as God, against invoking the finite as the Infinite, lies as truth. In Judaism, the guarantee of salvation lay in the rejection of any belief that would replace it. Redemption was the knowledge obtained in the denunciation of illusion and delusion. The consequence of the third commandment reaches not only into Schopenhauer's, Marx's, Nietzsche's and Freud's theory of religion, but also into that of the critical theorists of the Frankfurt School, which combines in itself the bourgeois as well as the Schopenhaurian, Marxian, Nietzschean and Freudian enlightenment movements.

Determinate Negation

Horkheimer and Adorno had to admit that the negation in Judaism was not an indeterminate, abstract or general one, but rather what Hegel had called in his *Phenomenology of Spirit* (1967a) and *Science of Logic* (1969) a determinate, concrete or specific negation. According to the critical theorists, the contesting of every positive element without distinction, the stereotype formula of vanity as used by Buddhism that Hegel (1987:303–316, 562–579) had called in his *Philosophy of Religion* the religion of inwardness, set itself just as far above the to be sure radicalized third commandment of the Mosaic law, the prohibition against naming the Absolute, as did its contrary, pantheism – be it Hindu, Greek or Spinozian – or its caricature, bourgeois skepticism. For Horkheimer and Adorno, explanations of the world as all or nothing were mythologies. All guaranteed roads to redemption were sublimated magic or fetishistic practices. The self-satisfaction, so the critical theorists explained, of knowing everything in advance and the transfiguration of negativity into redemption were untrue forms of resistance against deception. In Horkheimer's and Adorno's view, the justness of the image was preserved in the strictest obedience to the second commandment of the *Decalogue*: the faithful pursuit of the prohibition against making images of the Absolute. This pursuit, i.e. determinate negativity, did not receive from the sovereignty of the abstract concept any immunity against corrupting intuition, as did bourgeois skepticism, to which both, true and false, were equally vain. In the perspective of the critical theorists, determinate, concrete or specific negation rejected the defective ideas of the Absolute, the idols, in the different world-religions and world-philosophies differently than did rigorism. Such rigorism confronted these idols with what Hegel (1969) had called in his *Science of Logic* the "Idea," to which they could not possibly match up. On the contrary, the critical theorists' – what Marx (1961) had called in *Capital* – materialistic dialectic interpreted every image as writing. It showed how the admission of the falsity of the image was to be read in the lines of its features: a confession that deprived the image of its power and appropriated it for the truth. The critical theorists remembered that with the notion of determinate negativity Hegel had revealed in his *Phenomenology of Spirit* (1967a) and *Science of Logic* (1969) an element that distinguished the great bourgeois enlightenment from its positivistic degeneracy, to which he had attributed it. However, so the critical theorists argued, by ultimately making the conscious result of the whole process of concrete negation – the totality in system and in history – into an absolute, Hegel of course contravened the second commandment of the *Decalogue* and thus lapsed back into mythology. Hegel fell victim to the same dialectic of enlightenment, which he himself had discovered. The same happened to the enlighteners Schopenhauer, Nietzsche, Marx and Freud after him. As they negated the mythos merely abstractly, they prepared the return of the insufficiently negated mythology. The second and the third commandment of the *Decalogue* belong to the semantic material and potential which the critical theorists were willing and able to rescue from the depth of the already highly demythologized and disenchanted Jewish religion by inverting them into the secular dialectical method of determinate, concrete and specific negation, which enabled them to resist effectively re-mythologization, re-enchantment and re-barbarization in what Adorno called the late capitalist society. It is today – together with its business cycle – in the process of extreme globalization.

Anti-Semitism

The Dubrovnik discourse group did not only rescue from the Frankfurt critical theory of society the second and the third commandment of the Mosaic law and its secularization into dialectic into its own new critical theory of religion, but also took seriously Adorno's theory of anti-Semitism, or more precisely, anti-Judaism. Adorno developed his first design of a theory of anti-Semitism in a supplement to his letter to Horkheimer (1995a:760–764) of September 18, 1940. According to Adorno, the depth and the obstinacy, the stubbornness and the persistence of the many centuries old hate against Judaism and the Jews let the usual, more or less rationalistic explanations of anti-Semitism appear as being insufficient and inadequate. In Adorno's view, anti-Judaism did not only date back into a period of human history in which many of the rational reasons for its origin were not yet effective: e.g. the share of the Jews in capitalism and liberalism. In Adorno's perspective, anti-Semitism itself carried certain archaic traits in itself, which pointed beyond the usually identified causes for it. Particularly the fact that anti-Judaism was cordoned off against argumentative discourse, revealed to Adorno that very old motives had to be in play, which had long become a second nature to people. Adorno thought of such motives that immediately had nothing to do either with the relationship of the Jews to Christianity, or with the money – or market economy, or with the bourgeois, Marxian, or Freudian enlightenment movements. However, Adorno suspected nevertheless that these later motives of anti-Semitism themselves stood in a deep relationship to its archaic motives. According to Adorno, a sufficient theory of anti-Semitism that would go beyond the pluralism of particular reasons for the hate against the Jews and Judaism would depend on the success of an original, primordial history of anti-Semitism. Unlike Freud, Adorno was convinced that such an original history of anti-Judaism could not be developed and given as a psychological one. Rather, such an original history had to try to discover the origin of anti-Semitism, the hate against Judaism and the Jews, in archaic but nevertheless socially real movements.

The Image of the Jew

In Adorno's view, one indication concerning the archaic origin of the hate against the Jews possibly could be taken from the present image that anti-Semites made of them. Concerning this image, so Adorno argued, sociologists were usually accustomed to emphasize the moment of unfamiliarity or remoteness. For Adorno, this notion of the sociologists was too abstract and too unspecified. Adorno knew of innumerable strangers, or foreigners, who admittedly in particular situations had drawn the hate of the natives upon themselves. However, the position and the fate of those strangers could in no way be compared with that of the Jews. According to Adorno, in the whole folklore the girl from foreign lands, who was received through marriage, had played in a very positive sense a great role. Adorno thought particularly of the black-brown girl of the German folksong: who was praised even in fascist marching songs. In Adorno's view, there existed no corresponding image of the Jewess. On the other hand, so Adorno remembered, German folklore about the Jew contained traits which went far beyond those of the foreigner. They were traits of travels; of the very old; of the eternal Jew who cannot die; of the scrounger or cadger. Adorno suspected that the image of the scrounger implicated that of a rich beggar: of a beggar who carried over his shoulders a sack full of thalers.

From Nomadic Life to Agriculture

It seemed to Adorno, that neither all these traits of the image of the Jew in the consciousness of the anti-Semites and even more so the specific configuration that they constituted, nor the Jewish character as such could be explained out of the history of the Jews since the Diaspora, i.e. since the Roman victory over and destruction of Jerusalem and of the Temple and of the Fortress of Masada through Flavius Vespasianus and his son Titus between 67 and 74, or since the last Jewish insurrection against the Romans between 132–135 led by Simeon ben Koseba, who was greeted as Messiah by Rabbi Akiba, the most influential teacher of his time, and who was given the title Bar Kokebar or Kochba – i.e. son of the stars – and who was condemned by others, as witnessed in the Talmud, as Bar Koziba – i.e. son of lies, or seducer of the people. While Adorno rejected this explanation of the anti-Semitic image and real character of the Jew out of the experience of the Diaspora, he accepted nevertheless the following one as ultimately valid. In a very early stage of the history of humanity, the Jews had either disdained and spurned the transition from nomadic life to a settled state, to agriculture, and had held on to the nomadic life form, or they had performed this transition merely insufficiently and seemingly: in a kind of pseudo-morphosis. Adorno recommended that the Biblical history should be analyzed very precisely in terms of the Jewish relationship to the historical transition from nomadic life to the settled state. To Adorno, the Biblical history seemed to be full of indications in this direction. For Adorno, the most important indications were the Jewish Exodus from Egypt and its prehistory with the promise of the land, where milk and honey was flowing on one hand and the short duration of the Jewish kingdom and its immanent weaknesses, on the other.

Monotheism

For Adorno, the specific trait of the high age of the Jew seemed to hang together most closely with his holding on to the archaic nomadic life form in a world characterized by agriculture. In Adorno's view, the Jews were the secret Gypsies of world-history. Adorno was certain of the anti-mythological form of the Jewish monotheism and of its relationship to the Hellenistic and modern enlightenment movements. For Adorno, this monotheism was also a function of the Jews holding on to the nomadic life form. Likewise, so Adorno explained, those traits of the Jews that were generally called the progressive ones, were in truth not younger but rather older than the mythology. According to Adorno, there was only as much mythology in the world as there were ties, bonds, attachments and commitments to the earth and to a particular place of residence and fixed abode. In the perspective of our new Dubrovnik critical theory of religion, here Adorno came very close to the connection between the myth of origin on one hand, and nationalism and particularly fascism, on the other, which was deeply rooted in blood and soil, and which had become so important particularly in the 20th century, and which in that century served again and again as fruitful framework for the development of anti-Semitism and other forms of racism and which seems to continue to do so into the 21st century.

Jewish Patriarchalism

According to Adorno's anti-Semitism theory, the Jews had been pre-matriarchal in the sense of Johann J. Bachofen's (1967) mother right theory. Precisely therefore, so Adorno argued, Jewish patriarchalism was completely incompatible with the later one of the societies of the high Antiquity or those of Modernity. In Adorno's perspective, that the Jews refused to accept any partial, or local gods hung together with the fact that they refused to accept any one and limited homeland, or native country. It was vague and obscure for Adorno to what extent the homelessness of the Jews was the result of free will and decision, or rather of political failures. At any rate, it was at least thinkable for Adorno that the possible political failures of the Jews had their reason precisely in their holding on to the prehistoric nomadic times. That, in Adorno's view, would explain the peculiar extra-territoriality of the Jews in relation to the whole occidental history, which expressed itself today to the same extent in anti-Semitism as well as in the reaction of the Jews toward it. In the perspective of the critical theory of religion that we developed in Dubrovnik, Adorno went even further in his anti-Semitism theory than Fromm (1997) in his reinterpretation of Bachofen's, R. Briffault's and Henry Morgan's mother right theory, when he assumed a patricentric life form preceding the matricentric civilizations of Antiquity. We were even aware of modern scholars who assumed that the old Jewish pre-matriarchal patriarchal life form had been preceded already by a matriarchal culture including matricentric institutions and personality types. In Dubrovnik, we noticed that while the critical theorists at least of the first generation were mainly Jewish, none of them ever became a Zionist: the critical theory of society has been extremely non-Zionist. Horkheimer and the other non-Zionist members of the Institute of Social Research in Frankfurt a.M., New York and Los Angeles anticipated the political fallacies and failure of Zionism, which have become so obvious again in the recent most bloody Palestinian upheaval and in the landslide victory of Prime Minister Sharon, a farmer, in Jerusalem on February 6, 2001 in the midst of the most recent Intifada, which continues today in 2007. Will the Zionist political fallacies and failure end once more – against all the best intentions – nevertheless in Jewish homelessness?

The Occidental Notion of Work

According to Adorno, the survival of the nomadic life form among the Jews explained not only their own social character, but even more so the anti-Semitism of their enemies: the hate not only against their nationalism, or patriotism, or Zionism, but against them themselves as a nation. For Adorno, it was obvious that the giving up of the nomadic life for a settled state, for agriculture, was one of the most difficult sacrifices, which history has ever imposed on humankind. The occidental notion of work, so Adorno argued, and all the instinctual renunciations connected with it, might precisely fall together with the development of the settled state. In Adorno's view, the image of the Jew represented that of a condition of the human species, which did not know anything of hard work. All later attacks, so Adorno explained, against the supposedly and allegedly parasitic, snatching, grabbing, amassing and gathering character of the Jews were only rationalizations of his original nomadic image. The Jews were those, who did not allow themselves to be civilized and who did not permit themselves to be subjugated under the primacy of hard work. This is precisely what the non-Jews could not forgive the Jews. Therefore, the Jews became the bone of contention in the traditional and modern class societies.

Paradise

According to Adorno, the Jews did – so to speak – not allow themselves to be driven out of Paradise: or only very reluctantly and grudgingly. In Adorno's view, still the description that Moses gave in the Torah, in the Book Exodus, of the land, where milk and honey was flowing, was that of Paradise. This holding on, so Adorno explained, to the oldest image of happiness was the Jewish utopia. Here it did not matter to Adorno if the nomadic condition was indeed one of happiness or not. Probably the nomadic state was not one of happiness. However, so Adorno explained, the more the world characterized by the settled state reproduced itself as one of work, the more the older nomadic condition had to appear as one of happiness: that one had not to permit and the thought of which one had to forbid and to repress. In Adorno's perspective, this prohibition against the condition of happiness was the very origin of anti-Semitism. In Adorno's interpretation, the many attempts to drive out and chase away the Jews and to commit ethnic cleansing against them were so many attempts to complete, or to imitate the ejection, the eviction, the exile of Adam and Eve from Paradise in the Torah, in the Book Genesis. In the perspective of the comparative critical theory of religion, which we have been developing in Dubrovnik, Adorno, Horkheimer, Fromm and Löwenthal and the other critical theorists of the Frankfurt School allowed the semantic potential of the Paradise, of this oldest image of happiness, of this Jewish utopia, to migrate from the depth of the legends of the Torah and to be inverted into their secular critical theory of traditional and modern society. Their secularized Jewish social utopia of global alternative Future 3 – the realm of the freedom of all on the basis of and above and beyond the realm of natural and economic necessity – which originally they shared with the third volume of Marx's (1961) *Capital* – was sufficient reason for the national socialists to drive the critical theorists out of Frankfurt and Germany into their rather precarious life in Swiss, French, English and American exile: and in the case of Benjamin even into suicide.

The Lapse from Faith

In his letter to Adorno from Hollywood, California, on September 24, 1940, Horkheimer (1995b:765–766) believed that the former had formulated a decisive thought in his anti-Semitism theory. This thought, so Horkheimer specified, was maybe more decisive for the explanation of anti-Semitism than for that of Judaism. According to Horkheimer, the Judaism of today could be comprehended only negatively: out of the lapse from faith in its God. Of course, so Horkheimer argued, the value of Adorno's insight expressed in his theory of anti-Judaism proved itself also here concerning this lapse from faith in God. After such lapse, so Horkheimer argued, there was nothing left for the Jews any longer. The Jews were spoiled once and for all for the false gods of fascist or liberal civil society: nation, leadership, blood, soil, power, money, etc. Furthermore, nobody believed the Jews any longer, when they tried to kiss and cuddle with the idolatrists of globalized late capitalist society. Even in England the Jews had been put into concentration camps already by 1936. For Horkheimer, precisely that was grounded in the prehistory. Horkheimer was convinced that the question of the Jews was the fundamental question of the present modern society. In this Horkheimer and the other critical theorists were in agreement with Marx and Hitler. Otherwise, Horkheimer and his friends were as little in agreement concerning the Jewish question with Marx, or Hitler, as with Freud. Horkheimer thought that Adorno's design of a theory of anti-Semitism would best be put as excursus in the discourse with Freud: as the last theory of anti-Semitism. In this process Horkheimer wanted to cooperate with Adorno. In the perspective of the Dubrovnik critical theory of religion, the result of this cooperation was Horkheimer's and Adorno's (1972) *Dialectic of Enlightenment* and its specific analysis of anti-Semitism.

Jews and Germans

In his letter to Leo Löwenthal in Port Chester, New York, of July 24, 1944, Horkheimer (1996a:564–568) came back once more to Adorno's theory of anti-Semitism. In Horkheimer's perspective, in this context there existed a great similarity between Jewish and German pre-history. Both peoples were originally nomads: i.e. pastoral tribes. Both nations looked as such with great contempt on agricultural activities. Both, the old Germans and the old Jews, considered such working of the earth to be a curse. This was the case not only in the Genesis, the Jewish myth of origin, but also in the Germany described by Tacitus as well. If the critical theorists would have accepted Freud's or Jung's terminology, they could have said, that the two nations, the Germans and the Jews, shared certain traits of their collective unconscious with the Muslims in contrast to the Greeks. However, so Horkheimer argued, if both, Germans and Jews, showed a militant sort of patriotism, then the patriotism of the Jews was characterized by a longing for the soil which was lost, while the Germans wanted to win a soil which they never possessed. The unconscious of Germans and Jews was alike in so far as they dreamed of getting the fruits of the earth without laboring it themselves. According to Horkheimer, the land of milk and honey was represented in the German soul by the nostalgia for the South: e.g. Italy. Of course, in Dubrovnik we could not fail to notice that the Germans were longing for the East as well.

Patriarchal People

Following Adorno's theory of anti-Semitism, Horkheimer stated in his letter to Löwenthal, that the Jews were certainly the oldest patriarchal people in the Western World. The Jews' legend, however, celebrated the younger brother. Horkheimer thought of Cain and Abel, Esau and Jacob, Isaac's sons and Joseph, Aaron and Moses and others. Horkheimer reminded Löwenthal of his remarks, following Eric H. Erikson's (1942:475–493) article entitled "Hitler's Imagery and German Youth," on the role of the rebellious son in fascist psychology. In his article, Erikson had promoted the thesis that the person of Hitler corresponded to the confused rebellion of – what Fromm (1973:209f., 1980) had called – the authoritarian, or fascist character, which refused to accept authority and subordinated itself under it at the same time, in so far as he incorporated the rebellious son as well as the authoritarian father. Horkheimer asked Löwenthal whether anti-Semitism could be – even in this point – an unconscious imitation of Jewish structures? Horkheimer tried to understand the precise meaning of these structures in Jewish life.

Nomadic Traits

In his letter of August 4, 1944 from Port Chester, New York, to Horkheimer (1996b:583–587) at Pacific Palisades, Löwenthal found his ideas about the Germans, the Jews and the nomads to be very interesting. In Löwenthal's view, Horkheimer probably hit here on an important issue. However, according to Löwenthal, one of the psychological problems still to be resolved seemed to be, why – if Horkheimer's concept was correct – these two groups, the Germans and the Jews, preserved those nomadic traits in their souls since, after all, all ethnic groups and tribes once had passed through the nomadic stage. Löwenthal guessed that indeed the sun and the south played their role in this connection. According to Löwenthal, besides the Germans all European peoples, like the Dutch, the Scandinavians and to a certain extent even the Russians, who were deprived of southern country sides like France and Switzerland, had nevertheless also displayed the same urge for the South. That was at least true for their intellectuals. In any case, for Löwenthal this was a stimulating issue. Löwenthal thought of the specific German, fascist anti-Semitic slogan of the one-way ticket to Palestine. Since, so Löwenthal explained, the anti-Semite was the eternal persecutor and imitator of the Jew, it was not difficult to imagine, where the Jewish journey to Palestine would lead him, at least in imagination: the image of the Eternal Anti-Jew chasing the Eternal Jew. Löwenthal had no specific comment on Horkheimer's theory of the younger brother in Jewish legends except that he accepted it whole-heartedly. In Dubrovnik we had the suspicion, that the younger brother in Jewish legends may very well be a residual of a matriarchal order which was even older than the Jewish patriarchy.

The Battle of the Sexes

In the perspective of our Dubrovnik group, Adorno's, Horkheimer's and Löwenthal's theory of anti-Semitism was strangely connected with Fromm's theory of anti-feminism: the war between the sexes, which he expressed in the Italian magazine L'Espresso as late as February 1975 (Aleotti 1975:56–59. 94), precisely when we began to initiate our new critical theory of religion. Here the psychoanalyst Fromm stated that we shall never understand and comprehend the psychology of either women or men as long as we fail to acknowledge that a state of war has existed between the genders for approximately 6000 years. For Fromm, this battle of the sexes was indeed a guerrilla war. Fromm remembered that approximately 6000 years ago, the patriarchy triumphed over women and their matriarchy. The event is plenti-fully reflected in Babylonian, Hebrew and Greek mythology. From then on society became organized on the basis of male domination. From now on, women became the property of men and were obliged to be grateful to them for every concession. But, so Fromm argued, there could not be domination of one social class, nation, or sex over the other that did not lead to sublimi-nal rebelliousness, rage and hatred, and the desire for revenge in those who were oppressed and exploited, and to fear and insecurity in those who did the oppressing and exploiting.

Patriarchal Domination

In Dubrovnik, we had the suspicion that what had been true for the domi-nation of one social class, nation, or sex over the other, may also be true of the oppression and exploitation of one race by the other. Was there, so we asked ourselves, a similarity between the fate of the women under patriarchal domination and that of the Jews, or of the Blacks, or of the proletariat? Did the anti-Semitism correspond to an anti-feminism under patriarchal domination? Was there a similarity among the roles of the woman, the Jew and the proletarian in patriarchal civil society? In any case, we became convinced that there was a connection between the antagonism of the races in modern civil society and that between the genders and the classes, and that these contradictions were once more related to the modern dichotomy between the sacred and the profane. We noticed that all four antagonisms constituted a network in modern bourgeois society. It found its expression on the cultural, social and psychological and social-psychological level. It was continually reproduced from one generation to the other by its internalization from the cultural through the social – particularly the family – into the personalities and character structures of the individuals: their Super-Ego, Ego and Id and thus shaped their libidinous and aggressive instincts and impulses. Obviously, the solution to these antagonisms between the sexes and the races and the classes in modern civil society did not lay in the inversion of the roles in what Hegel (1967a) had called in his *Phenomenology of Spirit* the relationship between lordship and bondage: that the former lord would now become the bondsman and that the former servant would now become the master. For the Dubrovnik group, it was rather the relationship itself between lord and bondsman, between oppressor and oppressed, between exploiter and exploited, which had to be abolished once and for all in global alternative Future III.

III. Theodicy

As in our Dubrovnik discourse, we developed our new critical theory of religion, we were not only concerned with the Frankfurt critical theory of society, of Judaism, of anti-Semitism and anti-feminism, but we also penetrated into its innermost core: the theodicy problem (*theos* – God; *dikae* – justice): the question concerning the justice of God in the face of the injustices of his world. In our Dubrovnik circle of scholars we dealt even more broadly with questions concerning the fate of all still living world-religions in the face of the after Auschwitz and Triblinka, Hiroshima and Nagasaki newly arising, most dramatic forms of the theodicy: the problem of meaning.

Perils of Human Existence

Can – so we asked ourselves in Dubrovnik – those established positive religions further contribute to the well being of modern and postmodern societies by solving the theodicy problem on present levels of social evolution and learning as they had done in the past for thousands of years. Could they still deal adequately with the fundamental perils of human existence: the problems of finitude, suffering, loneliness, abandonment, alienation, guilt, meaninglessness, fear of illness, aging, dying and death? Will the traditional positive religions continue to be consoling in the moment, when non-everyday events break into the normal everyday life world: earthquakes, hurricanes, cancer, wars, sudden shootings in families, schools, offices, factories and even churches, airplane-ship-train-car accidents, divorce, etc.? We concentrated on the question, what will happen to traditional positive religions, their ideas, values, symbols, and practices in modern and post-modern society when their Gods, or God, or Divinity can no longer be justified and defended without illusion or delusion on the basis of this existing world of nature and history, in which most organisms and organizations maintain themselves only through the most painfully tearing to pieces and consuming of other organisms and organizations: except through its determinate, concrete and specific liquidation in the form of a Messianic, apocalyptic eschatology as announced by the Hebrew, Christian and Islamic prophets many centuries ago? We aimed at an eschatological theodicy.

The Apocalyptic-Eschatological Reservation

The Messianic apocalyptic-eschatological theodicy, so we argued in our Dubrovnik discourse on the basis of our studies of the still living world-religions – Taoism, Shintoism, Hinduism, Buddhism, Judaism, Christianity, Islam, Bahai, etc. – may very well be the only possible one after the talion-theodicy, the test-theodicy, the freedom-theodicy and the inquiring theodicy have become obsolete in the face of the horror and terror of the 20th century history alone, not to speak of 7 million years of human evolution and the billions of years of natural evolution, in which almost every organism survived only through the killing of others until it was torn to pieces itself by a stronger one: shortly, the Messianic eschatological-apocalyptic reservation, which reaches from Isaiah to the book of revelation. Particularly the

Abrahamic religions – Judaism, Christianity, and Islam – have moved toward the most extremely revolutionary vision, that the same God who created the first creation had admitted intrinsically, that it is beyond repair, by promising to make all things new: the new heaven and the new earth without death, mourning, tears, murder, robbery and lies. The prophetic image of the new heaven and the new earth is the precise, but nevertheless inverted mirror script of the old earth and the old heaven on which and under which we find ourselves. The Marxist revolution against the capitalist world is harmless in comparison to the revolutionary impulses in the prophetic Abrahamic religions, which aim not only at the overthrow of one particular social system – be it the slaveholder society, the feudal society, or the capitalist society – but of the totality of the old universe, to which they all still belong: even a possible global alternative Future 3 – a society characterized by the freedom of All and by justice and by friendly and helpful living together. The iron law of death would still not be broken.

The Aristocratic Principle of Nature

In Dubrovnik, we discovered that the Messianic eschatological-apocalyptic theodicy has for its most extreme opposition in civil society the Machiavellian, social-Darwinistic, fascist, Hitlerian aristocratic principle of nature as well as the very similar old-liberal and neo-conservative postulate, that there must be winners and losers in nature as well as in history. According to the Messianic law as expressed in Isaiah 11:6–7 and 25:8 and in Revelation 21:4

> the wolf lives with the lamb,
> the panther lies down with the kid,
> calf and lion cub feed together
> with a little boy to lead them.
> The cow and the bear make friends,
> their young lie down together.
> The lion eats straw like the ox......
> The Lord Yahweh will wipe away
> the tears from every cheek.......

To the contrary, according to the aristocratic principle of nature announced by Hitler (1971) in his book *Mein Kampf (My Struggle)*, who knew the Bible very well, the wolf must eat the lamb and the panther the kid and the lion cub the calf and the bear the cow and the lion must consume all of them, if – as he put it – humanity was not to be destroyed, annihilated and buried and if this planet was not – as it did millions of years ago – to move through the ether devoid of men. It affirms the right of the strong over the weak, of the predator over the prey. Might is right!

Three Loves and Three Hates

Hitler applied, incorporated and concretized the aristocratic principle of nature in three loves – for Germanism, for the workers and for peace – and in three hates – against Judaism, against Communism and against France. The aristocratic principle allowed Hitler to sacrifice his love for peace for his love for the workers and for Germanism, and finally to sacrifice his love for the workers to his love for Germany. The aristocratic principle allowed Hitler to sacrifice his hate against France for his hate against communism and the Jews, and finally to sacrifice his hate against Communism to his hate against the Jews. Hitler's final expression of the aristocratic law was his absolute, i.e. idolatrous love for Germanism and his absolute hate for the Jews. Ultimately Hitler hated absolutely not only the Jewish race but also and even more so the Jewish religion: the Jewish prophetic, Messianic, eschatological-apocalyptic vision of the new heaven and the new earth which was to replace the old heaven and the old earth, in which one organism preserves itself only through the destruction of another organism. Hitler's aristocratic principle affirmed the old heaven and the old earth, their blood and soil and their horrible food chain and opposed most passionately the eschatological-apocalyptic, creative nihilism (*mae on*) of Judaism and tried to replace it by his own false Messianism and destructive, deadly, suicidal nihilism (*ouk on*) without hope. For this malignant fascist nihilism the ruins of Europe became the most terrible metaphors. The essential explanation is *Apres moi le deluge!* In this deepest sense, Hitler and his propaganda minister Dr. Joseph Goebbels were indeed the arch-positivists which Horkheimer accused them to be: the most extreme metaphysicians of what is the case, i.e. the old heaven and the old earth. They would have become known and famous as the greatest positivists if they had won the war and if they could have established global alternative Future 1 – what Horkheimer and Adorno called following Weber the totally administered society, of course in fascist rather than in Stalinist, or positivistic-technocratic form. These three forms of global alternative Future 1 were anticipated already in the 20th century in aesthetical form: liberal-positivistic-post-modernist, fascist and communist architecture in European and American cities showed an amazing similarity of spirit pointing toward alternative Future I: total bureaucratization, mechanization, automation, computerization and robotization.

Exalted Ruin-Polluted Success

Hitler's destructive nihilism survived, nevertheless, his own destruction. In his letter from Pacific Palisades, California, of July 15, 1944 to Herbert Marcuse in Washington D.C., Horkheimer (1996c:560–561) observed that this year seemed to be brighter on his 46th birthday, which was on July 19, 1944. The enemy of humanity, Hitler and his form of fascism, so Horkheimer declared, were breathing their last. Of course, while Stalingrad and Kursk had happened already, the Arden Offensive and the Battle of Berlin were still to come. It, nevertheless, looked to Horkheimer, as if the chance of peaceful work would materialize once again. However, so Horkheimer argued, the critical theorists' triumph had been spoiled once and for all. In Horkheimer's view, torture, despair and death had come to so many people of their own kind: the Jewish people. Untold hecatombs of destruction had been the fate of so great a part of the spiritual and material things the critical theorists had cherished. Therefore, the good news of the destruction of fascism by the Western and Eastern armies found the critical theorists in a miserable shape. It was difficult for Horkheimer to enjoy the thought that the evil forces of fascism had now to experience what the good ones had suffered for over a decade, from 1933 to 1944. Horkheimer did not enjoy the deeply Jewish and Islamic *Lex Talionis* at work in world – history! Horkheimer felt as if ruin had been exalted and success had been polluted. What else, so Horkheimer asked Marcuse on July 15, 1944, could the critical theorists say on the days they celebrated but that they would make the best use of the time which, as an undeserved favor of fortune, was left to them. Horkheimer knew that he and Marcuse had the same image of such use: the continuation of their theoretical work and perhaps the effort to teach a few students who were worth while. This was not mere resignation.

The Messianic Law

As a matter of fact, for almost a century the critical theorists of three generations have stood continually, most heroically and most consistently with and
for the – to be sure, in secular terms inverted – Messianic law versus the fascist
aristocratic principle of nature and have aimed in their theory and praxis at
global alternative Future III – a society in which – as Hegel (1967b) had put it
in the "Preface" to his *Philosophy of Law* – the rational would be real and the
real would be rational and right would also be might. However, as the decidedly anti-fascist critical theory allowed Messianic eschatological-apocalyptic
elements to migrate from the depth of the mythos and to be inverted into
its own secular social-scientific discourse, it remained, nevertheless, always
rooted in critical autonomous reason rather than in revelation and faith. It
was not theology, but rather profane philosophy and critical social science.
Concerning the modern dichotomy between the sacred and the profane,
mythology and enlightenment, the critical theorists stood and still stand
decidedly and consistently on the side of the revised bourgeois, Marxian and
Freudian enlightenment movements. The critical theorists tried to overcome
the dialectic of enlightenment by not – like the positivists – negating religion
abstractly, but rather determinately, and thereby to avoid a new failure of
nerve and a consequent relapse into mythology and the revival of exactly
the same supernatural entities and forces, or rather spirits, whose exorcism
had been the core of scientific thinking as a whole for centuries Such relapse
into mythology and return to spirits of all kinds out of a failure of nerve do
indeed happen not infrequently today particularly in departments of comparative religion, which otherwise fall very much in line with the predominant
positivistic trend in American and European universities in the midst of late
capitalist societies: they happen even in the most primitive and archaic forms
of witchcraft, astrology, spiritualism and the occult in general.

Religions and Cultures

Our Dubrovnik discourse of the past 31 years assumed with some good
reasons, that the differentiation and even antagonism between the old world
religions on one hand, and the modern scientifically and technologically
grounded and formed civil and socialist societies and their cultures on the
other, will probably continue and will even deepen in spite of all the sporadic,

so called religious renaissances of the 20th and 21st centuries. It is, however, unlikely that the modern or postmodern societies and cultures will simply drown out or replace the positive religions, as magic and fetishism had once been replaced by science and technology: at least not as long as the latter can not yet produce unconditional meaning, ethical validity claims and – most of all – consoling theodicy answers as once had been done by the great world-religions as well as by the arts and by the philosophies originally intrinsic to them. We assumed, nevertheless, in Dubrovnik, that the global secularization process will continue independently from the atheistic agitation or theistic counter-agitation of unbelievers or believers, and that the world religions will be threatened by obsolescence to the extent to which they can no longer give adequate answers to newly arising forms of the theodicy question: e.g. Auschwitz and Triblinka, Hiroshima and Nagasaki and all the terror and horror these names have stood for in the 20th century. In case this will be true, there may, nevertheless, still be present in late capitalist or early socialist societies and even in alternative Future 1 or 3 religious ideas, values, norms, symbols and practices, without which a global humanity may not be able to continue to exist humanely and humanize itself further, but may regress into a new barbarism. In this case, the question arises, how certain religious semantic and semiotic contents and potentials, motifs and motivations can possibly be rescued for and preserved creatively in a more and more secularized modern and postmodern society and culture and how they can possibly be actualized through communicative and political actions and movements?

The Idealistic Paradigm I

In the perspective of the new critical theory of religion, as developed out of the old one intrinsic to the original critical theory of society by the Dubrovnik circle, there are two paradigms for such rescue and creative preservation of semantic and semiotic materials and potentials from the depth of the mythos: e.g. the creation of man in freedom, the fall of man, the second and third commandment of the Decalogue, exodus, resurrection, redemption, Messianic light, Providence, etc. There is an idealistic and a materialistic paradigm. The idealistic Paradigm I was rooted in the dialectical philosophy of Hegel, in the poetry of Johann Wolfgang von Goethe and in the music of Ludwig van Beethoven. According to this Paradigm I as the original traditional Medieval unity of religion and secular culture was in modernity further and further differentiated to the point of an extreme, even hostile antagonism, so in post-modernity it may be restored again through the reconciliation of a transformed religion and a likewise changed secular culture, without the destruction of religions' absolute content on one hand, and the modern or postmodern autonomous dialectical rationality. Hegel found the solution of the theodicy problem in the intrinsic dialectical rationality and teleology of the political history as well as of the history of art, religion and philosophy, which would ultimately harness and overcome all physical and moral negativity. Goethe (1961) renewed in his *Faust I and II* the test-theodicy of the Book *Job*, the most advanced theodicy answer of Judaism: far beyond its original talion-theodicy. Beethoven expressed his theodicy answer in his *Missa Solemnis*, in which he returned from secular to religious music and which he considered to be his greatest work.

The Materialistic Paradigm II

The materialistic Paradigm II was developed by the critical theorists Adorno, Benjamin and Habermas. According to this Paradigm II as the secularization of the modern and postmodern society and culture continued rapidly, the religious semantic and semiotic elements, which were necessary for the humane survival of humanity, may not be able to be rescued and preserved any longer in a religious form, but only in a secular shape: namely, through their migration and inversion into secular philosophical and social-scientific discourse and through it into different forms of corresponding communicative and political actions toward alternative Future 3 – a society characterized by the friendly and helpful living together of human beings with human beings and with nature. At the same time such migration would be a test for the religious semantic and semiotic contents, if they can survive or not in a substantial sense in the modern and postmodern world. Through their inversion and critical rescue into secular form the religious semantic and semiotic materials, motifs and motivations may still be able to make a difference in modern and postmodern societies through their steering them <u>via</u> the latter's media of communicative and political actions: in the immediate life world and maybe through it also in the political and economic subsystems of civil society. This could happen, in spite of the fact that only the immediate life world is still characterized my communicative and mimetic rationality and action and steered over ethical and socio-ethical norms, while the economic subsystem is characterized by instrumental rationality and action and steered over the medium of money and the political subsystem is also characterized by functional rationality and action but steered over the medium of power.

Empowerment

Maybe, so we thought in terms of the materialistic Paradigm II in Dubrovnik, the semantic and semiotic materials and potentials from the depth of the mythos could still empower people living in extremely profane environments to resist further barbarization in the 21st century and to engage in the great refusal against global alternative Future 1 – the totally administered society and against global alternative Future 2 – the entirely militarized society. While e.g. Freud rejected the semantic element of Providence, which is present in several world-religions, his student Alfred Adler wanted to rescue it for psychological reasons. Following the Nietzsche-disciple Vaihinger's as-if-philosophy, Adler suggested that it could contribute to the psychic health of people if they would act and live as if there was a Providence: at least until science would have found a substitute in the form of a universal steering system, which still has not yet been discovered. While Habermas rejected following Kant any philosophical theodicy attempt and suggested that we had to live disconsolately in civil society, Benjamin and Adorno replaced ontology by eschatology and followed something like an inverted Messianic eschatological-apocalyptic theodicy. It found its most beautiful expression in Benjamin's early *Theological-Political Fragment* (1978:312–313) and in his late essay *On the Concept of History* (1969:253–264) as well as at the end of Adorno's (1974) *Minima Moralia* devoted and dedicated to his older friend Horkheimer. In Dubrovnik we preferred Benjamin's and Adorno's inverted eschatological theodicy over Habermas's methodological atheism which suggested a life without any deeper consolation whatsoever. Of course all the time in Dubrovnik we were fully aware of the fact that the prophetic, Abrahamic religions, Judaism, Christianity and Islam, were suffering from a most painfully open flank – the non-appearance of the Messiah. It certainly could also not be easily closed or simply be ignored by the idealistic Paradigm I or by the materialistic Paradigm II.

IV. Alternative Futures

In our Dubrovnik group we were fully aware, that throughout the 20th century the Frankfurt School's critical sociologists of society and religion had observed trends in the civil societies, which constitute the present Euro-American civilization, pointing toward three global alternative Futures. They were: Global alternative Future 1: the totally administered, mechanized, automated, computerized, cyberneticized and bureaucratized signal-society; Global alternative Future 2: the more and more militarized society, leading to conventional wars or civil wars, NBC wars, and connected ecological disasters; Global alternative Future 3: a society, in which personal autonomy and universal, i.e. anamnestic, present and proleptic solidarity will be reconciled.

Chances of Religion

In our Dubrovnik circle, we tried to estimate the chances of religion in the three global alternative Futures. We thought that in global alternative Future 1, which is very probable and possible, if also not very desirable, religion or theology may or may not be able to coexist. In alternative Future 2, which after the collapse of the Soviet Union and its empire in 1989 has become a little bit less probable and possible, but in any case is still utterly undesirable, religion will – depending on the extension of destruction – have no chance to exist at all, or will be able to exist in an entirely crippled, or distorted, or regressive ideological form: ideology understood as false consciousness, masking of class and tribal or national interests, or simply as the untruth. In our Dubrovnik group, we explored as critical theorists of religion trends in the present religious substructure of the Euro-American civil societies, which seemed to point into three alternative Futures of religion and enlightenment: alternative Future 1, which were closely connected with the global alternative Futures 1, 2 and 3. Those trends pointed to alternative Future 1 – Further expansion of fundamentalism, alternative Future 2: total secularization, alternative Future 3: New reconciliation of the sacred and the profane. In Dubrovnik we considered alternative Future 3 to have the greatest chance to be realized in the context of global alternative Future 3, if it should ever come about and be realized.

The Totally Other

In Dubrovnik we thought that in global alternative Future 3, which is very desirable, but unfortunately at present rather improbable and impossible, a religion, which – in terms of the critical theorists – would understand itself as longing for the totally Other, or for the absolutely Non-Identical, or for the absolutely New, or as the hope for perfect justice or unconditional love, or as the longing, that the murderer shall at least ultimately not triumph over the innocent victim, could certainly have a chance of survival and coexistence. Here in global alternative Future 3 even specifically Judeo-Christian-Islamic elements may survive. Here man may still be defined not in terms of radical immanentism as a god, or a wolf to his fellowman, but rather in terms of Biblical thought by his relatedness to others as pointed out in Luke 10:28: *"Thou shall love thy neighbor because he is like you."* However, in Judeo-Christian-Islamic perspective, man, a finite being, neither defines nor comprehends himself by himself but rather is defined and comprehended by God, the Infinite, the wholly Other, who – in terms of the second and third commandment of the Mosaic law – can neither be expressed in images nor be named. Horkheimer and Adorno concretely inverted and superseded the God of Israel and the God-hypostases of other world – religions into their longing for the totally Other as the negation of the identity of this world, which is neither nothing or all there is, but which is rather in terms of Judaism, Christianity and Islam a process of becoming moving towards its Messianic redemption, from which end-perspective it must be seen and understood and comprehended. While the critical theorists were hoping for the entirely Other as the source of unconditional meaning and validity claims – like truth, honesty, rightfulness, tastefulness and understandability – and possible theodicy solutions, that did not mean that they were not fully committed to communicative and political action directed toward global alternative Future 3 – the right society. To the contrary, this longing for the totally Other as the negation of the fundamental perils of human existence, gave the critical theorists a motivating answer to the question, why one should follow at all one's moral insights and act morally not only in civil society's everyday life-world, but particularly in its economical and political subsystems. In this respect Horkheimer's (1985:207–212; Ott 2006:115–120) statement may still be valid, that to rescue an unconditional meaning without God is utter vanity, and the second verse of Psalm 91 on his grave stone in the cemetery of Bern, Switzerland, may still make sense: *"In You, Eternal One, alone I trust!"*

Original Formation

While Horkheimer found help from Schopenhauer, Kant and Hegel much earlier than from Marx, it remains nevertheless true, that the latter played an important role in the formation of the critical theory of society. Obviously, Marx allowed the semantic potential of Messianism to migrate from the Jewish and Christian prophets into his own historical materialism and critique of political economics. Marx's historical materialism contained a secularized materialistic Messianism. There lies in genuine Marxism the Messianic longing and hope for human happiness on this earth. Marx and Marxists represented this then as the longing and hope for global alternative Future 3 – the good society, in which freedom and justice are realized and reconciled. With all that Horkheimer's and Adorno's and their colleagues' critical theory of society has to do in so far as it shares the underlying Messianic longing of Marxism for an earthly happiness.

Difference

However, there is an important difference as well between Marx's historical materialism and Horkheimer's critical theory of society. Contrary to Marx, Horkheimer and Adorno allowed another semantic element from the Torah and the Hebrew prophets – besides the Messianic one – to migrate into and to penetrate the secular discourse among the expert cultures and finally their own critical theory of society and to let their dialectic of theory and praxis be guided by the former – namely the second and the third commandment of the Mosaic law as they appear in Exodus 20:4–7:

> You shall not make yourself a carved image or any likeness of anything in heaven or on earth beneath or in the water under the earth: you shall not bow down to them or serve them. For I, Yahweh your God, am a jealous God and I punish the father's fault in the sons, the grandsons, and the great-grandsons of those who hate me; but I show kindness to thousands of those who love me and keep my commandments.

and

> You shall not utter the name of Yahweh your God to misuse it, for Yahweh will not leave unpunished the man who utters his name to misuse it.

In modern radicalized language the two commandments meant for Horkheimer and Adorno shortly: You can not imagine or name the Absolute. All three Abrahamic religions – Judaism, Christianity and Islam – share not only the Messianism but also the Mosaic Decalogue and precisely therefore are extremely anti-idolatrous. The totally Other, who is to be loved, is nameless and imageless. This theological core of the originally Jewish, but otherwise extremely secular Frankfurt School is directed not only against religious, but also – and particularly so – against secular idols: the idolization of nation, race, leadership, property, science, technology, capital, sex, car and career, and most of all against the fetishization of all commodities in a more and more globalized civil society in which increasingly almost everything is commodified – even human embryos and the eggs of beauty queens. Consequentially, Horkheimer and Adorno and their colleagues directed their empirical and experimental and therapeutic work – e.g. the Berkeley Project – against fundamental social illnesses and evils in American and German civil society: nationalism, anti-Semitism and other forms of racism and the corresponding hate crimes, anti-communism, anti-democratism and other fascist diseases and evils. The second and third generation of critical theorists continue this critical as well as therapeutic and rescuing work in the Frankfurt Institute for Social Research and elsewhere today.

God, Freedom and Immortality

For Horkheimer, the second and the third commandment of the Decalogue became identical with Kant's prohibition in his *Critique of Pure Reason* (1929), *Critique of Practical Reason* (1956) and *Critique of Judgment* (1951) that human thought was not even allowed to merely roam into the world of the thing itself: the dimension of God, freedom and immortality. For Kant, God as well as freedom and immortality were merely postulates. Finite man could not judge about God's qualities. The same judgment was valid for the truth. One could speak only negatively about the truth. Therefore, no positive philosophical theodicy solution was possible. The critical theorists obeyed the first and second commandment of the Decalogue more radically and strictly even than Kant, Hegel, or Marx, or the Marxists, or even the old Jews themselves had ever done. In the final analysis, the critical theorists determinately negated Kant's as well as Marx's work into their own critical theory as they in general superseded great philosophers – from Plato and Aristotle to Hegel, Schopenhauer, Nietzsche and Heidegger – and as they concretely sublated great art – from Goethe, Beethoven, Richard Wagner through Charles Baudelaire, Franz Kafka, Brecht to Samuel Beckett, Gustav Mahler and Alban Berg, and as they specifically superseded the great world religions – from Buddhism through Judaism to Christianity.

The Fall of Humanity

For Horkheimer it was thinkable that through intuition a small piece of the truth could be experienced. According to Horkheimer, one example was what Schopenhauer had said about the mythos of the fall of man in Genesis 3. In Schopenhauer's view, the teaching of the original sin was the most marvelous and splendid one in Judaism and Christianity. The fall of man had determined the previous world history. For the thinking person the original sin still determined the world of today. The fall of man was possible only under the presupposition, that God had created man with a free will. In Schopenhauer's view, the first thing which man did in Paradise was to commit this great sin, on the basis of which the whole history of humanity was really to be explained theologically. Religion, so Horkheimer interpreted Schopenhauer, had once a social function that it has lost in the civil society of today. Religion stated: If you do what is good in the sense of the particular positive religion, then you will be rewarded. If you do what is evil, if you sin, then you shall be punished. Hell awaits you. That, of course, the enlightened Schopenhauer denied. However, so Horkheimer insisted, Schopenhauer taught something similar. According to Schopenhauer, who ever did something bad and who with his will to life negated the will of the other individuals and who ever was seeking his happiness for the price of the happiness of the others, had to be born again in some way without knowing of his previous life. He had to go through all the sufferings himself until the suffering of the others was so close to him as a true and genuine martyr as his own suffering: until he could feel compassion and co-enjoyment. For Schopenhauer precisely this affirmation of one's own self and the negation of the other individuals was the fall of man: the original sin. Adorno expressed what Schopenhauer had said about the original sin in this way: "All in the world stands under a curse." The critical theory of society, which determinately negates in itself Kant, Marx and Schopenhauer, preserves in itself this intuitive piece of truth, among others.

Unconditional or Absolute Truth

In his early *Twilight – Notes*, Horkheimer (1978) stated that only the most stupid ones among the philosophical bootlickers of capital attacked Marx openly today – i.e. in 1926. The other philosophers rather received Marx's words and took them into their own jargon and deepened, extented and increased them into the cesspool of the newest metaphysics until they finally spread the same stench as e.g. Max Scheler's original ground of being or order of precedence among values. Thus, Horkheimer could hear those other philosophers talk of socialism as the perfect society and he could discover from them that this notion had been for Marx identical with the unconditional truth. However, so Horkheimer argued, as far as the truth was concerned the better order of society differentiated itself from capitalism essentially through the latter's existing in truth while the former was only in the process of becoming the truth. In Horkheimer's view, for the time being the better social order was one goal only: not the goal of history, but the goal of certain human beings. For Horkheimer, the metaphysical praising to the skies of that goal of the better social order as the absolute truth, or as the Messianic realm of God expressed merely the soothing, calming, pacifying, easing, relieving, settling and reassuring certainty, that the socialist order stood only at the end of time, and that no historical reality could possibly suffice this high standard, or criterion: particularly not the present industrial or late capitalist society. In Horkheimer's view, in this way the goal of the better social order as absolute truth or Messianic realm of God turned into ideology as false consciousness, masking of class and national interests, i.e. as untruth. Precisely in this sense the critical theory of society is essentially ideology – critique: no matter if such ideology is of a religious, or a secular nature.

The Optimum of Theoretical Truth

The Dubrovnik circle was aware of the fact that if there was any great philosophy, which served particularly as methodological prototype for the development of the critical theory of the Frankfurt School, then it was certainly Hegel's dialectical philosophy. It was, according to Horkheimer and Adorno, the standpoint of the highest consciousness, which the bourgeois class had ever reached and achieved of itself in the past three millennia. In discourse with Horkheimer, Adorno stated that the determinate negation of the Hegelian position would be the optimum of a theoretical truth that he could imagine. This was so for Adorno, in spite of the fact that the Hegelian standpoint was for the critical theorists – themselves being members of the German and American bourgeoisie and longing for the high-middle class style of life – the highest form of bourgeois identity-philosophy. For the critical theorists, Hegel's philosophy was identity-philosophy in spite of the fact that in his logic, in his teaching on being, he had criticized the "first": the beginning. Hegel's critique of the "first" or of the beginning was simply not good enough for the critical theorists measured by their demand for a critical philosophy of Non-Identity: a philosophy of the totally Other, the absolutely New. In spite of the fact that Adorno, Horkheimer, Benjamin and the other critical theorists found Hegel's identity-philosophy unacceptable, they nevertheless did their best to reach the *optimum* of a theoretical truth in their critical theory precisely through its concrete negation.

Migration

In each of our Dubrovnik-discourses between 1977 and 2007 we were concerned with several religious semantic materials, potentials, motifs and motivations. When Benjamin, Adorno and Habermas spoke of religious semantic potentials, motifs and motivations, which were to be tested by their migration and inversion from the depth of the mythos into secular scientific and philosophical discourses and into the likewise profane language of the everyday life world and even into communicative and political practice, they thought of the following elements: paradise, freedom, tree of knowledge, tree of life, original sin, the original curse, exodus, diaspora, the love of the neighbor, the second and the third commandment, Messiah, the Messianic energy, the realm of God, the Messianic intensity of the heart, immortality, resurrection, eternity, Messianic nature, redemption, salvation, Messianic light, redeemed humanity, truth, remembrance of the dead, anamnestic solidarity, the Anti-Christ, the hope for the innocent victims, the monastic *acedia*, the poor, the angels, the redeemer, the *kairos*, Messianic standstill, the *Nunc stans*, or Now-Time, prayer, the Infinite, finitude, last judgment, hell, the martyrs, the saints, peace, bliss, blessed state, compassion, migration of the soul, perfect justice, fear, Transcendence, etc. While these and other semantic and semiotic elements are concentrated particularly in Benjamin's and Adorno's critical theories of society, they can be found in Horkheimer's and the other critical theorists' writings as well.

Great Dreams

In Dubrovnik we were very much aware that many of these religious representations, images and concepts indicate great dreams not only in the individual's
personal but also in humankind's collective unconsciousness, from which
they may be awakened some day in order to be realized and actualized in
the bright daylight of world – history. Some of those individual or collective
dreams and the wishes they present – e.g. the tree of the knowledge of good
and evil, or of the tree of eternal life – can be very old as well as very new
at the same time, because the unconsciousness and its archetypes know of
no procession of time whatsoever. It was amazing for us in the Dubrovnik
circle to see, how tenacious those individual and collective dreams and their
widely unconscious wish fulfillment – potentials had been even in the face of
massive historical and metaphysical disappointments throughout the centuries
and even millennia. We discovered that no great technical invention had ever
been made of which humanity had not first dreamed for a long time: e.g. its
dream to learn to fly since the old Greek myth of Icarus, or its dream to go
to the moon. Why could or should the same not also be true of great social
or cultural dreams, or utopias, as well: e.g. the possibility and probability
of global alternative Future 3 – a society in which the fundamental antagonisms of modern civil society between the sacred and the profane, between
the genders, between the individual and the collective, between the classes
and between the races would have been worked out and fought through and
finally reconciled and the master-servant relationship in all its forms would
be dissolved as e.g. Thomas More (1965) foresaw it in his great book *Utopia*.
In any case, Marx (1979:29–32) did not think – as he made perfectly clear in
his famous letter to Arnold Ruge from Kreuznach in September 1843 – that
global alternative Future 3 – a communistic society, the arrival of which he
predicted, was an entirely new idea. To the contrary, Marx thought of it as
a very old dream of humankind, which had been dreamed many times. That
had happened e.g. in Christianity. More had had no doubt in his *Utopia* that
Jesus of Nazareth made communism the precondition for entering the Kingdom of God. The early Church was communistic. All Western monasticism
had been as communistic as all Eastern monasticism before. In Marx's view,
for sure, men and women would emancipate themselves from all forms of
class-domination some day and would realize their great dream of global
alternative Future 3 – an un-alienated, free, communistic society.

Communism and Christianity

When the so-called communistic empire in Eastern Europe collapsed in 1989 and people told the great German, European, Left-Catholic journalist, Walter Dirks, in the German Federal Republic that now the dream of communism had been dreamed out and gone under once and for all, he warned against such all too hasty and abstract liquidation, be it of socialism, or also of Christianity. Up to his death, he asked how something like communism or Christianity could possibly go under, when it had hardly ever existed yet in reality in the first place. Positivism, of course, as the metaphysics of what is the case is very much the end of all great social and cultural dreams of human kind. Particularly since the neo-conservative trend turn in the 1970's the younger generation, which had been pushed back again into what Weber (1958:181–183) had called the "iron cage" of capitalism through the Nixonian counter-revolution and the shooting of students at Kent State University and elsewhere is continually told to stop dreaming and to adjust to the status quo. Yet, the younger generations continue to dream nevertheless in different countries around the globe in the midst of the globalization of civil society. The Jews pray at the Wailing Wall in Jerusalem and dream of the restoration of their Temple. A Palestinian who can not go to the next village without Jewish permission and who is forever checked by Israeli check-lists and who is not allowed to pollute the Jewish purity of Israeli beeches continues nevertheless to dream of the sea washing the shores of his ancestral home. The great dreams cannot be stopped.

Re-enchantment or Rationalization?

In our international Dubrovnik – discourses of the past 31 years our intent has not been the re-enchantment of the already disenchanted everyday life world in modern civil society, but rather its rationalization: not only in terms of instrumental or functional rationality and action, but rather in terms of mimetic, communicative and anamnestic-proleptic rationality and praxis. Our very discourse has stood in the service of such communicative rationalization of the social interaction of the everyday life world and of the acquisition of the corresponding competence of social understanding and interaction. We have continued our discourse on "The Future of Religion" in Dubrovnik in April of every year from 1977 to 2007 and we have planned and prepared already our meetings for April 2008. We met even throughout the horrible four years of the Yugoslav civil war, and in the following period of intense nationalism and bourgeois counter-revolution and restoration. We even put our critical theory of religion into praxis and helped the innocent victims of the Yugoslav civil war with money and medicine. Nothing taught us better than the Yugoslav war the necessity to rescue religious semantic and semiotic materials, potentials, motifs and motivations in secular form for the profane world and thus to put them into the service not of the re-enchantment of the life world, but rather of its – not instrumental – but rather communicative and anamnestic/proleptic rationalization, in order thus to enable it to resist the always new waves of re-barbarization. During the Yugoslav civil war such re-barbarization cost over 250,000 human lives. The following attacks by NATO air-forces, against the sovereign territory of the newly constituted Yugoslavia, which were elicited in terms of psychological warfare and propaganda through the deception by the OSCE concerning the alleged Serbian "massacre" in the Kosovan village of Racak and other atrocities in other places in 1999, and which made even out of critical theorists NATO – philosophers and – theologians, killed another 10,000 civilians.

Ideology or Truth?

In Dubrovnik we remembered that throughout the 20th century the critical theorists perceived with great astonishment positivistically oriented sociologists in European and American universities being concerned with social questions without asking at all, how global alternative Future 3 – i.e. a better, or the right society, could possibly be established. The positivistic sociologists seemed to show a certain wink – attitude. It seemed to say, that the positivistic sociologist knew of course that all this utopian thinking about a better society was nothing else than ideological swindle and cheat: that there were no revolutions and no classes. These were merely inventions of certain special interest groups. Sociology consisted precisely in that, to transcend such inventions and interest groups through this winking know-all attitude. On their part Western positivist sociologists, who since 1989 took over the chairs of the former Marxist professors in the former German Democratic Republic could not understand, why their students, e.g. in Leipzig, were not satisfied with simply what was the case in the newly reestablished civil society, but wanted to know how it could possibly be improved toward alternative Future 3 – a free society. In Dubrovnik we found out that what even into the 21st century puts on an act as resistance of sociology against alleged theologumena of critical-theoretical thinking in European and American universities was nothing else than the former gesture of wink elevated into a system, or scientific theory. In this gesture is present the assertion that for a sociologist there does not exist any truth, because everything in civil society is conditioned by special interests. This, of course, was the concept of sociology developed first by Vilfredo Pareto, the teacher of Benito Mussolini. In Dubrovnik we were convinced that this fascist concept of sociology is fundamentally untrue out of the simple reason that through the negation of the notion of truth, which is present in this fascist representation of the totally ideological character of all socially related consciousness, the differentiation between true and untrue is made entirely impossible. Furthermore, one cannot speak of false consciousness if there does not also exist the possibility of truth. Of course, it has in general been the main function of the positivistic sociology rooted in the tradition of Comte and Pareto, Weber and Durkheim, Parsons and Luhmann to prevent as much as possible the rise of socialism, not to speak of communism, in civil society. In our Dubrovnik discourse we were and are guided by a negative notion of truth: truth as the negation of ideology. Maybe we could not say, what the true society or religion was, but we could at least recognize the wrong one by measuring it by its own norms.

V. The Historical-Idealistic Paradigm

In order to deal specifically with the theme of "The Future of Religion," i.e. the alternative Futures of religion, my colleagues and I employed in our Dubrovnik – discourses first of all historical idealism as developed from Kant through Johann G. Fichte and Friedrich W. J. Schelling to Hegel. We also used historical materialism as developed from Ludwig Feuerbach through the young Marx to the critical theorists of the Institute for Social Research at the Johann Wolfgang von Goethe Universität in Frankfurt a.M.: to Horkheimer, Pollock, Adorno, Benjamin, Sohn-Rethel, Fromm, Marcuse, Habermas and others.

From Historical Idealism to Historical Materialism

As a matter of fact, we moved more and more from historical idealism to historical materialism. Not only the historical-idealistic but also the historical-materialistic approach of the Frankfurt School has been well known globally since at least 1936: e.g. in Kyoto, Japan, where some parts of this essay was presented first as a paper at the Bukkyo University on September 19, 1997. Already in June 1936, Dr. Masashi Nedzu, Professor for Literature in Kyoto, had proposed to Horkheimer to translate his essays into the Japanese language. In his letter from the Institute of Pacific Relations at Yenchin University, near Peking, China, of July 30, 1936 to Horkheimer and his collaborators in the International Institute for Social Research at Columbia University, New York, the critical theorist and China-specialist Karl August Wittfogel recommended Nedzu as translator of his essays. According to Wittfogel, Nedzu was a scientifically highly educated young scholar, who could transfer Horkheimer's work into the Japanese language and culture with as much insight as could possibly be expected. Wittfogel knew Nedzu personally. Nedzu had made a name for himself through his sociological and prehistoric work among the younger and more progressed scholars of Japan. Wittfogel did not know if Nedzu would be able to reproduce all the subtleties of Horkheimer's dialectical argumentation. Wittfogel wanted even to say that this was improbable. However, Wittfogel assured Horkheimer, that he would hardly find anybody else who at that moment – in July 1936 – could possibly do that better than Nedzu. Therefore, Wittfogel was of the opinion, that one should let Nedzu try to represent the fundamental structure of Horkheimer's work to the Japanese. According to Wittfogel, Nedzu would and could certainly do that. He would do that with respect and with honest effort. Wittfogel considered it to be correct, if Horkheimer would ask Nedzu for inspection and examination of the text before its publication. In Wittfogel's view, if this could really be done at that moment considering the thousand technical difficulties, only the God of time and history could decide. In Dubrovnik we speculated, that maybe such translation could have helped to stem the flood of "Asian Arianism," fascism and barbarism before it lead to massive human suffering in China, all around the Pacific Ocean and in Japan itself and finally to its own catastrophe and disaster in 1945. We are now turning to a more detailed consideration of the transition from the historical idealist to the historical materialist paradigm as it has taken place in our Dubrovnik discourses between 1977 and 2007, as we were in process to develop a new critical theory of religion, possibly including even a critical political theology.

Traditional Union, Modern Disunion, Postmodern Reunion

In 1977, the interdisciplinary group of scholars of the international course on "The Future of Religion" in the IUC, Dubrovnik, started out its exploration of the alternative Futures of religion first of all with the help of the historical-idealistic, mostly Hegelian paradigm. Following this idealistic dialectical model we moved from the Medieval unity between the religious and the secular consciousness, language and action, through their Modern disunion, to their possible post-Modern reunion in the American and/or Slavic World. In our Dubrovnik discourse we used the word "post-Modern" or "post-Modernity" not in the deconstructionist sense, as proposed e.g. by Emmanuel Levinas, Jean Baudrillard, Alain Finkielkraut, Jacques Derrida, J. Lacan, Bataille, Michel Foucault, C. Castoriadis, or Fredric Jameson, but rather in the original Hegelian understanding. While the deconstructionists mean with post-Modernism really a kind of anti-Modernism in the romantic tradition and thus have no real vision of a post-Modern world which would or could follow the present Euro-American life form, Hegel foresaw global alternative Future 3 in the form of a post-European, post-bourgeois, post-Modern American and Slavic World, in which the universal and the particular, the collective and the individual, the traditional universal solidarity and the modern personal autonomy and sovereignty would be balanced and reconciled the first time in world-history. In Dubrovnik many of our theoretical as well as empirical studies were concerned with the Modern dichotomy between the sacred and the profane consciousness, language and action and as such were placed into the perspective and the context of a post-Modern American and Slavic World in the Hegelian sense.

Theists and Atheists

From 1977 on, we found out in our Dubrovnik circle through mainly empirical studies, that the contradiction between the religious and the secular consciousness, language and liturgical and ethical praxis was continually deepening in modern civil society, no matter if it was resisted by theists in Europe and America, or if it was promoted by atheists or agnostics in the former communist Eastern Europe; if it happened in the revolutionary communist era, which did not particularly favor religion, or in the counter-revolutionary, post-communist, bourgeois restoration period, which once more tried to emphasize and cultivate it as a means of social control, integration, stabilization: shortly, as – in the words of the late Niklas Luhmann – contingency-experience-management subsystem of civil society. Those of us in Dubrovnik who had anticipated that after the breakdown of atheistic communism in Eastern Europe in 1989 there would be a mass-return to traditional religion, e.g. to the Orthodoxy in Russia or Serbia, or to Roman Catholicism in Poland or Croatia, or to Protestantism in East Germany were thoroughly disappointed. Even many of those people in Eastern Europe who gave up socialism, or communism, did nevertheless remain atheists. There were no more baptisms performed per year in Eastern European states after the fall of the Berlin Wall than there had been before. Of course, for the Dubrovnik circle the contradiction between the sacred and the profane did not only happen on the level of culture and social organization but was also deeply internalized by the individuals involved: here, on the level of the individual and social character structure it appeared as a spiritual schizophrenia in terms of the interpretation of reality and orientation of action, which is in need of psycho-and logo-therapy.

Threefold Dialectic

In our course on the future of religion in Dubrovnik, we discovered with the help of the historical idealists and through our own empirical research a three-fold dialectic being at work in the history of the Western Civilization. There was for us first of all the fundamental dialectic between the religious and the secular consciousness, language and action: their union, disunion and possible reunion. In his *Phenomenology of Spirit*. Hegel (1967a:73) had described first the original Medieval unity between the sacred and the profane in the following rather precise way:

> Time was when man had a heaven, decked and fitted out with endless wealth of thoughts and pictures. The significance of all that is, lay in the thread of light by which it was attached to heaven; instead of dwelling in the present as it is here and now, the eye glanced away over the present to the Divine, away, so to say, to a present that lies beyond.

Then Hegel identified equally exactly the development of the modern disunion between the secular, i.e. what is earthly, and the sacred, i.e. what is beyond, the Divine:

> The mind's gaze had to be directed under compulsion to what is earthly, and kept fixed there; and it has needed a long time to introduce that clearness, which only celestial realities had, into the crassness and confusion shrouding the sense of things earthly, and to make attention to the immediate present as such, which was called Experience, of interest and of value.

Finally, Hegel anticipated equally clearly a possible new reunion of the secular and the religious, the earthly and the heavenly:

> Now we have apparently the opposite of all this; man's mind and interest are so deeply rooted in the earthly that we require a like power to have them raised above that level. His spirit shows such poverty of nature that it seems to long for the mere pitiful feeling of the Divine in the abstract, and to get refreshment from that, like a wanderer in the desert craving for the merest mouthful of water. By the little which can thus satisfy the needs of the human spirit we can measure the extent of its loss.

Nothing made clearer to us that this loss had not yet been overcome in late capitalist society than the continual use of the abstract and as such completely empty expression of and demand for more "spirituality" in the midst of a positivistic wasteland, or of the likewise pitiful and impotent jargons like "authenticity", or "encounter", or "rediscovery of spirit" in different scientistic circles in late bourgeois society. In our perspective, the realization of such concepts would need a dialectical identity change in the antagonistic totality of civil society, which so far has not yet occurred. However, in our view there was not only a continuing dialectic between the religious and the secular going on in modern civil society, but there was secondly also at work a dialectic in the profane dimension itself, in the bourgeois, Marxist and Freudian enlightenment movements: a dialectic of enlightenment. Thirdly, there was a dialectic happening in the sacred sphere itself: a dialectic of religion. We were not only concerned with the continual broadening of the abyss between the religious and the secular in modernity – in spite of all kinds of sporadic religious renewals – but also with the deep dialectic of enlightenment – i.e. its turning against itself – as well as with the likewise dramatic and tragic dialectic of religion – its own inner contradictions with itself.

Attacks and Rearguard Struggles

The Dubrovnik scholars traced the attacks of the secular sciences against religion from Galileo, Copernicus and Newton through Schopenhauer, Darwin, Marx and Nietzsche to Freud. For 400 years, every enlightenment attack was answered by the rearguard struggles of the Churches, which again and again were broken off and an adaptation was – later rather than sooner – achieved by them to the progress of enlightenment: be it to the bourgeois enlightenment, the Marxian enlightenment, or the Freudian enlightenment. Only in very recent years, the Vatican declared, that Galileo and Darwin may have been right after all. Often we found a large culture lag on the religious side. Religious people seemed to be slow learners. To be sure, also slow learning has its advantage: one does not make so many mistakes! But the disadvantage was greater. A religious community that offers to the world a message of liberation and redemption makes this task difficult for itself through slow learning. The general resistance of religion against scientific and technological discoveries and inventions as well as against social revolutions and the final breakdown of it, had necessarily to lead to an enormous credibility lack, which made the acceptance of the religious message of salvation and liberation by modern people more and more difficult.

The Dialectic of Enlightenment

The Dubrovnik circle discovered, that there was not only a dialectic between religion and enlightenment, but also in enlightenment itself. With Hegel's (1984) *Philosophy of Religion* we understood religion as finite man's elevation to the Infinite, the Unconditional, the Absolute. For us, mythology was the attempt to present the world as a more or less harmonious totality, in which all negativity was interpreted away. Each mythology tried to solve the theodicy problem: the dichotomy between the justice of the Gods or God on one hand, and the injustice of their or his world on the other. As the myth appeared like a second nature, it chained people to the first one. Not only philosophy but theology as well were mythology critique from their very start: not only the theology of nature and the political theology but also – and particularly so – the theology of myths. Theology, as we understood it, was much closer to secular radical enlightenment than to mythology. Radical enlightenment was for us the attempt to free people from their fears and to make them into masters of their fate. Monotheistic theology and radical enlightenment were both the determinate negation of myths and mythologies. They both intended to liberate people from the boring repetitions and thus from the spell and the curse of the second nature, and thus also from the ban of the first nature, which was justified by the former.

Abstract and Concrete Negation

However, so we discovered in Dubrovnik, unfortunately often the enlighteners' negation of mythological religion had not been determinate, specific and concrete, but rather indeterminate, general and abstract. Often the enlighteners gave up religion altogether and completely. They threw out – so to speak – the baby with the bath water. They engaged in a bad reductionism of religious legacies. They did not ask, if there were not maybe present already pieces of genuine and radical enlightenment in the midst of myths and mythologies themselves, which were worthy to be rescued: as Hegel and others had proven particularly in terms of Taoist, Hindu, Buddhist, Persian, Syrian, Egyptian, Jewish, Islamic, Greek, Roman and Christian myths and mythologies. They did not engage in a good reductionism of religious legacies. It was simply not good enough when Nietzsche, the last great bourgeois enlightener, merely declared that Christianity had failed or that God was dead. Nietzsche should also have asked, which tasks the failure of Christianity – if indeed it was a fact – left behind for modern philosophy, or for the social sciences, or the humanities to articulate and to carry out and to fulfill. Also Marx's and Freud's enlightenment movements were not concrete enough and thus both fell – like that of Schopenhauer and Nietzsche – victim to – what Hegel, Adorno and Horkheimer had described and called – the dialectic of enlightenment. The result of the enlighteners' merely general rather than specific negation of religion turned over dialectically into what already Hegel had called the triteness and shallowness of knowledge, which then sooner than later produced the return of the repressed mythos.

Positivistic Enlightenment

According to the Dubrovnik circle, here following Hegel, Horkheimer, Adorno and the other critical theorists, the trite, dull, shallow and even dark knowledge of a merely positivistic enlightenment has finally lead to the end of enlightenment: to neo-conservativism and deconstructionism. It has ultimately brought about a regression into mythology, neo-paganism and neo-fascism: sometimes even in pseudo-Christian forms. Thus, the neo-conservative President Ronald Reagan reproduced more or less consciously the Persian myths of Ahura Mazda, the God of Light, and Arhiman, the God of darkness, who was to be conquered by the former, or of Mithras, the representation of goodness, and the Bull, the symbolization of evil, who was to be slaughtered by the former, when every Saturday he spoke to the American nation on the radio – in terms of a dualistic political Manichaeism – about the struggle between the realm of darkness or the evil empire, the Soviet Union, on one hand and the realm of light, or the good empire, the United States, the leader of the Free World, on the other. The dream and utopia of a Free World – in which All would be free – was transformed into the mythology and ideology of the Western World, in order to cover up and mask its rather unfree freedom of the Few: the owners of capital. In addition the President used the Hebrew myth of Armageddon, when he predicted the victory of the forces of the North, the American forces of light, over the Soviet forces of darkness. These Persian and Hebrew myths were used with the intent to kill: as have been the myths about the killer whales, or about the sharks, which the enlightened natural sciences have tried to demytholo-gize and thus to overcome, in order to rescue the fish. These Persian and Hebrew myths made it easier for President Reagan and Chancellor Helmut Kohl in 1985 to honor on the cemetery of Bitburg at the same time both: the SS – murderers and their Jewish victims. The counter-revolutionary political application of the Persian and Hebrew myths succeeded even, when in 1989 the "evil" Soviet Empire collapsed. There exists of course in late capitalist society the overall polytheism, with Mammon or Pluto being the supreme gods: who in the end has made most money has won! And what then: noth-ing! At the same time there happens in bourgeois society the general ten-dency toward global alternative Future I: a society which Weber had called already an extremely integrated, bureaucratic, iron cage and that George Orwell and Aldous Huxley had described in detail as an either Hitlerian-fascist, or Stalinistic-communistic, or positivist-technocratic dystopia, and which Adorno thought with extreme horror had already happened, and which Horkheimer considered as still being in the process of coming, and which the Parsonian Luhmann considered to be a trivial presupposition. Orwell

(1949:17, 228) characterized in his novel *1984* the global alternative Future 1 most adequately, when he stated:

> War is Peace! Freedom is Slavery! Ignorance is Strength! …Two and Two Make Five! God is Power! The Principles of Newspeak!

Today on February 13, 2001, even all the bourgeois mass media announce the newest gene discoveries as important steps toward alternative Future 1 – Huxley's (1946) *Brave New World*. Enlightenment as mass deception! Limits of enlightenment! Dialectic of enlightenment!

Providence

When we met in Dubrovnik during the bloody Yugoslav civil war and had to have our discourse in the basement of Hotel Argentina next to the room of the UN observers of the conflict and were even shot at while we brought medicine and money in order to help the innocent victims, we experienced once more the full realization of these cruel Persian and Hebrew myths translated into the 20th century. It was only a small step from the God-sent Ante Pavelic to the likewise God-sent Franjo Tudjman. According to Croatian political theologians, both nationalist dictators were – in spite of the fact of being 50 years apart – not only brought in and established through what Hitler had always called Providence, but were therefore also correctly supported by the Vatican and Germany as well: *Deus vult!* *[God's Will!]* Donoso Cortes and Carl Schmitt were still very much alive even at the end of the 20th century. Of course, only the Right, which makes plentifully use of the myths of origin as well as of Providence, seems to have God-sent leaders. Such regressions into mythology are the exact opposite of the critical theorists' attempt to let migrate and invert progressive semantic potentials from the depth of the mythos into the scientific discourse among the expert cultures and through them into communicative and political praxis in order precisely thereby to prevent any return into barbarism.

The Dialectic of Religion

In Dubrovnik we became aware that unfortunately there existed not only a dialectic of enlightenment, but also a dialectic of religion. Not only enlightenment can be perverted into ideology, but religion as well. We understood ideology not in the uncritical sense of a combination of ideas and values, but rather in the critical sense as false consciousness, as masking of national, class and race interests and in general as sinful social structures. To be sure, precisely because there has taken place such a dialectic of religion, religious people do not have the privilege to stand safely at the shore of the wild and murderous river of history, and criticize and judge comfortably the dialectic of enlightenment. Only too often the religion of truth has turned against itself and has become the ideology of slaveholders, feudal lords, and capitalists and of whole imperialistic nation states. Only too often the religion of love provided the ideological justification for hate crimes: for 200 years of crusades, for the murder of innumerable heretics, for the annihilation of 10 million so-called witches, and for the conduct of most bestial so called just or holy wars. Often religious wars were even more beastly than civil wars and even more horrible than any secular wars for economic purposes. For centuries, army chaplains blessed the soldiers and the weapons of opposing belligerent nations. For centuries, French and German Christian soldiers celebrated the mass early in the morning on both sides of the Rhine River and then marched against each other and shot and bayoneted each other: the *Corpus Christi Mysticum* butchered itself again and again. In August 1945, American army chaplains blessed even the most advanced murder weapons of World War II: the atomic bombs which destroyed the cities of Hiroshima and Nagasaki and killed over 100 000 civilians. Even the so called "God-believing" SS, Hitler's elite troops and administrators of his concentration camps, had its Catholic and Protestant chaplains. What indeed has Mother Theresa, the peaceful friend of the poor and the powerless classes in India, to do with the Indian or any other army, and the soldiers who carried her coffin through the crowded streets of Calcutta and saluted her with gun fire?

Fundamentalism

In Dubrovnik we did not only ask, how religion would be situated in case of the realization of each of the three global alternative Futures, but also which futures of religion we could possibly derive from the dialectic of the religious and secular consciousness, language and action, from the dialectic of enlightenment and from the dialectic of religion. We considered it possible, that people – being disgusted and alienated by the dialectic of enlightenment – could turn away from the project of secular modernity and could try to return to the religion of their fathers. After all, while so far modernity has fulfilled its promises concerning the development of power-guided instrumental-functional-technocratic rationality and action, it has disappointed most hopes concerning the evolution of a mimetic – communicative rationality and interaction: global alternative Future 3 – the right society characterized by the friendly and helpful living together of human beings with each other and with nature. Thus the turning away from the project of modernity happens today in liberal democratic societies not only in the deconstructionist movement but also on the fundamentalist wings of the great world religions: Hindu, Jewish, Christian, Islamic fundamentalisms. Often the religious fundamentalism is connected with a political fundamentalism: the religious with a political, authoritarian, fascist personality type. While such religious fundamentalism is felt to be valuable by millions of religious people today, there is nevertheless also a high human price to be paid for it. A consequential religious fundamentalism means the separation of believers not only from the project of modern enlightenment, but also from world – history as such, determined by its innumerable discoveries and inventions. There is the danger of hypocrisy: that religious fundamentalists, who turn their back to modernity and make no contributions to it, do nevertheless enjoy its fruits: cars, airplanes, electricity, weapons, medicine, etc.

Total Secularization

In the Dubrovnik community of scholars we also considered the possibility that millions of people, disgusted by and alienated from religion because of its intrinsic dialectic, aim at the destruction of religion and at the total secularization of society. For them religion has been a childhood affair of the human species, which has to be left behind without trace as fast as possible. Man has to grow up fast on his long march from animality to freedom. This is particularly true in the bourgeois and socialist upper classes and elites. Even the critical theorists have been tempted to plead for the destruction of religion, because it merely hides reality more than it reveals it: not only sexuality, but also death, and the processes of economical and political reproduction and control. The only reason, why the critical theorists wanted as radical enlighteners nevertheless to preserve semantic and semiotic elements from different world-religions was their most noble aspect: the remembrance of the dead. The only reason, why the critical theorists used theological categories at all and why they wanted to rescue some semantic and semiotic potentials, motifs and motivations from the depth of the mythos, was their desperate hope, not for themselves, but rather for the others: for the redemption of the hopeless, of the innocent victims of history, who had been destroyed without ever having had their day in court: the slaves, the serfs, the wage laborers, the slum-dwellers, the degraded, the exploited, the humiliated. Their desperate hope for the others made the critical theorists walk on a ground, under which there was nothing else than hell. Having been ashamed of having survived the *Shoah*, the holocaust, because of an undeserved favor of fortune, the first, mainly Jewish generation of critical theorists saw their main purpose in life in becoming the voice for the voiceless: the innocent victims, who having the sand of their graves in their mouths, could no longer speak for themselves, while their murderers triumphed over them in an already almost reached global alternative Future 1 – in the totally administered secular world without unconditional meaning, or love, or the longing and the hope for the entirely Other. Even during this approach to the very close global alternative Future 1 – so Horkheimer had argued during his last television interviews in Germany during the late 1960's and early 1970's up to his death – the critical theorists had, nevertheless, still to try to do the good, while one had to expect the worst. Sometimes the critical theorists compared their critical theory of society with the "mail in the bottle" which shipwrecked sailors would throw into the stormy Atlantic Ocean along the Latin-American coast in order to tell those who would find it on the safe beach maybe many years later, what their final fate had been.

Resource of Meaning

For the Dubrovnik group, no matter how advantageous the move toward the totally secularized society might be, also here massive human costs were definitely involved. For a long time, religion had given the answers not to how – questions, but rather to why – questions of the human existence. For a long time, religion had answered questions concerning the where – from and the where – to of human life: questions concerning the origin and most of all the goal and meaning of personal biography and collective history. At least in the Western Civilization up to Kant or maybe even up to Habermas and Apel, all morality and ethics and social ethics had been rooted in theology. Thus, religion continually replenished the resource of meaning and of the ethical validity claims in traditional and even still modern civil society. However, increasing secularization in bourgeois and socialist societies meant necessarily the depletion of the resource of meaning. In secular sociological perspective, modern humanity looks like a circus, which comes out of darkness, puts up its tent at the crossroads, does its acrobatics and clownery, takes its tent down again and then once more disappears into darkness. Nihilism! The further depletion of the resource of meaning leads to more boredom and more boredom to a higher demand for drugs. The abuse of drugs is not only a supply problem, but also a demand problem as well. From the rising demand for drugs in late capitalist society we can conclude the rising level of boredom and from the increase in boredom the degree of the depletion of the resource of meaning, and vice versa. Since the global alternative Future 1 – the totally administered society – will probably be even more boring than the present late capitalist society and will therefore need even more drugs, in Dubrovnik we could only hope that the chemists will invent drugs which are less damaging for human health than those which are used presently in large quantities. So far the positive sciences can not replenish the losses in the resource of meaning stemming from the departure of religion At least part of the Dubrovnik circle agreed with Habermas: we must live disconsolately. Positive science can not even tell us concerning the ethical validity claims, why it is better to love than to hate, except because it is better for business. But sometimes, of course, it has been better for business to hate than to love: e.g. to hate Jews in fascist Germany, or Blacks in the American South.

Reconciliation

Finally, the scholar's in Dubrovnik did not only discover the possibility and probability of alternative Future 1 – religious fundamentalism, and of alternative Future 2 – the end of religion in the totally secularized society, but also of alternative Future 3 – the possible reconciliation between monotheistic religion and radical enlightenment. Here the Dubrovnik scholars tended to follow Hegel's prediction, that positive science which had set itself apart from religion and had continually attacked it, would some day return to it again. In any case, the reunion between religion and secularity would have to happen in such a way, that neither the absolute content of religion nor the dialectical reason would be damaged. To be sure, the finite analytical understanding would have to surrender itself to dialectical reason as well as to religious faith in the Absolute. In any case, their post-modern reconciliation would mean change for faith as well as for reason. In Dubrovnik, scholars who wanted to overcome the dialectic of enlightenment met with scholars, who wanted to overcome the dialectic of religion and in discourse both partners thought about a new balance, or reconciliation, of the religious and the secular, in which both would change, but the dignity of neither religion or the enlightenment, revelation or reason, faith or society, faith or history would be imperiled, or damaged.

Isolated Priesthood

Already in Hegel's philosophy of religion the secular returned to the religious without doing any harm to its own dialectical comprehension or to the absolute content of religion Likewise Beethoven's already extremely secularized music returned again to religion in the form of the *Missa Solemnis*, which he considered to be his best work, and Goethe's (1961) extremely secularized Faust of Volume I returned nevertheless again to religious redemption in Volume II. As Hegel before, we were, of course, fully aware of the fact that this philosophical, musical or poetical reconciliation of the sacred and the profane was only a partial one: without external, sociological universality. Already Hegel had spoken – as later on Comte, the inventor of the words positivism and sociology – of an isolated priesthood of philosophers. Thus for us in Dubrovnik, philosophy, music and poetry were a separate sanctuary in antagonistic civil society. The philosopher, the musician and the poet constituted an isolated priesthood, which was not allowed to go together with and be conform to dichotomous civil society, and which had to guard and to watch over and to protect the truth. However, for the philosopher, the musician and the poet the question – as Hegel had put it – how the temporal, empirical bourgeois society, particularly the poor classes, was to find its way out of the modern dichotomy between the religious and the secular, monotheistic faith and radical enlightenment, not to speak of the modern antagonism between the genders, between the collective and the individual, between the classes, the rich and the poor, the bourgeoisie and the proletariat, between the races, and thus, and how it was possibly to constitute itself in its own subjectivity, and how it was to survive humanely, seemed to be left to itself and seemed not to be the immediate practical task and concern of philosophy, or art, be it music or poetry.

Unreified Transcendence

For 31 years believers have met in our international course in Dubrovnik, who have repented deeply the dialectic of religion, with enlighteners, who have reflected on and have overcome the dialectic of enlightenment and its ideology, in order to determine, if monotheistic religion and radical enlightenment have indeed become obsolete, or if they are still alive and thus can possibly be reconciled in terms of what they have in common – unreified Transcendence. They asked if thus together faith and autonomous reason could have a future into the 21st century after the disqualification both have suffered in the 20th century and in general in the cruel stream of world-history has been removed through repentance and reflection and the corresponding atonement-praxis. Doing so, the believers and enlighteners in Dubrovnik transcended already the historical-idealist model from which they had started out in the first place.

VI. The Historical-Materialist Model

Precisely concerning this alternative Future 3 – the reconciliation of monotheistic religion and radical enlightenment on the basis of unreified Transcendence – the Dubrovnik scholars felt driven by its obvious deficiency – its lack of sociological universality – to engage in a paradigm change. Following the guidance of the critical theorists, particularly Benjamin and Adorno, the Dubrovnik researchers concretely superseded the historical-idealistic paradigm into the historical-materialistic model.

Inverse Theology

At least some of the Dubrovnik discourse partners, who were particularly influenced by the Frankfurt School and its critical theory, broke out of the Hegelian, still very theological as well as very metaphysical historical-idealistic paradigm and its balance – or reconciliation – program, and began to follow what Benjamin and Adorno had developed and called inverse theology during their working-vacations on the Island of Ibiza from April to July 1932. According to this inverse-theological, historical-materialistic model, the secular did not any longer return to the religious, but, nevertheless, still critically rescued some of the latter's semantic materials, potentials, motifs and motivations for the secular world. Benjamin and Adorno expressed the relationship of inversion in matter of fact images and metaphors like brushing something the wrong way; the wrapping and the thing that is wrapped up; the pocket and its contents; the photographic development of a negative. The basic form of these reversals was what Adorno called secularizing theology in order to save it. Thus, according to Adorno's and Benjamin's inverse theology, one could hold on to theological and metaphysical semantic materials, motifs and motivations in late capitalist society only by bringing them wholly and completely into the secular dimension. If those religious semantic resources, motifs and motivations were expressed directly, they would be subject to a triumphant misunderstanding, which may then call itself negative theology. Thus, when Adorno and Benjamin and other critical theorists included theological semantic potentials, motifs and motivations in their comments on contemporary civil society, they did so not in order to transcend them, but rather in order to keep them alive in a worldly disguise. For all critical theorists undisguised theological discourse was past saving.

Salvation as the End of History

Benjamin and Adorno were searching for a lost age of a historical consciousness, for which salvation was not teleological, as the goal of history, but rather religious, as its end. Both critical theorists did not work in a logically consistent way, for their studies lived precisely in the paradoxical inversions of political and religious extremes into one another: e.g. the Jewish mysticism of Scholem and the Marxist poetry of Brecht. Benjamin and Adorno protected *theologumena* precisely by means of their inversion. The critical theorists' exodus from philosophy into commentary on bourgeois society can then indeed be referred to as inverse theology. For the critical theorists, particularly when theology stood face to face with all possible forms of fascism, particularly religiously interpreted fascism, or of positivism, it was forced into inversion. For Benjamin and Adorno, even a purely religious theocracy was related to the purely secular ordering of the secular. But this relationship of the sacred and the profane must not be misunderstood simply as secularization or profanation as it happened in the late Roman Empire in the process of syncretism. It must rather be conceived of as a paradoxical, mutual inversion of the religious and the secular realms of consciousness and action into each other. For Benjamin and Adorno, the kingdom of God was not the goal but rather the end of history. For the critical theorists, out of the alliance with the past arose the demand that revolution no longer be regarded as a goal, but rather as an interruption of the horrible historical continuum of force and counter-force, of crime and punishment, of guilt and atonement, shortly of the *Lex or Jus Talionis*. This was precisely what made it possible for the critical theorists to relate revolution to the end of history. The nameless and image-less Absolute, the totally Other, was the end of time: the end of history.

Three Assumptions

Adjusting to the massive secularization and profanation of civil society and its culture particularly since the end of German idealism with Hegel's death in 1831, the historical-materialistically inclined scholars in the Dubrovnik circle started from three assumptions. Firstly, the enlightenment – disenchantment – and secularization – process cannot be steered back again to traditional positive religion, and thus be stopped. The traditional positive religions have definitely become obsolete, because they are no longer able under modern conditions to solve the theodicy problem on the present level of social evolution, learning and experience. For masses of people there has been no divine counter-movement to the prayers of the believers in extreme distress throughout the 20th century, be it in Auschwitz or in Triblinka, in Hiroshima or in Nagasaki, or anywhere else. Secondly, religion contains, nevertheless, semantic materials, resources, potentials, motifs and motivations which have not only been necessary for the previous humanization of the human species, but which may continue to be needed also for the further humanization of humanity as it moves into the 21st century. Thirdly, those religious semantic potentials, motives and motivations must be rescued for the modern world, so that further regression into barbarism can be prevented. They can, however, probably not be rescued in a religious form, but only in a secular shape. At least some of the Dubrovnik researchers accepted the critical theorists' final resolution of the modern schizophrenia between the religious and the secular consciousness and action: the religious contents are to be critically tested and rescued by their migrating and thus by their being inverted into the secular argumentative discourse among the expert cultures and furthermore into communicative and political praxis in direction of global alternative Future 3: a society in which personal autonomy and universal, i.e. anamnestic, present and proleptic solidarity will be reconciled. Beyond that, this profane, not strategic, but rather practical discourse will on its part move toward the totally Other, the New, the Non-Identical, into which all past God-hypostases will be concretely sublated. The entirely Other is to negate radically, but still determinately, the perils of human existence which have constituted the theodicy problem from the very start of the history of the world – religions as well as of great philosophy and great art. In this sense, the totally Other contained indications for the ultimate solution of the theodicy problem: the murderer will ultimately not triumph over his innocent victim! While the critically oriented Dubrovnik scholars criticized religion in so far as it had covered up reality mythologically and ideologically, as indeed it often did, they tried nevertheless to rescue religious semantic materials, motifs and motivations in so far as they were still able to disclose and reveal reality.

Good and Bad Religion

What allowed the critically-oriented Dubrovnik scholars still to be concerned with religion at all, was their differentiation between – what Horkheimer (1978:163) had called – good and bad religion: between a religion, which changes things toward global alternative Future 3 – the right society, and a religion, which gilds the extant wrong society. Like the critical theorists, the Dubrovnik scholars remained interested in religion and its future because of their desperate hope for the others: the innocent victims of history. Here the Dubrovnik scholars were concerned particularly with Benjamin's good religion. Benjamin helped them most in their attempt to rescue religious semantic potentials, motifs and motivations into their secular psychological, sociological, philosophical, religiological and even theological discourse for the sake of global alternative Future 3 and beyond that the totally Other as source of unconditional meaning, validity claims and theodicies.

The Theological-Political Fragment

In the years 1920/1921, the by now 28/29 years old Benjamin (1979) formulated in his *Theological-Political Fragment* the first time the very core of his mystical – Messianic – eschatological – apocalyptic political theology in all clarity and precision: that history had not to be understood as development towards redemption, and that thus it did not have an ultimate goal in itself, but that it was dependent on a Messianic redeemer and interruption. Two years earlier, Benjamin's and his wife's only son, Stephan, had been born. In the same year 1918 Benjamin had become acquainted with the Schellingian Marxist Ernst Bloch and the Marxist literary critique Georg Lukacs, who both influenced him deeply. Only one year later, in 1919, Benjamin (1996:116–200) had received his doctorate at the University of Bern for his dissertation *The Concept of Art Criticism in German Romanticism* with *summa cum laude*. After his promotion, Benjamin returned again together with his wife Dora and his son Stephen from Bern to Berlin. Shortly afterward, in 1921, Benjamin (1996:292–296) started his journal-project *Angelus Novus*. In the same year Benjamin wrote his essays *Goethe's Elective Affinities* (1996:297–360) and *The Task of the Translator* (1996:253–263). During the Summer Semester of 1923, Benjamin went to the University of Frankfurt am Main to prepare for a Habilitation, i.e. a post-doctoral lecturing qualification, in contemporary German literary history. He began working on his Habilitation – dissertation *On the Origin of German Tragedy* (1977a). It was finally not accepted by the University of Frankfurt because of its mystical character and maybe also because of the rising anti-Semitism in Germany at the time. At the same time, Benjamin became acquainted with Adorno and Siegfried Kracauer. A year later, in 1924, Benjamin's friendship with the Marxist Lithuanian and Russian actress Asja Lacis started. She came from the Brecht circle. She reinforced Benjamin's positive attitude toward Marxism. When Benjamin (1979) composed the *Theological-Political Fragment* in Berlin, he found himself – as very often before and later on in Germany and France – in great economic and financial difficulties. Only a poor man could possibly have written such a Messianic document.

Philosophical-Theological Life Style

In his *Theological-Political Fragment* Benjamin summed up his whole philosophical and theological life style: as he had unfolded it since his early studies in the humanistic branch of the Kaiser – Friedrich High School in Berlin-Charlottenburg; since his stay in the country-educational-home Haubinda from 1905–1907, where he became acquainted with the outstanding educator Gustav Wyneken and was very much influenced by his pedagogical ideas; since his membership in the youth movement; since his return to

Berlin and taking his Abitur, i.e. his school-leaving exam, in 1912; since his philosophical studies at the Universities of Freiburg in the Breisgau and Berlin and his very active cooperation in the Free Student Movement there; since his becoming Chairman of the Free Student Movement in Berlin and meeting Dora Sophie Pollak, his future wife; since his friendship with the poet C. F. Heinle, who in 1914 committed suicide together with his girlfriend; since his retreat from the youth movement after the death of his friend and after the outbreak of World War I in August 1914; since his first meeting with his lifelong friend Gerhard, later on Gershom Scholem; since the continuation of his philosophical studies in Munich, particularly in the theory of language, which will become fundamental to his further thought up to the early essay *Theological-Political Fragment* and his latest essay "On the Notion of History" (1969); since his marriage to Dora in 1917 and his dispensation from military service and his move to Bern and the birth of his son Stephan in 1918. In his *Theological-Political Fragment*, Benjamin laid the foundation not only for his writings on Kafka, Baudelaire and Brecht, but also for his real life work, which admittedly remained fragmentary, incomplete, a torso: the great *Passage-Work*/Arcades Project (Benjamin 1999). Benjamin's *Theological-Political Fragment* was the very basis for his later attempt to connect and to reconcile the Jewish mystical theology of Scholem on one hand, and the historical – materialist poetry of Brecht, on the other. After Benjamin had unfolded his *Theological-Political Fragment* of 1920/21 particularly in his later essays and books on Kafka, Baudelaire and Brecht and in his fragmentary *Passage-Work* and in innumerable letters to like-minded scholars and friends, he finally tried in 1940, the year of his death, to unfold it once more and at the same time sum it up ultimately in the 18 Theses of his small work *On the Notion of History*. In his *Theological-Political Fragment* Benjamin had characterized his whole philosophical and theological life style as "Messianic Nihilism." What precisely did Benjamin's Messianic nihilism really mean?

The Order of the Profane and the Kingdom of God

Benjamin (1979:312) declared in his *Theological-Political Fragment*, that only

> the Messiah himself completes all historical happening, and, to be precise, in
> the sense that he first of all redeems, accomplishes and creates its relationship
> to the Messianic itself. Therefore nothing historical can want to relate itself

out of itself to the Messianic. Therefore the kingdom of God is not the <u>telos</u> of the historical dynamic; it can not be posited as goal. Historically seen it is not goal but end. Therefore the order of the profane can not be constructed from the thought of the kingdom of God, therefore the theocracy has no political but only a religious meaning.

Benjamin had learned from Bloch's (2000) famous book *The Spirit of Utopia* of 1919 to deny with all intensity the political significance of the theocracy. According to Benjamin's *Theological-Political Fragment* the order of the secular, or the profane, had to orientated itself in terms of the idea of human happiness. For Benjamin, the relationship of the order of the secular to the order of the religious, specifically the Messianic realm, was one of the essential tracts not only of the philosophy of religion, but also of the philosophy of history. In Benjamin's view, the relationship of the profane order to the religious order, particularly the Messianic realm, conditioned a mystical conception of history. Not entirely unlike Hegel in his mystical *Philosophy of History* (1956) and *Philosophy of Religion* (1984, 1985, 1987) as theodicy, influenced particularly by the Christian mystics Master Eckhart and Jacob Boehme, Benjamin started in his no less mystical and theodicy-like "Theological-Political Fragment," determined by Jewish mysticism, the Kabbala and Hassidism, from the modern dichotomy between the religious and the secular order, with the intent to resolve it.

Dynamic of the Profane and Messianic Intensity

In his *Theological-Political Fragment* Benjamin posed the problem of such a mystical conception of history in the form of a dialectical image of two opposite arrow directions. In terms of this dialectical image, one arrow – direction signified the goal in which was at work the dynamic of the profane. The other arrow – direction characterized the goal, in which was at work the Messianic intensity. Benjamin had to admit, that according to this dialectical image, the free humanity's search for happiness strove, of course, away from that Messianic direction. Benjamin's dialectical image only affirmed once more – like Hegel's *Philosophy of Religion* (1984, 1985, 1987) before – the modern disunion between the religious and the secular dimension of consciousness, language and action. However, as little as Hegel, did Benjamin remain standing with this modern disunion between the sacred and the profane realm. However, according to Benjamin's dialectical image, one energy was able through its own way to promote another energy on its way in the opposite direction. Thus, in Benjamin's view, the profane order of the profane could likewise promote the coming of the Messianic realm. In this sense, for Benjamin the profane was admittedly no category of the kingdom of God. However, the profane was nevertheless the most correct, justified and applicable category of the quietest approach of the Messianic realm. For Benjamin, that was the case because in the happiness of the profane all earthly things strove for their downfall. Only in profane happiness all earthly things were destined to find their destruction.

Messianic Nihilism

Benjamin had to admit in his *Theological-Political Fragment* that, of course, the immediate Messianic intensity of the heart, i.e. of the internality of the individual human being, had to go through misfortune in the sense of suffering, in order to reach the Messianic realm. To the spiritual *restitutio in integrum*, so Benjamin argued, which introduced people into immortality, corresponded a secular *restitutio in integrum*, which led them into the eternity of a downfall. According to Benjamin, the rhythm of this secular realm, which eternally passed away and disappeared in its spatial and temporal totality – this rhythm of Messianic nature – was precisely the core of human happiness. For Benjamin that was the case, because for him nature was Messianic exactly out of its eternal and total transitoriness. In Benjamin's view, it was the task of world-politics to strive for this Messianic, eternal and total transitoriness, also for those stages of man, which were nature. Benjamin called the method of such world politics: nihilism – Messianic nihilism.

Jewish, Roman and Christian Nihilism

As Hegel had stated in his *Philosophy of Right* (1967b) and *Philosophy of Religion* (1984, 1985, 1987), that only that person was able to pluck the rose of Reason from the cross of the present, who first of all was willing to take that cross upon himself, thus Benjamin had to admit in his *Theological-Political Fragment*, that the individual had to go in his heart, characterized by Messianic intensity, through misfortune and suffering, in order to reach the kingdom of God. In our Dubrovnik circle we had no doubts, that Benjamin's

Messianic nihilism had nothing to do with the bourgeois nihilism which Tillich experienced spreading through Europe and America after World War I and II. Benjamin's Messianic nihilistic method of world-politics was closer to the nihilism of the Gautama and of Eckhart and of Boehme than to that of Nietzsche. Benjamin's Messianic nihilism was closer to the philosophical and theological nihilism in Hegel's (1969) *Science of Logic* as Logos – theology, for which being and nothing were identical, than he, or his friend Scholem, or the other critical theorists were aware of, or would have been willing to admit. Certainly Benjamin's concept of Messianic nihilism has some affinity to the Greek – not *ouk on* – which Bloch translated as the nasty, sterile nothingness intrinsic e.g. to a dreadful cancer disease, but rather *mae on*, which he rendered as the positive not yet of productive potentiality. Certainly Benjamin's Messianic nihilism came close to the mystical nihilism of his friend, the cabalist Scholem (1992:123–124), who stated in his poem that was devoted to Kafka's (1956) *The Trial* and which was attached to his letter to Benjamin in Paris from 51 Ramban Street, Rehavia, Jerusalem, on July 9, 1934:

> The great deceit of the world
> is now consummated.
> Give then, Lord, that he may wake
> Who was struck through by your nothingness.
> Only so does revelation
> Shine in the time that rejected you.
> Only your nothingness is the experience
> It is entitled to have of you.

Hegel had shown in his logic that there was, of course, not only a Jewish, but also a Christian nihilism, which admittedly as a methodological and Messianic one, had also nothing to do with the malignant profane and substantial nihilism of Nietzsche, or of his fascist and deconstructionist disciples directed against it. According to Hegel, Christian nihilism went far beyond the Roman nihilism, which found its classical and most adequate expression in Horaz's poetry: *si fractur illabatur orbis, impavidum ferient ruinae*. More than an old Roman, so Hegel argued, a Christian had to confess, that when the edifice of the world would crash down, its debris would still hit a hero: when in the words of Isaiah and the book of *Revelation* the old heaven and the old earth would be annihilated in order to make room for a new creation, the new heaven and the new earth without mourning, tears, death and sin. While Benjamin's Messianic nihilism certainly survives in extremely secular form in Habermas's methodological atheism, it has nevertheless found its most adequate expression in what Adorno and Horkheimer have called the longing for Heaven, Eternity and Beauty or better still, the Non-Identical, the absolutely New, the totally Other than the horrible historical continuum of force and counterforce, which can easily be traced in the daily newspapers and television shows all around the globe: and the hope for the rescue of the hopeless.

The Notion of History

Precisely through his many discourses between 1922 and 1940 not only with the cabalist Scholem and the Marxists Bloch and Brecht, but also and particularly so with Horkheimer and Adorno and the other critical theorists Benjamin became rather paradoxically, or better still dialectically, not only one of the greatest theorists of modernity, who today is claimed as their own not only by critical theorists but also by deconstructionists and others, but also the most outstanding political theologian: the brilliant counter part of Carl Schmitt, Hitler's lawyer and political theologian and one of the most intelligent fascist theoreticians up to the present. Today his works are translated massively in the USA and Canada. Benjamin's mystical political theology which had been formulated first most shortly and precisely in his *Theological-Political Fragment* of 1921/1922, found its final, most mature expression in the 18 Theses of his last essay *On the Notion of History* (1969) of early 1940. The latter essay was symbolized most adequately by the story of the hunchbacked dwarf in Thesis I (1969:253) and by the *Angelus Novus* in Thesis IX (1969:257–258).

Portbou

The story of the hunchbacked dwarf had been told first by the Catholic romantic philosopher, Franz von Baader, a friend of Hegel. Benjamin's version of Baader's story is to be found in the Thesis I of his *On the Notion of History* which he kept most securely in his briefcase, as if his life depended on it, when he arrived as stateless refugee from Marseilles in the Spanish border town of Portbou in the evening of September 26, 1940 on his way to

Lisbon and New York. Benjamin kept the manuscript most tightly until he committed suicide through an overdose of morphine in the hotel Fonda de Francia during the night from September 26–27, 1940, after he had found out that the border had been closed for stateless refugees – and out of fear that the Spanish fascists would deliver him to the Vichy-French fascists, who would then give him to the German fascists, who would then imprison him once more in a concentration camp. For the fascist police in Portbou Benjamin was nothing else than an *apatrida*. He was – like so many Hebrew prophets before – a stranger in a foreign land.

The Hunchbacked Dwarf

Benjamin's (1969:253) version of Baader's story in Thesis I of his *On the Notion of History* reads in the following way:

> It is well known that there was supposed to have existed an automaton, which was constructed in such a way that it reacted to every move of a chess player with a counter-move, which secured victory for it. A puppet in Turkish attire, having a water pipe in its mouth, sat before the board, which rested on a spacious table. Through a system of mirrors the illusion was awakened, that the table was transparent from all sides. In reality a hunchbacked dwarf was sitting in it, who was a master in the chess game and who guided the hand of the puppet through strings.

According to Benjamin's interpretation of Baader's story, one could imagine a counterpart to the automaton or apparatus in philosophy. For Benjamin the hunchbacked dwarf was theology. The puppet in Turkish attire was historical materialism. According to Benjamin the puppet historical materialism should always be victorious. In Benjamin's view, the puppet historical materialism could be a match for anybody, if it took the hunchbacked dwarf theology into its service. Certainly it would be immune against all theological or metaphysical objections. In Benjamin's perspective, today theology had become small and ugly and was in any case not permitted to let itself be seen in public. Whenever Adorno saw theology go hand in hand with the modern civil society's dominant forms of positivism and thus betray itself, he thought of his 8 years older friend Benjamin's abyss-like smile when he characterized it as the out of sight hunchbacked dwarf.

Historical Materialism

At latest since 1989, the Dubrovnik circle asked, if not the same characterization, which Benjamin gave to theology in Thesis I of his "On the Notion of History" may not in the meantime also have become true for historical materialism? Had not also historical materialism become a hunchbacked dwarf like theology with the break down of the Marxist oriented Soviet Union? The Dubrovnik scholars argued that maybe historical materialism lost in Eastern Europe in 1989 because it had betrayed itself as it forgot or refused to let itself be guided by genuine theology and thus to take it into its service and thus to become immune against all theological and metaphysical objections: precisely by allowing theological semantic and semiotic material, potentials, motives and motivations migrate from the depth of the mythos into its own theory and praxis, as Marx had done. At least some Dubrovnik discourse partners hoped, that in the future the historical materialists would falsify Hegel's pessimistic statement, that the only thing people could learn from history was that they did not learn anything from it; and that they would verify and obey the statement, that not to learn from history means to be cursed to repeat it; and that they would learn at least – as Habermas put it – from history what not to do; and that thus the next time around they would take genuine theology as seriously as Benjamin, Adorno and also Horkheimer had done.

Angelus Novus

Benjamin's mystical political theology was besides by the hunchbacked dwarf also symbolized by Paul Klee's picture of the *Angelus Novus*, which the great painter developed out of a picture of the German Emperor Wilhelm II entitled the Iron Eater. Benjamin had bought that picture in Berlin shortly after it had been produced. Benjamin (1969:257–258) described the Angelus Novus in Thesis IX of his *On the Notion of History*. According to Benjamin the angel looked as if he was in the process to distance himself from something, at which he stared. His eyes as well as his mouth were opened widely. His wings were spread out. In Benjamin's view, the angel of history had to look like that. Klee's angel has turned his face toward the past. Where there appeared before us a chain of events, there the angel saw one great catastrophe, which heaped unceasingly debris on debris, rubble on rubble, wreckage on wreckage and threw it before his feet. The angel would like to stay. He would like to awaken the dead. He would like to put together again what had been smashed and shattered. However, a storm blew from Paradise, which got caught and entangled in the angel's wings. The storm was so strong, that the angel could no longer close his wings. The storm drove the angel irresistibly into the future, to which he turned his back while the heaps of debris grew before him into the sky. According to Benjamin, that what was called progress in society and history was precisely that storm. For the Dubrovnik circle, it was Benjamin's mystical political theology, symbolized in the hunchbacked dwarf and in the *Angelus Novus* or angel of history, which made it possible for him to see with historical materialism and in opposition to historicism the static element in the dynamic of his own biography and of his own life work as well as of the modern history in general, which he had lived through: the *Nunc Stans*, the Now-moment, the Now – time, the fulfilled time, the dialectic in standstill.

Messianic Redemption

The Dubrovnik scholars noticed that Benjamin always went in search of extremes. Unlike Hegel's dialectical philosophy that dealt authoritatively with the antagonisms in modern civil society, Benjamin did not shape these contradictions into an affirmative synthesis. Like Horkheimer, Adorno and Marcuse, Benjamin participated in the power of negative thinking: in the methodology of an open dialectic or of determinate negativity. Benjamin let the extremes in modern bourgeois society and its culture collide with each other in order to create space for the concept of a Messianic redemption, or salvation, that could not be understood positivistically as the result of social evolution, or in general of human planning and manipulation. Thus, for Benjamin Messianic redemption was not the outcome of a horizontal process of history, but rather arrived vertically without intermediaries, if at all: as Messianic interruption of the horrible historical continuum of force and counter-force. This theological idea of Messianic salvation occupied a central place in Benjamin's version of the critical theory of modern society. In any case, up to the end of his life Benjamin was convinced that today theology had to conceal itself in order to have any intellectual or political influence whatsoever. To be sure, Benjamin's mystical political theology should under no circumstances be confused with any form of church dogmatic: particularly not one that has betrayed itself to any type of positivism. Benjamin's theology rather constituted that extreme of metaphysical thought without which one could not possibly think about society and history. Furthermore, Benjamin's mystical-political theology was as such the necessary antithesis of historical materialism and vice versa. For Benjamin theology and political thought and praxis constituted a totality that had to be thought of as the coexistence of extremes. In Benjamin's view, such thinking required not discursive consistency but rather radicality. The Messianic redemption Benjamin as well as his friend Adorno were longing and hoping for was not one in history but rather one from history: the totally Other, the Non-Identical, the absolutely New not as *telos*, but as end of history. Even today Habermas's critical theory of society, which concretely supersedes Benjamin's work in itself, is sometimes in German newspapers criticized by his positivistic opponents – and that not without some good reasons – for being a disguised theology, in spite of the fact that he continually stresses his methodological atheism.

Two Theological Streams

In our Dubrovnik circle, we have been fully aware of the fact, that Benjamin's great theological influence not only on Adorno's and Horkheimer's, but also on Habermas's critical theory of society, came not only from his late essay *On the Notion of History*, but also already from his 20 years earlier essay *The Theological-Political Fragment*. In reality, two theological streams were meeting in the critical theory of society. Firstly, Horkheimer's political theology stressing the second and third commandment of the Mosaic law and their secularization in the method of determinate negation. Secondly, Benjamin's mystical-political theology emphasized the Messianic realm. Adorno combined in his work Benjamin's and his own inverse theology with his and Horkheimer's negative theology, without which he could not formulate the truth. Indeed, the two theological tendencies in the critical theory are dialectically related to each other. They are different as well as identical. They reproduce each other. Thus, the theological dimension in Horkheimer's and Adorno's critical theory of society, particularly its theodicy, can not be understood without the influence of Benjamin's two political-theological essays, and the latter can not be comprehended without the former. This is so, in spite of the fact, that the influence of Scholem's mystical theology prevailed very strongly against Brecht's dialectical materialism in Benjamin's form of the critical theory of society, and the influence of Kant's, Hegel's, Schopenhauer's, Marx's, Nietzsche's, and Freud's theories of religion remained powerfully present in Adorno's and Horkheimer's critical theory at the same time, and up to their death in 1969 and 1973. The critical theory of religion, as we have developed it in Dubrovnik, is essentially the result of the influences of Kant's, Hegel's, Schopenhauer's, Nietzsche's, Marx's, Freud's, Horkheimer's and Adorno's theories of religion on one hand, and of Benjamin's essays *The Theological-Political Fragment* and *The Historical-Philosophical Theses* and of Habermas's communicative theory of religion on the other: of negative and inverse theology.

Epimetheus and Prometheus Theology

Benjamin's political theology, expressed most adequately in his "Theological and Political Fragment" and in his *On the Notion of History* has not only influenced the philosophers and social scientists Adorno's, Horkheimer's, and Habermas's critical theory of society, but also the new Prometheus political theology of Johannes B. Metz and his many students and disciples in Germany, Europe, North, Central and Latin America, which from its very start in the 1960's was directed against the traditional Epimetheus political theology of Carl Schmitt. While the new political theologian Metz prefers Benjamin's mystical-political theology over Horkheimer's and Adorno's negative theology, the critical theory of religion and the critical political theology as its central, integral part, which to a large extent have been developed in the Dubrovnik circle and discourse since 1977 – in which not only Habermas but also Metz participated – have concretely superseded in themselves Benjamin's and Adorno's inverse theology and Adorno's and Horkheimer's negative theology as well as Metz's new political theology: the Messianic redemption as well as the second and third commandment and its secularization in the form of the method of radical but nevertheless still determinate negation.

Remembrance

Benjamin (1969:263) remembered in the final, concluding Thesis XVIII of his last essay *On the Notion of History* that the old Jews were forbidden to explore the future. To the contrary, the Torah and the prayer instructed the Jews in remembering. For the Jews, this remembrance disenchanted the future to which those fall prey who get their information from the fortune-tellers. However, for the old Jews, the future therefore did not turn into homogeneous and empty time, simply because in the future every second could become the small gate, through which the Messiah could enter. In spite of his passionate commitment to historical materialism – or maybe because of it – Benjamin came very close to the charismatic initiator of Chasidism, the Rabbi Elieser Baal Shem Tov, or simply and shortly to Bescht, who summed up the faith and the hope of the pious people of the East European Chasidim in his famous statement: *Forgetfulness leads to exile, while remembrance is the secret of redemption.* This became the motto of our Dubrovnik discourse from 1975–2007.

Historical Foundations

Chapter One

Constantine: From Religious Pluralism to Christian Hegemony

A. James Reimer

In this chapter I look at the fourth century as the period that gave birth to Christendom and was determinative in the shaping of Western law and church-state relations. There is a long minority tradition within Christian history that has identified the conversion of the emperor Constantine the Great in the fourth century, including the events leading up to that conversion and its subsequent workings out, as the Fall of the Church from the original intent of its founder Jesus Christ and his Apostles. Already in the fourth century, the monastic movement (anchorites and cenobites), in their retreat from the centers of power and culture into the desert to live out the teaching of Jesus, as expressed in the Sermon on the Mount, were implicitly if not explicitly protesting the Constantinian synthesis of Christ and culture, the Christian church and state.[1] Some early Christian

---

[1] I say implicitly if not explicitly because the relationship between these monastics and the urban centers is a complex one. There were individuals (such as St. Anthony) who escaped into a life of solitude into the desert caves of Egypt (anchorites), there were monastics who lived in isolated communities (cenobites), but there wee later also those who retreated into monastic communities in the middle of urban centers. In many cases there was traffic (physical or by means of correspondence) between these monastic communities and the centers of power. Rulers and others would seek the advice of desert fathers on any conceivable problem, from how to rule justly to how to deal with children. Sometimes rulers (political or ecclesiastical) would

groups that where anathematized as "heretics" by those who were able to define the nature of "Orthodoxy" – groups such as the Donatists and Pelagians, for instance – might be considered to be part of this anti-Constantinian tradition in their call for a purer, uncompromising church. In the middle ages, various "sectaries" like the 12th century followers of Peter Waldo in Italy (the "Waldensians"), Wycliffe and his 14th century followers in England, the 15th century Hussites in Czechoslovakia, and others denounced the Constantinian church, calling for a restitution of the early New Testament church. In the modern period, there are those dissenting groups that find themselves within the so-called "Free Church" tradition, beginning in the 16th century with the Anabaptists and Mennonites, and continuing with the dissenting groups from within the Church of England (Brownists [late 16th century], Baptists [early 17th century], Quakers [mid-17th century], Methodists [18th century]) and the later Church of the Brethren and Brethren in Christ (19th century), Pentecostals and numerous Evangelical groups (20th century). All would to a greater or lesser degree reject the Constantinian shift in favor of a return to pre-Constantinian, "primitive" Christianity.[2] The term "Free Church" that has historically been identified with this distinct set of churches derives from their insistence that the church must be free of (separate from) the state. With the collapse of Christendom in the contemporary period this designation becomes anachronistic because virtually no church traditions would consider themselves "state churches" in the stringent sense, most if not all striving for an autonomous existence apart from the state. This is the new situation in which the Constantinian question becomes much more complex.

---

themselves for a while seek monastic retreat, and sometimes contemplatives would leave their retreats to take over public offices. I will be proposing that the Christian community that wants to remain faithful to the ways of Jesus and the early church ought to conceptualize itself spiritually in the tradition of these varieties of monastic communities. Within this model there is a wide diversity of types, but all have a qualified, even tenuous, relationship with surrounding culture, never absolutely separating themselves from worldly responsibilities but never simply identifying with the world either. This is quite different from escaping into pure inwardness; it is a concrete corporate existence but it is a social existence lived on the margins of society with occasional forays into common public life. It is a recognition, that in the post-modern context referred to above, there is no such thing as common public existence as such, but all there is are individual and communal cultures that together constitute the public as a whole.

[2] For the classical treatment of these various Free Church groups see Donald, J. Durnbaugh, *The Believers Church*. Scottdale: Herald Press, 1958.

The Christian church's attitude toward war and peace is a litmus test for how it perceives itself in relation to the state and surrounding culture.[3] It is this issue which most clearly demonstrates the revolutionary nature of the change which occurred in the first centuries of the Christian era, culminating with the conversion of the Emperor himself. The change in the church's readiness to tolerate and even justify the use of violence in the protection of itself and the state against internal and external enemies is the most blatant departure from the earliest core teachings. Most scholars believe that the earliest Christians vigorously rejected all bloodshed and joining of the military. There is, however, some disagreement among scholars concerning the nature of and reasons for the early church's rejection of the military. The evidence in support of the pacifism of the church in the first few centuries are: a) the overwhelming evidence in the Gospels that Jesus himself denounced bloodshed of all kinds and taught the way of non-violent love and the way of the cross, as a fulfillment of the Torah and characteristic of the reign of God that he was inaugurating (see especially Matthew 5–7); Paul echoes similar views in Romans 12:10–21; b) strong anti-military pronouncements by early church fathers: Justin Martyr, Clement of Alexandria, Origen, Tertullian, Lactantius;[4] d) church document, like the Canons of Hippolytus, which declare that civil soldiers ought not to kill even if commanded to do so; e) in those cases where

---

[3] For studies of the Early Church s attitude toward the military see, among other works, Roland Bainton, *Christian Attitudes toward War and Peace*, 66–84; S. Cahill, *Love Your Enemies*, 39–54; Adolf von Harnack, *Militia Christi*; Tertullian, *On Idolatry* and *Apology*.

[4] Although these early theologians all denounced Christian involvement in the military they did so on different grounds. For example, Tertullian (C.E. 160–220), son of pagan centurion who came out of the Antiochene literal school of biblical hermeneutics, frequently sounds separatist in his denunciation of the world, including the military, but was not a string sectarian pacifist that is, he was critical of the state but he did not reject it. His pacifism was more than just a rejection of violence, and was directed more against idolatry, killing and immoral lifestyle of the military. Origin of Alexandria (C.E. 185–254) was more allegorical in his approach to Scripture than was Tertullian, and subordinated the literal reading of the text to the spiritual meaning when it was suitable. This was a way for him to handle disagreeable, violent Hebraic texts. He was, also, less separatist in his views to the world than was Tertullian the Christian life of virtue is realized gradually, as part of a movement toward reunion with the God of the whole cosmos, enabled by the *Logos* guided by the Holy Spirit. Like Tertullian he does not deny the legitimacy of government but rejects involvement with professional violence of the military. Non-Christians may be involved in necessary wars. His adherence to the Sermon on the Mount is not as rigorous as Tertullian s because of the fallenness of the world and the gradualness of the process of sanctification toward the kingdom of God. (Cf. Cahill, *Love Your Enemies*, 39–54.)

there was participation in the military it could be interpreted as a form of police protection or civil service: fire protection, care of prisoners, public transport, mail delivery, secretarial work; f) there is no official evidence of Christian militia until C.E. 170–180.

A case has also, however, been made against the view that the early church was pacifist: a) unclear statements by Jesus himself: "I came not to send peace, but a sword" (Matthew 10:34), "He that hath no sword, let him sell his garment and buy one" (Luke 22–35–38), "Render to Caesar the things that are Caesar's and to God the things that are God's;" b) other ambiguous New Testament texts: the conversion of the Centurion in Acts 10, where there is no indication that he was expected to give up his military occupation; Paul's injunction to the Romans to be subject to the ruling authorities who have been ordained by God to bear the sword in their task of restraining evil and preserving the good (Romans 13:1–7); and what appears to be a positive understanding of Roman authorities and militia in Paul's missionary journeys, his arrest and trials, and his voyage to Rome to appear before the Emperor (esp. Acts 21–28); c) Tertullian's strong opposition to soldiering seems to suggest a problem – a gap between the teaching of the church and practice; his *Apology* (C.E. 197) suggest that there were Christians in the palace, senate, forum and army; d) by C.E. 173 there exists the Thundering Legion of Christian soldiers under Marcus Aurelius; also, by C.E. 278 Bishop Paul of Samosata has a body guard; e) tombstone inscriptions and epitaphs show that soldiers were not denied Christian burials; f) the existence of Acts of Soldier martyrs who refused to obey orders; g) injunctions against participation in the military may have been for other than "pacifist" reasons: emperor cult (idolatry) adulterous life-style, prevalent homicide, Roman persecution of Christians, eschatological indifference. With Constantine's conversion in the fourth century the ethics of war and peace changed dramatically. The normative position of the church now no longer was the rejection of the military but participation in the defense of the Empire became a Christian duty. In the following pages I examine how this shift came about and what fateful ramification is had for the church and Western history.

The Constantinian watershed can be interpreted positively as the great finale of a successful missionary effort and therefore it is to be applauded. Christian values, after all, now permeated and transformed the Roman Empire, and civil laws were grounded not on polytheistic beliefs but in Christian divine laws. Or the great Constantinian shift can be viewed negatively as erosion that began shortly after the death of the first Apostles, possibly already with Paul, and gathered momentum in the work of the second century Apologists. These Apologists, particularly the Alexandrian school of theologians, combined Greek philosophical thought and Judeo-Christian theology in order to bring greater clarity to central theological doctrines, thereby contributing to the development of a distinctive Christian doctrine of God as Trinity, and to convince the pagan world of the truth of these doctrines. In their apologetic work they assumed a common, foundational rationality between classical philosophy and Christian revelation that made it possible to argue, for instance, as does Justin Martyr, that Plato had received his ideas from the Hebrews and that, truth being truth no matter where it is found, the great Greek philosophers must have been Christian before Christ.

It is this "rational foundationalism" (a contemporary post-modern turn of phrase) which provides the epistemological ground for a new Constantinian ethic, of which the Just War is the clearest, although not only, example. The philosophical assumption behind Just-War thinking is that it makes no common or rational sense to expect the Emperor, Caesar, or any ruler to run the world on the basis of the Sermon on the Mount. Sometimes war is necessary, maybe an evil but nevertheless a necessary evil. In such cases the teachings of Jesus (revelation) can be discarded or bracketed as a basis for ethical decision-making, and other forms of reasoning must take its place. This is where the Apologists had prepared the ground for a kind of "natural theology," in which the philosophical argumentation of the Stoics, Platonists and Aristotelians could be used for Christian ethics in a way that the earliest Christians had not done. The rejection of all bloodshed and violence is not defensible rationally. The usual rational, pragmatic, consequentialist and political arguments don't work. Nonviolence is ultimately a position based on faith, revelation and non-self-interest assumptions. Once one has joined the Apologists in their move to join faith and reason, theology and philosophy, it is argued, one can begin to justify anything even violence in the name of Christ. And this is what St. Ambrose and St. Augustine did in the fourth century. They were the first theologians to develop the rational principles of the Just War.[5]

---

[5] St. Ambrose (ca. 340–397) drew on Old Testament, New Testament and Stoic sources for his justification of war but had two conditions: that the conduct of war be just and the priest abstain. St. Augustine (–430) drawing on Hebraic, Christian and

The person from my own tradition who has thought through this problem most thoroughly is the late John Howard Yoder. Yoder was a theologian and ethicist, who before his death in 1997 taught for many years at the University of Notre Dame. He espoused a theological and ethical position that he called "Biblical Realism," in which he argued that the life and teachings of the biblical Jesus are socially and politically relevant even in today's complex world. He was outspoken in his denunciation of the wrong direction taken by the established churches ever since the time of Constantine. Many of his writings deal with the ethical implications of what he calls the "Constantinian shift," represented by the imperial decree of toleration toward Christianity in 311, the "conversion" and later baptism of Constantine, and the crucial role Constantine played in the formulation of Christian orthodoxy, especially at Nicaea in 325, the great negative watershed in Christian history. Although the shift took place gradually, beginning already with the Apologists in the 2nd century, Constantine's person and period symbolize a "great reversal" in the relation of the church to the larger society, which can only be thought of as apostasy. No longer is the church a critical, prophetic, and suffering minority within a hostile pagan world; it now takes a privileged role in justifying power, wealth and hierarchy.[6]

The heart of the matter for Yoder is ecclesiology. What happened in the Constantinian era was a reversal of the New Testament doctrine of the church. The three characteristics which, according to Yoder, were assumed by the New Testament Christian community were: 1) disestablishment (the church is neither governed nor supported by civil government), 2) voluntary adult membership (church membership is based not on birth {as in infant baptism} but on an adult confession of faith), 3) renunciation of all violence, wealth and imperial office. This all changed with Constantine, and mainline

---

Classical sources developed the following criteria or conditions for a justified war: 1) the intent (approximate peace) must be just, 2) the object or goal (vindicate justice) must be just, 3) the disposition (love of enemy) must be just, 4) the auspices (ruler) must be just, 5) the conduct must be just (no wanton violence), 6) there must be a just distinction between combatants and noncombatants.

[6] For an extended treatment of Yoder's views on Constantinanism, alongside those of another Mennonite theologian J. Denny Weaver, see Trinitarian Orthodoxy, Constantinianism, and Radical Protestant Theology, in my *Mennonites and Classical Theology: Dogmatic Foundation for Christian Ethics* (Kitchener and Scottdale: Pandora Press/Harold Press, 2001), pp. 247–271.

churches fell from faithfulness when they changed from a critical prophetic minority church into a privileged minority and gradually into a majority from the fourth-century onward. With the medieval synthesis of church and state, clergy and sword, ecclesiastical hierarchy and wealth, Christianity came to be identified with "violence, money, and social stratification." Jesus as revelatory norm for social ethics was gradually overshadowed by common sense, natural reason, and a sense of responsibility for society and history as a source for ethics. In other words, at the point where Christians and the Church took on responsibility for running history and the world, at that point the Constantinian problem takes effect (Yoder 1984a).

Yoder makes a great deal of the change in ecclesiological, theological, ethical and philosophical assumption behind the Constantinian shift. Before Constantine the church was a visible, persecuted minority waiting for the kingdom of God. After Constantine, the visible church is a privileged majority (a mixture of the faithful and the unfaithful), and the true church an invisible reality to be identified only in the eschaton. Now the pagans and the Christian heretics become the persecuted minority. Before Constantine God's way with the world and history (providence) was ambiguous and a matter of faith, only God's way with the church was clear. After Constantine, this is reversed: God's working within history and through the Empire is beyond dispute, imperial values and culture, legal tradition, and social structures are identified as Christian. One's duties as defined by station, office, and vocation within the civil government replaces Jesus and his teachings as the ethical standard. Power, efficacy, and utility replace revealed norms as principles of ethics. Behind all this is a new metaphysics" a neo-Platonic dualism between invisible spirituality and visible worldliness. Christianity becomes interiorized and individualized with a growing distance between Jesus and worldly authorities. Two levels of Christian with different ethical obligations come to exist: the religious monastics for whom the high moral claims of Jesus especially in regard to nonviolence continue to apply, and the average Christian for whom a lower, common sense approach to life suffices. Constantine represents this basic reorientation and lowering of standards for ordinary believers. The "Just War" as articulated by Ambrose and Augustine, a moral theory not based on Jesus' teachings but dependent on an extra-biblical common sense epistemology, is the ethical outworking of this new orientation (Yoder 1981:39–70, 1984b).

Constantine and the Jews: Cross and Sword

For my own tradition, along with other groups in the so-called Free-Church movement of Christianity mentioned above, "Constantinianism" has become a kind of shibboleth covering everything that's wrong with mainstream Christianity. While I find myself largely in agreement with the above critique of the so-called Constantinian compromise, especially as it applies to violence, I have in my own work over the years called for a more differentiated analysis of the Constantinian problem. A number of important new studies on Constantine have recently appeared, including James Carroll's (2001) *Constantine's Sword: the Church and the Jews*, Elizabeth DePalma Digeser (2000), *The Making of a Christian Empire: Lactantius and Rome*, and H. A. Drake (2000) *Constantine and the Bishops: The Politics of Intolerance*. In the following pages I will engage the important findings of these works in developing my own overall thesis. I begin with Carroll's *Constantine's Sword*. Carroll's main interest is in tracing the history and nature of Christianity's anti-Semitism leading ultimately to the 20th century holocaust (*Shoa*). Carroll (2001:164–231) lays the blame squarely at the feet of Constantine and his policies. I had come to the same conclusion earlier, in a lecture given on "Pius XII, Hitler's Pope? An Alternative View" at the University of New Orleans, February 28, 2000, and on "Ecclesiastical Responses to National Socialism," at Western Michigan University, Kalamazoo on February 20, 2001.

A Brief Historical Excursus

Before Constantine, Jews and Christians were rival but overlapping communities co-existing on the edges of the Roman Empire, says Carroll. Until Constantine, the boundaries between various groups, including Jews and Christians, and theology and politics generally were fluid and ill defined. Greco-Roman society was "pluralistic" in the polytheistic sense, with a relative degree of tolerance by the state and between the groups. Persecution of Christians, according to Carroll, was sporadic and rare. There was a brief period of oppression under Decius (249–251) and following 303 when Diocletian cracked down on Christians, ordering the destruction of Christian texts and churches, in his attempt to establish order in a chaotic and fragmented society.

The armies of Caesar Augustus and his successors expanded the Roman Empire throughout Europe west of the Rhine and south of the Danube into the Near East and North Africa. Up to the beginning of the third century, power shifted away from the Roman Senate to the military and the armies as the Empire was threatened by barbarian invasions, civil war and chaos. Militarism eclipsed all intellectual, cultural and political life. It was under these conditions of threat to the Empire from the outside, civil strife internally, and growing militarism that Constantine came to power and his conversion and policies, especially in regard to the religions of the Empire must be appraised.

In 285 the Emperor Diocletian divided the Empire into East and West, appointing Maximian as his fellow Augustus in the West, with a Caesar under each. Diocletian's own Eastern Caesar was Calerius, and Maximian's was Constantius, Constantine's father. In effect, Diocletian established a ruling Tetrarchy, although he himself was clearly the supreme ruler. It was a Tetrarchy in which laws were grounded polytheistically. Maximian moved his court from Rome to Milan, and his Caesar Constantinius ruled from Trier, closer to the threatened frontier of Italy. Under Diocletian's rule, Christians were threatened with death throughout the whole Empire, except in the territory of Constantinius, who valued religious toleration and freedom. In 305, Diocletian abdicated and forced Maximian to do the same, leaving Galerius as Augustus of the East and Constantinius Augustus of the West with his court in Trier. In our study of this period, we will have an opportunity to look at the important legal policies instituted by Galerius in the East through the eyes of DePalma Digeser in her book. Here we are most immediately interested in how Constantine gained power first in the West and then over the whole Empire. Constantius died in 306 while in Britain with his legions trying to maintain control of his unruly subjects there, with Constantine at his side. The troops immediately hailed the 18 year-old Constantine his father's successor.

What transpired in the next half a dozen years became a turning point in Western history. The ambitious Constantine defeated Maximian, who had regained control of the East, in a battle at Marseilles in 310, and killed him. In 312, Constantine moved against Maxentius' army in Italy – Maxentius, son of Maximian, had laid claim to the Western half of the Empire. It was the night before this definitive battle against Maxentius, at Milvian Bridge, on the Tiber river, that Constantine supposedly had his famous vision, and his subsequent victory, which became the basis of his "conversion" to Christianity. Carroll ranks this as the "second-greatest story ever told." "After the death and Resurrection of Jesus, the conversion of Constantine may have been the most implication-laden event in Western history. If we rarely think so, that is because we take utterly for granted the structures of culture, mind, politics, spirituality, and even calendar (Sunday as holiday) to with it led" (Carroll 2001:171). After his defeat of Maximian at Marseilles in 310, an oracle suggested to the young Augustus he had been accompanied in his victory by a vision of Apollo, identified with the sun god. It is known that before his conversion Constantine worshipped the supreme Unconquered Sun, a devotion expressed on his coins even after his conversion. There was already a religious revolution underway toward a type of monotheism in the Empire, which prepared the way for Constantine's conversion. Earlier, under Apollo, and later under Christ, he saw himself "divinely commissioned" (Carroll 2001:180–181). It was probably political expediency that led his to embrace the religion of an increasingly significant and power minority group within the Empire.

What happened at that moment in history was the fateful identification of "cross" and "sword." There are a number of versions of what happened on that night before the battle. The most common legend, according to Eusebius, is that "he saw with his own eyes the trophy of a cross of light in the heavens, above the sun, and bearing the inscription CONQUER BY THIS" (Carroll 2001:175). What now follows is even more critical. He is to have sat down with his army and described his vision, and had a new banner made for his soldiers to carry into battle, made, in the words of Eusebius, as follows: "'A long spear, overlaid with gold, formed the figure of the cross by means of a traverse bar laid over it'" (Carroll 2001:175). Whether historically accurate or not, this legend is what shapes the subsequent ideological identification of Christian cross and Imperial sword. Within a year after the Milvian Bridge battle, Constantine was in control of the Western half of the Empire. By 313, he and Licinius, by now the Augustus of the East, had jointly declared the Edict of Milan, which gave religious freedom to Jews, Christians and pagans. By 324, the year he called together the Bishops for a conference at Nicaea, he had defeated Licinius and gained control of the whole Empire.

Pagans, Jews, Christians and the Empire

Carroll's primary interest is in the consequences of Constantine's conversion, and the identification of "cross and sword" for the fate of the Jews. For me it raises much larger issues about the nature of religious pluralism and freedom generally in the face of the Christian hegemony that Constantine's conversion set in motion, and the ramifications of this period for the evolution of law and civil society in the West. Carroll's case study of how this Constantinian watershed affected the Jews is, however, an exceptionally illuminating instance of these larger questions.

By the time of Constantine there were an estimated three million Jews in the Roman Empire, while Christians numbered an estimated 10 percent of a total Roman population of between fifty and sixty million (Carroll 2001:166, 168). There had been for centuries many vital, urban *Hellenized Jewish* communities especially in Alexandria, Carthage, Roman and Asia Minor, as well as in fertile agricultural areas of Mesopotamia and Egypt. There were also strong *Rabbinic Jewish* communities concentrated in Palestine, with a rabbinic academy flourishing on the Mediterranean coast. By the late fourth century, Jewish scholars, working in schools, under the guidance of prominent rabbis, had codified the collected writings of the Mishnah, a literary tradition well established by 300. Although Hebrew and Aramaic were the primary languages used, Greek, Latin and Persian references were also found in the ancient texts, indicating an interchange with other cultures around them.

Prior to Constantine there co-existed a diverse group of religious communities more or less tolerated. Jews had their own arrangements with the Roman government, were exempt from military service, and given considerable autonomy, with their own patriarchate in Palestine, recognized by the Romans. This was the case even though, like Christians, they refused to associate with the pagan cults in Rome. Christians were not similarly tolerated. The reasons Carroll gives are the following: a) Jews had the status of being an ancient religion; b) they themselves had a separatist theology that tolerated the co-existence of other religions alongside them. Quoting Alan Segal, Carroll (2001:170) states: "'For the Jews, purity categories could remain strong without sacrificing universality because, even Jews distinguished between themselves and the Gentiles, they were not distinguishing between saved and the damned.'" Christians, on the other hand, were much more aggressive proselytizers. Based on their belief on "Jesus Christ as God-made-man," that only those who were baptized are saved, and in Jesus' imperative to go and make disciples of all nations, Christianity was seen by the Romans as a fundamental threat to religious tolerance within the Empire. Herein lies the irony. Up to the time of Constantine, Christianity was allegedly a threat to polytheistic pluralism and tolerance in Roman society. With Constantine and the official recognition of Christianity on the basis of the Edict of Toleration of Milan in 311 C.E., forces were set in motion that would eventually replace that very pluralism and tolerance with a Christian hegemony.

This hegemony, according to Carroll, is achieved by the identification of post and beam, cross and sword. The weakest part of Carroll's otherwise compelling narrative and argument is his interpretation of the history and meaning of the symbol of the cross itself. Carroll (2001:175ff) claims that the cross as representing the death of Jesus emerges a central symbol of the Christian Church only with Constantine, replacing the earlier emphasis on the life and Resurrection of Jesus, and it was this change that decisively shifted the balance against the Jews. Here I think Carroll is simply wrong. The passion and death of Jesus on the cross was decisive for the primitive Christian community, as were his birth, life, teachings, resurrection and ascension. But the earliest meaning of the cross was the opposite to what Constantine took it to be. For the earliest Christians, the way of the cross represented God's reconciling love for all of humanity, and embodied the way of non-violent, sacrificial love for the other, even the enemy. It was not Constantine's high-lighting the cross that was the problem. It was its identification with the sword. It is true that the cross was a stumbling block for many (not all) Jews in the first century. This was precisely one reason why there was such a rift between those Jews who accepted the messiah-ship of Jesus and those who did not, as recorded in the Pauline writings and the Gospels.

The consequences of this equation of cross and sword were dire not only for the Jews but for everyone: Jews, pagans *as well as* Christians. While earlier the boundaries between these three groups had been relatively fluid, now the lines quickly became clearly defined (Carroll 2001:184). In a 315 edict, Jewish proselytizing was declared a crime; a century later it was punishable by death. In 414, history's first pogrom against Jews occurred in Alexandria – the city's entire Jewish community was for a time wiped out. Palestine, the land of Israel came to be known as the Christian Holy Land. In 429, the Jewish patriarchate in Palestine was abolished by one of Constantine's successors. The very year of the Edict of Milan, declaring freedom of religion to all three groups (pagans, Jews, and Christians), Constantine began taking measures against the Donatists, a dissenting group within Christianity. Quickly after becoming sole Emperor, Constantine began moving against the pagans, ordering some of their temples burned, confiscating their temple treasures, and outlawing their sacrificial smoke. The pagans remained a majority until Constantine's death and he could not afford for political reasons to move too aggressively and violently against them – that had to wait until later in the century.

I find myself in serous disagreement at another point in Carroll's treatment of this period. He interprets the theological decisions made at the Council of Nicaea as almost totally driven by Constantine's desire to wipe out the diversity that had existed in the theological arena from biblical times onward for the sake of a unity that he required for political reasons. Tolerance of disagreements in theology and differences between churches had existed since the Jerusalem council (Acts 15) and were now suddenly, because of Constantine's political need to unify the Empire, deemed unacceptable and treason (Carroll 2001:188–189). I have argued at length in another context, that the decisions reached by bishops at Nicaea on the doctrine of the Trinity cannot simply be equated with Constantine's political program. The Christian doctrine of God as it developed in the first few centuries, not without serious controversy and never with total agreement, had its own independent momentum, and the decisions made at Nicaea in 325 and concluding at Constantinople 381 were a remarkable ecumenical achievement, despite their inadequacies (Reimer 2001:247–271).

To the extent that these theological developments to define orthodoxy were used to legitimate violence against internal and external enemies of the Empire, as they so often have been, they must be condemned. And there is no doubt that Constantine and his successors appropriated theological orthodoxy in support of their policy of *Gleichschaltung*: the creation by violence if necessary of a Christian hegemony unifying the Empire. The family of Constantine inherited a legacy of violence: the three sons battled it out in a succession struggle and in the end only two males out of numerous members of the family survived the blood bath. For two decades following Constantine's death there was what Carroll (2001:204) calls "murderous internecine chaos." In a short two year period, 361–363, Constantine's half-brother Julian, known as

"Julian the Apostate," the last pagan Emperor, tried to turn the clock back by unsuccessfully trying violently to return the empire to paganism. Ironically, he ordered that Jerusalem welcome back its Jews and the rebuilding of the Jewish Temple. Rebuilding began but was cut short by the premature death of Julian. Christians reacted with unprecedented vengeance against pagans and Jews. It was after this, under Emperors Valentinian and Theodosius, that Christian heresy was declared a capital crime and pagan worship was officially banned.

Ultimately, the Jews suffered the most: "Once church and state had agreed that it was righeous and legal to execute those Christians – Docetists, Donatists, Nestorians, Arians – who dissented from defined dogma on relatively arcane matters of theology, why in the world should stiff-necked persons who openly rejected the entire Christian proclamation be permitted to live?" (Carroll 2001:206). In 388, the Bishop of Callinicus burned and utterly destroyed a synagogue in the city. Theodosius objected and called for a rebuilding of the Temple, but bowed to pressure in support of the anti-Jewish action by Ambrose, the Bishop of Milan. In this case the Christian church had become more intolerant and violent than the imperial ruler himself.

Lactantius: The Legal Basis for Toleration, Forbearance and Concord

A much more favorable reading of Constantine is given by Elizabeth DePalma Digeser, in her book *The Making of a Christian Empire: Lactantius & Rome*. Lactantius was a Christian theologian who responded to the persecutions of Diocletian with a work titled *Divine Institutes*, written in response to lectures sponsored by Diocletian, and given in Nicomedia in the winter of 302–303 by two authors: Sosianus Hierocles on *The Lover of Truth*, and Porphyry of Tyre *On Philosophy from Oracles*. The Emperor Diocletian, who was determined to bring order into the chaotic patchwork of local laws and cults under a unified system of Roman law, and to do this by promoting traditional religious piety, had assigned these authors to bring dissenters into line. Both tried to undermine by argument the growing Christian threat. Hierocles tried to show that Apollonius was a better person than Jesus and his miracles were greater than those of Jesus. Porphyry did not encourage Christians to forsake Jesus but tried to show that faith in Jesus was compatible with traditional philosophy and religion. The error was in worshipping Jesus rather than following him as a guide. In their understanding of the supreme Deity (monotheism) the two were not that dissimilar from the Christian view. What they criticized in Christianity was their worship of a human being. The two philosophers were in effect developing a kind of political theology in support of Diocletian's persecution after 43 years of toleration and forbearance (Digeser 2000:4–8).

Lactantius was in the audience listening to these lectures. He decided to write a well-argued philosophical response. He felt the traditional defense or apology was not enough. What was needed was an attempt to change the system, to make a case to the Emperor for religious tolerance, and so he chose the genre of Institutes – an accepted way of setting the first principles of a field. In his argumentation he drew on classical religious and literary tradition rather than scripture, and was less polemical and more constructive and comprehensive than earlier writers like Tertullian had been. His basic argument is that polytheism, the basis of the Tetrarchy, is a corruption of an earlier Roman piety which was monotheistic, that only worship of the Supreme Deity can be an adequate basis for true justice in a society, and that true wisdom is found only through Christ. Lactantius claimed that the true innovators were not the Christians but the current emperors, philosophers and lawgivers. Christians were actually closer to traditional Roman law and theology. In the light of this, he argued, the rulers should not persecute Christians but inaugurate a policy of religious toleration and forbearance. Digeser cannot find a direct causal link between Lactantius' argument and Galerius' 310 Edict of Toleration, nor Constantine's rescinding of the edicts of persecution in his territory shortly after his succession. Nevertheless, Constantine did audit Lactantius' reading of the *Divine Institutes* in the Trier court in 310–311, and used its ideas after he became sole ruler in 324 (Digeser 2000:12–13).

For our purposes, the importance of Lactantius is that as a theologian who spanned the last period of systematic persecution of Christians under Diocletian and full toleration under Constantine after 311, he developed a new type of political theology quite different from earlier theology. At first, theology had been directed to Christian internally as a way of clarifying what it meant to remain faithful as a minority community within the Empire even if it led to martyrdom. In the second phase, theology becomes apologetic and turns outward. Using Greek philosophy it tried to bring coherence to its own central beliefs to persuade others and to defend itself before the Greco-Roman world. In this its third phase, with Lactantius, theology tries to shape the very legal and political structure of surrounding culture. This is a momentous change for Christians; now Christians begin seeing themselves responsible for running the world on the basis of Christian beliefs and values. Under Gallienus (253–268) Christian worship had been unofficially tolerated as part of a pluralistic religious culture. Christians had begun to co-mingle with others in palace, government, army and classroom without having to participate in religious rituals in worship of the Roman gods. Lactantius himself was given a chair in the imperial court. His vision, as he articulated it in the *Divine Institutes*, was the Christianization of Rome. The inner logic of that vision, although not clearly understood as such by Lactantius, was the unifying of the Empire under the set of "Christian" laws ("Christian" now understood in new ways) that would ultimately exclude non-Christian visions if need be by force, a reversal and perversion of the original Christian *kerygma*.

Using sophisticated argument, and drawing on traditional Greek and Roman literature and philosophy, Lactantius' political theology calls for a policy of *forbearance* as distinct from *toleration*. Toleration, on the one hand, assumed a state of affairs in which different religious groups co-existed side by side within a "pluralistic" state, with little hope of converting others let alone society as a whole. Since there is no such thing as a neutral pluralism and ideology of tolerance, such a world is always precarious and can erupt into persecution of one group or another. Toleration was the ideology of the Empire, relatively speaking, up to the time of Constantine. A policy of official pluralism was best based on polytheistic political theologies but there was always an element of legal chaos in such a society, and although allegedly the Roman state was one of tolerance, the Emperors up to and including Diocletian in actual fact were quite ready to use force against groups whose religious practices threatened fidelity to the laws (Digeser 2000:120). The drive for monotheism tended to coincide with attempts to unify and centralize the legal system, although Diocletian tried unsuccessfully to ground his systematization of law polytheistically. His successor Gelerius in his 311 Edict of Toleration officially made Christianity a legal religion for the first time, even though he himself objected to Christianity and the laws that they created for themselves.

Forbearance, on the other hand, as Lactantius envisioned it, allowed for the co-existence of different groups but with hopes of converting the other and even the state as such, assuming one's own religion to be the superior or the true one. In the Diocletian context, this would mean that even though officially Christianity was considered reprehensible yet it ought to be forborne without the use of force against it. Yet since, for Lactantius, Christianity was the superior religion, the drive to convert others and Christianize the whole was intrinsic to it. The critical point, however, was the Christian state should be achieved by persuasion not by force. Persecution of others and the use of force in religious matters is against natural law and violates the very essence of what it means to be religious. Here Lactantius draws on Tertullian who was the first to use the expression "freedom of religion." Lactantius' showed how on this issue the Christian law was identical with natural law as conceived by the traditional Roman legal tradition, consistent with the ancient philosophy of Hermes Trismegistus, considered to be the source of Plato's religious ideas (Digeser 2000:111–114).

Lactantius appears to have thought, and Digeser shares this opinion, that Constantine's state approximated this vision of forbearance and concord. Digeser disputes the twentieth-century assumption that a universalizing religion (Christianity) is fundamentally an intolerant one as distinct from the tolerant polytheistic theologies. The early Roman state was not particularly tolerant and there were ways of conceiving a universal Christian state that refrained from violence and practiced forbearance of other religions, such as that of Lactantius. "Lactantius's position may have been exceptional among contemporary Christian theologians [in contrast, for instance, to Eusebius], but it was concordant with the thinking of Emperor Constantine, whose court he joined in 310" (Digeser 2000:118). Digeser (2000:119) further states, "...nothing in the definitions of tolerance or concord requires a state to allow everything religious that it finds harmful. Even the more liberal constitutions can justify some sanctions against religion: the United States Constitution guarantees freedom of religion, but this guarantee does not protect every practice or action that is called religious."

Digeser bases her "benign" reading of Constantine partially on the fact that Lactantius became a member of his court in Trier in 310. There he tutored Constantine's son and regularly read from his *Divine Institutes* to the Emperor. The Christian theology of the *Institutes* that Constantine heard read to him was quite Jewish in nature. God was referred to as *summus deus*, an epithet common to older Jewish tradition and familiar sounding to the educated monotheists of Rome, but not as common among later Hellenized Jews and Christians. The Son is identified with the eternal *Logos* in a way that combines elements of Jewish creation cosmology and the Neo-platonic and Roman Hermetic tradition: his pre-existence, incarnation and salvific work. He insists that the *Logos* has become incarnate in Jesus the Christ but in such a way that Roman monotheists will not find offensive. Salvation depends more on divine teaching than on suffering and the Passion of Christ. The central historical event is the incarnation of the *Logos* in Jesus Christ as the great teacher of virtue and justice. "For Lactantius...people are brought back to a state in which they can achieve salvation not because Christ suffered on the cross as a way of redeeming human sin but through the content and example of Christ's magisterium" (Digeser 2000:74). The crucifixion was not a means of redemption but a heroic example of virtue that humankind was called to follow. Although this strong emphasis on the teaching example of Christ existed already in Alecandria, Lactantius was the first Latin scholar to stress this, following some part of the book of Acts, the *Didache*, and continuing later in Justin Martyr and Theophilus. Mainstream Christianity, however, beginning with Paul, continuing in the Apostolic Fathers, Clement of Rome, Ignatius of Antioch, Ireneaus of Lyons, Origen of Alexandria and virtually all of subsequent theology emphasized the redemptive nature of Christ's suffering. Christ as spiritual guide and conversion as a form of enlightenment went along well with Lactantius' attempt to bridge the gap between Christianity and Greco-Roman philosophy, which had no explicit views of original sin and grace and saw salvation as a series of stages toward enlightenment (Digeser 2000:66–79).

Digeser's analysis of Lactantius' political theology and its influence on Constantine throws a substantially different light on Constantine's own theological framework and political and legal policies than what we gleaned from Carroll's depiction above. Carroll, in stark contrast, for instance, claims that with Constantine there is a new emphasis on the cross and the symbolic importance of the death of Christ. While Digeser acknowledges that Constantine did, in addition to opposing the schismatic Donatists, express opposition to the Jews, he tolerated them. Overall in the middle period (312 to mid-320's), he fostered a milieu of religious liberty, as reflected in the Edict of Milan, which "granted 'both to Christians and to all persons the freedom...to follow whatever religion each one wished, by which [act] whatever divinity exists may be appeased and may be made propitious toward us and toward all who have been set under our power' in order that 'no cult may seem to be impaired'" (Digeser 2000:122).

Digeser claims that this ensures religious liberty not toleration, because it aims to treat all religions equally. Christianity was not to be favored but was to be brought up to the legal status that other religions had. His policy toward the Jews was an exception. He was harshly critical of them and threatened with death any Jew who harassed Jewish converts to Christianity. He nevertheless continued to practice traditional Roman tolerance toward them and gave them certain exemption, not limiting Jewish practice as long as it did not threaten the liberty of others. Digeser softens Constantine's later (after 324) increasing disparagement of traditional religious cults and establish Christianity as the official religion, with her distinction between liberty and concord. Within the earlier policy of religious liberty, traditional cults were not criticized. With the new policy of concord, there was a movement of forbearance toward these cults with the intention of converting them and achieving religious unity in the end. The shift to a policy of concord is reflected by Constantine in a letter to the Eastern provinces in 324 in which he expresses the hope that the erring ones will be restored to the "sweetness of fellowship" but without the use of any force: "All should try to share the benefits of their religious understanding with others, but no one should force his or her truth upon another, 'for it is one thing acting with free will to enter into the contest for immortality, another to compel others to do so by force through fear of punishment'" (Digeser 2000:126). It was a conviction that, Digeser claims, Constantine held to the end of his life.

Conclusion

Lactantius' vision of a new Christian-informed civil constitution and set of laws based on natural laws, themselves ground in Divine law, was actualized in the life and policies of the first Christian Emperor. The nature and understanding of citizenship, and one's duties to the state changed profoundly under Constantine. Whereas traditionally citizens demonstrated their loyalty to the state by performing ritual worship to the gods, now their loyalty was increasingly determined by their allegiance to the Christian god. Prayer for the protection of Rome replaced sacrifice to the gods but most critically, and this is seriously underestimated by Digeser, the protection of the new state involved the identification of "Christ" and the "Sword." Whatever good intentions Constantine may have had about not using violence or force in religious matters, at the point where Christianity was identified as the theological underpinning of the destiny of the Empire, the military defense of the "homeland" became a moral and ethical obligation also for Christians, and particularly for Christians. The "proof" of this came in subsequent years with the development of the Just War theory. Already Constantine had made a special case out of the Jews and the schismatic "heretics." Very soon this was also applied to the other religions. Between 325 and 381, State and Church became allies against heretics. In the time period of 390–392, pagan temples were closed. In 420, Augustine, the father of the Just War principles mentioned above, gave his approval to coercive-repressive measures against Christian dissenters. Whereas much earlier, Christians had been excluded from the army, by 436 non-Christians were excluded from the military.

If 1) the essence of the Jewish Torah is the *Shema* ("You shall love the Lord your God with all your heart, and with all your soul, and with all your mind" and "You shall love your neighbor as yourself" [Deuteronomy 6:5, Leviticus 19:18, Matthew 22:37–39], and if 2) the love of the neighbor includes the Jesus imperative to love the enemy (Matthew 5), and if 3) Jesus came not to abolish the Torah but to fulfill it (Matthew 5:17–20), then the moral and ethical problem for Christians is how this love of God and the other is to be lived out socially and politically in any age, but most immediately in the contemporary (modern and post-modern) culture of diversity and pluralism. To what extent has the above Judeo-Christian understanding of law shaped the whole Western history of constitutional law after Constantine? After the collapse of Christendom (the Constantinian synthesis of state and Christianity) is the Lactantius vision still a possibility or even desirable? How are religious and no-religious communities with diverse even mutually exclusive religious worldviews, each with hopes not only of living out their own vision separately but in transforming whole societies and cultures, to live and co-exist peacefully with each other? These are questions at the heart of my larger project, of which this is just one small part.

Chapter Two
Christianity and the Concept of National Guilt
Denis R. Janz

"The past weighs heavily on the present." This has almost become a cliché for many of us. Yet, the vast majority of thoughtful people would concede that it points to an inescapable reality. The more human beings understand the past, the more obvious it becomes to them that history is, to use Paul Tillich's words, "the depth of the present." Even the supremely pragmatic mind of a Henry Ford, who proclaimed that "history is bunk," senses at some pre-reflective level that the past makes a difference in the present. It is not the past as such which I wish to focus on here, but more precisely on the "heaviness" of the past. Those that experience this heaviness, at least in the West, are accustomed to calling it "guilt." It has for many centuries been entirely conventional for us to think of this in highly individualistic terms. We can all acknowledge that the negativity of our personal past impinges, sometimes in dramatic ways, on our present realities. Feelings of guilt can, for some people, be vague and ill defined and yet they are undoubtedly part of the tangled web of motives out of which people's decisions emerge. For others, these feelings can be so overwhelming as to cripple their lives. However, this is only a difference in degree. For all but a tiny minority, guilt helps to shape who we are and what we do.

It may even be one of the things that makes us human. This is suggested by Wislawa Szymborska [1995:124], the Polish poet who won the Nobel Prize for Literature in 1996. Her poem is entitled: "In Praise of Feeling Bad about Yourself."

> The buzzard never says it is to blame.
> The panther wouldn't know what scruples mean.
> When the piranha strikes, it feels no shame.
> If snakes had hands, they'd claim their hands
>   were clean.
> A jackal doesn't understand remorse.
> Lions and lice don't waver in their course.
> Why should they, when they know they're
>   right?
> Though hearts of killer whales may weigh a ton,
> In every other way they're light.
>   On this third planet of the sun
> Among the signs of bestiality
> A clear conscience is Number One.

With the poet Szymborska, we might say that memory – the kind of memory we call an uneasy conscience – humanizes us.

A problem arises, however, as soon as we begin to speak of guilt in a collective sense. In what way can guilt for some past horror be attributed to a group when not every member of that group participated in it? Can whole societies be said to bear the guilt of some massive social crime in their past? And what about major injustices perpetrated by a previous generation? Do the descendents carry any responsibility, and therefore by implication any guilt? In short, is there any such thing as "national guilt?" And if there is, can we also speak of national redemption?

I would like to approach these questions with the help of several concrete examples. However, first, a word must be said about the individualized notion of guilt in the Western world. It seems to me that the attribution of guilt exclusively to individuals is a product of the Christian tradition. With its concentration on rules of behavior for the individual, Christianity already in its earliest stage taught people to feel guilt almost exclusively about their own personal actions. In the Middle Ages, this was intensified by the penitential system of private confession to a priest. This in turn developed into what Jean Delumeau [1990] has called a "guilt culture," the influence of which is still felt today. Yet, throughout this development the focus is on the inculcation and alleviation of personal guilt. The vast compilations of canon law, the lengthy treatises on moral theology, the endless listings of "sins," the hundreds of catechetical manuals, and the innumerable sermons show scarcely a sign of any consciousness of collective guilt.

It is to more ancient sources that we must turn to find a concept of national or social guilt. In her book, *The Human Condition*, Hannah Arendt (1959) credited Jesus of Nazareth as the discoverer of social forgiveness (Shriver 1995:35). By implication then, his teaching includes a concept of collective guilt. To an extent, Arendt was right: the Gospels depict Jesus as preaching repentance to cities (Luke 10:13–15; Matthew 11:20–23) and even to nations (Luke 24:47). The notorious anti-Jewish polemic found in some of the Gospels (Matthew 13:15; John 8:44) rests on the supposition that the guilt of the Jews is a national guilt. However, Arendt was wrong to see this as something new in the teaching of Jesus. For the Hebrew Scriptures, more pointedly even than Jesus, speak of guilt's social and national dimension. Central to the prophetic writings, for instance, is the theme of national guilt and national repentance. Here is where we find the concept's origins in the West, and it is somewhat ironic that Arendt, a secularized Jew, did not recognize this in her own tradition.

It was this consciousness of a collective, national guilt that was largely lost in the Christian tradition. The only place it survived, it seems to me, was in the Christian attribution of guilt to the Jews as a people. For well over fifteen hundred years, "the Jews" were collectively blamed as "Christ-killers," and their "guilt" in this regard was used to justify a massive history of atrocities, even though the victims were centuries removed from the alleged crime. Yet, one looks in vain for Christian groups who attributed any kind of collective guilt to themselves.

However, today the concept seems to be making a comeback. While there is still great reluctance to speak of national guilt, the twentieth century has seen in various countries national days of repentance, for instance. It is also not uncommon for political and moral leaders to at least mention "national crimes" and the like. Many societies today are attempting to confront their own difficult past. Beneath all of this lies inescapably the concept of national guilt. Several examples will help us explore this theme.

The most advanced public discussion of this issue is undoubtedly the one that has gone on in Germany for the last half-century. In fact, here the discussion has been protracted and intense enough to produce its own specialized language – a set of words with no satisfactory English equivalent (Ash 1998:35–40). The first is *"Geschichtsaufarbeitung,"* which means something like working over or confronting one's history. The second term is *"Vergangenheitsbewältigung"* – dealing with, overcoming, or coping with a difficult past. The inevitable political dimension of the issue is covered by the terms *"Geschichtspolitik," "Erinnerungspolitik,"* and *"Vergangenheitspolitik."* The evolution of this unique German vocabulary suggests that here above all the issue has been treated as an urgent item on the national agenda.

I do not want to attempt to summarize the ways in which Germans have wrestled with the massive criminality of their past. This history has been adequately chronicled by others. Rather, I merely want to lift from it certain features which bear on the topic of collective guilt, and which might be instructive for the rest of us.

It seems to me that already during the war and immediately after, it was Christians who led the way in the acknowledgement of collective responsibility. One example of this is Dietrich Bonhoeffer, arrested in 1943 and executed in 1945. Already at an early stage he was writing of guilt and forgiveness as it applies to nations:

> …in the historical life of nations there can always be only the gradual process of healing…. The only question is whether the wounds of this past are in fact healed, and at this point, even within the history of the internal and external political struggle of the nation, there is something in the nature of forgiveness…. It is recognized that what is past cannot be restored by any human might, and that the wheel of history cannot be turned back. Not all the wounds inflicted can be healed, but what matters is that there shall be no more wounds…. This forgiveness within history can come only when the wound of guilt is healed, when violence has become justice, lawlessness has become order, and war has become peace (Shriver 1995:73, cf. 114).

What is interesting in this statement is that Bonhoeffer, who certainly had no personal, actual share in it, nevertheless can speak of a guilt that the entire nation must bear. Immediately after 1945, other theologians echoed this. Jürgen Moltmann, who was a prisoner of war in Glasgow, could speak of the German "solidarity of guilt." Martin Niemöller, Gustav Heineman, and others imprisoned for their opposition to Hitler, did not shy away from saying "we:" the fact that they were not personally involved in the atrocities seemed, in their minds, not to entirely exculpate them.

This inclusive "we" also found its way into the early collective statements of the churches. In 1945, the "Stuttgart Confession of Guilt" of the Evangelical Church acknowledged that, "Through us, infinite suffering has been inflicted on many peoples and countries" (Shriver 1995:85). The same can be said for the "Darmstadt Declaration" of 1947. In 1950, the Evangelical Church made this even more explicit:

> We declare that through negligence and silence before the God of mercy,
> we have shared in the guilt for the crime, which was committed by men
> of our nation against the Jews (Shriver 1995:88).

Obviously, not all in the church had been personally involved. Not all had been "negligent" and "silent." Yet what underlies these statements is a consciousness of collective culpability.

The Nuremberg trials that were going on in these same years (1945–1949) pointed in another direction. Here was a "justice of the victor," imposed from outside, and ascribing guilt now to individuals. Necessary as these may have been, their value in producing a kind of social catharsis seems to have been limited. We cannot calculate the impact they had on German society, but it is reasonable to assume that private, unexpressed resentment was substantial. It is in any case doubtful that a process of authentic *"Geschichtsaufarbeitung"* can be moved forward by outsiders. Their efforts and advice will inevitably be seen as self-righteous and uncomprehending.

Perhaps this sheds light on why, in the Adenauer years (1949–1963) a silence on this issue fell over Germany. The other reason of course is that the Cold War displaced it on the national agenda. A context of threat is clearly not conducive to social introspection. Yet, it was not only this. Some actively advocated a policy of forgetting as the healthiest alternative. This view continues to find defenders.

> The philosopher Hermann Lübbe has suggested that it was precisely the
> fact that Adenauer's West Germany in the 1950's suppressed the memory
> of the Nazi past, with both amnesty and amnesia, that permitted the social
> consolidation of democracy in West Germany. It helped Nazis to become
> democrats (Ash 1998:36).

On the other hand, there may be a steep price to be paid for silence. A strong case has been made for this by Gesine Schwan (1997) in her book, *Politik und Schuld: Die Zerstörische Macht des Schweigens.* When discussion of the horrifying past is stifled in the media, in schools and in homes, she argues, the psychological consequences are immense. The political consequence is the re-eruption of the issue with a new fury, as happened in Germany in the 1960's and 1970's (Ash 1998:36). Incidentally, Henry Rousso (1991) has made a similar case regarding the long French silence over the collaboration of the Vichy government in his book, *The Vichy Syndrome: History and Memory in France since 1944* (Ash 1998:36).

In the late 1960's and 1970's there were far fewer German citizens who had actually been involved in the war crimes of the 1930's and 1940's. Yet now this past came back with a vengeance. There was a renewed call for legal prosecutions: by 1970, there had been 12,900 such cases before the courts. The generation born after the war was now making restitution payments. By the year 2000, it is estimated, 100 billion DM in compensation will have been paid (Shriver 1995:82). A government statement in 1986 about this *"Widergutmachung"* said, "No matter how large the sum, no amount of money will ever suffice to compensate for National Socialist persecution...." (Shriver 1995:88). Yet, lurking behind all of this was the question of national guilt, all the more acute now that so many Germans had never been personally involved. Why was restitution necessary unless a debt of guilt had been somehow inherited? Germans more or less willingly paid, but "they were repelled by the notions of collective guilt and race liability (*Sippenhaftung*) on the part of people born after the war...." (Shriver 1995:98).

What began in this period and continues to the present was a long series of attempts to explain all of this. President Richard Freiher von Weizsäcker's famous speech of May 8, 1985 is an example. Weizsäcker began with an absolutely candid acknowledgement of German guilt for what he called "the unimaginably vast army of the dead...a mountain of human suffering." However, this guilt belonged to a past generation. About the present generation he had this to say:

> No feeling person expects [young Germans now] to wear a hair shirt merely because they are Germans. Yet their forefathers bequeathed them a heavy legacy.... [A]ll of us whether guilty or not, whether old or young, must accept the past (Shriver 1995:108).

Von Weizsäcker then went on to argue that the present generation does not inherit guilt, but it does inherit responsibility. This is a responsibility, he said, to remember and not to repeat the past (Shriver 1995:108–114).

Yet, the denials of collective guilt continued. In the heated debate surrounding the Reagan visit to the Bitberg war cemetery in 1990, journalists, scholars, and politicians largely "disdained the concept of 'collective guilt' spread from generation to future generation" (Shriver 1995:105). Chancellor Helmut Kohl repudiated "collective guilt" but he accepted "collective shame":

> Reconciliation with the survivors and descendants of the victims is only possible if we accept our history as it really was, if we Germans acknowledge our shame and our historical responsibility (Shriver 1995:99).

Even Elie Wiesel, the most eloquent witness to the atrocities, repudiated the concept. "I do not believe in collective guilt, nor in collective responsibility. Only the killers were guilty. Their sons and daughters are not" (Shriver 1995:97). A similar chorus of denials echoed through the furor surrounding Daniel Goldhagen's (1996) book, *Hitler's Willing Executioners*. So also today, in the debate about a national holocaust memorial in Berlin, the issue lives on.

The interesting thing about this litany of denial is that none of it is very convincing. If the thing in question does not exist, why does its non-existence have to be continually re-asserted, argued, defended? Why does what Martin Walser has called "the incessant presentation of our disgrace" continue in Germany? If responsibility, liability, and shame are to be accepted by the post-war generation, how precisely does this differ with what we ordinarily call guilt? What can it mean for Germans to "accept their history" except to shoulder the weight of its catastrophes? As for Elie Wiesel's blanket repudiation of the concept, has any writer done more precisely to foster German guilt? How can this repudiation be reconciled with his own religious tradition?

It should by now be clear that in speaking of guilt, we are not speaking merely about an objective status attributed to an individual, as for instance in a court of law. Guilt is above all a human feeling, an emotion. At least in this sense, there can be no doubt that we can speak of a collective guilt in the case of Germany. Were it not for this, how could one possibly explain the long and intense national debate, the multitude of books, the speeches, the memorials, the sensitivity to outsiders meddling in these issues? What Germans, even post-war Germans, feel is, I think, guilt. Whether they should or not is another question. However, that such a feeling exists is, I think, unquestionable. The long, difficult process of alleviating it is what is going on in the process of *"Geschichtsaufarbeitung."*

I have focused here at some length on the German example because it is, I believe, extraordinarily instructive for the rest of us. One further thing should be mentioned, and this also is, as far as I can tell, a German innovation. It has to do with writing a common history. After the Second World War, a "French-German School Commission [was] created to promote reconciliation between France and Germany." In 1970, a similar Polish-German Commission was established (Baum 1997:141). Their task was to write a mutually accept-able history for use in schools and universities. The supposition behind this was that antagonists have differing versions of the past. The version of the past that must be acknowledged is one that the parties agree on, one which neither downplays nor exaggerates the crimes committed.

A second and very different example of national guilt is Russia. Here, there occurred what was surely one of the great social crimes of the twentieth century. Here, perhaps as many as thirty million lost their lives in Stalin's planned famines of the 1930's. Countless more succumbed in the Bolshevik Revolution, the purges, the gulags, and so on. Why? They were sacrificed on the altar of an ideal that the Russian people finally, in 1991, saw was utterly bankrupt. The innumerable victims were to be the manure, as Dostoevsky called it, out of which would grow a future, more noble humanity. Yet, this society must now face the appalling truth that it was all for nothing: the dream of a future utopian society lies in ruins.

Already in 1990, the prominent Russian social philosopher Alexander Tsipko suggested that the shattering of this dream left the Russian people with an enormous burden of guilt. The seventy-five year Soviet experiment was in fact an utter "betrayal of humanity" for which this specific community of human beings must now bear the responsibility. The birth pangs of the "new Russia" are accompanied above all, he argued, by shame and guilt. In fact, Tsipko (1990) wondered if the Russian spirit was capable of bearing this crushing burden.

Today it seems that the Russian spirit is not ready to confront its recent past. Perhaps the memory is too fresh and therefore too painful. Perhaps the social chaos resulting from a faltering democratization process is not conducive to such a remembering. Perhaps the economic hardships accompanying Russia's "mafia capitalism" make the issue seem irrelevant. Perhaps the lawlessness makes the future too uncertain for remembering. In any case the hard, complicated, long work of *"Geschichtsaufarbeitung"* has not really begun in Russia.

This is not to say that there is no nostalgia in Russia today. Tatyana Tolstaya (1997:15) in fact confirms that there is indeed a widespread yearning today for "the peaceful, stagnant 1970's" with its dependable salaries and pensions, safe streets, affordable prices, and so on. As she puts it, "[when] it's dark ahead, you feel like turning back." However, nostalgia is not yet memory. Willful forgetting of the horrors of the past – this now seems to be the prevalent mindset in Russia. Michael Scammell (1998:40) sees the disfavor into which the Solzhenitsyn classics have fallen as a symptom of this:

> The crimes and enormities of the recent past get little attention in today's shallow and materialistic Russia.... [T]he Russians now seem to have emerged from party dictatorship untroubled by the horrors of the past. With no external force to pressure them, they prefer almost total amnesia, at least for the time being. And for them Solzhenitsyn is part of the tragic history they want to forget.

Yet, it is hard to believe that this Russian national amnesia will be permanent. Once chaos and hardship give way to order, stability, and prosperity, these memories will, I think, reassert themselves and demand a reckoning.

A third and very different example of a society dealing with the burden of its difficult past is South Africa. Here, as is well known, an openly racist social and political system prevailed throughout the colonial period. After that, in 1948, the system known as "apartheid" was imposed – strict racial segregation in order to maintain the dominant status of the white minority, together with legalized discrimination in education, housing, employment, public services, and so forth. Dissent and resistance were legally punished. The result was an appalling forty-year period of imprisonments, house arrests, spying, exiles, torture, maiming, executions, bombings, assassinations, and terror for countless human beings. Cruelty here was not incidental but rather a matter of national policy. Most nations of the world concurred when the United Nations called the apartheid system a "crime against humanity."

The system collapsed in 1990 when Nelson Mandela was released after twenty-seven years in prison. Almost immediately, South Africans on a large scale agreed that the nation's recent past could not simply be forgotten or ignored. One result of the consensus was that shortly after Mandela was elected President in 1994, the government established its "Commission of Truth and Reconciliation." The mandate of this commission was to document the "gross violations of human rights," to grant amnesty to "persons who make full disclosure of all the relevant facts associated with a political objective," to hear the stories of the victims, to restore "human and civil dignity" to these victims, to report to the nation its findings, and to make recommendations for preventing such violations in the future (Ash 1997:34). As a result, South Africans, and indeed the world, have now heard hundreds of stories from the victims and their relatives. We have also heard numerous confessions of guilt by those directly involved in the crimes and atrocities of the last decades. The entire process has of course been flawed and has come under heavy criticism from some quarters. Its long-term effect remains to be seen. Yet, perhaps it should be seen as a rather unique experiment in *"Geschichtsaufarbeitung"* from which the world community can learn.

Most of this, however, remains on the level of the individual. In what sense are we dealing in this case with a collective, even national guilt? Is there any acknowledgement of a corporate dimension to the guilt with which South Africans are dealing? First, when former President F. W. DeKlerk came before the Truth Commission, he spoke not only for himself but for his National Party, acknowledging its guilt and apologizing for it (Ash 1997:36). Others have spoken of the collective guilt of white South Africans. These understand of course that not every individual white South African is personally guilty: indeed some struggled valiantly against apartheid. Yet, it is frequently pointed out that all white South Africans were nevertheless beneficiaries of apartheid: they prospered, relatively speaking, in an enormously unjust social system, and in part because of that system. With this in mind, collective guilt and apology has meaning for many.

It was not only individuals that came before the Truth Commission. In 1997, provision was made for religious organizations to come before the Commission. For a week, leaders of churches publicly acknowledged on various levels their collective guilt and complicity (Christian Century 1997:1149–1150). Even the Dutch Reformed Church, once the dominant legitimizer of apartheid, has now confessed the sinfulness of white rule (New Orleans Times-Picayune 1998). Already back in 1991, as the structures of apartheid were beginning to crumble, a national conference of 230 church leaders representing ninety percent of South African Christians issued the famous Rustenburg Declaration. In it they confessed that "we have in different ways practiced, supported, permitted or refused to resist apartheid." They called "upon the Government of South Africa to join us in a public confession of guilt" (Alberts 1991:277–279). Guilt, according to the Rustenburg Declaration, was collective.

My last example, and the most difficult one for me as an American to speak about, is the United States. To a large extent it is true to say that here is a society that was built on the foundation of massive human suffering. For two and a half centuries, from the first slaves sold in Virginia in 1619 to the Emancipation Proclamation which went into effect in 1865, millions of human beings were held in bondage by white masters who saw them as barely human. Their sole purpose in life assigned to them by their owners was labor, and their work was the engine of early American prosperity. This is largely true even if we distinguish between North and South. Conventionally the North is designated as "a society with slaves" – a social and economic system abetted by slavery. The South is designated as "a slave society" – a social and economic system in which slavery was integral to the whole and which could not function without it. In any case, the economic success of the nation rested to a large extent on the institution of slavery.

The political foundation of the United States was also unthinkable without slavery. Had it not been for the slavery provisions in the Constitution of 1790, the South would surely not have accepted the Union. And this, despite the stark contradiction in the document between the slavery provisions and the liberal democratic rhetoric familiar to all. Both economically and politically then, the birth of the nation was inseparable from the institution of slavery.

It should not be necessary here to make the point that slavery was cruel and inhumane. Yet, there are sectors of American society today that constantly attempt to shift the focus. The phenomenon of "the happy slave," the "kind" slave owner, the fact that Africans themselves sold slaves – these familiar themes supposedly mitigate the true horror of the entire institution. It is enough perhaps to cite one piece of evidence. In the 1920's and 1930's, the Federal Writers Project interviewed scores of former slaves, all at that time in their eighties or older. George Rawick, in the 1970's, published a 41-volume collection of the interviews, the reminiscences of slave life. Those who have studied them agree that the happy memories are few and far between. As Edmund Morgan (1998:16) says:

> What stands out in all these interviews in grim monotony is the unrelenting dominance of masters, maintained by regular whipping and torture, sometimes by exemplary murder.

It may be true that, as some recent historians have argued, slavery was a "negotiated relationship." However, this "negotiation" was carried out by the lash and by terror, the defining features of slave life. The history of slavery is the story of a massive human suffering.

Today, of course, it's over, and it's been over for 135 years. There are those who now simply advocate forgetting: this past, in their view, is essentially irrelevant to America's business in the present. Outsiders sometimes point to this willful amnesia as an element in the American national character. Yet this, in my view, is superficial. Perhaps some Americans today would *like* to forget this painful past, but they simply cannot. For the legacy of slavery is inescapable. Southerners, at least, hear about it, see it, and feel it every day of their lives. In my local newspaper, almost every day at least one column deals with race. With unrelenting frequency, today's political debates over inner-city poverty, welfare reform, affirmative action, as so on, lead us back to the issue of our difficult history. Some are utterly impatient with what they see as a senseless and unproductive wallowing in the past. Yet this inheritance, despite all efforts to suppress and obliterate it, refuses to go away.

In part this is because of the lingering racism of American society. While slavery is over, racism is not – a fact that is far clearer to African Americans than it is to white Americans. Malcolm X's words sound extreme to white ears: "You cannot find *one* black man…who has not been personally damaged in some way by the devilish acts of the collective white man!" (Shriver 1995:206). However, even for more moderate African Americans, racism is obvious and self-evident. In Cornell West's view, "It goes without saying that a profound hatred of African people…sits at the center of American civilization" (Shriver 1995:215). Racism is the constant reminder in America of the burden of its past, i.e. slavery. Jack Miles speaks for many when he says, "…everything in America begins with that old and still unpaid debt" (Shriver 1995:214).

Here the question presses on us again: is there really such an indebtedness? If there is, are we not really speaking of a collective, national guilt? The fact is that many Americans would acknowledge this liability from the past. And many more sense its validity at some unspoken level. If this were not true, why would American society as a whole be making regular, if inadequate, payments on this debt? For surely the various social programs to benefit African Americans, from affirmative action to social welfare initiatives, are precisely such payments. Without a collective sense of indebtedness, without national guilt, they would be unthinkable.

So too would be the series of apologies American leaders have offered to the world on behalf of the nation. The latest was President Bill Clinton's statement of regret about slavery when he visited Africa in 1998. Despite an outcry from conservative circles, the vast majority of Americans seem to have seen nothing amiss in this. The consensus that such apologies are not out of place points to a collective sense of guilt long after the scourge of slavery has come to an end (Tavuchnis 1991).

Finally, I want to return to the question I raised at the outset. Can we legitimately speak of such a thing as "national guilt?" What sense could such a concept possibly have?

To answer this question, I want to appeal again to a basic distinction. Guilt can be conceived, on the one hand, as an objective or ontological or metaphysical or juridical reality. If we understand guilt in this sense, then the question of "national guilt" must be left open. It may be in some cases that the actual perpetrators of a massive social crime still exist and constitute a majority or dominant group in a society. In that case it would be appropriate to speak of a national guilt in the literal, ontological sense. Here the example of South Africa applies. Yet, more often the actual perpetrators are gone from the scene. Are their descendants "guilty" in this sense? Literally speaking, no.

But we can also understand guilt as a subjective state, as the phenomenon of feeling guilty. In this sense, "national guilt" is indeed real. This is undeniable, I think, when one considers the examples of Germany and the United States. To minimize or dismiss the collective reality simply because it is subjective is, I think, a serious mistake.

We all know, of course, that guilt feelings are highly problematic. They can be inappropriate – that is, they can be utterly without foundation. They can also be pathologically exaggerated, so as to cripple the individual or the society that is their subject. They can be politically exploited, used by social groups to further their own narrow self-interests. They can be subtly transformed, for instance, into new forms of racism, as George Rawick and Edmund Morgan (1998:16) have pointed out. These dangers are all real and should not be minimized.

And yet, I want to suggest, this kind of national guilt can also be appropriate, authentic and legitimate. I refer again to the example I know best. American national pride and patriotism is in large measure an assertion that the greatness of the American past is ours. Americans lay claim to the glories of the past as belonging to them. However, if they in this sense "inherit" the credits of the past, they also "inherit" its debits. Their regret about these liabilities is appropriate. To go one step further, white Americans could also concede that they have benefited, at least indirectly, from their oppressive past, and even from its continuing legacy of racism. In this sense, American national guilt is neither misplaced nor exaggerated, but healthy.

The phenomenon of national guilt can also have a transformative function. Such feelings, it seems to me, sensitize societies to the victims, in the American case, to the descendants of the victims, who continue to suffer at the hands of a dominant majority. To use only one example, it seems extremely doubtful to me that the Civil Rights movement (1955–1968) would have succeeded as much as it did were it not for the sense of collective culpability on the part of white society. Then too, this kind of moral memory that we call guilt steels the resolve of society not to repeat the sins of the past.

I have argued here that national guilt can be real, legitimate, and healthy. I want to end with an all too brief theological reflection.

Christian theologians have said a great deal about evil, sin and guilt. However, they have had little to say about collective, national guilt. Perhaps the closest correlative concept today can be found in liberation theology's emphasis on social or structural sin (Duffy 1993:362–365). Like national guilt, this is an imprecise concept which defies easy analysis. What is meant is the type of evil that embodies itself in institutions or inheres in the very structure of societies. This systemic evil perpetuates itself by creating a false consciousness in members of such institutions and societies. These people can be men and women of enormous good will while remaining utterly blind to the dehumanizing forces in their midst. The result can be a massive evil for which no individual, properly speaking, bears the blame. If we have in mind moral evil, and if moral evil implies guilt, then here it is the system, which is more than the sum total of individuals in it, to which guilt must be assigned.

At first sight, this concept of social sin that is thematized in liberation theology seems directly relevant here. Yet, further consideration casts doubt on this. For the liberationist concept deals with the assignation of what I have called objective guilt: who (or what) is to blame for the oppression, dehumanization and alienation endemic to a society? My concern, on the other hand, is the subjective feeling of guilt experienced by groups, societies, and even nations. Helpful as the liberationist concept may be in an analysis of the massive evils of modernity which transcend the individual, my focus here has been on the way in which groups and nations deal with a widely shared feeling. On this issue, it seems to me that what theologians have said is inadequate, especially now, when the subject presses itself upon us in new and forceful ways.

Perhaps a more promising path to follow would lead in the direction of a re-thinking of the traditional doctrine of original sin. For about thirteen hundred years, most Christians in the West believed that the first parents of humanity committed a monumental sin, and all human beings thereafter have inherited both the guilt and the punishment for it. Baptism, they held, removes the guilt while the punishment remains. Today of course any literal understanding of all this is obsolete.

Nevertheless, the doctrine was an attempt by this tradition to express its profound consciousness that we as human beings do not come into the world with a clean slate. We do inherit in some sense the liabilities of the past, the sins of our ancestors, if you will. The doctrine of original sin is social: not only individuals but society inherits the consequences for crimes of the past. Baptism then must be understood not as a magical and instantaneous lifting of the guilt of the past, but as the entrance into an alternative society, the church, which anticipates and works towards the reconciled society of the future. In doing this, it is precisely *"Vergangenheitsbewältigung"* which is the Christian community's first and ongoing task.

Yet, must it go on forever? When is the arduous work of *"Vergangenheitsbewältigung"* ever done? Who can pronounce an absolution so powerful as to lift the heavy burden of the past from the shoulders of nations or groups? If it is not society's priests, then is it the victims perhaps, or their descendents?

Can we ever let *these* bygones simply be bygones? Unfortunately, I think, the answer is no. The poet Szymborska, it seems to me, is right: a society which transcends its past by emerging from it with a clear conscience remains open to the recurrence of the bestial. True transcendence of the past must include a refusal to forget. Ultimately it is our burden of anamnestic sadness and longing, heavy as it may be, which opens for us the possibility of a more humane future.

Chapter Three
Pius XII and the Third Reich
Hans K. Weitensteiner

On October 31, 1997, the *Berliner Morgenpost* published an article by Andreas English with the title,
"Beatification for Pius XII Under Debate – Critique
Against the role of the Vatican during the Persecution of the Jews by the Nazis." The author reported
that in the Vatican State, Pope John Paul II rapidly
was losing popularity with many Cardinals. Despite
great resistance, the Papal Commission for the Cooperation between Jews and Christians organized a
colloquium with the title "Roots of Anti-Judaism in
the Christian Context." The Pope received about 60
participants in Rome. Particularly auspicious for the
experts concerning the situation was the complaint
of the Jewish community in Rome that expressed
their deep disappointment of not having been invited
to this discourse. Nevertheless, one could foresee
a clear condemnation of the politics of Pope Pius
XII coming. Yet, many Bishops and Cardinals, so
the author continued, urged the conclusion of the
beatification of Pius XII as a "heroic example." In
1949, with the excommunication of all Communists,
this Pope was supposed to have saved Italy from
the being integrated into the Soviet sphere of influence. Contrary to this, Jewish experts have criticized
the role of Pius XII for decades. Only recently, the
holocaust researcher Professor David Blumenthal,

has once more stated: "a third of all victims could have been rescued if the Pope had excommunicated the perpetrators."

The critics of Pope Pius XII consider it possible that under John Paul II the beatification procedure for Pius would be broken off definitely. Paul II was the first Pope to promote seriously reconciliation with the Jews. For the first time in the history of the Catholic Church, Pope John Paul II visited the Synagogue in Rome in 1986. In 1994, under John Paul II's guidance, the Vatican State began diplomatic relations with Israel.

On April 1, 1998, the *Berliner Morgenpost* made an alarming announcement again. This time it had the title "Despite Silence Concerning the Holocaust: Vatican will Beatify Pius XII." The newspaper reported that behind the walls of the Vatican State responsible people tried to reconstruct the history of the Rabbi Israel Zolli. This former head Rabbi of Rome, who died in 1956, had allowed himself to be baptized after the war and had converted to the Catholic faith. In his book, "Anti-Semetism", which was written before he had converted, the head Rabbi wrote: "The Jews of the world owe much to his Holiness Pope Pius XII." During his attempt to rescue the Jews of Rome from annihilation, the SS coerced and extorted the Jewish community. The SS promised the Jews that they would not be deported if they would deliver a ransom of 50 kilograms of gold to them. Despite making the greatest effort, the Jewish community brought together only 35 kilograms of gold. The Jews then turned directly to Pius XII. The Pope gave the order to deliver the missing 15 kilograms of gold. The gold of the Vatican however did not rescue the Jews of Rome. On the days of October 15–16, 1943, those Jews who could not escape in time were driven together by the SS and sent to annihilation camps.

The *Berliner Morgenpost* reported that the daughter of Israel Zolli, Miryam Zolli, who lived in Rome, defend the reputation of her father, who the Jews did not like to remember any longer since his conversion to the Catholic faith. Rabbi Israel Zolli let himself be baptized taking the name Pius. Already in his time as head Rabbi in Triest, Israel Zolli had learned to speak German perfectly and would later on discourse with Pope Pius XII in the German language about the crimes of the Nazis.

The statements of the Rabbi are supported through the Vatican sources, which were published in 1997. As a matter of fact, on September 20, 1943, the SS leader Herbert Kappler demanded the leaders of the Jewish community of

Rome to deliver 50 kilograms of gold to the SS in 24 hours. The head Rabbi of Rome, Israel Zolli, then turned for help directly to Pius XII. A memorandum of Commandant Bernadino Nogara, the chief of a special commission of the Holy See testified that the Rabbi Zolli had come in order to report that the 15 kilograms of gold had been delivered through "Catholic communities." A contribution of the Vatican was therefore no longer necessary (Blet 2000:200). Thus, the help of Pius XII for the Jewish community in Rome is without doubt.

Finally, the weekly *Freitag* that appears in Berlin reported on January 21, 2000 in a contribution by Jens Renner entitled "Christian Tragedy" that the Holy See still did not see any reason to distance itself from Pius XII as the most controversial Pope of the 20th century. Admittedly, the "greatest scandal of the Holy Year," namely the beatification of Eugenio Pacelli, would not take place. After many negative reactions, the Vatican saw itself compelled to postpone the beatification of Pius XII. However, it cannot be expected that the Vatican will revise its judgment about Pius XII.

In a crass falsification of history, the *Berliner Morgenpost* thought this Pope would be thanked for what he undertook personally or did through his representatives in order to rescue the lives of hundreds of thousands of Jews. The number of Jews who survived in the monasteries and also in the Vatican, however, was in fact much lower.

In March 2000, the *Berliner Morgenpost* entered anew in the discussion about Pius XII. Under the title "The Vatican Admits to Shared Guilt in the Persecution of the Jews – the 'Mea Culpa' of the Catholic Church." The newspaper reported that the Roman head Rabbi Elio Toaff suddenly dignified Rabbi Zolli as "a man of bridge building." Due to the guilt confession of the Pope, the will to reconciliation now determined and dominated the relationship between Christians and Jews in the Eternal City. With surprise, the Jews in Rome had received the confession of John Paul II that the Vatican did great harm to the Jews. Before that, an international theological commission chaired by Cardinal Ratzinger had arrived at the conclusion that the condemnation of the Jews as the murders of Christ, which was negated only by the Second Vatican Council, had essentially contributed to the spreading of anti-Semitism in Europe. At the same time, the Catholic Church conceded that during the Holocaust Catholics made themselves guilty by not having helped the Jews. The Vatican has admitted in the document *"Remembrance and Reconciliation"* that "the persecution of the Jews by the Nazis was facilitated through the anti-Jewish prejudices that were present in the hearts of some Christians." Despite the fact that the Catholic Church held on to the project of the beatification of Pope Pius XII against the protests from Israel, Karol Wojtyla conceded that there had been too much silence in regard to the crimes against the Jews from the side of the Catholic Church. The consequence of this world-wide protest was that in the Holy Year Pius IX and John XXIII was beatified instead of Pius XII.

However, on October 28, 2000 in the *Hamburger Abendblatt*, Andreas English entered into the discourse once more. Under the title "Has the Vatican Been Hiding Something? – Experts Should Clarify Why Pope Pius XII Was Quiet About the Holocaust." The beatification of Pius XII was once more thematized. There was the complaint that the Vatican did not open its archives. All the documents that came into the Vatican after the death of Pope Benedict XV, on January 22, 1922, have been placed into the secret archive. The *Hamburg Abendblatt* demanded that the Vatican should prove that the suspicion was not true that Pius XII wished for the victory of Hitler's armies because he was afraid of Communism. The newspaper conceded finally that a prejudgment against Pope Pius XII was not the intention of the historians. First of all, many documents still had to be analyzed until one could be found with an unambiguous statement to this question, one that could withstand any later test.

One answer to the question as to whether Pius XII should have broken his silence in order to accuse the Nazis publicly of mass murder had been given by John Paul II in 1996 when he beatified the Cathedral priest of the Headwigs church in Berlin, Bernhard Lichtenberg. The Catholic priest had called publicly for prayers for the Jews in the Third Reich. After two years of imprisonment, Lichtenberg died on November 3, 1943 on the way to a concentration camp. Lichtenberg was born in 1875 in Silessian Ohlau (*Berliner Morgenpost* November 6, 1997).

Admittedly already Rolf Hochhuth had directed attention to Lichtenberg in his drama "The Deputy." Hochhuth had dedicated his drama to the memory of Peter Maximilian Kolbe, who died in Aushwitz's hunger bunker and to Prelate Bernhard Lichtenberg, Cathedral Priest at St. Headwigs church, Berlin. In a free translation, Hochhuth gave expression to the acts and the goals of the Berlin Cathedral priest in the figure of the Jesuit priest, Riccardo Fontana.

He is a counter figure to Pius XII, who was silent when Lichtenberg accused the Nazi's publicly. When Lichtenberg was thrown into prison, he asked his captors if he could share the fate of the Jews in the East. The Nazi's did not fulfill his request. However, the respect of the executioners for the public reputation of the priest was so great that after his death they released his corpse and allowed a few thousand Berliners to participate in his funeral (Hochhuth 1963:16).

On Monday, March 3, 2001, under the category of "political books" the Frankfurter *Allgemeine Zeitung* published a book review by Konrad Repgen. Repgen directed the attention of his readers to a book by the French Jesuit Pierre Blet, which under the title "Pope Pius XII and the Second World War" had been translated from the French into German by Birgit Martens-Schöner and had come out the previous year in the publishing house Ferdinand Schöningh in Paderborn. Pierre Blet's work, with the original title "Pius XII and the Second World War According to the Vatican Archives," was presented for the first time in Paris in 1997. It belongs to the remarkable things of our media landscape that until today no one has taken this work officially into consideration. Somehow Blet's work seems not to be appropriate for the writers of the articles in the *Berliner Morgenpost* or in the *Hamburger Nachtausgabe*. Or should we maybe assume that one does not even know the book in the editorial offices of these newspapers? In any case, the discussion of Eugenio Pacelli does not seem to be free from partiality and prejudices that have been customary already for four decades.

In February 1963, the young author Rolf Hochhuth's drama *The Deputy* appeared, which changed the until then non-controversial, high reputation that Pius XII enjoyed to the negative. In this drama Hochhuth assumed that Pius XII had been quiet about the Third Reich at a point in time when a public declaration of the Pope would have put an end to the National Socialistic murder of Jews. Since that time, there have been innumerable articles and debates about the quotation "Silence of the Pope." Even prudent Jewish historians, such as the well-known, always critical Pinchas Lapide, who in the circle of the Johann Wolfgang Goethe Universität in Frankfurt am Main took the side of Pius XII, were not heard.

In this situation, Pope Paul VI [1963–1978], who in the Second World War had been one of the closest co-operators with Pius XII decided at the end of 1964 to counter the fictitious Pacelli in Hochhuth's drama with a large document addition about the factual activity of Eugenio Pacelli. This task was entrusted to four Jesuits, who as competent historians enjoyed a high reputation in specialist circles: these were Robert Graham from the United States [died in 1997], Angelo Martini from Italy [died in 1981], Burkhart Schneider from Germany [died in 1976], and Pierre Blet from France, who was born in 1918. Blet had received his doctorate at the Sorbonne and since then had taught at the Gregorian University in Rome as well as at the Papal Academy of Diplomats. The *"Actes et Documents du Saint Siège relatifs à la Seconde Guerre Mondiale"* (ADSS), as the editors of the Papal Secretariat of State signed as being responsible, have appeared in eleven volumes between 1965–1981. They contain 5,000 documents that have been printed in complete text and reveal in their footnotes many thousands of further texts.

Five volumes document the attempts of the Vatican to influence the course of the war actions, i.e. to prevent the entrance into the war by Italy, Spain and other States. Four volumes document the efforts of the Holy See to help the victims of the war. Two further volumes are devoted to the politically important correspondence of the Pope with the German and the Polish Bishops during the Second World War. The quality of the Vatican addition corresponds to the high standards of comparable document publications of Western States.

It is admittedly correct that so far the Vatican secret archive is open only to the year 1922 so that the testing of the Vatican addition is not possible in detail. The credibility of the Vatican document publication, however, can be easily tested through comparison with the archive pieces of participating States. Of historians of some standing, so far only the British scholar Owen Chaddwick has undertaken such comparison. In 1986, Chaddwick published a convincing investigation under the title "Great Britain and the Vatican in the Second World War" and he has thereby proven that the Vatican addition has not been falsified. Unfortunately, up to today, contemporary historical research has so far not taken into consideration the Vatican edition. So far, there is no significant monograph of high standing about the theme "Pius XII and the Second World War." Also, the book by Pierre Blet cannot fill that empty spot. Blet starts from the observation that the content if not even the existence of the Vatican document edition has by-passed many scholars, who write about and judge the politics of Pius XII. The review of his book in the Frankfurter *Allgemeine Zeitung* Conrad Repgen confirmed this conception and added "the ADSS gathers dust and remains unused to a large extent on the shelves of great libraries, while late night talk shows are concerned with Pius XII."

Blet wrote his book in order to change this condition. He took up again the extensive introductions of the ADSS and compressed and enriched them with greater source excerpts. In twelve strictly chronologically ordered chapters, he offers a highly interesting document presentation about the diplomatic activity of the Holy See in the Second World War and about the reports of Papal help of the victims of war and persecution. Blet reports *sine ira et studio*. He abstains from all apologetics. Only on the last pages of his final chapter does Blet openly stand on the side of Pius XII. Still in 1952, Pius XII was convinced that he did everything that was possible to help the Jews. Repgen supports this judgment. The Papal decisions were made neither blindly nor in fear for the existence of the Roman Catholic Church. They were "painfully difficult considerations." One is tempted with Bertolt Brecht to declare:

> You who will rise out of the flood
> in which we have gone under,
> remember
> when you speak of our weaknesses
> also the dark time which you have escaped.

We want to show through a few examples that contemporary history has up to today neglected the role of the Papacy in international relations. In the new Hitler biography of the British historian Ian Kershaw, the name of Pius XII is not even mentioned in the name register.

The Cardinal Secretary – Eugenio Pacelli – is chosen as Pope

On March 2, 1939, Cardinal Eugenio Pacelli was elected successor of Pope Pius XI. The new pope chose the name Pius XII. This was a confession to his predecessor to whom he had been the closest cooperator and whose politics he would continue. Pius XII had been prepared particularly well for his task. During World War I, Benedict XV had sent him first to Austria and then to Germany where he was supposed to look for possibilities of reducing the chances of war. During his twelve year mission as Nuncios in Germany, beginning in 1917 in Munich and then in Berlin in 1925, Pius XII had developed a preference for Germany that lasted his entire life. He was considered to be a Germanophile. That was particularly resented paradoxically by the German left after 1963.

As Cardinal Secretary of State, Eugenio Pacelli was responsible for the Concordat between the Third Reich and the Holy See on July 20, 1933. This Treaty was the first foreign policy recognition for Hitler. The Vatican affirmed and confirmed the Third Reich as an equal member in the circle of European Nations. In the Empire Concordat, the Pope sacrificed political Catholicism in order to defend the Church in Germany. This was a momentous mistake as would soon become obvious. Pius XI considered the thought up to his death to cancel the Concordat between the Catholic Church and the Third Reich, which was continually broken by the National Socialists.

However, Pius XI was convinced of the diplomatic and religious qualities of Eugenio Pacelli. For Pius XI, there was no doubt that Pacelli, whom he had recalled in 1929 from Germany and who he had made into his Secretary of State, would be chosen as his successor. Through missions in France, the Cardinal State Secretary found the opportunity to become familiar with the French culture. During a great round trip through the United States in the year 1936, Pacelli met President Roosevelt, who from then on he considered to be "an old friend and a good friend" and with whom he corresponded again and again. While the Cardinal Secretary of State traveled through the American continent, Pius XI said of him *"sara un bell papa!"* – He will be a wonderful Pope!

Cardinal Secretary of State Eugenio Pacelli was elected Pope on March 2, 1939. After his election, Pius XII called Cardinal Luigi Maglione to the post of the Cardinal Secretary of State. Maglione had been Nuncios in Paris for ten years. Immediately subordinated to him was Monsigneior Tardini. Since 1937, he was Secretary of the Congregation for Extra-Ordinary Ecclesiastical Affairs. On March 15, 1939, while diplomatic representatives of the whole world were still celebrating the coronation of the new Pope in Rome, Hitler broke the Munich agreement and marched into Czechoslovakia. In the eyes of all the world it became clear that Hitler was not concerned with the revision of the Versailles Treaty but with the conquest and the territorial gains in the East by the German Empire. With the invasion into Prague, Hitler lost all trust in England, who Hitler wanted up to the last moment in a kind of love-hate relationship to pull over to his own side. Chamberlain announced on March 31 before the lower House that England would help Poland in case its independence was threatened. On April 13, France guaranteed the integrity and existence of Poland. On the same day, both powers broadened and extended their guarantee declarations to Greece and Romania. The appeasement politics represented by Neville Chamberlain had broken down. Mussolini, who wanted to compensate himself for the gains of the German Empire in Central Europe bombarded Tirana on April 7. The Italians occupied Albania.

On April 9, 1939, in his Easter Sunday sermon in St. Peter's Cathedral, Pius XII saw peace threatened and deplored and lamented the armament competition, which made it more difficult every day to prevent the war. President Roosevelt directed a long message to Hitler and Mussolini. He demanded from the two dictators to commit themselves for a time of ten years to not attack thirty-one countries, the list of which he attached to the letter. Beyond that Roosevelt asked the Pope to intervene with Hitler and Mussolini in order to give his message a stronger emphasis. Pius XII answered that at the moment he was not able to introduce himself to Hitler in the desired way. The Vatican had estimated the situation correctly. On April 28, Hitler gave a speech before the Diet in which he sharply attacked Poland and ridiculed the message of President Roosevelt (Blet 2000:6).

In the midst of massive confusion, all of which pursued the same goal, namely to rescue the peace, the following demand was finally settled upon. The Pope should call for a world conference in order to facilitate a peaceful solution of the unresolved problems. The attempt of a Papal negotiator to win over the Duce for a common conference of the five European powers failed. Also a discussion in Berlin, which the Nuncios Cesare Orsenigo had with Hitler on the Berghof, was unsatisfactory. Hitler asked the Nuncios to express his real thanks to the Holy See, but he would have to get into contact with the Duce first.

Today, nobody will believe at all that Hitler would have allowed himself to be restricted in his will to annihilate Poland through the intervention of the Pope. Every historian who is concern with the foreign policy of the Third Reich knows that it belongs to the political strategy of Hitler not to get involved in multilateral conferences. Under all circumstances, Hitler wanted to avoid a second Munich. Despite that, Saul Friedländer (1965:27) imputed in his historical documentation, which was published in connection with

Hochhuth's (1963) *Deputy*, that Pius XII had only searched for a pretense when he answered the American President that at present the relationship between the Holy See and the German government was not favorable for such a step. Before the beginning of World War II, Hitler never shied away at any time from lying to the entire world about his will for peace despite the fact that the assault on Poland had long before been a decided matter. The initiative of the American President misjudged Hitler's intentions and was from the very beginning without any chance.

However, in the Summer of 1939, Papal diplomacy undertook everything it could in order to prevent the outbreak of the war. After a talk of the Nuncio in Italy with Count Ciano, the son-in-law of Mussolini and his foreign minister, Poland was warned against provoking Hitler in Danzig. As a matter of fact, Ciano met Hitler and Ribbentrop in Salzburg from August 11–13. Ribbentrop did not keep it a secret any longer that an attack against Poland was at hand. Nevertheless, the Vatican was successful in getting the Duce to declare to Hitler that Italy was not in a position to support him militarily in a conflict that would break out immediately after the attack against Poland. Finally, a Papal radio speech was prepared in the Vatican in which some people saw the *ultima-ratio* for peace. On August 24th at 7:00PM, Pius XII directed the call for negotiation and peace to the whole world.

> Only through the power of reason not weapons, will justice pave its way. Empires that are not grounded on the foundations of justice are not blessed by God. A politics freed from morality betrays its own author. Dangers are immediately threatening, but there is still time. Nothing is lost with peace but all can be lost with war. May the strong ones hear us in order not to become weak in the injustice. May the powerful hear us if they want their power not to mean destruction (Blet 2000:18).

Had the words of the Pope reached Hitler? Hitler, who had already given the order to attack for the night of August 25–26, hesitated once more. He wanted to make a last attempt to convince England and France to abandon Poland. In the last negotiation phase before the start of World War II, the Vatican tried through its Nuncios in Berlin and Warsaw to negotiate an agreement about the fate of the ethical minorities between Germany and Poland. On August 28, the Nuncio in Berlin had to admit that it was impossible to present a solution that would be acceptable to both sides.

On the same day, the French ambassador Monsignior Montini demanded the public gesture of the Pope in favor of the Poles, who for centuries had stood faithfully with the Roman Catholic Church. Pius XII refused. The ambassador was told

> His Holiness says that this was asking too much. One was not allowed to forget that there were forty million Catholics in the German Empire. To what repressive action would they be exposed after such an expression of the Holy See? The Pope had spoken already and he had done this very clearly (Blet 2000:18).

On November 9, 1939, the ambassador of Great Britain to the Holy See, Sir Osbourne, wrote to the Papal Secretary of State, Magilione,

> In the last talk that I had with you, you asked me if I believed that the Holy See has done everything possible for it in order to rescue the peace. I answered without hesitation that I was convinced of that. I have told Lord Halifax of this talk, who asked me to tell your Eminence that he is in full agreement with what I have said (Blet 2000:22).

Hitler or Stalin – Which Alternative does the Vatican have?

In the morning of June 22, 1941, Hitler's army attacked the Soviet Union. Pastor Rudolphi wrote in his parish chronical, (*Sankta Familia Chronike*, 51) the following confession:

> It is also furthermore clear and becomes clearer to me that only Hitler could complete this enormous achievement, to create an army, which could encounter this storm of Mongols – on a day like today a reflection on the last 23 years is necessary. Bolshevism would have let its army march, in 1941 or later, in this or another war. One may imagine the Germany of 1932 in the face of such an Asian army. It would have rolled over us like a steamroller. And while there in the East, Catholic fights beside Protestant, one like the other in the service of the Fatherland, one hurts us here at home all the time. Where is the meaning in all this? I am often questioned more or less nicely because I am too political in my sermons: What this meant by this is the demand to have a positive attitude to the great tasks of the time. When I spoke of the "Divine Providence" one expressed oneself ironically that I

am after all quoting the Fuehrer. Our believers are insecure and troubled and deeply embittered because of the manifold and radical interventions in the religious life.

In another place Pastor Rudolphi (*Sankta Familia Chronike*, 49) writes,

> In my two sermons, I related myself to this great and tremendous war against Bolshevism, in which are effective, 'Satan and the other evil spirits, who move about in the world for its perdition.' How will this opponent look? One does not think very highly of his military efficiency and ability since small Finland could resist him so long. However, Bolshevism is machine obsessed. He will probably be equal to us concerning instruments of war. If his masses are not fanaticized: …our great strength has been so far the combination between the soldier's efficiency and ability with the means of modern technology. What will the struggle look like, which the stubborn death defying Russian Muschik of the First World War will engage in after 20 years of Bolshevist formation?

This was one image of the mood from Catholic Germany in June 1941. Behind the public indignation about the attack of the German army against the Soviet Union, many British and French politicians were hiding in silent contentment. It was the general opinion that two hated powers had finally begun to struggle against each other. The hope was that they would annihilate each other so the rest of Europe could gain advantage from it. From the Vatican, the correspondent of the New York Times wrote: "the Vatican hopes that the German-Soviet war will give time to the British Empire and to the United States to improve its military preparations" (Blet 2000:116).

The Vatican had no reason whatsoever to deplore the fate of the Soviet Union, which was now under attack by the German army, particularly after Stalin and Hitler participated together in the annihilation of Catholic Poland. In his encyclical *"Divini Redemptoris,"* Pius XI had already signified Communism as being "evil in its innermost core." This attitude was known in Berlin and may have given the Nazi's the idea of presenting themselves as a kind of crusader for the rescue of Christian Europe. In Germany where the public was excluded from every critical commentary of the politics of Hitler by the Nazi's, many people believed like Pastor Rudolphi in this propaganda lie. As a matter of fact, Ribbentrop said during an audience with the Pope, already on March 11, 1940, that as he saved Germany from Communism so Hitler has also rescued the Church. However, Pius XII did not yield to this argumentation and he firmly rejected the National Socialistic ambition to present the German Empire as the defender of Christianity against Communism. From reports from the Papal Nuncio in Berlin, one knew that National Socialism and freedom of religion were not able to agree with one another. The harassment and dirty tricks of the Nazi's against the Catholic Church in Germany were carefully registered in Rome.

Despite of all that, the ambassador of Italy to the Holy See, Bernardo Attolico, asked on September 5, 1941 that the Church support the struggle of the Axis powers against Bolshevism. Secretary of the Congregation for Extra-ordinary Ecclesiastical Affairs, Monsignior Tardini answered Attolico's statement by saying:

> that the attitude of the Holy See against Bolshevism did not need to be clarified. The Holy See already had disapproved of Bolshevism with all of its errors and had condemned it and imposed the Church ban on it... There can be no question that the one who had ended friendship treaties with Russia in the past no longer had to explain his behavior [...] Tardini added, in consideration of the explanations, condemnations etc. of the Holy See, that he would be very happy if communism was put out of action. It was the worst enemy of the Church. Yet, it was not the only enemy of the Church. Nazism had organized a real persecution against the Church, which was still taking place. Correspondingly, the swastika was not [...] necessarily the cross [...] of the crusade. Yet, nevertheless, it was the Germans and not Mussolini who spoke for the first time of a crusade (Blet 2000:118).

In his Christmas message of December 24, 1941, the Pope announced principles, which condemned the methods of the National Socialists as well as those of the Soviets. In an order founded on justice, so Pius XII stated, there was no place for attacks against the freedom and the security of other nations, and finally, there also was no place for the persecution of religion and the Church.

Significant for the situation in which Pius XII found himself at the time, was also a rumor that Stalin had written to the Pope. The Vatican denied the rumor. Up to today, no writing of Stalin to Pius XII has been found in the archives of the Vatican.

After the attack of Germany against the Soviet Union, the question arose for President Roosevelt whether the United States should support the

Soviet Union and Stalin along with Great Briton. However, support of Stalin met with great objections in the United States. In the eyes of many people in the United States, the political dictatorship of Stalin and the religious persecution in the Soviet Union forbid such cooperation. On September 17, 1941, the ex-President Herbert Hoover stated:

> I believe and 99% of Americans believe that totalitarianism, be it National Socialistic or Communistic is abhorrent. These two forms are immoral because they reject religion and they do not know of a faithfulness to obligations. They go into error because of their unspeakable cruelty and their abhorrent killing of millions of human lives. I reject any kind of compromise or alliance of America with them. What would be the result, out of millions who are enslaved in Russia and in the whole of Europe and out of our own freedom, if we would have to send our own sons in order to win the war for Communism (Blet 2000:120).

Particularly, Catholics in America rejected every thought of cooperating with the Soviet Union. The encyclical letter *Divini Redemptoris* of Pius XI was remembered by Catholics in the United States. It became clear to Roosevelt that he needed the help of Rome in order to find a majority in Congress for such cooperation with Stalin.

Myron C. Taylor, personal representative of President Roosevelt to the Holy See, brought a personal message from the President to Pius XII. Taylor was received for an audience with Pope Pius XII on September 10, 1941. Since there is no direct witness about the talk with Pius XII, we have to depend on notes of the Papal Secretary of State Maglioni. Taylor said to Cardinal Maglioni that Americans were convinced that Hitler would lose the war. The United States had nevertheless prepared themselves for a defensive war. The United States' military potential had already reached a considerable strength. Yet, it would remain outside the conflict as long as Hitler would not provoke the U.S. and as long as the allies would not be in danger of being beaten. Taylor then explained to the Pope the Atlantic Charter, which had been concluded in August 1941. He added that Roosevelt and Churchill wished that the Pope would follow them and would support through his own declaration the ideas that had been expressed by Roosevelt and Churchill.[1]

---

[1] On August 14, 1941, Churchill and Roosevelt published a declaration concern-

Pius XII rejected the proposal with the relevant information that he could not mix his voice with that of Statesmen because then he would make himself suspicious of partisanship for the one or the other camp. Taylor then raised a question, which was of great significance for the American President. There were in America Catholics who interpreted the Encyclical letter *Divini Redemptoris* in such a way that they could not separate the Communism from the Russian people. If one would help the Russian people, so they argued, then one would also help Stalin. Therefore, there was the threat of a deep split among the American Catholics. The Pope was astonished by this. For the Russian people, the Pope continued to have only fatherly feelings. In other words, this meant that Catholics should have no scruples to support Roosevelt if he wanted to support Stalin against Hitler (Blet 2000:124). The Pope had condemned Communism not Russia, just as he insisted after the defeat of Germany on the differentiation between National Socialism and the German people. However, only too soon, Roosevelt was no longer dependent on the support on the Vatican in the question of whether the United States should fight on the side of Stalin.

On December 7, 1941, the Japanese sank the American Fleet in Pearl Harbor. On December 11, 1941, Hitler declared war on the United States. At the same time, the German attack against Moscow failed in the icy winter. Today, we know that in December 1941 the war was lost for Germany. From this time on, Hitler no longer succeeded in any thing.

The Vatican and the Holocaust

As part of my research on this topic, I once again after thirty years took Hochhuth (1963) from my bookshelves and read once more his drama *The Deputy*. We discussed this drama at the university in the 1960's and I still talked about it at the beginning of the 1970's in High School with our students. I am today, after thirty-seven years, still as shaken up as I was at that time, and I am inclined to contradict the whole apologetics for Pius XII.

---

ing the goals and principle of their common politics. The Atlantic Charter became a fundamental document of the United Nations. It demands, for instance, the nation's right to self-determination, free global commerce, and the erection of a world-wide safety system.

In the second act of *The Deputy*, Hochhuth (1963:83) dramatized the scene, which he dated on February 2, 1943. The location of the action is the house of the Counsel at the Vatican, Count Fontana, whose son, a member of the Jesuit order, Hochhuth gave traits of the Berlin Prior Bernhard Lichtenberg. Father Ricardo Fontana has come from the *Nuntiatur* in Berlin to Rome in order to convince the Pope to take publically a position against the Holocaust. Father and son argue about the silence of the Pope.

> Fontana: Ricardo please – that is unfair, That is already demogogical. Despite of all the coldness he tries nevertheless to help and to understand. And if he is also as egocentric as he may be, the victims…
>
> Ricardo: Do you really believe he has the victims before his eyes? The world press, the embassy, the agents – they bring all the details. You believe that he does not only study statistics, abstract numbers, seven hundred thousands dead – hunger, gassing, deportations,…but that he is with it, that he has once looked at it, that he has turned his new insight – that he has really observed: the deporation from Paris, three hundred suicides already before trip begins. Children under 5 years are torn away from the parents – And then, Konin near Warsaw: eleven thousand Poles, immovable gas chambers, their cries, their prayers – and the laughter of the SS criminals. Eleven thousand – but imagine I, you, we would be them. […]
>
> Fontana: Surly, surly, but what depends on it? He after all is not allowed to obey the feeling!
>
> Ricardo: Father! – What you say there, that cannot be – You cannot say this. Do you not comprehend here! – You, Father, you must comprehend…: A deputy of Christ, who has that before his eyes and is silent nevertheless because of state raison de'etate, who reflects only one day, who hesitates only one hour to raise the voice of his pain to a curse, which lets still the last person of this earth shutter –: such a Pope is…a criminal.

However, Pierre Blet provides another view of this situation through his review of the document publication of the Vatican. Before the beginning of the Second World War, the situation of the Church in Germany worried the Pope greatly. The military events in September and October 1939 sharpened the problems the Catholic Church dramatically. During a few weeks, the whole of Poland fell victim to the Third Reich and the Soviet

Union. Poland's Western territories were annexed by the Third Reich. The Southern part of Poland was transformed into a kind of colony, the so-called "General Government." East Poland – up to about the Curzon Line – was occupied by the Red Army. Poland was torn apart by two powers, which had made the annihilation of Christianity their task. What the Nazi's did not yet dare to do in the Reich, because there was a well organized Catholic population, they could put shamelessly into action in the conquered Poland. Beside the Polish Jews, representatives of the Catholic faith were also marked for extermination. Up to the end of the war, four Polish Bishops, 1,996 priest, 113 clerics, 341 simple Brothers, 1,117 Nuns were killed. On September 30, 1939, the Pope turned to the Polish people for the first time with a message of conciliation. However, he avoided every condemnation of the aggressors. A few days later, he said in his inaugural encyclical *Summi Pontificatus:*

> The blood of innumerable human beings, also of non-combatants, raises a terrifying lamentation, particularly also about a much loved people as the Polish people, whose ecclesiastical faithfulness and merit concerning the rescue of the Christian culture are written with inextinguishable letters into the book of history. And to give the Polish people a right to the human – brotherly sympathy of the world. Trusting in the powerful intercession of Mary, the help of Christians, the Polish people long for the hour of a resurrection according to the principles of justice and of a true peace (Blet 2000:69).

Cardinal Hlnold, Archbishop of Poland and Gnesen, thanked Pius XII. Already in the first month of the German occupation, hundreds of priests were arrested and shot. Catholic intellectuals, clerics and lay people were sent into the concentration camp Oranienburg.

Hitler wanted the vacancy of many Polish Bishop Sees to force the Vatican to nominate German Bishops in Poland. When he did not succeed in that, on June 10, 1942, Hitler denied the Vatican the right to appear before the German authorities because of these issues. After the attack against the Soviet Union, Poland became the field of experimentation for the Nazis. A large part of the Polish territory in the West was united into the Reichsgau Wartheland. At the head of all of this, Hitler put the former President of the city of Danzig, Arthur Greisler. Greisler acted very harshly against priests and Bishops and tried to establish a Catholic Church independent of Rome, first in the Warthegau, and later also in the German Reich and its satellites. The decree about the religious communities, which created a "Roman Catholic Church of German Nation" was promulgated by Gauleiter Greisler on September 13, 1941. Greisler's ultimate goal was a German Empire in which the Roman Catholic Church would be replaced by a German National Church. However, what was at stake ultimately was the annihilation of Christianity in general.

Maybe these processes are a explanation of the fact that the Pope did not dare univocally to protest against the crimes of the Nazis. The protest of the Papal Nuntius Orsenigo in Berlin was mostly not accepted by Ribbentrop as far as they concerned Poland. In any case, such protests remained behind the closed doors of the Chancellory. Therefore, many Poles believed that the Holy See was indifferent toward their fate (Blet 2000:79).

With the German attack against Russia, the persecutions of the Jews increased. In the occupied territories, terror commandos of the SS murder 370,000 Jews through mass execution. The first mass executions by poison gas took place in Chelmno, near Lodz in 1941. The plans for organized genocide climaxed in the Wannsee Conference on January 20, 1942.

The leaders of the Jewish communities in Europe and America asked the Pope to intervene on behalf of the deported Jews. In the meantime, it became known that in the death camps, hundreds of people died due to poison gas locked up in chambers. In his Christmas speech of 1942, the Pope condemned all the cruelties of the present war. He spoke of "hundreds of thousands, who being personally guiltless but due to their nationality or descent were given over to death or were committed to an increasing impoverishment" (Blet 2000:292).

In the night from October 15–16, 1943, the SS searched house after house for Jews in Rome according to prepared lists. There were many Jews living in Rome who were baptized Catholics. Also they were deported. All of this happened, as Hochhuth presented it extremely dramatically in his play "The Deputy" [Compare the third act, first scene], practically under the windows of the Vatican, even those of the Pope. Already on July 19, 1943, 500 airplanes of the Allies attacked and bombed the city of Rome for 3 hours. At the end of October 1942, Cardinal Magalione communicated to the American ambassador Taylor that the Pope would protest in the case of a bombardment by the Allies. Roosevelt was personally against the bombardment of Rome, but Churchill remained obstinate. On December 28, the British ambassador at the Vatican affirmed the declaration of Churchill that the British would not hesitate to bomb Rome if the course of the war demanded it. A protest of the Pope would be understood as standing up in favor of the fascist government. On May 16, the British bomb Ostia. During the bombardment on July 19, 1943, there were 1,500 dead and wounded. The Basillica of San Lorenzo fuori le muria, one of the oldest and holiest churches of Rome was hit. Pius XII went with Cardinal Magnilione into the corner of San Lorenzo in order to help the people there.

On July 25, 1943, the Italian King Victor Emanuel III let the Duce be arrested. Pietro Badoglio formed a new government excluding the fascist. Hitler was of the opinion that the Vatican had participated in the conspiracy against Mussolini. During the military situation discourse in the early morning hours of July 26, 1943, Hitler answered the question if one should occupy the Vatican exits by saying: "That does not matter at all. I will move immediately into the Vatican no matter what. Do you think that I'm worried about the Vatican? It will be taken right away. There is most of all the whole diplomatic Corp inside. That doesn't matter to me. We will take out the whole pig gang" (Heiber 1963:171).

Only with greatest effort were Goebbles and Ribbentrop able to keep Hitler from taking an unheard of action against the Vatican (Kersaw 2000:775). On September 8, 1943, the Italian army capitulated to the allies. At that time, sixteen German divisions had already been moved to the Italian mainland. 650,000 Italian soldiers became German prisoners of war. Only a part of the Italian Navy and the insignificant air force of Italy could escape. Only a few hours after the Italian capitulation, the allies landed in the Gulf of Salarno, about 50 kilometers South-East of Naples. The German army resisted fanatically. They fought for every kilometer of the Italian mainland (Kersaw 2000:780–781). On September 12, German paratroopers were able to free Benitto Mussolini from an Italian prison and take him to Hitler in Rastenburg. On September 15, 1943 at the Gardasee, Mussolini formed in Salo, a fascist counter-government with a cabinet of Badoglio in Rome, which a few days later on September 29 escaped to the allies in Bari.

That is the historical background against which the Jews of Rome were arrested four weeks later on October 12–13 by the SS. Despite that, thousands of Jews found protection in the Convents, Monasteries, and in the Vatican itself. Many were also able to escape to the South to the Americans. However,

1,259 Jews fell into the hands of the SS and were murdered in Auschwitz. Often they were baptized Jews who were not at all aware of the danger that threatened them. This is the scenario of the third act of Hochhuth's (1963) *Deputy*. Should the Pope have condemned in this heated situation the SS regime publicly, as Hochhuth and others demanded?

In a Consistorial speech, in July 1943, the Pope came back once more to those who had turned to him because they had been predetermined for annihilation on the basis of their nationality. At that time, Pius XII had admonished that the one who carried the sword was only allowed to use it in the sense of the law of God (Blet 2000:292–293). As urging as these words were for the one who was willing to receive them, they did nevertheless not satisfy those who demanded a clear condemnation of the crimes that were committed by the Nazis. The Pope spoke in diplomatically skillful language where what was at stake was to reach millions of people who waited for a clear condemnation of National Socialism's crimes. In the same speech, Pius XII declared that every word of his public declaration had to be well considered in the interests of those who suffer and had to be weighed with particular seriousness (Blet 2000:293). From now on, Pius XII held on to this reserved attitude.

There were several reasons for the silence of the Pope. While Hochhuth asserted that the Vatican was very well informed about the annihilation camps, the documentary report of Pierre Blet puts this thesis into question. A great insecurity with what happened to the Jews in the different camps can be read again and again in the published documents of the Vatican. Only in May 1943 did the Secretary of State receive a copy of the message that the world Jewish Congress had directed to the British and American Governments. In this copy it was mentioned that the annihilation campaign against the Jews had reached its peak. One spoke of death camps where the victims died from the effect of gas. According to Blet, the motives for the silence of Pius XII were obvious.

The Red Cross had validated these motives for itself in a very strong formula: the protests had no effect at all and could prove to be dangerous particularly for those who such protest tried to help. The only possibility to help the Jews, so answered the State Department, was to win the war. Concerning this argumentation, Blet (2000:293) relates himself to Robert M. W. Kempner, the representative of the United States during the Nuremberg Trial, who said "every attempt of propaganda by the Catholic Church against Hitler's empire would not only have been a self demanded suicide as Rosenberg had recently explained; it would have accelerated the execution of the Jews and the Priests."

According to Blet (2000:294), Pius XII acted out of consideration for the German Catholics and not at all out of consideration for the Regime or its leaders, because the Pope did not have any illusions about the real intentions of the leadership of the Third Reich. The persecution of the Church had become even worse through the war and continued into the last month. Pius XII said on June 2, 1945:

> [...the Nazis believed namely]...that they could finish up the Church forever right after the completion of the military victory. Believable and irrefutable witnesses have informed us continually about these plans.

While the Pope communicated toward the outside the impression of silence, through directives the State Secretariat urged the Nuncia and the Apostalic representatives in Slovakia, in Croatia, in Romania, and in Hungary to intervene with the government and with the Episcopate to give help. That the help of the Vatican was effective is witnessed by the repeated gratitude of Jewish organizations in 1945. The Israeli historian Pinchas Lapide estimates the number of the Jews saved by the Holy See to be 850,000 (Blet 2000:294).

I conclude this analysis, which could give only a few aspects of this upsetting discussion, with two more time witnesses, who relate themselves admittedly not explicitly to the silence of the Pope but to the role of the Catholic Church in the Third Reich and who in their position give indirectly also their own judgment about the silence of the Pope.

On April 25, 1945, Pastor Rudolphie wrote into the *Chronical* of the parish Sancta Familia (296), when the city of Frankfurt am Main was occupied by the Americans:

> Also we have become guilty but not as Churchill, the Americans and the Russians declare us to be guilty. We carry a guilt of weakness of faith, of a confusion of spiritual attitude. If in the year 1933, the Bishops would have called for broad opposition then this demand would have remained ineffective. Because the consequences of the Versailles Treaty, the fever of a terribly suffering nation had also among Catholics confused the spirits to a large extent so that they only saw the political hopes and underestimated the religious and moral consequences.

On February 23, 1946, Konrad Adenauer judged this completely differently in a letter to Bernhard Custodis, pastor of the Elisabeth Church in Bonn:

> In my opinion, the German people and the Bishops and the clergy carry a great guilt concerning the happenings in the concentrations camps. It is correct, that after 1933 maybe not much could be done any longer. The guilt lies earlier. The German people, also the Bishops and the clergy to a large extent, fell for the National Socialistic agitation. It could be adopted nearly without resistance, and partially with enthusiasm. In this lies the guilt. In general, one has also known – if one has also not known the process in the camps to their whole extent –, that personal freedom, all principles of right were stepped on, that in the concentration camps great cruelties were committed, that the Gestapo, our SS and partially also our troops in Poland and Russia have proceeded with unparalleled cruelty against the civilian population. The Jewish Pograms of 1933 and 1938 happened completely publicly. The murder of hostages in France were made know by us officially. One can also really not assert that the public did not know that the National Socialistic government and the leadership of the Army violated continually as a matter of principle the natural law, the Haag Convention, and the simplest commandments of humanity. I believe that if the Bishops all together had opposed this on a definite day publicly from the pulpits, they could have prevented much. That has not happened and for that there is no excuse. If thereby the Bishops would have gone into prison or concentration camps that would not have been a damage, to the contrary. All that has not happened and therefore it is best to be silent about it (*Frankfurter Allgemeine Nr4 Zeitung*, January 5, 2001:6).

Chapter Four

Tepeyac and Plymouth Rock: Pilgrimage and Nationalism in Mexico and the United States

Brian C. Wilson

Perhaps some of the best examples of the migration of the sacred from pre-modern religions into the new religions of modernity can be found in the rituals of nationalism as they developed in the early modern period. In this chapter, I investigate the origins and processes that led to the development of nationalist pilgrimages by comparing four pilgrimages that arose in the colonial periods of Mexico and the United States. As we shall see, the transformation of a pilgrimage into a stable nationalist ritual was not a simple or straightforward process, and many elements had to mesh precisely if such a transformation were to occur successfully. Of the four colonial pilgrimages discussed below, only three became the object of nationalist sentiment and of the three, only two have survived as nationalist pilgrimages to the present day. Although necessarily elliptical given restraints on space, I will endeavor in the following to explain some of the chief reasons why the migration of the sacred was successful in some cases, but not in others. I will conclude by discussing some of the key similarities and differences between nationalist pilgrimage in Mexico and the U.S.

Two Pilgrimages in Colonial Mexico

One of the most popular pilgrimages in New Spain during the sixteenth century centered on the image of the Virgin Mary venerated near Mexico City on the hill of Tepeyac. The origins of this pilgrimage site were ancient, as it was already a pilgrimage destination for the Indians before the conquest. There, it was said that the Indians venerated an image of Tonantzin, of whom the famous Franciscan ethnographer Bernadino de Sahagún wrote, "The first of these goddesses was called Cihuacóatl, which means wife of the Serpent; they also call her Tonantzin, which means 'our mother'" (Lafaye 1987:211). The shrine at Tepeyac attracted people from points beyond the valley of Mexico and was well known before the conquest (Marin 1972:166–168).

The association of Tepeyac with the Virgin Mary went back to the first days of the conquest. We are told by Bernal Díaz de Castillo in his history of 1568 that during the siege of Tenochtitlan, one of Cortés' lieutenants, the infamous Gonzalo de Sandoval, made his headquarters at Tepeyac, and it is supposed that he erected a shrine to the Virgin Mary there. After the conquest was completed, a statue of the Virgin Mary, copied from the Virgin of Guadalupe in Extremadura in Spain, was installed at the site (Lafaye 1987:232–233). Following church precedent, the Franciscans encouraged investing pagan sites with Christian symbols, and for a time the friars even seem to have encouraged the continuation of Indian pilgrimages to what was now called the Virgin of Guadalupe at Tepeyac (Lafaye 1987:215). Later, in the 1550's, this statue was replaced by the Indian painting, which can be seen there to this day. Late in the sixteenth century, pious legends began to grow up around the sanctuary and the painting, the earliest concerning healing miracles, with later legends recounting an apparition of the Virgin Mary to an Indian shepherd, identified as Juan Diego (Johnson 1981:25–48; Turner 1978:82–85). By this time, however, the pilgrimage site had long since passed out of the hands of the Franciscans and into the firm grip of their arch-rivals, the secular clergy.

Despite their initial promotion of the Tepeyac pilgrimage, the Franciscans ultimately became its most vigorous opponents. Since idolatry persisted in the valley of Mexico well until the second half of the sixteenth century, the Franciscans became paranoid about any practice that – however remotely – preserved pagan belief and practice. Thus Sahagún, for example, in his *Historia general* (1576), denounced the cult of the Virgin Mary of Tepeyac since the Indians who frequented it referred to the image there as the Aztec goddess, Tonantzin (Lafaye 1987:216).[1] Sahagún saw the pilgrimage as nothing more nor less than an insidious confusion of Christianity with paganism, or, worse, as a camouflage for purely pagan practices. Years earlier, in 1556, a prominent Franciscan preacher had denounced the Guadalupe pilgrimage from the pulpit of the church of San Francisco in similar terms. With the civil authorities present, Father Fray Francisco de Bustamente protested against the new cult, which he considered illegitimate and impure, and he singled out the archbishop of Mexico City, Alonso de Montúfar, for especially harsh criticism for his promotion of it. Bustamente argued in this sermon that

> nothing was better calculated to keep the Indians from becoming good Christians than the cult of our Lady of Guadalupe. Ever since their conversion they have been told that they should not believe in idols, but only in God and Our Lady...To tell them now that an image painted by an Indian could work miracles will utterly confuse them and tear up the vine that has been planted (Lafaye 1987:239).

Jacques Lafaye cogently argues that Montúfar and the secular clergy actually tolerated a certain amount of syncretism when it came to this pilgrimage cult since the cult tended to tie the *iglesia indiana* closer to the *iglesia española* by conspicuously bringing Spaniards and Indians together in an exceedingly popular form of worship within sight of the capital, Mexico City (Lafaye 1987:238–240). Thus the Franciscans, who sought desperately to retain control over the *iglesia indiana* by maintaining a policy of strict separation, lost no opportunity in attacking the pilgrimage to Tepeyac. For them, it now represented both a theological *and* a political threat.

This is not to say that the first Franciscans in Mexico did not encourage pilgrimage of any kind. Indeed, while they attacked the cult of the Virgin of

---

[1] Louise Burkhardt (1993:208) argues that Tonantzin was not an authentic pre-conquest goddess: "[In Tonantzin, the] Indians were not perpetuating memories of pre-Columbian goddesses but were projecting elements of their Christian worship into their pre-Christian past, conceptualizing their ancient worship in terms of Mary. Tepeyacac [sic] being holy to Mary, when questioned on ancient worship at the site they assumed that it had always been holy to a figure similar to her and named this figure Tonantzin." For Burkhardt, the Virgin of Guadalupe at Tepeyac is a synthetic figure because she represents the assimilation of the Christian Mary with Nahua notions of heaven, not because she was assimilated with a pre-existing Aztec goddess. Nevertheless, regardless of the origins of Tonantzin, it is clear that by the late 16th century, the reality of such a pre-conquest deity and her association with Tepeyec were accepted by both Indian and Spaniard alike.

Guadalupe, they themselves attempted to promote what they considered more "pure" pilgrimages throughout Mexico, carefully creating shrines where none had existed before. One of the most interesting of these Franciscan-inspired pilgrimages was centered on a town to the southeast of Mexico City, Ameca-meca (Wilson 2003:207–219). This pilgrimage found its focus on the personality of the famous leader of the first twelve Franciscan missionaries to New Spain, Fray Martín de Valencia. During the last years of his life, Fray Martín used to frequent a small cave on the side of a volcanic peak on the outskirts of Amecameca. Here he would meditate and practice what the Franciscans themselves called "frightful austerities." It was here as well that he tended to the wild birds and animals much like St. Francis. Indeed, Martín's earliest biographer enthusiastically played up the similarities between Fray Martín and St. Francis. It was even claimed that Fray Martín was routinely visited by the spirits of both St. Francis and St. Anthony at Amecameca (Jiménez 1926:48–83).

When Martín died, in 1534, the Franciscans seized on the potential of the cave of Amecameca as a shrine (Mendieta 1870:602–605). They constructed out of the cave an archetypal Franciscan pilgrimage site, investing it with a nest of mythological and spatial homologies which tied it back to La Verna, the Italian retreat of St. Francis, and even farther back to the Holy Sepulcher of Jerusalem. In the center of the cave, the Franciscans built a small stone receptacle in which to house the relics of Fray Martín – a reliquary that they called, significantly enough, "the holy sepulcher" (Mendieta 1870: 605).

The relics of Fray Martín themselves have a curious history. Before they could be installed in the reliquary in the cave, the relics suddenly disappeared. It turns out that they had been spirited away by the Indians of Amecameca who kept them hidden for some fifty years. Accidentally discovered by a Dominican in the 1590's, the relics were returned to the Franciscans, who installed them in the cave-shrine. Almost immediately after the installation, the shrine, which had been primarily popular up to this point with Spaniards, now also became a popular pilgrimage site for the Indians of the area. The Franciscans were especially gratified that the Indians of Amecameca posted guards at the entrance of the cave twenty-four hours a day and that processions of Indians ascended to the shrine every week without fail. In later Franciscan accounts of the pilgrimage, the Indians' veneration for Martín's relics were interpreted, naturally enough, in terms of European ideas about the cult of saints and the inherent power of saints' relics. The chroniclers assumed that the Indians of Amecameca, inspired by Fray Martín's saintly example during his life among them, now viewed him as their intercessor before the throne of the Christian God (Mendieta 1870:602–605).

Had the Indians of Amecameca really internalized the European cult of saints so quickly? Did they really respond to Fray Martín as a saint? This would be more than slightly ironic since the records left of Martín's life indicate that he came to hate the Indians over time and thought little of their spiritual state (Jiménez 1926:67). A year before he died, Martín de Valencia even tried to charter a ship to sail to China in order to find people he considered more worthy of Christianity (Mendieta 1870:594). When this failed, Martín, who never managed to learn an Indian language, retired to Amecameca to live out his life in solitude (Jiménez 1926:79). It is doubtful that the Indians of Amecameca had much interaction with him while he lived in Amecameca or that Valencia encouraged such interaction. Considering that a virtuous Nahua life was an intensely communal one, it would seem more likely that the Indians saw Valencia more as a slightly mad misanthrope than as a saint.

We can account for the Indians' behavior better if we interpret it in terms of indigenous categories. The historical anthropologist Jorge Klor de Alva (1993:178), for example, suggests an indigenous framework in which Fray Martín might have fit into the Nahua (Aztec) cosmology:

> As was the case for most sixteenth-century Christians, Nahuas experienced their religiosity primarily as a social phenomenon. Human ("civilized") existence was possible only in the context of participation in a social whole that expanded out from the lineage to the local community and finally to the regional polity that wove the various hamlets into a single unit. Spiritually speaking the moral community was made up of those individuals who recognized as theirs the sacred bundle, *tlaquimilolli*, made up of the relics and/or belongings of the divinized founder – tutelary deity or mythical hero. The physical remains of this man-cum-god were part of the supernatural powers of the universe and therefore functioned as a channel through which flowed the sacred forces that empowered, protected, legitimated, and gave a common identity to the village or town. Logically, the *tlaquimilolli* was housed in the temple that represented the sacred center of the community. Many of these sacred bundles were hidden, and others were destroyed after

the Spanish missionaries insinuated themselves into the local capitals and proceeded to destroy the ancient temples.

We know from indigenous records that the first Franciscans who came to Amecameca did indeed burn the local temple (Schroeder 1989:24), and probably the sacred bundle of the local divinized founder was lost. In a way this signaled an end to the identity of the town; however, the imaginative structures still existed in the minds of the Indians whereby a new divinized founder could be located, this time in the guise of a dead Franciscan missionary. The sacred power of this new "founder" was not based on any special relationship between the town and Martín de Valencia. Rather, it was based on the sacred power he embodied and channeled as a kind of shamanic figure since, although Valencia during his life may not have had a very good relationship with them, the Indians of Amecameca nevertheless understood him to be the Spanish imperial representative of the sacred and therefore some kind of a holy man. Hence, when Valencia died, his relics could be used according to indigenous categories to recreate an identity for the Amecameca area. Indeed, the fact that the Indians hid the sacred bundle from the Franciscans seems to indicate that their conception of it linked it to the older idea of *tlaquimilolli* and not necessarily with European ideas of saints' relics. After all, the Franciscans had destroyed the first *tlaquimilolli*, and if they knew there was a new one, they were likely to destroy that one too. When decades later the bundle was accidentally discovered, the Indians were exceedingly anxious to keep the bundle in Amecameca, and they were clearly relieved when they were told that the relics were to be deposited in the cave of Amecameca under lock and key (Mendieta 1870:605). Thus, it is highly likely that the Franciscans had unknowingly created not only a European-type pilgrimage shrine at Amecameca, but a kind of Nahua temple as well.

The examples of Tepeyac and Amecameca show how slippery was the whole colonial enterprise of converting the Indians to Christianity. The Spanish had an almost absolute faith that an acknowledgment of the sacrality of a Christian symbol necessarily meant a kind of mystical acceptance of the entire religious worldview behind it. However, changing the deep structures of a culture's religious worldview overnight is nearly impossible. As the work of the historical anthropologist Louise Burkhardt (1989) has shown, when the Spanish destroyed the indigenous system of sacred symbols in Mexico and imposed a Christian one, the Indians did not immediately abandon their own.

Rather, the evidence seems to suggest that they struggled to reinterpret as best they could Catholic symbols according to indigenous categories, a process facilitated when there was a formal correspondence between symbols, such as the correspondence between the *tlaquimilolli* and Valencia's relics, or the correspondence between the goddess Tonantzin and the Virgin of Guadalupe. This led to a circumstance typical of colonial situations in which two religious worldviews come to be expressed more or less using a single set of symbols. Anthropologist Michael J. Sallnow calls this "cultural schizophrenia," and argues further that pilgrimage shrines in Latin America are frequently the places where this "cultural schizophrenia" is manifested most acutely (Sallnow 1991:152). Here, the liminality and *communitas* of the ritual allow both the dominant and subordinate discourse about the shrine symbol to be expressed simultaneously, if only obliquely and usually through differing devotional practices at the shrine. If there is active dialogue at the shrine, however, mutual awareness of this "cultural schizophrenia" can result and occasionally this leads to conscious efforts to resolve it.

Returning to the example of the shrine of the Virgin of Guadalupe, we can perhaps interpret the myth of the apparition of the Virgin Mary at Tepeyac as a spontaneous and (unlike Amecameca) quite public effort in this direction. The myth, which arose among the Indians only very late in the sixteenth century and first appeared in Spanish only in 1648, tells the story of how an Indian, Juan Diego, was confronted on Tepeyac Hill by an apparition of the Virgin Mary (Brading 1991:353–354). According to the myth, Mary, speaking in Nahuatl, demanded of Juan Diego that a shrine be built there so that she could be a mother ("Tonantzin") to the Indians. When Juan Diego subsequently related the story to the archbishop of Mexico City, he was rebuffed as a liar. Nevertheless, the Indian was met again by the Virgin, who this time imprinted her image on his cloak as positive proof of her appearance. Now no one could doubt the authenticity of the apparitions and the shrine at Tepeyac was duly built.

Not only did this myth account for the indigenous origins of the image of the Virgin Mary at Tepeyac, but, as it was first narrated exclusively by the Indians, it gave them priority over the meanings of the place. It was an Indian, after all, who first witnessed the miracle, and it was Mary herself who used the Nahuatl name "Tonantzin," a name which tied together Tepeyac's pre-conquest sacrality with its post-conquest sacrality. The aggressive polemic intent of the myth was obvious, and it was no wonder that Church authorities ignored it for nearly seventy years, as they probably ignored too the myth of Amecameca. The image at Tepeyac would remain the Virgin Mary, the mother of Jesus, and not Mary Tonantzin, the mother of the Indians. These competing meanings endured for decades at the shrine, since, like the myth of Amecameca, the Indians' myth of Tepeyac remained unacknowledged (or perhaps simply unknown) to the Church and to the Spaniards in general.[2] However, due to the concerted and well-publicized exegesis of the apparition myth by the Creole elite of Mexico City in the seventeenth and eighteenth centuries, the myth came to be known and embraced by many sectors of the society, not just the Indians. This paved the way for the Tepeyac pilgrimage to become in the ensuing centuries an enduring symbol of Mexican nationalism (Brading 1991:343–361).

The Creoles (that is, Spaniards born in Mexico) of Mexico City had no particular interest in orthodox doctrine about the Virgin nor, particularly, in Indian culture. The Creole elite were, however, struggling to create an identity for itself which was every bit as prestigious as that of the Peninsular Spaniards who held the majority of power in the colony. The myth of Guadalupe at Tepeyac, properly and forcefully interpreted, yielded both the unique Creole identity and the prestige they craved. Thus, in 1648, we find published in Mexico City a book entitled *The Image of the Virgin Mary, Mother of God of Guadalupe, miraculously appeared in the city of Mexico*. Written by Miguel Sánchez, an ardent Creole patriot, the book was for many in Mexico the first time they had ever heard about the miraculous origins of the image of the Virgin at Tepeyac. Beyond introducing this myth to a larger non-Indian public, however, the importance of Sánchez's work was the interpretative spin he gave to the myth. Through long and tortured biblical typologizing, Sánchez saw in the myth a prophecy of the future millennial greatness of Mexico, a blessed blending of the best of America and of Europe that necessarily legitimated both native and Spanish understandings of the sacred.

Sánchez's inclusive vision is graphically illustrated by a seventeenth-century painting that beautifully elaborates his typological interpretation (Anon.

---

[2] Such is the case at many Latin American pilgrimage shrines: see, for example, Sallnow (1991).

1989:70). Midway between Europe and America, floating above the sacred Aztec symbols of sovereignty, the eagle, snake and cactus, the Virgin of Guadalupe is the object of wonder for the allegorical female figure, Europa, and a male Indian. The Indian, obviously by his clothing meant to be a noble, sums up the ultimate synthesis of the two cultures, saying in perfect Latin: *non fecit taliter omnia nationi*: "God has not done this for any other nation." The blending of Nahua and Spanish spirituality was therefore not a scandal, but a sign of God's plan, and Tepeyac the symbolic means by which God signaled Mexico's future millennial greatness.

That the Virgin of Guadalupe at Tepeyac has become the preeminent symbol of Mexican nationalism in the 20th century is a testament not simply to the endurance of indigenous categories of the sacred and Mexican Roman Catholicism, but, more importantly, to the enduring power of the nationalist vision encoded into it by early Creoles like Sánchez. Without this Creole exegesis disseminated throughout Mexico in pamphlets and in paintings like these throughout the late colonial period, it is doubtful that the Marian shrine at Tepeyac would have taken on such rich national importance on the eve of Mexican Independence in 1810, nor would it have survived the country's periodic bouts of violent anticlericalism in the late 19th and 20th centuries. It should be remembered that Amecameca was also endowed with a syncretic myth, one that celebrated one of the religious founders of Mexico, making it equally ripe for nationalist exegesis. That it did not perhaps has more to do with geography than anything else: for while Amecameca lies in an obscure corner of the Valley of Mexico, Tepeyac is within walking distance of the center of the Mexican capital.

Two Pilgrimages in the United States

Contrasted with colonial Mexico, the English colonies look pretty bleak in terms of pilgrimage. The traditional Protestant, especially Puritan, antipathy towards sacramentalism made the development of pilgrim shrines in the English colonies unlikely (Walsh 1980:79–95; Sweeny 1993:59–93; Juster 1994:21–28). Yet, during the transition from the colonial period to the early national period, we do find certain places in the United States attracting large numbers of visitors for religious motives, and these places bear comparison with Tepeyac. The most obvious example, of course, is Plymouth Rock.

Local historians from Plymouth dated the first celebration of Plymouth Rock – albeit rather ad hoc – to the year 1741 (Craven 1956:31–32). Two decades later, in 1769, the town of Plymouth officially organized an anniversary sermon to be read over the rock each year, and in 1772, the town fathers set up a corresponding committee to invite noted speakers of the day to come yearly to the rock and explain to the country and the world the importance of the landing of the first settlers at Plymouth. The sermons and discourses that resulted from these invitations were a varied lot. Many took the occasion to rehearse at length the Separatist history of the Pilgrims, while others in a more revolutionary mood made the Pilgrims the initial bearers of democracy and freedom to the New World. Many of the orators reminded their listeners of the important comparison between the Pilgrim migration and the exodus of the Israelites. On at least two other occasions, however, the speakers felt the need to address exactly why the rock continued to evoke such strong emotions in those who visited it. Significantly, both did so by claiming that it was because the Pilgrims themselves had consecrated Plymouth Rock. Daniel Webster, for example, in his *Discourse* of 1820, told of how the "Rock became hallowed in the esteem of the Pilgrims," just as the soil of New England was to become "sacred ground" for them (Webster 1821:44, 43). Thus, one still feels at the rock, Webster wrote, "a sort of *genius of the place*, which inspires and awes us," a genius that the Pilgrims themselves had invested in the rock generations before (Webster 1821:11).

Even more explicit about the Pilgrims' consecration of the rock was the Congregational minister James Flint's (1816:3–4) *A Discourse Delivered at Plymouth, December 22, 1815, at the Anniversary Commemoration of the First Landing of Our Ancestors at that Place*. Flint, too, felt that a kind of sacred aura pervaded the place:

> The rock, on which they first stepped, when they took possession of this land, is, with reason, piously preserved and visited by their posterity, an appropriate monument of that event. It is to their posterity, what that heap of stones upon the margin of the Jordan was to the children of the Israelites, a monument to remind them of the wonders, which God wrought for their fathers.

In the mind of Flint, therefore, Plymouth Rock had indeed become the gateway to the "Zion of America" (Flint 1816:20). Appropriately enough,

Flint (1816:5) took his model of ritual consecration from the example of the Israelites at the moment they entered into the Promised Land: "These and a crowd of kindred ideas throng into the mind when we contemplate the *rock of the pilgrims*, and while, as at this time, we are assembled upon the spot, which first afforded a resting place to the weary voyagers, on which they first erected their domestic altars, on which the first Bethel, in this land of idolaters, was consecrated with christian [sic] rites, by a rational and spiritual worship of the true God."

Of course, as strict Calvinists, the Pilgrims would never have considered ritually consecrating anything, but the orators' attribution of such a consecration to Plymouth Rock signaled the creation of what can only be called a pilgrimage shrine.[3] From the early nineteenth century on, New Englanders came to the rock in ever-increasing numbers, and not just on the Fourth of July, but throughout the year. Eventually, as if to make its religious meaning explicit, the rock was covered by a stone cupola surmounted by nothing less than the iconic scallop shell so evocative of the medieval Catholic pilgrim. Soon, the mythology of Plymouth Rock would spread far beyond New England, attracting Americans from far and wide to experience the "genius" of this holy American place. Moreover, like the Creole patriots of Mexico and the myth of Tepeyac, generations of New England historians would work tirelessly to firmly embed Plymouth Rock in the larger mythology of the founding of the United States. They were successful too: to this day, the myth of Plymouth Rock continues to be taught to every school child in the nation and ritually re-enacted in countless school auditoriums during the Thanksgiving holiday.

Plymouth Rock was not the only colonial pilgrimage to intensify in the early national period of the United States, however. As John F. Sears (1989:12–30) and Patrick V. McGreevy (1985:27–32; 1994) convincingly document, Niagara Falls must also be seen as such a pilgrimage destination. Before the European arrival in the area, Niagara had been a sacred border landmark between the Iroquois to the south and the Huron to the north (McGreevy 1994:68). After its discovery by the French in the 1670s, it became an object of fascination

---

[3] For a discussion of the return to the notion of consecrated space in New England in the late colonial and early national periods, see Wilson (2001).

by Europeans and generated a deal of fantastic lore about it size and power (McGreevy 1994:23–25). French Catholics were especially enthralled by the Falls and began investing it with overt religious meaning almost immediately: an engraving showing the Prophet Elijah, herald of the Messiah, ascending from the Falls in a fiery chariot, was done in 1700 by Sebastian Le Clerc (McGreevy 1985:28). This image became widely disseminated both in the Old World and the New. Even after the Falls were lost to the British in 1760, French Catholic interest in Niagara continued strong. Indeed, Niagara Falls actually did become an official pilgrim shrine for the Catholic Church in 1861, when Pope Pius IX consecrated the Falls, granting it an official status on a par with Jerusalem and Rome (McGreevy 1994:2, 34).

However, what is most striking about Niagara Falls is how many non-Catholic Americans, how many Deists, Transcendentalists, and especially Protestants of all stripes traveled to Niagara, each investing the Falls with their own (and others') symbols of transcendence. Such pilgrims reached a torrent in the years between 1800 and the Civil War (Sears 1989:12, 30). Thus, in the poetry of the period, we find that Niagara is the home of the Divine Architect, of Nature Eternal, of Jehovah, and of Manitou and the Seneca gods of O-ni-ah-ga-rah and Hi-nu (Dow 1921:714, 743, 745, 756, 780–81, 783, 805). Protestants often brought millennial meanings to the Falls, and more than one visitor remarked that the roar of the cataract was like "that great voice in Patmos heard by John" (Dow 1921:702, 726). Others thought of Niagara as the lost Eden or the new Jerusalem, or even a substitute for the Temple of Jerusalem. This last was best expressed in a poem by a Newark, New Jersey doctor named Abraham Coles:

O, Let my heart exult
That here she may consult, The Oracle Divine!
That at Jerusalem, no more
Is fixed as heretofore
Jehovah's Shrine!
That ancient ritual is past,
That temple to the ground is cast,
Those symbols and those semblances sublime
Endured but for a time.
Their everlasting prototypes, I ween

Their patterns on the Mount by Moses seen,

Were these, are here!

This much, at least is clear;

If, in th' immensity of space,

God makes one spot his special dwelling-place,

That sacred spot is this (Dow 1921:781–783, 812).

Visitors to Niagara more often than not chose the language of medieval pilgrimage to describe their journey and their feelings once there (McGreavy 1985:27; Sears 1989:13). Nathaniel Hawthorne (1876:105–114), for example, wrote that "Never did a pilgrim approach Niagara with deeper enthusiasm, than mine." Before setting out, Hawthorne bought himself a "pilgrim staff," "adorned with the carved images of a snake and a fish." Upon arriving, he threw himself to the ground in an abject posture, "feeling," as he said, "unworthy to look at the Great Falls." Moreover, by the 1820s, the Falls had become surrounded by a complex series of what can only be called devotional rituals (Sears 1989:18–24). Guides and detailed guidebooks directed the visitors to all the essential points of interest with explicit instructions on what order and what time of day they should be seen. There arose a common perception that there was a right way to do Niagara and a wrong way, and those who did not follow the rules would not reap the full sacred benefit of a visit to the Falls – a phenomenon found at many traditional pilgrimage shrines.

Niagara, like Tepeyac and Plymouth Rock, also became a potent symbol for American nationalism, as Elizabeth McKinsey has shown in her recent work on the Falls (McKinsey 1985a; 1985b:83–101). After the American Revolution, the spirit of American Republicanism strove to establish a sense of national identity, taking its symbols largely from America's most distinctive resource, its landscape. The power and freshness of the American landscape symbolized the power of the new "Republican man," as opposed to the effete subjects of European tyranny and the exhausted landscape of Europe.[4] It was especially those remarkable or awe-inspiring features of the American landscape – features such as Niagara – that marked Republican America alone as having a special destiny. America would, as one poet put it, "Niagarize

---

[4] For a discussion of Republican nature, see Albanese, *Nature Religion in America* (1990:47–49).

the world." A sermon delivered in 1860 by a Father Taylor in full view of the Falls, perfectly captures the melding of religious and nationalistic sentiments. "[L]ook at Niagara," Taylor exhorted his audience,

> What does it represent? What does it resemble? Does it not resemble our country, – our vast, immeasurable, unconquerable, inexplicable country? After you have said Niagara, all that you may say is but an echo. It remains Niagara, and will roll and tumble and foam and play and sport till the last trumpet shall sound. It will remain Niagara whether you are friends or foes. So with this country. It is the greatest God ever gave to man; for Adam never had the enjoyment of it; and if he had he could not have managed it. It is our own. God reserved it for us, and there is not a shadow of it in the world besides (McKinsey 1985a:107–108).

Interestingly, the iconography of American Republican nationalism associated Niagara with a goddess who, like the Virgin at Tepeyac, appears before an Indian (McKinsey 1985b:86).[5] First published in 1800, this emblem was destined to become one of the most popular Republican images of America. Framed against the backdrop of Niagara Falls, it shows a young Indian in worshipful (or at least submissive) attitude towards the goddess Columbia, who herself is surrounded by all the symbols of American nationalism: the flag, the eagle, pine trees, and, magically transported from Mount Vernon, even the sarcophagus of George Washington himself. In a more sophisticated vein, Niagara Falls would also become one of the most important subjects for American landscape painters, with depictions of the Falls becoming a staple in both private collections and public art galleries throughout the country. While their style of painting was uniformly naturalistic, many American artists nevertheless could not refrain from adding a bald eagle somewhere in their composition, just in case their audience might miss the nationalistic import of the picture.[6] American nationalism would remain strongly associated with Niagara Falls until the end of the 19th century. For many Americans during this period, celebrating the majesty of the Falls – either by traveling

---

[5] The emblem is in the private collection of Mrs. Robert B. Stephens and dates from 1809. The original 1800 emblem, identical in all respects to the 1809 version, is found in the Print Collection of the New York Public Library. For other versions of the emblem, see McKinsey (1985a:103, 105).

[6] See, for example, Thomas Davies *Niagara From Above* (1766) (McKinsey [1985a]: Plate 7) or William Constable's *Niagara Falls* (1810) (McKinsey [1985a]: 106).

there in person or by hanging a chromolithograph – was a powerful way of affirming and celebrating the strength and transcendent righteousness of the United States.

Comparing Nationalist Pilgrimages in Mexico and the United States

Several more interesting points can be made in this comparison of pilgrimages that bear directly on the theme of the migration of the pre-modern sacred into modern forms and practices. I will highlight a few of these in this section. One of the glaring differences between the Mexican and U.S. nationalist pilgrimages is the fact that, in addition to seeing it as a symbol of the state, contemporary Mexican pilgrims to Tepeyac still continue to see it as an explicitly sacred place, a place of supernatural power and an access point to God through the intercession of the Virgin Mary. Visitors to Plymouth Rock and Niagara Falls, on the other hand, no longer bring such overt religious expectations, and explicitly religious rhetoric almost never enters into contemporary discussions of these places. True, Plymouth Rock continues to be celebrated because it was the reputed landing site for the first Pilgrims, but this is a civic celebration of the Puritans as founders of the country, not as religious heroes, and certainly not because of their supposed ritual consecration of the rock. The rise of Liberal Christianity and Evangelical anti-sacramentalism in the late 19th century, followed by religious pluralism and deepening secularization during the 20th, makes both the attribution of overt sacrality to Rock impossible and acknowledgment of the Pilgrims' unabashed Calvinism unpalatable. Indeed, with Plymouth Rock we can truly see a migration of the pre-modern sacred into a modern form since the Rock remains indubitably a pilgrimage shrine to American nationalism, but one only very tenuously connected to religious concepts that earlier generations had originally invested it with.

The case of Niagara Falls presents an even more striking difference, for unlike Tepeyac and Plymouth Rock, both the religious *and* the nationalist meanings have fallen away. For a brief historical moment, Niagara became a lightening rod for religious and nationalist sentiments in this country, and then these fragmented and were largely forgotten. Visitors still come in droves, but the Falls are seen today as little more than a natural wonder –

even for American Roman Catholics for whom Niagara is an officially recognized pilgrimage shrine. History and geography have had a hand in this: while Tepeyac remains at the center of Mexico and Plymouth was the gateway to America, Niagara, it seems, was fixed upon in part because it marked the farthest western frontier of the U.S. at that time. However, not only did the western frontier move on, with Niagara soon straddling an international border with Canada, but the Civil War violently reoriented the nation along a fracture north and south. It was no wonder then that after the War nationalistic sentiment became invested more heavily than ever before in the buildings and monuments of Washington D.C., straddling as it does the line of that internal fracture (Meyer 2001).

Perhaps more important, though, is the nature of Niagara Falls as symbol. At Tepeyac, the power of the place is mediated through the personality of the Virgin of Guadalupe, while at Plymouth Rock, the power is mediated through the myth of the Pilgrims. And yet, at Niagara, no personality, and thus no myth, became permanently associated with the Falls. This was not for lack of trying, as we have seen: religious poets and nationalist iconographers tried repeatedly to endow the place with an anthropomorphic presence, whether it be Jehovah or the Goddess Columbia. In their failure to create a lasting connection, we can see one of the reasons why Niagara failed as both a religious *and* a nationalist pilgrimage. While sacred rituals may metamorphose into civic celebrations, key elements of the ritual must remain in the celebration if it is to remain powerful. One of these elements is an anthropomorphic presence, now seen by many theorists as crucial for any religion's staying power (Guthrie 1993). Thus, without such a presence, whether in the form of physical representation or a strongly associated mythology, a place will remain unsuitable for religious or nationalist pilgrimage regardless of how intrinsically interesting it may be aesthetically. Perhaps the best proof of this assertion is the fact that the next time Americans hallowed a natural landmark with all the nationalistic fervor they once had for Niagara, they had to blast faces in it first – Mount Rushmore.[7]

The above conclusion, that anthropomorphism is a necessity even in the case of nationalist shrines, entails an ironic corollary: one of the most "primi-

---

[7] For an interesting interpretation of Mt. Rushmore as sacred space, see Matthew Glass (1995).

tive" forms of religion – ancestor worship – is alive and well in the modern western world. Just as many archaic and ancient societies developed ranks of "superior ancestrals" in tandem with the development of a centralized state, so too did modern "secular" states develop such pantheons.[8] Moreover, the superior ancestrals associated with Plymouth Rock (the Pilgrim Fathers) and Mt. Rushmore (four U.S. presidents) function in the same way as premodern superior ancestrals the world over: as superhuman beings, they preserve and maintain the nation. However, unlike superior ancestrals in pre-modern societies, these ancestors do not evolve out of an actual kin group, and therefore one does not have to be a lineal descendent to approach them. Indeed, their democratic appeal accounts for the continuing popularity of the pilgrimage shrines dedicated to them. In the case of nationalist pilgrimage shrines, therefore, the migration of the pre-modern sacred into modern nationalist rituals depends on what, in the West at least, is an atavism, which, if recognized as such by those who practice the rituals of nationalism, would probably be rejected as abhorrent or irrational. But, as Marvin and Ingle (1999) have recently shown in the case of the cult of the American flag, nationalist rituals exert power precisely because their primitive religious mechanisms remain occluded. Thus, in these, perhaps the most modern forms of religious practice, the migration of the pre-modern sacred is not a move towards novel "secular" constructions of the sacred; rather, nationalist rituals in the West such as Plymouth Rock and Mt. Rushmore depend for their power on an unconscious return to a form of spirituality that is far more archaic than even that manifested in the miraculous appearance of the Virgin of Guadalupe at Tepeyac.

In conclusion, pilgrimage is alive and well in the Americas, and not just in predominantly Catholic Mexico, but in the highly "secularized" United States as well. The desire to perform pilgrimage transcends the pre-modern/modern dichotomy. Liminality and *communitas* are still valued experiences, but more importantly, so too are interactions with superhuman beings. However, a primary difference between the major Mexican nationalist pilgrimage, Tepeyac, and those of the United States is the acknowledgment of the involvement of superhuman beings. As the pre-modern sacred migrates into a thoroughly

---

[8] Dean Shiels defines superior ancestrals as those ancestors whose influence extends beyond their own descendants to all members of a society (1980:248). See also Fustel de Coulanges (1956 [1864]).

modern form such as American nationalism, the true source of its power, the presence of a superhuman being or beings, is repressed, and so successful is this repression that a visit to an American nationalist shrine is often interpreted by the pilgrims themselves as a simple act of tourism. And yet, remove the superhuman presence and the seriousness and respect with which the shrine is regarded would surely diminish. This, of course, engenders a larger question: how much more of modern culture in the U.S., beyond simply the rituals of nationalism, is informed by such phantom presences? In this vein, it would be interesting to investigate other reputedly "secular" areas of American culture that are accorded such interest and respect. Perhaps superhuman beings are lurking, for example, in the "hidden hand" guiding the free market economy, or in the modern "cult" of celebrity, or even in the obscure anxieties that fuel the United States' search for life on other planets.

Chapter Five

The Pains and Pleasures of Opium, Religion, and Modernity: A New View of Robert Owen

Anja Finger

The subject matter addressed in this chapter is the apparently contradictory views on religion held by the early British socialist Robert Owen (1771–1858): condemning all of religion while yet proposing a new religion at the same time. If this ambivalent attitude was not only the product of a benighted psyche, which would make it a bad subject for sociological research, there would have to be a substantial social reason for and background to the statements of this religious revolutionary. History, in the form of its representatives – the historians – has tended not to look kindly on those deemed failures. If asked whether the non-religious/religious Owen was a success one would have to give a negative reply. So why bother with this aspect of Owen? Certainly not in order to prove that the tolerant regimes of academia are broad enough to accommodate a history of Great Failures.

Owen's case is fascinating because it extends an invitation to think beyond (or below, down in the muddy grounds where logic fails) the classical giants of theory whose wisdom one is more often than not compelled to parrot, also beyond (or below) the manufactured clarity of textbooks that do not ask questions which could not be answered (by repeating the core text). The most important question in the research context mentioned is how Owen's views on religion could be grasped in theoretical terms. The idea of a constitutive ambivalence of religious phenomena derived from a re-contextualization and re-interpretation of Marx's opium metaphor is far away from any textbook portrayal of Marx, and the questions arising in the process will not be answered by repetition of the same. The Ambivalence here proposed is not a closed concept, for if it were it would erase the ambivalence pointed out.

Ambivalence is quite fashionable at present, but then again it already was a topic decades ago. Musil's narrator in his *Man without Qualities* talks about an understanding of love "as one of those contemporary bifurcated emotions that the latest trend calls 'ambivalent', which amounts to saying that the soul, as is the case with swindlers, always winks with its left eye while pledging an oath with its right hand" (Musil 1996:1315). This should not be true, of course, of those researching ambivalence.

That is why some remarks on the structure of this essay are in place. First, a couple of remarks on Robert Owens' life, also indicating the religious surroundings of his time, are made and the difficulties of putting Owen into one of those neat categories at hand in the Sociology of Religion are named, difficulties which have necessitated the theoretical search for an alternative in the second section. In the third section of this essay, Lenin's version of the metaphor and its context is presented, to be compared with Marx's, which is then structured according to its units of meaning. It will then be shown in section four how this metaphorical concept can be applied to Owen, including an excursus on the sigh as a crystallization of ambivalence. This will then lead to a more general, exploratory reading of what the metaphor could look like and what it might give to the Sociology of Religion. Finally, it is asked in which ways the Ambivalence of metaphorical opium offers insights concerning the contemporary religious situation.

Setting the Stage for Owen and Religion

Assuming that the celebrity status of Robert Owen is not extraordinarily high, some remarks about his life that are of a necessarily summary character will be made. In a second step it will be asked why and in what ways religion was important for Owen. This is a basic question because it will lead to the question of why and in what ways understanding and criticizing Owen's perspective on religion is helpful for sociologically dealing with contemporary religion/s.

A Few Short Biographical Notes. Robert Owen was born in rural Wales in 1771. His mother was a farmer's daughter, his father a saddler and postmaster. At the age of ten Owen left his parental home for London. Afterwards he went to Stamford in Eastern England where he worked as apprentice under a textile trader. Already in 1791 he became director of a Manchester textile factory. Eight years later, he married Caroline Dale, whose father was a banker, leader of an Independents' sect and the owner of the cotton mills at New Lanark, Scotland. Owen, with some partners, bought the mills and thus the conditions for all the legendary stories about the benign capitalist, who reduced child labor, shortened the working hours, and introduced all sorts of other social reforms, were established.

The publication of *A New View of Society* in 1813 shows the far-reaching ambitions Owen (1993a) was driven by: the reforms at New Lanark were to be only the beginning, an exemplary experiment, for changes that should affect the society at large. In 1816 Owen founded his "Institute for the Formation of Human Character" at New Lanark, one of the first efforts at elementary education. Since Owen's thought centered around the idea of social determinism, he was convinced that once humans were educated according to his principles from the earliest ages on all would be well. However much this may smack of an educational dictatorship today, Owen certainly was a pioneer in discovering the importance of childhood for later life.

The communitarian settlement of New Harmony, Indiana, was a relatively short-lived experience for its Owenite members: It lasted only from 1825 to 1828, probably due to insufficient planning and foresight including a lack of skilled workers. Back in England, Owen gained influence within trade unionism, yet this was not for long either. His critics claimed that he was never really able to do away with the paternalist attitude of the once factory owner.

The 1830s witnessed the founding of the "Association of All Classes of All Nations," the name of which was changed twice, and the opening of the "National Equitable Labour Exchange" under Owen's leadership and the Queenwood community, another attempt at communal living in Hampshire, Southern England. These years also saw the early socialist's withdrawal from trade unionism due to its politicization.

Owen's ideas for a "New Moral World" were published in the beginning 1840s. The cooperative movement drew upon some of his ideas, and his autobiography came out in 1857. One year later, Owen died where he had been born more than eighty-seven years earlier, in Newtown, Wales.

The Presence of Religion in Owen's Work

Robert Owen's life, his attempts, achievements and failures alike, have been studied from a multitude of perspectives, which is not very surprising. After all, he took part in many different movements and projects of his time. Yet, if we skim the well-researched subjects, from education to working conditions, communal living, trade unionism and cooperatives, there is one remarkable, conspicuous absence: religion. It is in fact striking that although Owen's open denouncing of religion at a public meeting in London in 1817 and his announcing of a new, Rational Religion are well-known historical facts, little has been made of this.

To be sure, as regards the so-called masses and the roots of their political awareness, social historians have shown the relevance of religion, especially Methodism. Yet, when it comes to Owen this has mostly been neglected, and attempts to trace the background of his thought were focused on philosophy. Questions such as: Had he read Rousseau, or maybe Helvétius, however, turned out to be hard to answer. Owen, in his autobiography, claimed that he had been a voracious reader in his young days, but his enthusiasm for books must have faded away later in his life. We also do not know much about what he had read, apart from Seneca and what then was classical English fiction. As a consequence of this situation, hypothetical models have been constructed, based on similarities and parallels in thought or taking as a starting point Owen's years in Manchester, where he was a member of the Literary and Philosophical Society and must have made acquaintance with rationalism and determinism somehow. Both of these philosophical theories were to become elementary features of his world view. Considerable detours are made when the library catalogue of another society, the Newcastle one, is used to infer what Owen could have come across (Dupuis 1991:32).

Why is it that one desperately needs to find sources in philosophy at all cost, instead of studying the religious influences which are easily at hand? In Owen's case, his parents were from the Church of England. Evangelical

Protestantism in Scotland was prevailing among the workers at the time when Owen was one of the owners of the New Lanark mills. His father-in-law was a head of the Scotch Independents. The Quakers were highly respected by Owen for their achievements in prison reform, the small-scale success that fuelled his belief in the malleability of circumstances and character as well as his skepticism on professionalization. In addition to that, there are to be named sects like the Shakers in the US, where Owen tried to establish the communal living project of New Harmony, the predecessor of which he had bought from the Rappites, German religious settlers. Of particular, life-long importance to Owen who as a youth was still part of the Church of England, was his relation to Methodism. John Wesley was impressed by John Locke's rational empiricism and tried to translate it into theology (Brantley 1984), which does not necessarily contradict the self-presentation of Methodism as a "religion of the heart" on Sundays. Reason and reasonability of experience were crucial for Wesley, as they became for Owen.

The later writings of Owen, from his spiritualist phase, were given to oblivion and not reprinted, not even in the 1990's four-volume edition of his works (Claeys 1993). Biographers tended to end their reports by admitting that Owen in his old age became more or less crazy, a turn that should not stain the heroic story for most of them. Certainly, the evidence of his religious imagination does not fit well into a one-dimensional portrayal of Owen as a rationalist and socialist in line with an unambiguous, progress-oriented Enlightenment tradition. Picturing Owen as a benign but cool capitalist philanthropist does not do him full justice either.

A prophecy of progress is certainly what he proclaimed for his followers. He was a prophet for the poor, as one is told by the title of a collection of essays published in his honor (Pollard/Salt 1971). Yet, Owen's idea of progress was strongly inspired by his religious imagination. It was often proposed that Owen had emptied religious language of its content by connecting it to political agitation. Once more, a reply critical of ideology has to be made: such a reproach rests on the assumption that religion and politics are and ought to be strictly separated, which they are not and certainly were not in those days. Given Owen's social background and his autobiographical statement that the day in 1817 on which he denounced all religions was the most important day of his life, Karl Mannheim's (1949:30) observation applies:

> The breakdown of the objective view of the world, of which the guarantee in the Middle Ages was the Church, was reflected even in the simplest minds. What the philosophers fought out among themselves in a rational terminology was experienced by the masses in the form of religious conflict. When many churches took the place of one doctrinal system guaranteed by revelation with the aid of which everything essential in an agrarian-static world could be explained – when many sects arose where there had formerly been a world religion, the minds of simple men were seized by tensions similar to those which the intellectuals experienced on the philosophical level in terms of the co-existence of numerous theories of reality and of knowledge.

In this context, it is noteworthy that one of Owen's favorite points raised against the possibility of the Christian believers' being right and their beliefs being true was the organizational fragmentation he witnessed. How could there be one Christian truth if all one could see were innumerable sects, predominantly occupied with fighting each other? In dealing with Owen's writings on religion and with secondary sources about the practice of the proclaimed new, Rational Religion, some research perspectives seem to be near at hand: historically, e.g., one could – as it has been done by Oliver (1971) and Harrison (1969) – conceive of Owenism as a Millenarianist movement. Systematically or typologically the early socialist utopian could be described as a prophet.

However, neither of those two ways of conceptualizing seems to adequately exhaust the specific qualities of the material. What is needed is a frame in which not only the multiple discrepancies and internal contradictions of the phenomenon could be grasped but also and foremost the fundamental difficulty of how to make sense of one who is a decided opponent of religion generally on one hand, while being a by no means less fervent proponent of (new and Rational) religion on the other hand. If it can be expected that there are good reasons for opposing as well as for proposing religion, depending on what the religion in question is, and assuming a difference between religion and religions, criteria are needed for further decision-making on the subject.

First of all, the unanswerable question of what religion as such is comes to mind if one should be able to oppose as well as to propose it, citing good reasons in each case. Suggesting the opium metaphor in this context may appear strange.

The Opium Metaphor

In this part, Lenin's and Marx's statements on religion as opium are presented and compared. The case is made for a re-contextualized reading of the Marxian version which focuses on the ambivalence of the judgment passed and the ambivalence of what is being judged, religion. Since religion is still with us, it has to be a concern for sociologists, and a fresh look at the opium metaphor could serve as a promising starting point.

Lenin's Version. Often, at times even in academic discussion, Lenin's version of the opium sentence is mistaken for Marx's. Lenin said: "Religion is the opium *for* the people," whereas Marx's statement reads: "Religion is the opium *of* the people." This difference in itself is not insignificant, but the full significance of what distinguishes both versions from each other clearly comes to the fore only when the respective contexts are compared to each other. Starting with Lenin's text consciously reverses the historical-chronological order which is not only done for the purpose of improving the point being made here.

> Those who toil and live in want all their lives are taught by religion to be submissive and patient while here on earth, and to take comfort in the hope of a heavenly reward. But those who live by the labor of others are taught by religion to practice charity while on earth, thus offering them a very cheap way of justifying their entire existence as exploiters and selling them at a moderate price tickets to well-being in heaven. Religion is opium for the people. Religion is a sort of spiritual booze, in which the slaves of capital drown their human image, their demand for a life more or less worthy of man (Lenin 1905).

The first sentence points out the calming and appeasing effects religion exerts on the workers, who are being consoled by the hope for a better life after death. In the next sentence, we are told that the exploiting class is served by religion, too; for its members it is good enough to give bread crumbs, bits of charity. The ideological influence of religion on the antagonistic classes works in a stabilizing way, i.e., to maintain the existing, unjust and unequal social order. Then follows the famous phrase: "Religion is opium for the people." One could expect an end at this point. The Marx quotation has been revised and religion is defined. Why not stop here? Instead, Lenin goes on by restating what has been said. Having spoken of "opium" along with Marx, he now talks about "spiritual booze." The forcefulness of this critique of religion attacking religion as violent is tied to the verb "drown:" "the slaves of capital drown their human image, their demand for a life more or less worthy of man." This sort of drowning, drowning in alcohol, of course, is derived from the drowning of oneself which is first evoked when the word is uttered. Its use rounds up Lenin's message: the content and consequences of religion are highly detrimental to liberation for justice, even in such a way that they have quasi-killing power.

Marx's Version. That a major change has occurred on the way from Marx to Lenin, which is far more than just an attempt to be up-to-date by supplementing "opium" with "booze" as done by Lenin, can easily be seen when the point of reference, the relevant quotation from the introduction to a *Critique of Hegel's Philosophy of Right* is examined:

> Religious distress is at the same time the expression of real distress and the
> protest against real distress. Religion is the sigh of the oppressed creature,
> the heart of a heartless world, just as it is the spirit of a spiritless situation.
> It is the opium of the people (Marx quoted from Pals 1996:141).

Faced with the striking contrast between the two quotations, we can ask: How could the popular confusion about Marx and Lenin have developed? Probably, because the Lenin phrase catches best that which in terms of common-sense is felt to be the Marxist attitude towards religion, namely, a wholly negative and decisively anti-religious position, exactly the one expressed in Lenin's text. Though he was certainly not a friend of religion, but one of its fiercest critics in terms of criticizing projection and its consequences for social praxis, the portrait Marx gives in the respective paragraph is much more balanced.

Observing this should not induce anyone to christen or sanctify Marx and historical Marxism and thereby depriving both them and us of the critiques of religion and ideology. It is to be emphasized that the aim of this whole exercise is not to give the really authentic and genuine exegesis of Marx – if there could ever be the one such account. Instead of this a more modest attempt is being undertaken, which is a more daring one, too. It uses the imagination kindled by Marx's one famous line and its textual surroundings in a rather free manner, thus claiming the durable inspiration of its wording. A heuristic use is being made here, not a definite report on what Marx really felt about religion.

Marx's statement looks like a play upon words, and that is what it is to a considerable extent. Binding together contradictory terms creates the impression of ambivalence on the part of the reader. Marx's judgment – in this paragraph! – is ambivalent. Maybe religion itself is ambivalent. If his judgment would turn out to be true, it surely would be.

Marx's Version Reconstructed. A closer look at the construction of the three sentences in question and their units of meaning could be of help.

> "Religious distress...
> is...
> at the same time...
> the expression of and the protest against...
> real distress."

Here, distress or misery (*Elend*) is the central category. Its being linked to religion is not surprising, keeping in mind Lenin's verdict on religion. What does surprise is the relation of "religious distress" and "real distress." Despite the underlying assumption that religious distress is somewhat un-real – the religious is the un-real – both religion and reality are by no means uncon-nected. If religion expresses the reality of distress it shares in its flaws and evils, which is the side historically later separated from the rest, stressed and condemned in "Opium for the people." If religion, as "religious distress," is also a "protest against real distress," the other side is touched. A critical perspective on religion faces two extremes, thereby positing an alternative.

Either, religion is only an "un-real" reflex of what is there, bad reality. Then, of course, it has to be abandoned by the knowing – and becomes, furthermore, extremely uninteresting as a topic for research. Then there are more important things to do than dealing with lunatic, religious idiots – this could be the slogan of the first group and its way. By contrast, the protest-oriented focus on religion as a form of resistance, liberation and justice-seeking in and demanded by religion is in permanent danger of forgetting about the distressful character of religion. Both paths have been trodden.

Marx's opium metaphor and its context can be regarded as a parting of the ways: Take the left, expression-oriented, negative road, and go away from religion in terms of personal as well as academic life; or take the right, protest-oriented, affirmative road obsessed with the idea of an innocent reli-gion as a liberating revolutionary and or emancipatory movement. Perhaps, although the term has become unfashionable lately, something like a third way can be paved, like the two other ways taking its starting point at the parting, Marx's opium metaphor. Due to this possibility, the remaining two sentences should be examined:

> Religion...is...the sigh...of the oppressed creature, the heart...of a heartless world, just as it is...the spirit...of a spiritless situation. It is...the opium of the people.

Real distress and its manifestation are expressed by the phrases "oppressed creature," "heartless world," and "spiritless situation." The other column, the protest function of religion, I would suggest, is to be seen in the terms of "sigh," "heart" and "spirit."

Certainly, there is irony in this: a heartless world is a world in which there is no heart, so how can there be one? A spiritless situation is a situation in which there is no spirit, so how can there be any spirit? In religion? At all? Is this not rather a point for those seeing in Marx's verdict on religion nothing else but opposition towards pure illusion? Religion, apart from whatever else can be said about it, is a social phenomenon: as such it is there, like it or not. It has developed its own practices and constituted its praxis. This is true not only for believers but also for observers. Observers are free to deny the existence of what the believers believe in – but they cannot deny the existence of the believers! Therefore, from a sociological perspective, working on religion is indispensable, however much the secularization thesis may be right or wrong. Diagnosing or even predicting within the foreseeable future absolute secularization would be illusionary itself, even though it is not "the people" in general who are using religious opium nowadays, at least not in Western Europe. Howsoever that may be, "opium of the people" is the conclusion drawn from and drawing on what has been said before.

Applying the Reconstructed Opium Metaphor to Owen

One of the advantages of this concept of ambivalence is the critical function it can have. Owen's thought presents a clear dichotomy of conventional religion – including all religion/s up to his day, yet in fact concentrating on the Christian environment he lived in – and the Rational Religion he advocated. From Owen's perspective "oppressed creature," "heartless world" and "spiritless situation" belonged to the sphere of conventional religion as an expression of real distress, while "sigh," "heart" and "spirit" form parts of the Rational Religion as a protest against real distress. These are not merely formal categories; they are content-sensitive. Thus, the units of the reconstructed opium metaphor will be applied to Owen's anti-conventional and pro-Rational views on religion and complemented by hints regarding the other side of conventional and Rational religion respectively, sides Owen could not acknowledge due to his strict dichotomizing.

Applying the reconstructed opium metaphor to Owen's views on religion, we can re-describe his critique of religion as a critique of conventional religion being the expression of real misery and his proposal for a new religion, the idea of a Rational Religion, as a protestation against real misery.

> But now farewell – a long farewell to happiness – winter or summer! farewell to smiles and laughter! farewell to peace of mind! farewell to hope and to tranquil dreams, and to the blessed consolations of sleep! I am now arrived at an Iliad of woes: for I have now to record the pains of Opium (De Quincey 1986:96).

Oppressed Creature, Heartlessness and Spiritlessness in Conventional Religion. More specifically, the aspect of the oppressed creature appears as a product of religious rule. This rule had decisive consequences: religious groups, each of which convinced of possessing the one and only truth, had emerged and fought each other bitterly, even causing wars. Despite all sectarian differences, Owen sees these fractions united by a belief in free will: religion burdened the individual with responsibility, when humans could not help how they acted. This was Owen's real dogma: that the character of human beings is formed for, not by them.

In his 1830 lectures on *The New Religion*, Owen (1993b) tried to sketch a list of religious types. Although this typology may not be brilliant, the four types Owen constructed can be read as expressions of the oppressed creature. There are: the sincere believer, whose intellectual faculties are generally low; the hypocritical non-believer; the anti-religious, yet not enlightened non-believer lacking sensibility for Nature; and, finally, Owen's favorite, to be sure: the new non-believer embodying all desired values and of benevolent attitudes. It is only the representatives of the last type who are able to defy the Trinity of Vices: Private property, the institution of marriage, and religion with its priests. Education is the key to the production of new and more numerous generations of the new non-believing type. They would practice what they would preach, not like the religious functionaries of his time – at least that was Owen's hope for an end of oppression.

The heartlessness of the religious world finds its Owenite pendant in his critique of self-absolutization and the ideology of punishment. Neither criminals nor politicians are responsible for their actions. Even for himself Owen rejected any idea of responsibility:

> Am I to blame for thinking thus? Those who possess any real knowledge of human nature know that I cannot think otherwise – that it is not in my power, of myself, to change the thoughts and ideas which appear to me to be true (Owen 1993a:208).

Consequently, the priests – who Owen liked to attack wholeheartedly – would not be responsible for their actions either. It is not them but the "Church" and "Government" Owen blames: not individuals but structures are outfitted with agency! Human beings are therefore always objects of society – a conclusion Owen is far from lamenting about. However, the additional intervention of religious violence is rejected. Humans should not be forced to believe or feel anything that they cannot do. Such a use of force justified by an ideology of free will and attached punishment can be reconstructed as a form of the symbolic heartlessness. Spiritlessness is also to be found as a target of Owen's critique: conventional religion is opposed to Reason, he asserts, and its ritual practices are economically dysfunctional.

Excursus on the Sigh. Turning to Owen's propaganda for a Rational Religion, the religious forms in which it was shaped reminds one of Marx's "sigh" – both are ways of externalization. Furthermore, given the triad of sigh, heart and mind, the "sigh" could be the most interesting one of the three in terms of theory. Heart and spirit may well be hidden and separated from the other in everyday life. The sigh is only through its being sighed, which is potentially being perceived by others. Sighing is not talking, and yet it can "say" and mean a lot. Those listening to one's sigh are charged with interpreting what the other's sighing means. Is she just tired, or fed up, or angry? As long as she does not tell us, we do not know. Ironically, even if she tells us we cannot be sure of the truth of her statement; maybe she is lying to us.

Anyway, the sigh is even more indefinite; it is an act of holding back oneself (from speaking out), and if sighed involuntarily it is not even an act. Most relevant is its dependence on the material, bodily aspects of life. A materialist sociology of religion may well be confronted with a crystallization of what the challenge is in the sigh. In this, the whole ambivalence of religious phenomena is captured: there is statement as well as non-statement, resistance as well as surrender, or – to repeat from what has been said before – protestation as well as expression. The internal logic of the sigh could be summed up as an address: You have to decide how to interpret what I have "said", but also what I have said by saying nothing at all.

Can religion be compared to the sigh in its being non-verbal? At least, religion has holy scriptures, creeds, dogmas, catechisms, hymns, and so on. It knows of and believes in powerful formulas or even the word(!) of God – a whole lot of phrases, but religious language, maybe more than most other languages, tends to be aware of the limited character it has and the difference between its talking and what this is (all) about.

Sigh, Heart and Spirit in Rational Religion. Owenites turned Christian religious holidays into their own celebrations. Instead of Christian baptisms, there were name-giving ceremonies, and often names of high-caliber Owenites were chosen for the children. In addition to that, Owenism was famous for its lavish burial ceremonies (Yeo 1971).

The Book of the New Moral World, published by Owen from 1842–44, "became the Bible of the Owenites, lessons from it were regularly read, as from the Scriptures, in the Owenite Halls and Institutes" (Cole 1965:296f). It contained reflections on a Moral Science, a Social Science, Happiness and its bodily, mental and social conditions, a Rational Religion with an agnostic position regarding a "Power", a Science of Society as well as a Constitution and Laws. In biblical words, Owen proclaims the change towards his new world as being "near at hand" and readable from the "signs of the time" (Owen 1993c:363). Yet the old order is still there, witnessed by the conventional religion as well as what is nowadays called a secular religion with Wealth as a God (Owen 1993c:372).

The Heart was touched by dance parties and the "Social Hymns" which were sung "to a sacred tune" (Brindley quoted after Royle 1998:111) to have a good laugh at church religion. The Hymns were also a participatory factor at the assemblies and furthered the cohesion of the group. They often centered around happiness and harmony in community. Harmless and dull as these songs may sound, they presented a considerable opportunity for marking off the community from the outside world. Repeating verses from 1 Corinthians 13 ("It [Love] suffereth long and is kind"), Owen proclaimed his as a Religion of Charity.

As for the dimension of Spirit, Owen's insistence on both "Reason" and "Nature" is most significant. It is closely connected to his social determinism: Once set into the right conditions, humans will act accordingly. The Rational Religion is an orthoprax rather than an orthodox type of religion. It will "consist in promoting, to the utmost of our power, the well-being and happiness of every man, woman, and child, without regard to their class, sect, sex, party, country, or colour" (Owen 1993c:232). Interestingly, it would be tolerant enough to grant freedom to those still bound by the beliefs of the various sects. Owen's model religion entails an awareness of the limits of speech, even of its own limits. There is room for wondering about the order of Nature, a quasi-mystical dimension.

Owen repeatedly stressed the divide between the conventional religion he attacked – as expressed in this reconstructive attempt as the religious forms of the oppressed creature, the mindless circumstances and a heartless world – and the Rational Religion he propounded – here expressed as its sigh-like externalizations, its spirit character and its speaking to the heart.

Protestation against Real Misery in Conventional Religion and Expression of Real Misery in Rational Religion

Yet, in order to fully reconstruct the ambivalences being constitutive for the religious phenomena under scrutiny, one would have to lay bare the aspects of sigh, heart and spirit in conventional religion as well as the elements indicative of oppressed creature, heartless world and spiritless situation in Owen's religion. Only some suggestions for accomplishing this task briefly indicating possible directions can be given here.

Sigh, Heart and Spirit in Conventional Religion. The ritual practices of conventional religion – for Owen symptomatic for economic dysfunction – may also be seen as sigh-like manifestations. Such a view would account for the ongoing attraction this sort of religion held for its believers (and probably still holds for quite a percentage of "believers" who have separated themselves from their respective religious affiliations ideologically).

Owen's borrowings from biblical passages and imagery give rise to the suspicion that he sensed something valuable in these, in spite of what he had to say about the traditions which laid a claim on them. As already mentioned, Owen quoted the Pauline song of love from 1 Corinthians 13, the poetic content of which can be interpreted as a manifestation of the heart.

Occasionally, Owen had to concede that not all was doom in the religion he criticized, though he never drew any major conclusions from these concessions. For example, he praised a Roman Catholic priest who conducted a school for the poor in Switzerland, for his "truly Catholic spirit" (Owen 1993d:174).

Of course, much more might be said about conventional religion if the frame of reading Owen against his own grain was left.

Oppressed Creature, heartless world and spiritless situation in the Rational Religion. On the other hand, not all was light in Owen's historically factual Rational Religion. In retrospect, its sigh-like manifestations, heart and spirit character display deficient traits. The intellectual anti-ritualism of the new founder of a religion – softened only by regional or singular events – promoted a lack of sensuousness which generally tends to limit the success of popular religious movements and therefore its sighing, which would bring relief to the oppressed creature.

Apart from the fact that many of Owen's ventures failed after a short period of time, certain properties of his and his doctrine in practice are closer to what he criticized than to what he proclaimed. Contemporaries complained about his authoritarian style, his arrogance that deemed all those skeptical of his plans to be ignorant. Owenite sermons were frequently perceived by listeners to be not at all in line with the idea of harmony (Royle 1998:108). All of this makes it hard to quote the Rational Religion as a splendid example for the heart in (a) religion, rather than as one for a heartless world.

At times, of course, heart and spirit – as well as the deficiencies in both – do overlap. The following example may be interpreted in terms of deficiency of the heart, yet according to Owen's standards for a religion of Reason and Nature, it offers a fit illustration for a lack of Spirit inside the reality of Rational Religion, a spiritless situation.

The Orbiston community in Scotland continued the class differences in its midst. The members of the higher strata received their meals separately from those of the lower ones, who also got food of a worse quality (Harrison, 1969:185). Inside Owenism, the secularist wing detected signs of clericalization among the Rational Religionists. Finally, the historical development of an Owenite sect contradicted the universalism of the message.

The Metaphorical Representation of Religious Ambivalence as a Provocation to Thought in the Sociology of Religion

> Opium! dread agent of unimaginable pleasure and pain! I had heard of it as I had heard of manna or of ambrosia, but no further: how unmeaning a sound was it at that time! what solemn chords does it now strike upon my heart! what heart-quaking vibrations of sad and happy remembrances! Reverting for a moment to these, I feel a mystic importance attached to the minutest circumstances connected with the place and the time, and the man (if man he was) that first laid open to me the Paradise of Opium-eaters (De Quincey 1986:70).

The opium metaphor invites doubt whenever just one side (expression or protest) is highlighted and ambivalence cut. It is critical in this respect because it does not stand by and indulge in the illusion of mere observation, but rather urges to taking an option. Ernst Bloch remarked that the opium passage once quoted in full and no longer half-cited would not be able to work miracles but at least open the forum for dialoguing among believers and non-believers who have liberated themselves from ideology and taboo (Bloch 1989:92).

Besides this practical usefulness, the opium metaphor revisited and reconstructed offers a new frame for methodically dealing with religion. Sigh, heart and spirit – oppressed creature, heartless world and spiritless situation, the metaphors within the metaphor can be understood as representing different aspects of religion in tension, the whole of which might be called ambivalent. Thus, the ambivalence of religious phenomena is not just accidental, and especially their dark nuances cannot be taken for mere deviations of religion. Interestingly, this perspective is currently rediscovered in theological discourse. There, after an epoch of highlighting God's love we can find a plea for the alien, incomprehensible God.

The opium metaphor encourages attempts at reconstructing both sides, while at the same time reminding us that it is not an equilibrium or harmony of contrasts, as Rudolf Otto expressed it for the aspects of Mysterium Tremendum and Fascinans in the Numinosum (Otto 1997:56). Reinterpreting the critique of religion entailed in the opium paragraph has to remain critical itself and should not lead to being content with some religion-friendly or even religious ideology that would be most happy to tame and incorporate the tamed Marx. Likewise, and other than Otto's approach, such an interpretation will not require of its interpreter any memories of (self-)experienced religious excitement (cf. Otto 1997:56 et seq.).

Heart and spirit signify two complementary modes of what human being means, of what being human means. The sigh stands for the ways in which the religious subject externalizes him/herself. Looking for facets of sigh, heart and spirit in religion is a demanding task. The triad of terms, heart – spirit – sigh, could offer a helpful set of metaphors: its components are not as abstract as Otto's moments of the Numinosum, nor are they as concrete, matter-of-fact-wise as historically derived categories. This reservation notwithstanding, they can be applied to the socio-historical process, as I have tried to show in this piece on Robert Owen.

Ambivalence Cut and Uncut: The Diagnosis of Religious (Post)Modernity

Finally, is there any sense in using this tool for critically understanding the changing role of religion in modernity and/or post-modernity? One of the probably most popular diagnoses of the present-day situation in Western Europe is that religion is chosen on the market. There is no longer one religion only for each, but a whole range of religious, quasi-religious or post-religious offers to choose from. The individuals are responsible for tinkering at a religion of their own, in some sort of a "do it yourself" manner. Though there are tendencies productive of religion, not everybody is a religious amateur constructor. There are e.g., those still holding on to the traditional pros in the business, the churches, those whose ethnic background plays a role for their religious affiliation, and there are those who do not care at all. For many accounts of contemporary religion this list suffices; one group is regularly left out and especially maltreated by those who see new religions springing up at every corner: those who have decided against religion and do not feel as believers in a community of TV talk show watching or in the football stadium. Labelling them as religious automatically puts them in a state of self-delusion: You may well say you're not religious; alas, in fact, you don't know (yourself).

Of course, the opium metaphor cannot solve all the problems arising from this complex situation – much would be gained if it could be a help in diagnosing these problems correctly. By virtue of its critical potential the reconstructed opium metaphor can support attempts at structuring what we see, as well as provide a relatively stable base for elaborating criteria on the social and moral qualities of religious phenomena. Revisiting the base and elaborating those criteria is a task to be performed in interdisciplinary cooperation. Watching the pluriformity of religion through the lenses of ambivalence is selective and simplifying, no doubt, but it keeps for oneself the ability to understand and judge, what the resignation to non-selection and indifference – which, by the way, is simplifying too – does not.

At the end of his essay "Postmodern Religion?" Zygmunt Bauman (1997:182) closes by surprising the reader by stating that there is a "specifically postmodern form of religion:"

> Fundamentalism is a thoroughly contemporary, postmodern phenomenon, embracing fully the 'rationalizing' reforms and technological developments of modernity, and attempting not so much to 'roll back' modern departures, as to 'have one's cake and eat it' and make possible a full enjoyment of modern attractions without paying the price they demand. The price in question is the agony of the individual condemned to self-sufficiency, self-reliance and the life of never fully satisfying and trustworthy choice.

Fundamentalism then is a form of religion of both ambivalence and forced unambiguousness: Having one's cake and eating it – choosing the pleasures only, not the pains of opium. However, to the non-fundamentalist outsider, fundamentalism appears as pains only, not pleasures. It is all so ambivalent.

Conceptions of the Future of Religion

Chapter Six

Max Horkheimer's Negative Theology of the Totally Other
Michael R. Ott

> The appeal to an entirely other [ein ganz Anderen] than this world had primarily a social-philosophical impetus. It led finally to a more positive evaluation of certain metaphysical trends, because the empirical 'whole is the untrue' [Adorno]. The hope that earthly horror does not possess the last word is, to be sure, a non-scientific wish (Horkheimer 1973:xii).

In December 1971, Max Horkheimer wrote this statement as part of his expression of appreciation to Martin Jay for writing a history of the Frankfurt School and the Institute of Social Research. This chapter seeks to explain this appeal to the totally Other in terms of Horkheimer's materialistic sublimation or inversion of this religious and theological notion into his critical theory as a catalyst for resistance to the continuing barbarization of modern society in its development toward a globalized, totally administered society.

Dialectical Methodology

In January 1930, Horkheimer became the third director of the Frankfurt Institute for Social Research since its beginning in 1922. It was under the directorship of Horkheimer, who Habermas (1993a:49) called its "spiritus rector," that the critical theory of the Frankfurt School began. Horkheimer's critical theory of society and religion was founded on the critical application of G. W. F. Hegel's dialectical methodology of determinate negation (Ott 2001). As another first generation member of Institute, Herbert Marcuse (1960:xi), has stated, "determinate negation" is the governing principle of dialectical thought. For Th. W. Adorno (1973:5ff), a close friend, colleague and ultimately successor of Horkheimer to the directorship of the Institute, dialectics is the consistent sense of nonidentity; the realization that objects of the status quo do not fit cleanly into their concept. The socially created objects, concepts, grammar, language, and definitions of the status quo leave out elements of the truth. In such limitation or even reification of both theory and praxis to what is created to be factual – the essence of positivism – that which is thereby becomes untrue. Dialectics is the critical awareness of this untruth; of the insufficiency or contradiction or antagonism between reason and reality, essence and existence, concept and content, the infinite and the finite, sacred and profane, religion and secularity, the individual and collective, as well as between the social classes, races, genders, etc. It confronts the given reality with that which it itself excludes and thereby seeks the determinate, concrete negation of this limitation for the sake of a greater possible concrete realization of truth, justice, goodness, peace, etc. Dialectics and its method of determinate negations translates everything into writing, as that which points beyond itself and in so doing admits of its own falsity, which can thereby possibly drive reality beyond itself toward its own better realization. Dialectical thought, then, critically recognizes, enters into, and seeks the specific or determinate negation of the *contradictions* that are structurally and systematically created by the antagonisms of modern civil society.

Unlike the dualistic methodology of modern natural and positivistic social science, which abstractly negates or simply brackets out this tension, the dialectical dynamic of determinate negation seeks a higher historical form of this tensions reconciliation beyond the mere existence of what is. The reduction if not negation of this contradiction and the suffering it produces is not just an issue of logic, methodology, or theory formation. Rather, the very concrete and historical goal of this dialectical method of the critical theory is the specific negation of those social systems, structures, and powers of the existing status quo that prevent if not oppose its own inherent potentialities of a new and more just, rational, beautiful, free and shalom-filled social totality from being realized. For Horkheimer and the other critical theorists, however, this inherent potential of what is remains merely a potential, merely a future possibility for which they longed but not a certainty. Unlike the negative and positive dialectics of Hegel (1967a:81), for whom "the truth is the whole" and who idealistically professed to know in advance the positive goal toward which history was moving, Horkheimer and the entire critical theory expressed only a negative dialectics, and sought only the determinate negation of the existing negativity that was/is producing the needless suffering and horror of humanity. The future is open toward something new, if at all, only in a negative not a positive way. The critical theory's negative dialectical method was summarized in Adorno's (1974:50) dialectical inversion of Hegel's statement in that "the whole is the untrue." Such a critical statement and the theory it expresses, however, avoids falling into the meaninglessness of absolute nihilism or from becoming mythological only by maintaining the tension with the falseness and negativity of what is by means of the notion of that which is "other" than what is; of that which is ultimately grounded in the religious notion of the totally Other than this false socio-historical totality.

Religion's Migration into Secular Form

Along with Adorno and Walter Benjamin, Horkheimer sought to allow the still relevant and meaningful, liberating and humanistic content of religion to migrate into a modern secular form, particularly into his critical theory of religion and thereby become a possible anamnestic, present and proleptic force of resistance to the development of an "iron caged," totally administered, cybernetic, dehumanizing and oppressive society. For Horkheimer, religion – particularly the prophetic and Messianic religions of Judaism and Christianity – was not merely a pre-modern, mythological expression of the antediluvian childhood of humanity, which thereby needed to be forgotten. Neither was religion only understood to be an ideological conservative force of control and legitimization of the existing social systems of class exploitation and domination. According to Horkheimer, religion also gives expression to the radical and revolutionary critique of such social systems that produce the oppression, suffering and death of innumerable generations of innocent victims. It is this inherent social critique of religion in its narrative form of human resistance and hope, which in the face of modern capitalist society's development toward a globalized/imperialistic totally administered society, needs to be negatively appropriated in the continuing struggle for a more just, humane, rational, free – in terms of both autonomy and solidarity, and a peaceful future society. It is in this context of the determinate negation of religion that Horkheimer's concept of the "totally Other" than this historical development toward such an administered world [der verwaltete Welt] is understood as a fundamental dynamic of his materialist theory of society and religion.

Longing for the Totally Other

From the mid-1960's to the year of his death in 1973, Max Horkheimer gave a number of interviews in which he addressed the question of the relationship between the critical theory and religion/theology. This fundamental and critical relationship was specifically the topic of a 1970 interview in Montagnola, Switzerland that was published under the title *Die Sehnsucht nacht dem ganz Anderen* [The Longing for the Totally Other]. Although as Horkheimer (1985b:431) states the specific expression "the Other" comes from Adorno, it is no less a fundamental dialectical notion of Horkheimer's materialistic critical theory of religion from start to finish.

Different Norms

In this 1970 interview with Helmut Gumnior, Horkheimer gave expression to the dialectical materialistic meaning of his notion of the "totally Other" in response to the question of how he as a Marxist and a revolutionary could be concerned with or write about "the infinite One" as he had already in a short essay entitled *Thoughts on Religion* from 1935. Echoing Marx's (2002:171) materialistic conception of religious suffering being at one and the same time the expression of real suffering and a protest against it; of "religion [being] the sigh of the oppressed creature, the heart of a heartless world and the soul of soulless conditions," Horkheimer stated that religion was originally the expression through which suffering humanity gave voice to their cries and longing for justice. True and good religion possesses different norms than those of either nature or society and, thus becomes the voice of accusation against the injustice experienced in life by countless generations of innocent victims. At the very same time that Horkheimer was writing this article on religion in exile in the United States, these unjust norms of nature were being forcibly nationalized in Nazi, Germany. In *Mein Kampf* Adolf Hitler (1971:65) named these norms of nature and the society built on it under the title "the aristocratic principle of Nature"; a Machiavellian or social Darwinistic conception of society in terms of the survival of the fittest, which eternalizes the privilege of power and strength of the one and/or the few over the resulting oppressed masses. It was this law of nature that Hitler (1971:63–64) understood to be the will of God for which he would fight to defend against all its foes; against the "veritable devils" and inhuman "monsters" whose contrary norms and organizations would bring about the collapse of civilization and devastate the world; in other words, against those who live by other, "unnatural", non-capitalistic norms, expressly Jews and Marxists. Frighteningly, with only a few changes of words and identifying names, we hear the same verdicts against people and call to arms today in the service of the perpetual war on terrorism.

Authoritarian Principle

Already in his writings of the early 1920's Horkheimer (1978:27–28) identified this dehumanizing and authoritarian norm developing in the post-World War I German society in the form of the tabooed principles of the nation and God, which are the culturally legitimating corollary of the more essentially tabooed and hidden capitalist system of production. In modern civil society, the State and religion are subsumed into the service of protecting, developing and legitimizing the aristocratic principle of systematic class domination and exploitation in the form of the antagonistic social totality of capitalist production. During this same period of time, Walter Benjamin (1996:288–291, esp. 288), another critical theorist and future member of Horkheimer's Institute of Social Research, wrote that capitalism itself is an essentially cultic religious phenomenon *"sans rêve et sans merci"* [without dream or mercy]. Capitalism as religion is a self-contained, identity producing cult with no dogma or theology [nothing "other" than itself], in which everything has its meaning and purpose in relationship to the antagonistic capitalist, utilitarian system of production and consumption. As Horkheimer (1989:78) asserted, "whoever is not willing to talk about capitalism should also keep quiet about fascism." Fascism as state capitalism is the further historical development of the cybernetic rationalization of the capitalist mode of production and the systematic reification of the extreme class antagonisms it produces. The aristocratic principle of nature is thus not to be understood as only the extreme, barbaric norm of fascism, which was not just a horrific aberration of bourgeois society. This authoritarian principle is the norm of capitalism itself, which in its reactionary, neo-liberal and neo-conservative form is being globalized imperialistically today.

Revolution

It was because of the increasing post-World War I danger of the development of this aristocratic principle in the form of National Socialism that led Horkheimer to the study of Marx and the advocacy of the need for a Marxist revolution as the means by which the totalitarianism from the right could be defeated. As Horkheimer (1989:94) stated, "Disrespect for anything mortal that puffs itself up as a god is the religion of those who cannot resist devoting their life to the preparation of something better, even in the Europe of the Iron Heel." However, unlike Marx, Horkheimer already knew that the *subject* of this revolution would not be the proletariat. The needed consciousness of their exploitation and oppression, which was to produce the solidarity of the proletariat as a revolutionary force, was becoming systematically dulled by the incremental improvement of their material well-being without the need of a revolution. The proletarian class did not and still does not have the solidarity of class consciousness nor resolve to be the revolutionary force that could overthrow the exploitive capitalist system.

Solidarity Through Compassion

By means of the determinate negation of Marx's theory with that of the brutally honest and pessimistic philosophy of Arthur Schopenhauer, Horkheimer attempted to critically identify a universal form of human solidarity, which could not be overcome by the capitalist system of production. This solidarity is established through the consciousness that all human beings are finite and will die. According to Schopenhauer, such consciousness of universal suffering and death of all living things can create compassion and empathy for the other. Such compassion can thereby overcome the "will to life," which is the ontological cause of all suffering as well as happiness in the world. However, Horkheimer (1978:38–39) also determinately negated Schopenhauer' metaphysics of compassion with Marx's class analysis, as he stated that not everyone suffers and dies in the same way in a capitalist class society. Baring the immediacy of tragic and accidental death, the circumstances surrounding the death of a millionaire is different than the death of a worker. A millionaire dies with the knowledge that his family and friends will be taken care of, whereas the poor die with the added weight of fear, anger, if not guilt at the conditions of those that are left to grieve. For such consciousness of death and compassion to be a liberating force of social change it must also become a consciousness of this social class differentiation. The suffering, pain and even death of a decent human being is directly connected with the social quality of that person's love and longing for a new, non-antagonistic society. It was this critical, social consciousness of a shared finitude, suffering, and death that has the potential of breaking down the socially produced solipsistic, monadic isolation and alienation of people from themselves, each other, and ultimately the products of their own labor in bourgeois society. Through the shared experience of suffering produced by the antagonistic society in which people live, people can break out of their isolated, compartmentalized selves and enter into solidarity with others in the attempt to overcome the causes of human suffering. The consciousness of shared suffering and the solidarity that it can produce is the catalyst for what Horkheimer (1970:56) called the "original human interest" to create a better, more beautiful, free, and peaceful future society.

According to Horkheimer, already in the 1920's and not just at the end of his career and life, the secret motivation of Marxist thought was this "*compassion*" for the innocent victims of the capitalist class antagonisms. Marxism's compassion is generally not acknowledged because it can become subjectively privatized and turned into a substitute, e.g. charity, instead of the class conscious, concrete revolutionary praxis of social change toward a more just, merciful, rational, good, free and solidarity future society. It is from this consciousness of shared suffering and the finitude of all worldly things that the radicalized notion of the Infinite One or totally Other comes for Horkheimer.

Absolute Abandonment

The notion of the totally Other thereby preserves the harsh reality of human-ity's unalterable abandonment and prevents the creation of any social power or form of knowledge from being made into a new theistic, bourgeois civil religion of consolation or salvation. Such a religion has the capability of not only distracting humanity from the truth of its ultimate aloneness, a distrac-tion which thereby eviscerates even the possibility of such human solidarity as a power of social change, but also functions socially to legitimate if not anoint the systematically produced social antagonisms that further create the fragmentation, isolation, suffering and horror of humanity.

This type of religious certainty of God's will, which gets translated into authoritarian social, political, and military policies and actions in the national and international realms, has been increasingly appealed to in the past few months in the U.S. A representative of the so-called Christian Right, the TV evangelist Pat Robertson has stated that God had spoken to him proclaiming that no matter what President George W. Bush does, either for good or evil, he will win the Presidential election in 2004 by a "landslide" because Bush is a person of faith. In reference to God's providential choosing of the U.S. for "salvation," the Reverend Billy Graham has recently stated that "paradise is none too roomy – no more than fifteen hundred square miles. The chosen will be few. Now guess which country has bought up all the entrance tickets?" (La Jornada 2003.)

The world also has experienced the deadly horror of such a religious knowl-edge if not certainty of God's will, of the Manichaean knowledge of "good" and "evil," through the policies and actions of President George W. Bush and his administration. In June 2003, the Israeli newspaper Haaretz quoted statements made by President Bush in a Summit meeting on the Middle East from transcripts it received from the meeting. Seeking to explain his moral authority for brokering peace in the Middle East, President Bush referred to his administration's pursuit of peace and justice through the United State's pre-emptive invasion and occupation of Afghanistan and Iraq. As quoted by Haaretz, Bush's exact words were:

> God told me to strike at al-Qaida and I struck them, and then He instructed
> me to strike at Saddam, which I did, and now I am determined to solve the
> problem in the Middle East (Floyd 2003).

The heinous and murderous ideological use of religion as a legitimization for the United States' pre-emptive invasion and occupation of Iraq, with the tens of thousands of innocent lives lost, is made crystal clear through a comparison with another personal appeal to God to justify murder. In March 2004, a woman in Texas in the United States, Deanna Laney, murdered her two sons, age 6 and 8, by crushing their heads with rocks because, according to her, "the Lord" wanted her to kill them. In the trial that ensued, five mental health experts who were consulted agreed that the mother met the standards for being legally insane. Ms. Laney was not convicted of these crimes by reason of insanity. She is now incarcerated as a patient in an institution for the mentally insane. If one is judged as insane by appealing to God for committing murder, why isn't the President of the United States, who made the same appeal to God to justify the U.S. policy of pre-emptive war against another sovereign nation and its people judged the same?

Throughout their later writings, both Horkheimer and Adorno called positivism the myth or the metaphysics of the way things are. Such proclaimed religious knowledge of God's will and purpose is nothing other than the positivistic perversion of religion into being a legitimizing tool of the neo-liberal globalization of transnational corporate capitalism and the resulting domination and exploitation of the so-called "peripheral" countries by a new form of Western imperialism.

No Knowledge or Proof of God

As Horkheimer repeatedly states throughout his writings, humanity has no knowledge of God, whose existence, thereby, cannot be proven. Not even the consciousness of humanity's abandonment in finitude can be used in a reverse manner to prove the existence of God. Quite the contrary, the experience and knowledge of human suffering – particularly the suffering and death of the billions of innocent victims of the "slaughter-bench" or "Golgotha" of history as Hegel (1956:21, 1967a:808) called it, makes the belief in Christianity's theodicy of an all-loving and almighty God most unbelievable. All that can be brought about by such a consciousness of the natural and socio-historical negativity is hope and longing for such a totally Other than what is. The consciousness or knowledge of the abandonment of humanity is possible only with the thought and hope of such an Infinite One that transcends the horror of this world. This notion of the totally Other and that which becomes "other" or "non-identical" to the identity or equivalence producing power of bourgeois society becomes an unrelenting "provocation" to "the rhythm of the iron system" – the absolute power of antagonistic, capitalist social totality (Horkheimer/Adorno 1972:120, 183; Adorno 1973).

Commandments of Judaism

However, this notion of the longing for the totally Other cannot be made into a proof of God's existence. There is and can be no absolute certainty of the existence of this thought of God, for if there were, then the knowledge of humanity's abandonment would be false. Such supposed knowledge of God thereby becomes a ideological reconciliation of the antagonism between the infinite and finite, the universal and particular, reason and reality; a legitimating theodicy for the slaughter-bench of history. As Horkheimer asserts, not only as a commandment of Judaism, which is his own religious heritage, but also as an essential principle of the critical theory, absolutely nothing can be stated about the totally Other. All that can be said, due to the thought of the Infinite One, is that this world is finite. Thus, it is in regards to this contradiction between the notion of God and the world that Horkheimer's critical theory of society and religion radicalizes the prohibitions of the Judaism's Decalogue, particularly that of the second and third commandments (Exodus 20:4–7, Deuteronomy 5:8–11). It is in this radicalization of the Judaism's prohibitions concerning God wherein the connection between the critical theory and Judaism lies. The second commandment of the Decalogue of Judaism prohibits humanity from making any image or likeness [an idol] of God. The third commandment upholds the ancient taboo of pronouncing and thus misusing the name of God, which equates with dragging the transcendent and holy infinite into the corruption of finitude; of equating truth with falsehood. According to Horkheimer, Judaism prevents any word or act that would ultimately alleviate the consciousness and despair of humanity's abandonment. These negative commandments, i.e. "You shall not...", are to lead the followers of Judaism to a dynamic, socio-historical praxis expressive of the longing for the totally Other, which rejects all knowledge or guarantees of salvation as utter delusion. In this way, "Israel" – meaning those who wrestle with God and humanity and have prevailed (Genesis 32:28) – is to become the light of the nations, who will come to Israel in search of wisdom and thereby change their weapons of war into implements for human well-being (Isaiah 2:2–4). The truth and justness of the image and/or name of the totally Other is thereby maintained by such negation, by its prohibition. This negativity of the totally Other, however, is not abstract or a total negation, which is equally a delusion. Such abstract negation of that which is other than what is the case of the given status quo is, as Horkheimer and Adorno (1972:x) called it, the metaphysics of positivism.

Radicalization of Kant's Critique of Reason

Horkheimer's critical theory is rooted negatively not only in proverbial "Jerusalem" – the religious foundation of Western Civilization, but also in "Athens" – the rational, humanistic, secular Enlightenment heritage. It is the negative dialectical synthesis of "faith" and "reason" that seeks to determinately negate both forms of human experience and thought into a dynamic critical materialism of human liberation, both subjectively and objectively. Thus, Horkheimer not only radicalizes the commandments of Judaism in regards to finite images or names of the infinite, but also radicalizes Kant's *Critique of Pure Reason*, in stating that humanity does not and cannot have any knowledge of anything that transcends human understanding based on experience and intuition. Humanity has no knowledge of anything noumenal, and thus does not need to bother with it. This rejection of the noumena of theistic religion, of metaphysics, of idealism is, however, quite different from that of positivism and bourgeois skepticism/agnosticism, which dualistically "brackets out" all questions of anything other than what is the case in human experience. However, unlike Kant, Horkheimer does not attempt to "make room for faith" and religion in the face of the development of human reason and science. Rather, Horkheimer materialistically grounds the truth of religion not in the noumena, as a separate entity or sphere of being and value that can be thereby disassociated from all matters of this world, but in the cries and longings of the innocent victims of this world for a better future society and the totally Other.

Truth of Religion

For Horkheimer, the truth of real or good religion does not come as consolation to a person who is unjustly suffering and in need, but rather is that very concrete suffering and need not only of the individual but of the oppressed social class as well. The truth of religion, for Horkheimer therefore, is to keep alive the critical, compassionate impulse for social change, to break the dehumanizing, ideological "spell" of capitalism, which could open the future up toward the creation of a non-antagonistic society as well as toward the unknown totally Other. As Horkheimer (1978:163) states, "we have religion where life down to its every gesture is marked by this resolve." This materialistic, negative dialectical "resolve" is grounded in and expressive of the prophetic, Messianic, critical notion of the "totally Other" than this world. Horkheimer's critical theory of religion negatively and materialistically embodies both notions of the *malum physicum* – not only the terror of nature but the horror of the antagonisms of the capitalist social totality – and the *malum metaphyisicum* – not Schopenhauer's ontological notion of the "will to life" but the consciousness of humanity's absolute abandonment; that human history is a socially created hell for billions of innocent victims of its horror, with the dialectical, materialistic "resolve" to lessen if not negate this horror with the given technological and scientific means available to create a better future society.

Focus on Human Praxis

There is no other religion that has this commandment of not making any image or name of God. According to Horkheimer, this is due to the fact that the central focus of Judaism is not on the metaphysical question of God's existence but that human beings become godly, holy, just, good in their praxis of life, both personally and socially. The religious concern of Judaism – and I would say, of Christianity as well – is not on what one believes to be true but on what one does for the sake of truth. As Horkheimer (1993:14) stated in his inaugural address on becoming the third director of the Institute for Social Research in Frankfurt, Germany: it is this indomitable will to serve with single minded devotion this negative, dialectical materialistic notion of the truth that is the guiding principle of the entire critical theory. It is thus dialectically both important and unimportant, according to Horkheimer, whether there is a God or not. It is unimportant since nothing can be said or known about God in either terms of faith or of reason. However, as Horkheimer (1970:60) states, the existence of the totally Other is nevertheless important because theology stands behind all genuine human action. Without the meaning and purpose of theology as a motivating power of human praxis, such activity collapses into being nothing more than mere business and stratagem.

Negative Theology

Theology for Horkheimer is not understood in metaphysical or ontological terms as the science of the divine or knowledge of God. Rather, from the critical perspective of dialectical materialism, theology means the consciousness that the world is finite, appearance, and that it is not the absolute truth. Theology is the hope that the injustice and horror of history will not have the last word. It is the expression of the longing that the murders may not ultimately be victorious over their innocent victims. Again, as he stated in the mid-1920's, one of the most important functions of religion is to give oppressed and suffering humanity such a theological vehicle through which they can express their misery and their longing for its end in terms of the newness of that which is totally Other. Religion did not always distract people from the injustice of society and the world but functioned to expose such horror and enabled people to resist it. An example of such a theological longing is expressed in the mythical notions of the resurrection of the dead and the Last Judgment. Through these beliefs, the idea of an absolute and disinterested justice was expressed; a justice that holds everyone accountable for what they did or did not do to overcome the causes of human need and suffering. A biblical expression of this is found in the gospel of Matthew 25:31–46, where the verdict of inclusion in the community of God or exclusion from it is based on what the "nations" did to alleviate the conditions and causes of the suffering of the least in society: the hungry, the thirsty, the stranger – the "other", the naked, and those imprisoned.

By means of such a negative theology, which begins not with the notion of God but with the horror that is experienced in this world that brings about the necessity of a God, such religious beliefs as these can become a critically reflective and dynamic concept that could be applied as a standard to judge and thereby negate the reified class antagonism of capitalist society. According to Horkheimer, the content of such religious ideas must not be abstractly negated and thus discarded with their mythological form. Rather, the religious or mythological form of such theologically expressed ideas of human suffering and hope needs to be determinately negated so as to allow such expressions of indictment of unjust social powers the possibility of becoming critically effective and liberating in a different, i.e. modern, secular form. Religion developed and contains, albeit in inadequate form, the longing and the struggle for the totally Other of past generations, which needs to be negated, remembered and preserved, and furthered into a this worldly, revolutionary theory and praxis that longs for the creation of a new and better future society and the totally Other. It is this materialist, negative theology of the totally Other in which there is a similarity between the critical theory and theology.

As Horkheimer (1985b:431) stated in another interview in the early 1970's, the critical theory is founded on the thought that the Absolute, the totally Other, or God cannot be made into an object. All that can be said is that the critical theory cannot express nor does it want to express the belief that this present antagonistic world experienced as a slaughterbench is identical with the totally Other. This Other is completely unknown, and it is in this negativity of the Absolute that the critical theory differentiates itself from every positive theology and religious doctrine. For the critical theory of religion, the unbelievable Christian theodicy of the existence of an all-loving, almighty God, who is providentially working God's purpose out in the horror of history should be materialistically transformed into the longing for the existence of such an Other, which will not allow the suffering and death of the innocent to be the last word of history. For the critical theory of religion, true theology expresses prophetically and Messianically the dialectical materialistic notions of justice, of the Good and Right, of liberation of the oppressed and exploited, of resistance to the crushing and "grinding the face of the poor in the dirt" (Isaiah 3:15) by the powerful. These ideas must be critically differentiated from their distortion in the history of religious institutions, e.g. the church. This is the fundamental thought of a negative theology of the totally Other to which both Horkheimer and Adorno have granted a right within their critical theory of society and religion.

Morality

For the critical theory of religion, such theology is the foundation of all morality, particularly in Western civilization. Based on this dialectical understanding of a negative theology of the totally Other, Jürgen Habermas (1993b:134) is correct in stating that the essential trait of Horkheimer's critical theory of religion is morality. The longing that the murder will not ultimately triumph over the innocent victims is the foundation of morality in both its rational and, as stated above, "non-scientific" form. According to Horkheimer, this non-reified, non-fetishized, materialistic longing for that which is totally Other than the socially created barbarity and horror of existence was the original understanding of theology and morality in both Judaism and Christianity.

As examples of this theology and morality, Horkheimer (185:432) looked to the Jewish and Christian martyrs – to those who have given themselves completely in the service of humanity's emancipation from all forms of exploitation and domination as they professed the totally Other. However, Horkheimer differentiates between the Jewish and Christian martyrs based on their theological motivation. The martyrs of Christianity – who resisted the power of the status quo in the hope of the totally Other – endured their torture more easily due to their belief that their suffering was only a brief stage before they personally entered paradise. Jewish martyrs, however, believe something completely different. Theirs was not the issue of a personal reward in heaven but that they would live on in the memory of the faithful. They sacrificed themselves not for personal salvation but for the welfare of the people. In Judaism, the particular subject does not play as large a role as it does in Christianity. In the Pentateuch of the Jewish scriptures, the word "you" applies to both the individual and to the whole people as subject, of which the individual is a part. The subject's identity and autonomy is bound up dialectically with the solidarity in and of the community. In Judaism, this relationship cannot be separated or differentiated clearly. Horkheimer's illustrated this point through the work of one of his doctoral students who retranslated the Jewish moral law, which is also the second part of Christianity's "greatest commandment" – "You shall love your neighbor as yourself" (Leviticus 19:18, Matthew 22:39) – in terms of this Jewish collective understanding as being its original intent: "Love your neighbor, for he/the other is you" (1970:63). This is the moral corollary of Judaism's theological prohibition of naming and making images of the Absolute that interests Horkheimer. Morality in theory and in praxis is found in this dialectical identification of one's autonomy and sovereignty in the love and solidarity with the fate of others, particularly "the least" of humanity. Morality is the expression of the dialectical dynamic between personal autonomy and social solidarity wherein one is truly a member of humanity. It is for the well-being and life chances of others that martyrs and enlighteners of all ages have thus sacrificed themselves.

Such a notion of morality cannot be found in the solipsistic bourgeois, instrumental, strategic and positivistic rationality, in which there is no transcendence beyond what is. As Horkheimer asserts, in the thought of positivism, there is no compelling reason why a person should not hate rather than love the other, particularly if such an action is enjoyable or beneficial to the one acting. Morality is grounded in actions that put into praxis the longing for that which is Other than the antagonisms of the existing status quo. In the critical theory of religion, human actions are moral when they transcend the self and its concern for self-preservation for the betterment of life of the others. Morality can not be justified in terms of positivism, which appeals only to facts, to science as a means of capitalistic production and the knowledge of the world as it is. According to the critical theory of religion, all attempts to ground morality in the theory and praxis of positivism – which is the reifying metaphysics of what is – becomes nothing but an insidious and harmonistic false consciousness.

Free Will

In terms of Horkheimer's critical theory of religion, that which is good and moral in this world comes not from God but from human beings, who act freely for that which is Right – a better, more just, beautiful, kind, rational, free and peaceful world. Human beings can do good or bad due to their freedom of will. Horkheimer grounds this understanding of free will in terms of Jewish and Christian theology, which asserts that human beings are created in God's image and thus, have free will (Genesis 1:27, John 1:1–5). This religious notion of the freedom of will leads Horkheimer to what he terms the greatest teaching in both religions – the doctrine of original or hereditary sin. Following yet determinately negating Schopenhauer's pessimistic ontological interpretation of this teaching, Horkheimer explains the demythologized truth of this doctrine of original sin in terms of the sacrifice of the other's happiness and life chances in service of one's own interests and wants. In terms of the materialistic, negative theology of the critical theory of religion, the personal and social forms of sin, immorality, selfishness, greed, the domination of one individual, class, or nation over another which creates the antagonisms, injustice, suffering and horror of history are all expressive of this notion of the original sin – not as an ontological given of human nature but as a matter of free will. This materialist notion of the mythological original sin is expressive of its concrete socio-historical realization through the exploitive capitalist class system of production and its ever-increasing need for cheap resources, cheap labor and greater market share, all for the maximization of profit for the capitalist power elite. It is this latter, capitalist system imperative for the maximization of profit, which also creates the horrendous suffering and chaos for entire nations, that is the propulsive engine of the dominant form of what is known as globalization. This antagonistic social and historical development of modern society has taken the liberal principle of the autonomous subject to the social Darwinistic, survival of the fittest extreme of an monadic, privatized notion of self, which is isolated from, fearful of, in competition with and against any other.

The Totally Administered Society

In terms of Horkheimer's critical theory of society and religion, it is this modern, immoral, systematic and globalizing development of capitalist class antagonisms that is leading toward a totally administered and dehumanized future society. As Horkheimer states, as long as people continue to live as isolated, monadic egos, seeking their identity and autonomy only by satisfying their own desires according to the exploitive system imperatives of capitalism, the world will remain as it is. Then, the terrifying neo-conservative pronouncement of capitalism being the "end of history" and the self-centered bourgeois being the "last man", who for the moment might have autonomy but no chance of solidarity, becomes reality (Fukuyama 1992). According to Horkheimer and many other critical social theorists, it is "the immanent logic of history" that leads inexorably toward the totally administered, bureaucratized, instrumentalized, integrated and controlled society. In such a society, human individuality, autonomy, love, longing for that which is other than what is will be increasingly diminished through the necessity of conforming to demands of the social cybernetic iron cage system, from which no one can escape. In fact it is questionable to Horkheimer whether humanity even will be conscious of the loss due to the rhythm of the iron system becoming instinctual. Not only will serious and liberating theology but aesthetics and philosophy too, whose true social function is also the criticism of what is in light of that which is other and socially realizable, will be thrown on the trash heap of history as mere expressions of humanity's childhood and forgotten. Life in the totally administered society will be boring.

Horkheimer does hold out that there may be also a positive side to the development of a totally administered society, namely that the material needs of humanity may be satisfied in this society, the administration of justice might be better served in the abolishment of world conflicts, and a consciousness of universal solidarity may also arise. I do not share Horkheimer's qualified optimism in regards to these issues, for even if these positive affects were possible, the question must be asked: at what and at whose cost were these developments made? As Benjamin (1969:256–257) stated, there isn't a historical act in or document of the development of civilization that isn't at the same time expressive of barbarism; that isn't developed on the labor and sacrifice of multitudes of unknown workers. The critical theory thus has a double task: to designate that which is to be changed, and to name that which is to be preserved. It has the task of showing what the price is that has to be paid for progress; what the effect history or *"Wirkungsgeschichte"* is for any action. It is the task of critical theory of society and religion to rub against the grain of history's development and remember, reveal and possibly redeem the hopes of the past as history moves toward the totally administered society.

Resistance

In 1970, Horkheimer stated that we do not yet live in a totally administered society. Although the dominant social productive forces of globalizing capitalism, its increasingly administered national and international bureaucracies, and its imperialistic military might have moved the world closer to its realization, we today in the early 21st century can still say we do not yet live in a totally administered society. Here in the United States, which presently is leading the charge in the direction of this cyberneticized social, global totality, a truly humanistic theory and praxis can still be done albeit in the face of the violations of the US Constitution and the Bill of Rights by the Patriot Act I & II, the Board of Homeland Security, the Total Information Awareness program of John Poindexter, etc. As Horkheimer and the entire critical theory of society and religion acknowledges, the historical development toward a totally administered society cannot be prevented or abstractly cancelled. The critical theory does not offer any reprieve from this historical development. It also, however, does not fall into nihilistic despair and resignation nor positivistic conformity to this trend. The task of critical thought remains the remembrance, preservation, and critical furtherance in theory and praxis of human autonomy and solidarity in resistance to the historical trend that leads to the totally administered world. The urgent task remains of keeping alive the critical theological and materialistic notion of the totally Other than that which is ideologically justified as the "real" world by positivism and its economic, political, military and cultural system power brokers; a socially created world weighed down by the gravity of facts that has the capability of killing the human consciousness or spirit for anything other than what is. By means of the critical notion of and thus longing for the totally Other than what is the possibility of revolutionary social change in a new historical direction of a better, more communicatively and aesthetically rational, less antagonistic, more humane and shalom-filled future society exists.

Critical Theory as Successor of Religion

According to Horkheimer, religion has lost its social purpose of being an actual force for social change in today's world through its betrayal of any critical, prophetic notion of transcendence and the longing for the totally Other. Religion, particularly Christianity, has given up its prophetic and Messianic critique of existence and has been sublimated into the reified social function of ideologically legitimating the development of the capitalist society toward its totally administered fulfillment. In terms of the critical theory of religion, true religion is the critical consciousness and expression of humanity's finitude of suffering and death, which thus, produces the longing that this world is not the absolute end. Such religious or theological longing for the totally Other can then be put into the moral praxis of resistance against the making of anything finite into the Absolute. Religion, therefore, cannot be secularized – brought into conformity as an ideological social function of any existing social totality – without giving it up. It is thus a futile hope that the churches will ever reclaim its original negative, prophetic, Messianic and eschatological critique of longing for the totally Other and its revolutionary social praxis. According to Horkheimer, due to religion's betrayal of itself, of its critical function of negatively expressing this longing for the totally Other and its ideals of justice, truth, freedom, etc., this critical content has thrown off its religious form and has transformed itself into a secular, materialistic theory and praxis of historical struggle for a more rational, just, free and solidary future society. Horkheimer's critical theory of society and religion is such a modern, dialectical materialistic heir of this theological longing for the totally Other.

Chapter Seven

The Functional View of Religion: Limits and Dangers. Some Remarks and Directions

Gottfried Küenzlen

The humanities and the social sciences are part of the theoretical apparatus that serves for the enlightenment of Western societies. Sociology, in particular, has become a hermeneutic authority, whose concepts and images concerning human existence and the world govern our understanding of the external and internal factors of human life. Lurking behind the endeavors of Sociology, we can make out a hypostatic view of society that is reduced to a world-view that determines – as a metaphysical variable – the rank and destiny of the people living in it:

> In society as a social system human existence has become a being determined entirely by society, meeting in it its destiny. Accordingly, sociology has become a key science, which alone can enlighten people with regard to the powers making them act like puppets on their strings. At the same time it would provide them with knowledge about the law-like regularities that bring about changes in human existences by changes in society itself (Tenbruck 1986, 1984).

Now, this sociological world-view has put its spell also on a theology that conceives itself as being open-minded toward modernity. It has put its spell especially on the ecclesiastical activities influenced by such theology, as we have been able to make out from the relevant publications and ecclesiastic practices of the past thirty years. The historical irony in this is theology's striving to join a scientific tradition that in turn has been striving from the very beginning to overthrow traditional religion or any religion whatsoever. So, the motivation of this movement, still immanent in the mainstream of current sociology, is essentially one that is critical of religion.

To be sure, the cultural importance of sociology as an hermeneutic authority has by now decreased – whether because sociology, in a process of self-enlightenment, silently stepped back from its own former motives, or because science in general has lost its cultural significance. In any case, it is striking that analyses and diagnoses of the present, as well as discussions about them, are now rarely carried out by sociologists but increasingly more by literary personalities, historians or philosophers. This could be witnessed ten years ago already in the so-called "historians' dispute" (*Historikerstreit*), and more recently in the Walser-Bubis controversy as well as in the controversy around the philosopher Peter Sloterdijk.

Now, it is remarkable in this situation that theological attempts of self-determination as practiced in ecclesiastic academies and in scholarly departments as well as in theological and ecclesiastical pronouncements – if not, perhaps, in academic theology – continue to make use of sociological interpretations and explanations of the world. Concerning this we may first of all state that certainly, theological speech and ecclesiastical activity do depend upon hermeneutic devices that are partly sociological in character in order to achieve an adequate understanding of current social situations. Also, any secular society is in the long run dependent on sociology in order to be able to reflect on itself adequately. However, the danger lies where analyses and interpretations provided by science are not taken heuristically, but in a dogmatic way, as unconditionally true statements of the situation and nature of human existence in general. Such a view is problematic already because of the enormous rapidity of the process in which sociological insights become outdated. This shows already, why we should not make use of such insights too freely and naively.

Moreover, even sociologists make mistakes and have done so before! We must grant them their right to be in error, for this is an essential aspect of science, which has always – particularly in the person of its most famous representatives – been conscious of its own perpetual susceptibility to error. The problem begins just where statements of the social sciences, originally intended as hypothetical approximations to social reality only, are taken to be reifying descriptions of that reality as it is in itself.

More specifically, let us look at notions like "change of values" or "no future generation," like the progress from "late capitalism" to "post-modernism," like "consumption society," "risking society," "adventure society" and so forth. All of these petty or big sociological theories have often been received in an extremely naive directness just in order to secure the actuality of theological speech and ecclesiastical activity. This has been done despite their dubious explanatory value and epistemic basis. Phenomena like these force us into critical self-reflection, if we consider that many of the sociological certainties once dealt with dogmatically have either become wastepaper after a certain period of time or have never really achieved academic appreciation at all.

For years, a particularly successful figure of thought has been appealed to in order to prove the so-called functional view of religion. This view, which follows the tradition initiated by Durkheim (Küenzlen 1995:85–100), regards religion as a "social fact" according to its effects, use and function for society. The leading question is hereby not the nature and content of religion, but rather what impact and functions it ought to have. Or, even more specifically: The meaning of "religion" is to be determined with regard to its function for society. I do not intend to give here a detailed analysis of particular theories and their differences, as they are found especially in the writings of Thomas Luckmann, Niklas Luhmann and Hermann Lübbe. Neither do I intend to present a survey of the history or of the theoretical location of the "functional argument." This has been done already succesfully in a recent comprehensive study by Heinz Theo Homann (1997). Rather, in what follows, I would like to focus on the fact that the sociologically functional conception of religion has, to a large extent, entered even theological thinking and ecclesiastical practice itself.[1] My aim is to lay bare, as briefly as possible, some of the limits and potential dangers of the functional view.

---

[1] Even the Evangelische Zentralstelle für Weltanschauungsfragen (central Protestant office for questions of ideology) has proved, in some of its publications, impressed by the functional argument.

What are the reasons behind this development of the functional view in the theological and ecclesiastical fields? My thesis is that one of the main impulses is a certain apologetic tendency, a special interest in finding an answer to the diminution of the social and cultural significance of Christianity and of the churches.

Apologetic Tendency

First of all, we may get an insight into the practical impact of functional thinking by taking a look at the church's official arguments concerning the abolishment of the German Protestants' Day of Prayer and Repentance. Another example is the current debate in Germany about whether or not to keep Sunday as an official working holiday. To begin with, we should consider that public discussions about official religious holidays are themselves already a sign of the cultural diminution of Christianity and the churches. Not long ago, an issue like the abolishment of the Day of Repentance would have been unthinkable. Nowadays, however, the church's reaction to such considerations – as shown in the case of Sunday – is based on a functional argument. Holidays, it is argued, are socially serviceable days, the abolishment of which would bring with it a loss of their relevant social effects. Now, this argument is bound to be a deadlock. For, the political pursuers of the abolishment of certain holidays have always argued functionally themselves. The social benefit of financing health care insurance, for example, would have to be rated much higher in social value than an official holiday. Moreover, though it might be deplorable to abolish official holidays at all, still it would be much easier to do it with Protestant holidays, since the Protestant church is socially much more marginalized than the Catholic Church.[2]

The above example shows already where the limits and problems of functionalism in questions of religion can be found. If the official representatives of religion are basically ready to argue in functional terms, perhaps even justifying their own role functionally, there will immediately arise a question as to possible functional equivalents to which one may believe in religion. If

---

[2] It is remarkable that three decidedly Catholic Prime Ministers in Germany have stood firmly against the abolishing of Protestant holidays. In Saxony, this opposition even proved successful.

functional equivalents to religion are thought possible at all, then they might as well turn out to be, in some respects at least, even more serviceable, e.g. more economical than their religious counterparts. So, finally, there will be no striking argument left at all against neglecting or abolishing religion.

Dangers

I would like to illustrate two aspects of the problem or even potential danger of functional religious thinking. The first facet of the danger is that the determination of religion in terms of its serviceability, which goes along with a typical neglect of the difference between ethics and faith, gives a clue to an influential process in the history of Western modernism. According to post-enlightenment theory, if the question of religious truth, particularly within the Christian faith, cannot be answered by means of cognitive reason, then there still ought to be practical life itself where the truth and nature of religion may be found. So, religion would prove to be true at least by being made functional in real life, that is in ethics, according to a main stream of enlightened thinking. In addition, we must consider the dominance – mentioned already in the beginning – of the status quo of society as a world-view. If it is society only, as an ultimate and so quasi-metaphysical power, that determines peoples' actions, thoughts and feelings, then religion as well is to be valued exclusively according to its serviceability in society. Its identity and purpose would then entirely depend on this criterion.

Now, the reception of this figure of thought in theology and ecclesiastics can easily be recognized as an apologetic reaction to the social diminution of Christianity and the churches. Although the messages and dogmatic contents of Christianity are culturally evaporating in light of peoples' ways of life, the social serviceability of religion may still be maintained. This serviceability is to show itself programmatically in social politics, social technologies, social therapies, or social deaconry. Although the churches as institutions have lost their former dominance, still their traditional religious service of uniting society would suffice to secure their acceptance and continuance. At least this would be the case if they took refuge in communitarian and civil religious ideas.

However, this way certainly leads to a standstill. It suffices to call upon two important insights to prove this. First, we should remind ourselves that where functional arguments are brought forth, we are immediately faced with the question of functional equivalents. For example, what if secular programs should turn out more profitable and easier to be integrated into peoples' understanding than Christian-based programs? A religion that depends for its acceptance and support on social profitability is forced to retreat as soon as other social institutions are able to take over the same social tasks with even greater effectiveness.

Again, we ought to remember that, from a religious point of view, questions of utility should always remain secondary, but not neglected. Christian Reformation theology, in particular, has always insisted upon charitable and in the wider sense social-deaconary activities as being the *result* of faith and not the other way around. Although, according to the letter St. James, faith is not practicable without deeds, it nevertheless must precede them. As soon as the theoretical substantiation of religion goes beyond a mere utilitarian and functional view, it will arrive at this very insight as it is summarized tersely by the Japanese theoretician Nishitani (1982:42f):

> Just as little as life itself should religion be measured under the aspect of its utility. If a religion does lend primacy to such considerations, then this already shows how much it is degenerated. (...) What is essential for religion, and what renders religion essential for human existence, is that it makes us return to the point of origin in life. There, life is something beyond functionality or utility. That is to say, there we transgress our everyday way of living and let behind our usual mode of being. (...) When the nature of religion is at stake, the question 'what use does religion have for us?' is in itself wrongly put. There is another very simple question that turns the first one over: 'What is the purpose of our existence?' That is why the question 'why do we need religion?' from the beginning blocks its own way to any possible answer. It blocks the way in which we can become a question to ourselves.

Once having left behind the utilitarian and functionalistic paradigm, the question of religion's use and function is put in a very different and new way.

> (religion's) 'secular use' has always been the greater the more unperturbably and exclusively it fulfilled its real task, the more unequivocally it preserved its 'religious peculiarities'. (...) The factum of religion itself is its true service to the world (Schaeffler 1973, Homann 1997:497).

Paradoxically, from the standpoint of theology and religious sciences, religion is serviceable to society only when it is not practiced for the sake of its services only.

Now, a second effect of functional thinking in the theological field is this typically enlarged notion of religion that allows us to unite most disparate phenomena under the heading of "religious." Here as well, the apologetic intention is obvious. Declaring esoteric techniques and all those varying streams within the current market of ideologies, as well as rock sessions, football, Love-Parade, consumption of drugs and so forth, to be religious acknowledgments of existence may serve in itself as an apparent proof that the world on the whole is still imbued with religion – even though it gradually and steadily loses the influence of Christianity and the church. Such a strategy, however, turns out to be nothing but a theoretical, ultimately theological short-circuit. Although one succeeds in explaining all those non-everyday events and explanations of meaning as "religious," one has not asserted anything about their possible ecclesiastic Christian impact. For, what is here called "religion" comes with its own specific contents and ideas about human nature and existence. The explicit or implicit dogmatics of such phenomena are still waiting to be explored.

In any case, from the Christian standpoint our view of current spiritual situations remains shortsighted as long as we are looking only for problems of language, of communication and of hermeneutics. As Max Weber has pointed out emphatically, authentic religions are themselves based upon and determined by different conceptions of humanity and the world. Likewise, those spiritual phenomena which are called "religious" today are grounded on *their own* implicit views of being and, for this reason, cannot be incorporated in Christian ecclesiastic strategies of thought. The issue is, therefore, not one of different ways of religious orientation, as the functional argument would make us believe, but one of an altogether different kind of faith. As Georg Simmel (1989:58) has put it:

> In religious faith the mutual independence of content and function does not exist. Belief in another God is a different kind of belief. It is like with our emotional attitudes towards other people: When love is taken away from one and turned towards another, it has not only changed its object but has also – according to the extent of depth and to how much it will touch our own being – become another kind of love. Whether one believes in Jehovah,

or in the Christian God, in Ormuz, Ahriman or Vitzliputzi – this makes a difference not only in content but also in function, it means a different way of humanly existence.[3]

In all this, I do not want to question the fact that the functional view of religion may serve as a limited heuristic instrument for comprehending the whole of socially effective spiritual orientations, even in the field of Christian apologetics. Yet again: Even in this case, the religious peculiarity and the specific claim to truth combined with it must be perceived and considered. We should avoid those short-circuited doctrines that operate with concepts like "everyday religion," "implicit religion," "invisible religion," etc. in order to turn everything that shows a social meaning or can be identified through non-every-day experiences into "religion." Doing this means to subscribe to a functional understanding of religion that has lost its capability of making differences altogether.

There is another reason why we should keep distance from such conceptions, especially in the light of a Christian theological and ecclesiastical treatment of the many current spiritual orientations and exotic happenings. Functional thinking is a temptation to value human beings themselves in functional and economic terms only. It continues the de-personalization of human beings, which is the specific dynamics of modernity. More specifically, the one who goes to a rock concert goes there and finds what he or she is looking for. To turn him therefore into one who is "looking for religion" or even into a "tacit Christian" is not only at best a helpless apologetical attempt, but it even deprives the person who is functionally so treated of his or her own personal dignity.

There would still be plenty of other aspects to consider, but I will restrict myself lastly to two of them. First, functionalism does not recognize any history. In this as well it proves the heritage of Durkheim's work, in which religion's function for society was regarded as eternal, whereas its contents were nothing but a historically transitory, ultimately substitutable side aspect. The result is that religion in its historical genesis, as well as in its very power

---

[3] See also my attempt to characterize "secular religion" according to its specific pecularities in Gottfried Küenzlen, *Der neue Mensch. Eine Untersuchung zur säkularen Religionsgeschichte der Moderne*, München 1994, esp. pp. 269ff.

to influence culture, society and history, is altogether neglected. Now, if we today take a look at the world beyond Europe, we realize how much religion is still – or now again – able to control people and has come back into history. What is nowadays misleadingly squeezed into the formula of "fundamentalism" can not be explained in its potential cultural significance within the functional theory of religion. That is why Christian apologetics should, in their attempts to understand current religious culture, strive to keep in view the latter's location in history.

In all this, we have not yet treated the decisive insight concerning where any considerations about functionalism must of necessity lead; considerations, which also have been lurking behind all of the above arguments: Functionalism simply cancels the question of the truth of religion. It is not possible in this essay to get into this thesis any further than this statement. Be that as it may, a caveat can be made to such an assertion in the form of the question: What is truth at all?

There is still something we may add in this context, however. Functional thinking is not even able to *ask* the question of truth or falsity. According to an exclusively functional understanding of religion, that which is "true" in religion can only be what fulfils the demanded social function and thereby prove itself socially necessary. Everything dysfunctional must be untrue, then, and therefore unnecessary. From the external perspective of the theory of religion as well as from the internal theological perspective, however, we have not only reduced the nature of religion then but entirely missed it. *Homo religiosus* knows about the commitment to truth, even when it is viewed as something unnecessary and negligible according to the functional account (Jüngel 1979:45–75).

Finally, a functionally enlarged notion of religion, which excludes the question of truth and declares everything socially identifiable by its subjective sense to be religion, is not able to avoid the question of how to tell sense from nonsense.

> The danger which lies in the equation of human religious being with human's being affected by sense consists in the simple fact that there might be also false sense. If the subjective experience of sense could suffice to grant the truth of what is experienced, then the difference between sanity and insanity would have been dispensed with as well (Rohrmoser 1975:126).

In a process of critical self-reflection, it is time to rethink the pattern of understanding offered by the functional view of religion, which superficially appears so easy to be handled within the theological field with respect to its limits and dangers.

Chapter Eight
Religion within the Space of Reasons
Helmut Fritzsche

Religion is – and should be practised as – a motivation to free oneself and others from internal and external barriers that hide the truth that life is worth living and is capable of actions that are worthy to be undertaken.

Keeping in mind the many connotations of the word religion, I do not pretend to provide a timeless and comprehensive notion of religion. Rather, my thesis focuses on some contemporary issues due to the revival of traditional religions in many regions in the world today. Related to this are the issues of the rapidly growing loss of religious education in Europe, and of the world-wide threats to the physical, socio-political and mental conditions of life and a growing loss of awe of life.

I take my starting point with William James' pragmatic understanding of religion as a variety of mystical experiences of the value of life. In order to discuss the importance of religion for practising a life worth living within the circumstances of our life today, I take up the metaphor "space of reasons" as a symbol for the truth that a life worth living is surrounded with "motivational reasons" in form of desires stimulated by value experiences on the one side, and with "normative reasons" providing critical and self critical standards for life worth living on the other one (Halbig 2002:961–972, 2003:133–149).[1]

Finally, the importance of religion for life worth living and actions worthy to be undertaken will be demonstrated in the context of some contemporary schemes of the philosophy of religion, as well as in the framework of a philosophy of personality and, at the very last, in view of public debates about some issues of justice and morality.

Introductory Remarks: Religion in Contemporary Contexts

The revival of the world religions and a growing interest for religious questions in the public opinion formation processes is a widely known phenomenon today and it has many reasons. Of course, first of all, it happens because of the invocations of "jihads" and "crusades," reminding us of religion as a motivational power as well as the ambivalent role religions have played in the past. Bloody wars and sacrificing charity, mental pressures and struggle for intellectual freedom, wishful thinking and cultivating rational discipline, were at all times closely held together. There is scarcely a religion or a religious cult to be found without being tempted to follow these ambivalent practices in one or another way.

To discover the ambiguous character of religion is by no means a new approach. I mention only some of the most prominent examples. It was one of the concerns of Kant's philosophy to praise religion in the form of one's being guided from the heuristic ideas of God, freedom and immortality of the soul as the highest practice of a reasonable way of life, while also understanding religion as a form of fanaticism, credulity and superstition, which thereby belongs to the darkest sides of human history. Whitehead (2001:17) spoke very openly about the double role of religion in saying, "Religion is by no means necessarily good. It may be very evil." Further, William James – about whom I will say more – extensively dealt with the double face of religion within personal life and within the theological and philosophical theory formation as well.

---

[1] To the importance of and the relatedness of both these notions see the survey of regarding literature given by Christoph Halbig, Motivierende Gründe in: Deutsche Zeitschrift für Philosophie, Berlin 50 2002, pp. 961–972, and Normative Gründe in: Deutsche Zeitschrift für Philosophie Berlin 51 2003, pp. 133–149.

Further, the religious come back today plays an important role in the contexts of politics. It is no longer true to take power politics and economic interests to be the only working factors for making wars and the formations of treatises. Cultural identities and, in this context, religious traditions are increasingly coming out as additional factors. Certainly, Samuel Huntington's (1996) well known thesis of an already ongoing and for the future determining "clash of civilizations" is a fatally oversimplifying theory, because cultures are not closed firm units capable of acting as a political subject. Nevertheless, considering the diminishing of the importance of nation states following the globalisation in politics, nation-state identity feelings based on cultural and religious values are not to be overlooked. The "World of Islam" or the "Transatlantic Value Community" are obviously working as identifying factors and probably other similar identities will follow. Given that these tendencies are continuing – and there is scarcely anything to plead for the contrary – the mental climate changes drastically in our age. To deal with the importance of religion in this dimension is more than a special issue for politicians. It concerns more or less all of us.

Furthermore, there are deep connections between the revival of the religions on the one side and the many disappointments of people in the different regions of the world coming from their experiences of the practices of democracy and the increasing power of the globalisation of a no longer softened capitalism. Scarcely any doubts are possible that the revival of Islam started with the worsening of the conditions of life of the people in those regions and their growing fury about the drastic rise of poverty and starvation on the one side, and corruption and immense wealth among the ruling elite, on the other one.

Notwithstanding the incomparably higher living standard of the average person in the Western world, feelings of social precariousness are rising here too. This has motivated people to question religious institutions, such as churches and their messages, about the social relevancy of religious practices with regard to the problems within the Western world and in global dimensions as well.

Yet, concerning our reflections about the contexts of religious revivals, there is still another aspect to be mentioned that also has to do with cultural frustrations. In his article "Two Concepts of Freedom" Isaiah Berlin (1958) already opposed the triumphalism of the freedom of the individual and the promises of everlasting eudemonism, symptomatic of the self-understanding of modern people in those days. Berlin pointed to the underground fears that make people bend to a form of paternalism, which trusts higher order authorities who promise a man-made paradise. Berlin recommended the Enlightenment principle of thinking for oneself in order to live responsibly in a culturally pluralistic civilization.

Charles Taylor (1997:418–429) took up Berlin's idea of the two freedoms. He criticises the notion of "negative freedom" that goes back to Hobbes and Bentham. According to them "freedom is the absence of external obstacles, physical or legal." Berlin convincingly states that the possibility to do what one's deepest desires and wants are willing to do would be a very poor notion of freedom. Real freedom, "positive freedom", starts – so states Taylor (1997:423) – with one's capacity to discriminate between uncritically working wants and desires within our feelings and "second order desires, desires about desires...making...some of our desires and goals...intrinsically more significant than others."

Of course, in this article Taylor did not deal with religion as such, but with the question that I will address below: what makes the space of freedom with a real chance to develop a higher order personality or self in search of a life worth living? This is one of the context questions in which religion becomes interesting again.

Finally, globalisation in cultural life and global politics brings the powerful secularisation theory and what William James mockingly called the "survival theory" into some troubles. One point of the secularisation theory is the irreversibility of the principles of the differentiation between state and church; respectively between the realm of public opinion building about fundamental constitutional state affairs and justice on the one hand, and the realm of opinion formation within the language games and institutions of the various religious communities on the other one. No doubt, this distinction has in principle proved to do justice to both; to the interests of the states to include the citizens irrespective of their comprehensive world views on the one side, and to the churches interested in freedom from state-based prevalence of certain religious or profane world views on the other.

But in detail, irritations and confusions are rising. Where exactly should the line be drawn between religious reasons for this or that moral claim and public reasons acceptable for all citizens in a culturally pluralistic society?

The ongoing debates about birth control, genetic engineering, and euthanasia are only some examples of many others regarding the conflict lines in public reasoning.

Yet, the global situation is still worse. In the minds of many Islamic people, the distinction between state and religion is not acceptable – of the neutrality of the state in favour of religious freedom, but it is evaluated as support for power claims of the Western Christian tradition. The insight that a global order for the religion-state relation is far out of reach is one of the more accurate understandings about realities in the fields of religion today.

Using the term "revival theory", William James was amused about people thinking religion and religious practises to be something like a fossil surviving in niches without relevance for life. The hasty debates in Europe, particularly in France and in Germany, about the importance of religious symbols, such as the cross in public institutions and head-scarves in classes, and the different cultural connotations of religious symbols witnessed in public life, highlights the ongoing and increasing importance of religious traditions for both the traditional centres of secularised nations as well as for people without any religious ambitions.

What I mentioned briefly in the foregoing – the ambivalence of religion, the many mixtures of religion and culture, the different social and cultural frustrations in the world today, and finally the new problems of speaking religiously in public affairs – belongs together and forms what I like to term the context problems of religion today.

The concept "religion within the space of reasons" attempts to catch some essential points of the new position of religion in the contexts mentioned. However, considering the complexity of the problems, some methodological decisions are unavoidable to make.

First, I take the viewpoint of religion within the Western cultural tradition. Speaking of religion in general terms and claiming validity for people in the 21st century in principle, irrespective of the conditions of their life, would not make any sense. The subject as such would be lost.

Secondly, I will take the perspective "from below," from the experiences, from the interests of people watching their personal concerns about a life worth living under the circumstances today. What the world religions are teaching about culture, justice, life and personality is another issue and cannot be taken up adequately in my reflections.

Thirdly, the social dimension of religion, meaning the role of religion for improving the conditions of life in global dimensions, seems to me the most important dimension in all of the issues at stake. Yet, to deal with religious activities for improving life conditions in separation from the sources of religion as such, only theoretically raising claims for what would be the best for man according to the religious traditions, seems to me absolutely pointless. I attempt to aim at the social relevance of religion from the sources of religion that can be experienced within life.

Fourthly, in order to place religion within the contexts mentioned, to bridge over the gap between the seminal, personal, individual religious experiences on the one side and the intellectual standards of a Western styled society on the other, seems to me the core issue. The concept "religion within the space of reasons" serves as an instrument for proposing some steps in the direction of bridging the gaps.

According to these methodological decisions the itinerary of the essay goes from religious experience via philosophical standards for practical reasoning to some ideas about traits of a personality that is capable of making sense of religion within the cultural and social life within the Western world and with regard to the intercultural exchange as well.

Religious Experience and its Philosophical Significance

In a recently published collection of lectures about the appearances of the religious today, Charles Taylor (2003) introduced some illuminating thoughts about tendencies in the development of the religions. He focussed on the "North-Atlantic region", well aware of the differences between the situations in Canada – his home –, in the USA, and in Europe. Taylor also concentrates on the intercultural tensions of today. Taylor develops his thoughts in the form of an interpretation of William James (1958), particularly of his *The Varieties of Religious Experience*.

Taylor reads James as a prophetic voice anticipating a "post-Durkheimian world" and a "post-Durkheimian system of believing", both terms meaning a religious practice without taking seriously the levels of communal life and the concerns of the political society. Taylor delineates an interesting panorama of two sides of James's work: the one, helpful for vindicating our contemporary tendencies in and needs for religious practice, and the other, of shortcomings we should try to avoid in our practice.[2] I will refer shortly to both of these aspects by the means of which Taylor highlights the actuality[3] of James' thought and take Taylor's half way asserting and half way critical view of James as a starting point for my own – in some aspects – different interpretation of James.

Taylor beginnings by quoting the famous passage from the *Varieties* containing James's (1958:42) notion of religion: "Religion...shall mean for us the feelings, acts, and experiences of individual men in their solitude, so far as they apprehend themselves to stand in relation to whatever they may consider the divine." In his further analysis, Taylor underlines the religious individualism with James and his emphasis that religious experience transposes the healing forces of the divine into the individual's life. In this regard, Taylor agrees with James exactly in what people today are expecting when they share a religious community.[4]

Taylor, however, is not content in stating only the proximity of the Jamesian individualism to the life expectations of people in our age. Taylor goes

---

[2] "It might seem that our post-Durkheimian world is a paradigmatically Jamesian one. Individuals make what they can of their 'religious experience,' whithout too much concern for how it all fits together at the level of society or how it affects the fate of different churches. In one way, James is very close to the spirit of contemporary society. He was already living in his own post-Durkheimian dispensation. But in another way, he is still missing something important. I want to mention three key phenomena today, which we might miss if we went away with a too-simple notion of James's undoubted prescience." (Taylor 2002:111). Taylor differentiates between a durkheimian world in which the sacred, the divine or God are present in holy places, holy times and/or in the institutions of the state and the body politics on the one side, and a post-durkheimian world, in which God, respectively the divine are present mot indirectly, namely in the moral values and the moral rules valid for all the member of the correspondent social unit. Different to both these ideal-typical frames of state-religion relations is according to Taylor the post-durkheimian scheme in which a plurality of religious practices is living more or less besides the concerns of the correspondent political societies. But Taylor emphases that this scheme of state-religion relation only serves for analytical purposes, namely to point to contemporary tendencies, which could be change in the one or the other direction. Nevertheless, the post-durkheimian model is – according Taylor – one of James' centre points.

[3] To quote from Taylor's (2003:3) Introduction: "In fact it turns out to have a lot to say. It is astonishing how little dated it is. Some of the detail may be strange, but you easily think of examples in our world that fit the themes James is developing. You can even find yourself forgetting that these lectures were delivered a hundred years ago."

[4] "The religious life or practice that I became part of not only must be my choice, but must speak to me; it must make sense in terms of my spiritual development as I understand this." (Taylor 2003:94).

further and diagnoses a cultural revolution in the West starting after World War II and continuing up to today. What is developing in this revolution is a new quality of an "expressive individualism" culminating in slogans such as authenticity, self-realisation, self-experience, or self-presentation. Essential to this excessive use of what "negative freedom" allows to happen is the practice of mutual self-presentation. To demonstrate one's self seems to be meaningful first when it is practised in the view of others who are also probing their self-realisation in more or less public spaces. In these tendencies, Taylor sees traces of a new form of social life.[5]

Taylor's approach to this development – given that I understand him correctly – does not go along with a simple cultural-critical pessimism. His point is to compare the Jamesian and the expressive individualism according to the insight that alternatives are needed to consider the strengths and the weaknesses of both sides. No doubt, comparing Taylor's analyses of expressive individualism with James's thought about the importance of individuality, there are deep commonalties but decisive differences as well. Exactly these confrontations make Taylor's methodological approach attractive as it points to the importance of James's ideas. Considered in the context of expressive individualism, the Jamesian perspective discovered a dimension of life that scarcely can be grasped adequately by the means of expressive individualism. Thus, James can be understood as a critical alternative to the new individualism. On the other hand, one has to question the importance James gives to religion as an essential part of a full-fledged human individual.

Taylor's assessment of the religious situation of our age – viewing the West – includes both kinds of individualism. On the one hand, by pointing to James, he states that religious experience has never before been so important for life.[6]

---

[5] "And so the new, more individualized pursuit of happiness, loosening some of the ties and common lifeways of the past, the spread of expressive individualism and the culture of authenticity, the increased importance of these spaces of mutual display, all these seem to point to a new way of being together in society. This expressive individualism, which has been growing since the war, is obviously stronger in some milieus than in others, stronger among youth than among older people, stronger among those who were formed in the 1960's and 1970's; but overall it seems steadily to advance." Ibid. p. 88.

[6] "In some sense religious 'experience', the beginning intimations and intuitions that we feel bound to follow up, is crucial as never before, wherever we end up taking them in our divergent spiritual lives. It is because he saw this with such intensity, and could articulate it with such intensity, and could articulate it with such force, that James's book lives on so strongly in our world." (Taylor 2003:116).

On the other hand, he identifies three points that "James has not seen" (Taylor 2003:111). First, he points out the continuance of the socio-political relevance of religious practice. Secondly, he expresses the importance of collective forms[7] of the religious life, and thirdly, the mediation between religious "feelings" and religious "conversion"[8] with the rest of one's ways of life.

In principle, I agree with the contents that Taylor is pointing to when criticising some shortcomings of James. Indeed, religion without including the social-political dimension, religion without sharing religious communities, and religion exclusively focussed on some biographical highlights, would be a very deficient kind of religion. However, I contest Taylor's opinion that this deficient practice of religion is what James has presented in his works. On the contrary, the three points mentioned, belong – besides some other aspects particularly concerning the truth of religion – to the essentials of James's thought. At the end of my interpretation of James, I will come back to these points.

My interpretation of James's (1958) *The Varieties of Religious Experience* including his earlier essay "Is Life Worth Living?" (James 1956:32–62) is aimed at the following assertion: True religious experience – respectively the truth that the divine or God is accessible for us in religious experience – on the one hand, and practising a life worth living – respectively the truth that life is worth living – on the other hand, are different terms for one and the same thing. I take the reasons for this assertion that this is the essence of what James wanted to express, particularly from the chapters about "The Sick Soul," "The Divided Self," and both chapters about "Conversion" in the *Varieties* (VI till X) and also from his "Is Life Worth Living." This essay was originally an address to the Harvard Young Men's Christian Association and published first in 1895. This relatively rare noticed essay (but mentioned by Taylor) is so to speak a shorthand of the *Varieties*. Because of its brevity and precision in drawing the lines of thought, this essay seems to me particularly suited for an introduction into the essence of the *Varieties* and of James's philosophy of religion as such.

---

[7] "What James can't seem to accommodate is the phenomenon of collective religious life, which is not just the result of (individual) religious connections, but which in some way constitutes or is that connection." (Taylor 2003:24).

[8] "...the foregrounding of feeling, and the moment of conversion and inspiration, take him away from the kind of religious life that may start in a moment of blinding insight, but than continues through some, perhaps very demanding spiritual discipline." (Taylor 2003:115–116).

"Is Life Worth Living?" is focussed on the issue of suicide, not suicide because of illness or in panicky situations, but on reflective suicide and the reflections before and about suicide. James, who had studied medicine, was well aware about physically conditioned psychic states in which people are tempted to commit suicide. Yet, the point of interest for James was the mental background, the so to speak world-view which brings "reflective people" to think about making an end with life. His speech about suicide is addressed to young reflective people, students; most of them "are devoted, for good or ill, to the reflective life."

James's (1956:37) position on the issue of suicide is summed up in the following assertion: Suicide is a kind of demonstration, namely "that life is not worth living the whole army of suicides declare." The sincere practice to raise the question "Is life worth living?" is one, and ultimately seen, the only way to free oneself from the internal barriers of metaphysical pessimism preventing oneself from catching the truth that suicide may be the wrong decision. James's final advice, backed on the grounds of a philosophy of religion in nuce, is: "Be not afraid of life. Believe that life is worth living, and your belief will create the fact."

But the significance of James's essay goes much further than giving advice on how to respond to suicide ideas in one's consciousness. The importance of the essay lies in the fact that James makes the suicide issue, together with the theodicy problem, the reference point of a philosophy of religion, and – as far as I see – there is scarcely a comparable approach in the long history of the philosophy of religion. Going still further, suicide thoughts in one's conscious life, the idea of a would-be-suicide, is taken by James as an ideal-typical mental scheme for the mental habituation of people who have spirit-ualised the scientifically "agnostic positivism" on the one hand and have lost any trust in the traditional way in religion and metaphysics. In no other place within the work of James does the influence of Nietzsche become so evident than in the context of the suicide issue. However, James does not share the Nietzschean pathos and triumphalism regarding the coming of the Overman. James keeps in his mind the enduring force of the religion tradition and the ongoing needs for religion within humanity.

All these ideas come out in James's (1956:39) reflections about suicide. His starting point is the "nightmare experiences" of metaphysical pessimism, and says: "Pessimism is essentially a religious disease. In the form of it to which you are most liable, it consists in nothing but a religious demand to which there comes no normal religious reply." This experience of religious reply reminds one of Job and the traditional theological teaching of temptation (*Anfechtung*), but James has in mind the failures of the traditional rational theology glorifying God's Spirit ruling the world to the best of law and order and the well being of the creatures, of the human beings first of all.[9]

The "bankruptcy" of natural theology – and obviously, James felt himself at one with the majority of the students he was addressing in his lecture, and many other contemporaries[10] as well – is the broader spiritual background for the ideas of the would-be-suicide. In the view of James, the first step on the escape route out of the nightmare of a life not worth living to the "daylight experience" of a life worth living, is the protest against the natural theology of the traditional religiosity. James (1956:44) states very clearly:

> I cannot help, therefore, accounting it on the whole a gain (though it may seem for certain poetic constitutions a very sad loss) that the naturalistic superstition, the worship of the God of nature, simply taken as such, should have begun to loosen its hold upon the educated mind. In fact, if I am to express my personal opinion, I should say (in spite of its sounding blasphemous at first to certain ears) that the initial step towards getting into healthy ultimate relations with the universe is the act of rebellion against the idea that such a God exists.

---

[9] Referring to the question why he is calling "pessimism an essentially religious disease", he states: "The nightmare view of life has plenty of organic sources; but is great reflective source has at all times been the contradiction between the phenomena of nature and the craving of the heart to believe that behind nature there is a spirit whose expression nature id. What philosophers call 'natural theology has one way of appeasing this craving; that poetry of nature in which our English is so rich has been another way." (James 1956:40). Pointing to the hollowness of the traditional natural theology, he writes: Now, I do not hesitate frankly and sincerely to confess to you that this real and genuine discord seems to me to carry with it the inevitable bankruptcy of natural religion naively and simply taken. There were times when Leibnitzes with their heads buried in monstrous wigs could compose Theodicees.... But those times are past; and we of the nineteenth century with our evolutionary theories and our mechanical philosophies, already know nature too impartially and too well to worship unreservedly any God of whose character she can be an adequate expression." (James 1956:43).

[10] "It is this natural religion (primitive still, in spite of the fact that poets and men of science whose good-will exceeds their perspicacity keep publishing it in new editions tunes to our contemporary ears) that, as I said a while ago, has suffered definitive bankruptcy in the circle of persons, among whom I must count myself, and who are growing more numerous every day." (James 1956:52).

Opposing the authoritarian approach of the traditional religiosity to the issue of suicide, namely "God alone is master of life and death, they say, and it is a blasphemous act to anticipate his absolving hand," James (1956:38) emphatically states that in his view the would-be suicide is emerging not as a thought of blasphemy, but quite on the contrary, as an immense relief.[11] The relieving function of the very individual and personal experience of this "I can", and "it is allowed to commit suicide" comes out – according to my understanding of the religious heart of James's essay – as the beginning of one's feeling of being taken seriously by God as one's partner in a life-long dialog about the life worth living.[12] It is a feeling of one's being freed out of the grips of a divine tyrant and provides a free space for fighting the battles of life, "Life is worth living, no matter what it brings, if only...combats may be carried to successful terminations..." (James 1956:49).

Beyond and after this first "destructive" step of freeing oneself from the grips of the traditional authoritarian religion follows the second, the "constructive" step, namely the continuing of the already mentioned internal dialog of one's own heart with the divine about possibilities how to master the difficulties of one's life, which had thrown oneself in the metaphysical nightmare. James describes this turn in one's life from the "night" to "daylight" in terms of dreaming and supposing spontaneities stretching one's mind in the direction of the realities of the unseen divine partner working within the realities of our life but not available in terms of our scientific "naturalism."

Is this "unseen" reality thinkable? James's (1956:61) essay about the suicide issue ends without giving any other answer than the assertion that the practice

---

[11] "Here, then, on this stage of mere emancipation from monistic superstition, the would-be suicide may already get encouraging answers to this question about the worth of life. There are in most men instinctive springs of vitality that respond healthily when the burden of metaphysical and infinite responsibility rolls off. The certainty that you may step out of life whenever you please, and that to do so is not blasphemous or monstrous, is itself an immense relief. The thought of suicide is now no longer a guilty challenge and obsession." (James 1956:46).

[12] Here, a fundamental difference between James and contemporary theologians of maturity (*Mündigkeitstheologen*) is to be noticed. What James is emphasizing has scarcely something to do with the pathos of theologians praising humanity – or at least the part of it – to rule the world according to being mandated from God. In the view of James, partnership with God within one's being bounded in a deeply conflict-burdened life-situation, in which – I will return to this point – the presumption is allowed that God may be helpless too. It is a point one may take recourse to the importance of Christology, beyond the traditional swearing to the dogmatic formula.

of hoping, feeling and supposing in the direction of help coming from the "unseen" divine. "I confess that I do not see why the very existence of an invisible world may not in part depend on the personal response which any of us make to the religious appeal."[13] Of course, this basing the unseen divine in one's spontaneous energies that fight for possibilities of making life worth living under the "given" condition that the worth of life is a "metaphysical" truth, brings James into much intellectual trouble. It confronts him with the accusation of making the psychological technique of self-fulfilling prophesy into an ontological principle.

Here, we are at the basic problem of James's philosophy of religion, to which I will come back at the end of the following interpretation of the *Varieties*. What I wanted to make clear in these reflections about James's essay "Is Life Worth Living?" was the close connection between the question of the value of life and the ontological truth question regarding the divine or regarding "God." James – I suppose – was not really satisfied with the answer to the ontological question he attempted to give in the essay. Again at the end of the *Varieties*, he mentions that the gravity and difficulty of the subject are in need of being taken up in further books,[14] a plan James could not fulfil[15] in the rest of his life-time. Anyway, the thematic lines of thought developed in the *Varieties* reflect James's fighting with the issues at stake.

In his *Varieties*, James (1958:22) pursues two strongly different but closely related questions, namely "What are the religious propensities? And…what is their philosophical significance?" The first question is taken up in the form of extensive, very detailed descriptions of religious experiences, mostly taken from biographies or letters of people speaking freely about what they hold for their religious experiences. James was very concerned to report only, and

---

[13] He continues: "God himself, in short, may draw vital strength and increase of very being from our fidelity. For my own part, I do not know what the sweat and bloody tragedy of this life mean anything short of this. If this life be not a real fight, in which something is essentially gained for the universe by success, it is no better than a game of private theatricals from which one may withdraw at will." (James 1956:61).

[14] "That of course would be a program for other books than this; what I now say sufficiently indicates to the philosophic reader the place where I belong." (James 1958:394).

[15] To the "incompleteness" of the *Varieties* see the illuminating essay from Richard R. Niebuhr, William James on religious experience" in: *The Cambridge Companion to William James*, ed. by Ruth Anna Putnam, Cambridge University Press 1997 pp. 214–236, particularly p. 216.

not to falsify the original opinions of the people quoted. The second question about the philosophical significance refers to conclusions, which under philosophical aspects should be drawn from the reports about the varieties of religious experiences and is focused on the question of truth, and closely related to this – with the value experiences of life. I will follow the lines of both these questions before coming to a concluding assessment of the importance of James's thought, providing some basic points for religious-philosophical reasoning under our contemporary circumstances.

As far as I see, James pursued various goals when quoting from the biographical sources gathered in his "documents humain" concerning religious experiences. First of all, I presume, he wanted to document the empirical reality of religious experiences in the past and the present and oppose the prejudices mentioned in the foregoing, according to which religion can be taken as the survival of a fossil only. Irrespective of all reflections about the truth-value of what people take for religious experience, the fact as such belongs to the world in which we live. Nearness to the realities, empiricist pathos, seem to me motives behind the uniquely rich gathering of sources concerning the religious dimension of life. Of course, James's describes religion from his own point of view, focussing on the perspectives of the individual. He has his stand – taking up the phrase of Taylor – in the North-Atlantic edge of the world.

A second and more sophisticated aspect comes out in the preference given to religious witnesses of persons close to mental diseases, people such as George Fox, who is well-known for his pathologically exaggerated temperament, and many others who freely speak about experiences that every psychologist would categorise under psychotic disturbances. This trait in James's method to illustrate religion in her psychic reality is thought through very well. Probably one of the reasons for this is an ironic turn against those of his contemporaries who used to blame religious people for being mentally disordered, and then, it is like saying: why not? Religion is such a deeply moving experience in the psyche of an individual that exaggerated people may be more congenial for religion while mentally cool tempered people are more frequently to be found among scientists. Anyway, the subjective state says little or nothing about the truth-value of the opinions they are uttering. Religion, under the viewpoint of the psychic state of the individuals, is a borderline issue, but by far not the only one. Realistically seen, living a human life is happening in a broad "between", nobody can really and objectively define the border between sane and insane, psychical and physical as well.

Another reason for James's preference for exaggerated and disturbingly tempered witnesses is the motive to illustrate the deep ambivalence of religious experiences. They cannot be taken as true on the bases of subjective experiences alone. On the contrary, what people are feeling as absolutely true and secure in their own mind, can be exactly both: divine and diabolic. Therefore, the philosophical proof – meaning personal rational reflection – about the significance of religious experiences is absolutely indispensable. Religious experience can be a very bad thing.

A third and far reaching point in James's psychological description of the experiential base of religion is his differentiation between the two temperaments, namely, optimism or healthy-mindedness on the one hand, and pessimism, sick soul or morbid-mindedness on the other. Both types of character are organically conditioned but culturally developed and in a certain sense are the individuals responsible for the formation of their characters, more in the one or more in the other direction. Of course, both these types are ideal-typically descriptions, and the "antagonism…between the healthy-minded way of viewing life…and the morbid-minded way" (James 1958:137) comes out particularly significant when people tending more to the one or to the other type meet and observe each other. Then "…to the morbid-minded way…healthy-mindedness pure and simple seems unspeakably blind and shallow. To the healthy-minded way, on the other hand, the way of the sick soul seems unmanly and diseased" (James 1958:137).

This mutual reflection (overlooked for example in Taylor's essay mentioned in the foregoing) seems important to me. It shows James's intention to come to a well-balanced judgement, and further, both these temperaments are basic traits for a life worth living. However, what James considers with uneasiness are attempts to reconstruct a religious experience in favour of only one of these types, particularly the optimistic trait. Essential to this type is the psychological ability to close one's eyes against seeing the evils and sufferings in the world and in nature. James (1958:137) writes:

> The method of averting one's attention from evil, and living simply in the light of good is splendid as long as it will work. It will work with many persons; it will work far more generally than most of us are ready to suppose; and within the sphere of its successful operation there is nothing to be said

against it as a religious solution. But it breaks down impotently as soon as melancholy comes; and even though one be quite free from melancholy one's self, there is no doubt that healthy mindedness is inadequate as a philosophical doctrine, because the evil facts which it refuses positively to account for area genuine portion of reality.

In the view of James, the morbid-minded people – with whom he saw himself – are closer to reality.[16]

With regard to James's thought of the religious and philosophical importance of the two temperaments, I would like to make two comments. First, religious experiences have roots in the biological-cultural conditions of life, which demeans all attempts to place religion in a space of the "totally other." Secondly, religious experiences do not depend only on one's practising religious customs, rites and religious language games but depends also of one's propensities to develop one's own character by means of other practices, such as training in arts, politics, or the sciences. This is a point to which I will come back in the context of reflections about a philosophical anthropology.

The fourth point in James's psychological description refers to the topic of conversion. According to my understanding, it is the heart of the *Varieties*, at least when reading this book from the perspective of a life worth living.

---

[16] To be mentioned in short in this connection is James's strong polemic against the "mind-cure" and the "mind-curers". Meant is a very popular contemporary movement in the USA, namely to "cure" the morbid minded by means of a psychological technique from the essential character traits and to transform their way of life in direction of the healthy minded. James (1958:90) speaks with regard to the mind cur of a kind of a new religion (an "entirely new religious turn"), and writes: "The leaders in this faith have had an intuitive belief in the all-saving power of healthy-minded attitudes as such" (James 1958:88), further: "The mind-curers...have demonstrated that a form of regeneration by relaxing, by letting go, psychologically indistinguishable from the Lutheran justification by faith and the Wesleyan acceptance of free grace, is within the reach of persons who have no conviction of sin and care nothing for the Lutheran theology. It is but giving your little private convulsive self a rest, and finding that a greater Self is there. The results, slow or sudden, or great or small, of the combined optimism and expectancy, the regenerative phenomena which ensue on the abandonment of effort, remain firm facts of human nature, no matter whether we adopt a theistic, a pantheistic-idealistic, or a medical-materialistic view of their ultimate causal explanation." (James 1958:99–100). James's strongly opposition against the mind-cure theory (there many parallels to efforts made today in the USA and in Europe too) may prevent from a frequently uttered misinterpretation of James's pragmatism and pragmatism in the philosophy of religion at all. The psychological fruits are by no means the ultimate arbiter for a well thought pragmatism in the philosophy of religion. Without taking seriously the evils and sufferings no fruits!

Conversion means the transition from the "divided self," the self divided against itself, to a state of one's feeling carried by or being one with the divine. In the description of the interrelation of life and experiencing the divine in one's own life in the *Varieties* is an expanded version of the essay mentioned, expanded by means of the biographical material James held in his hands. He refers particularly to Tolstoy in explaining the transition from the sick soul's feeling emptied of life being worth living to the "mystical state" of living a life worth living. In explaining Tolstoy's divided self, James (1958:129) writes: "In Tolstoy's case, the sense that life had any meaning whatever was for a time wholly withdrawn." To express the reborn mystical state, James (1958:154) quotes from Tolstoy's "My Confession": "To acknowledge God and to live are one and the same thing. God is what life is. Well, then! Live, seek God, and there will be no life without him."[17]

A fifth point to be mentioned briefly is "saintliness." It is the possible but never automatically the resulting outcome of conversion. In his quotations of witnesses of saintliness, James underlines the character traits well known from the history of Christianity, particularly charity, tenderness, and asceticism. Two points seem to me worth mentioning. First, all saintly virtues are liable to corruption, a fact underlining again James's awareness of the ambivalence of religious experiences and religious ways of life. Secondly, in his reflections about saintliness as an outcome of conversion and as a way of life in which the new spiritual centre of one's subjectivity comes to bear, James avoids any hint of making prescriptions for religious ways of life. It is up to the "reborn" individual what "fruits" may be the outcome of his or her conversion. The only thing to evaluate as necessary is the fact that the fruits are expressive of the truth that life is worth living.

Finally, in the view of James, the varieties of "mystical states" and their expressions in prayer, are the vital center-point in practically all of the witnesses he had gathered and used in the *Varieties*.

---

[17] These words are the end of a longer context, beginning with "'I remember,' he says, one day nearly spring, I was alone in the forest, lending my ear to its mysterious noises. I listened, and my thought went back to what for these three years is always was busy with – the quest of God. But the idea of him, I said, how did I ever come by the idea? And again there arose in me, with this thought, glad aspirations toward life. Everything in me awoke and received a meaning…why do I look farther? A voice within me asked. He is there: he, without whom one cannot live. To acknowledge God…" (James 1958:154).

One may say truly, I think, that personal religious experience has its root and centre in mystical states of consciousness; so for us, who in these lectures are treating personal experience as the exclusive subject of our study, such states of consciousness ought to form the vital chapter from which the other chapter get their light (James 1958:292).[18]

In order to explain the importance of prayer for the expression of the mystical states, James extensively quotes "liberal French theologian" Auguste Sabatier, saying "Prayer is religion in act; that is, prayer is real religion."[19]

Now I will turn to the second question to which James wanted to give an answer in the *Varieties*, namely, to the "philosophical significance" of the varieties of religious experiences, which he illustrated in the book. I will focus upon two closely related aspects, first, to the ontological question: what is to be said from a philosophical point of view about the truth-value of the feelings of being moved from a divine force? Are there reasons to place the divine into the universe in which we are living? Secondly, what is the importance of the value experience of life as worth living in the context of the ontological question? What about the logical stringency of the indissoluble connection between the ontological and the value question?

My argument will be: James refuses to give academic answers to the questions mentioned, answers in terms of making "dogmatic" conclusions from logical premises[20] that would amount to a philosophical position of "foundationalism," which has lost its plausibility in the course of the development of thought. James's philosophical approach is pragmatic. He feels entitled and

---

[18] With these words James explains the role and function of the chapter about "Mysticism" within the *Varieties*.

[19] This quotation continues as follows: "It is prayer that distinguishes the religious phenomenon from such similar or neighbouring phenomena as purely moral or aesthetic sentiment. Religion is nothing if it were not the vital act by which the entire mind seeks to save itself by clinging to the principle from which it draws its life. This act is prayer, by which term I understand no vain exercise of words, no mere repetition of certain sacred formula, but the very movement itself of the soul, putting itself in personal relation of contact with the mysterious power of which feels its presence." (James 1958:352).

[20] "The intellectualism in religion which I wish to discredit…assumes to construct religious objects out of the resources of logical reasons alone, or of logical reason drawing rigorous inference from non-subjective facts. It calls its conclusions dogmatic theology or philosophy of the absolute…" (James 1958:331); further: "We must therefore, I think, bid a definite good-by to dogmatic theology. In all sincerity, our faith must do without that warrant." (James 1958:341).

committed to making a personal decision to believe in the divine or in God as both the motivational reason and the normative reason for a life worth living. He freely uses some Peircean concerns when talking about his own pragmatic approach to the questions at stake: "The true is what works well, even though the qualification 'on the whole' may always have to be added" (James 1958:348). According to James, what the pragmatic way of thinking discriminates from the arbitrariness of a so-called "decisionism" is the awareness of one's being fundamentally in connection with the divine because of the common "interests" of the divine and of human beings, namely, the value of a life worth living.

Considering the unbelievable abundance of thoughts James has broadened in his *Varieties*, I can use only a very limited selection of viewpoints, making my choices according to the methodological decision to take the value experience of the life worth living to be the point of departure.

The answer that James has in his mind to the ontological question – where the divine, or God, or the unseen reality are to be placed in the reality of the universe – is reminiscent of Spinoza's ideas of a multi-dimensional matter on the one side and the human spirit as only capable of a small selection of dimensions of the universe, on the other. James (1958:389) writes

> ...the so-called order of nature which constitutes this world's experience, is only one portion of the total universe and that there stretches beyond this visible world an unseen world of which we now know nothing positive, but in relation to which the true significance of our mundane life consists (James 1956:51). Further: 'So I will call this higher part of the universe by the name of God.'

With this equation between God and the higher part of the universe, James is confronted with a dilemma. He strongly refuses the traditional solutions of the ontological difficulty, namely, absolute idealism or pantheism, which says that the universe is in God, at least its ideas, laws or plans. However, in order to make the truth of the religious experiences plausible from a philosophical point of view, James has to state both the divinity's continuity with the reality at hand, and its discontinuity as well. In purporting the line of continuity, James is compelled to refer to a kind of naturalism. Yet, this term is fixed for signifying the scientifically decodeable order of nature only.

The simple negation of naturalism, for example, by the means of a Kantian "thing-in-itself," cannot provide a resolution for James. Other than with Kant, the divine must be signified as able to be experienced in its being a partner in experiencing the value of life in an process of hoping and fighting. Otherwise, the whole project to justify religious experience in principle by means of philosophical thinking sinks down in an abyss of sheer subjectivism. Thus, the only escape route seems to be a higher naturalism, a "supernaturalism", and "If one should make a division of all thinkers into naturalists and supernaturalists, I should undoubtedly have to go, along with most philosophers, into the supernaturalist branch" (James 1958:392). Unfortunately, the usual kinds of supernaturalism[21] are inclined to a partisanship with, or a relapse to, crude naturalism or materialism, and – paradoxically speaking – also to a partisanship with crude idealism, which takes the laws of nature to be the thoughts of the absolute.

The dilemma faced by James in searching for an answer to the ontological question is the seemingly unavoidable choice between two equally bad and for his purposes pointless solutions. Thus, James prompted a new term for his pragmatism: "piecemeal supernaturalism".[22] It means that the divine – God – is not accessible in its entirety, but only piece by piece. This piecemeal ontology fits exactly to James's philosophical significance, which he is ready to grant the varieties of religious experiences culminating in the experiences of being empowered and authorized from the divine to keep life worth living free from the abysses of the divided self. By means of making experiences to live a life worth living, each person has access to a piece of the divine.

James's piecemeal approach to the ontological question prompts two significant conclusions, namely, pluralism and hypothesis as guidelines for one's understanding of the divine, the unseen reality, or God. Speaking in terms of piecemeal supernaturalism amounts to the assertion that the truth of the divine, the truth of God's existence cannot be said other than by means of a

---

[21] Universalistic supernaturalism surrenders, it seems to me, too easily to naturalism. It takes the facts of physical science at their face-value, and leaves the laws of life just as a whole, sentiments which may be admiring and adoring, but which need not be so, as the existence of systematic pessimism proves. In this universalistic way of taking the ideal world, the essence of practical religion seems to me to evaporate." (James 1958:393).

[22] After reflecting some different "refined" versions of supernaturalism, James (1958:392) states: "Refines supernaturalism is universalistic supernaturalism; for the 'crasser' variety 'piecemeal' supernaturalism would perhaps be the better name." Further: "I believe that a candid consideration of piecemeal supernaturalism and a complete discussion of all its metaphysical bearings will show it to be the hypothesis by which the largest number of legitimate requirements are met…" (James 1958:394).

"pluralistic hypothesis" (James 1958:396). Speaking or thinking about God in terms of pluralism is unavoidable – logically and empirically – because of the plurality of religious experiences in the context of the value experiences of life. Furthermore, speaking and thinking about God in terms of witnessing a hypothesis is unavoidable also because one is not entitled by one's religious piecemeal experiences to make one's own view a claim for others.

> Who says 'hypothesis' renounces the ambition to be coercive in his arguments. The most I can do is, accordingly, to offer something that may fit the facts so easily that your scientific logic will find no plausible pretext for vetoing your impulse to welcome it as true (James 1958:395).

Thinking forward he writes at the very end of the *Varieties*: "I think, in fact, that a final philosophy of religion will have to consider the pluralistic hypothesis more seriously than it has hitherto been willing to consider it" (James 1958:396).

Pluralism and hypothesis in the understanding of James's piecemeal pragmatism are by no means positions of a withdrawal of religious thought in the face of the triumphant advancement of the sciences. Rather, they are implications drawn from the decision to take seriously and as being true that life is the meeting point between individuals and God, i.e., the divine as the unseen reality.

In view of James's intention – considered in the limited framework of my interpretation of the value experiences – the ontological question about God's being present in the universe and the moral question about the value experience of life are indissoluble. Thinking and speaking about God implicitly is speaking and thinking about life worth living and capable of actions worthy to be undertaken. To say it the other way around: Thinking and speaking about the value experiences of life implicitly is thinking and speaking about God. Or, to express it in more general terms: the epistemological and the moral viewpoints in philosophising about reality are bound essentially together. According to this connection of philosophically reflected religion and life – described from the very bases in the realities – Taylor's questioning James's approach and fearing his intention of isolation from the contexts of life seems to me at least not congenial to James's intentions.

In these concluding remarks two further issues are to be briefly mentioned. The one is the use James makes with the metaphor of the "magnetic field" in order to describe the empowering force of the divine influencing the individual in its "energetic centre." The other point is James's reference to the subconscious in order to interpret the "incursion" of the divine into the self and moving the self in the direction of conversion.

Both of these points can be read in two very different ways, namely, as relapses into the strands of foundationalism on the one hand, or as illustrations of the anti-foundational piecemeal practice. There is nothing to say against an illustration of the "energetic centre" of an individual in his or her striving for a life worth living using the old idea of Schelling to make "magnetism" a metaphor for ones being under external influences. However, when the metaphor "magnetic field" is used – as Schelling did throughout – to mean a "naturalistic or "super-naturalistic" proof that the divine is really working, than we have "foundationalism," which amounts to what James explicitly rejected when stating: "The world interpreted religiously is not the materialistic world over again, with an altered expression" (James 1958:390).

The case of the subconscious is somewhat more complicated. The assertion that the divine comes into the personality via the subconscious – simply understood – also would amount to foundationalism. The subconscious is indeed an interesting and important aspect of one's being in the hope and fight and belonging to a life worth living. It is important to mention that James by no means takes partisanship with Hume's idea of the unconscious as the working of the lower instincts within one's mind. For James, the subconscious – when using the metaphor for the incursion of the divine – is illustrating the "higher part of the universe." The best non-foundational use of the metaphor of the subconscious that I know is from Rorty. Rorty (1986) states that the idea of the subconscious may be used for the practice of speaking with a partner's voice in one's own mind, a partner of equal intelligence who provides reflections about alternative resolutions in different situations in one's hoping and strife torn life.

I wanted James's thought to be going along with the non-foundational strands of thought, but I cannot exclude that he to a certain extent was wavering between both; between the consequently taken piecemeal supernaturalism or – what I would prefer to say – the piecemeal pragmatism on the one hand, and the temptation of relapsing into the incoherent position of foundationalism, which seeks for implausible footholds for the divine in the universe. Anyway, notwithstanding the actuality of James's founding insights regarding religion, his conception is in need for further reflections in order to provide efficiently guidance for religion today. One reason for this need is the linguistic turn in philosophising of the 20th century, which has provided some further going capacities for dealing with the dilemma of the ontological question. The other reason for the need of further reflections refers to the moral question and amounts to a more concretely interconnection between the individual aspects of the value experiences and the socio-political circumstances.

The Metaphor "Space of Reasons"

In his reflections about a practice of life that meets the realities of life, James underlines the motivational reasons for one's striving for a life worth living, while the normative reasons remain more in the background. Within the works of both the contemporary philosophers Robert Brandom (1944, 2000) and John McDowell (1996, 2002) the normative reasons are placed in the foreground. The thought of both these philosophers is pragmatic and thus non-foundational. Their points of departure are the great shift in philosophising marked by the symbol "linguistic turn" personified first of all in Ludwig Wittgenstein, and furthermore in the philosophy of Wilfrid Sellars, the teacher of both.

It goes back to Sellars to speak about the ontological question in terms of a dilemma between the "myth of the given" on the one side, and one's being captivated in the limits of coherence, on the other one. The first horn of the dilemma means that for humans as language users, there is no access to a reality as such that isn't always already interpreted by means of language-based symbols, perspectives and feelings. Therefore, the promise of classical Empiricism to provide access to reality as such is nothing but a myth.

Yet, and this is the other horn of the dilemma, any attempt to turn away from the fraud of the given, seems necessarily leading to another equal bad thought. This thought would be that all of our notions and feelings are nothing but interpretations of other notions and feelings to be measured whether and to what extent they are in "coherence" with what we already know and feel. In other words: we are captivated in the pre-given schemes of thought, which Wittgenstein already called "the limits of language are the limits of our world." Nevertheless, the realities of everyday life convince us permanently that there is really a world "outside", a mind-independent reality.

With this dilemma in mind, "experiencing the world" (McDowell 1999) in terms of a responsible answer to the realities independent and outside of our consciousness has advanced to the philosophical problem par excellence. Consequently, to meet reality as such has become a normative claim. Both, McDowell and Brandom provide promising points of departure for coming to terms with this "post-analytical" normativity concerning our relations to the world. They both renounce the traditional mental construction of a world behind our world and propose different versions of practical reasoning in order to meet the normative claims.

The different conceptions of McDowell and Brandom are interesting for a philosophy of religion, which attempts to continue James within the framework of Wittgenstein's but also a post-analytical way of philosophising. The dilemma that James was confronted with when he attempted to think the divine in continuity and discontinuity with the world at hand, returns in the dilemma mentioned between the myth of the given and the principle of coherence. Therefore, Brandom and McDowell's attempts to provide an escape route out of the dilemma continue the philosophical concerns of James.

The difference between the classical pragmatism held by James and Peirce and the pragmatism of the contemporary philosophers mentioned amounts – in the particular perspective of the interests of the philosophy of religion – to the fact that Western philosophical thought has taken a further step on the way of becoming emancipated from the tradition. Religion is based on the decision of the individual and thus, the philosophical concern is no longer the divine's continuity and discontinuity with the world at hand, but the question how to answer responsibly to the mind-independent reality.

For the purpose of transposing James's thought of living a life worth living and capable of actions worthy to be undertaken into the circumstances of our present, McDowell's and Brandom's concepts about practical reasoning seem to me very helpful. Here, I seek to demonstrate the essence and the importance of these concepts. In what follows, I will raise the question to what extent religious practice today may profitably use these new philosophical thoughts.

Brandom uses Sellar's phrase "a game of giving and asking for reasons" and his concern is to thematize the normativity within our linguistic practice as reasonable language users. With regard to the philosophy of religion, a particular matter of interest is Brandom's dealing with the issue of belief, meaning the actions of people who believe in this or that event in the world. He displays the commitments that are to be taken when people are acting as believers. McDowell uses another of Sellars's phrases as his point of interest, namely, the "space of reasons." McDowell's concern is to provide "reasons" that may cause a reasonable practice suited for opening our eyes for the "greater" nature accessible not by means of science but in terms of value experiences. The relevance of this thought for contemporary attempts to deal with the subject "nature" religiously seems obvious to me.

Going more into the details, I begin with McDowell (1996:77). He explains his philosophical project as follows:

> We need to bring responsiveness to meaning back into the operations of our natural sentient capacities as such, even while we insist that responsiveness to meaning cannot be captured in naturalistic terms, so long as 'naturalistic' is glossed in terms of the realm of law.

This position clearly provokes the "holy cows" of analytical philosophy and marks a full turn back to the world in which James was at home. It strikes me that McDowell does not refer to James. When arguing against "bald naturalism," the ideology of modern scientism, McDowell (1996:123) goes totally along with James's protest against naturalism. When recommending a "naturalistic Platonism," which does justice to both our watching nature with the eyes of a scientifically trained reasonableness and the readiness for value experiences, McDowell moves in what James has called "piecemeal supernaturalism." According to McDowell's scheme of thought, there are "reasons" in the mind-independent nature that cause humans to make value experiences of meaningful contents in the world which is the living place for plants, animals and rational animals such as humans and their building up civilisations. Furthermore, there are "reasons" working within the human mind, namely, within the cultivated wants and wishes structured in a moral "habituation," which cause people to search for appropriate experiences of the values "outside" in the world.

Alongside the polemics against bald naturalism and the recommendations favoring a naturalized Platonism, McDowell develops his interpretation of the metaphor "space of reasons." By means of this simile, McDowell wants to illustrate that the human mind is to be thought as being placed within a "re-enchanted nature," which is giving "reasons" for seeing nature correctly. He is arguing against the Max Weber tradition of absolutizing the natural scientific interpretation of the nature in which humans are living, and states that there is a wider or richer nature beyond the narrowness of seeing only the laws of nature and ignoring the values of the nature, meaning the richer realm of the universe. What is needed in order to become receptive to the stimulating power of the reasons working in the re-enchanted wider nature is the development of a "second nature" in which humans acquire in their reasonable ethical upbringing[23] the model that is provided by the Aristotelian notion of *phronesis*.

According to this scheme of thought, humans are living in two realms. Humans' first nature is their animal like endowment, biologically seen, and open to become the object of the sciences. Humans' second nature is their openness to the "space of reasons," the richer nature, and a part that is an element grasped by the sciences. McDowell is convinced that this return to the interests and symbols of the classical philosophy of nature is possible without using the means of classical idealism. The following quotation may illustrate the perspectives and interests of McDowell's (1996:192) use of the metaphor "space of reasons" in its entirety:

> And there is nothing against bringing this richer reality under the rubric of nature too. The natural sciences do not have exclusive rights in that notion; and the added richness comes into view, not through the operations of some mysteriously extra-natural power, but because human beings come to possess a second nature.[24]

---

[23] McDowell (2000:188) speaks about "the thought that the second nature acquired in moral education is a specific shaping of practical logos…"

[24] McDowell's conception of the two natures is an outstanding target of criticism. Jens Timmermann (2000:807) for example questioning the success of McDowell's attempt to bring to bear both "…the differences and connections of first and second nature" states "In Mind and World, he fails to do this, which draws his project as a whole into question." Indeed, an explanation of the notion of the two natures more detailed than it is possible in the frame of this essay would have to mention some open questions. Nevertheless, the proposal as such, McDowell wants to give by means of these terms, namely to provide a philosophical outlook beyond the limits of the natural sciences when dealing with the issue of nature seems to me clear and highly valuable and meaningful within the particular frame of McDowell's interests. Therefore I do not see the whole project to be endangered. But the term "second nature" – taken out of the frame of this project – is very problematic. The only foothold for it is Hegel

As already hinted, the prima facie intention of McDowell's thought is to provide escape routes and alternatives to the narrowness of so-called scientism. More interesting for the purposes of the philosophy of religion are – in my perspective – the following three concerns directly or indirectly pursued by McDowell with the metaphor "space of reasons."

A first point of interest is McDowell's concern to build up a wall against the disastrous implications of a Humean styled philosophical anthropology. According to Hume, man is living on two floors, the first and determining one is the realm of the desires, wishes and wants symbolising the more animal drives. The second floor, the realm of rationality, is thought of as being the servant of these drives. Following the Humean picture of the world places the will to power in the foreground and humans are taken as subject promising their values and meanings on the world. McDowell's space of reasons brings humans' "passivity" to bear. It means the sensitivity for values coming from outside and placing humanity in a broader universe.

Following this line of thought, a second point comes out in McDowell's discussion of the internalism/externalism issue in ethical theory formation in response to Bernhard Williams. Essential to internalism favoured by Williams is the idea that moral actions and performances are in need of being grounded in the household of motivations. Without being motivated, moral and other actions cannot be understood other than being dictated from outside. Thus, internalism secured the thought of humans' maturity.

Notwithstanding the fact that humans are motivated from the network of wishes, desires and the wholeness of their habituation, McDowell counters that the most important impulses comes from outside. Internalism – so argues McDowell – threatens to limit moral activities to the framework of

---

speaking about the Spirit of the world in similar terms as the world's second nature. But viewing the history of the European thought under the influence of Christianity and its performances of sin, the term second nature was used for humans' status of fallen into sin. McDowell obviously well aware of this history of thought seeks his foothold for the second nature as the "higher" quality of humans' mind within the philosophy of Aristotle, what is causing further troubles (see: the essay of Timmermann quoted in the foregoing), because Aristotle's notion of nature clearly is pre-Enlightenment, and McDowell has made many efforts to discern between an outdated Aristotleism and a re-interpreted Aristotle suited for us within the frame of practical philosophy. Considering all these troubles may be when using the naturalism terms at all, similes such as the piecemeal supernaturalism term of James prove to be helpful. To the problems of the term "Second nature" see (Gubiljic 1999:42–49).

what is already taken for granted. Externalism brings to bear that humans are in their best capacities reasonable subjects, capable of the wider horizons of values within the "space of reasons." Externalism symbolises openness to the world.

But the most impressive application of the simile "space of reasons" come out in McDowell's using another metaphor, namely Otto Neurath's symbol of a boat afloat and in need of repair in order to keep balanced in the stormy sea. This picture is taken up by McDowell to illustrate some basic essentials of the human condition. First of all humans – individuals, collectives, the civilisation as such – are living permanently in need to change something of being equipped with notions, feelings, perspectives, the whole know-how of coming to terms with life. Yet, it is impossible to change the equipment in its entirety. As the people in the ship are able to change something of the navigation but cannot change the ship, so the human condition is open for piecemeal change only (McDowell 2000:37).[25]

Secondly, the ship on the sea symbolises that the safety of a closed comprehensive world view is not available, be it either by means of the empiricism (the myth of the given) or through reliance on the coherence of what is trustworthy according to the experiences of the world up to now. The need to balance the ship and the stormy sea reminds us of our being in a reality that gives us reasons to respond to the "outside" and to use the means of tentative reflections, using first and second nature's capacities.

Finally, Neurath's symbol demonstrates that hopes and predicaments arising from the human condition are social and at the last political ones. In order to keep balance, co-operation of the different perspectives from different "lights" from the sciences, the philosophers, the artists and other capacities is needed.

To sum up: McDowell (1996) is using the metaphor "space of reasons" to provide practical reasoning in order to keep one's or our mind open for experiencing the world. Openness for the world is the point of his book-title, *Mind and World*.

---

[25] "Neurathian reflection on an inherent schema of values takes place at a standpoint within that scheme; the scheme can be altered piecemeal, but not suspended in its entirety, with a view to rebuilding from the ground up" (McDowell 2000:37).

At this point, Brandom's notion of belief joins excellently McDowell's concern for openness and responsivity to the facts. The Sellarian "game of giving and asking for reasons" places language users into a social practice, in which the interlocutors mutually are watching – score keeping – the rules of the game. The watch that the give and take of reasons is practiced rightly by all the participants in the discursive practice as the intellectual home of humans as "sapients."

In the philosophy of Brandom, belief – respectively the practice of believing, the practice of what people are doing when acting as believers – is identical with the notion of the give and take of reasons. Thus, Brandom (2000:158) states fundamentally: "Sapients are believers."

The equation of belief and the social practice of giving and taking of reasons is a complete turning away from the traditional notion of belief. Two points are essential to the conventional notion of belief. First of all, believers – according to the subject/object scheme – are thought to be in an "intentional state," watching, hoping, and trusting performances by the object of their beliefs. Secondly, believers trust the promises given from others, the believers take for granted the trustworthiness of the opinions of others in relevant situations, and further, believers are trusting to a certain extent the reliability of their own convictions and promises as well.

Of course, trust, reliability and the capability of one's own principles to enable one to lead a life worth living, play an important if not central role in Brandom's notion of belief too. However, different from the traditional ways, what he wants to work out philosophically are the "rational" commitments, which are implicitly presupposed when people are rightly acting as believers. In order to make the implicitly given commitments "explicit," Brandom places the practice of believers between two regions of commitment.

The first, the grounding one, is given in the network of premises, which provide the social and intellectual base for one's life. It is the entirety of social bindings, obligations, and commitments, the norms and rules for life, the knowledge of the relevant facts of the realities. The other region, one is committed to take into consideration for one's acting as a believer the consequences of one's actions, the reality of life that has changed in a certain sense because of the inferences the believer has made in acting, in doing something in the world. It is important for Brandom to consider the interpersonal and the historical dimension of the circumstances. The region in which one's interferences are working and prompting certain effects, is a network again, namely, that of one's future life. As "rational animals", as sapients, one is responsible for what will follow from one's doing and not-doing for oneself and for the whole social-political environment.

Yet, obviously, nobody is able to look through the entirety of one's premises as well as the consequences of one's actions. These facts ground the importance of the reasonable belief-practice. Brandom describes the practice of believing as a moving back and forth between one's premises and one's conclusions to be made in the form of interfering in the common world. The reflective move – the practice of the belief – consists in questioning oneself whether or not and to what extent one is "entitled" to act in this or that way. One also questions oneself whether or not and to what extent one is "committed" to the action one is doing. This is the most important point of Brandom's notion of belief, that this questioning one's entitlements and commitments is a social practice. One lets oneself be questioned from the perspective of an "other," represented as the perspective of a "second person,"[26] whose judgement about the correctness of my doings is judged by me under the same aspects: is he really entitled and committed to judging.

In Brandom's practical philosophy, belief as the practice of believing is fundamentally envisaged in the perspective of a rational normativity. It has nothing to do with traditional prescriptions for what people should have to believe. Believers carry the norms and rules for rationally believing within

---

[26] Habermas (2003:161–162) has criticised Brandom's use of the perspective of the "second person" for providing a controlling partner for proving one's entitlements and commitments. He states: "Aber bei näherer Betrachtung zeigt sich, daß der Akt des Zuschreibens, der für die Diskurspraxis grundlegend ist, nicht wirklich von einer *zweiten* Person ausgeführt wird. Eine zweite Person kann es ohne die Einstellung einer ersten zu einer zweiten Person gar nicht geben." Of course, Habermas argues correctly within the frame of his own philosophy of communicative rationality that culminates in consensus-formation among people who are in need to find common resolutions in this or that issue. But Habermas does not do justice to Brandom's use of the second person perspective within his frame of discursive practice in which consensus formation does not get the place at the sun, but it is more interesting to make one's beliefs rationally clear in a social discursive practice accepting that a rationally cleared difference of opinions and thus a pluralistic discursive practice is needed, what by no means excludes that in everyday political and moral practices consensus formation is that what is needed. But this is an other game. I do not see the need for establishing a unified philosophical understanding of the world and the normativity of rationality. A plurality of philosophical language games seems to me more promising, and I think within the limits of his practical philosophy, Brandom's use of a second person's perspective is well taken.

their capacities to participate in language, or in playing the game of give and take of reasons.

In order to determine the "normative fine structure of rationality" and thus the normativity of believing in more detail, Brandom (2000:43) states: "we can discern and distinguish at least three fundamental ones (i.e. inferential relations): commitment-preserving inferences, entitlement-preserving inferences, and incompatibilities." All three kinds of inferences are working together in the practice of believing. However, the third kind plays a particular role for understanding the whole project, and I will come back to it in a moment.

To begin with I will interpret briefly the first two kinds of inferences. A believer, when wanting to do this or that action or when reflecting on distinct performances of one's acting reasonably in a distinct situation of life, has to question whether or not and to what extent the would-be action would "preserve" what one is convinced to be one's entitlement or commitment. Otherwise, one has to prove to what extent one's convictions of being entitled or committed are to change. Brandom's notion of belief practice – exactly because of its rational normativity – is very open for change. In principle, nothing in one's convictions about entitlements or commitments is to be taken as infallible. The status of a believer is not a stand still but a status of permanently being open as learning processes.

The third kind of inference, namely, incompatibilities, mean the possibility that the contents of one's inferences made on the base of one's trustworthy premises do not harmonise with the convictions of others and maybe even with one's own system of what else one believes. Due to the possible discord with regard to the formation of human opinions as already stated above, fundamental disagreements are possible and this the more so when the opinion formation has to do with questions that are bound to comprehensive worldviews.

The substantiation of disagreement can scarcely be satisfying in the perspective of believers, who are rationally concerned to prove their beliefs in a discursive practice. In order to come to terms with fundamental disagreements rationally, Brandom (2000:169ff) introduces the differentiation between speaking and thinking ["*de re*"] on the one side, and speaking and thinking ["*de dicto*"] on the other. Agreement between interlocutors referring to the rightness of what is said and thought is possible in principle. Quite possibly, the burden of coming to terms with the comprehension of language utterances takes a lot of time.

The practice of remaining in rationally clarified disagreements has an important ontological background. It is an expression that "objectivity" – reality as such – remains the ultimate arbiter judging human opinion formation and furthermore that all of our beliefs are to be taken as "vulnerable."[27]

Summing up the interpretation of some of the thoughts of Brandom, I would like to state that the importance of Brandom's notion of belief – particularly considering its relevance to religion to be dealt with explicitly in what follows – lies in the close relationship between commitment and openness. As a believer, one is committed to keep one's mind and one's actions open toward a rational linguistic practice and not – as was done mostly in philosophising before the linguistic turn – in one's sentiments.

Some further reflections about the importance of this notion of the linguistic practice of believing may be briefly added. They concern the inter-personal, and the intra-personal dimension of life. Turning to the first point, Brandom (2000:69) illustrates the practical, political importance of the normative status of entitlements and commitments by means of an evaluation of misleading propaganda slogans such as "Germans are boche" and black people are "niggers." The question whether people make such statements due to some bad experiences with Germans or with black people, depends on the inferences to be made from others in present or future. Because of the generalizing "thick" terms "the Germans", or "nigger", there is no space to make differences, and one has to state such generalizing terms are wrong ones and cannot stand the test of responsibility.

Further, the move back and forth reflecting one's being entitled and being committed – essential to the belief practice of making inferences – is used by Brandom (2000:94) to highlight the internal activities of the individual in developing their personalities and thus their capacities to use their volition rationally. "Kant defines the rational will as the capacity to derive performances

---

[27] It is impossible to deal in the frame of this essay with Brandom's notion of objectivity and its ontological implications adequately. The far-reaching importance comes out for example in an Interview with Susanna Schellenberg in: *Deutsche Zeitschrift für Philosophie 1999*, 1005–1020. Ruferring to the "Begriff of Objectivity" Brandom states: "Es geht darum, wie wir zu dem Punkt gelangen können, an dem wir davon auszugehen vermögen, daß sich unsere Handlungen und Äußerungen objektiv an den Dingen in der Welt messen. In: Von der Begriffsanalyse zu einer systematischen Metaphysik." P. 1017. To the problem of objectivity with Brandom see: Lutz Wingert: Genealogie der Objektivität Zu Robert B. Brandoms "expressiver Vernunft" Deutsche Zeitschrift für Philosophie 48, 2000, pp. 738–761.

from conceptions of laws. I am suggesting that we can replace 'conception of a law'...by 'acknowledgement of a commitment.'" According to both the normative states of people acting in discourse, a person acting rationally is committed to "acting with reasons, which is being entitled to such a commitment" (Brandom 2000:96). And an individual acting rationally is also "acting for reasons, which is the case where reasons are causes" (Brandom 2000:96). This double perspective highlighting one's volitional disposition is, it seems to me, very illuminating for understanding the practice of the individual in its socio-political environment. Acting with reasons and acting for reasons are two different but also related motivations. Luther, when stating in Worms "Here I stand. I cannot do otherwise. God, help me. Amen." acted with good reasons because he knew about the matters at stake, but he acted – first of all – because his will was lead by premises essential to his personal identity.[28]

Practicing openness to the world rationally is common to both McDowell and Brandom. The heritage of Sellars is "sublated" ("*aufgehoben*" in the Hegelian sense of this term) and furthered in the interpretations of both the images, "space of reasons" and "give and take of reasons." My intention to transpose James' notion of religious experience into the framework of contemporary post analytical thought could use both these metaphors saying: religion within the give and take of reasons or religion within the space of reasons. In the concluding remarks, I will make use of the second phrase.

Religion within the Space of Reasons

William James's notion of religious experience within living a life worth living, combined with the concerns of rational reasoning mentioned in the foregoing chapter, amounts to the thought that religion – philosophically seen – is a matter of practice, a way of life using the entirety of humans' capacities. In these concluding remarks I will refer to some thoughts in the contemporary debates in the fields of philosophy of religion. Further I will provide some suggestions about the project to include religion into the frame of a philosophy of personality, and finally I will refer to a point issued in the "Introductory Remarks, namely the inclusion of religious viewpoints into public debates.

---

[28] To Luther's acting in context with the issues of judgement and reflective judgement see: Christine M. Korsgaard, *The Sources of Normativity*, Cambridge MA: Cambridge University Press 1996.

This very last paragraph serves also a short summing up the whole project to speak arbour religion within the space of reasons.

Issues in the Philosophy of Religion. In the philosophy of religion, Hilary Putnam's[29] philosophy is focussed on the relationship between faith/religion and reason.[30] His line of thought follows particularly William James, Ludwig Wittgenstein, Kant, and the Jewish tradition. Putnam states his agreement with James and Wittgenstein asserting that the relationship between religious faith and reason may be made explicit by means of the formula: faith is neither rational, nor irrational but a-rational.[31] It is a phrase which particularly refers to the Wittgensteinian concept of religion as a way of life in terms of the practice to "organize" one's life in order to live by means of the importance of the "picture" of God one has in, or takes into one's mind.[32]

Wittgenstein's notion of a way of life is closely related to his understanding of "language games" underlining the thought that our words – principally seen, but not in all cases – get their meaning out of the contexts given in the life worlds and our living in them. Consequently, without partaking in a religious way of life, one is scarcely suited to understand what the religious

---

[29] Important publications of Hilary Putnam with regard to religion are: *The Many Faces of Realism*, Open Court LaSalle Il 1991[2]; *Renewing Philosophy*, Harvard University Press 1998; On Negative Theology", in Faith and Philosophy 14, 407–422; God and the Philosophers, in Midwest Studies in Philosophy 21, 175–187. To Putnam's philosophy of Religion see: Klaus Oehler, Hilary Putnams Religionsphilosophie, in *Hilary Putnam und dies Tradition des Pragmatismus*, ed. By Marie-Luise Raters and Marcus Willaschek, Suhrkamp stw. 1567, Frankfurt 2002, pp. 325–343, further: Michael Quante, Exstentielle Verpflichtung und Toleranz, in ibid. pp. 344–362.

[30] Other than in the Sellars-tradition, Putnam's philosophy does not deal so much with reasons (in plural) as causes for doing this or that, but with the other meaning of the word reason (in singular), namely reason in the sense of Reason writ large particularly following Kant's differentiation between Vernunft in difference to Verstand. Nevertheless, both connotations of the word reason, namely "cause" used for explaining what causes someone to act in a certain way, and Reason writ large meaning humans' excellence, are close to each other. With regard to the philosophy of religion, the Kantian phrase and tradition to speak about religion in terms of "religion within the limits – or boundaries – of reason, and in terms of religion within the space of reasons can be taken as different phrases for the same subject, namely religion after the European Enlightenment."

[31] "James believed, as Wittgenstein did, that religious belief is neither rational nor irrational but arational." (Putnam 1998:192).

[32] "What Wittgenstein means to bring out…is that one's life may be organized by very different pictures. And he means to suggest that religion has more to do with the kind of picture that one allows to organizes one's life than it has to do with expressions of belief." (Putnam 1998:146).

person really has in mind when speaking – for example – about the belief in a "Last Judgement." According to Wittgenstein's language game *contextualism*, one has to be very cautious in judging the meanings of utterances at home in other cultures – particular alien "primitive" cultures. Furthermore, one cannot make judgements about the referent of the word God, used in a religious language game, out of the perspective of a scientific language game. Religious beliefs expressed in a religious way of life, are in principle not shakeable from the scientifically organized perspectives or ways of life.

Putnam refers to these Wittgensteinian reflections about religion and reason as different kinds of approaches to reality and he emphasises that the religious person may feel one's being connected with God, but she neither can nor is in need to "explain it by means of science or philosophy."[33] Notwithstanding the moral obligation to refuse and to protest against religiously founded utterances of fanaticism, superstition and credulity – in principle, reason and faith can tolerate each other, they are not in conflict with each other. On the other hand, again referring to Wittgenstein, Putnam takes a position against the theory of "incommensurability" as an approach, according to which religion and the rest of one's life have no links to each other. In the view of Putnam, they have links based on one's personal decisions to be made in one's way of life. A mature individual is capable of using religion and the other propensities of one's behavior to the profit of flourishing the well being of one's life.

In this regard, Putnam's reference to William James' pragmatism comes to bear. Issuing from the relationship between faith and reason, the "fruits" of one's right conduct come out in an external pluralism or tolerance, and in an internal (intra-personal) pluralism and tolerance as well. Putnam argues pragmatically, stating our reasonable understanding of the whole history of humankind tells us that religious intolerance is a thoroughgoing evil and

---

[33] "That religious language connects us to God is something one can feel with one's whole being, not something that one can explain. Pace, Maimonides, it is not the theoretical intellect that connects us to the Divine." (Oehler 2002:334). In an autobiographical remark Putnam (1998:1) says that the taking of religion and science as two different approaches to reality was a way very usual for himself: "As a practicing Jew, I am someone for whom the religious dimension of life has become increasingly important, although it is not a dimension that I know to philosophise about except by indirection; and the study of science has loomed large in my life…I was a thoroughgoing atheist, and I was a believer. I simply kept these two parts of myself separate."

therefore to offend. On the other hand, religious people are fit – using rational thinking and the meaning of religious thoughts as well – for relating within their own life practice, religious and non-religious reasons to each other, holding a balance based on their own responsibility. In other words, the principle of pluralism is valid also for one's personal decision making.

Pursuing this thought further, in his *The Many Faces of Realism* Putnam draws an interesting line from the Jewish Biblical tradition via Kant to the problem of conduct of an individual life worth living after the Western divide between pre-Enlightenment and post-Enlightenment time periods. The "value of Equality" – writes Putnam (1991:44) – symbolised in "the idea that all human beings are created in the image of God…is, perhaps, a unique contribution of the Jewish religion to the Culture of the West." It amounts to the idea that every human being is of equal value. Putnam writes, however, that historically "the idea of equality was detached from its specifically religious roots." This idea was philosophically rediscovered by Kant, who opposed the traditional efforts to explain religious belief by means of reasoning and any kind of blind faith.

> This leaves him (and us) with a problem, of course: where do we get any content for religion, if neither reason nor blind faith can provide it? Kant's own answer is that the only content on which we are justified in relying is our right to hope; understanding the legitimacy of that hope is still a use of reason (Putnam 1991:50).

And this hope rationally refers to what is the essence of a post-Enlightenment reconstructed understanding of the value of equality, namely,

> that we have to think for ourselves…and that fact is itself the most valuable fact about our lives. That is the characteristic with respect to which we are all equals. We are all in the same predicament, and we all have the potential to thinking for ourselves with respect to the question How to live (Putnam 1991:50).

Summing up the importance of the thought of Hilary Putnam with regard to the project "religion within the space of reasons", Putnam teaches us to consider pluralism in different stages. The first stage is the pluralism of different ways of life as what follows from the religious tradition to respect dignity and equality of every individual. The second stage is the external pluralism of religious traditions informing people to their ways of life. The third stage is an internal pluralism allowing the individual to make his or her own balance between faith and reason.

What makes Jacques Derrida (1996) interesting in the context of this essay is first of all Putnam's emphasis on the relationship between life and religion, and Derrida's *"aporetic"* plead for a rediscovering the "holiness of life" and the mystical dimension in which holiness or sacredness of life is grounded. I take Derrida's approach as an encouragement to pursue the close connection of religion and the evaluation of life worth living that I interpreted first of all by means of James's connection between experiences of conversion from the divided soul to the experiences of a mystical union with the divine.

Of course, there are deep differences between James and his thought of prayer as a mystical state of consciousness on the one hand, and Derrida's notion of "mystical foundation" of life, meaning its holiness, on the other. Very different to James, in his understanding of mysticism Derrida follows the Jewish tradition of thinking in terms of the totally other and he follows Heidegger's claim for a rediscovering of the voice of the being beyond the present world. Nevertheless, there are also some common roots. Henri Bergson, one of Derrida's points of reference when speaking about the "two sources of religion," belongs to the European *Lebensphilosophie* and – irrespective of the long history of rivalry, there are important links to American pragmatism (Joas 1996:173).

Unlike Putnam, Derrida's goal is not to recommend a religious practice in a purified way of life freeing oneself from the vessels of superstition. Derrida takes a fundamentally critical stance to what is called world religions, to Islam, whose fundamentalist streams he is very well informed about due to his Algeria origin, but no less with regard to Christianity. In a certain sense, Christianity works as Derrida's main target of criticism. He mockingly blames the pope-cult, using the high tech-means of tele-communication and wonders about the capacities of religious institutions using modern means for proclaiming a very old thing.

What Derrida fundamentally opposes is what he states with the phrase "religion and reason develop in tandem." This means that religion, particularly Christianity, co-operates with the modern "tele-technoscientific machine, this enemy of life in the service of life." Of course, in the background stands Heidegger's phrase (taken as wording from Whitehead) Christianity should be interpreted as functioning as a "footnote" to Platonism, understanding Platonism as a symbol for the practice of ruling the world by means of a reason that comes from another world above.

However, Derrida does not criticise one-sidedly. He knows very well, life needs rationality, technique, economy, law making, law application and many other acquisitions of modernity. He speaks about the "promise" of developing life worth living implicitly working in the development of the modern conditions of life. What he is opposing – first of all – is the uncritical blindness with regard to the aporetic fact that the development of life is indissolubly mingled with the use of tele-techno, scientific power, which causes the permanent loss of life worth living. Further, Derrida opposes the uncritical claim for the values of life in the mass media, in policy-making, and public opinion formation, making people more and more blind or "forgetful" of the origins of the sacredness or holiness of life, which are to be heard only in a place like a "desert" beyond all the talking – and gossips – about life. Derrida thinks here consequently in the line of his *"differânce"*. Yet, the retreat into such a desert is not practical way. It is a philosophical construction. This construction, being in a philosophical sense of the phrase a "fundamentally critical" voice or in some sense a prophetic voice, belongs to our thought about life worth living in the perspective of religion. This is because it points to the "aporetic" situation and refuses to give recommendations how to escape this situation in practice.

The relationship between religion and reason or rationality is expressed in the work of Habermas (2002) from its very beginnings up to the present. I would like to distinguish two lines of thought regarding the links between religion and rationality in the work of Habermas. The first line may be called the "translation line" because it is a central intention of Habermas (1981, 1987), particularly in his main work, *The Theory of Communicative Action*, to transform or to "translate" religion in its pre-modern function to provide consensus into the modern democratic practices of opinion formation. Habermas introduced for this step by step removal of public life from religion the term "linguistification of the sacred," pointing to the importance of linguistic communication within the modern democratic societies.

I think, within the framework of his "project" to interpret the way from pre-modern societies to modern "Western" life, the translation line can be taken for at least an important historical perspective. Whether or not and to what extent the idea of a universal discourse community in the sense of the optimistic outlooks of Peirce can be used as the historical objective goal of the transforming of religion in principle into the universal discourse community may be an other question. Anyway, we have reasons to remain very sceptical today about any alleged irreversible historical tendencies.

The other line of thought in Habermas's wrestling with the links between religion and rationality may be called "the coexistence line," which means that Habermas is well aware of limits of the any translation of the function of religion into the functions of rational opinion formation. Until now, religion preserved at least one function that cannot be taken over by philosophy, namely, the function of providing "consolation" considering the contingencies of life and to provide a substitute for the experiences with this issue of life preserved in religious tradition. Habermas (2002:164) clearly says: "…it would be the worst kind of intellectualism to expect that philosophy's 'way of translation' could completely appropriate the forms of experiences preserved in religious language."

How do both lines of Habermas's thought, "translation" and "coexistence", exist together? In a similar perspective, Eduardo Mendieta – in an interview with Habermas (2002:147) – referring to utterances of Habermas to Max Horkheimer's famous statement "an unconditioned meaning without God is a futile undertaking" comes to a fundamental observation of "two conflicting tendencies" in the work of Habermas (2002:161–162):

> in one tendency, religion is liquefied and sublated in discourse ethics…in
> the other, religion is given the function of preserving and even nurturing a
> particular type of 'semantic' content that remains indispensable for ethics'
> and morality, but also for philosophy in general.

Confronted with Mendieta's question about the conflicting tendencies, Habermas (2002:162) answers: "I see no contradiction here."

According to my understanding, there remains at least a tension between these lines of thought. Yet, this is not meant as a criticism. Quite to the contrary, this tension refers to reality, but it remains the question about the importance of the fact that it seems to be impossible – also in the particular philosophical concept of Habermas – to create an unified model for the relationship between faith and reason. In the framework of my project, I would like to interpret Habermas in the direction of Putnam. By this is expressed a plea for an ongoing pluralism in which the philosophical translation of traditional religious functions goes hand in hand with a new evaluation of religion as a capacity of the human character that cannot be lost without damaging the quality of life.

Issues in Contemporary Philosophy of Personality. In what follows, I will relate the issue of religion within the entirety of life and consequently of religion within the space of reason, to some problems debated in the contemporary philosophy of personality. Two matters are of interest in my context. The one comes from the tradition of George Herbert Mead and the development of a responsible self focussed on both the personal dimension of the "I" and the "Me." According to this tradition, the development of a responsible self happens in the course of taking up one's own I-perspective in response to the Me-perspective coming from outside. Habermas, engaged in a philosophy of personality that gives expression to intersubjectivity as the most important point for regulating one's way of life after the demise of religion, follows this line. Ernst Tugendhat (1981), also following Mead in principle, stresses the issue of motivation and states the wish to become accepted from one's relevant social environment should be taken as the grounding motivational reason for efforts to live a life worth living, while Erich Fromm focuses on "true self-love."

Of course, all these conceptions are pointing to motives and perspectives essential for living a personal valuable life in Western societies. Following some ideas of Charles Taylor, according to which alternative conceptions may be helpful or necessary for a self-understanding that transcends internal barriers, I will explore possibilities of re-introducing religion and religious experiences into the motivational reasons for striving for a life worth living.

I take my starting point with a book published more than eighty years ago, namely, Eduard Spranger's (1928) *Types of Men.*[34] The centrepiece of

---

[34] In German: *Lebensformen.* The book is placed within the German cultural, political, and philosophical situation between the end of World War I and 1933, relatively close to Dilthey and to the Lebensphilosophie. The book shows significantly that the author lived in a situation in which the emancipation from the traditional religious bindings was a subject of very controversial public debates, and Spranger took a clear conservative position. Further Spranger took in this book and other publications a sceptical approach to the values and the practices of democracy like most of his academic contemporaries in the so-called Weimar-time. (For more details to these

Spranger's argument is the explanation of six "Ideal Basic Types of Individuality", namely, the theoretical attitude, the economic attitude, the aesthetic attitude, the social attitude, the political attitude, and the religious attitude. His sophisticated efforts to ground these six types in a *"geisteswissenschaftlich"* conceived psychology can scarcely be very convincing today, considering the much more expanded empirical investigations about the psychic states of modern people. Yet, the kernel of his thought is sound and still speaks to us today. Spranger refers to the "old theory of Temperaments", the "Characters" of Theophrastus, and understands his conception of the six types or characters of individuals as a renewal of the ancient intuitions of character-properties according to the circumstances of the modern differentiation of cultural spheres and the developed education system.

The six types of man describe six combinations in the formation of one's individual character due to different genetic endowments – temperaments on the one hand, and the appropriation of cultural goods (*Bildungsgüter*) on the other. Some people are quasi "born" theorists, other "born" social concerned characters, others artists, and so on. The point is that everybody participates biologically in all the six grounding character traits and everybody participates in the culturally developed capacities to develop these traits. It depends on one's upbringing and then one's own efforts to develop a very special unique combination of the six traits. One of the character types dominants and makes the individual represent this one type. Yet, all the other capabilities remain in a more or less supporting position to the type leading. There are – Spranger gives a lot of examples from the *Geistesgeschichte* – theorists, scientists, philosophers whose works are very "economical", i.e. practical, pragmatically oriented, while others are deeply typed toward artistic concerns.

Spranger´s pluralism works as a character centered pluralism of distinct normative value experiences. The real point in order to understand the importance of this idea is the following: Value experiences in one of the types mentioned are in need of becoming broadened by an ongoing exchange with normative value experiences in the other five types. This exchange is accomplished in the way one's character works growing up to higher standards of sensitivity for the good and the evil in one's own life and in society as well.

---

issues see my: Bildung als Lebensform – Erwägungen zu Sprangers "Lebensformen" forthcoming in Croatia.)

Two points seem to me particularly important. First, Spranger's conception of the individual's placement within the biological and cultural factors and their combination in developing one's personality provides a very concrete understanding of the connection between the motivational and the normative reasons in one's life. The appropriation of cultural goods motivate to this or that particular effort in one's life sharpens one's consciousness of the normative reasons one has to respect for a valuable life. Further, in principle, Spranger's concept provides the possibility of speaking about the individual's habituation in terms of value consciousness for which one is to a certain extent responsible.

Secondly, in Spranger's conception religion emerges twice. On the one hand, religion in its infinitely manifold combination with the other character traits belongs to the human condition, but the typical expression of one's religious capacities is unique in every individual. According to Spranger's conception, religiosity as such is not bound to traditional forms of religion. It can take forms that, from a traditional point of view, seem to be irreligious. Besides this pluralistic understanding of religion and its development in the individual, Spranger holds to a conservative reading of the traditional substantial conception of one's soul, close to the Lutheran, Protestant teaching of the justification of the sinner. Furthermore, he was interested in providing an alternative to Scheler's first Catholic and than pantheistic religion and his use of these conceptions in thought about the developing of one's personality, which was similar to Spranger.

What Spranger sought to provide with his conception of the soul as the individual substance that could directly experience God's consolation for one's being a sinner, is – according to my interpretation – to point to religion as the central motivation for developing the plurality of one's endowments and cultural given capacities. Following James, I would like to take from Spranger his conception of religion as both a part of one's *Bildung* and as a central motivation to develop one's capacities. I do not agree with Spranger's substance soul conception.

However, his founding insight of placing religion within a pluralistic internal frame of reasons, influencing one's motivational and one's normative reason, seems to me stimulating – given the chance that the development of the notion of the soul from its substantial to a functional and metaphorical use of the term will succeed.

Religion in the Realm of Public Reasoning. Finally, I will attempt to place religion into the realm of public reasoning. It is impossible to deal in detail with the role of religion, meaning in this case the role of churches and other religious institutions, within the realm of public debates.[35] My goal here is a very limited one and serves first of all to confront a frequently expressed misunderstanding when speaking about religion in terms of the individual. This misunderstanding consists of the notion that one could in principle separate the private or the personal reasons for one's action from the public reasons brought forth in public debates. In this regard, Wittgenstein's insight concerning the impossibility of creating and using a "private language" comes into play.

Our words and our thoughts too are placed within language games, which function to allow people to act within the context of certain life worlds, and life worlds are in principle social and political realms. One's personal feelings, because they are always already mediated by the means of using a language game, are by no means "only" private; they are common and private too.

What is valid for speaking and thinking people in principle is true for religious speaking and thinking persons as well. It is one of the mistakes of the traditional secularisation theories to conclude – from the possibility of making individual choices with regard to one's approach to religion – that religious motives, ideas and normative claims can be taken as a "private matter" only, without consequences for actions in the public realm. Religious motives, because of their being mediated through cultural traditions shared by religious and non-religious people, are also always part of common motives.

My intent of speaking about religion in terms of religion "within" is to place religion into the common world. By this I mean that the public realm of reasoning is a space in which people live together, holding different and divergent views of what makes life worth living. According to their different value experiences, they are differently motivated for acting in this or in that way. Also, according to their different worldviews they think differently about the normative claims.

Tolerance and the ground rules of modern Western societies to keep the public realm of opinion formation on the one hand, and the opinion building institutions of religious communities on the other, separated, is not the

---

[35] To this issue see: Robert Audi (2000).

terminus ad quem but the *terminus a quo* for living and acting together in Western society. Recalling the metaphor of the ship afloat, co-operation of the people onboard is a rational precondition for coming to terms with the common situation, but the goal to keep the ship balanced in the stormy sea brings to bear different value experiences. In this context, the individual counts as well as the voice of particular groups and collectives.

From the perspectives of the socio-political sciences and social ethics, John Rawls' (1997:273–287) concept of an "overlapping consensus" provides, in my view, an appropriate frame for speaking about religion, religious motives, and previously interpreted normative claims within the space of public reasoning. By means of the simile "overlapping consensus," Rawls is saying that a modern liberal society needs at least a large majority of citizens to agree with the constitutional rules of a liberal democracy – of course respecting the particularities of a distinct state – and with the basic values of a democratic society, expressed in the ground rules of human rights. Overlapping consensus takes into account the socio-political value of pluralism. Therefore, the overlapping consensus limits that which for the purposes of stabilising the political systems has to be respected by all the citizens to the grounding institutions and values mentioned to "the political" to use the phrase of Rawls. What should be overlapped is the diversity of comprehensive worldviews, non-religious and religious ones, which are held by the citizens, individuals, groups, churches or humanistic organizations. The content of the overlapping consensus is – as said – "the political" or in other words, what is of common political interests and as such acceptable for all.

The overlapping consensus, in the sense of Rawls (1997:275), is the reasonable base for opinion formation in a liberal society, and as such the *terminus a quo* for taking up the "burdens of reasons," which occurs in the many disagreements between the reasonable members of a certain social unit with regard to how the basic rights and values should be applied in the changing of the social, of the political and of the mental circumstances as well. In Rawls (1997:282) words: "We know from the burdens of reason that even in a well-ordered society where the basic freedoms are secure, sharp political disagreement will persist as their particular interpretation."

The essential point with regard to speaking religiously in public is the fact that the burdens of reason include the fact that it is not possible to state in principle what kinds of argument are helpful for making applications of the values due to the circumstances given. Therefore, the overlapping consensus does not exclude but includes to argument the perspectives people bring from their comprehensive world-views – but given that they accept the rules of the game and give opinions only to those issues which are political ones.

Reasonable disagreements belong to the values of public reasoning. What Rawls has in mind when pleading for the acceptance of reasonable disagreements is the fact that the space of reason in a democratic liberal society cannot be limited to the realm of policy making in a narrow sense, limited to parliaments and other official institutions. This was a tendency in his *A Theory of Justice* (Rawls 1971). In his newer publications about "Political Liberalism," he expands the realm of opinion formation that is relevant for the application of "justice" to a broader spectrum including universities, churches, other institutions, and also the realm of "private" reflections and actions, such as voting for this or that party.[36]

Rawls' overlapping consensus functions like a normative rationality: people speaking and acting in the public realm, irrespective of their particular comprehensive world view, are to bring only such issues that are in principle acceptable for all members of the society including themselves in the overlapping consensus. Consequently, holders of religious worldviews – individuals and collectives as well – have to respect the rules of the game and are to bring up issues that are only "political" ones, i.e. issues concerning the political foundations mentioned above. Other issues, for example theological question as such, belong to particular opinion formation institutions. This differentiation remains the true kernel of the secularisation theory. However, it is not the whole truth, but rather the precondition for bringing into the public one's particular value experiences, grounded in one's particular value horizons, and value experiences, one's own and those preserved in the traditions one is using as one's premises. Everything depends on the capacities of the speakers to demonstrate convincingly – understandable and acceptable – for people holding different views, experiences and traditions.

Remembering Brandom's action theory, one could say that people have to act "with reasons," bringing up what is acceptable as reason for all within

---

[36] Regarding the improvements of Rawls' thought after *the A Theory of Justice* and the importance of "overlapping consensus" I am indebted to (Ferrara 2002:925–9430).

the political frame. Accordingly, Rawls' overlapping consensus functions as a normative reason from above. Yet, Brandom's second principle – "acting for reasons" – expresses a normativity from below, from the motivational premises of one's network of convictions. Therefore, people practising religion within the space of reasons are entitled to act for reasons that bring up their being motivated to this or that evaluation of what a human life worth living should include. What counts with regard to such an action for reasons is the capacity to make the action understandable or acceptable as an action with reasons. Yet, that is scarcely possible without taking up the burden of reason and thus, the readiness to accept the facts of rational disagreements about what would be needed for furthering human beings' well being in a certain situation.

Chapter Nine

Spiritual Culture: Transcendence of the Fundamental Problems of Life

Reimon Bachika

> Only the universal is rational. The particular and
> the concrete baffle understanding.
>
> (Durkheim 1964:31)

The Telos of Culture

Life in modern societies is more and more differentiating and individualizing at the same time. Social classes are disappearing, but other lines of social subdivision are coming into existence through growing numbers of organizations and associations, growing work specialization and professions, acquiring or not acquiring computer literacy, differentiating ways of life, leisure activities, differentiation of gender roles, various forms of youth cultures or subcultures. The driving forces of the dynamic cultural expansion are quite varied: the still growing knowledge explosion, the new techniques of communication, the advent of the information society, growing intercultural communication, economic and political globalization. It appears to be natural and unproblematic that all development is expansion and change, but there seems to be a problem when change is unharmonious among collectivities that can no longer act independently. It is a fact that the world as a whole grows towards more and more interrelated collectivities. Within this situation it should be meaningful to look for what these collectivities could have in common and what would affect more balanced relationships. This is the goal of the present paper. Our core question is: do universal aspects of culture already exist or can they be developed? Could one discover a *telos* in the developments of culture?

In the search for cultural commonality, I propose to discuss universal spiritual culture. In this regard I will assume that spirituality must be sought in those aspects of culture that contain holistic meaning and in instances of culture where human beings surmount states of mind and action that have only limited meaning for life as a whole, intellectually, emotionally, and morally. In particular, I will argue that the important aspects of spiritual concern transcend material and limiting socio-cultural conditions of human life and its fundamental problems. Ultimately, I take the spiritual to be an important dimension of human well-being. "Physical" well-being cannot be the only way of human happiness.

A crucial and problematic part of our subject matter is religion. Religious believers usually see it as the paramount area of the spiritual, but nonbelievers do not engage in the same way of thinking. Religion is a matter of latent controversy, which is not likely to be resolved soon. The categories of religion have evolved over long periods of time into different species and subspecies that in practice, more often than not, do not recognize each other. Partly due to this situation, many people are wary about religious matters, while others reject religion as a genuine form of culture. Acceptance and rejection of religion is part of theories and identities. Because of its controversial nature, I do not wish to be concerned with religion directly.

In outline, I shall start the discussion by reviewing some manifestations and signals of transcendence as pointed out by Thomas Luckmann and Peter L. Berger, and continue with a discussion of the physical and socio-cultural conditions of living and the fundamental problems of life: ignorance, suffering, and evil. The last part of the paper concerns the inherent mechanisms that make spiritual dimensions of life possible: symbolization and valuation.

Different Views of Transcendence

As can be seen in particular writings by the two sociologists of religion, Luckmann and Berger, the meaning of the term transcendence is considerably different when used anthropologically or theologically. This difference may also be expressed by saying that the latter use is substantially religious and the former functionally religious. The 'substantial' meaning is narrower than the 'functional' one. In other words, both stand for a maximum and a minimum possibility of transcendence respectively.

Luckmann (1967) utilizes the term transcendence in a 'functionally' religious or an anthropological sense, to indicate a quality of religion, that is, the *"transcendence of biological nature,"* which is a key proposition in his theory of religion. His general goal was to criticize theoretical positivism in the sociological study of religion during the 1960's, which centered on superficial problems of secularization, such as the decline of ecclesiastic institutions and church attendance. The sociology of religion, according to Luckmann, has theoretically more important tasks, for instance, theorizing the relation between the individual, society, and religion.

Luckmann (1967:69) neatly summarizes his view as follows.

> Religion is rooted in a basic anthropological fact: the transcendence of biological nature by human organisms. The individual human potential for transcendence is realized, originally, in social processes that rest on the reciprocity of face-to-face situations. These processes lead to the construction of objective worldviews, the articulation of sacred universes and, under certain circumstances, to institutional specialization of religion. The social forms of religion are thus based on what is, in a certain sense, an individual religious phenomenon: the individuation of consciousness and conscience in the matrix of human intersubjectivity.

Thus, Luckmann maintains that, by becoming conscious of one-self and by appropriating a structure of meaning, the individual transcends the abilities of his or her biological nature. The development of consciousness, as is clearly the case of the newborn, does not take place without assistance of other humans. Because mental development does not occur without external stimulation, it can be said that this form of transcendence is not given in the "raw" biological nature. Luckmann concludes that its development is a universal, "religious" phenomenon.

In turn, Berger (1970), as a sociologist, reflects on the possibility of theology producing a kind of theodicy in order to offset the far-going trends of the present-day age, which are profoundly secular, utilitarian, and hedonistic and which dismiss the supernatural. Resurgent forms of religion notwithstanding, Berger observes that religious believers are becoming a *"cognitive minority."* Being concerned with the fate of religion, he then discusses several *"signals of transcendence"* drawing on philosophical and sociological literature. By signals of transcendence he denotes "phenomena that are to be found within the domain of our 'natural' reality but that appear to point beyond that reality" (Berger 1970:70). He derives these signals from the following: social order, human play, hope, humor, and the idea of damnation. First, Berger argues that order is a basic and necessary condition of social life, which may suggest the existence of a higher form of order in the universe. Secondly, human play, as part of the reality of life, suspends the rules of the 'serious' world. This, too, eventually points to the existence of another reality. Thirdly, in his argument concerning hope, Berger points out that human existence is always oriented towards the future, possibly a future beyond death. Though not validated by empirical reason, people continue to hope. Fourthly, humor, or the comic, reflects the imprisonment of the human spirit in the world. It also relativizes the 'serious' business of the world. Lastly, the idea of damnation presents itself as a form of negative reasoning. In other words, a refusal to condemn monstrous evil is a fatal impairment of *humanitas*. Either one denies that there is truth, or one looks for validation beyond this world, transcending the human world (Berger 1970:66–96).

Berger (1970:92) mentions that many philosophical considerations can be brought forward to underscore his view, but, ultimately, he concedes that a transcendental dimension cannot be proven. Its possibility rests on an act of faith. This he calls "a possible solution to the vertigo of relativity."

The views of transcendence discussed by Luckmann and Berger differ in the sense that the former does not discuss an explicitly religious reality while the latter explicitly relates his signs of transcendence to religious beliefs. Yet, to me, both seem to discuss similar phenomena, that is, general human conditions that are requisites for having religion. Thus, in Luckmann's view, qualifying the aspect of transcending individual biological nature as 'religious' indeed can be said to be religious in the sense that this transcendence is a condition for the formation of religious attitudes. Yet at the same time it is also a condition of being human. In other words, Luckmann's transcendence concerns subjectivity and inter-subjectivity, the most basic properties of human existence. Subjectivity evidently is the common condition not only of religion but also of all other forms of human culture. As for Berger's view, his signals of transcendence are expressions of human life that manifestly exceeds animal existence. Sensibility to order, relativizing overly rational attitudes, hope, humor and a sense of righteousness must be evaluated as human sensibilities and expressions of subjectivity, of which animals are not capable.

In sum, one can say that both the above authors' notions of "transcendence" merely denote a generic human phenomenon, which evidently is not religious in the narrow sense. A question that might be raised here is whether all forms of transcendence are equivalent, and, in the same breath, whether all forms of spirituality are similar in nature.

A term similar to transcendence is "enlightenment," which, though not exclusively, is much used in the context of religion. Transcendence is primarily a Western, religious term, originally presupposing a radical break between nature and what is called the supernatural. Eastern religious thought predominantly presupposes the oneness or immanence of all reality. In the latter worldview, human life is merely a manifestation of Life in the universe. Enlightenment in Buddhism concerns the possibility of overcoming the contingencies of human life (ignorance) and of realizing the buddha nature (*bussho*) that permeates all forms of life and is somehow contained even in inorganic matter.

Both terms, transcendence and enlightenment, appear to have been devalued lately, partially because of the rejection of religious attitudes and partially because of a new religious thought that does not rely on these terms. This seems to be the case of the New Age Movement or, more broadly, "the new spirituality movements and culture" (Shimizono 1996; Maekawa 2001). The aim of these movements roughly seems to be self-realization and seeking a more authentic self. However, inasmuch as the terms transcendence and enlightenment denote human phenomena, they need not be suspicious or fundamentally problematic. The same regards the term "the spiritual" and the religious itself. In my view, all these terms are metaphors that express a specific, more or less distinct, characteristic of our subject matter: spiritual culture.

The Conditions of Human Life

Human life is conditioned by the physical and socio-cultural, environmental factors on which it is dependent to the extent that dependence and contingency are characteristics of human nature itself. Obviously, all life is conditioned by its physical existence. Needless to say, individuals must fulfill physical needs in order to live and to act. The same is true for the proper functioning of the human mind. It is conditioned in two ways, 'internally' by the physical qualities of the human brain, and 'externally' by the existence of objects and other subjects to which it relates.

Basically, the material world is a world of usefulness for fulfilling physical needs. It is lately seen as an organic-inorganic system in its own right. The usefulness of the physical world in our age has become enormously enhanced by means of science and technology. Yet, for all its practical usefulness, the significance of the physical world is not limited to fulfilling physical needs. Humans also have non-physical needs that are served by observing the physical world as an object of thought and contemplation for intellectual and emotional enjoyment.

Further, human life is conditioned by belonging to collectivities. As referred to earlier, humans are basically *social* beings to the extent that they cannot become humans without stimulation by other humans and internalizing culture. Initially, in primary socialization, the internalization of culture proceeds more or less in an unconscious way. In secondary socialization, one internalizes culture through conscious identification. Both forms of socialization engender a sense of belonging. However, to the extent that collectivities are static, belonging may be experienced as a limiting condition.

Mental interaction with the physical and socio-cultural world is the most basic condition of mental growth. The human self is essentially a growth-process. To repeat, humans *become* humans through socialization and the internalization of culture via communication with and through recognition by others. Self-identity is a social product. Dependence is as pervasive as it is profound. Dependence is further complicated through the fundamental problems of human life: ignorance, suffering, and evil, three forms of chaos with which humans are ill at ease (Geertz 1972:100–110).

Humans at birth lack consciousness and are totally 'ignorant'. No knowledge emerges from within an individual organism. Having only a certain amount of potential, all knowledge has to be gained from external sources.

In this respect, humans are quite different from the lower forms of life. Plants almost automatically realize their potential and animals develop theirs without much learning.

Human ignorance as a problem is well recognized by most religions. Human foolishness is a theme in the wisdom literature in the Bible, but Buddhism has dug deeper in this terrain. Buddhism sees ignorance as lying at the core of the Law of cause and effect in the human world. It is the first link in a series of twelve that determine human existence (*ju ni engi*) (Mizuno 1973; Dalai Lama 2000). In a different way, foolishness in Buddhist teaching is seen as one of the three human "poisons" together with greed and anger. Buddhism concluded that there is "no-self," exposing a fundamental human dependence and the lack of self-sufficiency of individual human nature.

The second basic human problem is suffering, which comes at least in two varieties: physical and mental suffering. Some instances of physical suffering are quite natural, especially sickness and death. It is again Buddhism that has chewed most on this difficult to digest human condition. Suffering (*issai kaiku*), after dependency and the characteristic of no-self, is the third peculiarity of the Law of all living. Other instances of suffering are inflicted by fellow human beings and eventually by oneself. These constitute the third category of fundamental human problems: evil. It is a special kind of suffering on which I will comment below.

Lower and Higher Forms of Experience

If the human self constitutes a process of growth and self-fulfillment, one can distinguish different forms of experience, lower and higher forms, depending on whether growth and self-fulfillment are impeded or enhanced. Let us look at some examples.

With respect to physical conditioning, experience seems to be of a low quality when the means for fulfilling one's physical needs are lacking, when usefulness is non-existent, when physical harm occurs through bodily dysfunction, accidents and natural disasters. In respect to social conditioning, particularly at a time in history when self-realization is highly evaluated, becoming aware of merely 'existing' within a social group cannot be rated as very significant in terms of experience. Again, a form of lower experience seems to derive from attempts to maximize self-satisfaction as in the case of addiction to alcohol, drugs, and sex. Addictions often lead to depression and suicide (Giddens 1992:65–70). Maximizing collective self-realization tends to cause forms of lower experience to other collectivities. Other forms of lower experience occur, e.g., in conflict situations and instances of discrimination, resulting in harm to one's sense of self-respect. Further, experience is of low quality when higher experiences turn "sour," when one experiences the absence of enjoyment, e.g., when one is confronted with ugliness, when internal confusion is too great to enjoy even the best of physical conditions.

The fundamental problems of life evidently denote a low quality. Becoming aware of ignorance can be very painful. The same is true for mental suffering in the face of adversity and evil. For most people, evil denotes harm done by others, constituting an injustice. A deeper problem is that "[T]he problem with evil is concerned with threats to our ability to make sound moral judgments" (Geertz 1973:106). Casting doubt on our ability to judge what is good and what is not, and having to accept judgments of others in this matter may hurt our sense of self-worth.

In contrast, bodily feelings of well-being mostly lead to higher forms of experience. Other examples of higher forms of experience are the positive enjoyment of culture, of uncalculated acts of kindness, endearing emotional relations, creative contributions to social and cultural life, and so forth. Thus, one's family life and work may occasion higher forms of experience, yielding satisfaction and stimulating mental growth.

However, here we seem to have stumbled on a fundamental theoretical problem. Even though many experiences are clearly understood as having either a certain degree of positive or negative significance, it is uncertain when such is the case and under what circumstances. Cause and effect is not easily discernable. That it is not clear what exactly constitutes lower and higher forms of experience is due partly to the fact that the boundary of these experiences is not clear. Ignorance in many cases cannot be helped; there are necessary instances of suffering such as the ultimate deterioration of health and dying; on the other hand, suffering may be evaluated positively from a religious point of view; it may be inflicted on purpose. Further, it seems curious that it is easier to locate lower forms of experiences than higher ones. Are lower experiences in reality more frequent?

Indeed, uncertainty about the outcome of these fundamental facts of life is both an existential and theoretical problem. In the following I will attempt to clarify two mechanisms of transcendence that may shed some light on those problems: symbolization and valuation. This clarification should be the more meaningful if indeed lower forms of experience are more in evidence than higher forms.

Mechanisms of Transcendence

As mentioned above, humans at the beginning of life lack an innate behavioral orientation but have potential to develop orientations by learning patterns of behavior. I assume that symbolization and valuation are basic human faculties that lie at the basis of learning behavior. Starting from this premise I further argue that symbolizations and values are core elements of culture, forming distinct mechanisms, responsible for the dynamism of culture. In reality, these mechanisms are closely interrelated. They function in combination but are analytically distinct.

Symbolization seems to be a mechanism responsible for extensive cultural development. It is a source of meaning construction and a means of establishing meaning. In contrast, valuation as a mechanism denotes evaluation of meaning. Speaking analogically, meaning construction can be said to be *linear* and evaluation of meaning *circular*, moving in and out of the former. Symbolizations (all forms of symbolizing) accumulate differently from values. Subjectively, valuation is more subject to change. Similar to the above case concerning the awareness of lower and higher experiences, *value coordination* is as yet not understood well. Valuation therefore is the greater problem. Let us first consider symbolization.

Symbolization

All symbolizations are basically simple and similar. Symbolization works through substitution. One thing so to speak is the "cultural" doppelganger of another, or, the meaning of one thing is explained by some implications of another. Differences among symbolizations seem to derive from a lesser or greater degree of analogy. In other words, some symbolizations are mere substitutions while others are analogies that have more "weight," more "depth." The latter I would like to call metaphors. It is these that generate new meaning.

Language basically is a symbol system. One can imagine that somewhere at the beginning of civilization and the initial development of speech, objects were "substituted or represented" by means of "words," that is, sound-formations. In the later development of speech, words were subsequently "substituted" by means of written symbols, pictures, hieroglyphs, "characters" (as in Chinese and Japanese) and combinations of letters. Thus, objects were "substituted or represented" in two ways: phonetically and graphically. Not only objects but many other things were subsequently represented in the same way: actions, thoughts, feelings, the properties of things, relations, functions, the dimensions of place and time, different modalities and dimensions of actions, and so forth.

Obviously, we are touching on complex problems of linguistics and semiotics about which my knowledge is limited, but, I hope sufficient for present purposes. Partly I am relying on Julian Jaynes' (1993:48–49) view of the significance of metaphor for language. To quote:

> The most fascinating property of language is its capacity to make metaphors. But what an understatement! For metaphor is not a mere extra trick of language, as it is so often slighted in the old schoolbooks on composition; it is the very constitutive ground of language. I am using metaphor in its most general sense: the use of a term for one thing to describe another because of some kind of similarity between them or between their relations to other things. There are thus always two terms in a metaphor, the thing to be described, which I shall call 'metaphrand,' and the thing or relation used to elucidate it, which I shall call 'metaphier.' A metaphor is always a known metaphier operating on a less known metaphrand. I have coined these hybrid terms simply to echo multiplication where a multiplier operates on a multiplicand. It is by metaphor that language grows...

Leaving aside the precise role of metaphor in the system of language, I totally ascribe to Jaynes' conceptualization of it, that is, symbolization in the narrower sense (Jaynes does not distinguish between symbols in a narrow or broad sense). In the following I will give some examples, some borrowed from Jaynes.

The formation of some words clearly reveals a symbolic origin in the broader sense. Good examples are: person, role, structure, system, status. "Person" originally denoted the mask of a stage performer, "role," a rolled up scroll, and so on. The new meaning of these words, the new concept that results, is an extension of their referents. Though differing in formation, some Chinese characters are symbolic in the same sense. They are simplified pictures of objects and till today show reference to the concrete, external reality that they represent. No new meaning is affected in the latter case.

Some words, the very metaphors, are symbolic in a special way. They generate new meaning. Interesting examples are the words father and mother, which are curiously similar in seemingly all Indo-European languages. Recently I checked them in Sanskrit, where they read *pitri* and *matri*. I was amazed to find that they are derived from words that denote heaven and earth respectively, implying that the father figure from ancient times was symbolized with the "metaphier" heaven, while the image of a mother was derived from the "metaphier" earth. This 'vision' was retained in Roman and Greek mythology. The Roman Ju*piter* is the god of the sky, one of the principal gods. Its relation to the Sanskrit *pitri* is evident. The Greek gods of heaven and earth, Ouranos and Gaiya, are personified as a father and a mother figure but these words have a different origin. Further, it is revealing that some words in Germanic languages related to "earth" clearly are similar to the word mother (*Mutter* and *moeder* in German and Dutch respectively). For example, the Dutch "*modder*" and the English "mud," (both meaning the same) are of the same origin. Similarly, *Murast, moeras*, denoting a swamp in German and Dutch respectively are of the same origin.

A very interesting example of an unmetaphorical sounding word is the verb "to be," that together with its irregular conjugation was formed analogically. "To be" derives from Sanskrit *bhu*, "to grow, or to make grow." The English "am" and "is" have evolved from the same root as the Sanskrit *asmi*, "to breath." Jaynes (1993:51) mentions: "It is something of a lovely surprise that the irregular conjugation of our most nondescript verb is thus a record of a time when man had no independent word for 'existence' and could only say that something 'grows' or that it 'breathes.'"

There are many pleasant or unpleasant surprises, depending on one's mindset! Christianity teaches that God is like a father figure, because Jesus taught to pray to God as *"Our Father who art in heaven."* (He used the Aramaic *abba*, in a meaning and use similar to the English "daddy" as the best word to speak to God). Jodo-Buddhism believes in Amida-Buddha, "who" is represented by a benign, dignified, mysteriously looking manlike figure sitting in meditation position. "Amida" made vows to the extent of saving all people first before entering nirvana. Yet, in a different way, Amida-Buddha is thought to be the Eternal Life or the Eternal Light contained in the universe. Taoism believes in Tao, the unfathomable essence contained in the universe, constituted by Yin and Yang. Taoists symbolized this invisible existence with the character for Way.

The ancient people who fashioned these representations did not claim to have seen the Tao or God or the eternal Buddha, but they thought they had experienced something surpassing sense perception and expressed those feelings analogically in various ways. The manner of "approaching" unseen realities or the supernatural, in its Western sense, is basically similar to the conceptualization of the words for father and mother in Sanskrit. It is also basically similar in the case of action-symbols and ritual.

Action-related symbols are much less numerous than word-symbols. The Buddhist wheel of the Law and the Christian cross are primary examples. The Buddhist wheel of the Law represents a stylized wheel of an ancient war chariot that was made and used to charge the enemy. Blades are attached to the axle at both sides of the chariot for more fighting efficiency. At the time Buddhism became a religion, it probably was the most effective piece of weaponry. The early Buddhists chose the wheel of a war chariot to represent the central theory of their religion, the eternal Law of cause and effect that shows the fundamental interdependency of all living things. Understanding the Law was thought to facilitate enlightenment. Through the understanding of the Law and acting accordingly, people would be able to destroy all human passions (*bonno*) like a chariot destroying the enemy. As such, the wheel of the Law is a powerful symbol. The same holds true for the Christian cross that was originally a cruel instrument for torturing and killing criminals. It was transformed into a symbol of redemption. Both the wheel of the war chariot and the cross acquired new meaning. Symbols apparently are more powerful, the greater the difference between the original meaning and the new meaning.

The same can be said for the "degree of transcendence" of metaphorical symbols, that is, the new meaning they introduce, although it is difficult to judge to what extent, the transferring of meaning is different in each case. However, the more important point is that a transfer of meaning *effectively occurs* and that there is a gain in meaning. The *metaphiers* of metaphorical

symbols add a new dimension of meaning to the *metaphrands*. This constitutes transcendence. As in our examples, a "heavenly Father" is not quite an
earthly father but the image lets one imagine God in a specific way. Amida-
Buddha is the Eternal Life of the universe, or its Eternal Light, which we
can imagine when thinking of the life and light that we know. There is no
guarantee that these symbols are "true" in any literal sense. Except for the
fact that evidently there is a gain in meaning as in the case of the wheel of
the Law and the Christian cross, this meaning cannot palpably be verified.
The latter symbolizations suggest the possibility of redemption in one way
or another, and, therefore, they represent an advantage, for example, when
confronting mental and physical suffering.

Valuation

Valuation, too, is basically simple. It is evaluation of action, of choosing
what is useful, meaningful, gratifying. In other words, humans can judge
and choose what is of use, what is good, and reject what is useless or bad.
By acting and experimenting they find out what is most effective and what
is most satisfying.

In attempting to theorize about values, I would like to maintain, first, that
a value is an aspect of an act, that is, the component of gratification for oneself, for others, or for both. Often, though not always, evaluation involves
choosing between different ways of action. If a value is an aspect of an act,
a value can be seen as the reward that results from acting that is internalized through acting itself. The successful act tends to be repeated because
of its gratifying effect. As is often mentioned in theories about values, it is
for this reason that a value functions as motivation for action. Yet, contrary
to what is often assumed, the fact that a value is an inherent aspect of the
action implies that acting not necessarily involves choosing between different
courses of action. In many cases, action seems to propel itself, even to the
extent of overcoming external constraints. In case choice is affected, it tends
to be a choice between various rewards.

A second important point is that, prior to the internalization through
autonomous action, values are learned from significant others. Successful
internalization of values therefore depends on primary socialization. A "good
start" is supposed to be vital for having a more or less well balanced set of

personal values; total balance is impossible since total socialization is impossible. Individuals growing toward adulthood of necessity must experiment with their set of values. Since action in daily life is varied, one's collection of values will be varied respectively. It is for this reason that ambivalence is characteristic of human action. Choice between different rewards will never be a settled matter.

Complexity of Valuation and Symbolization

The two mechanisms of valuation and symbolization, taken separately, are as plain as they are fundamental. The differences in their functioning also appear to be clear-cut. To repeat, symbolization involves meaning construction and its fixation. Valuation is evaluation of meaning. In reality however these mechanisms do not function separately but together. In daily life we are not conscious of the differences between symbolizations and values, between rational and symbolic action. In most cultural studies, symbols and values are not distinguished, not even in studies of religions where symbols and values (commandments) are notably different elements. The main reason for not isolating these core elements, no doubt, is the fact that in reality they are closely related phenomena that show almost infinite variation in individuals, in collectivities, and within various patterns of social action. Tackling this complexity cannot be our present concern.

Finally, I will attempt a few considerations about the possibility of universalization of symbolizations and values and their role in creating spiritual culture.

Spiritual Culture and Transcendence

All knowledge functions as a means of transcendence of "raw" biological nature in the sense discussed by Luckmann. None is given within biological human existence. Nothing emanates internally from the brain itself. A normally functioning human brain is a prerequisite substratum for the development of consciousness and subjectivity, and, as Jaynes (1993:129–137) eloquently argued, language has been of great consequence in the development of consciousness.

Similarly, Berger discussed manifestations of human transcendence that involve symbolizations and symbolic action: the creation of social order, human play, expressions of humor and hope in adverse situations, and the condemnation of evil. Whether these things point to a higher order of reality is not important in the present context. As suggested earlier, the more important point is whether transcendence is affected or not.

The point I am advancing is that transcendence is created by metaphors, through the formation of concepts and new meanings. Due to being embedded in the concrete, symbols are essentially particularistic, even though they have a transcendent quality, shown in the birth of new meaning, including religious meaning. However, because of their being embedded in the concrete and the particular, symbols are not apt to be universalized. For example, there are various views of enlightenment and many religious symbols like the Buddhist wheel of the Law and the Christian cross, each of which is important for the religion concerned. Each religion can remain unique by retaining its own symbolizations. Another pertinent example is language as a symbol system. Language must not "globalize." If the whole world would come to speak only one language, culture will ultimately deteriorate.

Also, values originate from concrete behavior. Values are aspects of acts. Yet, as elements of culture, values are ideas about behavior and being. As such, values are shareable and better suitable to become universal elements of culture than symbolizations. Social values have the greater transcendent meaning the more they are shared. The same does not hold for symbolizations, since they consolidate meaning. In the introduction I stated hypothetically that the universally spiritual culture must be sought in those areas of culture that have transcendent meaning for life as a whole, intellectually, emotionally, and morally. Admittedly, this hypothesis sounds tautological. However, it will be easily agreed upon that lower forms of experience and situations involving the fundamental human problems of ignorance, suffering, and evil are not evaluated as meaningful. They are experienced as painful in various ways. Overcoming these problems and being again able to enjoy life leads to higher forms of experience. Although we cannot be certain about what actually is of a lower or higher degree in a state of mind, we can find out how it is affected. The pain of ignorance can partly be overcome through humility, that of suffering through patience, compassion and sharing of grief. Evil can be overcome through forgiveness. Thus, humility, patience, compassion, and forgiveness are values that are significant as unique means of "transcending" the respective problems.

However, the problem of ignorance is quite different from those of suffering and evil. Ignorance can more easily be overcome by means of symbolizations and knowledge than suffering and evil. All instances of metaphorical transcendence, originating in thinking, are little steps, little glimpses of spirituality. Transcendence in this case is affected through thinking that stops as it were when something new is found or created. All symbolizations create and fix meaning, although thinking itself does not become fixed. Values, on the other hand, are aspects of action. They are a matter of attitude, which is never fixed. Attitudes may change from one moment to the other. The transcendence of values is affected through will and the degree of transcendence will depend on the degree of will exercised. Suffering and evil can only be overcome minimally through knowledge but more through action that incorporates those values. While symbolizations are particular, limited in meaning or applicability, social values seem to have more applicability, paradoxically because the range of action is more limited than the range of thinking. Every day life is similar for all humans. Because all share the fundamental problems of life, all could share the same values to overcome them.

Universal spiritual culture then must be sought in those aspects of life that are common to all people. Overcoming of the fundamental problems of suffering and evil appears to merit the greatest consideration in this respect, because the ways of overcoming these seem few in number and common to all people. Transcendence in this area is more vital than overcoming ignorance. Concern for reducing suffering and evil is possibly the place to look for the *telos* of culture.

Human life has an open dimension that develops through symbolization and valuation. Both processes produce spiritual culture. Both have a transcendent quality, but only valuation can produce universal spiritual culture. In other words, the greatest possibility for universalization appears to be given in the area of morality. Its primary condition is the inclusion of the Other. Durkheim's phrase *"Only the universal is rational"* takes on a paradoxical meaning. Coping with suffering and evil is usually not perceived as rational action.

Chapter Ten

The Future of Christianity as a Question about the Future of Europe

Gottfried Küenzlen

If all the signs are to be believed, the century that lies ahead of us will, *among other things,* be characterized by the power of religion. After the end of secular ideologies, the great world religions are returning as powerful guides of how to lead one's life, as guarantors of cultural identity and as creative powers of religiously influenced policy. This also applies to non-western Christianity, which will soon comprise over a billion believers.

The tragedy about Western European Christianity is that in spite of such a return of the religions, it will not take a place in public that will afford it any influence – as far as we can see. The fact that Christianity has lost its cultural power and that secularity has been allowed to take its place is too deeply rooted in history and continues to exert too much of an influence at the present time for even the slightest suspicion of a reversal of this process to seem justified.

When analyzing the present situation in Germany, one of the most astonishing observations to be made is that this finding does not unsettle people's minds in the least. Among others, it is particularly today's cultural intelligentsia – who are free to dedicate themselves to reflecting on the situation and fate of the social and cultural conditions of our nation – who seem completely un-moved by this erosion of Christianity. As far as religion is concerned, they seem to have found themselves a nice little place at the liberal center from where they mildly criticize religion or remain indifferent towards it. They consider the question about the future of European Christianity unimportant since the matter is deemed to be closed or of a secondary nature. This issue has a meaning only for those rare remnants of society who still cling to their Christian background and Church.

Admittedly, such convictions, which reflect the mood of the Enlightenment and partly continue the tradition of the religious criticism of the nineteenth century, have by now themselves become strangely antiquated and stale. For one thing, such an attitude of Euro-centric conceit makes people close their eyes to the worldwide return of the religions as an influencing and politically realistic factor. In addition, it also renders them helpless since they lack any sort of reference system and thus do not know how to deal with this development. What is more, in Europe itself, the remaining traces of religious criticism rooted in the Enlightenment or religious indifference will no longer be mental attitudes enabling people to face the new developments either. This will become true, at the latest, when the religion that has long since started immigrating to Europe and is absolutely sure of itself will increasingly gain public standing and recognition – namely Islam.

However, apart from these facts, it is important to realize: *For the time being*, the decisive cultural question is actually not about the future of European Christianity but about the future of European civilization itself. More precisely: What future does European civilization have? Where is it heading since its original religion, which used to shape it, has let itself become culturally marginalized?

To at least keep asking such questions, even without finding an answer, is what our memory compels us to do if we think about the fact that almost all "Western" world views and images of humanity, that is, the sum of all we by now refer to as Western "values," originated in our Christian past. This does not mean mere reverence for a heritage exhibited in museums that has lost its meaning for our lives. It rather implies learning to see that civilizations and thus also societies are certainly also very much characterized by the ideas, conceptions of the world and images of humanity that are generally accepted and predominant in them. Let it be repeated once more, *the reason why* the question about the future of European civilization is such a pressing one is that Europe, at least its Western part, only has a residual awareness of its spiritual and religious heritage or even has shed it completely.

Of course, we have become completely alienated from and can no longer understand the ideas Freiherr von Hardenberg, known as Novalis (1986:287), had of a bygone "Christian Europe" he romantically dreamed about and yearned for:

> Beautiful and splendid were the times when Europe still was a Christian land, with one Christianity living in this part of the world where humane values prevailed; one great common interest united the most remote provinces of this vast spiritual realm. – Without large worldly possessions, one religious leader directed and united the big political powers...

However, already in 1799 and for Novalis (1986:296) himself, these times had long since become a thing of the past and Europe was shaken by frenzy and new wars resulting from "modern unbelief" as the "key to all dreadful phenomena of recent times." However, Novalis (1986:301) was convinced that the "New Europe" would develop as a home to "new human beings" once Christianity would become resurrected as the soul of this Europe:

> Who knows whether there have been enough wars; however, war will never end if one does not grasp for the palm leaf that can only be offered by a spiritual power. Blood will continue to stream across Europe until the nations become aware of their dreadful madness that keeps them going in circles and finally hear holy music that calms them down, causing them to assemble around altars of times past, with people from different nations standing side by side, doing deeds of peace and joining in a great love feast where hot tears are shed on the smoking battlefields in celebration of peace. Only religion will be able to resurrect Europe and provide security to the nations and install Christianity in its former pacificating office with new glory for all the world to see.

For us today, all this is in fact only a testimony to a lost spiritual world, and that the dream of Novalis of an imminent "Christian Europe" has become a mere illusion. This contrast becomes very obvious when looking at the present consultations held on the wording of a constitution for the European Union. So far, no answer has been found at all to the question whether even the term "Christian" may be included in a future preamble or agreement can be reached only on the much more vague term "spiritual heritage." However, whether this will suffice in the long term to preserve what we call "Europe" – in particular with a view to the present global situation – is a question that, let this be repeated, may at least be asked. It may well be that Novalis's works, despite all their romantic and Catholic nostalgia, are in fact of a certain relevance to the present situation and the future. This means that also Christianity, as a cultural power, makes its contribution to building the Europe of the future and helps "provide security" to its "nations."

Nobody asked more explicitly the cultural question about the future of Christianity as a question about the future of Europe than did Friedrich Nietzsche. Admittedly, literature on Nietzsche and his relationship to Christianity is relatively abundant. The following short comments and notes cannot even be an attempt at interpreting Nietzsche; they are only meant to more clearly define from Nietzsche's point of view the possible dimensions and dramatic implications of the question mentioned before.

That Nietzsche was the most radical critic of Christianity of modern times is a well-known fact. Ever since, all criticism of Christianity has been in the shadow of Nietzsche's work. The momentum of this criticism of Christianity by Nietzsche of course only reveals itself if it is understood to be a statement about the fate of European civilization itself. Those who only know Nietzsche to have stated the "death of God" and proclaimed Europe's parting from Christianity have merely understood half of what he wanted to say, which amounts to nothing at all. Rather, for Nietzsche the question about the future of Christianity also provides an answer to the question about the future of European civilization: The end of Christianity also marks the end of Europe's previous culture.

Two short aphorisms may serve as examples that also afford a glimpse of the dramatic dimensions of the process as described by Nietzsche (1988a:85ff):

> At the deathbed of Christianity. – The truly active people now have no Christian belief, and the only Christian belief to be found among the more moderate and thoughtful people of the intellectual middle class is one that has been adapted to their very needs and thus is of a strangely simplified nature. A God who, in His love, will ordain what is finally best for us, a God who gives and takes our virtue and luck alike so that, all in all, the things that happen are always right and good and there is no reason left to take life hard or even complain about it – to put it in a nutshell: elevating resignation

and modesty to a divinity; this has become the best and most fervent that has been left of Christianity. However, one should not fail to notice that this means that Christianity has turned into some kind of gentle moralism: What has been left is not 'God, freedom and eternal life' but goodwill and virtue and the belief that also in the entire universe goodwill and virtue will be omnipresent: This amounts to the euthanasia of Christianity.

Thus, for Nietzsche, Christianity lying on its "deathbed" does not only imply the fading and death of Christianity but its "euthanasia." This "euthanasia" also means that Nietzsche, as he repeatedly emphasizes in numerous other passages, does not claim that everything "Christian" has disappeared; he rather maintains it lives on, transformed into more trite and trivialized manifestations, for which Nietzsche coined the special term of the "decadence" of Christianity. However, what Christianity used to be when it still was founded on "God, freedom and eternal life" ceased to exist once these pillars of Christian faith had collapsed. As a result, Christianity also lost its power to shape European civilization.

Much as this aphorism suggests reflection on the present situation of Christianity and the Church ("gentle moralism!"), it only formulates one side of Nietzsche's diagnosis. Nietzsche (1988b:480; Rohrmoser 2000:276–286) again and again sought to describe what the end of Christianity as a cultural power *meant* to him. Let me quote a few sentences from the famous aphorism "The Mad Man" in order to at least indicate briefly what he meant. "The Mad Man", who goes out into the marketplace with his lantern to look for God, cries:

> "Where has God gone?...I will tell you! We have killed Him!" Then he continues: "But how did we do this? What enabled us to drink the sea dry? Who gave us the sponge to wipe away all of the horizon? What were we doing when we unchained this Earth from its sun? Where is it heading now? Where are we heading? Away from all suns? Aren't we forever falling? And backwards, side-wards, forwards, to all sides? Is there still an above and a below? Aren't we wandering about as if through an infinite void? Don't we feel the cold breath of empty space? Hasn't it turned colder? Doesn't night fall upon us more and more? Isn't it true that lanterns must be lit in the morning? Don't we hear the noise of the gravediggers yet who are burying God? Don't we smell divine decay yet? – Gods do decay, too! God is dead! God remains dead! And we have killed Him! How will we

find consolation, the murderers of all murderers? The most sacred and powerful that the world hitherto had possessed, it bled to death, stabbed by our very knives...

With his description of God's death in this aphorism, Nietzsche describes what he experiences as a most dreadful loss, that is the loss of the "most sacred and powerful." Nietzsche uses three images to illustrate this loss: The sea, the horizon and the sun. Taken together, this means: All that used to give a civilization of more than two-thousand years, which comprise the ancient world and Christianity, metaphysical depth ("sea"), cultural shape ("horizon") and a spiritual center ("sun") disappeared with the killing of God. What remains is the expectance of the "most frightening of all guests", nihilism ("Aren't we wandering about as if through an infinite void?")

Let me repeat this once again: We do not need to determine whether Nietzsche is "correct" about his cultural criticism and even less do we have to consider or evaluate his personal approach of overcoming nihilism, such as announcing the coming of a superman as the "true sense of earth." Rather, Nietzsche's diagnosis of the development of European civilization *compels* us to again recognize the question inherent in the cultural erosion of European Christianity. What will the future of a civilization look like whose original religion has lost its former power to shape society?

Open Questions

Most of the studies I just talked about were based on two fundamental realizations. For one thing, Western European Christianity, the original religion of Europe, has lost its "power of life" (Max Weber) that used to exert a decisive influence on culture and society. However, also the gods of the secular culture that have determined the history of the Western modern age to a considerable degree have turned old. Just like the fading Western European Christianity, the modern age, which has become tired of its secular convictions, is no longer sure which way to go.

This, however, leads to the question: *Which* spiritual sources will give us the power to meet the challenges we are already facing? This question is a very serious one that will not be answered by a cultural criticism, which consists in mere lamentation about the "decline" or even the "end" of Western civilization. The matter requires much more careful consideration. For sure, no civilization or religion will last forever, and history is also the story of the rise and fall of civilizations and religions. However, whenever cultural and religious ways of explaining life and the sense of our existence had lost their meaning, cultural struggles followed until new ideas and convictions about the world, humanity and civilization finally gained general recognition. Those who still mourn over the "decline of the Christian West" are pretty late in doing so. The latter has come to an end a long time ago, and the question that matters now is: Where is Europe heading after it has started getting rid of its original traditions, and which spiritual forces are driving this process?

Another reason why the question mentioned before is not taken as seriously as it should be is to be found in an attitude that seems to be rather common today and which exerts a far-reaching influence on political action and even on science. One no longer knows nor wants to know about the power of culture and blindly believes in the myth that the world is moved simply by the fact that people pragmatically pursue their interests and merely seek to gain maximum profit, with the required "values" automatically resulting from this. This belief is blind because it forgets that people will always feel the need to and actually *will* find explanations with inner meaning for their actions, thoughts and feelings. Therefore, the question must be: *Which* explanations and interpretations of our existence will prevail and finally shape our society and civilization? The "values" that are talked about so much do not just fall out of the blue, either; they are in fact founded on religions, ideologies, conceptions of the world and philosophies of life and are propagated by their religious – or today secular – priests and prophets. As a result, today's dominance of a simple pragmatism focusing on people's interests and pure economical rationalism is *in itself* the result of a certain way of explaining our civilization, which does neither develop "innocently," that is without human interference, nor naturally. Rather, it is the result of the way the secular culture of modern times has developed and the world-view and image of humanity that have come to prevail in it.

The fact that it seems impossible today to find alternative ways of explaining the meaning of our existence makes the question about the "spiritual sources" even more urgent: How will we be able to meet the challenges facing us if the only thing our civilization provides us with is mere utilitarianism and vague talk about "values" which, of course, are no longer founded on religious belief?

Finally, I would like to mention a few of the "challenges facing us," which are regarded as particularly pressing when considering the present situation and which inevitably lead to asking questions about the situation and the fate of religion. It will not be possible for me to talk about the challenges the *individual* and his personal way of life will be confronted with in the secular, Western and liberal societies or how the present situation will affect him, also psychologically. Neither will I talk about the possible meaning and future *religion* might have in this context.

However, if we look at Western European civilization and societies as a whole, there are good reasons for the following thesis: We, the people in Europe and Germany, are faced with the task to *find out what it is that makes up our own civilization today*. A nation which sees a new civilization and religion moving in must inevitably ask about its *own* cultural and national identity. The question is: Who are we and who do we *want* to be – as Europeans, as Germans?

In the past few years – in particular after September 11, 2001 – there has been a lot of public discussion about Samuel Huntington's thesis of the "clash of civilizations." It is no coincidence that Huntington's work was mostly met with repudiate or even refusal to talk about his theories at all by the intellectual elite who deal with such questions, particularly in Germany. Asking questions about the survival of one's own civilization, about the identity of "a people" and "a nation" in Germany always is suspicious since this might imply the acceptance of "a superior race" and "nationalism" as the highest values whose disastrous recent history keeps following us like a shadow.

Nevertheless, we – as Europeans, as Germans – will not be spared the question about ourselves, who we are and who we want to be, either. Whether we want to admit it to ourselves or not – whenever we look back into the past we see: Only those civilizations will survive that know who they are and have not lost faith in themselves in the course of time. The fact that communism no longer exists as a negative counterpart to the Western world, the process of internationalization and the global omnipresence of all culture compel us to ask about the special characteristics of *our* civilization and our view of society. In this context, the dreams of "one world" that obviously so many are moved by are no real help, either. Consequently,

> the outlines of a global confrontation can be seen whose outcome is unclear and will be determined in the distant future. However, one thing is certain:

The civilizations will neither mutually enrich each other and promote each other's development by give and take nor will their exchange make them grow into one single global civilization to which all of them have contributed their best. Such hopes have been nurtured before at a time when one big nation used to subjugate all other peoples and nations except for a few unimportant tribes at the outer fringes. However, sooner or later, a large number of different civilizations, peoples and languages used to develop all the same. Should our future indeed be one single global civilization this time that would unite all free civilizations, it will certainly not be the result of free amalgamation but bear the stamp of the one civilization which has shaped, distorted, pushed aside, converted or soaked up the others. This is what history tells us, and there are no exceptions (Tenbruck 1996:276).

However, those who seem not touched by this lesson history teaches us will still find that they have to face the seriousness of the *present situation*. A clash of civilizations? It is not important whether Huntington's thesis is "correct" since one may well disagree on the diagnostic and, even more, prognostic relevance of his explanations. The question is: Do we even have a choice? What will we do if *others* challenge us to this fight, maybe even in the name of their faith? Then we, that is the people living in the open, liberal societies of the West, won't have any choice but to rediscover what *our* spiritual and cultural roots are. We will have to find out whether we are prepared and still able to newly appreciate and, if necessary, defend the values of our constitutions, which must not be taken for granted at all: The protection of life, the dignity of the individual, the renunciation of violence whilst strictly ensuring that the use of force remains an exclusive right of the state, the freedom of religion and ideology, and so on. It is thus the seriousness of the present situation that forces us to learn virtues, which had almost disappeared, anew: Moral courage and perseverance, determination of mind and an awareness of the importance and dignity of our own cultural foundations.

However, this makes the question I have put at the beginning even more urgent – the question about the future of Christianity as a question about the future of Europe. Will Europe's new awareness of its values and cultural foundations be able to hold its own, also in the future, if it won't *also* entail a new awareness of its religious origins, of Christian faith?

Such new cultural awareness also includes another question of an equally fundamental nature: Which image of humanity shall be the predominant one for us in the future? This question is too compelling to be evaded by pointing to the pluralism of images of humanity and philosophies of life that is an essential characteristic of liberal Western societies. Whatever the exact meaning of "pluralism" may be, however valuable or threatening we may consider it to be, pluralism is not merely a place of peaceful encounter and free discussion of the many different philosophies of life that our society offers but also a battleground of truths striving to gain cultural and thus finally also political dominance.

At present, an irrefutable example of this is the possibilities opened up by biotechnology. These might mean the end of everything Western civilization had thought about humanity so far. Once we have reached the point where we must ask the question whether therapeutical cloning, which naturally leads to reproductive cloning, should be allowed or not, we will no longer find an answer by pointing to the pluralism that exists in our society with respect to the images of humanity. Then, the decisive question will be: *Which image of humanity will prevail?*

The very day I wrote these last sentences, two big articles appeared in the feature supplement of the *Frankfurter Allgemeine Zeitung*. In the first article, the head of the Protestant Church of the Land Berlin and Protestant expert on social ethics, Wolfgang Huber asks: "May man create a human being in his own image?" In his article, in which he weighs the different arguments, Huber not only warns of the biotechnological possibilities of reproductive medicine but also pleads for rediscovering the biblical image of humanity:

> Christians profess their faith in the God who frees them from themselves in their search for transcendency. They know that they will not find perfection in themselves but only in Him... This relieves believers from thinking they themselves have to create a life that is not subject to finiteness (Frankfurter Allgemeine Zeitung 2003:33).

The other article is by Ray Kurzweil, one "of the most eminent contributors of ideas to the debate in the United States on how to deal with the consequences of modern science" (Frankfurter Allgemeine Zeitung 2003:41). The heading of the article already reveals its message: "Beyond all limits." In a mood of almost breathtaking optimism, Kurzweil praises the revolutionary biotechnological possibilities that will, in particular, be opened up by cloning methods. They will not only cure us of diseases that have been terminal up to now. We will also be continually renewed and rejuvenated by them. Yet the power of such promises made by science, and particularly their *cultural implications,* can only be fully understood once one becomes aware that Kurzweil does not even feel the need to ethically justify himself but instead is convinced of the ethical dignity and even superiority of his message.[1]

Which image of humanity will prevail? The dream of creating a "perfect," "new" human being, a dream that has always been alive throughout the history of secular modern times – has it now become a real possibility? In this dream, humanity is both its own creator and the very being that is created. Or, will the other image of humanity gain general acceptance, one which acknowledges humanity's finiteness as something that in fact constitutes humanity's dignity and worthiness, an image preserved in the Christian faith, which, according to Kierkegaard, says that humanity's greatest perfection lies in its imperfection, in the fact that God is needed?

Any kind of civilization must have an answer to the question: what it is that makes a human being. What answers we will finally find in our civilization of today with its many different secular and religious tendencies remains a secret to our eyes, which are fixed upon the present.

Translator's note: The English quotes and titles of reference material are not taken from the published translations of the respective works.

---

[1] Also for animal conservationists, Kurzweil offers promising new options in the "new world" that lies ahead of us: "Finally, another exciting new aspect made possible by cloning is the possibility of producing meat without animals. Like in the case of therapeutical cloning, we would not create a whole animal but only the desired parts, that is the meat...Meat production that does without animals will also reduce the suffering of animals."

Conceptions of the Future of Society

Chapter Eleven

Civil Society and the Globalization of It's "State of Emergency:" The Longing for the Totally Other as a Force of Social Change

Michael R. Ott

In his last work entitled *"Theses on the Philosophy of History,"* written before his suicide in Portbou, Spain on September 26, 1940 as he fled Nazi Germany, Walter Benjamin (1969:257) stated that the existing "state of emergency" due to Fascism was not an aberration of history. Rather, this crisis was the result of the systematic principle and historical development of modern capitalist civil society. As Benjamin stated, this inherent and intensifying crisis of capitalist civil society is a reality that the socially disenfranchised, exploited and oppressed know all too well. Benjamin advised that a critical notion of history as a whole be developed, one that is expressive of this systematically created and perpetual tragedy not only so it can be comprehended but also resisted and hopefully changed toward a more humanistically rational and reconciled future society.

The ever-present barbarous reality of this globalizing state of emergency of capitalist civil society has once again imperiously raised one of its deadly Hydra heads through the preemptive strike, invasion and now occupation of Iraq by U.S. and British military forces; an act that by many accounts is in violation of International Law and United Nation

Charters. Following the critical theory of Benjamin, Max Horkheimer and Theodor W. Adorno, however, this "regime change" and the resulting destruction of human life cannot be seen as something unique, but rather as yet another barbaric expression of the historical development of the state of emergency that is capitalism. This war, once again, raises the urgent and bewildering question, the answer to which is foundational for the development of the entire critical theory of society and religion as a theory and praxis of liberation and social change toward the creation of a better future society. Erich Fromm expressed this question from a social psychological perspective, which was derived from his childhood experiences of the cruelty and insanity of the First Bourgeois World War. Fromm (1966a:56) asked "why decent and reasonable people suddenly all go crazy. How is it that men stand in the trenches for years and live like animals – and for what?" This was the foundational experience and consequential question that led him into the critical study of psychoanalysis. Due to this war, which he describes as "one of the most cruel and irrational events in modern history," Fromm became aware not only of the irrationalities of human behavior but also of *social* behavior in modern civil society. As Rudolf Siebert (www.wmich.edu/religion/siebert/critical_theory.html) states, the critical theory of subject, society, culture and history came into being through these theorists' attempt to make sense of the insanity or the First World War. In the midst of the Second World War and its madness, Horkheimer and Adorno (1972:xi) rephrased the question and sought to discover "why mankind, instead of entering into a truly human condition, is sinking into a new kind of barbarism."

In the present socio-historical context of this preemptive if not imperialistic war of aggression by technologically superior First World countries against the Third-World country of Iraq – with threats now being seriously made against neighboring Syria and Iran as an evolving expression of U.S. aggression in the imperialist, racist, and xenophobic "war on terror" that has no known object and no known end, this question needs to be critically addressed anew. Why has modern, so-called enlightened Western society, with all the technological and scientific capabilities of overcoming the vast majority of social problems that cause such horrific suffering and death to billions of people in the world, collapsed into a new form of barbarity? In this enlightened society, what has happened to humanity – to what it means to be "human" in terms of human agency and social system, of the individual and collective, of personal autonomy and social solidarity, of being and becoming – so that people in the so-called First World offer little resistance if any to the dominant system imperatives of capitalism that produce not only war but also the grinding poverty, hunger, thirst, sickness, anger, hopelessness, alienation, exploitation, suffering and death of the vast majority of the world's population? In terms of Herbert Marcuse (1964:x), such a question concerning the notion and reality of humanity is founded on the value judgment that real human life, which is created through the constantly becoming, dialectical relationship between personal autonomy and social solidarity, is or at least can and ought to be made worth living, not only for the 1 to 5% of the world population who make up the capitalist class but for all people. What socio-historical role does religion, particularly the prophetic and Messianic religions of Judaism, Christianity, and Islam, play in the midst of these antagonisms, which are being "globalized" by such international institutions as the International Monetary Fund, the World Bank, the G8/G7 of Western political leaders, the World Trade Organization, the World Economic Forum, and now by military might? Do these religions have anything concretely liberating, hopeful, "new," and revolutionary to offer for the redemption of humanity from these conditions and for the creation of a better future society? Or, are these religions merely legitimating and harmonizing functional systems within the given antagonistic social totality?

In an effort to make a contribution to the contemporary struggle in both theory and praxis toward answering these extremely relevant, meaningful and critical "emergency" questions, this article will be divided into two parts. The first part focuses on Horkheimer's and Adorno's research on the above question that they posed concerning the collapse of bourgeois society into barbarity. The second part gives expression to Horkheimer's critical theory of religion and the longing for the totally Other as a way by which humanity can free itself from the reifying mythical spell of the enlightenment in the form of positivistic science and the increasingly cybernetic production and consumption process of capitalism.

I.

Dialectic of Enlightenment

In their attempt to address the anthropodicy and the sociodicy question of why humanity in modern bourgeois society has collapsed into a new stage of barbarism, Horkheimer and Adorno (1972) sought their answer in the analysis of the bourgeois Enlightenment movement and the development of capitalist civil society. This is the focus of their co-authored *Philosophical Fragments* or *The Dialectics of Enlightenment*. In these philosophical fragments, Horkheimer and Adorno critically exposed the catastrophic, dialectical development of the Enlightenment into its very opposite, i.e. the modern mythology of positivistic science being a means of production of capitalism. As they state, the Enlightenment was originally a movement in both theory and praxis that was to set humanity free from all forms of fear, superstition, and ignorance as well as from the resulting social structures of domination and establish humanity's sovereignty: personal autonomy in social solidarity. The Enlightenment was to be a liberating movement of disenchantment – of revealing and thus, removing from both the natural and social worlds all forms of hidden and frightening power that kept humanity subjugated in fear to the unknown of existing reality. According to them, the program of the Enlightenment was the critical dissolution of all superstition and mythology, which in their attempt to give expression to the unknown and terror-producing powers of existence legitimated them in their mystery. Such mythology was to be overcome by the development of scientific knowledge, through which humanity was to find its sovereignty and power. However, as Horkheimer and Adorno (1972:3) stated after one World War and with the approaching end of World War Two, "the fully enlightened earth radiates disaster triumphant."

Trends

Already in 1944, when the authors wrote this text, they critically identified the sinister dominant historical trend "of the transition to the world of the administered life" (Horkheimer & Adorno 1972:ix). As noted above, in the past 60 years this ominous trend toward a totally administered and antagonistic society has been increasingly developed. The most dominant and commanding trend of history is not developing in the direction of a more humane nor enlightened and free future. It is developing conversely toward a totally integrated, identity producing, leveling of all difference, hierarchically administered capitalist class dominated world system. Although Horkheimer's and Adorno's (1972:x) theory does not offer any reprieve from this historical development, they nevertheless do state that the task of critical thought is to rescue, gather together, and represent anew those "residues of freedom" that resist such "identity" production and conformity to the status quo. This is to be done especially when these sparks of reason and freedom seem powerless in the face of society's "state of emergency" and the continued development of history as a "slaughter-bench" (Hegel 1956:21) and a gigantic "Golgotha" (Hegel 1967:808) in which humanity is sacrificed. The purpose of the critical theory is the dialectical preservation, maintenance, and furtherance [*Aufhebung*] of human freedom as the dialectical relationship of personal autonomy and social solidarity, rather than participating in the further development of society and the world toward total administration.

There is a general, insidious and unmitigated trend toward total integration in the totally administered society, to which everything in modern history is connected, either through it being a force for or resistance to this future. This historical development threatens to advance beyond dictatorships and wars into a systematized "iron cage" of one dimensionality; a computerized, pragmatic, technologized, instrumentally rationalized society and consciousness that is hopeless of anything other than what is. An expression of this development is the perversion of the Enlightenment into positivistic science – "the myth of things as they actually are" – which is "the identification of the intellect and science with that which is inimical to the spirit" (Horkheimer & Adorno 1972:x).

According to Horkheimer and Adorno, the collapse of modern, bourgeois society into a new form of barbarity is grounded in the perpetual self-destructiveness of the enlightenment itself, a destructiveness that is celebrated by neo-conservative reactionaries and naively furthered by liberal humanists. Such liberals do not critically penetrate behind the veil of bourgeois society to reveal the deadly "Medusa head" (Marx 1976:91) of the capitalist social totality and its antagonistic process of production. Critical thought has to jettison its purportedly innocent usage and conformity to the dominant positivistic theory and praxis of modernity – its "specialist axioms," (Horkheimer

& Adorno 1972:xi) which destroy the critical heritage of science and makes thought into a "commodity" and language a means of advertising and selling that commodity in the marketplace. Positivism instrumentalizes language, conceptual thought, and science itself and enslaves it to what is given in both nature and society. However, as Horkheimer and Adorno state, even those movements of resistance to this commodification of life are affected by and expressive of the reified capitalist production process. There is no longer any language of resistance that does not already participate in the trend toward conformity with the dominant social theory. Such liberally defined meaning of the language of the antagonistic status quo is merely the other side of the coin of positivism. Where the theory of positivism doesn't control such language, the system imperatives of the instrumentally rationalized capitalist "iron cage" provide the automatic and unconscious censorship to any act that is outside of the administered status quo. This is the task of the educational institutions, to make such external social control needless through the strict emphasis on the analysis and verification of what is/the "facts." Any other non-positivistically anchored theoretical approach to life is considered to be in danger of falling behind the development of the modern sciences and world and thus, back into superstition and myth. Such positivism itself, however, becomes such superstition, delusion, myth and their corollary of human alienation, fear, domination, enslavement. Thought has to give up the positive or affirmative language of contemporary science as well as its liberal opposition. Both are equally instrumentalized and effected by and expressive of the antagonism of the capitalist production process. The hidden, antagonistic societal process of civil society demands and systematically creates conformity and identity production. Strict limitation of science to the verification of "facts" of "what is," knowingly or unknowingly, covertly or overtly, naively or intentionally keeps the social antagonistic system of capitalist class power and its purpose of the maximization of profit for that class hidden behind the facts. Thus, just as the mythologies of pre-modern time, such positivistic science becomes equally a producer of fetishised myth and superstition. Through its limitation of thought to the given facts, positivism denigrates critical theoretical thought to the level of pre-science and thus, rejects it. By so doing, however, positivism itself becomes a metaphysic and mythology of what is, of the existing status quo, hiding all the while the capitalist class interest of domination and exploitation of both nature and humanity for the sake of increasing market share and profit. This myth is furthered by the external and *internalized* social imperatives of censorship, which locks people more fully into the iron cage of the existing society. By means of such positivistic socialization mechanisms as education, media, culture, as well as the administrational "chain of command" methods [Scientific Management/Taylorism, Fordism, computerization] of the work place that absorb the worker into the system's maintenance and furtherance, individuals and even the entire working class end up furthering the system of their own domination, exploitation, alienation, suffering and death. Positivism is not liberational of humanity or nature. That is not its intent nor purpose. Positivism as a "science" is a recidivist theory and praxis that fetishizes the "facts" in the service of a capitalistically dominated civil society, to the catastrophic detriment of billions of human beings.

How did this happen? According to Horkheimer and Adorno, the hard knowledge sought by the Enlightenment, which was based on the success of the so-called revolution of the natural sciences in the 17th century, was to be attained by the human mind penetrating into the very nature of existing things. Through such knowledge of how the natural world functions, "humanity" – as the subject of this knowledge – would not only be liberated from its mythologically induced and maintained immaturity and reifying fear of the world. Humanity would also be able to dominant nature to meet its own developing needs. As Horkheimer and Adorno state, the essence of this enlightened knowledge is both the instrumental rationality of technology and the domination of nature and humanity. Such knowledge does not seek answers to questions that critique and point beyond the existing social status quo, e.g. questions of meaning, substance, truth, justice, life, suffering and death; nor is its methods directed by concepts, images, critical thinking or discourse. Such things as these are abandoned by enlightened thought as being anachronistically rooted in and a continuance of myth and pre-history. As the authors states, there is to be no unknown, no mystery, no uncontrolled transcendent "other", and thus, "no wish to reveal mystery" (Horkheimer 1972:5). Rather, such *techné* focuses on the given facts, particularity, and the existing reality and probability of what is, for the purpose of "doing business", and its tools of research are number, formula, method and function. Such positivistic, technological knowledge thus became and continues to be a means of capitalistic social production and reproduction. The ultimate "subject" of this intended liberating yet technological enlightened knowledge was and is the bourgeoisie, i.e., the capitalist class, which makes up 1–5% of the population of the world. Those who own and/or control the means and relations of economic production control this technological knowledge and its use for the domination not only of nature but of humanity itself for the purpose of maximizing their profit. The betrayal of the Enlightenment and its intent of emancipating humanity from fear, ignorance and domination is rooted in this positivistic narrowing down of knowledge to technology out of fear of the unknown, which thereby becomes a powerful instrument of the capitalist class domination of both nature and the working class – in both body and mind.

The Disenchantment of the World

The Enlightenment's program, according to Horkheimer and Adorno, was to rid the world of animism; of the hylozoistic unknown "other," of Gods and spirits that give form and meaning to the inanimate objects of this world. It was deemed that such superstitious belief in unknown essences, qualities and beings that lie behind and yet in nature is what kept humanity trapped in childlike fear and alienating submission to the natural and social forces that claimed control of these forces, i.e. the magicians, the seers, the myth makers, the priests, philosophers, the kings and princes. The scientific knowledge sought by the Enlightenment was not understood to be "the crowing glory of a spiritual world" as it was for Hegel (1967:76), but a knowledge that could control/dominate a disenchanted world to meet the needs of humanity. All quests for meaning beyond such instrumental use of the objects of the natural and human/social worlds were abandoned. Nature was now understood to be nothing more than inanimate objects that were to be known through human analytic research and use. Such instrumentalized scientific knowledge becomes irrevocable and absolute as all things natural and human become its objects.

Projection

All former questions of substance, of the inherent meaning of things if not of life itself, of human fears and hopes, are now reducible to the systematic answer that such things are nothing in and of themselves but are mere projections of the human subject. As expressed in his *Critique of Pure Reason*, Immanuel Kant's (1929) attempt to make room for and thereby salvage faith in the face of this continual and victorious onslaught of enlightened scientific knowledge gave expression to this indomitable progression of the Enlightenment and the increasing antagonistic bifurcation of human experience. As Horkheimer and Adorno state, this development of the Enlightenment is *"totalitarian."* Such a statement, however, is still abstract as it hides the fundamental question of the "subject" of this development; *"cui bono"* – for whom and to what end is this science an irrevocable tool of production?

Number

As matter now became understood as a chaotic multiplicity of forms, with no inherent meaning or purpose, knowledge would be attained through this multiplicity's *quantitative* calculation and organization toward unity and identity. "Number became the canon of the Enlightenment" (Horkheimer & Adorno 1972:7). Everything including humanity itself becomes reducible to the abstraction of number. Individuality, difference and uniqueness are leveled. Through the subsumption/reduction of all things to number and ultimately to the unity of one, the particular object or being loses its identity as it is absorbed into an abstract collectivity of unanimity or identity. The Enlightenment and the bourgeois society that it reflects and reproduces is thus ruled by the harmonizing abstraction of "equivalence." Anything that is not quantifiable or reducible to fact, number and statistical analysis is considered to be an "outlier", an illusion, narrative, or literature.

Dialectics of Myth and Enlightenment

As Horkheimer and Adorno state, the program of the Enlightenment and the development of modern science is the cancellation of all myth, which thereby gives expression to the self-repetitiveness of nature. The mythical, reified, and universalizing expression of experience is exploded by the systematically vigorous and unrelenting empirical scientific research and calculations. However, the Enlightenment's principles of unity, universality, the beginning differentiation between subject and object resulting in the subjective influence and/or control of objectivity are already contained in the development of myth, through ritual and magic. The rationalizing, universalizing process of explaining events and experiences in life is historically expressed: From Animism to Magic to local epics to national myths to pre-Socratic cosmologies to religious theologies to metaphysics and to philosophic categories, e.g. *logos*. The development of the Enlightenment is rooted in the universalizing progression of mythology, in which every former specific mythological expression is negated by another as being only a errant belief. Ultimately, the experience of life is bifurcated in this development as the ultimate meaning, truth and reality of creation – the Logos – is separated from the multifarious objects and beings of creation. The world of things, i.e. matter, becomes subjected to God, Spirit, the Logos and ultimately to humanity, who, as religiously expressed in Judaism and Christianity, is created in the image of God and has been commissioned by God to dominate nature. It is in this development of mythology into the legitimization of domination that myth turns with fatal necessity into Enlightenment. It is also by this same principle of fatal necessity that the Enlightenment itself becomes mythological.

Alienation of the Human "Subject"

Through such domination, humanity becomes further alienated from the "object" that it dominates – both nature and the "self." The knowledge and science of such objective manipulation and control thereby become tools of domination, producing and reproducing such domination *ad infinitum* in accordance with the interests and needs of the imperious subject. Everything that is deemed the material of such domination is united and identified by its sameness as "object." The "subject", spirit, reason is identified and known by its power of dominance over any and every other. Objects – matter – are identified by their shared lack of such power and reason; the undifferentiated unity of meaningless, interchangeable matter and utility. The multitudinous qualities of inanimate and animate objects are now reduced to their use by the dominate subject, who thereby becomes the creator of the objects meaning and purpose. As Horkheimer and Adorno state, the modern industrial development of technology and the exploitation of natural and human resources first required the advancement of an instrumental rationality that divided and reified Being into the dualistic realms of spirit and world, idea and nature, subject and object.

A corollary development of this process of Enlightenment is that human beings pay for the evolvement of the abstract and isolated autonomous self/

Ego through its increasing alienation from of the objective "other" by means of the Ego's exploitation and domination of it. Thus, the experience and dialectical notion of human "empathy" for the other – the ability to "take the role of the other", to share discursively in the other's suffering or joy and thereby be able to enter into solidarity with the other in their experience – has to be taught today to students (The Lanthorn 2003:1). As Horkheimer (1978a:18) states, it is only though such empathy or "shared suffering" that the socially created, enlightened walls of separation if not antagonism between subject and object, spirit and matter can be broken down.

The program of the Enlightenment sought to free humanity from the mythic power of fate and retribution and the reified cyclical understanding of life – the myth of eternal repetition. However, in its attempt to negate myth, the Enlightenment reproduced in scientific and technological form the very same imprisonment of humanity to the reified laws of immanence and repetition, which are the principles of mythology itself. With the world now being understood to be a meaningless plethora of objects that are ruled by the mechanical and thus knowable eternal laws of nature, which are then replicated by the "meta-nature" of modern technological and computerized society, humanity becomes locked into an a-historical, mythological repetitive cycle of cybernetic system imperatives that must be followed for the sake of its own "survival." What was different and unknown, and thus out of human control, is now scientifically objectified, harmonized, and mastered. There is now nothing new nor different under the Sun (Ecclesiastes 1:9b). All is known and under control, or will be in the near future. This is the reifying and deadly meaning of the modern notion of "progress." What fate was for myth, abstraction accomplishes for the Enlightenment: it completely levels and equates all forms of objective difference. The world and thus humanity, which is now created in the image not of God but of its meaningless natural object, is frozen in a repetitive cycle with no hope of qualitative change or transcendence to something other than what is the case.

Enlightenment becomes the modern form of mythology, and positivistic science becomes the modern, albeit far more precise and systematic, form of the old magic, which teaches humanity how to conform and thereby survive by appeasing the hidden powers of the existing status quo. As stated above, Marx identified this hidden power of modern civil society in both its mythological and social scientific form, as the "Medusa head" and capitalist class dominated production and reproduction process for the ever-increasing maximization of its own profit and power. Through the scientific and rational equalization of all things so that there is no unknown difference or "other" to fear, nothing is identical with *itself* any longer. By means of the principle of equivalence, human beings lose their unique identity and autonomy and are absorbed into a false and oppressive collectivity. The enlightened, free subject of modernity has become little more than a replaceable automaton in the technological production and reproduction process of civil society. This development is not a return to the barbarism of old, according to Horkheimer and Adorno (1972:13), but a new, enlightened form of "the triumph of repressive equality." It is the continual triumph of this enlightened myth or metaphysics of positivism that has produced the new forms of barbarism in the 20th and now 21st centuries.

Mass Culture

This alienating, dehumanizing, objectivating and enslaving development of a "one-dimensional" positivistic Enlightenment, which has become a tool in the continued reproduction of the antagonistic capitalistic social totality that is now being "globalized" through world financial and political institutions as well as militarily, is further reproduced, reinforced and legitimated by a supporting ideology, i.e. false consciousness, manufactured by modern mass culture. This is accomplished not only through the constant bombardment of commodity and service advertisements, movies/videos, television programs, "popular" magazines and music disseminated through the mass media. The invasion and socialization of the human "life-world" – now seen as nothing more than a market place for the advertisement and selling of the insidious "system" of capitalist class interests – also takes place by means of the continued cybernetic leveling of language to the mechanics of "signals" as well as through the instrumentalization of various other aesthetic, religious, and philosophical forms. This continuing modern social dynamic toward a "totally administered," cybernetic future society has been analyzed quite profoundly and positivistically in the structural functionalist theory of Talcott Parsons and in the autopoietic system theory of Niklas Luhmann.

Economic Basis

As Horkheimer and Adorno assert, the scientific act of abstraction, which is expressive of the dualistic notion of subject and object, is concretely grounded in the very real distance in the economic production process between the master/owner/subject and the final commodity/object that is mediated by the workers in civil society. There is a reciprocity between the idea and theory of domination and its actual systematic occurrence in society. Those that are considered to be the "subjects" of the socially created structure and system of the status quo, i.e., the capitalist class, are the ones that establish, define, maintain and develop the class system of exploitation and domination. The lower classes thereby learn not only to honor and respect their authorities in the capitalist class but also learn how to subject themselves to the established system for the purpose of survival. In a social system of domination, a social Darwinistic "authoritarian personality" (Adorno 1950) becomes an almost endemic necessity for the purpose of survival. Issues of truth, of right and wrong are defined by the capitalist class interest in the maintenance and furtherance of the given system of exploitation, to which the masses accommodate themselves. Questions of meaning and transcendence or standards for action other than what is socially established and normalized are tabooed, e.g. questions of God and the nation (Horkheimer 1978a:27).

The essential liberational and humanizing intent of the Enlightenment, to educate humanity – to lead humanity out of ignorance to knowledge/wisdom, out of slavery to freedom, out of fear and submission to what is toward personal sovereignty and social solidarity through the creation of a better future peaceful society – is betrayed by its own fear of the unknown and its transmutation into an instrument of exploitation and domination. As Horkheimer and Adorno state, Enlightenment is mythic terror of the unknown other radicalized. This fear is combated through the bracketing out of all otherness as mythological chimera, which thereby gives primacy to the positivistic categories of the immanence and the equivalence of given objective reality. Enlightenment is thereby transformed into a technological rationality and the instrumentalization of existence, which becomes the theory and praxis of domination.

According to Horkheimer and Adorno, myths give expression to self-repetitive nature, which is the essence of the symbolic. In terms of the theologian Paul Tillich (1957:41–43), a close friend and colleague of Horkheimer and

Adorno, a symbol points beyond itself to that which is other and more than what is, while yet participating in that transcendent otherness. In this case, a symbol not only points beyond itself to that which is other, but also by means of the symbol itself brings that otherness into present existence. Unlike Tillich's transcendent notion of symbols, for the critical theorists, the symbol by its very nature reifies the other in its relationship to existence, which too is frozen in time. This is the eternal repetitiveness of symbols and myths and thus, of nature itself. This mythological and symbolic repetitiveness is shattered by the Jewish creation story in Genesis and through Judaism's prohibition of making any images or names of God. The Jewish creation story introduces history, change, and purpose into the relationship between the sacred and the profane, God and creation. This religious story expresses a radical distinction between creation and God as its totally "Other", who cannot be absorbed into or identified with creation in any fashion. A negative, dialectical, historical, yet prophetic, Messianic and eschatological relationship between creation and its God now is expressed in Judaism's notion of a nomadic, moving, becoming God that cannot be seen face to face – one may only see the back of God (Exodus 33:18–23) as God is moving purposefully away from the now into the future – or known and thus, possessed and controlled by existence.

The mythological notions of the transcendent "other" of nature, of the sacred or God, are the continuance of one of the pre-animistic religious notions, that of *"mana."* *Mana* is understood to be the dark, unknown and terrifying animate spirit that is behind yet in inanimate nature. This notion is not a fetish or projection of humanity but an expression of the very real power of nature in relationship to human beings. As Horkheimer and Adorno assert, it is from this dialectical experience of nature that the frozen divisions between animate and inanimate, sacred and profane, spirit and nature, subject and object began. Unlike the bourgeois conception of this division that originates due to the consciousness of the Ego, the critical theorist's materialistically invert this notion and understand the division to arise out of inanimate nature itself.

It is also from this experience of that which transcends existing reality that words, concepts, and language are derived as they seek to give expression to and thereby control the surprising if not terrifying dialectical experience of this transcendent other in nature itself. "Through the deity, language is transformed from tautology to language" (Horkheimer & Adorno 1972:15). An object's *name* is derived from the experience of this transcendence in nature itself, which is more than what was previously known of the existent. Myth is the expression of this repetitive relationship between that which is and its transcendent "other." The "fatal necessity" of enlightenment within mythology continued to separate these two realms from each other to the point of creating a division of labor between this world under the sway of reason and science and the fantastic sacred world expressed in myth, poetry, story.

Yet, the power and terror of *mana* is not just of an unknown, transcendent realm but is made into a terrifying tool of social control as well, wielded by the society's power elite and dominant class. The unknown and substantial *mana* becomes an instrumentalized means of social class domination and punishment for the lower classes and non-conformists via religious authorities, police and the court systems. It becomes further translated into the "invisible hand" not only of the economic market now but of the system imperatives of the capitalist social totality that becomes concretely developed through the military, Homeland Security Departments, Patriot Acts, Total Information Awareness Computer spy systems, etc. In all of this, the *mana* or power of nature and of its social agents becomes the governing norm of society to which all people and classes must acquiesce. Thus, the eternal, repetitious cycle of nature that is made into a concrete expression of the power of the sacred becomes the rhythm of technology and labor as well as the permanence of the dominant social class who are the authorities of this system of domination. The scientific and technological mimesis of nature, including the instrumentalization of the modern representatives of *mana*, e.g. bourgeois aesthetics and privatized religion in the service of the status quo, does not create a social totality expressive of personal autonomy and social solidarity. Rather its creates a society based on a false and repressive collectivity whose entire goal is the production of conformity for the sake of personal survival and social stability. This is what Horkheimer and Adorno call the irrationality of what has become of reason – its instrumentalization in the form of technology and the social class domination of the status quo.

Words, concepts, thought, language itself are also instrumentalized by this positivistic process of enlightenment into a system of signs and mathematical formula expressive of the power arrangements of the status quo, as the *noumena* – from which language arose – is now bracketed out as being superfluous. Through the theoretical and practical division of labor in modern society, the masses are socialized, incorporated and sealed into their own systematically produced alienation and exploitation. Out of a radicalized fear of the mythical "otherness" of mana, of the sacred, gods, transcendence, of *"kairos"* rather than *"chronos"*, and thus, of the unknown, the enlightenment and its positivistic science abstractly negated any and all "otherness" outside of what is naturally and socially given and established. The Enlightenment turns into mythology itself as it forces people anew into the eternal repetition and domination of what is the case through the metaphysics of positivism. "In both the pregnancy of the mythical image and the clarity of the scientific formula, the everlastingness of the factual is confirmed and mere existence pure and simple expressed as the meaning which [enlightenment] forbids" (Horkheimer & Adorno 1972:27).

Thus, the positivistic mythology of given "facts" and the corollary, necessary ideology of social Darwinism legitimate as being immutable the social antagonisms of modern capitalistic society, e.g., the antagonism between the various classes, races, genders, ages, nations, between the individual and the collective, between the religious and secular, etc. Thus, with no alternative to the status quo and thereby losing or never having hope for anything other than what is, individuals are socialized to survive in the midst of such an antagonistic social totality through conformity to what is; to "fit in to" as best they are able to the status quo; to become a "cog" in social machinery of production. Such acquiescence of the individual to the established antagonisms of the capitalist social totality is thus considered to be not only natural but also the only rational and right choice. Any alternative even suggested to this method of self-survival in the name of achieving autonomy and the good life is disparaged as being irrational and regressive. However, if such foolishness begins to gather adherents and is seen as threatening the status quo, the survival imperatives not only of the individual but of the social system itself kick in to invalidate if not destroy the alternative. Like the circle that protected the magician into which the threatening powers of the enemy could not enter, so functions the system imperatives for survival of the cybernetic, technological society and culture of capitalist class domination. "By subjecting the whole of life to the demands of its maintenance, the dictatorial minority guarantees, together with its own security, the persistence of the whole" (Horkheimer & Adorno 1972:31). The exchange for such conformity and self-alienation is the arbitrarily decided equivalence of having one's material needs possibly satisfied based on one's class position in the production process.

How then can this renewed and normalized barbarism of the enlightened, scientific, modern society be resisted? The *petitio principii* of the critical theory is that social liberation and the development of a more human society is founded on enlightened thought. However, such enlightenment and the social institutions created through it contain within themselves their very opposite, the seeds of its own destruction. This is the inherent dialectic of enlightenment, upon which such enlightened thought must reflect so as to prevent the flipping over of such thought into a new, modern form of barbarism. The primary reason for the enlightenment flipping over into the myth of positivism was the fear of the truth, which paralyzes the entire human project of enlightenment and liberation. It is a "fear of social deviation", from leaving the facts that have been socially created by the dominant social powers of science, economic pursuit of profit, advertising ideology, and political legitimization and reification of the existing status quo, and which are culturally promulgated. In such a society, any critique or attempt to negate the "facts" is condemned as being taboo, irrational, a violation of social norms and values, and thus, "condemns the spirit to increasing darkness" (Horkheimer & Adorno 1972:xiv). This fear and its resulting conformity to a reified, dominated, dehumanized and alienating social system is a "sickness." The language and the categories of this sick society cannot be used in an attempt to create a better future society. To do so merely conforms to the sickness and furthers it in the name of reform.

To overcome this tragedy of humanity, the Enlightenment must reflect critically on itself. The work that needs to be done is not the conservation of the past, of historically conditioned traditions, rituals, institutions, etc., but "the redemption of the hopes of the past" (Horkheimer & Adorno 1972:xv). What is happening is the betrayal of cultural and its human values and hopes/longings in the name of economic progress in the production of more and more commodities. Humanity thereby becomes itself such a dead and meaningless commodity. What it means to be human and thus, humanity as such, is no longer the subject and thereby purpose of the system, structures, and production of society. The elite capitalist class, which controls the means and relations of societal production, has become the contemporary social subject. The iron logic and necessity of such progress becomes real historical human regression. Such positivistic progress in science and its modern systems of social domination and production have become the modern metaphysics, "an ideological curtain behind which the real evil is concentrated;" (Horkheimer & Adorno 1972:xv) the evil that alienates, desensitizes, dehumanizes, exploits, kills, ideologically distorts enlightenment so that the masses acquiesce and thereby perpetuate their own destruction.

II.

In his inaugural address upon his becoming the third Director of the Frankfurt Institute for Social Research, Max Horkheimer (1993:1–14) stated the tasks of the Institute's endeavor, which has become known as the Critical Theory. The task of the critical theory was the investigation of

> the contemporary version of the oldest and most important set of phi-losophical problems: namely, the question of the connection between the economic life of society, the psychical development of individuals, and the changes in the realm of culture in the narrower sense (Horkheimer 1993:11).

The Institute's research was to focus on the old philosophical question of the relationship between the Universal and the particular, the Idea and the reality, Reason and existence, only now reformulated to express the conditions of modernity. As Horkheimer (1993:14) stated, the driving and guiding force of the critical theory was its unyielding determination "to serve the truth." Within the critical theory, truth was and is not conceived in terms of metaphysical absolutes but rather means the concrete, particular realization of the Idea, of Reason for the highest possible attainment of human need satisfaction, happiness and freedom for all within the productive capabilities of the existing social totality.

Unlike the metaphysical approaches to such questions in the past, the critical theory *inverted* its analysis materialistically to address this relationship from the side of the existing socio-historical reality. The critical theory scrutinizes the dynamic inter-relationship between a society's productive base structures, its cultural development, and the conditions of the psyche of individuals in the various social classes. In the socio-historical context of the development of capitalist civil society, this translates into critically investigating the causes of the systematic class antagonism that has created and continues to unfold the horrifying state of emergency as described above. In terms of the dialectical relationship between Reason and existence, one fundamental task of the critical theory is to expose the social forces that produce, reify, legitimate, and perpetuate the social antagonism between Reason and reality, between the social classes, races, genders, etc. Such interdisciplinary, scientific analysis and identification of the forces of social domination is the dialectical catalyst for the revolutionary purpose of the critical theory, which is the negation of the antagonism for the possibility of the creation of a better, more just, equitable, good, happy and shalom-filled future society. A fundamental element in the theory's service of the truth in the revolutionary struggle for a better future society, particularly for the first generation of critical theorists, was the liberational truth content of religion. This was particularly true for Horkheimer's critical theory of society and religion, to which I know turn.

The Class Formation of Religion

According to Horkheimer, religion can be either a liberating human expression of critique of the existing conditions of life and of hope for a better future society, or it can function as a conservative, reactionary force of social integration and legitimization of the existing status quo. Religion is a human creation, the content of which is conditioned by one's location in the class hierarchy of the given society. As Horkheimer states, neither the socially dominant, capitalist representatives of civil society's base structures or of its cultural realm give any critical expression to the exploitation and suffering of the masses. Such complaint is voiced by the society's poor and dispossessed, and with their critique develops the critical religious and eschatological idea of eternity. The idea of eternity, according to Horkheimer (1978a:111), "manifests itself with greater purity and sublimity in the most naïve, the most crudely sensuous hope, than in the most spiritual metaphysics and theory." It is this earthy and raw type of religious complaint against social injustice and the resulting hope of an eternity, expressed in Christian form as the resurrection of the dead, a Last Judgment, the New Creation of God – in which the innocent victims of the injustice and horror of this world can receive justice, that dialectically contains a critical, materialistic potential for the praxis of social change and human liberation.

Such religious, dialectical materialism is not the approach to nor the purpose of the society's official religious theorists' expression of eternity, which has been stripped of its critical human and social content and made into an abstraction; a myth that negates and rationalizes the notion of eternity's condemnation of the unjust social totality from which it arises. In bourgeois deistic terms, the socially critical notions of God and eternity become completely separated from human history. The notion of God becomes now not merely transcendent to the natural and social worlds, but totally emptied of any concrete socio-historical substance or relevancy, e.g., the cries of the innocent victims of the horror produced by nature, society, and history. Such nominalistic disemboweling of the originally critical social concepts of God and eternity leaves this world in the hands of the dominant, capitalist class, who thereby have filled in these notions with the standards and practical expectations that legitimate the exploitive capitalist system. Walter Benjamin (1996:288–291) described this same social process in terms of a competition between two "religions:" capitalism itself and Christianity. According to Benjamin, the religion capitalism – which is pure cult without any dogma – has attached itself parasitically to the history of Christianity in Western civilization. In so doing, the capitalist class has replaced not only Christianity's history but also its critical, liberational, Messianic, eschatological hope and praxis for a better future society with its own legitimating ideology and exploitive history. The critical voice and inspiring hope of such a prophetic and eschatological religion for anything other than what is thereby becomes eliminated. All that remains and is religiously hallowed is the "iron cage" of a systematically class dominated present. In terms of the neo-conservative, right-wing Hegelian Francis Fukuyama (1992), such a parasitic assimilation of Christianity into the cybernetic service of capitalism is part of the system that brings about "the end of history" in the form of a totally administered, capitalist dominated class society. It also legitimates the bourgeois, or capitalist as being "the last man" – the pinnacle of humanity's historical development.

Psychic Elaboration

According to Horkheimer (1972:58), the ambiguity of religion is a consequence of this antagonistic society, since the entire content of religion is derived from "the psychic elaboration of earthly data," which is produced, experienced, understood, and systematically reinforced by the structures of a class society. However, in this psychic projection of social class position and the resulting experience of life, the dominant class's religion and their "interests" become an objective force of the existing society itself, which dialectically turns around and influences the development of the human psyche as well as the entire social totality. Thus, as a fundamental form of mediation of the society's class domination and coercion to conformity, religion in the human psyche becomes an independent, specific power, which can lead people to conform to or resist the existing social conditions. It is in the tri-fold, dialectical relationship between the foundational economic mode of production, the cultural/religious forms and institutions that are thereby created, and the human psyche that religion obtains its potential liberational, critical, good quality, as well as its reactionary, pattern maintenance function. It is in the historical context of this dialectical relationship between these three realms of the modern antagonistic social totality of capitalism that Horkheimer's critical theory of religion is developed.

Thoughts on Religion

Horkheimer's dialectical theory of religion is not treated in a positivistic manner as an isolated, particular theme that is the focus of only one of his many theoretical works. Rather, as a fundamental element of his entire critical theory of society, his critique of religion is expressed in most of his writings and interviews. However, it was in his 1935 essay entitled *Thoughts on Religion* that Horkheimer (1972:129–131) gave precise expression to the inherent dialectic and thus, ambiguity of religion as well as to his materialist critical theory of religion. As he states, religion is understood to express different, transcendent yet very concrete and historical values. Religion is the cultural realm that possesses different norms, e.g., love, justice, peace, solidarity, hope, mercy, truth, than those of either nature or society. Religion, thus, contains the voice of accusation against the worldly conditions that produce the antithesis of these values as experienced by the masses of humanity for countless generations. Since these religious values were not experienced in the natural or social worlds, they were thought to exist in a transcendent place, e.g., heaven, or with a transcendent God.

According to Horkheimer, in counter distinction to people's experience of injustice and oppression, suffering humanity's religious projection of justice, truth, righteousness, etc., to a transcendent God originally served a critical and negative function. However, as Horkheimer asserts, it was Christianity in both its Catholic and Protestant forms that perverted religion from expressing the critical ideal of justice – an ideal which according to materialism can never be identified with reality – into a religious harmonization of this ideal with the existing power structures of the status quo. Christianity, in its modern bourgeois religious/Constantinian form, gave up its prophetic/Messianic function of social critique and took on the positive function of legitimating the domination of the socially powerful class in the form of the State. This turn over from its negative function to a positive one expresses the inherent dialectics and ambiguity of religion.

The Ideology of Nation and Religion

Horkheimer asserts that just as there is the *economic* base structure of bourgeois society that does not change, i.e., the exploitive relations of production, so there are also certain *cultural* principles of the society that are guarded equally against any change. Throughout his writings, he gave expression to the developing ideological relationship between the two fundamental notions of domination in bourgeois society: religion and the bourgeois nation-state. According to Horkheimer, religion enters into a historical conflict with the bourgeois nation on the essential issue of whether it will act in a structural functionalist manner, in which it inculcates pattern maintenance and thereby legitimates the State's authority and the society's antagonism, or whether it will resist such an antagonistic State and become the voice of social change on behalf of the oppressed and exploited. Already in his *Notes of 1926–1931*, Horkheimer (1978a:27–28) exposed the reactionary quality of a "positive" religion that performs a legitimating, cybernetic function of social control in bourgeois society. According to Horkheimer, the bourgeois nation and religion serve the same master – capitalism, the exploitive social system in which the collectively produced surplus value of human labor is privately appropriated/stolen by the ruling class.

For bourgeois society, the concepts of religion and the nation are considered sacred and are thus placed under the ban of taboo since they are fundamental, ideological tools for the domination of the masses by the ruling elite. As Freud (1950:18) explains, that which is labeled as taboo is considered to be something ineffable and unapproachable yet experienced as extremely real, and is thereby expressed in the negative terms of prohibitions. These prohibitions are not derived from the cultural realms of religion or morality. These socially constructed prohibitions appear to have no known foundation for their existence but are nevertheless generally accepted by the members of the society. This unknown origin of the taboo prohibition, such as that applied to the concepts of God and nation, corresponds to the hidden antagonistic mode of capitalist social production and reproduction process, i.e. Marx's image of the "Medusa's head" that hides behind the veil of the social facts and cultural ideology of capitalism.

A Collective Ideology

Through these religious and nationalistic notions, the social domination of the ruling class is legitimated and made into a national, collective ideology in which the individual finds his or her identity. This ideological identity formation dynamic can be seen quite clearly in the recent patriotic and religious fervor in the USA since the horrific, retaliatory strikes against the globalization of capitalism on September 11, 2001. Through these tabooed totems and their supportive ideological relationship, the psyche of the individual is incorporated as a dynamic force into the process of its own social domination. Thus, these notions of the nation and religion are to be taken with the utmost seriousness. As Horkheimer (1978a:28) states, if these sacred social structures are criticized, the person doing the critiquing will quickly become "personally acquainted with the very direct interest capitalism takes in the inviolability of the concepts."

Academic Freedom or Treason?

Since the attacks of September 11, 2001, the question has been raised once again about just where academic freedom ends and misconduct – or even treason – begins. In terms of Horkheimer's analysis, the critique of the hallowed, totemic social structures of religion and nation is the paradigm for such judgment. Jonathan Knight of the American Association of University Professors in Washington, DC, states that the intensity of attacks on academic freedom have increased since September 11 (The Daily Vidette 2005). The most recent demonstration of the inviolability of these system totems against any form of critique has been the social and academic denunciation of Ward Churchill, an American Indian activist and scholar who has been at the University of Colorado as a Professor for the past 26 years.

After television networks characterized the attacks of September 11, 2001 against the World Trade Center and Pentagon as unprovoked and senseless, Churchill wrote an essay wherein he stated that the attacks were the logical, retaliatory result against long-standing U.S. foreign policies. Also, in response to the one-sided, "romanticized," and thus, diversionary focus of the media and U.S. Administration on the horrific deaths of those who died in the World Trade Center, Churchill switched the focus from the personal tragedies of the individuals to the imperatives of the capitalist system in which these people worked; imperatives, which for Churchill and many others, were the cause of the attacks and their deaths. Churchill also stated that the World Trade Center victims should have known the violent consequences of their role in driving U.S. foreign policies, which he said have killed hundreds of thousands of Iraqi children. Churchill reminded his readers that some of these victims in the World Trade Center functioned as "technocrats" in the globalizing system of capitalist world trade that was one of the fundamental causes of the retaliatory attack. To make his point, he likened these white-collar technocrats in their bureaucratic roles to Adolf Eichmann in the Third Reich. For daring to transgress the hallowed boundaries of God and Country in the midst of a national catastrophe and to identify their exploitive history and policies in the service of capitalism as the cause of September 11th attacks, Churchill had to resign as Chair of the Ethnic Studies department and defend himself against calls for his being fired from the university by members of the academic community as well as by Colorado Governor Bill Owens (Clark 2005). Colorado lawmakers even suggested reducing the University's funding, unless action against Churchill was taken (USA Today 2005).

As the inherent contradictions and barbarism of the dominant, globalizing neo-liberal form of capitalism becomes more and more exposed and thereby less stable, the authoritarian enforcement of capitalism's system imperatives and its legitimating totems becomes more insidious and brutal.

Functional Conception

Horkheimer further expresses the pragmatic, functional conception of religion by illustrating its change of importance in the historical development of bourgeois society. As he states, atheism was tolerated in the nineteenth century because of its strategic and functional use in helping the bourgeoisie break the religious legitimization of the traditional feudal society. Such atheistic critique, however, is no longer tolerated in the modern capitalist society now under the domination of the bourgeoisie. Such critical atheism has the capability of exposing the hidden exploitive reality of the capitalist social system and its structures, which bourgeois religion and culture is to obscure and protect. Particularly in post-September 11 US society, where the official yet abstract line of demarcation has been declared by President G. W. Bush, "Either you are with us, or you are with the terrorists," (Bush 2001) such anti-bourgeois, anti-capitalistic atheism can carry a harsh social and legal threat if not punishment. As Horkheimer (1978a:28) states, the person who criticizes these ideological concepts of religion and the nation "lays hands on (the society's) very foundation."

This functionalistic service of the positive world religions to the given social system of which it is a part is what Horkheimer (1978a:123) calls the "profound pragmatism at the core of world religions, the lack of illusions." This is the transparency of positive religion, i.e., its lack of any real substance and depth that seeks to critically address the injustice of the given, capitalist social system for the purpose of envisioning and creating a more just, rational, free, and humane future society. The world religions' pragmatic lack of illusions expresses religion's real lack of hope for anything other than what is as it has capitulated to the historical masters of the world; conformed to the facts of reality. As Horkheimer states, even the most sincere believers today have no illusions that the purpose of their religion is just such pragmatism, such realism, such pattern maintenance and conformity to the social status quo.

For Horkheimer (1978a:123) this "synthetic, artificial, manipulatory, and trashy" characteristic of world religions is why the form of religion has to change. Again, for Horkheimer, there is a dialectical tension between the form and content of reality that provides its historical dynamic and revolutionary potential. For Horkheimer's critical theory of religion, the anachronistic form of religion needs to be determinately negated in order to allow the dynamic revolutionary, emancipatory, and enlightening content of religion to be expressed in a new secular form of hope and motivation for the creation of a new future society. Horkheimer (1978a:123) expressed the dialectic nature of his critique of religion by saying that such religious conformity to the national systems of human domination "was least true for the poorest and most naive believers, and perhaps for Jesus of Nazareth." As Horkheimer (1978a:111) also stated twenty years earlier, the liberating, historically empowering, critical hope of eternity, for the totally Other, is to be found amongst this world's "wretched in their despair." Giving a new, relevant and secular voice to the religion of the poorest is the purpose of Horkheimer's critical theory of religion.

Modern Form of Animism

Through his critical theory, Horkheimer expressed another ideological aspect of religion as the projection of humanity's autonomy to other people, events, or to a similarly viewed divine will that is active in all worldly events. This is religion as fetishism, i.e., the religious attribution of humanity's strengths, abilities, hopes, etc., to a finite or infinite "other," which disables and alienates humanity from its historical potential. As such a projection, religion is understood to be independent of the human mind and thereby outside the critique of reason and science, which furthers the bourgeois division of labor between religion and science.

Horkheimer described this modern, fetishized religion as a form of animism. Due to their innocently suffering the socially created and maintained horror of poverty, hunger, homelessness, loneliness, alienation, exploitation, and death, the suffering masses themselves wish for and create a transcendent, divine other who will protect and save them from the hard, cruel reality of capitalist society. As Marx (1964:42) had stated a century before, tormented people themselves create their own assuaging yet illusory "opium" in the form of religion. As Horkheimer states, although a more adequate, critical and liberating understanding of people's innocent suffering is possible, an understanding which then could be turned into a social praxis to stop such socially created horror, the capitalist power elite, who are responsible for such suffering, make sure that nothing disturbs the animistic religious dreams of the masses.

Thus, on the psychological level, according to Horkheimer, religion is a survival mechanism – a projection of oppressed humanity's wish, desire, longing, hope of something totally other than what is – within an unjust, oppressive, and death creating society. On the sociological level, religion in capitalist society is used as a justification of violence and state terrorism.

Horkheimer (1978a:42; Mark 11:15–19) uses the biblical story of Jesus driving the moneychangers and sellers of doves – the sacrificial animal sold to the poor – from the Temple to illustrate his point. That Jesus took a whip and drove the moneychangers from the Temple is used distortedly as a legitimating rationale of the dominant class's use of violence to realize their goals or to maintain the social status quo. Yet, as Horkheimer (1978a:42) ironically states, "it is curious how rarely the purpose of the biblical act is discussed." By driving out the moneychangers and sellers of doves who cheated the poor, Jesus was destroying the religious legitimization for the continued exploitation of the poor by the religious system of his day. According to Horkheimer, this story of liberation is ideologically turned around to justify the continued exploitation of the poor by the capitalists. Such bourgeois religion and its morality, thus, sanctify the antagonistic class structure and horror of capitalist society by giving the rich and powerful the appearance of being religious and ethical according to the status quo of capitalist society. Those on the bottom of society – the proletariat, as well as those who seek the liberation of humanity from domination and who thus seek to overcome the injustice of capitalism – are seen as being irreligious and immoral for they resist and deny the divinely established and blessed laws of capitalist society. As Horkheimer (1978a:54) states, "bourgeois morality and religion are nowhere as tolerant as when they judge the life of the rich, and nowhere as strict as toward those that want to eliminate poverty."

The Future of Religion?

According to Horkheimer, the question of religion can be addressed unambiguously only when it has been freed of its ideological social function. In the antagonistic social totality of capitalism, religion takes sides and can be either good or bad according to Horkheimer's (1978a:163) analysis. Religion as a means of explanation, rationalization, pattern maintenance, and/or legitimization of life in society and history is religion in a bad sense; it is ideology, i.e., a socially created false consciousness. For the thinkers of the Bourgeois Enlightenment, particularly those in France, who understood religion in this bad sense to be the metaphysical and superstitious attempt to explain the unexplainable and thereby keep humanity in infantile servitude to the masters of the feudal first and second Estates, religion needed to be completely negated. Thus, religion became increasingly useless the more scientific reason explained the functioning of the natural world. Now, by the means of the myth of positivism, the modern, enlightened, administered society no longer needs religion as society itself has become self-sufficient. It is only in emergency situations, when the inherent contradictions of capitalist society cause the cybernetic system to break down, that contemporary society still returns to religion as an ideological form of social mystification, integration, and harmonization. According to Horkheimer, modern bourgeois society has experienced a failure of nerve and will in continuing the Bourgeois Enlightenment's revolutionary vision and project of creating a society that was autonomous and solidary, just, humane, and good. Modern bourgeois society has returned to the past form of this bad religion as its attempt to save itself from its own annihilation. However, as Horkheimer states, such a return to religion does not mean a belief or trust in God or anything transcendent of itself. Such a fearful return to an empty religious form is only an expression of the disbelief in and rejection of a better future.

Critical Theory of Religion

However, according to Horkheimer, there is another aspect of religion besides its structural, functionalistic role as bourgeois ideology of domination and social integration. Religion is also a concrete expression of human hope if not struggle for emancipation and justice. This is the good theory and praxis of religion. As Horkheimer (1978a:58) states, "in its symbols, religion places an apparatus at the disposal of tortured men through which they express their suffering and their hope. This is one of its most important functions." According to Horkheimer (1978a:58), "a respectable psychology of religion" is needed to differentiate between religion as the legitimization of the capitalist system and structure of society, and religion as the expression and longing for human emancipation. As he states, the religious, mythical form of humanity's cry against the world's injustice has to be transformed into a this-worldly, revolutionary praxis to overcome the causes of this injustice. This is the very purpose of Horkheimer's critical theory of religion. This sublimation of the truth content of religion – of humanity's cries and struggle for liberation, solidarity, happiness, redemption – from its inadequate, co-opted religious form is based on the historical fact that religion did not always ideologically distract people from such praxis. At times throughout history, religion functioned to expose and resist the injustice done to people and nature. These dynamic, religiously cloaked impulses for justice, truth, goodness, love, etc., that arose out of people's experience of the antagonistic and brutal "ways of the world," are still very much alive in modern society, albeit in a more secular form. As Horkheimer states, the life and praxis of the revolutionary can be such an expression.

Horkheimer's revolutionary critique of religion as ideology seeks to free religion's emancipatory impulses from its limited mythological and religiously distorted form that is created by and for the legitimization of the antagonistic economic mode of social production. This socially assimilated and thus distorted form and content of religion is what distracts humanity from its purpose and goal of realizing its psychic, social, economic, political, cultural, and historical emancipation. Such critique of religion illustrates the dialectical process of determinate negation as the obsolete and repressive form of religion is negated so as to allow the dynamic, emancipatory content of religion to migrate into the modern secular struggle for human enlightenment and emancipation. According to Horkheimer, the truth content of religion is found in its concern with and historical praxis for the liberation of humanity from all forms of oppression, injustice, and alienation, for socio-historical creation of a new, more just, free, reconciled, humane, peaceful future society.

Unlike the critical theory, the bourgeois critique of religion – that does not contain this goal of human emancipation – is a lie; a dirty trick that gives the appearance of concern for the religious content of humanity's liberation while enslaving people even further to the exploitation of the capitalist system. This lie is the social function of the church in bourgeois society, according to Horkheimer, as it ministers to and classifies the poor. As Horkheimer (1978a:59) states, "these days, Christianity is not primarily used as a religion but as a crude transfiguration of existing conditions." The most recent expression of this capitalistic distortion of Christianity is President G. W. Bush's "Faith Based Initiative" (Ott 2001:131–133).

Bourgeois Christianity

Through his appeal to the very ideals professed by Western civilization Horkheimer exposes the cruel lie of bourgeois Christianity which legitimates the very misery, despair, injustice, imprisonment, torture, and death of the innocent victims that its professed founder sought to negate. At the very beginning of his ministry, Jesus identified the concrete subject of his

prophetic and messianic praxis of announcing the coming of God's kingdom: the poor, the captives, the blind, the oppressed (Luke 4:18–19). The lie
of religion, particularly that of bourgeois Christianity, in modern capitalist
society is that this prophetic, Messianic, revolutionary, emancipatory character
of Christianity is compromised and thus, destroyed by it being made into a
soporific salve that dulls and soothes away the horror of existing conditions
in capitalism rather than being a dynamic force that seeks to determinately
negate these conditions. Through such class distortion of the content of religion, the concrete, historical and religious distinction between the oppressed
and innocent victims of society and their oppressors is thus erased. Quite
abstractly then, Jesus becomes the Messiah/Christ, the Savior of all people.
Through the class domination of the capitalist society and its ideological
process of abstraction, now all people can be justified in their life-style with
no concrete repentance or discipleship, as long as their actions are in accord
with the interests of the dominant, capitalist class. As Horkheimer states, in
this contemporary, capitalist society the very rich are thus also considered
especially devout persons.

The Seriousness of Religion

According to Horkheimer, religion is not taken seriously in capitalist society.
In this society, religion has a cybernetic, pattern maintenance function to
perform that helps keep the masses subservient in their own exploitation to
the antagonistic capitalist mode of social production. Since the critical, prophetic, Messianic, eschatological if not apocalyptic teeth of Christianity have
been knocked out by capitalism, bourgeois Christianity has become merely
another comforting support and justification for the systematic and structural
domination of the few over the many, the rich over the poor, the powerful
over the weak, the owners over the workers, the "wolves" over the "lambs"
(Isaiah 11:6). It is this compromising religious lie that grants religion a place
in modern, capitalistic society. As Horkheimer (1978a:91) states, it is also this
compromising lie that prevents the critical "implementation of religion" or
its "expedient abolition."

However, as Horkheimer states, this antagonistic, dehumanizing society
and its religion contradict the essential teachings of Christianity, which this
society professes as its foundational heritage. Horkheimer (1978b:439) states
that it was inevitable that the contradictory principle of Christianity to the

economic and social way of life in bourgeois/capitalistic society would be willingly sacrificed to the development of capitalism, as "the vulgar positivism of bare facts along with the worship of success" would be raised up as the highest truth. As Horkheimer states, the dominant intellectual and cultural concern over the past few centuries was not to expose this contradiction but to hide and mystify it. Through such evisceration and perversion of Christianity's dangerous prophetic and Messianic content, religion became compatible with any and all practices in capitalist society – which Horkheimer (1978b:440) called "this atheistic reality."

Due to Christianity's betrayal of its prophetic and Messianic content through its functional assimilation in the antagonistic capitalist social totality, Horkheimer held no hope for the church to become again as it was in its beginning a liberating agent of social change. Rather, Horkheimer (1972:130) asserted that the original dynamic and liberating content of religion had freed itself of its religious form and had taken on the historical, secular form of social praxis through lives of progressive people. Horkheimer (1972:131) states that as humanity develops historically, religion is something that is left behind as no longer needed. However, this historical negation of religion is not something abstract but is a determinate negation, for in this historical movement, so Horkheimer states, religion leaves its mark. Those desires, wishes, longings, and accusations that first gave rise to religion and the concept of God are not only negated but preserved and furthered as they shed their religious, spiritual form and become forces of a critical social theory and praxis for the creation of a more just and humane future society. According to Horkheimer (1978a:163), this living, progressive dynamic is the essence of good religion, which is the spiritual force and motivation that "sustains…the impulse for change, the desire that the [mythical] spell be broken, that things take the right turn. We have religion where life down to its every gesture is marked by this resolve." Thus, a truly progressive person takes the liberating truth content of religion and translates it into social action for "the happiness of people who come after them and for whom they know how to die" (Horkheimer 1972:130).

As Horkheimer (1972:130) states, "true discipleship" does not lead back to religion but to social praxis for the creation of a happier, freer and more rational future society expressive of human solidarity; a society for which such disciples know how to live and to die. Christians, Horkheimer (1972:130–131) states, who take the religious meaning of the love of one's neighbor seriously, may once again be called as they were originally to such praxis by the increasing barbarism of a monopoly capitalist society. This is even more so the case today as the antagonism and horror of capitalism are being imperialistically "globalized" by means of the neo-liberal programs of the International Monetary Fund, the World Bank, the non-democratic rulings and procedures of the World Trade Organization, and by war, e.g., the "war on terrorism" in Afghanistan, the Philippines, and of the US led invasion and occupation of Iraq. This transformation of the original religious negative, emancipatory content into a secular, revolutionary form of resistance and praxis for a better future society is the very heart of Horkheimer's critical theory of religion.

Second & Third Commandments

The fundamental and guiding notion of Horkheimer's critical theory of religion is the materialistic determinate negation of the second and third commandment of the Jewish Decalogue: the prohibition of making images and naming the Absolute. Adhering to this prohibition as well as to I. Kant's philosophical rejection of human reason knowing the noumenal, Horkheimer's dialectical theory of religion cannot identify the Absolute, the Good. According to Horkheimer, that which is evil primarily in the social sphere can be identified but the good cannot. The concept of evil also implies by its very nature its opposite and the action one could take to resist or counteract the negative. Thus, the critical theory of society and religion focuses on the negative. The negation of the negative is the only quality of the good that can be said or known. This is the teaching of the entire critical theory: to define the good by the evil that is to be negated. Through this method of negative dialectics, or "inverse theology," (Adorno 1999:67) the critical theory of society and culture seeks to avoid the dialectics of Enlightenment process inherent in the naming of anything as good.

It is in this that "the role of faith becomes central" for Horkheimer's (1978b:158) dialectical theory of religion. His notion of faith expressed in the concept of the unknown and ineffable Absolute however is not expressed as a positive dogma that is to be believed but as a longing that unites all people in the hope that the horror of history will not be the ultimate end of its innocent victims. The longing for this totally Other than what is is the materialistic determinate negation of the Jewish and Christian, prophetic and Messianic teaching of the coming reign of God into hope and longing and struggle for a better, more reconciled and just future society.

This longing for the totally Other than the world that is a socially and historically conditioned representation – and thus changeable – is the right granted to theology in Horkheimer's critical theory of religion. The critical theory of society and religion rests on the thought that the Absolute cannot be made into an object and that the theological assertion of the existence of God should be transformed into the longing that such a God exists who will not allow injustice to ultimately triumph over the innocent victims of society and history.

Secular Mimesis

Throughout the centuries, the church in both its Catholic and Protestant forms has removed from its teaching the danger that the prophets and the Messiah might have caused society so that the masses would not be tempted to imitate the radicality of their love, hope for the totally Other God, and desire for justice in solidarity with the socially disenfranchised. However, as Horkheimer (1978a:208) states, such mimesis of Jesus as the Messiah is "the core of Christian teaching," by which the life of the Christian is distinguished from life that imitates nature's aristocratic law of conformity to what is for the purpose of survival at all costs. Mimesis of the Messiah is the motive and spirit for Christian ethics. Such mimesis sets people free from the limitation to what is – the myth of positivism – as it seeks what is possible from the facts of the present with an eye toward a better future. The church and its theology have given up the emancipatory power of the negative, which can break the mythic spell of domination. As Horkheimer (1974:87) states, "when a doctrine hypostatizes an isolated principle that excludes negation, it is paradoxically predisposing itself to conformism." The lack of negation in any theory, be it religious, philosophical, or scientific, implicitly if not explicitly identifies the Ideal, e.g., that which is good and true, with reality. There is then no hope and no transcendence but only conformity to what is socially and historically created. This sacrifice of its foundational prophetic and messianic dialectical negativity of society which thereby constantly pushes toward a better, more humane, just, free, happy, and reconciled future society is what Horkheimer (1978a:219) calls the "weakness of theology."

This weakness is the ambiguity of religion itself, whose content in its Judeo-Christian form expresses both a revolutionary indictment of the existing society in the empowering hope for a better future society as well as the longing for absolute justice of the totally Other God, as well as a conservative if not reactionary sanctification of the existing social totality and its system of social domination. It is due to this ambiguity that Horkheimer seeks the determinate negation of the historical form of religion, i.e., its positive social form of institutional structure, dogmas, rituals, the role of priests and ministers, religious language, etc., which have become obsolete in the historical struggle for human emancipation so as to allow that religious prophetic and Messianic content that is still relevant in the existing socio-historical context to migrate into a new secular form. This new secular form of the emancipatory and thus negative content of religion is Horkheimer's critical theory of religion, which does not thereby become a new religion itself. As Horkheimer (1985:434) states, "the critical theory rests on the thought that the Absolute, that is God, cannot be made into an object." In a post-religious, post-metaphysical, positivistic society that is developing toward its fulfillment in a hermetically sealed, totally administered social totality, Horkheimer's entire critical theory becomes the secular heir of the critical, negative, emancipatory content of religion in the historical struggle for a better, more enlightened, just, and reconciled future society, in the light of and hope/longing for a totally Other who will not allow those who grind humanity's life into the dirt to ultimately be victorious over their innocent victims.

Chapter Twelve

Social Philosophical Reflections on the Concepts of Culture and Multiculturalism in the Context of Globalization

Kjartan Selnes

I want to present for you some thinking about culture and multiculturalism in the age of globalization. Particularly, I want to address how cultures have to change and develop in order to adapt themselves to the global process of modernization, and how cultures often have to fight to preserve what they find valuable in their own traditions and uniqueness. I will hardly surprise you with any sensational news about this, because so much has been said by so many scholars for such a long time. So, what I seek to do is in a more humble way to select, connect and combine some perspectives which I perceive as important and illuminating in this rather bewildering and noisy field of discourse. I will do this in a somewhat provocative and simplified manner. At least that is my intention.

Before starting to elaborate my points, I will list them as follows:

1. I am concerned about the fact that the big diversity of relatively unique and distinct cultures are under an enormous pressure from the leveling and homogenizing forces of a worldwide technological and commercial mass culture. That is:

The economical, informational and industrial globalization includes a thorough going cultural globalization. However, the question I will ask is: is there only a pressure towards making the whole world uniform and similar? At least we can see that globalization has created a stronger consciousness about the value and importance of diversity. In fact, some essential aspects of globalization stimulate both preservation and further creation of variety.

2. *Cultural imperialism* is a well-established term. If we look at the actual power structure in the world, it should not be difficult to characterize fundamental aspects of globalization as a kind of cultural imperialism. This entails a strong, one-sided pressure of one culture – Western civilization's – towards all the others. "The West over the Rest," as some phrase it. However, let me hasten to say that not everything in imperialism needs to be negative. There can be liberating, rationalizing and progressive elements in certain kinds of cultural imperialism. Of course, this depends upon the ideological content and the political strategies. I will say more about this later.

3. In the ecology of nature, biological diversity is considered of utmost importance for the vitality and creativity of the whole biosphere and of nature as a dynamic totality. Variety of species and ecosystems is considered to have an absolute value in itself, (of course, within certain limits). The dramatic decimation and reduction of species and forms of life is today considered the biggest danger for the balance in the global ecosystem as a whole. Could we extend this to the field of cultures? In my opinion: Yes! – and not only as a picturesque analogy.

4. To continue the parallel with nature and ecology, I will also discuss if it may have some meaning to talk about cultural pollution in analogy with pollution in the world of nature and biological systems. In this context, I am thinking of the sudden invasion of commodities, attitudes and mentalities into different cultures that, as a result, create alienation, anomie and conflicts. I am primarily thinking of the world wide commercial system of mass-production, advertising, entertainment and so-called "info-tainment," which aggressively invades every culture. The primary motive of this system is profit maximization and expanding markets of often rather artificial demands. As such this is a manipulative motive quite the opposite of being seriously concerned about the genuine and authentic needs of

peoples and cultures. I think the word *pollution* could be quite appropriate in this setting.

5. The ideas and ideals of universal progress, rationalization, modernization, humanization, enlightenment, liberty and global solidarity put strong demands on different cultures to modify and change. In this context then, the important thing is to make it happen on the positive and creative premises of their own traditions. Perhaps one also has to realize that quite often a lot of elements in some cultures are not worth survival and continuation at all.

6. The attitude of postmodernism and cultural relativism has brought some sensitivity and insights to the problematic project of stating a universal form of rationality and progress. However exaggerated to the extreme, this relativistic position must be considered rather absurd and untenable. Rational Science and Human Rights are not possible without the idea of an underlying intellectual universality in diversity: the universality of well argued knowledge and the universality of well argued values. The hope to succeed sometimes in reaching a cross-cultural consensus about the fundamentals of life is a regulative idea we by necessity cannot be without if we want a betterment of the global human condition.

Culture

I begin with some thoughts about the concept[s] of culture. The word culture, as it is used in different settings, is a very manifold and rather unclear term. All over the world, the term is strongly and frequently used in politics to legitimize and mobilize a multitude of interests and actions, and in this way often generates severe conflicts. We may suspect that exactly this blurring of the term makes it so well suited for political and demagogical manipulations by the ruling elite and by different kinds of ideological intelligentsia.

It is often said that this problematic situation for the term "culture" in Sociology and Social Anthropology is the same as for the word "energy" in Physics: Nobody can give a good definition of the term but nobody can manage without it. In one of the most authoritative and widespread university textbooks in Social Anthropology since the 1970s, called *New Perspectives in Cultural Anthropology*, Roger Keesing (1971) started his exposition of culture with the statement that

> The anthropological concept of 'culture' has been one of the most important and influential ideas in twentieth-century thought. The usage of 'culture' adapted by nineteenth-century anthropologists has spread to other fields of thought with profound impact...Yet, paradoxically, the notion of culture implied in such usage has proven too broad and too blunt for carving out the essential elements in human behavior.

To take another reference, the opening lines of a recently published book about culture by the well-known Oxford literary professor and cultural critic Terry Eagleton (2000:1) frankly states that

> Culture is said to be one of the two or three most complex words in the English language, and the term which is sometimes considered to be its opposite – nature – is commonly awarded the accolade of being the most complex of all.

I think this is valid for most modern languages. I also think it is really worthwhile to reflect on this condition, because it ought to be a large philosophical puzzle that we try to talk about something in the reality we experience and perceive to be very important, but we never succeed in creating clear concepts about it. Must we for ever live with this situation? In this case, I think so – more or less.

Let us take a quick look at the concept of culture as usually applied in the Social Sciences. I think the following short formulation catches the essence:

> Culture is learned patterns of thinking and behaving, which one generation transfers to the next generation in somewhat modified form.

This can be expressed in a little more elaborated form:

> Culture is composed of ideas, values, rules, norms, codes and symbols, which one generation inherits from the preceding generation and hands over to the next one with more or less alterations. Culture is a more or less ordered system of meaning and symbols, in terms of which social interaction is structured. Culture makes models for behavior.

All of this sounds very good and adequate until we try to identify and make descriptive demarcations between cultures or subcultures within a main culture. The problem is to identify and individuate one culture from another.

We don't need to delve deeper into definitional sophistication or subtleties here. Let me simply state my point. The tendency to reify cultures as something substantial and solid with rather rigorous borders has been and still is a worldwide tendency. Reflections upon the relation of cultures in the world – and subcultures within them – show us a quite fluid, gradualistic and continuous overlapping of different styles of thoughts, attitudes and behavioral habits. The reality of culture is much like that of other realities: full of floating shades and gradual continuities, where we with our concepts cut it up and try to put it into neat definitional boxes, but we never really catch it's meaning. Dynamic and fluid processes can never be adequately depicted in the static structures of concepts. As a saying goes: Cultures are not like islands scattered around in the ocean but more like the streams between them in the ocean.

The reason why people are so concerned with drawing and defining cultures as something with clear borders has to do with psychological needs for cultural and group identities, which create unity and clearly distinguish them from other groups in situations of conflicts and competition for scarce resources. There may be other reasons, but I only emphasize this one.

Globalization

I now turn to globalization, which of course also is an extremely multifarious and strongly debated concept today. It refers to the whole world becoming more and more interconnected economically, politically, culturally, technologically, and so on. The same kinds of institutions, technical equipment, consumer products and patterns of thinking and behaving are expanding to all the different countries and cultures. A process of homogenization and diminishing differences takes place, which consolidates the existing power structures in the world, for good and for bad. A vast multicultural world is becoming more and more a mono-cultural world. This is one dominant part of the globalization picture; a real and frightening picture in many respects, which we should strongly try to moderate and counteract.

I will not discuss here how bad or good the process of globalization may be considered in general, but concentrate my comments on the role of mass media and the global informational network, because of their enormous effects on our cultural and political consciousness. Globalization has created in a dramatic way a consciousness of the world as a whole. Through the modern media, the world has developed more and more in the direction of becoming one single place, principally visible to all people.

This extended visibility of the world is an extremely important feature of the globalization of our time. It opens the possibility for developing a kind of critical global conscience, a democratization of the responsibility for the world as a whole, and perhaps a global ethics.

The exercise of political power today is increasingly open to critical view, not only locally but also on a global scale. Actions such as military interventions, massacres and suppression of demonstrations in distant places are actions which take place in a new kind of mediated global arena: they are visible, observable, and capable of being witnessed simultaneously and repeatedly by millions of individuals around the world. The exercise of political power is thus subjected to a kind of global scrutiny, which simply did not exist before. Given the possibility of such scrutiny, political actions carry unprecedented risks and may expose a regime to international condemnation and to political and economic isolation.

The really revolutionary, contemporary change in this is the extent to which the media not only makes the world more visible and gives reports of events and actions on a worldwide scale, but that the global media in a fundamental way has become a main actor in creating and constituting political processes and current events. As a classical example, it has often been pointed out by media-analysts that the extensive and vivid coverage of the Vietnam War was to a considerable degree responsible for the strength and concerted character of the anti-war movement. Since World War II, the Vietnam War was the first major American military involvement overseas, which was covered in detail by television. More than that, in the world history of warfare, it was the first war with television continuously acting on the battlefield.

Another and somewhat different example of modern media as a powerful actor in world politics is the revolutionary upheavals in Eastern Europe in 1989, which shows the ways in which the media messages can stimulate and nourish collective actions by individuals located far from each other. It seems utterly unlikely that these revolutionary upheavals of 1989 would have occurred as they did – with breathtaking speed and with similar results in different countries – in the absence of extensive and continuous media coverage. Not only did television provide individuals in Eastern Europe with a flow of images of the West, portraying life conditions that contrasted sharply with their own, but it provided Eastern Europeans with a virtually instantaneous account of what was happening in their neighboring countries, as well as in neighboring cities or areas in their own country. Collective actions grew like a rolling snowball, and when the Berlin War fell on the night of November 9, the images of young people celebrating beneath the Brandenburg Gate and hacking at the wall with pickaxes were transmitted live around the world.

We could continue to mention a lot of more recent examples about everything from the disasters of the Aids epidemic and hunger catastrophes in Africa, to the situations of the aboriginal and indigenous populations around the world, the destruction of the rain forests, etc.

In the evening of September 11, 2001, while I sat in a village-like suburb in Norway and was writing this paper, I turned on the television. I was shockingly confronted with the apocalyptic horror of terror-attacks on the World Trade Center, New York and the Pentagon, Washington, and reports about reactions from all corners of the world. How the pictures of this vividly visualized nightmare – directly transmitted to billions of TV screens around the world. – will affect the minds of people, we can only imagine to a certain extent. The complexity of this, however, is unimaginable and unforeseeable.

These examples illustrate some of the ways in which the global development of communication media, and especially television, has introduced a new and fundamentally important element into social and political life. By providing people around the world with instantaneous and simultaneous images of, and information about, events that take place beyond their immediate social milieu, the media may stimulate or intensify forms of collective action, which may be difficult to control with established mechanisms of power.

This phenomenon of concerted responsive action highlights the fact that the media is not simply involved in reporting on a social world that would, as it were, continue quite the same without them. Rather, the media is actively involved in constituting the social world. By making images and information available to individuals located in distant places, the media shape and influence the course of events and, indeed, create events that would not have existed in their absence. The global media create enormous new possibilities for spontaneous collective and coordinate actions in an unprecedented grand scale. Whether such possibilities are for good or for bad is largely influenced by the decisions of those in power as to how realities are presented. Even more important and expressive of such power is the decision on what realities are presented.

Critically analyzed, we have some rather sinister and oppressive sides of the global media world that are exposed when we look at the power and ownership structure of this advanced technology. A sad and difficult aspect of this is the extremely asymmetrical flow of communication materials and cultural commodities between the advanced capitalistic countries and the so-called developing countries. This is not simply a commercial exchange, but rather a part of the process whereby the latter are dominated by communication ideologies of the major capitalist countries. Also integral to this process is the incorporation of these countries into the market-oriented, consumer-capitalist economies of the western transnational corporations through the apparently neutral or harmless media products, such as entertainment, advertising and the selections of what is considered to be worth presenting as news.

From this cultural imperialist perspective, there are levels of dominance and dependence among nations: there are exploiting metropolises or centers, and exploited satellites or peripheries. While there is conflict between them, the latter are never really in a position to challenge the former successfully, since the cultural-ideological strength of the former is part of, and flows from, their advanced means of production and ownership, which is built up through a long colonial history.

Glocalization

In the activity of thinking we are in a way prisoners of our concepts. Yet, when we become uncomfortable by such constraint, we can try to break out by constructing new and better concepts or redefining the old ones. In thinking about the different aspects of globalization, a new word appeared on the scene during the last decade: glocalization. This word – as you easily suspect – is composed of the two component words: global and local. In order to give a more adequate picture of the manifold processes in globalization, this term was elaborated as a social scientific tool, especially by the British sociologist Roland Robertson. The concept of glocalization wanted to tell something about the often rather complex and dialectical relationship between the local and the global, the universal and the particular. Robertson observed that the usual debate on the topic took it for granted that globalization was the same as a massive homogenization of the world, that the heterogeneity of all the local cultures were becoming more and more uniform and standardized under the pressure of globalization. However, this simplified view did not fit very well with what one could observe in many cases. Globalization could often promote and create greater heterogeneity both intentionally and unintentionally.

When different cultures meet and communicate, they become quite conscious about their differences and peculiarities and become more concerned about their own traditions and cultural identity. When different cultures feel the pressure from the homogenizing forces of globalization, they may react by strongly consolidating their own cultural particularity and identity, to the verge of fundamentalism as self-defense in extreme cases. The general rule is then that different local cultures adapt to and integrate the global influences in different ways according to their own traditions and mentality. Yet, this presupposes that they have dynamic cultural powers of their own, which are able to confront and transform the influences in a constructive way.

One could also mention that globalization of an institution, as for example, the Nation State or the norms of Human Rights, is explicitly to globalize institutions and values that protect particularity and diversity. To put it another way, it is the globalization of heterogeneity. The international collaboration for developing legal rights to protect the integrity and identity of indigenous people is a consequence of globalizing processes. The global tourist industry, to put it bluntly, is an example of the case that diversity sells. People travel around in order to experience the very different and exotic.

So, expressed in a simple way, glocalization is how the local culture reacts and adapts to the influences of globalization. It may be of interest to know that the term glocalization was first used in business and advertising to signify that efficient marketing of a global product in different local markets must take local customs and values into consideration. This is called micro-marketing, which adapts a global product, e.g., Coca Cola, to local circumstances. In keeping with this example, one could say that it involves the efforts toward the coca-colization or coca-colonization of the whole world, with some local variations in order for it to sell even better. This exemplifies, of course, glocalization used as a manipulative commercial strategy by the big transnational corporations. To state this quite politically, these corporations together with the religion of neo-liberalism and the deification of the unregulated markets as sacred institutions constitute veritable threats to the sovereignty of both the national states and the viability of democratic institutions and local autonomy all over the world. Nobody has made this so eloquently clear, in my opinion, as the eminent sociologist and neo-Zapatista leader, the so-called sub-commandante Marcos in Chiapas, Mexico.

Multi-Culturalism

I now turn to the problems of multicultural – or multiethnic – nations and the relationship between majority and minority cultures within states or regions. The question I address is: What are the political challenges for multicultural nations?

Most countries today are culturally diverse. They are more or less multi-cultural and polyethnic. According to recent estimates, the world's nearly 190 independent states contain over 600 living language groups and 5000 ethnic groups. In very few countries can all the citizens be said to share the same language, or belong to the same ethno-national group.

This diversity gives rise to a series of important and potentially divisive questions. Minorities and majorities within nations increasingly clash over issues of language rights, regional autonomy, political representation, educa-tion curriculum, land claims, immigration and naturalization policies, etc. and they strongly use arguments of cultural identity. To find ethical, well-reasoned and politically viable answers to these issues is the greatest challenge facing democracies today.

In Eastern Europe and the Third World, attempts to create liberal democratic institutions are being undermined by violent national conflicts. In the West, high-tempered disputes over the rights of immigrants, indigenous people, and other cultural minorities are throwing into question many of the assumptions that have governed political life for decades. Since the end of the Cold War, ethno-cultural conflicts have become the most common source of political violence in the world, and they show no sign of improving.

The globalization and wide acceptance of the United Nation's Universal Human Rights document, that establishes ethical, legal and political standards all nations are obliged to follow towards their citizens, is a powerful instru-ment toward establishing a global ethic and international mutual understanding. However, human rights are the rights of individuals, of persons, not of groups, not of collectives and cultures. It has become increasingly clear that this mainly individualistic approach is quite insufficient in effectively handling the real and acute problems cultural minorities and culturally conflicting groups are experiencing. Minority rights cannot be subsumed under the category of human rights. Traditional human rights standards are simply unable to resolve some of the most important and controversial questions relating to cultural minorities and conflicting cultural groups.

Yet, the trend in international legal thinking is clear. It is legitimate, important and indeed unavoidable to supplement traditional human rights with collective rights for cultural minorities, which are able to regulate their relationship to the majority culture and the authority of the state. A comprehensive theory of justice within a multicultural state and in a multicultural world must include both universal human rights, assigned to individuals regardless of group membership, and certain collective rights assigned to cultural and minority groups. One could say that the foremost, universal criteria for judging the civilized level of a state is in how the state and the majority treat their minorities.

The most important task in this is that a well-argued theory of cultural minority rights must explain how these group rights may, without contradictions, co-exist with universal human rights, and how cultural minority rights must be limited by principles of individual liberty, democracy and social justice. This is, for example, an acute practical problem today as to how tolerant the state should be towards some religious groups, according to freedom of religion as a human right, when it is obvious that these religions violate other rather basic human rights.

The big question is really: are there unavoidable contradictions between individual rights and group rights? The Canadian political philosopher Will Kymlicka, who has done some interesting research in this field, points out that most liberal and humanistic thinkers believe that collective rights are inherently in conflict with individual rights. As a kind of solution, he makes a very important point that in this context it is necessary to distinguish between two meanings of collective rights. On the one hand, collective rights could refer to the right of a group to limit the liberty of its own individual members in the name of group solidarity or cultural purity. This Kymlicka calls "internal restrictions." On the other hand, collective rights could refer to the right of a group to limit the economic or political power exercised by the majority over the minority group in order to ensure that the resources and institutions on which the minority group depends are not vulnerable to external majority decisions. This Kymlicka calls "external protections."

This second kind of group rights need not conflict with individual liberty. Indeed, what should distinguish a liberal humanist theory of minority rights is precisely that it accepts some external protections for ethnic groups and national minorities, but is very skeptical of internal restrictions.

When cultural or ethnic minorities within a state demand the right to restrict the basic civil and political liberties of their own members, then this cannot be accepted from the viewpoint of universal human rights. The idea that it is morally legitimate for a group to oppress its own members in the name of group solidarity, religious orthodoxy, or cultural purity must be strongly fought, because it violates the basic rights of individual autonomy.

As we know, some cultures – and especially religions – far from enabling autonomy for individuals, simply assign particular compulsory roles and duties to people and prevent them from freely questioning or revising them according to their conscience and rational ideals. Other cultures allow this autonomy to some, while denying it to others, such as women, low castes, or stigmatized subgroups. One could then ask the question if democratic and liberal states should have the right to force or impose liberal norms on their illiberal cultural and religious minorities?

This raises complicated issues about the meaning of tolerance and its limits. In our time of post-modernism and cultural relativism there could also be difficult discussions about how to define what liberty and freedom really is in different contexts, or if other values are of a higher order in certain contexts, and so on. We must remember that some commentators from non-western cultures accuse the notion of human rights to be a western invention, which in a culture-imperialistic way is being imposed on the rest of the world as something said to have cross-cultural and universal validity. These critics also point at – with some justification, it must be admitted – that there is something biased in the western concentration on political and civil human rights at the expense of economic, social and cultural human rights. To make progress in these matters needs a lot of very patient cross-cultural and inter-faith dialogues and a lot of time for trying to reach a minimal rational consensus about the basics.

Generally, one should be aware that liberation of a culture must always come from within the culture itself to be dynamic and effective. You cannot force people to liberation, but you can stimulate. Though people are living in authoritarian and suppressive cultures, they may be bound to and identify with it in many complicated psychological ways. As a saying goes: People want to be ruled by their own kind, even if they are unkind.

It is worth remembering that all existing liberal nations have had illiberal pasts, and that their liberalization required a rather prolonged process of institutional reform. To assume that any culture is essentially and inherently illiberal, and quite incapable of reform, is an untenable ethnocentric and a-historical position. Moreover, the liberality of a culture is a matter of degree. All cultures have illiberal strands, just as a few cultures are entirely repressive of individual liberty.

This issue of how to promote liberalization in illiberal cultures, and how liberal states should treat their non-liberal minorities, is a really large and complicated topic. An argument can be made that the rise of Islamic fundamentalism is partly explained as a counter-reaction to the too rapid and too overwhelming influences of modernity and western culture.

Cultural Identity

Dynamic cultures create positive identities for people and are resources for a meaningful life. They constitute historical traditions and frames for feeling allegiance and solidarity with a continuous and substantial community. They create meaningful options for how to organize the future.

Particular cultures are valuable because it is only through having access to a societal culture that people have access to a range of meaningful options and ways of arranging their lives both individually and as collectives. People internalize culture as a shared vocabulary of traditions and conventions. As expressed by a moral-philosopher: "We inherited a cultural structure, and we have some duty, out of simple justice, to leave that structure at least as rich as we found it." Well, it depends of course upon how you feel about what is valuable in your culture and what you feel worth transmitting to the future generations.

My last question is this: Should we let non-modern, static and 'unfunctional' cultures that are not adapted to the dynamics of modern development disappear? I end this chapter with my answer to this question.

Many cultures in danger of disappearing, that are weakened and oppressed, can regain and enhance their richness if they are given the appropriate conditions. There is no reason to think that indigenous and aboriginal groups cannot become vibrant and diverse cultures, drawing on their cultural traditions while incorporating the best of the modern world, if given the requisite preconditions. It is the potentiality of societal cultures that matters, not just their actual current state. It is even more difficult for outsiders to judge the potentiality and future of a culture than to judge the conditions of its current and actual state.

It has been stressed by many social analysts that national, ethnic and cultural identity is particularly well suited to serve as the primary focus of people's identification because it is primarily based on belonging, not of accomplishment and merit. Hence, cultural identity provides a kind of anchor for self-identification and belonging. However, this in turn means that people's self-respect is bound up with the esteem in which their national, ethnic and cultural group is held. If a culture is not generally respected, then the dignity and self-respect of its individual members will also be threatened. Here we have many tragic examples from the indigenous populations around the world confronting modernity.

A main precondition for fruitful developments of cultures in liberal and vibrant directions is that they consider each other as resources for mutual learning and new creativity. History shows that dynamic creativity of cultures often is the consequence of adaptive confrontations and cross-fertilizations between different cultures.

Conclusion

We should strongly avoid a notion of culture that sees the process of interacting with and learning from other cultures as a threat to 'purity' or 'integrity', rather than as an opportunity for enrichment. The aim and ideal must be a societal culture that is rich and diverse, and much of the richness of a culture comes from the way it has appropriated the fruits of other cultures. Dynamic cultures need other dynamic cultures quite different from itself with whom to interact, both for inspiration to develop in new directions and as a way of becoming conscious about what is peculiar in one's own culture. We need people different from ourselves in order to become aware of the uniqueness of ourselves. This is a type of psychological logic. Although we all on a general and abstract level will move into a kind of overarching global culture as a consequence of global communication, we still and strongly need the firm anchorage in our concrete and specific local cultures as sources of vital personal identities.

Lastly, the variety of cultures may be looked upon – as hinted on several times – like the variety of forms of life in nature. They are inter-linked and are preconditions for each other's existence, identity and development. They are preconditions for the vitality and creativity of the whole. This analogy of nature and culture is of course strongly partial, because in nature species eat each other, and cultures should not do this. We must confess that the natural is amoral and, in contrast to that, the essence of culture is morality.

Chapter Thirteen

Ethics and Religion: From Modern "Aufhebung" to Post-Modern Revival

Mislav Kukoč

Abolition of Ethics in the Croatian Praxis Philosophy

The intention of abolishing morality and ethics as the theory of morality appears in the Croatian praxis theory as a part of the Marxist revolutionary concept of *"Aufhebung"* (abolish and overcome), which was promoted as the instrument of revolutionary change of the world with the aim of realizing the eschaton of the new history. The issue here is thus the well-known demand of Karl Marx for the realization of philosophy through its abolition, and the abolition of all of its disciplines: ethics, esthetics, gnoseology, ontology, anthropology, the demand that was consequently, even radically implemented by Croatian praxis philosophers. However, the postulate of *"Aufhebung"* did not concentrate only on philosophy. In line with the same revolutionary aspirations, there were demands for the abolition of science, art, religion, law – that is the whole 'ideological superstructure' – as well as the abolition of work, nation, state and all other institutions of the existing world.

The principle of *"Aufhebung"* – as the tendency of abolishing or overcoming of all and everything, was corroborated, on the one hand, by Marx's original work (as is the case of abolishing work or philosophy, for example) and on the other hand, by the fact that Marx had never in his opus established those disciplines; he had never set up "ethics," "esthetics," "gnoseology" or any other such particular philosophical discipline.

Among all the above mentioned attempts of abolition in the Croatian praxis philosophy, that which is most theoretically interesting, original and philosophically developed is the concept of the abolition of ethics and morality. This problem was analyzed and elaborated on in detail in the major part of Milan Kangrga's (1963; 1966; 1970a; 1970b; 1975; 1983) abundant opus.

Although the tendency of *"Aufhebung,"* as we have already mentioned, related to a wide range of phenomena of the existing world, which was insisted upon by the revolutionary radicalism of the Croatian praxis philosophy, the abolition of ethics and morality as a philosophical problem had not appeared earlier in the Marxist philosophy. On the contrary, the opposite tendencies were present – that of establishing positive Marxist ethics, starting with the intention of implementing Immanuel Kant's ethical theory in the philosophical system of Marxism by "revisionists" of the Second International, and all the way up to later attempts of interpreting Marx's concept of a humanity and revolution as normative ethics (Compare Fritzhand 1961; Stojanovic 1969). Indeed, that was more or less the case with other disciplines as well; some Marxists in their revolutionary aspirations wanted to overcome them consequently and radically, while others, "positivistically" inclined, tried to establish them as a part of the Marxist philosophical system.

What differentiates the problem of morality and ethics from other philosophical disciplines and theoretical and social phenomena comprised in the *"Aufhebung"* postulate is the fact that the demand for the abolition of morality and its theory – ethics, was philosophically established and developed by Marx's predecessor G.W.F. Hegel. Another interesting fact is that Hegel's criticism of moral consciousness and his overcoming of ethics were accepted neither by the "bourgeois," nor by the Marxist post-Hegelian philosophy. Kangrga explains that Hegel's criticism of Kant's and J.G. Fichte's ethics, and of a moral perspective in general, is "so thorough and radical that that thoroughness and radicalism are precisely among the main reasons for which it was later by-passed." Yet, on the other hand, one of the main reasons, at least when it comes to the adoption of Hegel's criticism of Kant's ethical stance, could be the insurmountable contradiction of Hegel's and Marx's *"Aufhebung"* of morality.

In the view of Hegel's criticism and philosophical overcoming of Kant's moral stance, the place and limits of Kant's and any other ethical position have been marked. Kant's human being as a *moral being* is a typical bourgeois individual, divided into dimension of *Sein* and *Sollen*, into real material and abstract ideal life. Therefore, a human being's ideal freedom in the sphere of morality cannot be realized in the real world because the postulated need or necessity (*Sollen*) is understood as a progress into infinity, which contains the essential contradiction of Kant's (and any other) stance on morality. Sainthood, perfection – which cannot be achieved – is nevertheless at the same time postulated as practically and morally necessary.

This infinitely postulated separation of *Sein* and *Sollen* is based on the absolutizing of the current and past condition of humanity as an alienated being before whom a completely different dimension of the future is never put. So, as Hegel would say, we are talking about "bad infinity" (*"die schlechte Unendlichkeit"*).

Solving the problem of morality and its contradictions is not possible within the framework of philosophy as a pure contemplative activity. It is necessary to cross over into the field of real historical practice, to which, as a precondition, points Hegel's criticism of Kant's (and any other) conception which is within the framework of morality.

Kangrga gives full attention to Hegel's criticism of moral consciousness, reproaching to both post-Hegelian bourgeois and Marxist philosophy the complete disregard of Hegel criticism of moral phenomenon. In contrast to philosophical tradition, Kangrga follows Hegel's analysis, which "reaches the core of moral phenomenon" showing that it is unreal and alienated from ethos – the homeland, the historical world of man – and abolishes it in that manner, placing its postulate in the concrete life of Being.

The author problematizes Hegel's position by presenting in detail several modes of contradiction in the morality itself. Hegel is not criticizing the moral stance from an ethical but from a philosophical point of view. Having overcome the radical separation of *Sein* and *Sollen*, he positively establishes morality, first in religion (in *The Phenomenology of Spirit*), and then in *The Philosophy of Law* morality is realized in the state as Morals (*Sittlichkeit*).

Having rejected Kant's ethical conception of *a man as a moral being* ,in accordance with Hegel's philosophical criticism, Kangrga criticizes Hegel's concept of *a man as a philosophical being,* confronting it with Marx's definition of *a man as a historical-practical being*. While according to Kant, a man realizes himself only in morality, for Hegel a man is "real and true only as a philosopher" – in both cases a man realizes himself only theoretically, that is abstractly and contemplatively. Kangrga believes that the true realization of a human being within the framework of historical practice was established only by Marx. While for Hegel the Being of humanity is a phenomenologically-anthropologically defined act of alienated work, from which a person returns to himself as to self-consciousness, for Marx humanity's Being is an act as self-acting, as a possibility directed towards the future.

Apart from Kangrga, the criticism of moral phenomenon, from which, in accordance to Hegel and Marx, follows the demand for the abolition of ethics, was also developed by Gajo Petrovic. Confronting the normativist ethical interpretations of Marx's thinking as "consequences of humanistic-anthropological interpretation and reduction of Marxism," he interprets the ethical stance as a "self-alienated form of a man's Being in which his animalistic-inhuman potentials are realized, while his human potentials take a form of impotent wishes and moral norms." Since he is not satisfied with the simple ascertaining of the split of a real man into spheres of "facticity" and "need," he poses a "question of its surpassing," that is, he calls for the abolition of ethics.

Thus, both Kangrga and Petrovic demand abolition of morality as ethical phenomenon, the substance of which is "comprised of *absolute opposition between Sein and Sollen*." "A dualist nature of the ethical," that is "dualism between what is and what should be" is prevailed over by the real-historical praxis which, in the Croatian praxis philosophy, is defined as the essence of man.

Difficulties of substituting the moral postulate as abstract ideal paradigm of the behavior of a real imperfect man with the concrete practice of an acting man were already indicated by Kangrga's question:

> Why overcome dualism at any price, if maybe it already lies in human nature, and if that human nature itself is dualistic and contradictory in its substance? On what is the *necessity* or *indispensability* for setting such a demand or task based? And finally, where is the *very capacity* for accomplishing such a task, when ethics itself cannot move from there on? Isn't that a *proof* in itself that there is a contradiction in human nature which cannot be overcome?

The author has a ready answer to those rhetorical questions and defines a man as a historical-practical being which realizes his freedom by de-alienating himself in the eschatological future.

Although he believes that he has overcome the dualism of the *Sein* and *Sollen* and has prevailed, Kangrga has really only replaced it with the dualism of the true and the untrue, un-alienated and alienated man, leaving the criterion of definition of true humanity unclear, since the moral postulate as a paradigm has been abolished.

Even in the previous elaboration of his criticism of morality that was inspired by Hegel, Kangrga concludes that the "postulatory" "unreal" human essence is – "actually his true alienation, one form of his alienation." Thus, he decisively and explicitly rejects normativism as a definition of a postulated de-alienated man. Nevertheless, his own understanding of the essence of man, that is, of the authentic human nature, is very close to a certain type of ethical normativism, as much as he tried to avoid it.

In the practical act of a self-producing world, there is a person's Being, so he *is* only when "he becomes it." It is only in the process of producing objectively of a man's becoming that his self-alienation is possible, which appears when in that process "a man is not become a man." Kangrga talks about two modes of a man's self-alienated existence, that is, of his "non-becoming a man:" his self-alienation happens when he lives by the criterion of survival, in the present and the past as the only possibility given in advance, and on the other hand, when a man becomes, for example, a criminal, so he confirms not his human but his criminal nature.

However, even a man as a criminal, by his criminal practice, realizes his essence. Kangrga says not human but criminal essence. However, couldn't it be said, in contrast to this and on the basis of the historical experience so far, that a man as a criminal realizes precisely the genuine human essence, or one part of it, which Machiavelli also discusses in his own way? Kangrga's vision of "authentic man" does not postulate realization of a genuinely human, but "saintly" or moralistic essence.

That is, how can the "bad infinity" of the historical manifestation of "inhumane nature" in increasingly cruel wars and other forms of violence be avoided, and what can "the true human nature" be based on so that it does not come down to a simple moral postulate? Nevertheless, the category of active future as the horizon of humanity's emergence does not give any guarantees, all the more so since the issue at stake is always, as St. Augustine (1987:268) would say, humanity's view of the future as "the present of the future."[1]

Similarly to Kangrga, Petrovic (1973:94) defines the human essence as the "totality of historically created human potentials which at every stage of a man's historical development can be and really are different."

In this respect, a person alienates himself from his own essence when he is alienating himself from "realization of his historically created human potentials," and by their realization "he always creates new and more."

Such stipulation by Petrovic is a bit more concrete than Kangrga's definition of the essence of humanity, which we examined earlier. It nevertheless is burdened with the same difficulties. Unlike Kangrga, Petrovic is aware of these difficulties and is trying to face them.

Kangrga's definition of humanity's essence as an active realization of his own future, as well as Petrovic's understanding of the essence of humanity as a realization of "historically created human potentials," requires an answer to the following question: which of these "historically created potentials" are human, and which are inhuman? This "hard question" cannot be answered in a satisfactory manner by simply saying that, for example, "war crime" is not an essence of humanity, or by "agreeing that this is a *inhuman* potential of humanity." Does this mean that *human* potentials are 'good,' 'just,' 'virtuous,' 'moral' and *inhuman* potentials are 'bad,' 'unjust,' 'criminal,' 'immoral' and so on? This would certainly be a satisfying answer to which not many persons could object, if this wasn't a decisive rejection of praxis philosophers to define their own understanding of the essence of man, that is, of the alienation and de-alienation, as axiological, normative, moralistic.

This can, however, hardly be avoided which is evident in Petrovic's attempt to try and give an answer to this "hard question." Differentiating between the essence of man – defined as "totality of historically created human potentials" – and the essence of inhumane beings, he is wondering: is there "a difference in principle between all other beings and a human so that a man's essence

---

[1] "There is no future nor past.... There are three times: present in the past, present in the present, present in the future. They are situated in my soul as some three things and I cannot find them elsewhere: present in the past is memory, present in the present is watching, present in the future is expectation." (St. Augustine 1987:268).

is not that which is common to all people, but that which a human being can and has to be." "The question may seem to be difficult" – says Petrovic, cautiously and with a certain reservation – "but *if* our answer is affirmative, there *does not have to be* any contradiction in the notion of alienation."

There is, however, a contradiction in the definition of the essence of a man through the use of the "has to," the Kantian *"Sollen,"* which points to the fact that despite all reservations, the essence of a man understood in such a way, just like the concept of de-alienation, necessarily has a moral and postulatory character. Judging by his twisted hypothetical-problematical formulation (if yes ... than it does not have to), instead of his usual, categorical and apodictic formulation of previously posed rhetorical questions, Petrovic was certainly aware of this contradiction.

In other places as well, the more Petrovic tries to adequately and persuasively answer the question of the definition of the true human essence and its attributes, for example, humanism, the more he gets entangled into normativism and moralism. Dismissing the possible objection to humanism for being "too naïve and optimistic in its theses because it sees only the 'positive,' 'good,' 'virtuous' side of a man and overlooks the 'negative,' 'bad,' 'sinful' one," he, on the contrary, claims that "humanists consider a man to be a free, creating being which progresses to ever higher forms and enriches his own life by transforming himself and non-human world in human ways." However, Petrovic does not question the possibility of realization of a man with such superlative qualities. Instead, he allows "self-alienated" existence of the real man; indeed, "if a man was only 'good' and if he didn't have any 'inhumane' side, humanist demands for radical change of man would make no sense."

Therefore, the inhumane and self-alienated reality of man and his world is necessary in order for the humanist demand for de-alienation and radical change to be possible! The imperfect real man and world are a necessary and an eternal prerequisite for the existence of the abstract sphere of morality as a paradigm of the man's desirable "moral" behavior, which is – according to Hegel's and Marx's criticism, as well as the criticism of the praxis philosophers – perpetuated in the "bad infinity," since the realization of morality in reality would abolish its *raison d'être*. Isn't the above mentioned Petrovic's recognition of discrepancy between the alienated reality and humanistically de-alienated paradigm actually a confirmation of the normativist-moralistic definition of the postulated essence of the man which, as an abstract paradigm, is necessarily perpetuated in the 'bad infinity?'

Another important objection to the demand for the abolition of morality and ethics relates to the questioning of the basic reason for that demand, and the reason is: impossibility of the realization of the moral paradigm. In that sense, the question arises: why is the realization of the moral paradigm at all necessary, as *conditio sine qua non*, in order for the moral phenomenon to be admitted as something desirable and needed by humanity?

The praxis philosophers are right when in the analysis of Kant's definition of the morality and its autonomous, formalistic and universalistic ethics they conclude that the moral postulate necessarily exists as an abstract, unreal paradigm which can never be realized in practice. Yet it is precisely this eternal dualism between the *Sein* and *Sollen* that is necessary and suits the true nature of humanity as an imperfect being, who always needs a regulation and a model for his own behavior, regardless of whether it is defined by heteronomous or autonomous ethics, by the ethics of values or discursive ethics. Compare, for example, Jürgen Habermas's (1985:761–773; 1991:9–30) problematizing of Hegel's objections to Kant's ethics, and in this context the comparative analysis of moral postulates of different ethical concepts.

Finally, Kant (1974:79) himself was completely aware of the impossibility of the realization of the moral law, regarding which, in his *Critique of Practical Reason*, he explicitly says: "Indeed, the moral law, according to the idea, transfers us in a nature where pure Reason, if it was accompanied by adequate physical powers, could produce the highest good, so it defines our will in order to give a form to the empirical world as a whole." Thus, the lack of "physical power" – that the moral law, according to its own transcendental nature, cannot have, unlike the empirical, heteronomous for the mind, laws that rule in an empirical world – defines in advance the sense of the moral law which, according to its fundamental definition, always needs to be the basic criterion of the good, directing the regulation and in reality unattainable paradigm for the man's appropriate behavior and acting.

Abolition of the moral activity, that is, its replacement by the historical, revolutionary practice, represents at the same time the abolition of the autonomous moral law and, with regard to the complex nature of man, implies a real danger of nihilism and voluntarism. Non-existence of the moral paradigm – as the historical experience up to now has shown, and as the current practice of desubstantialized modern world clearly demonstrates – opens a possibility of justification of any, even most inhumane act. In this context, it is enough to remind of the shameful role of some of the leading representatives of the Belgrade wing of the praxis philosophy (Mihajlo Markovic) as the closest collaborators of the "Balkans Hitler" Slobodan Milosevic during the war in former Yugoslavia.

Every moral action, in the necessary discrepancy between the *Sein* and *Sollen,* remains forever unfinished and unfinishable, just as the human world remains forever unfinishable. Moral action, as a real historical development, is perpetuated into infinity. Only, the issue at stake is not the bad infinity – *"der schlechte Undentlichkeit"* – (Hegel 1975:184, compare with p. 243 where Hegel says that "with executed act the bad infinity is nullified"); the infinity of the abstract perfect moral paradigm as a necessary and eternal regulation of the behavior of an imperfect being – this is *"die gute Unendlichkeit!"* In that sense, the role of religion as a necessary carrier and guarantor of the eternal moral paradigm has been fulfilled. Because, as the Great Inquisitor of F.M. Dostoyevsky (1950) says: If there is no God, everything is allowed!

Bioethics as a Post-Modern Ethics

In conclusion, we can say that the Hegelian and Marxian demand for the *"Aufhebung"* of morality, ethics and religion that was elaborated in the Croatian praxis philosophy cannot endure neither theoretical nor historical criticism. After the historical collapse of the Marxian project of communism, both ethics and religion find confirmation as enduring factors of social life at the global level. Moreover, they develop in their new forms suitable to the spirit of the new age. Bioethics is one of the new disciplines that is getting an increasingly important place in the contemporary world and becomes the focus of interest of religion.

Ethics, together with logic and physics, appears even in the pre-Socratic period of the development of the ancient Greek philosophy as one of its three basic parts, that is, at the very beginning of the emergence of European science and philosophy. What characterized the development of ethics, as the theory of morality, throughout history is its division into heteronomous and autonomous ethics. While the heteronomous ethics, as the main component of all the world's religions, found the paradigm of the moral acts of man in an authority outside and above him, in the *vis vitalis,* in *God,* in *Nature,* autonomous ethics, starting with Kant, bases the moral activity of man on the causality of freedom, of his autonomous mental will.

Bioethics goes beyond those differences and divisions of the traditional ethics. It uses philosophical questions and problems in order to obtain valid and defendable answers and practical solutions. In this matter, we have to highlight practical solution that bioethics, unlike the abstract discourse of traditional philosophical disciplines, resolutely demands now and right away. One of the founding fathers of bioethics, Peter Singer, gives a paradigmatic example of a case relevant to bioethics in medicine: out of two seriously ill newborns, only one had a possibility to survive and this under the condition that he receives the transplant of the other baby's heart. What is necessary here, as with other new issues that bioethics deals with, such as AIDS, euthanasia, abortion, contraception, genetic engineering, in vitro fertilization, etc., is a prompt and concrete ethical instruction, and not unproductive debates that prevail in traditional ethical approaches. It is precisely from this perspective of the need for practical action that the bioethical approach clashes with the usual approach of different traditional ethical trends and philosophies of life, from discourse ethics, hermeneutic philosophy, Marxism, feminism, all the way up to catholic ethics (Singer 1996:523–532). The above mentioned and similar bioethical problems, like cloning, eugenics, medically assisted prolongation of human life, and even theoretically presumed immortality, will surely be the main focus of ethics and religion in the future.

Chapter Fourteen

The Ethics of Interpretation after Postmodernism

Hans-Herbert Kögler

Has 'postmodernism' changed our understanding of the human and social sciences? In particular, has it affected the conception of social theory and its role with regard to the human sciences, especially with regard to the normative assumptions involved in cultural and social interpretation?

Postmodernist theorists[1] are engaged in the rejection of trans-contextual notions of truth and truth claims, moralities that speak in the name of all, and grand theories, so-called, 'meta-narratives' that construct historical and social developments imposed on and alien to the cultures discussed. To be sure, since we are dealing here with a postmodern *discourse* challenging classic modernist assumptions, we might immediately raise the well-known objection that those positions themselves involve commitments to truth, expressive normative perspectives, and engage in theoretical generalizations. In thinkers like Foucault, Derrida, or Rorty, those truth claims are often denied or, rather unconvincingly, 'dissolved' in allegedly playful gestures of

---

[1] The use of 'postmodern' and 'postmodernism' might, with good reasons, be contested on grounds of vagueness and over-inclusiveness. My use is as a heuristic umbrella term for precisely those conceptual and methodological positions that contest the modernist positions discussed below.

self-contradictory statements; furthermore, normative commitments are not explicitly justified, but rather 'shown' or 'displayed' in political action; and theoretical assumptions, while constitutive of the disclosure of concrete phenomena, are not clarified with regard to their general scope and explanatory power. Since these presuppositions do inform the 'postmodern' positions, however, one could be inclined to reject them as inherently incoherent.

A different, more promising road would consist in taking seriously the postmodern critique of situated reason, and to inquire whether, instead of necessarily implying a total rejection of reason, a reformulation of the scope and nature of truth claims and normative commitments is possible and needed. Such a project would involve a commitment to certain so-called 'postmodernist themes,' such as the context-dependency of theoretically articulated truth positions, the sensitivity to the cultural embeddedness of moral attitudes and rules, and the caution necessary for adequately integrating conceptual frames and empirical-hermeneutic processes. In what follows, I want to prepare such a re-conceptulatization with regard to the issue of normativity. The aim is to sketch the possibility of a normative commitment build into our interpretive practices, if understood as the dialogical reconstruction – and thus recognition – of the other's beliefs and assumptions. Dialogical interpretation, defined as a methodological core-principle of human science, entails a *situated normativity* that takes up the new (post-modern) sensitivity toward the concrete and contextual without succumbing to sheer relativism and reductionism.

To make the case for this proposal, I first present, by means of a comparison between modern and postmodern conceptions of social science, an interpretation of the relevance of the postmodern challenge with regard to modern social theory. Based on this, I will sketch a fourfold discursive field of positions addressing the justification of normative perspectives. This discussion will serve as a backdrop against which the concept of a hermeneutic competence of dialogical perspective-taking can emerge as a plausible candidate for the grounding of our normative intuitions.

Postmodern Challenges vis-à-vis Social Science and Theory

At the inception of modernity, *human and social sciences* were conceived after the model of the natural sciences; their task was to discover and accumulate laws concerning 'facts' of history and society (Comte's positivism). Yet, this methodologically positivistic picture was similarly tied to a *normative notion* of social and cultural progress. (See Condorcet, Comte as the founder of sociology; in Marx and Marxism, the normative force is obvious, and still deeply tied to a scientific understanding of society; detachment of the normative (as an attitude of the theorist) begins in Durkheim, Weber, fully with Parsons).[2] The features that define the original Enlightenment idea of a human or social science thus include:

– positivism/empiricism as the scientific self-understanding
– an evolutionary conception of human progress (both in science and, in turn, in history and society)
– a universal conception of human nature and values.[3]

Postmodern or post-structural thinkers radically oppose all three features of the positivistic Enlightenment conception of human science; postmodernism is:

– *anti-positivistic*: there is no unbiased, unmediated, or nonpolitical understanding of meaning and social life;
– *anti-evolutionist*: evolution-theories are criticized for using ethnocentric standards as yardsticks to devaluate others; they 'universalize' and ideologically justify their own contextual practices through evolutionary accounts of progress, positioning their own values as the highest cognitive and moral stage;
– *anti-essentialist*: theories of 'human nature' are shown to be ideological, discursive constructions that turn into 'essence' what is socially shared and symbolically constructed in concrete, and thus limited, social and cultural contexts.

The anti-positivism is grounded in the claim of the symbolic mediation of all experience and understanding. This fundamental assumption, supported by endless analyses of culturally mediated experiences, encounters,

---

[2] For the positivistic conception of social and human science, the fact that society entails value-orientations does not mean that social science has to be evaluative; norms, it is assumed, can be stated just as neutrally as any other thing; they are 'social facts' (see Weber's distinction between Value-orientation and Value-relatedness).

[3] Accordingly, the classic modernist conception of *social theory* has been conceived (a) as data-explanation, i.e. as synthesis and explanation of empirical knowledge (positivistic theoretical generalization), (b) as epistemological foundation and justification of social-scientific knowledge, defining its conditions of possibility, its basic concepts, major methodological strategies, etc. (philosophical grounding), and (c) as mediator between public social spheres and scientific knowledge by developing a moral-political vision of contributing to social change (critical social science and theory).

and scientific claims, in turn fuels the anti-evolutionism. Because intentional experiences or cognitive processes draw necessarily on a rich and 'thick' background understanding, particular concepts, ideas, or values cannot simply be abstracted from their original contexts and employed as trans-cultural standards of judgment and evaluation. This furthermore supports the rejection of essentialist conceptions of human or cultural identity: since the symbolically mediated processes of meaning-constitution are revealed as constantly transformed, contested, and reinterpreted, they are taken to resist theoretical objectification and fixation.

Normative Justification after Postmodernism

What, then, are the consequences of postmodernism? As we saw, we are dealing here with a totalizing rejection of reason (including universalistic normativity), which is seen as symbolically oppressive, metaphysically naïve and false, and politically devastating. If, however, this critique itself implies a certain normative perspective – displayed, for instance, in its evaluation of Enlightenment conceptions as false, morally wrong, and theoretically unac-ceptable – then what are the normative grounds (or a least intuitions) that inform postmodernism? Could there be, at any rate, a normative attitude that could be articulated and justified? In this section I shall sketch a conceptual field map delineating the four major positions that have emerged as responses to this problematic.

Anti-Normativism. The necessity to provide an articulated normative posi-tion, or the possibility to do so, are rejected. Deeply Nietzschean in spirit, this position denies the usefulness of moral theory in practice, which is seen, when realized, as intrinsically harmful. Normative values are infused with existing power and thus never pure; they will, once expressed as universal, be used for oppressing difference and marginal voices. Major figures of this position are: (Nietzsche), Foucault, the early Frankfurt School (Horkheimer, Adorno, Benjamin). The problems that this approach faces include:

- The critical intuitions and 'values' remain unjustified (thus leaving open why certain power-relations are worse than others, why equality is better than non-egalitarian social arrangements, etc.);
- the critical-normative stance thus is not developed and remains largely

unarticulated (possibility of alternative ethical modes (i.e. of a less universalistic-oppressive approach) are not explored;

– no political-ethical orientation, no 'regulative ideal' as to how to change social practices (critique remains negatively tied to the status quo as that which is rejected, no utopian potential).

Normative Relativism. Here, it is granted that we do evaluate and judge (and should), but do so always according to our basic vocabularies and values (those of, say, the liberal Western democratic constitutional scientific tradition). All is seen through our lenses, especially norms and values of others and other cultures. A major figure of this position is Richard Rorty, who coined this position 'frank ethnocentrism.' Problems include:

– a relativism of values that ultimately collapses logically the distinction between 'their' values and 'our' values, because all values become constructions of our perspective;

– others are judged and evaluated without a deep effort to understand them 'on their own terms,' or to see oneself with the eyes of the other; interpretive potential of perspective-taking and radical interpretive dialogue are not explored or pushed;

– why one should be open and sensitive to the other's perspective remains ultimately unjustified, because it is just 'grounded' in "the way we feel about that here," not because there is anything really wrong with, say, torture, political imprisonment, sex slave trade, etc.

Moral Neo-Universalism. This position tries to redefine a universal-normative stance capable of avoiding the oppressive and essentializing flaws of classical Enlightenment conceptions of morality. Instead of a solitary subject, intersubjective relations based on communication are taken to imply certain normative structures that are universal, and still realized differently in different social contexts. Also, those universal forms allow for recognition of differences and particularities as valid and important. Major representatives of this position are the second and third generation Frankfurt School – Habermas, Benhabib, Honneth; more politically concrete: Public Sphere theorists, Chicago Cultural Studies Circle. Problems with this theoretical position consist of:

– Distinguishing what is considered only contextually valid from what is universally valid cannot be captured by formal rules, with which this normativity is identified.

- Mediating between often highly abstract moral reflections and theories and concrete political theory or social science dealing with issues like globalization, democracy-theory, multiculturalism, social movements, reflexive agency, equally transcends the scope of a formal grounding of reason.

The Normativity of Otherness. This position can be considered the positive postmodern response to the normative challenge. It is concerned with developing an ethics of concern and concrete recognition for others consistent with the postmodern rejection of universalism and essentialism; concrete experiential phenomena highlighting the ethical experience of others are articulated as entailing ontological claims to respect and recognize the other. Major figures and movements are: Levinas, Derrida; feminist ethics (Carol Gilligan); multicultural ethics (Charles Taylor). Problems here include:

- The grounding of ethical claims remains ultimately ambiguous, because of a metaphysical foundationalism (Levinas: ethics as first philosophy) gleaned from phenomenological experiences (seeing the face of another), or references to quasi-theological foundations, or community-based experiences (why should those be valid for members of other traditions, or 'deviant' members?).

The Dialogical Recognition of the Other

While the stance against any normative justification as well as the ethnocentric position are inherently flawed, both moral neo-universalism and the normativity of otherness entail important insights. Indeed, the neo-universalist position realizes that some account of a universal structure of normativity is needed, if philosophically self-refuting and politically self-debilitating implications with regard to normative judgments are to be avoided. And the new sensibility toward otherness emphasizes correctly that a more pronounced orientation toward the other is needed if we want to overcome the pitfalls of classic modernist theory. Such a concrete orientation toward the other is found, so my thesis, in the methodological core of hermeneutic interpretation if understood as dialogical perspective-taking. A dialogical conception of interpretation entails a comprehensive fusion of universalism and concrete recognition, since the hermeneutic recognition of the other's self-understanding is both grounded in a general hermeneutic competence at understanding and, as such, tied back to concrete cultural contexts. We can thus circumscribe the detached formalism still haunting neo-universalism, but also abolish the predicaments of either foundational or contextual groundings of recognition, as in the otherness-paradigm. The dialogical approach entails

- the theory of a universal hermeneutic competence, defined as the socio-psychologically grounded capability of perspective-taking in the medium of articulated linguistic contexts;
- the strong acknowledgement of the contextually specific mediation of all beliefs and assumptions, displayed (a) in the reflexive account of the interpreter's or speaker's pre-understanding, and (b) the reflexive recognition of the other's or hearer's cultural background assumptions;
- an acute sense of the actual social constraints placed upon such universal capacity, which requires a structural approach toward social conditions and power as unintentional influences on symbolic and intentional contexts.

I will now briefly clarify what each of these points involves.

The Social-Psychological Origin of Identity as Perspective-Taking. With regard to the source of a radically reciprocal dialogical attitude, the task is to show how the potential (which is not necessarily developed, and thus might not represent the actual hermeneutic competence of agents) for a truly reciprocal dialogue is build into the agent's general socio-psychological identity. This approach assumes that the capacity to engage in meaningful human and social-scientific interpretation is grounded in a basic hermeneutic competence that is acquired by becoming the member of a social community. This, in turn, is basically mediated by language, but it is also embedded in a variety of cultural and social practices, and incorporates and embodies practical skills and habits.[4]

---

[4] The approach roughly belongs to a long tradition (Dilthey, Heidgger, Gadamer) that attempts to ground our interpretive methical attitude in a pre-scientific, more practical and cultural attitude. For an analysis of the hermeneutic background as a both enabling and constraining condition of interpretation, see H.-H. Kögler, *The Power of Dialogue*, Cambridge: MIT Press 1999. While there the background is described as encompassing symbolic assumptions, social practices, and individual experiences, I here foreground the agent-related competence to breach one's background and to take the perspective of others.

Recent research in cognitive science, more specifically in the field of social cognition, provides ample evidence that the capacity at role-taking is a very basic psychological mechanism. It belongs to the earliest skills of humans, and makes human interaction possible from the very start.[5] While it seems also to lie at the root of language learning, the move into language equally transcends earlier mimetic stages and allows for a symbolically mediated perspective-taking that can articulate another's view-point; it can reflexively thematize perspectives, both in their difference and consensus with regard to a subject matter. The hermeneutic competence of perspective-taking can be seen as a basic requirement to participate in everyday communication, and can be studied as crucial for psychological development and social integration. Higher forms of reflexive and reciprocal dialogue through interpretation can be achieved by interpreters in the human and social sciences.

The Normativity of Interpretation: Recognizing the Other's Self-Understanding. Perspective-taking is normatively oriented at the other's self-understanding. In order to make adequate understanding of the other possible, I introduce as a normative constraint that interpretation be based on the other's self-understanding. This normative point involves two dimensions, one epistemic, the other ethical.

Interpretation is supposed to reveal the meaning of an act or expression. Such interpretation is grounded in language as the encompassing medium of social action and symbolic expression. The linguistic meaning, in turn, can only be reconstructed if we orient ourselves at the subject matter, at 'what it is' that is meant in the purposive or expressive act (Gadamer 1989). Yet understanding the meaning expressed by another in linguistic form involves aiming at her perspective, which we have to profile and delineate with regard to our beliefs and assumptions regarding the subject matter at stake. Interpretation is thus constituted as a dialogue in which I am compelled, if I want to understand at all, to understand how the other sees what I (or better:

---

[5] For a good overview of the literature with an eye on its relevance for social cognition, see Davis, M./Stone, T. (eds.), *Folk Psychology*, Oxford: Blackwell 1995. Insightful with regard to different modes of empathy and their relation to moral experience, see M. Hoffman, *Empathy and Moral Development. Implications for Caring and Justice*, Cambridge, Cambridge U.P. 2000. For the application of these ideas to social science and theory, see Kögler, H.-H./Stueber, K. (eds.). *Empathy and Agency*. Boulder: Westview Press 2000.

we) take to be at issue; it thus involves necessarily the recognition of other's self-understanding concerning something we both relate to.[6]

Interpretive dialogical practices thus point to the existence of an ethics of recognition, based on the mutual perspective-taking of speaker and hearer about some subject matter shared. Taking account of the other's viewpoint, acknowledging thus the potential importance, relevance, and meaningfulness of his or her beliefs and cultural practices entail a sense of openness toward the other and reflexivity with regard to one's presuppositions. Openness toward the other and reflexivity vis-à-vis one's own interpretive assumptions define essential cornerstones of a new normative conception of intersubjectivity.[7]

The Methodological Profile of Perspective-Taking in Dialogue. Dialogical interpretation commits us to a perspective that takes seriously how the other understands the subject matter – the best way to organize the meaning one encounters, and a method that responds to the ethnocentric and anti-paternalistic criticisms of much of intercultural discourse. Reconstructing the other's view will involve reconstructing assumptions that the other takes for granted, which make sense in the context of the other's cultural practices and institutions. However, since we do not belong to such contexts, our reconstruction will explicate the ground on which they are based – without necessarily generating the same force of acceptance. Indeed, the reconstruction of such premises might do the opposite even for the other if he or she becomes aware of the contingency and mere habituation that might form the source of his or her beliefs and assumptions.

---

[6] This point can also be explained with regard to the intentionality of human action-interpretation. Interpretation in the human and social sciences is oriented at reconstructing *intentional human agency*. The behavior of an agent can be described in a potentially infinite variety of ways. However, since we are aiming at understanding another, we now have to specify which description of the situation actually captures the underlying meaning of the observed act or symbol. In order to do this, we have to orient ourselves at how the other sees and interprets the situation. This can be accomplished the closer we are to the other in interpretive communication – given that such communication is oriented at the other's own perspective.

[7] It is probably impossible to detach this ethical intuition from the ontological assumption that there is another *human being* encountered here – but this is, first, not an assumption that essentializes the other (as Levinas has shown), and, second, one can argue that it is indeed the ethical experience of the other which grounds our conception of intersubjectivity here. Furthermore, the ethical orientation at the other's self-understanding has the advantage that it grounds agency in a socially and culturally situated context without reducing the individual to such contexts. It situates the self, but it preserves the concrete recognition as an agent that can interpret her situation, and thus can reflexively take a stand toward it.

Interpretation thus involves two different processes, two dimensions of perspective-taking, and both take part in a productive and truly mutual dialogue in interpretation. At work is

- an orientation at the internally posited *value-perspective*, which is what we aim at in understanding that is focused on the subject matter and which targets what we previously called the intentional self-understanding; and
- an orientation at the underlying *symbolic assumptions and cultural practices* that unconsciously provide a backdrop for explicit acts and beliefs, and might both enable and constrain the possible knowledge and experience of situated agents.

Both attitudes begin from our own identity, and then lead back, through the refraction created by the view of the other, to a reflexive reconstruction of that identity. The fact that interpreters are not situated within the other´s meaning perspective *forces them* to make sense of that perspective, and *allows them* to see what constraints are involved in it. It thus enables a look into the social and political contexts of power, precisely by emphasizing the need to normatively recognize the other.

Chapter Fifteen

Toward a Naturalistic Foundation of Community: How Science Can Solve the Spiritual Crisis?

Werner Krieglstein

When we consider human history, especially as it played out during the past centuries, there appears to be little hope for a resurgence of healthy communities. Yet I contend that vital communities are the single most important factor in achieving the kind of global society that can produce healthy individuals and inspire human life on earth to be creative and fulfilling. Societies must help each person, not just the privileged few, to be the best he or she can be, and each person must in turn help society to be the best it can be. This simple truism was at the base of the Greek masters' ethical ruminations and must be considered again today as the world moves toward increased globalism and away from the nation state system, which dominated the recent past.

A revitalized concept of communities is indispensable if we ever should hope to reach Rudolf Siebert's vision of a reconciled society, what he has called Future III. Instead we are coming ever closer to living in societies resembling Siebert's horror vision of Future I, the totally administered society. In the developed countries of the industrialized West, participation in the democratic process is ever decreasing, as citizens feel more often than not being manipulated, cheated, and even tricked into wars. They often feel their hard earned wages being wasted, as their tax contributions, far from helping their needs and the needs of the *polis*, are turned into weapons of mass destruction or used to feed the hungry coffers of multi national corporations.

On the other hand, the project of Western moral philosophy, I believe, has by and large failed, having not been able whatsoever to anchor ethical reasoning within the confines of the individual's ontology. While the latest attempts of prominent philosophers such as Jürgen Habermas to develop an ethical framework from an analysis of communicative praxis are promising and point in the right direction, I believe that to achieve a real paradigm change it will require a new foundation of community. Such an idea of community can only come from a reevaluation of our current philosophies of nature and the development of a naturalistic approach to the necessity of community as a prerequisite for human happiness.

Globalization today is on everybody's mind. Which of three alternative futures will this global society ultimately resemble? Reflecting on philosophical, political, and religious problems of globalization, Tatiana Alekseeva, head of the Department of Political Theory at the Moscow State Institute of International Relations, in a recent publication on Democracy and the Quest for Justice (Gay 2004), developed a bold vision for a future global society, well worth considering. She claims that a global society must be based on the "principles of cooperation, mutual help, and justice" (Gay 2004:18). Alekseeva continues:

> Not competition between ideas and ideologies, but solidarity, not the clash of civilizations, but their mutual supplementary, not the "balance of power," but mutual help in terms of Martin Heidegger's existential of human being ought to become the main features of the new international order (Gay 2004:18).

This vision in mind, Alekseeva analyses current trends in Russia and America. For the immediate interaction of nations, Alekseeva envisions a development along the lines of Rawls' concept of "overlapping consensus" rather than the development of a new meta-ideology, which would be the result of different opinions and ideas flowing together into a unifying whole. In spite of this caveat, Alekseeva concludes that the 'breakthrough' to a new understanding of the world order may not be possible at all on the level of the so-called theories of the 'medium level.' What is needed is a revolution in philosophies and world views (Gay 2004:18).

Alekseeva contends that "many Russian philosophers have started to reflect on the problems of paradigms of world society and global problems." On the international stage, Alekseeva believes that a number of prominent philosophers such as Noam Chomsky, Jürgen Habermas, John Grey, and Klaus Hoffe have all expressed a renewed interest in the sphere of world politics. But perhaps a little discouraged she concludes that "for now such reflections are only the beginning of a new paradigm" (Gay 2004:19).

In this article I will explore how a new scientific understanding of the processes within the natural world could reshape our understanding and need for community and promote a spiritual stance. The traditional understanding of community limits the usefulness of the communal concept to human beings who live in communities for mutual support. According to the Abrahamic religions, man was created as an individual and as such lives as a separate unit before God. Woman was given to Adam almost as an afterthought. This creation story goes against any naturalistic foundation of community. In spite of overwhelming evidence indicating that the vast majority of primal people have lived in and valued communities, in the mythological context of the Abrahamic world religions, community is simply not important.[1]

The real sources of the Ten Commandments could, with a more refined historical interpretation, be understood as the culmination of the condensed wisdom of the ages. But instead of being conceived as an outgrowth of communal wisdom, the Decalogue is reported to have been delivered directly from God to one man, Moses. In spite of the distinct efforts of the Christ of the New Testament to rescue what he could of a sense of community among his followers, Christianity has not succeeded in fostering and developing a vital concept of community. Christian communities have sprouted, of course, and spread to

---

[1] Islam might be mentioned as an exception. The Quran and especially the Prophet's interpretative texts give detailed instructions about the operation and conduct within a Muslim community. But community here is also not so much seen as the source of the ethical norms, but its enforcer, not as an end but as the instrumental means to otherworldly fulfillment.

all corners of the globe. But because of Christianity's otherworldly orientation, the Christian concept of community has not been able to survive the unconditional victory march of enlightenment and secularization. Over time the civic community was able to replace the religious community, confining any rests of a former community spirit to religious activities on Sunday's, and ultimately preparing the way for the totally administered society, Siebert's Future I.

On its march toward individualism and in full conformity with the enlightenment goal to promote the autonomous individual, Western style civic societies set out to support their individualistic standpoint by founding an ethics on the basis of rationality. But in the totally administered, alienated societies of the industrialized world of the twentieth century reason itself quickly turned into instrumentalized rationality. Within the frame of this instrumentalized rationality it suddenly even appeared reasonable when the subordinated individual when ordered so by society commits horrific crimes against humanity. Society on the other hand sees no wrong in neglecting the plight of the poor and hungry masses. In the name and under the pretense of spreading democracy they invade sovereign countries only to appropriate their national resources and setting up shopping malls and industrial parks to feed the ever demanding needs of the multi nationals. Such behavior is defended by referring to Darwin's law of survival and justified by declaring one's own version of democracy to be "on the right side of history" and as "part of God's plan." In other words, those in power declare themselves the good guys while declaring the other side as evil.

With no hope on the horizon, people everywhere, perhaps sensing a lack of healing community, flee back into the arms of nearly forgotten institutions and old religions, only to find them hollowed out and meaningless, victims of the same process of secularization. But instead of looking back in an attempt to rescue ancient values I sense hope in looking forward and employ science itself on the road to a society of tomorrow.

Scientific methodology with it emphasis on openness, empirical testing and trust in falsification could help in developing and promoting a concept of community, free of ideological force. Such a society could focus again on providing a good, decent, and happy life here on earth, not unlike the kind of life secular society, at least in principle, had at one time attempted to provide, as enshrined in the so-called American Dream. However, far from promoting the acquisition of material values only, this new society, after the paradigm shift in regard to our concept of nature is completed, would also emphatically be able to fulfill Siebert's Future III, especially its other part, namely keeping open the door to the totally Other. This new society would balance and reconcile the material thrust toward happiness with the scientific recognition of the inherent spirituality of all of nature. In not being limited to one nation, or even to one culture, not even only to human beings, but rather being recognized as a common quality of all animals, plants and even the so-called inanimate world, this new spirit would clearly be different from Hegel's concept of the spirit of the people (*der Geist des Volkes*). This new spirituality would also be different from the nature soul (*Natur Seele*) of the romantics because far from being a romantic notion, it would be thoroughly scientific, thus within reach of empirical verification or at least successfully withstanding the pragmatic test.

This new philosophy will not only keep "the door open to the wholly Other" but also offer a bridge for our emotional involvement with the world as the Other and with others qua human beings, animals, and plants. Such an involvement I claim is the basic ingredient for spirituality if spirituality means entering into a compassionate dialogue with the Other in all its shape and forms. Vaclav Havel once described this dialogue with the totally Other as the only means of survival for the human race. He said:

> ...in today's multicultural world, the truly reliable path to coexistence, to peaceful coexistence and creative cooperation, must start from what is at the root of all cultures and what lies infinitely deeper in human hearts and minds than political opinion, convictions, antipathies, or sympathies: It must be rooted in self-transcendence. Transcendence as a hand reached out to those close to us, to foreigners, to the human community, to all living creatures, to nature, to the universe; transcendence as a deeply and joyously experienced need to be in harmony even with what we ourselves are not, what we do not understand, what seems distant from us in time and space, but with which we are nevertheless mysteriously linked because, together with us, all this constitutes a single world. Transcendence as the only real alternative to extinction (Krieglstein 2002:5).

On first sight, science, community, and spirituality seem to belong to entirely different worlds. Scientists often cringe when their vocabulary, their discoveries, and their inventions are used in what they consider the softer academic fields and worth yet, in the public arena. But, without its specific consent perhaps, science always was used to support and explain claims that were made in the social realm and the humanities. Thus Newton's contribution to science, which became known as Newtonian Science, birthed the philosophy of Deism. A totally mechanical universe was presided over by a disinterested deity who had started the world like a giant clock, but now left it alone and to its own devices. This made the classical understanding of the universe as a machine possible.

In the introduction to Ilya Prigogine's (1984:xii) ground breaking book *Order Out of Chaos*, Alvin Toffler depicted the world of classical science as "a world in which every event was determined by initial conditions that were, at least in principle, determinable with precision. It was a world in which all the pieces came together like cogs in a cosmic machine." During the nineteenth and most of the twentieth century, the image of a "simple, uniform, mechanical universe" not only shaped the development of science, but influenced most other areas of human development. We even shaped our social orders (the large bureaucracies that governed most modern industrialized nations) like giant machines, their "checks and balances clicking like parts of a clock." The achievements of the technological mind confirmed "the image of the universe as an engineer's giant Tinker toy."

Within this framework of Newtonian science, there was no room for spirituality and no sense of community. God could be declared dead without causing uproar. As Newtonian mechanism on the one hand inspired a rational concept of society, it on the other hand encouraged the idea of a rational ethics, serving the individual by providing meaning, and serving the state by producing law abiding citizens.

During the first part of the twentieth century, the mechanical interpretation of nature resulting from Newtonian science was first challenged by new insights into the smallest particles of nature called quanta. Quantum Theory seemed to say that, contrary to Newtonian certainty, nature at a fundamental level appeared to be quite inconsistent. Observations made on quantum objects such as photons and electrons seemed to contradict the laws of traditional physics. What was observed could not be explained with the tools of that physics. The most famous example is the dual character of the smallest particles, which in experiments appear to be waves and particles alternatively, depending on what the observer set out to find. Under traditional laws of mechanics this is not possible. A particle in the macro world of our experience cannot also be a wave. In the famous Copenhagen Agreement (1932), a considerable number of scientists of that period agreed to settle the question about the true nature of microscopic particles such as electrons and protons by accepting this contradiction as unsolvable. Even though several recognized scientists of the time disagreed with this solution, among them most prominently Albert Einstein, this interpretation of the quantum world became a cornerstone of the so-called standard model.

Another important influence of quantum theory on the general worldview of the time was what became known as observer dependence. Classical physics is objective. There is no place in Descartes' theoretical explanations for an observer or even a subjective mind. Processes in classical physics develop regardless of whether they are observed or not.[2]

Quantum Theory seemed to offer a completely new role for the observer. Referring back to the famous wave/particle duality, it was generally assumed that the quantum world behaves like a wave when not observed, and turns into particles when observed. The moment of observation became known as quantum collapse: The collapse of the wave into a particle through observation. This phenomenon placed a completely new emphasis on the importance of the observer, and thus on the subject in an otherwise objective, physical world. This led to far reaching research into subjectivity and a reevaluation of the role of consciousness.

Another observation at the quantum level has had great impact on every day world views. At the quantum level the whole world appears to be intrinsically connected. This phenomenon came to be known as quantum wholeness. Scientifically this is derived from the fact that certain quantum systems appear to communicate with each other over spatial distances instantaneously, at a speed faster than the speed of light. Much has been made of this phenomenon. In a world dominated by rampant disconnectedness, super individualism, and alienation, wholeness and connectedness are values we all yearn for and even cherish. In the recent aftermath of the Asian Tsunami for instance, scientists scrambled to find an explanation why so few animals died in the

---

[2] This is true in spite of the enormous role the observing self in the Cartesian world. Descartes anchored his proof of existence on the absoluteness of the observing mind. By placing the Self in the realm of spirit his philosophy created the ultimate ideological split, known as Cartesian dualism.

disaster when compared to the human toll. The question whether animals are somehow closer connected to natural events than we human beings are was on every ones' mind.

For many, especially those in the New Age movements, the implications of quantum theory, especially what it seems to say about wholeness and connectedness are easily aligned with one of the key elements of the Eastern Buddhist experience. At the depth of the spiritual experience of *nirvana*, the encounter with emptiness is often associated with a simultaneous experience of total connectedness with the universe. The self-conscious mind, which even pre-philosophically continuously asserts "I am not the Other", is seen as the strongest obstacle to the goal of Eastern enlightenment. In the extreme, this view leads to the denial of the natural world, whose center, of course, is my own self. According to ancient Hindu tradition, which is becoming ever more popular among certain groups in the West, the world is *maya*, a veil of illusion. Enlightenment can be reached when we lift the veil and experience everything as one. This same experience of emptiness and simultaneous connectedness is reported and verified by numerous mystics in the Western tradition as well. Mystics are people who have experienced the divine in the world of things by submersing their minds into the world, rather than escaping from it. While this kind of mysticism and the mystical tradition in general are certainly valuable parts of the human experience of transcendence, they can add little to our experience of community.[3]

Interestingly enough, a number of key scientists around the formulation of quantum mechanics have also come to the conclusion that the nature of the quantum world supports the idea of things as an illusion, Werner Heisenberg being the most prominent among them. This, too, was interpreted by many to

---

[3] Thomas Merton who as a trappist monk saw the contradiction between individual mystical pursuit and the need for community. When discussing the Desert Fathers Merton once said: "They were among the few who were ahead of their time, and opened the way for the development of a new man, and a new society...The eighteenth and nineteenth centuries with their pragmatic individualism...prepared the way for the great regression to the herd mentality that is taking place now. The flight of these men to the desert was neither purely negative nor purely individualistic...They did not reject society with proud contempt, as if they were superior to other men. On the contrary,...they fled from the world of men (because) in the world men were divided into those who were successful, and imposed their will on others, and those who had to give in and be imposed upon. The Desert Fathers declined to be ruled by men, but had no desire to rule over others themselves." (Merton, 1960:4–5).

mean, that everything outside of myself is not really real, and that the most important spiritual task consists in eliminating concerns for one's own self. The goal is to reach a state of mind in which nothing matters. Non-attachment promises to be the ultimate liberation. This kind of philosophical stance does not lead to spirituality or community, but rather points toward a dark pessimism a la Schopenhauer.

The end of the nineteenth century had seen a tremendous decline of enlightenment certainty and trust in reason. Intellectuals had lost their confidence in the power of the human mind and succumbed to irrational fears of a dooming end. This was a direct result of the implications of the Second Law of Thermodynamics. This law, discovered during the nineteenth century, said that any system, left to its own devices, will go toward decreased order, a virtual death sentence for the universe. In the twentieth century, this sense of general pessimism was again supported by an uncertainty governing the objects of the quantum world, a fact that was formulated in the famous Uncertainty Principle. This principle states that a quantum object can never be described with any sense of accuracy when stating its location and its velocity at the same time. Even though quantum theory deals with an utterly strange world, seemingly far removed from our experience, quantum uncertainty was quickly interpreted to be a direct blow to the understanding of physical principles in the macro world, the world we intimately know, as well.

On the surface this effect would seem utterly strange and unexplainable. Why should the one have such an effect on the other? But on closer inspection these two worlds are not at all separated. There is not such a thing as the macro world independent and away from the micro world. The two worlds are intricately interwoven, one nested inside the other. What sense could it possibly make that the two were ruled by a completely different set of natural laws, but yet, there it was. It is well known that Einstein himself never accepted this and to the end of his life searched for a hidden solution to the quantum conundrum. His famous edict: God does not play dice, has become proverbial.

A final scientific discovery toward the later part of the twentieth century was the formulation of what became known as chaos theory, introduced by the Nobel Prize winning Russian physicist Ilya Prigogine in *Order Out of Chaos*, in 1984. The most important implication of chaos theory resulted yet again in a sense of general unpredictability of natural phenomena.

To the great dismay of many scientists, who would have liked science to provide the kind of security that philosophy had given up searching for, this new scientific theory now most definitely extended the uncertainty of the micro world to virtually all processes taking place and defining the macro world. Many scientists hasted to soften the damage by pointing out that their conclusions from chaos theory are not at all anti deterministic, but the damage was done. The new concept of deterministic chaos was supposed to counteract the fact that chaos theory indeed was a theory that showed the general unpredictability of natural phenomena at all levels. The idea of a deterministic chaos never captured popular imagination like chaos theory itself. In fact, on closer inspection, deterministic chaos only seems to state the obvious; once a quantum event has run its course, all individual steps become totally causal and logical, exactly as in an event of classical nature. But that is a little bit like saying, once the bad guy has killed, I know he is a killer. Classical predictability strives for something much more causal and convincing. The classical scholar would like to be able to determine by analyzing the DNA of a person, whether he has the potential to be a killer, and indeed eventually will kill. That is meant by classical determinism.

As a direct result of chaos theory, physicists now had to admit that even those systems studied by classical mechanics can behave in an intrinsically unpredictable manner. In principle, such a system may be perfectly deterministic, but in practice its behavior is completely unpredictable. In broader terms, a system is chaotic if its trajectory through state space sensitively depends on the initial conditions; that is if small causes can produce large effects. This phenomenon became popularized as the famous Butterfly Effect. In fact, it now became evident, that all living systems belong to this group of open dynamical systems that can be subject to chaotic disturbances under the influence of the Butterfly Effect. Therefore classical mechanics can predict the trajectory of mechanical objects, but is incapable to fully predict the actions of any living systems such as the flight of a bee or the path through a day of any human being, simply because living things can alter their path.

According to classical physics, scientists assumed that small causes will always produce small effects and large causes large ones. With this assumption many small conditions in the observed world could be ignored, and yet, scientists believed they could make reliable predictions. Today we know that natural systems are non-linear, which means that they are sensitive to initial conditions. But to know all initial conditions of a process is impossible. Therefore scientific theory had to accept a level of uncertainty in all its predictions. So when we look today to science to provide answers to global questions, we must keep this distinction in mind: theories derived from scientific observation and scientific facts cannot claim to be universally true in the old, traditional sense. In fact, it is clear today that universal, absolute truth claims have always been vehicles invented and used by those in power to establish and maintain control. Such truth claims have rightly been called ideologies, and as tools for power are in need of deconstruction.

Many of the implications of quantum theory and chaos theory can perhaps only indirectly be used to support a naturalistic approach to community and spirituality. New Age and some feminist theories for instance have taken from quantum theory's concept of wholeness and connectedness to assist their causes. More often perhaps the combined effect of unpredictability and uncertainty found both in quantum theory and chaos theory produced an irrational fear of the future and a totally pessimistic stress of life's general meaningless that would rather negate than support the idea of community and spirituality.

At the same time, the legacy of Western civilization with its history of totalitarian systems, disregard of individual freedoms, and mass exploitation appears to be also pointing away from collaboration, collectivization, and connectedness, though these are obviously necessary features of any functional community. The global village applauded when not so long ago the walls came down that had separated a collective and totalitarian system from the rest of the world. The momentous dissolution of one of the two superpowers is almost old history now, but the fear and resentment of forced wholeness and top down orchestrated cooperation lingers on.

But over the past few decades, almost unnoticed, these same scientific theories that seem to provide support for a pessimistic worldview, have also changed the general focus of research from individual components to a research into systems and wholeness itself. When in 1944, Erwin Schrödinger (1967) first published his short, but consequential, essay *What is Life?*, little was known about collective behavior of individuals and particles at a small and at the large scale. Reductionism was the standard of scientific inquiry. By investigating and analyzing the smallest member of a group, scientists expected to get information about the composite set they were investigating.

The principles of System Theory, Cybernetics or Synergy were not yet understood (Ashby 1956; Bertalanffy 1968). No one had heard of a Science of Complexity either.

Asking the same question today, over sixty years later, new theories, and whole new sciences have been developed to assist us in understanding complex phenomena such as life, community, and perhaps also spirituality from equally complex perspectives. Instead of trying to understand the riddle of life and communal practices by reducing the problem to its individual components, for Schrödinger this was the individual cell or the DNA within each cell, we have learned to investigate complex arrangement of those smaller units in a holistic way. Today we should have a better understanding of how the very complexity might be the source of sophisticated new and dynamic properties such as life. We should be able to develop new insights into why community is a vital part of each natural system. We should also be able to provide detailed reasons why communication, the essence of spirituality, is present at all levels of the natural world, and why this will also help the human community to fulfill its ultimate cosmic mission.

When investigating the structure of complex systems we realize more and more that the world is comprised of layers and layers of such complex systems. Each is nested within myriads of others and all are interdependent in more ways than we can fathom. Each individual system is a whole on one level and a part of a larger whole on another, as Arthur Koestler (1978) pointed out many decades ago.

My first insight into wholeness and systems came from aesthetics. Studying at the Frankfurt School with Theodor W. Adorno during the Sixties, I learned about theories of classical and modern art and music. One of Adorno's main aesthetic questions was this: What makes a piece of art whole? Was this only a subjective matter of experience or was there something inherent in the piece of art that suggested wholeness? With his attention firmly focused on the transition from classical to modern music, the question of wholeness in Adorno's aesthetic theory was paramount. Wholeness was one of those ancient qualities, which Aristotle had required from a good piece of art. To express their opposition to such ideological aesthetics (an aesthetics that insists on wholeness even if life seems everything but whole), modern artists and composers had often made it their mission to destroy, structurally and through content – or lack thereof, the very wholeness of a piece of art. What was this elusive wholeness and could one really ever escape it?

Following Aristotle's command to achieve wholeness and believing in the mission, classical composers had laid down structural and mathematical requirements to guarantee the completeness and wholeness of a musical piece. Was it possible to leave out certain requirements or contradict them? Would a piece of art then be less than whole? To describe the transition of a piece from the level of disconnectedness to a level of wholeness Adorno used a new terminology. This he called a qualitative transition (*qualitativer Umschlag*).

Qualitative transition was also used to explain the emergence of a synthesis when in the dialectical triad two opposites combined to jointly emerge as a new unit, but now at a higher level, containing the earlier opposites and somehow superceding them (*Aufhebung*). The dialectical model was a first conceptualization of a collective process that today is called phase transition by physicists and bifurcation by system theorists. Philosophically this model might still be useful as an explanation or a visualization of qualitative advance of natural systems when a certain critical mass or threshold is reached.

During a discussion at a theater festival in Poland in the Seventies the question came up whether dialectics could last beyond death. At the time I intuitively affirmed this question, but had no real grasp of its meaning. I have now come to the conclusion that in nature there exists a system of qualitative advancement quite independent of human cognition. In some sense then, this would be a natural dialectic that persists beyond death. In a paper delivered at the Consciousness Conference in Tokyo[4] in 1999, I began using the term Collective Orchestration to describe the largely functional aspect of such a dialectical transition. Further inspired by Hiroomi Umezawa's (Yibu 1995) use of the collective mode to explain complex collective brain functions, I began exploring Collective Orchestration as a mechanism of qualitative advance occurring in all natural systems. Collective Orchestration is synchronized behavior of otherwise independently existing individuals for the purpose of achieving tasks that are not achievable to each individual in separation. Through Collective Orchestration individuals collaborate to achieve a qualitatively higher state of existence. Collective Orchestration describes a system of evolutionary advance that as of now has not been fully explored.

---

[4] Werner Krieglstein, *From Aristotle's Universals to Umezawa's Collective Mode. Is the Vacuum really a Proper Locus?*

In *What is Life? The Next Fifty Years, Speculations on the Future of Biology,* a number of evolutionary biologists reflect on Schrödinger's heritage. The biologist Stuart Kauffman (1995:83–114) emphasizes the importance of collective dynamics in the emergence of life. He says: "The ultimate source of order and self-reproduction may lie in the emergence of collectively ordered dynamics in complex chemical reaction systems" (Kauffman 1995:85). Kauffman (1995:84) asserts that

> ...development and evolution, while requiring the stability of organic molecules, may also require emergent ordered properties in the collective behavior of complex, non-equilibrium chemical reaction systems. Such complex reaction systems, I shall suggest, can spontaneously cross a threshold, or phase transition, beyond which they become capable of collective self-reproduction, evolution, and exquisitely ordered dynamical behavior. The ultimate sources of the order requisite for life's emergence and evolution may rest on new principles of collective emergent behavior in far from equilibrium reaction systems.

This is the kind of Collective Orchestration I had in mind. Collective Orchestration can be understand as the process not only for life to emerge, but for qualitative advance of all dynamical systems, beginning with the continuity of space/time to the complex organizations of corporations and galaxies. This will also have profound implications for our discussion of community.

Chaos theory put the concept of self-organization into the center of scientific discussion. Self-Organization is a key concept in understanding processes of Collective Orchestration in the so-called inanimate world. Scientists currently explain events of self-organization when they occur among inanimate things as a simple move of a system toward a state of lower energy consumption. They use this description of an otherwise difficult to explain process in order to preserve the traditional materialistic view of nature.

In order to be able to fully integrate the process of self-organization into the inanimate world I like to propose to accept a view common to virtually all primal people and most non-Western traditions. This is the view that the whole world, including the so-called inanimate world, is indeed permeated with some level of mind or consciousness. It has alternately been called "panpsychism," "panexperientialism," or "quantum animism." In this view, awareness does not start at the level of one-cell organisms, animals, or even only with human beings, but a rudimentary level of awareness exists at the deepest level of the material world. At the basic level, this awareness of a particle may be as little as having a preferred state, being on rather than off. It might mean being open to certain combinations, and being closed to others. Within the terminology of Transcendental Perspectivism, I have called this awareness an inside/out view, a minimal kind of perspective present at all levels of the natural world.

The idea of locating consciousness within *materia* is not new. In *The Spirit of Materia*, the French nuclear physicist Jean Charon (1979) identified electrons as the most likely carriers of mind and spirit. Charon claimed that the basic building blocks of materia and spirit directly connect on a material level. As an extension to Albert Einstein's theory of relativity, which, according to Charon, left no room for spirit in the universe, Charon proposed a "Complex Theory of Relativity," which includes the possibility of consciousness.

According to the traditional mechanistic view of the universe, the laws of nature causally determine and therefore predict everything. This view, according to Charon, failed to address spiritual phenomena, driving out the last of whatever spirit remained from mythical times. Only after the more flexible quantum theory replaced the mechanical worldview were we able to rethink the position of consciousness or spirit in the composition of the universe. Quantum theory replaced the stringent logical order proposed by the strict geometrization inherent in traditional science with a new order of probability.

Charon claimed that another space-time complements the space-time of our immediate experience. In that complementary space-time the coordinates are reversed. Every electron is an entity with its bulk existing in that other space-time. Charon used the image of an ocean and the airspace above it to explain his speculation. The ocean corresponds to our world. The airspace above the ocean reflects this other reality, the realm of spirit. Each electron, according to Charon, lives in the airspace above the ocean and only touches the surface of the ocean at one point. This single point is the only appearance of an electron in this world. This other space is a spiritual world where information is stored by the infinite multitude of electrons. Each electron, according to Charon (1979:85):

> represents an autonomous individuality, which has its very own space-time. This space-time differs from ours substantially. Each electron forms a

separate micro-universe. Its time is cyclical, which allows it to recollect all past events of the space it consists of. All events within this micro-universe develop with increasing negentropy. All this is evidence for our conclusion that the electron contains a spiritual space-time.

Electrons, according to Charon (1979:88), have the ability to form systems with other electrons without any external help, and they can develop hierarchical orders of ever-higher complexity through increased information. He claimed that his research into the physics of elementary particles showed that electrons have the ability to store information. They have a system of remembering and retrieving such information, and they communicate and cooperate with other electrons to create and operate complex systems (Charon 1979:90). This creation and operation of systems counteracts the entropic decay that otherwise rules the material world. Negentropy is the ability of mind to overcome the disintegration of *materia* by systematic organization. Similar to the binary model of storing information that computers use, Charon suggested that the negative or positive spin within each electron constitutes the mechanism of electrons to store information. The exchange of information between electrons, said Charon, is connected with the electric magnetic properties of electrons. Contrary to the functional character of computer chips, however, electrons have the freedom to enter into relations with other electrons. The free exchange of information and affection between the elementary particles of *materia*, Charon (1979:182) said, is similar to the exchange of affection human beings experience as love.

When Charon's book was first published in 1979, scientists had not yet discovered the science of chaos. Charon had little support for his thesis of a self-organizing tendency among elementary particles. Chaos theory put self-organization in the center of the discussion as a common property of chaotic systems, which includes the systems of smallest particle. Today the idea of a self-organizing quantum world does not seem so far fetched. In *The Life of the Cosmos*, Lee Smolin (1997), a physics professor at Pennsylvania State University, connects self-organizational processes observed on the large scale of galaxies with those observed on the quantum scale. He asks,

> Is it not possible that self-organization through processes analogous to natural selection is, indeed, the missing element without which we have so far been unable to construct a quantum theory of cosmology? (Smolin 1997:292).

Philosophically the idea to allocate consciousness to all nature, even at the level of the smallest particles, is not at all new. In 2003, the *Journal of Consciousness Studies*, dedicated a whole issue to the topic of panpsychism. David Skrbina (2005), the editor of the journal issue and researcher at the University of Michigan, is in the process of publishing a book on the subject. In his introductory remarks Skrbina (2003:5) says:

> ...the view that all things have a mind, or a mind-like quality – has been held by a surprisingly large number of the greatest thinkers in the history of western civilization. And not just in ancient times, but virtually throughout the whole of the past 2500 years. Even in the modern era of philosophy (since 1500 C.E.), one finds nearly three dozen major philosophers advocating some variation on the panpsychist theme. Additionally in the twentieth century we find another two dozen or so prominent physicists, biologists, and others supporting a similar view. Clearly these individuals found something compelling about panpsychism.

Skrbina then discusses the various forms of panpsychism and how throughout the history of Western philosophy various philosophers expressed panpsychic views and tendencies. It is perhaps needless to say that within the newly emerging studies of consciousness this discussion has become of vital importance because the panpsychist solution could bridge the age old gap of mind and matter and avoid further dualisms. From Plato, through Leibniz to Whitehead and Chalmers, philosophers of all times have defended this view, but panpsychism remained at the fringes of Western thought.

Looking into the 21st century, Skrbina notes a considerable increase in discussions around this topic, seeing it as the "very hallmark of a new anti-mechanistic worldview." Skrbina (2003:43) concludes:

> ...panpsychism has much to offer even beyond the confines of academic philosophy. It is not only a viable alternative conception of mind, but it promises to realign our thinking toward a more compassionate and ecological outlook on nature. Certainly one of the contributing factors to our present environmental (and some would add, spiritual) crisis is an entrenched system of mechanistic values, and any value system that sees nature as consisting of dead and insensate particles is ripe for exploitation. As many have observed, a panpsychic world view can serve as the conceptual framework for a new system of sympathetic and ecological values, one that may form a new basis for action.

Panpsychism, when it refers to the awareness of the smallest particles is often called, quantum animism. It sets the basis for a compassionate relationship with the universe. Scientifically quantum animism makes the phenomenon of self-organization in the inorganic world much more plausible. Some level of self-organization has also been observed in computer simulations that mimic fundamental systems. As in the game of life, some basic logical units are programmed to relate to each other following a set of very simple rules. But all these systems operate only after an outside mind or control center, in most cases a computer operator, has designed the system according to those rule and then set the system in motion. This is not unlike the deistic universe in which God has set the parameters and then in an initial bang set the whole thing in motion. Without this outside originator the system would be utterly incapable of self organization.

The whole thing changes when we assume that at the basis logical units operate and relate to each other without outside impulse. Charon demonstrated this by using electrons as examples. This is quantum animism in action. Self-organization then makes immediate, intuitive sense. Quantum animism provides the background for the possibility of a meaningful communication with the natural world. What is lacking still is an organizational principle that explains how less developed units evolve into ever higher ones of increasing complexity and flexibility, which will set the foundation for a new theory of community.

Traditional wisdom would suggest that evolutionary forces are the motor of advancement at the micro level as well as at the macro level of life. But traditional science only allows evolution to set in at the level of life. Blind tumbling of particles, following the laws of nature is supposed to be the norm for the rest. With the acceptance of quantum animism, we are able to extent evolutionary forces to the inanimate world.

We are able now to take a closer look at Collective Orchestration and how this organizational principle will affect a naturalistic understanding of community. Collective Orchestration is based on cooperative aspects of systems and advancement of systems through cooperation. Cooperative organization among living individuals has been observed in various forms. Take for instance a small a volvox, which has been called one of the seven wonders of the micro world (www.microscopyuk.org.uk/mag/indexmag. html; www.microscopyuk.org.uk/mag/artdec03/volvox.html). A volvox is a small, round animal that lives in the water and is made up of individual cells of algae. When food supplies fall short separate algae cells have been observed organizing into a volvox. This gives the individual cells an advantage in survival. Connected they are able to propel themselves in a way similar to an octopus and capture food inside the sphere. The algae cells operate in a unified manner, just as the cells in a larger organism do. Even staunch defenders of evolutionary survival theory admit that this is a clear example of increased complexity. Increasingly complex organizations of cells, combined with favorable mutations, can result in higher forms of life.

A similarly stunning example comes from the same murky world of one-cell organisms. At the threshold of what we generally call life, at the level where chemistry meets biology, one-celled organisms called dictyostelium live alone and isolated for most of their existence. As individual particles they do not even qualify as "alive." Like a virus, they have hardly an existence of their own. As much as scientists can tell, each of these tiny particles is identical with the other. But a strange mutation occurs when a qualified number of these creatures experience a deficiency in food and space. Scientists have observed how they suddenly group together to cooperate in a formerly unknown way. Collectively, they form one large multi-celled organism with head, tail, and digestive system. Each cell takes over a specific function within the new organism. They evidently group together to achieve goals that they could not achieve by themselves. In the case of the dictyostelium, the new body enables this collection of individual cells to move to new feeding grounds. They accomplish this in several metamorphic stages:

> After several hours, the Dictyostelium slug goes through another change. The back end catches up with the tip, and the slug turns into a blob. The blob stretches upward a second time, and now some amoeba produce rigid bundles of cellulose. They die in the process, but their sacrifice allows the blob to become a slender stalk. Perched atop the stalk is a globe, bulging with living amoebas, each of which covers itself in a cellulose coat and becomes a dormant spore. In this form the colony will wait until something – a drop of rainwater, a passing worm, the foot of a bird – picks up the spores and takes them to a bacteria-rich place where they can emerge from their shells and start their lives over (Zimmer 1998:88).

Today scientists have no idea what makes some cells become tail, others head, and yet others, digestive organs. There is no observable DNA in the original units. As far as science can say, they are identical. Yet, at the moment of unification they "know" or perhaps even "choose" their places. Scientists have speculated much about this phenomenon. Is there a hidden variable, something that has so far evaded the observing scientist?

In nature, it appears autonomous individuals can collaborate in a synergistic way, when natural conditions make such collaboration advantageous or necessary. Once they achieve this cooperation, development levels off and can remain static, at least for some time. We can observe such plateaus in evolutionary development at all levels. They have been called forms, universal categories, class, species, or populations depending on the cognitive frame and the theory behind it.

What are the energies behind synergistic behavior? What natural power orchestrates such community formation? Is it possible that one day an organized colony of these amoebas, did not disperse again after they had found new feeding grounds, but stayed together as one organism, forming the new beginning of a higher form of life? Remarkably, scientists have noticed that dictyostelium are similar to the cells that make up the human system. Millions of other bacteria and microbes have not become part of our complex system. Why is it that these community creating dictyostelium have become part of the success story of life? Could this collective orchestration be the tool with which nature proceeds and climbs up the evolutionary ladder to ever-new plateaus?

Collective orchestration is also a well-known occurrence among insects. When a new hive forms, bees join together in a swarm. They leave the old habitat and collect around the queen, often hanging from a tree. The collective slapping of the bees wings produces a temperature in the center of the blob that differs from the temperature of each individual bee. This is the optimal temperature for the queen to conceive new life (Krieglstein 2002:79–85).

For living organisms the traditional interpretation of such organizational phenomena, on the surface at least, appears adequate. Why is there a need for a new approach? While it is intuitively correct to assume that living creatures have a tendency to organize, for the very purpose of survival, this is, according to standard theory, not at all intuitive to assume at the inorganic level. Here blind chance, governed by the laws of nature, is the general rule.

Stephen Strogatz, a mathematician who recently published a book on the subject of synchronized behavior, observed that Collective Orchestration occurs in nature on many levels. Technically such synchronized behavior is made possible through so-called oscillators. An oscillator is a pulsating device mostly used for the purpose of generating a signal. Coupled oscillators are systems of such devices with two or more members that are communicating with each other. Often their communication results in synchronized behavior. Strogatz (2003:3) observed:

> Groups of fireflies, planets, or pacemaker cells are all collections of oscilla- tors-entities that cycle automatically, that repeat themselves over and over again at more or less regular time intervals. Fireflies flash; planets orbit; pacemaker cells fire. Two or more oscillators are said to be coupled if some physical or chemical process allows them to influence one another. Fireflies communicate with light. Planets tug on one another with gravity. Heart cells pass electrical currents back and forth. As these examples suggest, nature uses every available channel to allow these oscillators to talk to one another. And the result of those conversations is often synchrony, in which all the oscillators begin to move as one.

Synchronicity in its simplest form occurs when two things keep happening simultaneously for an extended period of time. According to Strogatz (2003:2), "such persistent sync comes easily to us human beings, and, for some reason, it often gives us pleasure. We like to dance together, sing together, play in a band." The surprising fact is that this includes synchronized behavior among non living, non animate things. He says:

> ...when sync occurs among unconscious entities like electrons or cells, it seems almost miraculous. It's surprising enough to see animals cooperating – thousands of crickets chirping in unison on a summer night; the graceful undulating of schools of fish – but it's even more shocking to see mobs of mindless things falling into step by themselves (Strogatz 2003:2).

Strogatz observes that all these occurrences of synchronized behavior follow the same mathematical pattern described by oscillators. They are also perfect examples of how natural systems, animate and inanimate, self organize into more complex creatures: Strogatz (2003:13) observes:

> ...the fireflies organize themselves. No Maestro is required, and it doesn't matter what the weather is like. Sync occurs through mutual cuing, in the same way that an orchestra can keep perfect time without a conductor.

What's counterintuitive here is that the insects don't need to be intelligent. They have all the ingredients they need: Each firefly contains an oscillator, a little metronome, whose timing adjusts automatically in response to the flashes of others. That's it.

Elsewhere I have collected evidence for Collective Orchestration at virtually every level of the natural world, from the level of space/time quanta to the organization of human beings in economic and spiritual communities.

In my book *Compassion* I asked:

> Could collective orchestration also drive human collaboration? Could the same collective orchestration cause human beings to form communities? Is there a subconscious awareness that through collective orchestration the whole human race will reach a level of realization, a new dimension of awareness, which we cannot reach individually? If so, nurturing human communities could be one of the most burning missions of humanity on earth" (Krieglstein 2002:85).

Once panpsychism, quantum animism, and collective orchestration have become part of the way science views the universe, I am convinced, humanity will finally evolve to a new level of cooperation, among each other and with the rest of the natural world. This just might help bring about the bold vision of Tatiana Alekseeva in her dream of a new global community enabling a new non-ideological philosophy that is based on the principles of self-organization, cooperation, solidarity, and mutual respect. It may finally bring about the kind of reconciled society that Siebert envisioned in his Future III. Even if today we still seem to be far from realizing such a vision, the tools are at hand to move toward it.

Chapter Sixteen

Socio-Economic Basis for Religious Socialization and Youth Issues in Croatia

Dunja Potočnik

Fundamental Social, Demographic and Economic Indicators

Considering a high level of economic and social development, a substantial private sector and a significant strategic position, Croatia had a good starting point at the beginning of its national transition. What brought Croatia back into the process of development was the war for independence that caused severe infrastructure and economic damages, not to mention over a half of million people exiled from their homes (at times, more than 8% of the total population) and the loss of over 10,000 human lives (Mendeš and Potočnik 2003). Taking the cohort of 15–29 years of age (as a most common limit for the youth cohort), even the youngest of them were relatively young when the war started. Thus, we can conclude that these turbulent changes marked the greatest part of their socialization period. Existing problems in our society, generated by the structural economic crisis, intensified by unsuccessful policies for its solution, affect the lives of the youth and prolong their social and economic dependence and social marginalization.

When talking about youth in transitional societies, one must keep in mind that they are in a more disadvantaged situation than their peers in the developed countries or the previous generations of youth in the modern transitional countries. The statement that they represent an irreplaceable economic, political and social resource is as valid for them as it is for the youth from the stable democratic countries, but they are going through a unique historical period and social transformation at that. This means that the maturation of young people in transitional societies is characterized by a double transition. On the one hand, they are passing through the universal period of growing up and preparing to assume permanent social roles, and on the other hand, this process is taking place in a society itself in transition from one social system to another. Their socialization is occurring in the conditions where the institutions, processes and social norms, which alleviate the transition in the world of adults, have weakened, become disabled or are in the process of transformation (Ilišin and Radin 2002). Basic determinants of the social position of the majority of youth and the degree of their integration are as follows:

- inclusion into educational or working process,
- family support,
- local community and
- peer groups.

Croatia shares some of the same trends that have occurred in Europe: during the 1990's youth became the poorest population group in the countries of Central and Eastern Europe. Countries in transition are exposed to additional risks of social differentiation, of social welfare level reductions, and to the appearance of new risks (organized crime, juvenile delinquency, drug addiction, human beings' trafficking and commercial sexual exploitation). Young people as a whole are in an unfavorable socio-economic position in comparison to other age groups. This means that young persons do not own property (real estate, savings and stocks); they have difficulties in finding employment and obtaining housing, and are dependent on their parents' support. Transitional processes increase the.degree of uncertainty for the young persons who, having completed their education, have no clear perspectives on the opportunities for employment, professional development and leading independent and productive lives.

The main aim of this paper is to give a short review of youth problems in Croatia, and the ways in which youth NGOs and youth Church organizations deal with these problems. Reference will be made to some research on religiosity in Croatia, which were conducted on the youth population. The specific group that is focused on are young Catholics, since the Catholic population in Croatia encompass more than 90% of the population. Also, reference will be made to some examples of positive practice in youth issues, both inside the Church and inside the Croatian NGOs.

There were several associations related to youth, which were expressed by youth in a focus group research conducted by the UNDP team in five Croatian regions in December 2003. These were: change, education, fun, optimism, future, tolerance, subcultures, creativity, ideals, mistakes, courage, freedom, unemployment, disinterest, apathy, initiative, drugs, and sexuality. Following these were advantages and disadvantages of being young. Advantages were: easier studying and training, young people are not burdened with the past, nowadays society is making efforts in helping young people to make progress, young people have an ability to make things better. Unfortunately, disadvantages and problems were significantly predominant. These included: young people were complaining that the adults do not take young people seriously; financial dependence upon parents and the wider society; too many expectations from parents and society as a whole; lack of experience; leisure activities are to expensive; unemployment; intolerance among youth (there is no sensibility for differences, especially between different subcultures); violence; use of drugs and alcohol; lack of sound information on youth rights and possibilities in Croatian society; underdeveloped communication between youth and institutions of official policy, as well as between institutions of official policy and civil organizations; adults are very often expressing prejudices towards youth (i.e. young people are unable to make things better, they only think of fun, they are drug-addicts); the post-war period is still not ended; many families suffer from war consequences, as well as from bad financial situation; education is not organized and there is too much pressure on pupils and students; the media are not focused on youth issues and there is a rigid and strict control of people who hold the most power in society, as politicians and entrepreneurs.

Summarizing everything stated above and the results of the UNDP research (Bačić, et al. 2004), we can divide youth issues into several groups. The main youth issues are: (1) youth and economics; (2) youth participation in society; (3) leisure time; (4) information, communication and media; (5) youth marginalization; (6) education; (7) health; and (8) conflicts, violence and discrimination. The actual situation in Croatian society compounds most of these youth problems, e.g. economic underdevelopment and regional disparities joined with bad or no communication between various governmental and non-governmental institutions mean lack of resources for better education and employment, which leads to social tensions and lower quality of life both in official institutions, like schools and universities, and in leisure time and culture. Existing data on young persons indicate a trend toward prolonging youth and the socio-economic lack of independence. The causes lie, among other factors, in the extension of the educational process, more difficulties in finding one's first and permanent employment, more complex conditions for access to material goods (regular incomes, credit, ownership of real estate property, etc.) and the marginalization of youth in the decision-making processes. The UNDP focus group research showed that the youth problems are very serious. Youth have many interests but they feel frustrated because they very often have no means for accomplishing their goals, and sometimes it seems that society and the official policy have no understanding for youth issues.

Problems related to the lack of leisure time activities for young people and areas for creative self-expression of the young, as well as lack of cultural programs, especially those originating from the focus groups, are fundamental in their essence precisely because it is the mode of using and the quality manner of spending one's free time that are in question. For young people, the shaping of their free time is certainly one of the basic segments of their everyday life, from the classical boredom and flipping TV channels to taking a walk into town. Nobody doubts that the young have enough free time on their hands; although somebody who would doubt the fact that the young are creative and that they wish to use their free time usefully could still be found. Contrary to their belief, most young people agree with the fact that there is not a sufficient number of programs and areas that could help them adequately fill the emptiness in their lives. If this is the feeling that prevails in Zagreb, just imagine what it must be like in the smaller communities; an indicator of some statements given by the young people who participated at the focus groups held at Vukovar, Karlovac or Pula. If you do not have the possibility to express your own creativity in the right way and you spend your time inadequately, there is an increased possibility that you will spend that time in socially less acceptable ways.

According to the latest data from the Croatian Bureau of Statistics', Croatia had $6,968 per capita. Using the internationally comparable standard for transitional economies ($4.3 per capita per day), the absolute poverty rate in Croatia is quite small (about 4%). However, the Croatian Bureau of Statistics' Household Budget Survey found that almost 10% of the population fell below the national poverty threshold. According to the Croatian Employment Service, the rate of youth unemployment in the year 2005 was 32.9%, double than the total population rate unemployment (14.0% according to the International Labor Organization standards, and 18.0% according to the CES standards). The eruption of unemployment and economic problems clearly indicates that young people are well aware of the fact that the basis for social progress lies in economic stability. However, it was surprising to see the low percentage of young people who were dissatisfied with the education system (Bačić, et al. 2004), which was similar to the results obtained from focus groups where young people placed education only in sixth place of their priorities. The participation rate in compulsory primary education is 98%. The data on secondary education participation is ambivalent. It is interesting to see what people think about education, and for this purpose there was a study on youth and education in 2002 (Baranović 1999). Youth see education as a resource for meeting their intrinsic needs. They partially regard school as a resource for solving their existential problems, but it is interesting that school as an institution for providing them with prerequisites for easier integration in society is listed in last place. In general, the data indicates that they are very rational in their expectations (primarily turned to expectations in solving the immediate existential problems upon completion of education). The data, namely, indicates that the young are aware of the limited influence of education in solving their life problems, that it is not appreciated enough in the society and that there are other factors that influence the social and economic status of the individual and possibilities of their promotion. These findings compared with UNDP research indicates that comprehensive changes are needed in Croatian educational system. The frustration that comes from the inability to fulfill one's goals at work, as the major socialization factor in the transitional process from youth to adulthood as well as apathy that grips the young people is understandable. This apathy is manifested in the escape from social and political engagement and loosing faith in the important institutions of the system, but also in the increased readiness to leave the country in the search for employment.

Health problems among young people are primarily linked with the problem of drug addiction and problems with reproductive health. Here we are concentrating only on the problem of drug addiction, or more specifically, "dance drugs", the case here being mainly ecstasy, speed (amphetamines) and other substances popular among the younger population in techno-rave parties (Bačić, et al. 2004).

The post-war and the transitional period in Croatia and the neglecting of the youth as a specific group caused sustainability and transition of prejudices, discrimination and violent behavior patterns among the young. The social and political context in Croatia does not yet provide sufficient support from the institutions, and there is no awareness and willingness among the citizens for their active involvement in changing this situation. The willingness of government institutions to deal with the issue of discrimination and violence, especially in the war affected areas, does not offer systematic and methodical work for promoting the values of non-violence. The climate that suppresses and approves violence, pre-supposes violence as a legitimate way of dealing with conflict, which may result in a long-term adoption of these value patterns by the young.

Young people perceive the marginalization they experience by their social surroundings as one of the facts of young people's status in the society, which was also confirmed by the research and the focus-groups reports. Marginalization is manifold and proceeds on several social system levels. Primary, marginalization applies to young people in general, to their actual inferiority in the social stratification system and to specific forms of exclusion based on the permeability of societies age limit (society, in our case, being rather impermeable). Additionally, on other levels, appears the marginalization of those young people who belong to diverse sub-cultural groups. Furthermore, young people have to face the marginalization belonging to their parental environment (for example, the rural one), additionally burdening their already difficult situation with additional marginalization based on age and possible sub-cultural "protrusion." The case is similar with other marginalized groups, which include both young and mature people – for example, disabled persons, minorities (the Romany) or members of same-sex unions.

Due to the traditional consciousness and the traditional patriarchal, cultural heritage (well described in the best works of Croatian ethnology, like the one authored by Dunja Rihtman-Auguštin), youth have to face the individual psychological and social processes that make their position more difficult and have an effect on different forms of marginalization. In Croatia, the issue of autonomy and growing-up, as well as the separation from the parental home issue, are accentuated on both the cultural and economic levels. This results in the fact that youth stay under the same roof with their parents for a long time, where the potential of successfully dealing with cultural and psychological barriers to independence still does not include the actual, economic and housing independence. If we were to search for the traditional consciousness in the public dimension, if we were to analyze the media world and the dominant public discourse regarding young people, we would then be able to understand the way in which the transitional and capitalistic elements have empowered the possibilities of labeling and stigmatizing youth, especially in the light of the bare and brutal sensationalism of the media. In fact, youth most often appear in public as participants in the deviant phenomena. In public, perception of the youth culture is most often characterized by stereotypes and prejudices. Threatening campaigns are present in Croatia as everywhere else in the world. Sometimes they resemble the textbook examples, especially when the media hysteria really wishes to reintegrate certain lost values of the parental/dominant culture, pointing the finger to the "common scandals", that is, to young participants in sub-cultures and kindred phenomena. The media sensationalism of youth culture – of trying to find one's own identity through music, clothing, slang, attitude – most often reduces all of that to sex, drugs, violence, cults, extremisms, vandalism, etc. Apart from the profitable business endeavors connected with this, for the Croatian public youth cultures are a topic depicted with a prevailing "criminal" character (Bačić, et al. 2004).

Religious Socialization in Croatia

From the sociological perspective, religious changes are connected to various social changes and imply an analysis of the extensive socio-cultural and political context and its relevance for the position and role of religion, the Church (churches) and believers in the society. In the transitional period, most post-communist societies of Central and Eastern Europe share some common characteristics regarding religious changes. That is, in the first place, the revitalization of religion and religiosity, followed by an increase in the number of the new religious movements, the connection of the religious and nationality/ism, the connection of religion and politics and the aspirations of the churches to take up the positions they had in the pre-Communist period, etc (Borowik 1997). The rapid de-Christianization in Croatian society until the mid-1980's was connected with the decline of social autonomy and not with development. Social instability, apathy, the breakdown of the moral system, the crisis in human relations, etc. were some of external indicators of social anomie. Many parts of Croatian society started to feel free of political pressure in 1990, so we can tell that religious culture presented a strong element in reconstruction of the society (Zrinščak 2001:1–2, 19–40). According to some authors, the revitalization of religion in Croatia did not take the same course as in the western countries, in a rapid expansion of some type of religion a la carte. The Croatian revitalization of religion took place much more within the framework of the re-traditionalization, re-totalization and re-collectivization of decisions, and in the return to the faith of the ancestors and its type of embedding (Vrcan 1999:45–64). The assumption that was expressed by the Catholic theologian Bono Zvonimir Šagi follows from this. He describes current religiosity as folk Catholicism that will most certainly have a greater influence then the conscious faith and its ethnical strength. He defines this folk Catholicism as a habitual belief of the people from one region (one nation or its parts) who are spontaneously attached to catholic principles, and these are often just a sign of national identity (Šagi 1995:82–90). Territory occupation, unemployment, political instrumentalization of religion together brought about the re-traditionalization of society. Turbulently, tragically, burdened by war, social and political events, unbalanced social and political "development," poverty and confusion, with narrowed perspectives especially for the young, these are characteristics of the society in which this generation grew up. In the value sense, except for national-religious identification, the society did not offer them any coherent value basis that would prepare them for the further development of a democratic, pluralistic, civil society (Marinović 1999). During the war, for many people belonging to a religion was a matter of survival; politicians took an advantage of this and incorporated such religious observance with nationalism.

Regarding the Catholic Church, we should emphasize the process that the western societies experienced much earlier, and that is the confrontation with modernity and pluralism. This process was delayed in the post-communist societies due to (different levels) or repression of religion, the Church and religious people, and due to the oppositional nature of religion under those circumstances (Hornsby-Smith 1997). This phenomena, processes and tendencies can be recognized as the elements of religious change in Croatia. Youth represents a crucial developmental in the transition from childhood to adulthood, and so can disclose a tremendous amount of knowledge about religious socialization and change in the life course. Young people are a population that many religious organizations, both congregations and para-church ministries, particularly target in order to exert influence in their lives. Youth and young adulthood is also a life stage when religious conversion is most likely to take place. The goals of these religious institutions encompass ritual, the socialization of members, the internalization of values, attitudes, behavioral norms, and creating a sense of belonging to religious group (group cohesion) (Tadić 1999). In the last ten years, with the introduction of religious instruction into the official school curriculum, including the sacrament of first communion, the process of the institutional support of religious orientation has turned to young people. On the other hand, religion, especially in its traditional forms, was also widely spread in the earlier period in Croatia, especially on a family level, and amongst young people in Croatia, together with youth from Slovenia, who were the most religious part of the young people in the former Yugoslavia. Therefore, the increase in their religiosity in the changed social conditions is not unexpected (Marinovic 1999). Finally, the problem of the role of religion in social integration is projected to the background of a possible development of Croatian society into an advanced complex society. A strong secularization paradigm was noticed in Croatia, some evident change concerning the religious role in society were interpreted by a theory of crisis, namely the crisis of secular culture and politization of religion.

In a social context as described above, the Church dominated the public space. Regarding this, data on religiosity was not only a subject of social or spiritual search for identity, but also of the Church dominating the public space. This is not contradictory to the fact that most believers do not accept Church dogmas on morality or sexuality, which is a result of the de-Christianization and secularization that had been on going during communism. Thus, we can suppose that differences in religiosity between the young and the other age cohorts explain the rebellion of the young against church domination. Actually, youth in a clearer way express their attitudes, while other age cohorts reject their attitudes due to their incorporation in a traditional *Weltanschauung* of social conformity. Regarding the reasons of religion acceptance, there should be noted a slight difference between students and the overall population. 22.6% of the adult population accept religion from personal convenience in respect to 27.8% of student. 27.8% of adult population and 39.2% of students accept religion from personal convenience, but not actively. Tradition and upbringing were reasons for religion acceptance in 40.4% of the adult population and 18.7% of students (Crpic 2000:1–63).

From this research, I conclude that there was some kind of a value vacuum that happened in Croatia, which led to a religious socialization just on the surface. Role performance was restricted to some behavioral patterns without real values being incorporated. These behavioral patterns were like empty codes, and young people performed their religious roles without asking themselves why they are really doing so, what was their aim. They were convinced that it was the only way and that they should do so. This pattern continues to be perpetuated during the post-war period since 1995 to the present. Young people on the value level (as they after all accept church and non-church beliefs in parallel) obviously do not find it contradictory to consider themselves religious, and have attitudes opposed to those of their religion and Church in the area of sexuality and morality. Secular ideas and values are adopted and exist alongside religious values, which indicate a kind of relativism of values, or the parallel existence of value orientation. However intensely "immersed" in the traditional, semi modern, confused society under the assumption of a greater pluralism, democratization, and development of civil society, a new and different value system will become evident, but so will different models of spirituality as well. The developed religiosity of young people will be faced with such changes. To the degree that the religiosity of young people is a part of the family and wider cultural and national stabilization, a stabilizing of religious structure for young people can be assumed. However, at the same time, such religiosity could be faced with great challenges with which western modern society is already facing (Marinovic 1999).

The indicator of the identification level shows how the young identify themselves on the religiosity – non-religiosity continuum, or rather on the scale mentioned from the convinced believers to the ones opposed to religion. It was determined that religiosity of the young increased by 40% compared to 1986. In the first two categories of religious identification in 1999, 66% of participants were recorded. With that number, the group of convinced believers almost doubled. This increase was primarily at the expense of the decrease of the non-religious participants, from 47% to 14% (Goja 20001, 148–160). In 2004, research of Croatian youth identified that 41.5% were convinced believers and that 32.1% conceived themselves as being religious. Also, there were 10.6% of young people that were not sure whether they believe or not. Since in 1999 there were 33% of young believers, 34% being religious and 14% of youth that were not sure, we can conclude that the Croatian youth are more religious than five years before. So, there is a task for some future research on youth religiosity in Croatia to explore the reasons for this growth of religiosity.

Religious affiliation, as a fundamental indicator of traditional religiosity, indicates whether some (specific) religion is present as a factor of the individual's identity. It can, in that sense, only serve as an initial guideline that may, when combined with other different indicators, indicate the content and the extent of their religiosity, or rather the presence or absence of certain aspects of it. The high level of religious affiliation among the Croatian adult population is a fact (Marinović 1999). Due to the high degree of religious affiliation of the participants and their parents among all the groups of religious self-identification, there was interest in the issues of religious socialization in the family. Namely, the family has the most important role in the inclusion of children in the religious congregation, the transmission and initial forming of their religious life. This is related to the religious upbringing in the family and enrolling children in religious instruction as well as the performing of the sacraments tied to birth, childhood, and early youth; therefore, to the period of primary socialization in the family. The comparative data for the Zagreb region from the 1970's to the end of the 1990's indicates the greatest distribution of the forms of religious practice, which transfers traditional religiosity in the family (Marinović 1999).

While in 1986, 55% of Croatian youth attended mass/church (more or less frequently), in 1999, 80% of them were doing so. The percentage of those that never go to Church decreased by more than half – from 45% in 1986 to 20% in 1999. The highest increase was determined in the weekly attendance (by 12%), and less than monthly (6%) and attendance at major religious holidays (4%). A slight increase was observed in the attendance of a few times a week (by 2%). The data indicates that occasional "practitioners" (those that go to church only in major religious holidays) are still dominant while the weekly attendance, which is the obligation of believers, is practiced by 24% (Ilišin and Radin 2002).

The Study of Religious Identity of Zagrebian Adolescents was conducted on 904 respondents (26 schools in Zagreb) in 1997 (Mandarić 2000). Church and institutional models of religiosity are going through a crisis. Adolescents in transitional countries like Croatia, in a process of forming human and religious identities, face the challenges of religious pluralism, syncretism and indifference. Every day or frequently during a week, 4% of adolescents participate in a Mass. This increases to 27% of adolescents who attend Mass every week, and again to 28.6% of those who attend once or more times a month. According to this Study, 29.1% of adolescents rarely attend Mass and 10.4% never do. In Croatia there is a much extended phenomena, especially with young people, not to enter the church during the Mass, but to stay outside and discuss non-religious themes. For them, a Mass is an opportunity to socialize, and they very often, after the Mass, continue their socializing in a pub, park, or some other place. Research data indicates that 8.3% of adolescents do so. 16.6% of adolescents cannot focus during the Mass. A reason for that may be that 19.0% of adolescents feel bored with the content of the Mass. 31.1% of them are interested and consciously and willingly participate in the Mass. 15.7% feel spiritually in contact with the God. 9.3% of adolescents did not answer the questionnaire.

What is most noticeable is the fact that 90% of young people agree with the statement that people go to church more often today, due mostly out of conformity but also because of they have the freedom to express their religious beliefs and feelings (Marinović 1999). The young have obviously recognized the expression of religiosity as a desirable conformity pattern in society, but also think that religiosity is used for repression. It is interesting to give expression to some results of the Youth in Transition 2004 research, conducted by the Institute for Social Research in Zagreb in the beginning of 2004 on 2000 respondents under the age of thirty measuring trust in church and state institutions.[1] In this research, the church won the highest trust – 23.9% – nearly twice that of the other highest values. Second was the President of Republic with 12.9%, and then came the military with 11.0% and national TV with 10.6%. The adult population had a very similar ranking of institutional trust; church was in first place with 27.9%, the President of Republic was second with 18.1%, and then the military with 15.6% and TV with 10.6%.

New data from the Youth in Transition research gave us plenty of data on youth leisure time activities. Youth leisure time was investigated mostly by a set of variables relating to the frequency of doing certain activities in their free time. Most frequently youth spend their time socializing with their friends (83.1%), listening to the music (64.4%) and going to the coffee shops (64.0%). Regarding activities connected to religion, 21.7% of youth spend their free time going to the Church, which is similar to their going to the cinemas (21.8%), but less than participating in sport activities (20.7%). Recently the Apostolic Nuncio in Croatia stated that Croatia was the most Catholic country in Europe. In the interview he gave to the one daily paper, he was surprised how much the politicians and the Croatian population respect the Church's opinion. He agreed that the Croatian youth attend Mass relatively regularly, but show no interest in social issues.

Church and Youth Problems

Social support has been conceptualized as the tangible or intangible assistance provided in times of need by family members, friends, neighbors, colleagues, self-help groups, and others. In addition to such tangible forms of support, there are intangibles such as the feeling of security that results from being loved and cared for by others in addition to education, socioeconomic status, and social support, one's involvement in religion was identified as a contributor to reduced vulnerability. The church and its members provided individuals in need with two forms of support: tangible assistance such as financial aid, and intangible support such as feelings of security and belongings trial societies (Stone, et al. 2003:327).

---

[1] The research data has not been published yet.

Analysis of the data shows that religious beliefs and the support provided by the religious community were seen as extremely helpful in times of crisis. A crisis is often described as a turning point – a time of danger as well as an opportunity for growth. In the present context it is the term for an individual's internal reaction to an external hazard (Tomić-Koludrović 1999). New ecclesial movements, as a reaction to radicalized secularization and external hazard do not keep believers inside the church; they do not create attachment to the church. It is a reason why priests do not accept new forms of acting in Church, which lead to the break in communication between priests (hierarchical structures inside the Church) and laics. The changes of hierarchical structures were not the key motives that led believers to do "something", but actual situation in Church and society. Nobody tended to hold some hierarchical position, but to gain their place and role in broadening Church's place in wider society. Strict hierarchical situation in Church lacked dynamics. It is a noted fact that religion and religiosity, despite their numerous specific traits, are not phenomena isolated from society, social processes, cultural and the historical achievements of human civilizations. Ecclesiastic movements are an example of reaction to a radicalized security of the world (secularization) and even neglected authentically religious elements in religion institutions, as a process of anti-secularization in the contemporary society (Tadić 1999). Congregations of ecclesiastical movements do not build new religious lives. Their ecumenism is not about dialogue concerning different doctrines, dogmas, declarations, attitudes or orientations, but first and foremost about concrete everyday religious living, conviction and religious experience.

Croatian Bishop Conference – Youth Office organizes activities which aims are to educate youth animators. It also has a section for communication, internet technology and media. Volunteers are a very important part of Youth Office that is oriented to ecological and social actions (especially in helping to the poor and socially deprived). Project "Youth for Youth" aims at helping young people to grow in their belief, actions in local communities. The basis for this project is a statement form the Second Vatican Council Project that emphasizes a role of the people in shaping their society. Project tries to: 1) Empower catholic identity; 2) Develop personal talents; 3) Support to different programs inside the religious community; 4) Exchange of information and experience; 5) Form new groups of youth animators. We should mention

Catholics at Work who run catholic soccer leagues, from which donations go for charitable purpose – mostly as a help to socially deprived families, and H. Epicenter organizes youth free time in a way that foster social sensibility and solidarity and promote volunteerism. An area that Church has proved its important role on is organizing communes for drug addicts, for a new high or an intensified religious experience plays an important role in stigmatized roles such as alcoholic, or drug user. Destroyed functional role/relationships, caused by alcohol and drug abuse can very successfully be recovered during people's staying in communes, so a person can (re)take their position in society. Church also plays a role in organizing volunteers' network for disabled people support and inclusion of disabled people in local community.

FRAMA movement is another one dealing with youth inside the Church. A word FRAMA is an abbreviation for a movement, i.e. community of young believers – Franciscan Youth. Members of this movement are people between 14 and 30 years of age. They are mostly active in the areas where there are Franciscan monasteries. The idea for Franciscan Youth developed twenty years ago in Italy, and it spread to Croatia in the beginning of the nineties. Franciscan Youth mainly act in charitable activities; preys; art groups (like vocal-instrumental band); sport and ecological activities and they publish a paper Tau (Franciscan Cross).

One of the objections to the youth movement inside the Church is their neglecting of gender and sexual discrimination that are still a taboo in the Croatian Church. Also, there have been done very little in the field of peer discrimination and violence, and youth discrimination from the side of broader society. Church very often helps to the media in stigmatizing some aspects of youth search for their identity (like belonging to subcultures). There is not exact data on peer discrimination and violence inside the cohort of 15–29 years of age that is a subject of our paper. Most data is based on single cases of violence and discrimination. There is more data on peer violence inside the cohort younger than 15 years, especially bullying, but it is not a subject of our paper. We can say that the basic reason for Church's neglecting of discrimination and violence is for they hope their message of peace and love is easily reachable by everyone, but it is rather inaccessible for the young in the country that have undergone war and consequences of turbulent political, social and economic changes. For instance, NGOs provide youth with opportunity to express themselves in a way that is different to official political level. In his respect, NGOs have more active approach to the youth issues, and we are going to say a few words about it in our next chapter.

Nongovernmental Organizations and Youth Problems

Starting with education, as a considerable youth issue we can say that non-formal education responses on different principles that are very often attractive for youth. Approaches and methodology in non-formal education motivates youth towards critical thinking and self-initiative and nurtures proactive approaches to life. Due to restricted resources however, non-formal education cannot be a panacea for all existing problems in formal education. In recent years, an increasingly large number of associations with educational programs have appeared, but they are not provided with significant support. However, such programs are particularly acceptable to youth because they do not experience them as imposed or compulsory. But, young people are usually poorly informed about the opportunities for informal education because there are no information on available resources and programs.

The needs of a cultural or sub-cultural nature are something that a project called Clubture (www.clubture.org) gives us an answer to. It has developed from a fundamental idea of "culture as an exchange process." Clubture gathers many non-profit and non-institutional organizations, clubs and initiatives related to the cultural projects and programs in Croatia. The purpose of Clubture is strengthening of an independent and non-profit cultural scene, with a special emphasis on connecting the clubs/alternative scene as well as other various initiatives resulting from this co-operation. Clubture is a project that functions as a network and a program exchange platform. What makes it different from the other networks, is the fact that Clubture members are all those who participate in the program exchange. Connecting of various NGOs and initiatives are encouraged, with a special emphasis on the independent youth clubs which offer a different cultural product. The strengthening of sectors and the recognition of the wider public are being encouraged up to the governmental institutions on a national and local level, as is the cooperation between different parts of Croatia stimulated through information exchange, various contacts and partnerships. Action is also being taken on the policy level – by creating fields on the non-institutional scene, or in other words, on a completely new type of cultural production. The network is dynamic and not hierarchically based, i.e. not based on a centre that co-ordinates the work of all the members, but every action planner – a member – develops his/her own network. Today's level of co-operation is based on several interconnected levels, both on program and co-operative level, with a common tendency and characteristic of developing and implementing joint projects. It should be specially mentioned that the focus is placed on the co-operation of small NGOs, which has proven to be more effective than co-operation between some big organizations (Bačić 2004).

Organisation of blind and partially sighted students started the fight for public recognition of the problem and for the actual changes that would smooth the progress of studying at the University and the everyday life of physically disabled students in general. The situation today, when public shows more consideration for problems of physically disabled students, was preceded by the two-year long efforts of Korak (Step) and Šišmiš (Bat). To make a step out of the margins meant to print leaflets and posters, to proclaim "the year of disabled students", to create a WEB site, to start an "open telephone", to organise a conference on the quality of life of disabled students, to found a project of the "office for physically disabled students", to fight for the transport of students, for university enrolment quota, scholarship possibilities (Bačić 2004).

Youth health problems in Croatia, that are perceived as more easily reachable if they are covered by informal youth organizations are that mainly connected to sexual and reproductive health and drug abuse harm reduction. Harm reduction refers to measures which have for a purpose the reduction of damage related to drug use, and which do not necessarily entail reducing consumption. In short, harm reduction is the approach that tries to identify measure and minimize negative consequences of drug use. This approach is controversial and suspicious to many people because it does not cultivate the typical stigmatization and mystification of drugs. On the contrary, it accepts the existence of drugs as a given condition, as well as the young who use it, but at the same time it raises awareness among young people about the damage that drugs cause. In this sense, minimizing the damage is more useful than trying to permanently (violently) remove the damage. The basic characteristics of the harm reduction program are: pragmatism, humanistic values, focus on damage, balance of expenses and benefits, and the hierarchy of goals. Some harm reduction programs are: exchange and availability of needles and injecting equipment, substitution programs, education of drug users and the so-called outreach work, cooperation with the legal system, areas of tolerance, programs for reduction alcohol induced damage, programs for reduction of nicotine induced damage.

This context requires the work on affirmation, promotion and implementation of values and ideas of the civil society, culture of non-violence and tolerance, human rights, dialogue, cooperation and trust as well as arousing the awareness for possible social change. It is important to inform and stimulate young people to get involved; to question and educate themselves about value based work and life in order to contribute to social improvement. These issues are the main focus of the organizations like CESI and Theatre of the Oppressed.

CESI is a women's non-governmental organization that deals with building gender awareness, promotion of women rights and offers support and education to all civil initiatives. Many of the direct or end-users of their services are young people as well as professors, educators and members of the medical profession. CESI has been working with the youth and for the youth since its foundation, when the need for working with younger population became evident during the first experiences in implementing the program of prevention of violence in the family (Bačić 2004). The goals of this program include promotion of gender equality, promotion of knowledge and skills through non-institutional educational programs, promotion of the values of non-violence, tolerance, solidarity and gender equality and introduction of appropriate sexual education and the education of gender equality in schools. These goals are realized through encouraging voluntary work of the young with the young, through informing the public about the problems of sexuality and violence among the youth, through professional training of the experts working with the youth, and through active cooperation with the institutions, non-governmental organization and civil society. The aim of the direct work with the young is their education about the issues of gender and sex, violence in adolescent relationships, human rights, reproductive health, sexuality, and co- education – the work of the young with the young on these issues. Of course, there are many tendencies in the opposite direction in Croatia.

Conclusion

The objective basis for sociological analysis of youth is a specific place that this socio-demographic group takes both in a system of social reproduction and development. A specific characteristic of youth is that they are still not completely integrated parts of society. Thus, the young can be seen as a subject of social reproduction on the material, intellectual and social level. Young people in Croatia have more, or less, the same problems as youth in other transitional countries. The Government has started with the implementation of a new National Program of Action for Youth in 2001. But, there are many areas where the state cannot be efficient enough, and that is why there should be a strong system of civil support developed. The church in Croatia holds a very strong position. There are more than 41% of convinced believers among youth.[2] Although the Church in Croatia has developed a very strong organizational network across the country, due to the traditional role of the Church, there are some youth issues that are not covered by Church programs and activities. It is the moment where NGOs can show their efficiency, and they have showed it since they have done a lot thanks to the large amount of creative energy and good ideas, despite poor financing and, very often, disinterest from the Government. Croatia is still a developing country and we can hope that both the Church and the NGO will go on with their programs for youth, at the same time making the rivalries that are still very strong, weaker.

---

[2] *Youth in Transition* research, conducted by the Institute for Social Research in Zagreb in the beginning of 2004 on 2000 respondents under the age of thirty.

Chapter Seventeen

The Serbian Orthodox Church and the Serbian National Identity: Some Relations and Controversies

Alexandra Basa

Religion has a special place inside the culture, and by its meaning and signification, it very often took, in smaller or greater degree, a dominant position. If the culture is defined as the way of life of one community or society, and if religion in that community or society has the main position, one can conclude that religion significantly defines the way of life for the people who live in that society. During Serbian history, religion has always colored everyday life, although the intensity of that relation was different through time. The relationship of faith and the nation is dedicated to its inheritance, so their division is a complete utopia. That which is religious and that which is national can easily take the place of one another, especially if nationality is not determined enough or confirmed, so that it leans on the religious identity or arises from it.

National culture can't be separated from the nation, and it doesn't have an equal meaning in each period of the national history, neither on the whole territory on which the nation lives. Serbs have always been living in numerous territories, more or less connected or separated. Therefore it is difficult to talk about a unique national culture of Serbs, because they accepted the elements of the cultures of the territories in which they lived, more or less, and kept their national ones too.

The culture of the Serbs in Vojvodina, Serbia, Bosnia and Herzegovina, Montenegro and Croatia has numerous different and sometimes opposite models. From all the facts that determine nationality, particularly for the Balkans, religion is one of the most crucial. It means affiliation to certain cultural circles: the Western (Central-European or Mediterranean-Latin), the Eastern (Byzantine and Slavic-Orthodox), Islamic.

In the circles where there is a developed tradition of laicization, which is not the case for those territories in which the Serbs live, the question of religious affiliation loses national character in its narrow sense, and enters into the district of human rights. The relations between faith and nation differ from those between religion and state or state and nation. Since the national and religious picture of Balkans is a very complex one, it is not easy to generalize or reduce it to the models familiar to Europe, which are derived from its own experience.

While Serbia was under the Turkish government, one could not speak about the national culture, but only about some forms of the folk culture that sometimes met with the humanistic one, either domestic or foreign, through the clergymen or rare educated people of that time. In the part that has been under Austria-Hungary, culture and politics have mutually supported one another as well as opposed to each other. Determination for some cultural project often expressed the impossibility for political action in the true meaning of that word.

In the 19th century, nation-states were created and confirmed, so separate national cultures were formed. Their development depended, besides other things, on the unity of a nation and the fact of whether or not the nation had its own country. Religion had an integrative role.

Institutions based on national or state grounds help different cultural creations to unite. They directed the national culture towards the needs of the nation or the nation-state and harmonized with them. National history, together with national religion and literature, explored and described the past of the state-nation, glorified patriotism and encouraged members of the nation for their new acts.

Cultural acts could be politicized in a special way, so national cultures became marked by those politics. Culture became only a means in the hands of the state or elite, which used it for their own interests. Religion was not spared from such manipulations, especially in the last 15 years.

Today, 15 years after the Serbian Orthodox Church (SOC) returned to the societal scene of Serbia, it can be said that it still hasn't found its place in society, nor has the state clearly declared its position on that question. Although by the Constitution, the Church and the state are separate, the factual situation is often quite different, because of the lack of functional laws and the desire of the Church to take the place that it had before.

The Past

There are 2 different institutions in Serbian society that lived on through the centuries – the Serbian Orthodox Church and the monarchy. Medieval Serbian countries were elevated twice, in the 11th and 13th centuries, to the level of kingdoms. When, during the 19th century, a modern Serbian state was created through rebellions, its population was, as the historian of Balkans Trojan Stojadinovic said, closer to the Neolithic age then to the Middle-Ages. Still, creation of the monarchy has been the most important pillar of the whole idea of the reconstruction of the state. However, the beginning of the connection between the Church and the national identity we find much before those events in the 19th century.

The Serbian Church was formed in a turbulent period, at the beginning of the 13th century. Conditions for the independence of the Serbian Church from the *Archepiskopy* [Archbishop] in Ohrid were realized when the Western crusaders destroyed Byzantine in 1204 and created their small states. Then the church and state started coordinated action: Nikkei and Constantinople were, as Byzantine political and spiritual centers, in conflict about the reconstruction of the Byzantine, so the leaders of the Serbs took advantage of that split and mutual controversy. They asked the Emperor of the Nikkei and the Patriarch to legalize the newly formed autocephalous *archepiskopy*. That took place in 1219, and Sava Nemanjic became its first Archbishop. Since that time, the Serbian church was more the carrier and the keeper of the national consciousness of Serbs then it was the religious institution. On the other hand, Serbs respected in their church only what was theirs, independent and special. Therefore, one can say that the Serbian Church was the oldest proof of the consciousness of the Serbs to themselves.

After the division of Christianity, the Serbian state turned towards Ortho-doxy so the strategic and tactical needs of closer relations with the West disappeared. Accelerated homogenization of the people on ethnical and religious basis was started, without foreign political and churchly interfer-ences. Undisturbed in that time, the Serbian State and the Serbian Church developed their political and ideological connection.

In the period of the rule of Tsar Dusan, Serbia got its first written law that arranged the life of the society and the state. According to that law, caused by the influence of the Byzantine, in which the rulers were coming and going, the state existed independently from the dynasty and the ruler. During all these shifts, the Roman meaning of the state remained. Byzantine's understandings came through that church and through the very close touch with the Byzantine.

The King's duty was to secure the general good and the welfare of the people, with the feudal Lords in the first row. The general good, general interest (understood strictly in terms of classes) and the term of the state are clearly emphasized. Further on, legal and state life was limited to the certain territory – Serbian monarchy for the Serbs of the period of Nemanjic. On that territory, the supreme government belonged to the ruler in cooperation with the privileged classes; the unity of the Serbian country was confirmed by the sameness of the language in which people speak and write – the Serbian lan-guage. At the end, the Nemanjic family itself believed that the Serbian country (terra, patria) was not their legacy and that others could rule in it, too.

Nemanjic's dynasty was not one of the absolutists as the Byzantine emperors were. They had to count on the limits of the government that were placed not only by religion (canonical law) and ideas of Byzantine law of the Tsars, but also by the common law borders.

One of the essential constitutional principles was independence of the country, both towards Byzantine and the Constantinople patriarchy from 1219 until its approval by the autocefalousity. That principle was reflected through the formula "according to the mercy of God."

In the structure of the society of that time, feudal Lords took an important place. They had relative independence towards the ruler because they were successful in gaining inheritance and free legacy, i.e. feud. Feud could be taken away only by a court decision. From one side, feudal Lords were economi-cally independent, and on the other, they had to take part in wars for the ruler, so they became an important factor in the state. The main function of the state was a military one. The ruler himself was first the military leader, and then the chief of the administrative and court government. In public life, the feudal Lords also had an important role because they surrounded the ruler. They performed the service in the palace, formed the ruler's closer and wider Council, and took part in assembly.

Council is a very old institution, formed by the feudal Lords of the court. The Council surrounded the ruler, but also the dynasties and aristocrats. Without that board, it was impossible for the management and the court itself to function. Each political act had to be first analyzed by the Council, which depended on the importance of the laws and the circumstances in which the action was planned.

There were 2 groups of the feudal Lords on the court. One was formed by those who had specific functions in the state-management, and the other, by those who (according to an old custom – feudal obligations) arrived in court and performed court service in the wider sense, i.e. helped the ruler in the court, in the management, especially in military actions. Aristocrats from the leadership of the Church also took part in the Councils. Sometimes, the ruler would widen the Council with domestic feudal Lords, or even invite in strangers.

Another important institution is the *Assembly*. The common law was stabilized during the rule of Tsar Dusan, although as an institution it dated from the 12th century and earlier. The Assembly developed from the usual gatherings of the aristocrats, both church and civil ones, in the ruler's court. The characteristic of the Assembly was participation of privileged classes-feudal Lords and the Church – invited by the ruler. Assembly was the factor of the public life. As far as the clergymen in Assembly, the Church was not only a privileged class, but the main ideologist of the state and the social order. The Church justified the division of the Assembly into the privileged and non-privileged ranks by God's will and considered it as the relationship given by God. The only thing that the Church demanded was that the non-privileged ones had to be treated rightfully and in a compassionate way. That point of view was accepted by the others in the country.

Protest of the non-privileged, if it occurred, was not aimed at canceling class privileges and social order, and never was it against the Church. Such protest was directed towards canceling new taxes and soothing out a difficult situation, or towards the rise from non-privileged position to the privileged class of the society.

Assembly made decisions about all important questions of the society and the state: it met before and after war, during negotiations, when military help was to be sent to Byzantine. Also, Assembly chose the *archyepiskop*, as the head of the Church. Such gatherings were not a formality because the Assembly would meet several times before they would choose an *archyepiskop*.

When the Assembly was divided into its participants, the main position surely belonged to the ruler of the state, the greatest landowner, the chief in command, who, besides that, owned the whole state property and had a squad of workers under him, that showed not only his significant possibilities, but his ability to rule even above the greatest feudal Lords, and puts him far above everyone in the state.

Another privileged class was the highest representatives of the Church. The episcope, *iguman* (head of a monastery) and church were not only representatives of God but worldly feudal Lords, too. The Church owned feudal properties with a dependant population. On the Church and monastery property even the priest was in patrimonial dependence. Therefore, the Church was a powerful factor in the country. The ruler had a certain support in it, he saw not only the source of its power in the Church, but also his higher force. The Church, with the episcopes, *igumans*, and the priests that were more educated then the feudal Lords, represented a huge force in the society as the creator and the preacher of ideology of the strong ruler, the anointed of God, therefore one that couldn't be hurt. The model was the rulers of the Old Testament, and, of course, the emperor of Byzantine.

The ruler was, by the teachings of the Church, the embodiment of the state, the representative (defender) of the tradition. According to the Church, the ruler was obliged to have "warm love" and to "give and distribute" to the Church, to preserve the old laws in the country that have been confirmed, to bring laws favorable to the Church, as also for the whole country that belongs to the Orthodox community.

That coincidence of the ideology of the Church and the State had a practical role. Huge and long-lasting fights with Byzantine for freedom, attacks of neighbors on the Serbian state, at the time created a special connection and affection of the whole society for the dynasty of Nemanjic family. The Church writers describe the Nemanjic dynasty as the carriers of the Orthodoxy, as the lawful rulers of the state. In that cult of Nemanja and his son Sava, the Church saw acts and a weapon for the

> religion of the Orthodoxy, liberation from heresy, truthful baptism, building of churches, the gracefulness of the saints, combining of the Tsar wreaths, bringing laws for humanity, the science of remorse, collection of icons, wonderful miracles during the life and after death.

In that way, in the class-divided society of 14th century, the Church was the main pillar of the ruler and his authority, as well as an ideologue of state patriotism. The Church had great merit for literacy and for developing language: the Church belonged to Eastern-Christianity so it had the opportunity to adapt religion to Serbian language. Also, there was some kind of Church patriotism: it was reflected in the "Serbian church", "Serbian saints", "Serbian episcope", later Patriarch, and all of that contrary to Constantinople.

The state and the Church have been restricted about the boundaries of the Church, and came together due to general feudal interests. The Church decided on its own in matters of canonic-legal branch, dogma and liturgy. Assembly made discussion and decision in church-political, social and administrative branch, both important for the state and for the Church (choice of archiepiscopate, later patriarch, struggle against heresy, protection of Orthodoxy as the state religion, etc.).

Although the ruler and the Church aristocracy came together in Assembly, it did not change its social-political and legal essence and position on the head of the state organization. Dignity of the Church was very important considering the role that Church played as preserver of the state order. The Church aristocracy took part in state legislation and participated in passing all important laws. State legislation has protected the institution of the Church, so each attack on Orthodoxy was a criminal act against the state and the Church.

After gaining independence, the Church become stronger institutionally, religiously and politically, multiplying its episcopes and also the field of its influence. So, it gained religious, but also political and ethnical significance. It strived to remove centers of heresy, with the help of the state, and it nourished the consciousness of the people towards the merits of Orthodoxy. The influence of the Church, in ideological and political ways, was huge because it included both classes of the medieval society: feudal Lords and the dependant population – landless peasants. The social order was considered as inevitable, so it was accepted with submission. The Church influenced the society to accept the norms of Christian morality and Church justice and to seek for its spiritual and moral freedom.

The state was clearly defined and so was the Church. The Church was the base of the national identity and its carrier. Although the Church was not formed as the national one but as an Orthodox church, by this time it had become national. Therefore, the following opinion became established: *that every Serb is an Orthodox and that every Orthodox is Serb.* This belief was so intense that it resulted in the following position: if in the second generation individuals were not Orthodox, they stopped being Serbs too.

This period, mostly called "the Nemanjic era" was one of the most stable periods in the history of Serbia. The Church glorifies that period, calling it its "golden era." Nevertheless, although the Church had a good position in that time, its place and all its activities were strictly defined by the law. Each violation was harshly punished – the Church was not allowed to interfere in the fields of the state, and the state respected the autonomy of the Church in return.

Today

Today, it is difficult to say where the state begins and where it ends. The average citizen of Serbia (without consideration of the religious and national identity) today does not know whether he lives in Serbia or Serbia and Montenegro, or both in Serbia and Montenegro, and does not know the difference between these two. If one does not know to which state one belongs, the confusion becomes even greater during state holidays. Some while ago, when the basketball team of the Federal Republic of Yugoslavia won the World Championship, on the reception preformed for the team there were 9 different flags that claim to represent the nation and/or the state, so whistles during the national and/or national anthem were not surprising. As the new Constitution is being prepared, conflicts about the definition of the state as the national or the civil one become only more profound. The position of the Serbian Orthodox Church in the new Constitution is also an issue of dispute.

After 10 years of Milosevic's government, the so-called average citizens of Serbia have found themselves in a transition that they do not understand. Many have lost their jobs and their employment has been brought into question. Many feel that they do not have the perspective, and also feel a huge injustice because many passed through the period of Milosevic very easily and got rich. As there still does not exist the desire or the consensus around the question of the critical insights of the 1990's, the feeling of injustice has become even greater.

Consensus still exists around the question that some changes are necessary, but there is no consensus around the issue of what has to be changed and who should make those changes. So, the Serbian Orthodox Church found itself called out publicly, both by the highest state officials and the sector of NGOs, as the institution that inhibits the development of the society to which the reforms are necessary.

The Serbian Orthodox Church does not agree with those demands. A professor of the Theological University in Belgrade, Dr. Radomir Popovic mentions that the term "reform" itself is a little bit strange to the Serbian Orthodox Church, because the Church does not operate with that term since there is no need for such reform. It would be acceptable if under the term "reform" one considers some change of the form of behavior, essential transformation of individuals or some institution. Yet, if that word is used in a political, non-clerical sense, as it usually is, it doesn't have any connection whatsoever with the essence of religion. Also, he points out that Christianity has a bad experience with reforms and reformations and that the Church on the West has lost more than it has gained.

A professor of the same university, Dr. Ljubivoje Stojanovic has a similar attitude.

> Constant transformation of each man, from sin to justice, from evil to good, is a 'reform' that does not cease, so the question of the "new" in the Church is something that involves constant renovation of everyone and everything, and not something that is occasional and temporary (NIN, NIN d.o.o. Belgrade).

Dr. Dragoljub Zivojinovic, historian, dealt with the themes of the Church's history. He thinks that there are plenty of things that could be done and improved in the Church, and even without big impact and serious break downs. He says:

> For many years, the Church was possessed by the fight for survival, on the physical level, regarding its destruction in the World War Two, then the pressure of the communistic regime, material problems, lack of educated people, but also non-existence of the relations with the other churches, the Orthodox ones in the first row (NIN, NIN d.o.o. Belgrade).

Therefore, numerous reforms remained unrealized in the Church, so some forms of its life and work stayed old-fashioned, because the society moved on. According to professor Zivojinovic, "the Church needs much more time to bring its forms of life and work into harmony with the contemporary life" (NIN, NIN d.o.o. Belgrade).

The Church can do the following: improve the education of clergy and improve theological education in order to form "people who are educated enough to understand the world around them," and who could take elevated theological positions. Also, in order to solve controversial questions that remain from the past, constant dialog with worldly authorities is necessary. Improvement of the relation with other churches is also requested: as Serbia is a multi-confessional country, the Serbian Orthodox Church should establish and develop relations with other churches and religious communities (Catholic and Protestant churches and the Islamic Muslim community).

Apart from that, during 1990's, the Serbian Orthodox Church found itself in a cycle of the wars in the Balkans. In that process, the Church was an institution that had an active role. The Serbian Orthodox Church accepted that role out of its free will or did so under the pressure of the elites that used the Church to accomplish their political goals. Considering the historical part of the Serbian Orthodox Church in the preservation of the identity of Serbs and its return to the public scene in that time, that was not at all difficult.

Among those who seek reforms in the Church, one can hear demands for the re-examination of its actions during the wars in the Balkans during the 1990's. However, to such demands the Church remains silent. As this is the issue that the Church has to decide for itself, and as everyone in Church are still highly positioned men from the 1990's, that is not a realistic expectation.

The connection between the Serbian Orthodox Church and national identity is historical, so this present state of the Church resembles the identity of the nation. Although the Church doesn't show its schisms publicly, they still exist. It is divided into the hard wing (traditional one) and so-called liberal wing (the modern one). According to that, the nation is divided into so-called traditionalists and Europeans. The gap between them still exists, as it appeared in 18th century.

Sometimes the Church brings in confusion. For example, during the last year there were several such events. Bishop Nikolaj Velimirovic was proclaimed to be a saint. This high clergyman led quite a turbulent life, and his attitudes disturb the public even today. Patrons of his cult call himself "the greatest Serb after Holy Sava, another Christ." On the other hand, opponents of Bishop Nikolaj do not miss to opportunity to remind people that he compared Adolf Hitler with Holy Sava. Europe was the "synonym of death" for him. He feared the European culture, and considered democracy, tolerance and capitalism as the "Devils deeds." His personality was extremely controversial, and his work full of contrasts. Therefore he is a potential moral model, but also a possible moral anti-model.

Zoran Djindjic, the Prime Minister of the government of Republic of Serbia, was murdered in March of last year. Many polemics were caused by the speech that Bishop Amfilohije held during the ceremony in the Temple of Holy Sava, in which he brought out numerous remarks on the account of international community. The government reacted, stressing that the speech was inappropriate. One part of the public accused the Bishop that he took advantage of that opportunity and the presence of numerous foreign representatives to point out his extremely worldly attitudes. The other part of the public considered that the speech was appropriate to the situation and that something like that was necessary.

When it comes to the relation between the state and the Church, SOC moves in a circle of the ideas that are closest to organists' concept. Individualistic guidelines are rejected, and the principle of collectiveness and solidarity is accepted. Society is an organism, a national organism and the individuals represent its cells that insure its functioning and stability.

An optimal solution, according to the Church, is an "organic-orthodox monarchy," that is founded on the trinity of "God-king-householders." Therefore, the Serbian Orthodox Church stresses the reconstruction of the Monarchy that was canceled in 1943. Identification of the Serbian nation with the Serbian Orthodox Church is a function of such vision. Nourishing the patriarchal culture, which is opposite to democratic principles today, (to which modern Serbia is moving in some cases), is proclaimed by the Serbian Orthodox Church.

There are individuals in the Church that have rejected such ideas as anachronous and harmful for the interest of the Church itself. A priest Nenad Ilic said: "That the Byzantine symphony between the Church and the state today is totally absurd and an obstacle for the Serbian Orthodox Church to take its actual place" (Blic News). The Church should be separated from the state and then it can return to its primary purpose.

One of the divisions that can be seen even today in the society of Serbia arose in 19th century. Then the society met the ideas of citizen-politics and the culture that came from Europe. At that time, there were more and more such ideas. They were rationalistic and did not fall under the influence of the Church's merits or horizon. It was then that the first quotation marks on the line "church – state" appeared. During the government of Turks, the Church was so emerged in the role of the builder and the keeper of Serbian national and Orthodox thought that every sign of possible movement from that spot was seen as the historical misunderstanding and the impact of foreign forces.

Civil class did not limit itself to the Church, but took parts of its tradition that were considered usable and acceptable, e.g. symbolism of the myths, in its efforts in forming the state. The appearance of socialistic thought at the end of 18th century, accompanied by the appearance of the first deeper class and social crises, additionally made the scene complex. Nowadays, apart from the division of the European and traditional vision, there is now a socialist one that is atheistic. This is in conflict with the Church and also in ideological conflict with the European vision. The Serbian Orthodox traditionalism is also disturbed by this socialistic vision. This conflict continues to today.

Since the end of the World War Two, when the Church was definitely separated from the state, there was a hope in the Church circles that there will be "spiritual regeneration" and some forms of social restoration. However, society itself passed through huge changes: World War Two and the civil war that followed it; 50 years of socialism with the communistic ideology of self-management; explosion of mass communications; roads, cars, phones; urbanization, migrations and the drastic change of population. Fifty years ago the relation of the rural and urban population was 90:10, and today it is 50:50. Many of these problems the Serbian society did not solve until today in generally accepted and satisfactory way. The Church also has not managed to handle them.

The Serbian Orthodox Church, just like all other Orthodox churches, collides with challenges for which it is not ready. Today's modern world is based on laity and the separation of religion and the social sphere. An open question arises: *will Orthodox people, who resisted pagans, Muslims, and communists for centuries, resist the harsh demands of the modern times?*

Some facts are not encouraging. In the Orthodox world, religion and the nation represent a kind of active symbiosis in terms of mutual supplementation. Even the most eminent Orthodox scholars admit that by sequence of historical events, Orthodoxy closed itself to the social and historical scene. It composes a mental combination that resists the changes of the modern world.

In the end, after one pays tribute to the Church and the faith for everything they did for their people, it is on them to judge themselves what they should have done, and didn't do, and what they could have contributed to the nation. On the other hand, the nation that attached its identity only to one institution has the historical task to try to spread the basis of its identity, because this one institutional support of the nation has always proved itself to be an unstable solution.

Chapter Eighteen
Education Toward Humanity[1]
Aurelia Margaretic

The following is based on my attempt to educate female and male students of the sixth grade in the framework of a project orientated education toward humanity. In this attempt, I start from the first demand of Theodor W. Adorno on education: "...that Auschwitz may not happen again" (Adorno 1981:88–104; Winkel 1987:325).

The first part of this work constitutes a coming to terms with the past and the "burden" (Giordano 1998:17) of being a German. Here, my own thoughts and experiences flow into this discourse with the history of inhumanity, because they should be made fruitful for the present. The outline of problems should make transparent my claims on education: I orientate myself throughout this essay according to the tradition that reaches from the Socratic demand for truth and justice over F. D. Schliermacher to Herman Nohls claims on education. I try always to connect their claim – to be the "advocate of the child" (Funk Kolleg 1970:56–68) – with the modern demand for orientation according to the "key problems" (Klafke 1991:178) of our society. Today, among those

[1] This chapter is an edited version of a larger work. It was translated from the German by Rudolf J. Siebert.

key problems is the revival of nationalism, the wars originating from it [the Yugoslav civil wars] and the question of refugees as a consequence of these wars.

When I confront the female and male students with the questions of nationalism, war and refugees, I have to transform "the claims that grow out of the objective culture" (Funk Kolleg 1970:58) in a way so that they do justice to the demands which result from the life connection with these children. Thus, I must always again ask myself the question,

> what sense does this demand make in the connection with the life of this child for his or her structuring and the escalation of his or her energies, and what means does this child have in order to deal with them adequately (Funk Kolleg 1970:58).

In order to make this transformation meaningfully, I have selected the stories of refugee children and of children who go on the basis of their different nationalities between the fronts of nationalism. They are the stories of Anna and Duro, Nils, Zelka, Tihana and Borna. The goal of this education is to educate the children against the coldness of the "social monad" (Adorno 1981:88–104; Winkel 1987:329) toward the empathy and warmth in the relationships among human beings. What matters is also always a "higher development of man and world" (Hänsel 1987:89).

Children who have an idea of what a refugee child has lost will be able to counter him or her with humanity and warmth and they will facilitate and make his or her integration easier. Young people whose heart has already once touched the pain of the "foreigner" will also not be able to decide to ignite and burn down emergency quarters and the homes of asylum seekers.

The part "my own understanding of the war," i.e., the war between Croatia and Serbia, is destined for the reader of this work. I considered it to be necessary to take into this work the completely different experience of the war, which deviates from the interpretation in the Croatian or Serbian mass media because my engagement to "educate toward humanity" originated certainly out of the experience of the "inhumanity" of the Yugoslav civil war.

Thoughts about the Necessity of an "Education Toward Humanity"

> If all the seas of the world would turn into ink and the globe were covered
> with paper, both would not be sufficient to describe the agonies.

With these lines ends Ella Liebermann-Shibers (1997) book *"On the Edge
of the Abyss."* I begin this work with these ending lines, which refer to the
futility of the attempt to grasp into words or into images the suffering and
the agonies through which people in Auschwitz lived. Liebermann-Shibers
(1997:190) wrote:

> I tried to put everything down that I felt and saw in my youth and which
> darkened the world for me to express in my designs in order to give witness
> to these things....I drew their faces, their cold murderous eyes. I depicted
> their relatives in the KZ, their wives and children. At home they were
> affectionate fathers and married men – and nevertheless they murdered
> women and children.

The authoress was born 1930 in Berlin and in 1943 was deported with her
family to Auschwitz-Birkenau. She was a five year old child when she was
pulled out from her dwelling, environment – childhood – family. Shortly
after her release, with pencil and coal she tried "to draw her innermost being
revealed" (Liebermann-Shibers 1997:190). During this time, a book was
published. It appeared also as a school edition. A name emerged, which was
unknown to me. It was the name of a man who experienced the hell of the
inhumanity, who perhaps had to live through again and again the innumerable night mares, in order now after more than 50 years to become public.
Why only now – after such a long time? Perhaps it was because in view of
its incomprehensibility every attempt to make what was experienced com-
municable to the others had failed. Those, who survived the hell, at that time,
died a quiet death – and probably for the rest of their life waited in vain for
those who would offer them a hand so that they could bring the dead back
to life again. "Show us slowly your sun," demands Nelly Sachs (1961:50) in
the lines of the second strophe of the poem "Choir of the Rescued." The
poem continues:

> Lead us in step from star to star
> Let us again quietly learn life

It could otherwise a bird's song,

Filling the bucket at the fountain

Could break into the open again our badly sealed pain

And foam us away –

We beg you:

Do not show us the biting dog –

It could happen, it could be

That we fall into dust –

Before your eyes disintegrate into dust.

What after all holds ours texture together?

We who have become breathless,

whose soul fled to him from the middle of the night

For a long time before one rescued our body

In the ark of the moment.

We rescue,

We press your hand

We recognize your eye –

But what keeps us together is only departure,

The departure from the dust

Holds us together with you.

However, instead of taking and holding on to the hand of the "rescued", it was repressed, denied, forgotten. Ralph Giordano (1998:17) writes in his book: *The Second Guilt or the Burden of Being German*:

> Every second guilt presupposes a first one: the guilt of the Germans under Hitler. The second guilt: the repression and denial of the first guilt after 1945. It has substantially codetermined the political culture of the Federal Republic of Germany up to the present day. This is a burden that will still have to be carried for a long time.

"Inability to Mourn" (Mitscherlich [1977]/1990:115–121), the ignorance and self-satisfaction with which we live today, the way, how one is not ashamed about arguing the claims of the victims, who on the basis of their biological age of having only a few years left to live has little to do with humanity. A first goal of education must be therefore the fact that such inhumanity never again repeats itself through working against such forgetfulness.

The First Demand of Education

In 1966 in his lecture on "Education after Auschwitz – ... In Search for Human-ity," Adorno (1981:88–104) said:

> The demand that Auschwitz should not happen again is the very first
> one concerning education. It is so much presupposed by any other that
> I do neither believe that I have to or should give reasons for it. I cannot
> understand that up to today one has concerned oneself so little with it. To
> give reasons for this demand would be something outrageous in the face
> of the outrageous that took place.

In the meantime, more than 30 years have past. From the student protests on the campus of Berkley University against the war in Vietnam, a development originated which in the time of the Cold War and the Adenauer coalition in Germany produced the extra-parliamentary opposition under the leadership of Rudi Dutschke. On June 2, 1967, that is a year after Adorno's lecture on "Education after Auschwitz" which he had given for the first time on the Hessen Broadcasting System, the student Benno Ohnesorg was shot. The shooting was the initial spark for the "hot fall" in Germany. The protest in Berlin and other large cities was directed against the repressive State.

Educational Policy and Co-Responsibility

During the 1960s, also falls the critique of an educational system formed by social structures, of the pure quantitative principle of Wilhelm Picht , who speaking about the catastrophe of education demanded the further develop-ment of teacher education, and of Ralf Dahrendorf's social critical principle with its demand for education as the right of every citizen. Both principles change radically the system of education. The "new" Klafki puts into question the contents of the classical humanist education. He made the effort toward educational reform. Klafki's educational, theoretical didactic constitutes an integration of the hermeneutical, experiential, scientific and social scientific principle. Klafki (1991:20f.) stated,

> My thesis states: Education or better, general education means in the
> indicated perspective to have gained a socially mediated consciousness of
> central problems of the common present and the predictable future. General

education means to gain insight into the co-determination of all in the face of such problems and the readiness to deal with them and to participate in the effort for conquering them. I am of the opinion that a sufficient consensus could be established about such central problems, so-called 'key-problems,' of our present and of the immediate future at the level of administrators, teaching plans, curricular, but also on the level of the concrete teaching process under co-determination of parents and students with open discourse. Such agreement would of course always have to put the discussion again in new ways according to the changing historical conditions.

For Klafki, there belongs to the key problems, also

the peace question, the democratization as general orientation principle of the formation of our common affairs,...right and boundaries of natio-nal identity formation in the face of the unconditional universal responsibilities,...German and foreigners,...the scientific reality consi-deration, the so-called 'scientification' of the modern world and the everyday relationship of man and reality.

On the Actual Situation in the German Federal Republic: Key Problems

A few days after the entrance of the extreme right winged party DVU into the State legislature of Sachsen-Anhalt, the President of the German Federal Republic Herzog called upon the German people to oppose decisively the right-winged radicalism in all sections of society. In his Berlin office in Kasel Bellevue, on the occasion of a Symposium of the Robert Bosche Foundation on the theme "School and German Unity," Herzog said that school could make a decisive contribution to the resistance against right-wing radicalism. The-matic points of emphasis of my project oriented teaching "education toward humanity," which thematizes the concern of the phenomena of inhumanity like nationalism and war and the actuality of the refugee question that arises out of them, have been moved into the center of the actual public discussion through the shocking events of the present. The demand for "humanity"[2] has

---

[2] "Unsere Schulen sind noch immer viel zu sehr auf die reine Wissensvermittlung ausgerichtet...Es ware übrigens schon viel geholfen, wenn das Gruppenverhalten der Schüler, die Fähigkeit zu gegenseitiger Rücksichtnahme, die Bereitschaft zur Hilfe

become the object of many speeches of politicians that mirror their concern and helplessness but also their ignorance and hypocrisy.

In spite of all of this, the phenomena of this "right-wing radicalism" did after all not arise over night like a "horrible ghost." It is rather connected as Ralph Giordano (Heitmeyer 1993:9) has proven with the "not adequately dealt with history" (Heitmeyer 1993:7). Added to this is that immediately after the German unification there appeared in the states of the former German Federal Republic an "open hate against foreigners" (Heitmeyer 1993:8). Wilhelm Heitmeyer stated that "it must be feared that the fundamental restructuring of the states of the former German Federal Republic and the insecurity concerning the consequences of the unity for the people in the states increase the sources out of which the hate against foreigners and the right-wing fanaticism is fed" (Heitmeyer 1993:8). We do not need to look merely to the new Federal States because in East Westphalia right-winged radical organizations have been established for many years.

Right-Wing Terrorism

Will we also in the future be in a position to grant to people the right of asylum and to guarantee their physical and psychic integrity in our country? Or do those who have experienced the "inhumanity" and who decided to leave behind everything that they loved in order to rescue themselves and the lives of their children still need to be afraid for their lives in the narrow housing projects in which they are exposed to incendiary attacks and other terror acts without any protection? Again, there are victims, both dead and survivors, who live the rest of their lives with the consequences of force, like

---

für Schwächere und außerfachliches engagement mehr als bisher in der Notengebung und in den Zeugnissen berücksichtigt würden...Unsere Erziehungsziele dürfen nicht einseitig an der Wirtschaft, sondern müssen am Menschen orientiert sein." Aus das Interview: "Ich gehe gern nach Bethel, um den Einsatz der dort tätigen Menschen zu würdigen." ("Our schools have always much too much fallen in line with the teaching of the pure knowledge...There was, however, already much help given whenever the group behavior of the students, their ability for mutual re-acceptance, their readiness to give assistance to weaker ones and to become engaged in extra-curricular assistance beyond note-sharing and this evidence must be taken into consideration...Our educational objectives must not be permitted a one-sided emphasis on the economy, but must be oriented toward humanity." From the interview: "I gladly go to Bethel, to the entrance there of worthy human activity." Trans. M. R. Ott.) Roman Herzog, Zeitgeschehen, Neue Westfälische, Nr. 131, Dienstag, 9. Juni 1998.

the victims of the attacks of Mölln and other places: there names and there are also names of children are this time not Hanna, Ruth, Rachel, and David. However, their names are now Seinab, [heavily wounded after incendiary attack in Hünxe]; Ayse, fourteen years old [burned on November 23 in Mölln]; Yeliz, 10 years old [burned on November 23 in Mölln]; Bahide, 51 years old [burned on November 23 in Mölln]; Silcio, [murdered on November 21 in Berlin]; Nguyen Van Tu, [murdered on April 24 in Berlin]; Torsten [murdered on May 9 in Magdeburg]; Dragomir, 18 years old [murder on March 18 in Saal]. All these victims of right-wing terror were slaughtered, stabbed, burned and died in 1992. The girl Seinab Saabo, whose wounded body was like a crater landscape, has stated that she is still today afraid when she is sleeping that incendiary bombs will be thrown into her housing (Floren 1994:45, 46, 47). The father, who carried his daughters like "living torches" out of the asylum application housing, is now afraid due to the threat of deportation, despite the fact that his daughter has to be treated because of her burns for the rest of her life. Here one proceeds with German thoroughness.

Death – "A Master from Germany"

Why do I speak about "inhumanity" when I write a work about "education toward humanity?" Is death a "Master from Germany?" [Paul Celan] On October 9, 1994, the writer Jorge Semprun (1994) wrote words of thanks at the occasion of the giving of the Peace Prize of the German book commerce in the Paul's Church in Frankfurt am Main.[3] In those thank you words, Semprun described his first reencounter with the Buchenwald concentration camp:

> a life later I stood again in the dramatic empty space of the gathering place
> of Buchenwald. The birds had returned, the same wind blew again of the
> Ettersberg...when I stepped further over the gathering place and when I
> stood opposite of the massive chimney of the crematorium I remembered
> a poem by Paul Celan. A volume of poems by Celan had accompanied me
> on this trip:

---

[3] "Demokratisierung ist die Wurzel des Friedens – und nicht umgekehrt." ["Democracy is the root of the peace – and not in reverse."]

...then you rise as smoke into the air,
then you have a grave in the clouds
there you lay not confined.

In this poem, the "Death Fugue," we all remember there is a terrible verse, which returns like a guiding motif: death is a "Master from Germany..."

> On that wonderful Sunday in March 1992, there in Buchenwald, opposite to the chimney to the crematorium, I remembered the rough and angry voice of the SS storm troop leader who, in the night with air raid alarm wailing, demanded that the crematorium stove be turned off: 'Turn off the crematorium!' Here I asked myself if this terrible verse [Is death a master from Germany?] was true: did it really contain an absolute truth that existed above all historical conditionality. Quite obviously it did and does not. That death, which devastated Europe and which was the consequence of Hitler's victory march was indeed a master from Germany. However, we all have recognized the death that sleeps in the interior of the totalitarian beast with different clothing, in the decorative glitter of other national origins. I myself have known death as Master from Spain and I have sometimes come close to it. And the persecuted and deported French Jews have known death as Master from France. The truth of the verse from Paul Celan is therefore a necessary, unforgettable truth. However, it is relative and historically conditioned. Death as a Master from Humanity would be the fitting philosophical formulation because it would emphasize the permanently present ability of the human being, from the beginning immanent freedom, to decide for the death of oppression and of servitude – against the life of freedom: the freedom of life. (Semprun 1994:7)

Jorge Semprun reformulated the lines of the Celan "Death Fugue" into "Death is a Master from Humanity" for today.

My Own Understanding of the Theme [Including Biographical Connections]

In 1991, during the Yugoslav war, I also came close to death[4] in a completely unexpected way and had to recognize that death is not exclusively a Master

---

[4] I appropriated the formulation of J. Semprun here. (Semprun 1994:7)

from Germany but that it can become a Master everywhere in the world: a Master from Humanity. Already in 1966, Adorno (Winkel 1987:330) pointed to the possibility of: the change of location of that which expressed itself in Auschwitz:

> Tomorrow another group other than the Jews can be in line, for instance the old people, who already in the Third Reich had just been left out, or the intellectuals, or simply non-conformist groups. The climate – I pointed to it – which most of all promotes such resurrection is the reawakening nationalism. It is therefore so bad because it can in the age of international communication and of the supra-national blocks not believe in itself so well any longer and must exaggerate itself into the measureless in order to persuade itself and others that it was still substantial.

With horror I had to experience that this nationalism was fed again by fascist thinking and that it carried anti-Semitic traits and that it used the lie with unbelievable skill. The peaceful location at which I lived transformed itself into a dark suburb of hell through which day after day hundred of soldiers marched, who called themselves "the Black Legion of Death," with that look – this really ice-cold look, which could only lead one to imagine how many "sub-humans" they had already murdered. For each death, there was a notch in the gunstock. The reputation of every individual grew with the number of the notches. I had the fear of death when I saw them.

They encountered me with distrust as if they had a premonition of what I was thinking. But when they heard from others that I was a German, then their cold faces changed and they radiated: Germany would help them to achieve their independence – now they would execute what Hitler could not finish – to make the land "Jew and Serb free." They would need only more weapons. What I saw was so unbelievable – it was as if Hitler still lived.

I saw grown up men weep when the hordes passed by – powerlessly they had to watch the dark spectacle. When I arrived in Germany and told my story, I found that nobody believed me. The lie of nationalism had been effective: liberation, independence, democracy were the masks for war, oppression and dictatorship. Yet, still I have to point out at this place that I would not like to have the arrogance to compare in the least my experiences of nationalism and the war with the horror that Jorge Semprun experienced. I feel gratitude today toward those who gave me their hand, which everybody needs in order to be able to live again after the experience of the super power of death. I also would like to carry the responsibility for future generations together with female and male students to work for the goal that these experiences will never repeat themselves. My highest goal of education is therefore, the decision for life – against the powers of death. An "Education Toward Humanity" is always a decision for the life of the other and therefore also for one's own life. It is an education toward mutual respect, responsibility and solidarity. However, what is equally important is the "Education of the Heart" (Flaubert 1979).[5]

The speech of Jorge Semprun gave expression to his deep emotion and struggle in a moving way for the German language despite the fact that this language had after all been associated with so many terrible things. This impressed me most deeply. The fact that a human being comes back to the location of his suffering and breaks his silence and does not neglect to say that he had come close to death also in other countries appeared to me as a great human accomplishment.

On the "Burden to Be a German"[6] and the Attempt to Escape this Burden

In 1994 after I heard the speech of Jorge Semprun, I asked myself what had influenced me so strongly in my own biography so that this speech moved me so much. I had a happy childhood. When I came home from playing toward evening, then my mother told me often from the past. She called this time between day and night: the blue hour. Sadness and the consciousness to have lost something which could not be brought back again shaped these hours. My mother had the ability to grieve – in the midst of an environment that wanted to forget. She lost as a young girl both parents in one year. My grandmother died at 46 years of age in the struggle with an SS man. My grandfather died in the same year alone in Bethel. He was a brave man who

---

[5] "The Education of the Heart" is the title of the famous novel from Gustave Flaubert: "Die Erziehung des Herzens. Geschichte eines jungen Mannes" (The Education of the Heart: History of a Young Man.) This first appeared in November 1889 under the title: "L' Éducation sentimentale. Histoire d'un jeune homme." It was first translated by E. A. Reinhart in List Verlag, Leipzig 1926; copyright 1979 by Diogenes Verlag AG Zürich.

[6] The phrase "Von der Last Deutscher zu sein" (Of the Burden of Being German) was spoken by Ralph Giordano (1998:14) in "Die zweite Schuld oder Von der Last Deutscher zu sein" ["The Second Guilt or Of the Burden of Being German."]

helped Jews to immigrate and was bound later on to a wheel chair due to inoculation damage. Before he died, one had declared his life as "unworthy." My mother told me that he wrote always in long sentences, which he posited as a personal protest against Hitler, who ordered sentences and the language as a whole to be shortened. Such shortened, code-word language was intended to transport commands and orders. I longed as a child for grandparents and I searched for myself in the neighborhood for a grandmother, a lonely old woman from Leipzig. She was a war widow and her two sons had not returned from Russia. In spite of this, she never gave up the hope that they were still alive. My mother took her into our family. To the other neighbors, my mother entertained a courteous but distant contact. As a child, one remembers such things precisely and one questions behind that which appears to oneself as unusual. My mother showed me the houses of those who in the Reich's Crystal Night (Gatzen 1993) were quite full of enthusiasm that the houses of the Jews were burning. She also showed me the house of the neighbor who on this night called in sick. She told me that the little store in which I bought sweets as a child, had once belonged to Jews, who were deported and did not return.

My parents had given me not a German name but an Italian one. We traveled to Norway, Italy and France and there visited also the family who had received my father like a son during his prisoner of war-time in the Provence, France. I loved it – to speak foreign languages – no body was supposed to notice that I was a German. I dreamt of having being born in another country. I became sad and angry, when an Italian youngster once greeted me with *"Heil Hitler."* The mimicry did not succeed. Later on I began to read everything that I could find about the Holocaust. The stories of eyewitnesses did not let me go. I never traveled to Israel – I considered it always to be an almost arrogant undertaking to go there as a German. The sadness of my mother – the stories of the eyewitnesses, the woman, who had lost her husband and her sons – one thing they had in common: one had robbed them of the human beings whom they loved. One had deprived them of their life with them. Men had been deprived by men. Now, she had to deal alone with her grief. "The war" was her answer to everything that had happened to them. And it lasted for many years until I could comprehend that the war, which I considered to be unavoidable and powerful, was made by men.

Studies: Teachers and Examples

During my studies at the Free University of Berlin, I heard through Professor Helmut Gowitzer and his Jewish wife Brigitta and Professor W. F. Marquardt, what had been lost for us really with the annihilation of the Jews and with their exodus from Germany. We lost with them precisely that warmth of the heart, the Hassidic tradition shaped love, piety, joyfulness and vivacity, the unbroken immanence of the transcendent – the wonderful relationship to the heavenly and the earthly, which formed the so lively Jewish life – this warmth which shines forth for us still from the pictures Chagall and the Legends of the Balscheem (Buber 1949).

> There is a weeping in the world
> As if the dear God had died.

Thus sounds the first line of the poem of the great German poet – Else Lasker-Schüler (1977:88) – who was able to leave Germany in time for the price of a homelessness that lasted to her death (Schultz 1990:77–98).

In the following years, during my studies at the Free University of Berlin, I dealt with the works of Martin Buber under the Guidance of Professor Gollwitzer and Professor Marquardt. In 1922, after reading the writings of Ferdinand Ebners, Hans Kohen, and Franz Rosenzweigs, Buber had himself noticed that they all searched for a "buried good." This buried good, the discovery of the other, appeared to Buber to be so revolutionizing as the discovery of new sun systems. In the works of Rosenstock, Gogarten and Brunner, this discovery expressed itself in Protestant theology (Casper 1967; Cohen 1961:163).

The dialogical thinking fascinated me and protected me at the same time so that I would not give myself too willingly to all those appearances of the new for which one could fall prey easily in this time in a big city like Berlin. Afterwards, I asked if behind everything there was a concern with real relationships or if the personal *"du"* was said while in reality *"es"* was really meant. During my studies in Berlin, I found the writings of the Jewish doctor and pedagogue, Janusc Korczak, whose pedagogy of love was expressed powerfully in his book *"How One Should Love a Child"* (Korczak 1974). The pedagogy of respect and love, the demand of freedom and autonomy of the child, was something completely new but also provocative for me. Some of it shocked me, like the first of his demand: "I demand the "Magna Charta Libertatis" as fundamental law for the child. Maybe there is another one – but these three fundamental rights I have found:

1. The right of the child for his death.
2. The right of the child for the present day.
3. The right of the child to be as it is (Korczak 1974:40).

Only after a long time of confusion, I had the premonition of what Janusz Korczak wanted to say with this first demand. I reflected upon my own action and I saw that out of this fear of the death of my child that all mothers[7] have, I took from the child all freedom. Korczak appeared to me often like a hard and unlovable critic. One day, I was able to understand him: he demanded the freedom of the child – life. What inhumanity this man had to experience, who had to look on when his children starved to death in the "Dom Sierot",[8] before one sent him broken on his last trip toward Triblinka. The possibility that he rejected the possibility of his own rescue that was offered to him and that he accompanied the two children on their trip to death, made him for me into a real living and trustworthy pedagogue – one, who not only carefully wrote a diary every night about pedagogical progress in the orphanage but who was also able to really love the children – very much in the sense of his pedagogic of love, the fundamental tone of which expressed itself in the last lines of his prayer of an educator:

> My thoughts have no wings to carry a song up into heaven.... Tired am I
> and exhausted. My look is weakened and my back is bent under the heavy

---

[7] "Die heiße, einsichtige und ausgeglichene Liebe der Mutter zu ihrem Kinde mußdiesem das Recth auf einen frühen Tod zugestehen, das Recht zur Beendigung seines Lebenslaufes nicht nach sechzig Umdrehungen der Erde um die Sonne, sondern nach einem oder nach drei Frühjahren" [The hot, understanding and balanced love of the mother for its child must grant the Right to this child of an early death, the right for the completion of his personal record not after sixty revolutions of the earth around the sun, but after one or after three springs – Tr. M. R. Ott] (Korczak 1974:40).

[8] "Dom Sierot" ist das Haus der Waisen im Warschau, das Januscz Korczak gründete und bis zu seiner Deportation leitete: "Im Haus der Waisen, 'Dom Sierot' in Warschau, wuchsen seine Ideen zu einem Erziehungsprogramm, das auf 'Achtung' gründete: 'Kinder werden nicht erst zu Menschen, sie sind schon welche'" ["Dom Sierot" is the house for orphans that Januscz Korczak founded and directed until his deportation. "In the house of orphans – 'Dom Sierot' in Warsaw – his ideas grew into an education program based on 'attention' to the fact that 'children do not only become humans, they already are.'" – Tr. M. R. Ott] (Korczak 1996).

burden of duty but nevertheless I present an intimate request, O God, and nevertheless, I possess a treasure which I would not like to entrust to a brother – to men. I'm afraid that man does not understand, does not feel, does not pay attention that he laughs at it. If I am gray humility before your face, Lord, in my request I stand before you nevertheless – a flaming demand. If I also whisper quietly this request I express with a voice of an unbending will, commanding look, I fire above the clouds with a lifted head I demand, because it is not for me. Give to the children a good fate, grant help to their efforts, bless their efforts. Do not lead them the easiest way or the most beautiful one and as additional payment for my request, accept my treasure: my sadness, sadness and work" (Korczak 1997:41).

Chapter Nineteen

The Human Being Called "Homo Techno-Sapiens": A Note on a Post-Human Perspective

Jan Fennema

I.

Homo techno-sapiens is the name, as used by some people, of the human being of the coming epoch. To mention a case, in March/April 2002 the European Society for the Study of Science and Theology organized a conference with the noteworthy title "Creating Techno-Sapiens." The homo techno-sapiens as referred to in this title is generally considered as a product of the evolutionary process. It therefore follows that a reflection on this being should take place in the framework of evolutionary thinking, more specifically in that of a hypothetical evolutionary perspective focused on the notions of cosmos and morality. The present text constitutes a short commentary in this connection.

Starting from the idea of an evolution, "cosmos" is the first word that must be looked at more closely. The cosmos as we know it today is mostly considered to be in evolution, and, upon reflection, this consideration generates a basic anthropology. It reminds us, among other things, of the so-called Archimedean point: "Give me a place where to stand and I will move the earth." This phrase characterizes the human being that considers him-/herself to be autonomous, able to take a position – that is a point of departure of his/her choice – and, starting from this position, "to move the earth." In our time this must be interpreted as referring to the autonomy of the researcher who investigates the cosmos scientifically, given his point of departure. This point of departure is a primordial space-time point defined by a supposed Big Bang.

Continuing this line of thinking, the second word to be looked at is "morality." This term refers to human conduct and to the rules that must be observed in order to do what is considered to be good and to avoid what is evil. Knowledge of these rules, how they are or were originated and how they change, can be obtained by carefully investigating human behavior and the relevant traditions. In the sphere of morality, however, there is more which is of particular importance. For a special distinction has to be introduced when using the term "knowledge." In addition to studying human conduct following the procedures of the relevant sciences, there are, for instance, also the conduct that is mine and the rules that I actually observe. Evidently, to be well informed on human conduct and on rules that are followed is not the same as practicing a specific conduct and personally observing particular rules. Indeed, as we all know, to practice a conduct and to observe rules is not necessarily the consequence of being well informed, of being conscious, aware of the rules that are to be taken serious. It rather has to do with a presence that is first of all felt, namely the presence felt in this person – in the person I am – of a specific conduct and of particular rules that, apart from their inherence in human conduct, may also be objectified as facts and studied afterwards, for instance by this same person or by others. And, when subsequently analyzing this presence, one finds aspects of conduct that can be traced back to past times as well as aspects of conduct that clearly antici-pate future times.

II.

The preceding general remarks have a specific impact. The idea of a cosmic evolution implies the idea of the evolution of the human being as a process of nature (encompassing culture), that is, it implies biology, and even sociobiol-ogy, including whatever the results may be of the (future?) manipulation of the human genome. In this reductionist perspective – which one has to face if the development of science and technology is left to itself – the acme of sociobiology seems to be the human being of the distant future, tentatively called today "homo techno-sapiens." Assuming that it is certain that the future epoch will be dominated by information technology, its applications, and its uninterrupted streams of information, what kind of human being may we expect to be most likely in those coming times? Will that human being – homo techno-sapiens – be a conscientious being, physically and mentally free because of mastering all there is to be mastered? Or will this being have internalized the laws, the logics of whatever things he masters, to such an extent that he will virtually have become their robot-like appendage? In that case his striving for autonomy would fatally have ended in slavery.

Though it is perilous to venture an answer to these questions, an attempt will be made nevertheless. In this connection the following must be taken into consideration. As everyone may experience, the logic of the systems, which are invented and used, do not reside only in the hardware and the software of the systems, but also in the interiors of the human beings concerned. Working effectively in the realm of information technology requires that any inventor, operator or user of the systems in question, each in their own way, are intimately familiar with the pertinent logic. Such logic depends first of all on what is considered as the present and labeled accordingly and, further, on the notions of "before" and "after" in relation to this present. This dependency entails that the present and the consequent all-over instantaneity will be predominant, as the information currents come to permeate and envelop the global society. This will affect the human beings that take part in this society, whether they are conscious of it or not. Thus, the human beings that actively take part will be immediately aware of anything that happens, and, in the long run, what is communicated to them by the information currents will be the only reality of which they actually accept the presence.

However, a responsibility that is carried implies that there is a reality of the past – a past that may be long ago already – which persists in the present and has its weight. Analogously, a hope that is entertained implies that there is a reality of the future – a future that may be distant still – which is sensed in the present and anticipated. Without doubt, the human being of the coming times will be conscious of the past as well as of the future, but, *in principle*, he will not be able to accept the possible reality of a part of this past or, analogously of this future, as something the presence of which – a "real presence" [!] – cannot be denied in the present. Thus, being factually confined to the present and its reality, the human being of the coming times, by consequence, will not be in the position to carry the weight of a responsibility or to live in response to a hope. Hence, the fundamental question becomes, whether that human being is still to be considered as a truly human being. In my opinion, homo techno-sapiens will certainly not constitute the apotheosis of the human being. In all probability, he will be post-human instead!

III.

Homo techno-sapiens is believed to be the successor to homo-sapiens, the human being of the present time and of the period which is historically accessible for us. In his moments of extreme pride, homo sapiens was convinced of his autonomy, of his – free – choice of a point from which to define his position in order to be able to "move" the earth, that is, to grasp the world, the cosmos, in order to understand and to exploit it. But, in his aspirations towards autonomy, homo-sapiens never was free from criticism. His presumed autonomy has always been counterbalanced by experiences, which transcended his basic feeling of personal autonomy. Thus, from time to time throughout the years of his life, he experiences heteronomy. For, naturally, what one does or does not, is not always and exclusively the result of one's deliberate decision. It is not always the consequence of one's so-called autonomous considerations or acts. On the contrary, as everyday life teaches us, a deed, a physical or mental act, may just as well constitute an answer to an appeal that is irresistible or it may be a reaction generated by, say, a provocation of whatever kind that cannot be ignored!

Clearly, the autonomy of the human being often meets its limits and, in this way, opens to his possible heteronomy. Experiences as above indicated constitute a most fundamental criticism with regard to the idea of autonomous man, a criticism that should not be forgotten. For if the earth – the world, the cosmos – is still considered to be humanity's empire, the experience of heteronomy teaches him to accept this empire as the place given to him in which to live. Human life requires keeping the balance, which means asking for the wisdom of ecosophy, the fundamental wisdom that bears any true ecology. It is a basic wisdom indeed. Yet, I fear that this wisdom will have been lost when the time of homo techno-sapiens has definitely come.

Chapter Twenty

Theology of Revolution versus Theology of Counter-Revolution

Rudolf J. Siebert

A. The Principle of Hope

In our international course on the *Future of Religion* in the IUC, Dubrovnik, Croatia, we became familiar with Thomas Müntzer's theology of revolution, particularly through the work of the Schellingian and Hegelian Marxist philosopher Ernst Bloch (1972; 1970a:7–18, 19–30): the teacher of the Catholic theologian Johannes, B Metz, father of the new political theology and indirectly of the Central and Latin American liberation theology, and of the Protestant theologian, Jürgen Moltmann, the initiator of the theology of hope, and of the American liberal Protestant theologian Harvey Cox (Lortz 1964:569, 589; 1962a: 237, 315–318, 323–324, 351, 374, 379, 410; 1962b: 17, 24; Küng 1994:624, 643–645, 1010; Kogon 1967: 616–630; Bloch, K. 1978:62–67, 70–74, 78–90; Habermas 1978:11–32). All three theologies constituted the counterpart to the traditional fascist theology of counter-revolution by Carl Schmitt, the disciple of Hobbes, and the jurist and political theologian of Adolf Hitler, and the teacher of Samuel Huntington (1996), the prophet of the *Clash of Civilizations*, and Pentagon advisor.

Dubrovnik

During his American exile from Nazi Germany, Bloch worked as a custodian in a high school. Long before his American exile, in 1921, Bloch had written already his famous book on *Thomas Müntzer, the Theologian of Revolution*. During his American exile, Bloch wrote his most influential work *The Principle of Hope*, which only decades later appeared in an English translation in the very conservative United States, where it had originated in the first place. Thus, in the past 30 years in our international course on the *Future of Religion* in Dubrovnik, we discussed not only Müntzer's theology of revolution, guided by Bloch, but also Bloch's very Müntzer-influenced philosophy of hope, philosophy of religion, historical materialism, philosophy of the future, and particularly his theodicy: the abyss between God's perfect justice and the horrible injustices in his world – e.g. Auschwitz and Treblinka, Dresden, Hiroshima and Nagasaki, and the cruel wars in Vietnam, in the former Yugoslavia, in Afghanistan and in Iraq (Bloch 1970b; 1970a; 1971; 1972; Kogon 1967:616–630; Oelmüller 1990; Colpe 1993; Rosenbaum 1999). We discovered the theodicy to be the very core of the theologies of revolution as well as of the theologies of counter-revolution.

Theodicy

Particularly after the cancer death of my wife Margaret, on October 20, 1978, the mother of eight children and a devout believer in God's Providence, in Dubrovnik we discussed most intensely the different forms of the theodicy: especially the talion theodicy and the test theodicy, which all three Abrahamic religions have in common (Siebert 2001:chapt. 3; 2002:chapts 2, 6.) We remembered that some of the Jewish mystics, the Cabbalists and Hassidim had taught that the infinite God could not *double himself up* and that God could thus not create another Infinite. Even the critical theorist, Jürgen Habermas, found this mystical theodicy to be plausible and acceptable. Yet, we were aware that this mystical theodicy threatened not only the metaphysics of immortality, but also the Jewish, Christian and Islamic hope in resurrection and the eternal life of *finite* human beings. Thus, like Bloch, we had problems with all traditional theodicies. It seemed that the development of the theodicies went from religious orthodoxy, through mysticism, to modern secular bourgeois, Marxian and Freudian enlightenments, and ended there – at least in their religious form – for the time being. We nevertheless continued to look at new religious theodicies that arose particularly with and through the Shoa or the Holocaust experience: e.g. the love – theodicy, or the shame – theodicy.

Shame-Theodicy

The shame-theodicy has most recently been newly re-formulated by Paul Viminitz (2005:397–408), the author of *Defense of Terrorism*. According to this theodicy, God and his people shame each other intersubjectively into raising the moral bar of mutual recognition. However, shaming was not meant to show the other to have fallen short of the formal ethical minimum, but rather to challenge the other to raise that minimum, e.g., though God was entitled to the sacrifice of Isaac, Abraham's willingness shamed God into withdrawing the demand for human sacrifice. The shame theodicy challenge to the other can also be seen in the biblical story of the Flood, the conclusion of the Book of Job, Jesus on the cross, etc. Maybe such a shame theodicy at least could give the *People of the Book* the means to mitigate the cycle of predation among them. According to the shame theodicy, it was Christian Anti-Semitism that gave rise to Auschwitz, Auschwitz to the State of Israel, the State of Israel to Sabra and Shatilla, and Sabra and Shatilla to 9/11 and 9/11 to the new crusades against Afghanistan and Iraq and the so called war against terrorism. If by availing itself of this theodicy of shame, Jerusalem could be persuaded to issue a *mea culpa* to Mecca for Sabra and Shatilla, and then maybe Rome and Wittenberg could be persuaded to issue its *mea culpa* to Jerusalem for Auschwitz and Treblinka.

Eschatological Theodicy

In Dubrovnik we were most deeply inclined toward an eschatological-apocalyptic theodicy in the sprit of Thomas Müntzer's theology of revolution: in spite of the *parousia delay* – the most painful open flank of all paradigms of Judaism, Christianity and Islam. Thus, we searched further, if not for a theoretical theodicy solution, of which there is none, then at least for a practical one, which would allow us to deal humanely with the perils of human existence. Once when I returned from the cruelest Yugoslav civil war, which cost the lives of 200,000 people, I told my Father Confessor in Frankfurt about it and asked him: *Where is God*? He reminded me of the passion of Christ. While that was not a theoretical theodicy solution, it was at least a practical one. While on the cross Jesus cried out the first verse of Psalm 22 in Aramaic – *Eli, Eli lamaha azavtani?* – *My God, my God, why hast thou forsaken me?* – the Messianic Psalm ends with the enthusiastic and universal proclamation: *Posterity shall serve him; men shall tell of the Lord to the coming generation; men proclaim his deliverance to a people yet unborn, that he has done it* (Matthew 27:45–50; Fromm 1966b:231–236).

Counter-Revolution

Thomas Müntzer became, so to speak, the Patron Saint of our international course on the *Future of Religion* in Dubrovnik as well as of our friendships. In the meantime, we have met 30 times in Dubrovnik, even during the horrible Yugoslav civil war. We spoke often about Müntzer's theology of revolution and related issues and engaged in time diagnosis. When shortly before the victorious neo-liberal, or neo-conservative counter-revolution of 1989, I crossed the border between the German Federal Republic and the former German Democratic Republic in order to teach in the Protestant Theological Faculty of the University of Rostock. In exchanging my money, I noticed on the East German 10 Mark Bill the head of Thomas Müntzer. To be sure, Thomas was a great religious figure. He had lived what he believed. He reconciled the usual discrepancy between theory and praxis in religion as well as in secular philosophies. Thomas's partisanship for the poor classes became an ethical and socio-ethical climax in the history of Christianity. However, against the advice of his military experts, Thomas led thousands of peasants with scythes, sickles and bare fists against General Frundsberg's very modernized, highly equipped troops, whom Charles V had called up from Italy. In the spirit of the *Imitatio Christi*, Thomas trusted unconditionally and absolutely in God's Providence and help. Thomas hoped and expected the arrival of the Messianic realm *now*: in his own, all too short life time. In Thomas, faith and hope overwhelmed military-technical rationality! Thomas, the *dreamer*, the saint, and the martyr of truth, liberation and redemption, unfortunately did not prove himself – like Joseph in the realm of the Hyksos-Pharaoh, not to speak of Moses later on – likewise as a man of technical and practical affairs. Thomas was abandoned by God and men. Theodicy! The revolution-ary God, who once had liberated the Hebrew slaves from their Egyptian and Babylonian masters, seemed to have moved to the side of the House of Habsburg and the princes and the nobility and their counterrevolution. Thomas and his revolutionary farmers were abandoned. The theology of counter-revolution won over the theology of revolution. Almost 400 years later, in 1918, historical judgment would reach the House of Habsburg and the whole European aristocratic ruling class. Maybe world history is after all – as Hegel put it – *world judgment*: not only for slaveholders and feudal lords, but also for the bourgeois owners of capital. While at the East German border, shortly before its cancellation and liquidation by the neo-conservative counter-revolution, I remembered that in 1525 Frundsberg had slaughtered mercilessly the insurrectionist farmers, and thus their revolution had come to its catastrophic end, and Müntzer's head had been stuck up at the door of Mühlhausen in Thüringia, Germany. I looked at Müntzer's image on the East German 10 Mark Bill and said to myself: *Poor Thomas, you have lost another revolution!* (Bloch 1972; Lortz 1964:569, 589; 1962a:237, 315–318, 323–324, 351, 374, 379, 410; 1962b:17, 24; Küng 1994:624, 643–645, 1010.)

Annexation of the Farmer and Worker State

Soon afterwards, the East-German *farmer and worker state*, the German Democratic Republic, collapsed and was annexed by its bigger, economically and militarily much more powerful bourgeois counterpart: the German Federal Republic. This time it was not the Emperor of large parts of Europe, Charles V, and the aristocratic ruling class who won the feudal counter-revolution over the farmer and worker proletariat. Rather, this time, it was President Reagan and the globalizing bourgeois ruling class of the West who won the capitalist counter-revolution over the farmers and workers of Eastern Europe and beyond, after having tried this twice before with many sacrifices and without success. If individuals, groups, or whole nations avoid, or ignore, or lose the continual historical struggle for recognition between master and servant, they get the ruling class that they deserve. However, as in man's freedom history, the slaveholders were once determinately negated by the feudal lords, and the feudal lords by the bourgeois, so the bourgeois will someday be concretely superseded by the globally united farmers and workers, the real producers of the wealth of the nations, into post-modern alternative Future 3 – the realm of the freedom of All on the basis of the realm of natural necessity. That will happen, if the process is not interrupted by alternative Future 1 – the totally administered society, or by alternative Future 2 – NBC wars and/or environmental catastrophes. Ultimately, no counter-revolution will be able to prevent the arrival of alternative Future 3, not to speak of the Messianic realm – in terms of the Abrahamic religions – without death and tears, and without continual stealing, murder, and lying: the radical Messianic inversion of the horror and terror of past and present society and history.

Longing for the Totally Other

Through the past 30 years in Dubrovnik, our discourses and our actions have been driven by the same longing that had moved the Pastor Thomas Müntzer to become a leader of the farmer revolution on the basis of the *Sermon on the Mount*, a longing which has survived him. It was the longing for light, friendship and love. It was the longing for perfect justice. It was the longing for a free society. It was the insatiable longing for the totally Other than the horror and terror of nature and history, for which the Abrahamic religions had reserved the name of the *Messianic Realm*. It was the longing that the murderer shall not triumph over the innocent victim – at least not ultimately. It was the longing that the finitude of the finite life may not be the last word of history. Shortly, it was the trust and confidence in the imageless, nameless and notionless Eternal One. For us in Dubrovnik, this longing for the entirely Other became a kind of definition of religion.

Theory and Praxis

However, we did not only renew this longing in theory, but also in praxis. Thus, we brought medicine and money to the innocent victims of the Yugo-slav civil war and sometimes even helped some of them to escape the terrible situation, and to settle in Canada, with the help of the most generous Mennonite Community and the Canadian Government. Unfortunately, late capitalist society is continually producing masses of narcisstic, socio-pathic, *me-me* individuals, who are sexually detabuized and desublimated, and who are without any ability to empathize with, to recognize, and to include the *other*; who sometimes even murder others without any further motivation than doing the act itself, and in whom all longing is suffocated, except maybe the desire for the American dream, i.e. sex, car, and career, and of course for the money, without which such items cannot be bought.

Socialist and Fascist Theology

One outstanding member of our Dubrovnik circle was the Canadian scholar, Jim Reimer. Before my family and I met Jim and his young family the first time in July/August 1976, we had already become known to each other indirectly through the mediation of his teacher and our common friend, Gregory Baum, who at the time taught at Toronto University. When I met Jim, he worked hard with Gregory on his doctoral dissertation The *Emmanuel Hirsch and Paul Tillich Debate. A Study in the Political Ramifications of Theology* (Reimer 1989:i–iii, iii–xii, xiii–xv). Obviously, Tillich and his existential and socialistic theology was closer to Thomas Müntzer's revolutionary theology than the conservative-revolutionary or better still counter-revolutionary, fascist theology of Hirsch. I think, at the time Jim found me interesting, because I had grown up in Nazi Germany, where Hirsch had been one of Hitler's theologians together with Gerhard Kittel, Paul Althaus, Carl Schmitt, and my teacher Joseph Lortz, and which Tillich had left in protest together with his friend, the Jewish scholar, Max Horkheimer, the founder of the critical theory of society, for exile in the United States (Erickson 1985; Meier 1994; Groh 1998; Krieg 2004). All of Hitler's theologians appreciated the apologist Tertullian, the lawyer, who in his apologetics described to the Roman officials and courts, what wonderfully conformist citizens the Christians would make for the Roman state: the same state, which by the time had executed not only Jesus of Nazareth, but also many of his followers for almost 200 years. *Christus aut Caesar!?* It is not accidental that the Latin word *fasces*, – the bundle of sticks with an ax in the middle, which symbolized Roman *justitia* – became the linguistic root for the modern word *fascism*. All the fascist theologians, Catholic as well as Protestant, represented a *Constantinian* Christendom, which was in bed with even authoritarian states, and which therefore could no longer criticize Caesar, if necessary, and which, also, was no longer able to announce the totally Other than nature and history, and thereby denounce what Hitler had called the *"aristocratic principle of nature,"* the right of the predator over the prey, and to promote the high ideals of perfect justice and unconditional love.

Brothers on the Christian Left

On my part, I – having been like Eugen Kogon (1965), the author of the *SS-State*, and my friend Walter Dirks, one of Europe's most honest and truthful journalists, a member of the Left Wing of the Roman Catholic Paradigm – was very happy to have found a brother and his family from the Left Wing of the Reformation Paradigm: from the Mennonite Community. As brothers on the Christian Left, Jim and I had a lot in common from the very start. We spent hours in discourse remembering: my experiences in a Catholic parish in Ginnheim, Frankfurt a.M., Germany; the Pastor Georg W. Rudolphi who had resisted fascism and suffered much for it; my membership in the Catholic Youth Movement and in the Hitler Youth; my service in the German Air Force, defending German cities against the Allied saturation bombings; my participation in the fight against the tank army of General Patton as an infantry lieutenant, originally trained for the *crusade* against *atheistic* bolshevism at the Eastern Front; my surrender to General Patton and American and Canadian officers near Alzenau, Germany, in March 1945; my time as prisoner of war in Camp Allen, Norfolk, Virginia; my selection there as Anti-Nazi; my education there to be an agent for the democratization of post-war Germany; my political work in post-war liberal Germany; my final immigration into the United States in 1962, my teaching at Loyola College and St. Agnes College in Baltimore, Maryland, and finally at Western Michigan University's Department of Comparative Religion (Siebert 1993; Weitensteiner 2002). Together Jim and I looked at movies about fascism and the Second World War and the suffering of the Jews: e.g. the movie *Conspiracy* about the Wannsee Conference in Berlin, in which SS General Heidrich and SS Colonel Eichmann made representatives of the State and Party accept the most radical and final solution of the Jewish question: the gassing of the Jews with the insecticide Cyclone B, which was invented by the Jewish-German General Fritz Haber, the father of the gas war in 1915, and produced by I. G. Farben, Frankfurt a.M. Höchst, in the 1940's. Jim was so terrified by the movie that he left early. My experiences in Nazi Germany were, nevertheless, tremendously informative, interesting and moving for Jim, who had grown up in peaceful Canada. I hoped that my experiences would also be useful for Jim's dissertation on Tillich and Hirsch. However, our long existential and academic discourses in Dubrovnik and elsewhere, and Jim's hard work on his dissertation never prevented him and his dear wife Margaret from inviting me and my large family – my late wife Margie and my seven children – for the most delicious meals, which he even cooked himself personally and most skillfully and most scientifically. Jim has been one of the few people with whom one could still speak seriously about serious issues in theology and metaphysics: God, freedom, and immortality.

Religious Socialism or Clerico – Fascism?

In our discourses in Dubrovnik and elsewhere, I urged Jim continually to stress in his dissertation Tillich and his religious socialism and his theology of revolution rather than Hirsch and his clerico-fascism and his theology of counter-revolution. I pointed to the absolute incompatibility between Tillich, the theologian who resisted German fascism, and Hirsch, the theologian who conformed to it and even supported it. How could one get them both into one dissertation? Yet, Jim always pursued the high ideal of political, historical and theological impartiality and objectivity. I was continually worried that Jim's soul would be infected by Hirsch's fascist theology, and that he would neglect Tillich's existential and socialistic theology, because the former seemed to him to have had such a high sexual ethics, and the latter was supposed to have been such a *womanizer*. Jim, like I, thought very highly of family values. Of course, Hirsch had been so little blessed by natural beauty or sexual attraction that he was spared Tillich's pleasurable but also most painful and sometimes even demonic sexual attractions and temptations. It was my opinion that there were still other ethical and particularly socio-ethical standards than those of sexual morality, as important as they may be. The German Bishops had trusted in the *conservative revolutionary*, or better still counter-revolution-ary Chancellor Adolf Hitler, because they believed that he would purify the German soul through forbidding pornography, nudist beaches, homosexuality, lesbianism, and the bathing together of men and women. However, the Bishops overlooked completely the concentration camps as work and later on as death camps. Why are sexual deviations so bad and mass murder for the fatherland is taken so lightly, or is even considered to be heroic? As late as the 1990's an American President was impeached for a sexual deviation and for lying about it, but not for the killing of thousands of civilians in Serbia – "collateral damage" – and being silent about it. Something had gone wrong in the evolution of Western Christian and secular ethics and social ethics, not to speak of the fact that for a long time these Christian and secular ethics have served more for the harmonization of the present status quo than for the formation of the future (Horkheimer 1987:138–144, 145–157).

Positive or Negative Metaphysical Theology?

Of course, there was never any real danger that Jim would have fallen for the clerico-fascist Hirsch. It is true that Jim had sometimes certain conservative tendencies in his wonderful personality. That accounts for his friendship with Catholics. However, at least two of these Catholics, Gregory Baum and I, were on the Left of the Roman Catholic Paradigm and thus precisely were not conservative Catholics. Maybe the Schellingian and Hegelian Tillich – who as a good Lutheran belonged to the Reformation-Protestant Paradigm of Christianity, and who at the same time was the great friend of the Jewish critical theorists of the Frankfurt School, and maybe also of the last Marxist metaphysician, Ernst Bloch – motivated Jim more than friends from the Roman Catholic Paradigm to think about the possibility of developing a *metaphysical theology* for the Mennonite community. Admittedly, this thought was, if not precisely conservative, nevertheless certainly also not really contemporaneous in a modern or even post-modern culture, which considers itself in the spirit of August Comte, the father of modern positivism and positive sociology, to be not only post-theological but also post-metaphysical. Particularly the horrible theodicy experiences of the 20th and of the beginning of the 21st centuries – be they the theodicy experiences with nature like the recent Tsunami in the Indian Ocean, or the hurricanes of New Orleans, or the earth quake in Pakistan, which cost the lives of hundred thousands of people including ten thousands of children; or be they the theodicy experiences with history – the two world wars, Auschwitz and Treblinka, Dresden, Hiroshima and Nagasaki, the cold war, the Vietnam War, the Yugoslav war, the two Iraq wars, the Afghanistan war, which all together killed close to hundred million people, and possibly next Iran, or Syria, or North Korea – have made it difficult for the Western civilization to accept the theological presupposition of the Hebrew prophets, that divine Providence governs the world, or the metaphysical proposition of Anaxagoras, that Reason governs the world. Yet, it was precisely Jim's great intention to make the non-contemporaneous contemporaneous: to bring a metaphysical theology into the post-theological and post-metaphysical modernity and possibly post-modernity. That was, indeed, a most courageous intention and plan. As expression of his great intention, Jim gave me August 14, 1978 a wonderful gift: an English translation of the *Science of Logic*, or better still Logos-theology, or dialectical metaphysics of the last great Lutheran theologian and metaphysician, Georg W. F. Hegel

(1969), who had once more and a last time reconciled the modern antagonism between Jerusalem and Athens, Jewish, Christian, and Islamic religion on one hand, and Greek philosophy and metaphysics, on the other, and who had thus stopped for a moment the de-Hellnization of all three Abrahamic religions and of the modern world. The dedication read very sternly: "*Rudolf, In appreciation for teaching me Hegel, Jim.*" While I was certainly fascinated by Jim's idea of a metaphysical theology, I nevertheless also suggested to him that maybe our common friend Thomas Müntzer and maybe also Conrad Grebel, the spiritual fathers of the Mennonite Community, could through their revolutionary theologies show us the way to a theology without a positive metaphysics, but maybe, instead, with a negative metaphysics, or with instead of a *prima philosophia* an *ultima philosophia*, one which was not concerned with the first *things*, but rather with the *last things*, not with Alpha but with Omega (1983). It could give us an eschatological perspective in which the world would alienate itself and would manifest its antagonisms and abysses as it shall lie prostate as needy and distorted in the Messianic light on Judgment Day (Revelation 21, 22; Adorno 1980:333–334; Benjamin 1977b). It could thus help us to interpret present day antagonistic civil society, and most importantly it could show us how to act in a Christian and humanistic way in the present turbulent transition from Modernity to Post-Modernity. Such negative metaphysical theology would certainly correspond to and could fulfill what once Thomas Müntzer intended to do in his theology of revolution.

Conservative Culture

While our historical friend Thomas Müntzer had lived, worked, fought and died at the beginning of the modern Western culture, Jim and I and our whole Dubrovnik Circle were very much aware that we were situated toward its end, and that we had to struggle for the recognition of our rights and freedoms in the context of the transition from Modernity to Post-Modernity, which Hegel had predicted already four generations earlier. In this process and against it, the modern Western civilization had become a very conservative one in terms of the neo-liberal trend turn, particularly in America. In the 1990's, Jim and Gregory Baum were upset, disappointed and saddened, that in this conservative culture I had not been recognized academically, in spite of all my articles, and books about the critical theory of society and of religion, as well as about a critical political theology, and my lecturing at many American, Canadian and European universities, and the organization of international courses in Dubrovnik and Yalta, etc. Jim, therefore, composed a wonderful *Festschrift* in my honor together with Gregory and many of my colleagues from the international course on the *Future of Religion* in Dubrovnik (Reimer 1992). Jim gave me the *Festschrift* in 1992, during a very dignified ceremony at Conrad Grebel College. Later on, Jim and his wife Margaret came all the way from Kitchener and Waterloo to Kalamazoo, Michigan, in order to celebrate my 70th birthday and to give me a wonderful recognition speech in the circle of my family and friends and present me with his Blue Grass CD, which I have been listening to ever since again and again.

No Awards for Critical Scholars

When several years ago, I visited on my way to Dubrovnik the critical theorist Ludwig von Friedeburg, then still Director of the Frankfurt Institute for Social Research, he asked me rhetorically in the office of his predecessor, Theodor Wiesengrund Adorno, the student and friend of Paul Tillich and the real genius of the Frankfurt School: *"What do you think, Adorno never received any academic award, in spite of the fact that the libraries are full of his great works?"* I was amazed that von Friedeburg could ask me such a question, because from long experience I was convinced of the fact that in antagonistic civil society and its conservative and sometimes even reactionary culture, be it liberal, neo-liberal, or fascist, a scholar would be less recognized, the more critical he or she was, and vice versa. Adorno had certainly not been a conformist. He had for some time been the leader of the third youth movement in the West, directed against post-World War II liberal civil society. There had been such a youth movement for *new love, new politics, new religion* and against – what Max Weber (1958:181–183) had called – the *iron cage of capitalism* before World War I, and another one between World War I and II In 1969, shortly before his death, the judges in Frankfurt made Adorno responsible for the whole student rebellion from Tokyo through the United States and Germany to Italy. The great critical theorist received no academic awards, but he rather got a police file. When Adorno died in 1969, the obituary in the New York Times mentioned only that he had written once an essay about the *jitterbug*. It forgot completely that the great pianist and composer had also written a whole sociology and philosophy of music, which could have easily been found in most New York libraries even in the English translation. To the contrary, admittedly, Adorno's teacher Tillich (1977) did receive awards and honors in the United States, but only because he was able to hide so well his *Socialist Decision*, which he considered to be his best book, and because of which he had to leave Nazi Germany. Not even his closest assistant, who helped to translate and edit his *Systematic Theology* (Tillich 1967), my former Dean and Vice President at Western Michigan University, Cornelius Loew who hired me in 1965, knew anything about it. Since Tillich (1966) could not introduce himself to the conservative American audience with his *The Socialist Decision*, which criticized the class antagonism in bourgeois society and pointed beyond it, he presented himself with the book *On the Boundary*, which tried to reconcile the modern antagonism between the religious and the secular. That was more harmless, and therefore more plausible and acceptable in America's conservative culture. When Tillich visited Kalamazoo in 1963, he asked his former Assistant Loew *what would remain of his theology*? Corney answered honestly: nothing! Corney gave as reason for his prediction that Americans could not think systematically and therefore could not find plausible and accept his systematic theology. In reality, conservative Americans could accept Tillich's religious socialism as little as the humanistic socialism of his friends, the critical theorists of the Frankfurt School – Adorno, Horkheimer, Walter Benjamin, Erich Fromm, Herbert Marcuse, Leo-Löwenthal, etc., – with whom he shared his exile in America from fascist Germany, not to speak of the Marxist playwright Bertolt Brecht and his epical or dialectical theater. The conservative American culture is more conducive to the development of a theology of counter-revolution than a theology of revolution.

The God above the God of Theism

Yet, Jim and I knew that something did remain of Tillich after all. When the pastors of Kalamazoo visited Corney Loew, the former army chaplain, in the hospital after his terrible car accident in which on the way to Lake Michigan he was seriously injured and his beloved wife – a wonderful organist and pianist – died, he told them: *it* [the accident] *was absolute contingency*. Corney meant the absolute absence of God's Providence. However, in spite of this terrible theodicy experience, Corney continued – following his teacher Tillich (1972:186–190) – to have faith in the power of the *God above the God of theism*, and to trust in the *God, who appears when God has disappeared in the anxiety of doubt, meaninglessness, and death.* When in the summer 2005 at Oxford University, some older Professors looked at me as I was lecturing and thought that Paul Tillich was sitting there and speaking with his heavy German accent, I was very much honored by this observation and remembrance. Finally, forty years after his death, Tillich's student Adorno also has received some recognition after all: a street in Frankfurt has been named after him. Something similar happened to his older friend and teacher, the critical theorist Walter Benjamin. Sixty years after Benjamin had been driven by Spanish, French and German fascists into extreme despair and committed suicide in the French-Spanish border town of Port Bou, the German Federal Republic was shamed by the poor, small town into paying an Israeli architect, to build a wonderful monument in remembrance of Benjamin in the town's cemetery right above the Mediterranean. It takes conservative bourgeois societies and cultures a long time to finally recognize a critical thinker. That as such, of course, does not yet mean that the critical scholar has finally been understood, not to speak of being comprehended and followed in theory and praxis, but is only the recognition that he is now dead and can no longer disturb the harmony of the conservative culture.

Expectation

Thus, how could Jim and Gregory possibly expect that I could be recognized and awarded as a critical theorist of society and religion in a conservative culture, which still remembered and honored the Anti-Semite Henry Ford, a friend of Adolf Hitler, and the Clerico – Fascist Father Charles Coughlin (1932, 1933), the spiritual leader of the *German Bund* and of the fascist *Christian Front* in Detroit? (Ward 1933, Baldwin 2001:chapt. 19; Brinkley 1982:chapt. 4). Father Coughlin had originally come from rich parents in Ontario, Canada, and as a priest had been stationed in Kalamazoo, where this essay is being written, before he finally took over a parish in Detroit. Coughlin left President Roosevelt's liberalism behind, which had been socially modified by the introduction of the *principle of subsidiarity* taken from Pius XI' social encyclical *Quadragesimo Anno* of 1931. Coughlin turned against the New Deal. Coughlin became a friend of Ford and of Dr. Joseph Goebbels, Hitler's propaganda minister. Ford and Hitler appeared in different issues of the Times as *Man of the Year*. Coughlin was even known to Hitler personally. Coughlin told Hitler through Goebbels, that if he would only be less hard on Christianity, the Americans would be very open for his national socialist ideas and message. As a consequence, Hitler planned to change his propaganda strategy toward the United States. In the conservative American culture, Coughlin was a smaller version and edition of the heavy weight intellectual Carl Schmitt. During the 1930's and 1940's, Father Coughlin preached over the radio to over 40 million Americans and Canadians every Sunday afternoon at 3:00pm. There are still people living in Michigan and Ontario today – in 2006 – who remember that their parents made them listen to Father Coughlin because he was such a great man. Father Coughlin was celebrated and honored by American Cardinals up to his death in the 1970's. In the conservative American culture it is easier for a theologian of counter-revolution to find broad recognition than a theologian of revolution.

Police File

Jim and the whole Dubrovnik Circle had a hard time understanding why, in the conservative and sometimes reactionary American culture, I as an anti-fascist received instead of academic awards a long police file, with all informers blacked out, for my resistance against the Vietnam – and other unjust wars (Bonfiglio 2005:266–288). My friend, the good father John Grathwohl, who in his youth had heard Coughlin on the radio and who had served Catholic parishes in Kalamazoo for 40 year, and who had even been an army chaplain in Vietnam, was marginalized by many conservative Catholics in Kalamazoo and Michigan, after he went with other priests and nuns to Iraq, shortly before the second war against this country in order to prevent it. Today, there are still present at the reactionary extreme of the conservative American culture the Rightwing militias, with whom McVeigh was connected, the terror – bomber of Oklahoma City. In November 2004, a majority of Catholics and Evangelicals voted once more for President G. W. Bush, who through Orwellian lies had led the country into the second Iraq war, in spite of the fact, that Pope John Paul II and many members of the World Council of Churches had called the first and second Iraq war *unjust*, and in spite of all the wonderful Papal and Episcopal peace and justice encyclicals and letters of recent decades. There is finally the Government-conformed, extremely Rightwing Fox News, which promises continually to be *"fair, balanced and unafraid,"* but which only seldom lets the truth break through, and then merely accidentally and unintentionally particularly through more enlightened guests appearing on the show. The anchor men and women speak so fast and loud that not any thought can possibly form in the audience. They often come close to a Huxleyan and Orwellian dialectics pointing to post-modern alternative Future 1 – the totally administered society, and alternative Future 2 – an entirely militarized society. According to Fox News, Huntington's collision of the Christian and Islamic civilization has already moved into World War III: self-fulfilling prophecy! In addition, Fox News continually feels the urge to defend Christianity. A religion must indeed be in bad shape if it needs the O'Reilly Factor to engage in its apologetics. The neo-liberals Bill O'Reilly, Rush Limbaugh and Michael Savage try to establish an alternative and thus balance to the so-called "liberal" standard national media, particularly the New York Times, who they consider to be as far on the Left as they are on the Right. While the standard national media constitute the very center of the conservative American culture, O'Reilly, Limbaugh and Savage represent its reactionary extreme.

Assassination

The same is true in the American conservative culture of Pat Robertson, one of Coughlin's successors, who recently called for the assassination of the social-ist President Chavez of Venezuela and even for war against his county, and who declared that Prime Minister Sharon's stroke was a punishment by God for having divided Palestine and having shared it – the Gaza strip – with the Palestinians in a unilateral move, in spite of the fact, that the land had been promised to the Jews alone: a talion – theodicy. Robertson's Catholic counter-part, Father Robert Sirico, agrees with him, but would like to transform his irrational nationalism into a *critical one* – a *contradictio in adjecto* – on the basis of the Roman Catholic natural law tradition. In such conservative or even reactionary atmosphere critical thinking in general and a theology of revolu-tion in particular, has certainly a hard time to survive, not to speak of being recognized, rewarded, and awarded, while the theology of counter-revolution is blooming in many religious radio and television stations.

Conservative Opposition

In 1978, after the death of my wife Margaret while I was teaching in London, Ontario, I considered returning from a secular state university to a Catholic college in London, Ontario. However, the conservative opposition to such a move was too strong. My neo-liberal colleagues particularly in the Department of Economics voted me down. I simply talked too much like Gregory Baum! In the 1980's an Associate Dean and a Registrar closed our Humanistic Future and Peace Studies Program at Western Michigan University, which continued the work of the critical theorist Ossip Flechtheim and his critical futurology, for the reason that it contained *too many foreigners*. In reality, the program was repressed because we studied the possibility and probability and undesirability of post-modern alternative Future I – the entirely administered society, torn off from the human potentials of mutual understanding and reciprocal recognition of human dignity, freedoms and rights. Flechtheim, who was in exile in America from Nazi Germany, and his critical futurology had already been rejected by 100 American universities in the 1940's. Maybe it would have been helpful for native and foreign students to discuss future and peace long before September 11, 2001 happened. When the progressive liberal theologian Hans Küng came to Western Michigan University as a Visiting Professor, the Catholic Bishop wrote a letter to all priests and nuns admonishing them not to attend his lectures. They came anyway. When the critical political theologian Johannes B. Metz came as a Visiting Professor to Kalamazoo College, the conservative and fundamentalist theological questions that came from the audience depressed him so deeply that he was unable to celebrate the mass in remembrance of my late wife Margie, which we had planned. The critical theorist Jürgen Habermas was not invited as WMU Visiting Professor, because *he had not written enough*. Shortly before the hurricanes, a Catholic college in New Orleans wanted to give me on the initiative of a Mennonite colleague from the Dubrovnik Circle an honorary doctorate for my work for peace and justice, but the neo-conservatives colleagues prevented it. I never had any Sabbatical in 40 years. I had to write all critical articles and books while often teaching three or four semesters a year.

Culture of Death

To the contrary, the pop-singer Madonna danced herself out of the working class of Flint, Michigan and finally out of the United States into England's bourgeoisie, through many sex shows. She then had no problem in finding wide recognition in the porno culture of the West. Oliver North, who was indicted for his involvement in the Iran – Contra Affair has no difficulty in appearing every night on Fox News with his war reports, and to find wide recognition in what recent Popes have called the *culture of death*. Yet, it is more difficult for critics of such cultures, who rather aim at a culture of life and of love, to find recognition in the national or international discourse of the West. It is not really functional for civil society and its conservative culture to fulfill Jim's good expectation and to give awards to critical theorists of society and religion, or critical political theologians, or theologians of revolution, who criticize its humanly most painful and costly antagonisms, and whose recommendations for their resolution cannot possibly be found plausible or acceptable, without it being willing and able to change its identity, not toward post-modern alternative Future 1 or 2, but rather toward alternative Future 3 – a reconciled society. Such a reconciled society is characterized by mutual understanding and symmetrical recognition, in which personal autonomy and universal, i.e. anamnestic, present and proleptic solidarity, would be reconciled and a friendly, helpful and solidary living together of human beings would be possible.

Unconditional Fairness and Justice

Yet, Jim's uncompromising sense for unconditional fairness and justice has always been to his greatest honor and most admirable. He has continually followed most intensely the non-conformist spirit of Müntzer and Grebel. It may console Jim, that also I was once recognized and named among the excellent teachers of my University, and that once I even received a grant for one of my books from the Mary Knoll Congregation in New York, when it was still critical, and when its members were martyrized by the Arena Party in El Salvador and other fascist organizations and their death squads. However, those awards came all before the neo-conservative and neo-liberal trend turn. One must be grateful for little things for the sake of the *critical spirit*, which Jim and I and the Dubrovnik Circle have shared for three decades, and the preservation of which is the greatest reward in itself. Tillich's friend, Max Horkheimer (1974:chapt. 4), was right when he stated, that the image of *perfect justice* – as the core of the great world religions, as well as of the critical spirit, the spreading of which brings neither power nor recognition in this world and maybe not even in the Beyond, and which at the same time may be accompanied in globolizing late capitalist society by a growing awareness of its own vanity – may, nevertheless, be more attractive to modern genuine and disillusioned believers as well as to secular humanists than the empty self-satisfaction, which religion in the 19th century and sometimes even still in the 20th and 21st centuries did either not see within itself, or which else it tolerated as well intentioned. Jim and I and the Dubrovnik Circle did not share this religious self-satisfaction, but rather Müntzer's and Grebel's and the Chiliasts' and the critical theorists' insatiable longing for the wholly Other than what is the case in nature and history and the often cruel laws of natural and social evolution, and for perfect justice and for unconditional love. Throughout my 44 years in America, I have always tried to falsify one of the most ironical and cynical statements of Emmanuel Hirsch's great charismatic leader Adolf Hitler: that Germans, who emigrate to America are mere cultural manure, and that the Americans don't even notice it. It was not easy! Yet Jim, no matter if we were meditatively melancholical or hilariously humorous and happy, pessimistic or optimistic, desperate or hopeful, was a continual consolation for me together with our common friends in the Dubrovnik Circle and beyond it in Canada, the USA, and Europe throughout the past 30 years.

B. Critical Political Theology

During the long years of our successes and setbacks, the Dubrovnik Circle turned very often to the mystical, radical, and enthusiastic Pastor Thomas Müntzer to consider his biography, his theology of revolution, and his historical significance. Who was Father Müntzer really, and what really happened to him and his Christian revolutionary movement at the beginning of Modernity?

Political Revolutionary

Father Thomas Müntzer appeared between 1523–1525 in Zwickau and Mühlhausen, where he received little recognition and suffered much (Bloch 1972; Lortz 1964:569, 589; 1962a:237, 315–318, 323–324, 351, 374, 379, 410; 1962b:17, 24; Küng 1994:624, 643–645, 1010.) As early as 1519, Thomas had listened in on the Reformer Martin Luther's disputation in Leipzig. Contrary to Müntzer, Luther was not a political revolutionary, but rather merely a religious reformer, and did not want to be anything else. Therefore, Luther turned passionately against the revolution of the farmers of 1525, and soon also against their theological leader, Thomas Müntzer. Not Luther, but Müntzer can be compared with the great revolutionaries of world history from Spartacus through the English Puritans and the French Jacobins to Marx, Lenin and Mao, who from the very start aimed at a violent overthrow of the old and unjust social order and its values and its representatives. The farmer rebellion of 1525, led by Thomas Müntzer, was not an early bourgeois revolution, as some Marxist authors have asserted. The majority of the city-bourgeoisie stood on the side of the feudal lords. However, Müntzer's farmer movement can be identified as an early socialist revolution out of genuine religious, Christian sources. Thomas was indeed a Christian political revolutionary.

Mysticism and Apocalyptic

Father Thomas Müntzer referred and appealed with many others to a person-ally experienced, immediate revelation and spirit experience – to an inner voice and an inner light – and connected them with apocalyptic-social-revo-lutionary ideas. Thomas's goal was the radical enforcement of the Reforma-tion here and now. That was his motto. If need be, this enforcement of the Reformation had to happen with violence, and without consideration and respect for the extant law, which after all belonged to the old oppressive and exploitative and thus unjust feudal order, which was to be overthrown. The radical competitor of Luther, Thomas Müntzer, wanted to put up and erect the thousand-year realm of Christ on earth. Pastor Müntzer was deeply rooted in the medieval mysticism and apocalyptic.

Farmer War

The farmer war broke out two years after the Empire-Knights Insurrection of 1523. Müntzer saw in the farmer war the approaching judgment over the godless, and the beginning of the new social order. In the face of the extremely unjust economic conditions of the farmers in the feudal system, the farmer war was a more than understandable political-revolutionary area – fire, which cost the lives of a hundred thousand farmers. Certainly the farm-ers could with good reasons appeal to the *Evangelium* for the legitimation of their political-economical-social as well as their religious-ecclesiastical demands (e.g. free elections of pastors). Thus, the connection between the farmer war and the Reformation is indisputable. Thomas Müntzer and his revolutionary movement must be seen as part of the Reformation-Protestant Paradigm of Christianity.

Reformation or Revolution

Martin Luther was afraid that his Reformation would be compromised in the eyes of the feudal lords by Thomas Müntzer's revolution. First, Luther tried to mediate. He admonished for peace. However, Luther became more and more startled by news reports about horrible terroristic excesses of the farmers. Strangely enough, he did not hear about any terroristic excesses of Frundsberg's counter-revolutionary army. Luther reacted with his extremely passionate and impertinent writing: *Against the Murderous and Thieving Gangs of Farmers*. Luther sided with the counter-revolutionary feudal lords and the bourgeoisie. Luther demanded that the feudal lords should intervene inconsiderately, recklessly, and ruthlessly, and that they should use the sword against this – in his eyes – reprehensible indignation. The princes should cut, thrash and stab the insurrectionists, the farmers and their families. Luther became a theologian of counter-revolution. Luther had to pay a high price for his counterrevolutionary theology and activities, i.e. his earlier popularity. Without Luther's counter-revolutionary theology, it would not have been possible for Adolf Hitler to win so many Lutherans over to his conservative revolution, i.e., counter-revolution against socialism, and even establish the Lutheran Empire Bishop Müller in Berlin in 1934.

Tragic Development

The Lutherans and the Catholics have repressed for a long time this tragic development of Thomas Müntzer's farmer revolution. They did this until finally after the bourgeois revolution of 1848, Friedrich Engels wrote the first history of the farmer war and revolution of 1525. After World War I, in his book of 1921, Ernst Bloch appreciated Thomas Müntzer as the founder of a socialist revolutionary tradition. It is quite obvious that this Lutheran repression of the memory of Thomas Müntzer and his farmer revolution had something to do with Luther himself: with his theology of counter-revolution. Luther was biased politically and theologically in terms of an authoritarian perspective from above, from the position of the ruling class, the princes, and the feudal lords, and even the higher bourgeoisie. Luther was not willing to draw from his radical demand for the freedom of the Christian likewise the radical political and social consequences, as Thomas Müntzer did as a theologian of revolution. Luther was as hypocritical as the fathers of the American Constitution, who in Philadelphia announced the freedom of all, but kept their African slaves. Jefferson continued to own his 250 slaves even after the Quakers had liberated theirs. Luther did not want to support the justified demands of the farmers against the princes and the feudal class with the same corresponding clarity and distinction as Müntzer did. There was no doubt that there existed extremely rational and justified demands of the farmers, who were threatened by the feudal ruling class in their independence, and who were increasingly exploited, and who were humiliated by such arrangements as the *lex primae noctis*, which remained valid in Austria up to 1918. Even Luther could not deny the economic, ethical, and legal distress of the farmers and their families. Even in 1525 a social reform concept would not have been illusionary. The cooperative order of the Swiss Confederation, which was for the farmers of Southern Germany the ideal of a new order, would certainly have been a doable model. Maybe the realization of such a reform model would have diminished the tension of the class antagonism to such an extent that Müntzer's revolution would not have been necessary, or could at least have been postponed. Several years ago, I recommended the Swiss Confederation model even at Haifa University for Israel, Lebanon, Jordan, and Palestine. Of course, Luther was caught in his narrow Thüringian perspective. Thus, the Swiss model remained foreign to him. In any case, the House Habsburg had always been afraid of the spreading of the Swiss cooperative organization principles into Southern Germany, and thus had resisted it. Thus, Thomas Müntzer and his farmer revolution became historically necessary. However, left alone and betrayed by Luther and the Lutherans, the farmers suffered not only a crushing defeat at Frankenhausen, but also a terrible judgment and punishment. Thomas was tortured and beheaded, being only 36 years of age. However, that was not the end of the radical-reformatory stream. To the contrary! In consequence of Müntzer's farmer revolution, Conrad Grebel began his activity in Ulrich Zwingli's Zürich.

Faith

Already in 1520, Müntzer had become a preacher in Zwickau, near Bohemia, where the Hussitic movement had developed side by side with the extremes of the war-like and violent-revolutionary Laborites on one hand, and the Brothers, who quietly and most patiently endured all social injustices. The clothing and the mining industry of Zwickau produced a proletariat and thus, offered a particularly favorable breeding ground for eschatological-apoca-lyptical and mystical thoughts. Here arose also those creative personalities, who could activate a universal but anonymous possibility for the necessary unity as a unequivocally and revolutionary push and thrusting force. Among these personalities excelled the preacher Thomas Müntzer. He became one of the leading figures of what Luther called the religious enthusiast move-ment. Thomas was full of distrust not only against the Papacy, but also against the great reformatory slogan and catchphrase of the Lutherans – by faith *alone*. On the question of faith, Müntzer, the mystic, thought very soberly. Here the extreme spiritualist made demands like a strict moralist. Thomas sought for the psychological process for the act of faith. He showed it through the highest examples of the Bible: e.g. through Mary, the mother of Jesus. Through his counter – questions concerning the first knocking of the revelation, Thomas preserved completely and definitely his justified independence. He came to faith only through the internal overcoming of the objections against it. That happened through the direct witness of the Spirit, and through the inner word, which was almost virtually the opposite of the dead word of the external Bible. Luther ridiculed Müntzer and the so-called enthusiasts: They talk directly with God! What lead Müntzer to the decisive rejection and refusal of Luther's Wittenberg, the dangerous corner, was the fundamental difference between the just out of spirit and the *professional*, proper theologian. Unlike for Thomas of Aquinas, and like for Luther, faith was for Müntzer not merely a holding as true certain statements of faith, but rather the unconditional trust in the God of Abraham, Isaac and Jacob and the Father of Jesus the Christ.

Social-Revolutionary

Thomas Müntzer was entirely a social-revolutionary type of a man. Thomas's endeavor was completely directed toward the poor classes, the common man, whom he spoke to and appealed to innumerable times. Müntzer's speech went to the poor of Christendom. Thomas saw history from the perspective of its victims. According to Thomas, the laypeople must become prelates and pastors. They had to be empowered. Müntzer had lived in Wittenberg with Luther. However, Thomas escaped Wittenberg, because of its adder-like scribes. Thomas taught that Jesus gave to John no other justification of his teaching than that he pointed to the common people. Thomas criticized the scholars of his days, who liked to bring the witness of the Spirit to the universities. They wanted to judge the faith with their stolen scripture without having any faith whatsoever, neither with God, nor before men. According to Müntzer, everybody could see and perceive that the contemporary scholars were striving for honors, and awards, and material possessions. Therefore, so Thomas argued, the common man had to become learned and a scholar. In Thomas's view, the true *Evangelium* was only for arduous and laborious people, and for those who were excluded from education. The disinherited people were the chosen ones. They must separate themselves from the world and from the official and organized Church as the *small flock*. Yet, nobody could be a member of this small flock, who had not come to his faith in his own seriousness and independently. For Thomas, the *Evangelium* had not negated the *law*, but had carried it out and made it happen with the greatest seriousness.

Bible Exegesis

The *unprofessional* theologian Müntzer had gained a deep insight into the fundamental demands of the Bible exegesis, which Luther had lost to a large extent. Thomas started from the elementary fact of the complexity of the truth, and thus also from the plural possibilities of the interpretation of the word. For Thomas, all judgments had the highest opposite with themselves. Where they were not taken together, none of them could be completely understood, no matter how bright and clear they may be. Thomas was a true dialectician. In Thomas's view, the consequence of the lack of such dialectic was the fundamental soup of all evil separation. The dialectical approach was indeed a most correct and important principle of a truthful Bible exegesis, equally valid for the Roman Catholic Paradigm as for the Reformation-Protestant Constellation of Christianity. Unfortunately, Thomas was sometimes not dialectical enough: not only in terms of the balance or mediation between revelation and tradition, but also between faith and reason, etc. However, his theology of revolution was, nevertheless, a dialectical one.

Christian Humanism

For Thomas Müntzer, the internal reception of faith in the abyss of the soul and through its inner witness alone created the right faith. In contradiction to this principle, it was admittedly after all the Bible, which gave the external confirmation and acknowledgement to the *spirit*. Faith was bound to the Christianity of the crucified Christ in the fundamentally tolerant way of the great Erasmus of Rotterdam, the father of modern Christian humanism. Thomas agreed with Erasmus that the Christian faith was compatible with the faith of all chosen people, be they Jewish or an Islamic Turk, in spite of all separations, or races with a plurality of faith positions. In general, at this point Erasmus was the clearest parallel to Müntzer, the spiritual father of the so-called enthusiast movement. In the agreement between Müntzer and Erasmus lay admittedly also the strongest differentiations. Erasmus was primarily philosophically-humanistically orientated. He was a carrier of education. He was a champion and defender of rest, peace, quiet, calm and tranquility. Erasmus's moralism had a soft tendency toward a spiritualistic evaporation and fading away. To the contrary, Müntzer was through and through a religious and strongly ready-to-fight potentiality. Like Andreas von Karlstadt or Bodenstein, Thomas struggled against the education of the upper classes. Thomas knew himself as its adversary, since he spoke to the uneducated people, to the poor and miserable community of farmers. Müntzer's moralism was of a *Torah*-kind. The threats of the law and fear have their accent inside the life of the faith and in the external mode of life down to the willingness to use violence in the class struggle, if necessary. Müntzer was not at all opposed to the raging uprising and revolt of the farmer proletariat against their oppressive and exploitative feudal lords. The principle of simplification, which belonged to the fundamental forces of the transition from the Middle Ages to Modernity, expressed itself through Müntzer in the radical form of universal equality in terms of socialism and democracy. While our Dubrovnik Circle agreed with Müntzer's combination of faith, humanism, tolerance, the principle of equality, democracy and socialism, in the present transition period from Modernity to Post-Modernity with all its aggressiveness and death – friendliness, we had a problem with Müntzer's notion of the *wrath of Yahweh*, and his willingness to use violence. We were rather scholars and practitioners of peace. We were more on the side of Martin Luther King and the Berrigan Brothers in Baltimore, Maryland, than on the side of Malcolm X of Lansing, Michigan, or the Cardinal Brothers in Nicaragua. We took seriously the first, fourth and fifth commandment of the so-called *Sermon on the Mount*. We were thinking of a non-violent theology of revolution.

An Erasmian Bishop from Farmer's Stock

In Thomas Müntzer's century, there existed only one Catholic Bishop in Germany, who was from farmer's stock: Michael Helding, a Suffragan Bishop of Mainz and the last Catholic Bishop of Merseburg (Siebert 1965). All the other Bishops came from the nobility or from the bourgeoisie. Helding had been 19 years old, when Müntzer was executed in Mühlhausen. He became a follower of Erasmus of Rotterdam. He was a teacher in Mainz and was married and had a son before he was ordained in Mainz. In the 1530's, he preached in the Cathedral of Mainz on the basis of the New Testament and the Church Fathers, particularly Augustine. During this time, Helding participated in the ecumenical discourses between Erasmian Catholic and Protestant theologians, who tried to prevent the further schism of the Western Church. Helding also went to the Trent Council, where in the beginning he was the only German Bishop. He was critical of the Pope and he was sympathetic to the lay chalice and priest-marriage, which were permitted for a few years in the Roman Catholic Church, until the Jesuit Counter-Reformation canceled them again. Helding finally became Bishop of Merseburg and a member of the Empire Court of Charles V in Vienna: the same Emperor who's General and troops had butchered the farmers from whom Helding came. Helding was an Erasmian reformer, not a Müntzerian revolutionary. In the highest court of the land, Helding, the son of farmers, served well his Emperor and the feudal class, the murderers of his people.

German Service

Müntzer's simple consideration that in many places in the Roman Catholic Constellation the ceremonies of the Mass did not agree with each other, and that some nations or groups of nations celebrated it in their own language, motivated him as the first theologian to arrange vernacular, i.e., German services in Germany: in Allstett. For Thomas, the reason for this action was that it was given to the servant of God to do his office openly and not to hide it under a cunning and crafty cover from Christendom and from the whole world. Thomas referred to Paul, who let his letters be read in public before all the people. Also, so Thomas emphasized, Christ, our Savior, had ordered his friends to preach the *Evangelium* to all creatures. That was to be done plainly and bluntly, not tangled up, involved, and complicated, and, not in Latin nor in any other foreign tongue, but in the language that every believer could understand, i.e. in the vernacular. Thomas's principle to share everything with everybody had a great impact, particularly after the believers had suffered under a narrow clerical-ecclesiastical leadership for centuries in the Medieval Roman Catholic Paradigm, and also after the massive clerical exploitation of the laypeople in the midst of their social discontent. Only 400 years after Thomas Müntzer, the Second Vatican Council finally re-introduced the vernacular together with the lay chalice, but not with the priest marriage, into the Roman Catholic Church, from which Müntzer and Luther departed, while Erasmus remained a member.

Obligation of the Law of God

Pastor Müntzer concentrated his theses into a few thoughts, to which he came back again and again in his sermons and in his writings in an exciting, infuriating, and provoking language, and which he continually transformed forcibly and urgently, and vividly. He made a tremendous impression, particularly on the poor masses. Müntzer composed and wrote popular songs, which carried his excitement beyond the 16th century into the 19th and 20th and even 21st centuries. Always again, Thomas returned to the thought of the strict obligation of the law of God, which he searched for more in the Torah – the Halacha – than in the New Testament. As Luther since the first indulgence thesis in Wittenberg of 1517 had fought the false security and convenience and comfort of the way to salvation in the Papacy, so Müntzer found Luther's reformation on its part not at all serious enough. According to Thomas, Martin made salvation too easy for people. According to Thomas, Luther preached only the honey-sweet half Jesus. Thus, so Thomas argued, whoever did not want to have the bitter Jesus, would gorge his head off on the honey. For Müntzer, Luther was the Father Pussyfooter and the *Devil's sure Archchancellor*. To be sure, Thomas overlooked somewhat Luther's *theologia crucis* and likewise the seriousness of his Christian life style. Yet, Müntzer's fight of 1524 against Luther, the softly living flesh of Wittenberg, flowed easily into the more embracing social revolution of the farmer proletariat. There was no connection with the petite bourgeois revolutions in some cities, which were mainly anti-clerical. As late as 1521, Luther still rejected bravely the use of governmental means of force in the struggle against Müntzer and pleaded for his freedom to teach. According to Luther, the struggle against Müntzer was to find its limit in the spirit that he had preached: love, joy, peace, patience, benevolence, faithfulness, gentleness and meekness (Galatians 5:21). Unfortunately, at the end that did not happen because of the overwhelming fear in Luther and his friends of the violent tumult of the farmers and the so-called enthusiasts.

Social Revolution

Thomas Müntzer was not only the exponent of the enthusiastic splitting of the Biblical religion, but also the theologian who completed the social revolution, and who engaged in and embraced the tumultuous self-help of the farmer proletariat. Thomas preached iconoclasm and did not stop his protest before the rights of the princes and the nobility. For Müntzer, the princes were not the lords, but the servants of the sword. Therefore, the people had to be there, when one was judged according to the laws of God. For Müntzer, the lords and princes were the ground soup of usury, theft, and robbery. The lords and the princes took all creatures for their property in order to maltreat, drive too hard, sweat and strain fish, birds, plants, the poor farm worker and the poor craftsmen and artisan. With the prophet Jeremiah (1:10), Thomas preached the uprooting and dispersion against the kings, princes, clerics, and parsons. Müntzer predicted that the victory will be odd and peculiar toward the downfall of the strong, godless tyrants. Thomas expressed clearly the sounds and tones and the wishes that accompanied the march of the revolutionary farmers. Thomas would put himself at the disposal of the farmers and would go under with them and their just cause, still being a very young man. Thomas undersigned his documents symbolically and correctly as *Thomas Müntzer with the sword Gideonis* or *with the hammer*. At the time, the sickle was still missing. The intervention of the Zwickau Council against the increasing unrest turned Pastor Müntzer into a homeless migrant preacher. Finally, Müntzer found in Allstett a new place for intensive work. However, the Electoral Prince drove him out of the town. Thomas came to Mühlhausen, where he was able to transform the City Council completely according to his wishes into an Eternal Council. Here then Thomas experienced his horrible downfall in the farmer war.

Sola Scriptura

As political and social revolutionary and leader of the farmer revolution of 1523–1525, Thomas Müntzer, in spite of all emphasis on the *inner light, the inner voice,* and *the inner word,* nevertheless, stressed most radically the fundamental position of the new Reformation-Protestant Paradigm: *sola scriptura* – the external Bible. It had been neglected for so long in the Medieval Roman Catholic Paradigm in favor of tradition and authority. Now for Thomas as for Martin this external Bible was alone the source of faith: i.e. without the guarantee of a universal ecclesiastical teaching office. The radicalization of this fundamental position quickly exploded the Reformation-Protestant Paradigm. Müntzer was a philosophically-exegetically, highly educated man. He stressed the Sermon on the Mount as the basis of his revolution for the recognition of the rights and freedoms of the farmers. He claimed the office of a *prophet.* Müntzer's radicality revealed itself most intensely in the final religious-socialistic-democratic insurrection of the German farmers. Müntzer and Luther had been priests in the Medieval Roman Catholic Paradigm. Now, both were married and had families. Both initiated the new Reformation-Protestant Constellation. Also Luther's preaching on freedom had promoted powerfully the rebellion of the farmers. However, Thomas, not Martin, became a theologian of revolution and thus a martyr of freedom and truth. Thomas's wife and his two children got lost in the turmoil and aftermath of the lost farmer war and revolution. Luther survived Müntzer by 21 years, while he adjusted himself to the power of the princes, in order to rescue his religious movement.

Underground Movements

However, also the repressed enthusiastic religiosity of Müntzer lived on in underground movements of different forms, of which the Mennonite and

Amish Communities constitute two. It was decisive that with the repression of the farmer revolution and its enthusiastic religiosity that had motivated it, the socialistic and democratic ideas were defeated and overcome as well. They were subjected to the power of the princes for centuries, which then quickly accelerated into absolutism. The theology of revolution lost out against the theology of counter-revolution. Finally, when the democratic and socialistic ideas broke through into the open again in the form of the bourgeois revolutions of the 17th and 18th centuries, and in the socialist revolutions of the 19th and 20th centuries, they did so no longer in a religious form, as with Thomas Müntzer and his movement, but rather in a totally secular form, in which, nevertheless, his theology of revolution was concretely superseded.

C. Critical Theory of Religion

Thomas Müntzer's theology of revolution had not only been dialectical but also materialistic. Even the greatest idealist, the Lutheran Hegel, had in 1807 materialistically inverted the statement from the Sermon on the Mount – *"Set your hearts on his (God's) kingdom first, and on his righteousness, and all these other things (food, clothing) will be given you as well"* (Matthew 6:33) – into: *Set your hearts first on food and clothing and the kingdom of God will fall to you by itself.* Likewise, Hegel's greatest student, Marx, a Jew baptized as a Lutheran Christian, inverted Jewish and Christian Messianism into the historical materialistic notion of alternative Future 3 – the true realm of freedom beyond the foundation of the realm of the necessity of nature (Amos 3:1–8; Marx 1961:III:873–874; Benjamin 1977b:chapts. 10, 11 esp. 252; Horkheimer 1985c: chapts. 4, 5, 9, 10, 13–18, 20–23, 25–30, 32, 34–40, 42–43; 1988, chapts. 2–3, 5–7; 1972:chapt. 4; Adorno 1980:333–334; Marcuse 1962:6566; Raines 1970. 3–10; Bloch 1072; Habermas 2001:9–31; Küng 2004:19–27, 29–43; Siebert 2001:chapt. III; 2002: chapts. 2, 6; 1993; Mendieta 2002; 2005).

Class Struggle

In the perspective of the critical theory of religion, which is very much obligated to the spirit of Thomas Müntzer and the other Chiliasts, and which I have developed in the past 30 years out of the critical theory of society of the by now globalized Frankfurt School in discourse with our common friends and colleagues in Dubrovnik and Yalta and elsewhere, Marx's or

Bertolt Brecht's atheistic historical materialism can be rescued in terms of an inverse theology. According to the critical theorist Walter Benjamin, the class struggle, which was always before the eyes of a historian who was educated by Marx, was admittedly a struggle for the raw, material things, without which there are no refined and spiritual things. In this sense, Thomas Müntzer and his farmers were involved in a class struggle against the feudal lords. However, for Benjamin, these fine and spiritual things were present in the class struggle in a different way than the representation of a booty or a loot that falls to the victor. Rather, these fine and spiritual things are expressed in the class struggle as confidence, courage, humor, cunning, and daring, all of which have a critical historical past and dynamic. In this – admittedly mostly religious form – the fine and spiritual things were present already in Müntzer's and the farmers' class struggle for the raw and material things, e.g. for the hunting and fishing rights of the farmers. These fine and spiritual things continually put into question again and again every victory which has fallen to the ruling class: e.g. the counter-revolutionary victory of the feudal lords over the farmers in 1525, or the counter-revolutionary victory of the bourgeoisie over the farmers and workers in 1989. Like flowers that turn their heads toward the sun in the power of a heliotropism of a secret kind, that which has been – e.g. Müntzer's farmer revolution and all revolutions before and after him – strives to turn toward that sun that is in the process of rising at the horizon of history. The historical materialist and the critical theorist of society, the heirs of Thomas Müntzer and of all the Chiliasts, must be sensitive for and must understand and comprehend this most insignificant of all changes: the slow arrival of alternative Future 3 – a society in which people can be happy, and ultimately the Messianic realm of redemption. While the direction toward happiness and the direction toward redemption are certainly opposed to each other in world-history, the former does, nevertheless, support the silent realization of the latter.

Perfect Justice and Unconditional Love

In the perspective of the critical theory of religion, the productive kind of criticism of the status quo, which found expression in the farmer revolution against the feudal lords during the transition from the Middle Ages to Modernity as a belief in a Heavenly Judge and his Perfect Justice and Unconditional Love, today in the transition period between Modernity and Post-Modernity often takes the secular form of a struggle for mutual understanding and reciprocal recognition against the globalizing capitalistic establishment, and thus, for more rational and peaceful forms of societal life than the late bourgeoisie can possibly offer. Yet, just as reason after Immanuel Kant, even though it knew better, could not avoid falling into – what Karl Marx and Sigmund Freud had called – shattered but nevertheless recurring illusions, so too, with the transition from the religious longing of Müntzer and his followers to the conscious social praxis of the historical materialists, there continues to exist a so-called illusion that can be exposed but cannot be entirely banished. This so-called illusion is the image of Perfect Justice and Unconditional Love. Mankind may lose religion in the sense in which Thomas Müntzer and the Chiliasts and the whole Left of the Reformation-Protestant Paradigm had still understood it, as it moves through the present transition from Modernity toward Post Modernity, be it alternative Future 1, 2 or 3. However, in any case, the loss of religion in the understanding of Müntzer has left and shall leave its mark behind. Part of the longings, drives, and desires that Müntzer's and his friend's belief in the Heavenly Judge and his Perfect Justice and Unconditional Love preserved and kept alive have in the meantime been detached from the often inhibiting, all to conservative religious form, and have become – in terms of Kant, Schelling, Hegel, Marx, Engels, Freud, Bloch, Horkheimer, Benjamin, Adorno, Marcuse and Fromm, etc. – *productive forces* in social practice. In the process of the modern and post-modern enlightenment even the immoderation characteristic of so-called shattered religious illusions has often already acquired a positive form, and thus has been truly transformed. After those great thinkers, in a really free mind the concept of the Infinity or the totally Other – what was once called in the great world religions and systems of metaphysics Heaven, Eternity or Beauty – has been preserved in an awareness of the terrible finality of human life and of the unalterable abandonment and aloneness of human beings. Up to the present and into the future this concept of qualitative Infinity can keep antagonistic civil society from indulging in a thoughtless optimism, an infla-tion of its own scientific knowledge and technology into a new religion. Every new theodicy experience stimulates anew – in the sense of a combination of Jewish and Christian negative theology and Kantian agnosticism – the long-ing for the imageless and nameless wholly Other than the horror and terror of nature and history, and for Perfect Justice and Unconditional Love.

Libertarian Radicalism

In the view of the critical theory of religion, a libertarian radicalism seems to link Thomas Müntzer and the other Chiliasts with Marx and his followers, and vice versa. This Müntzerian radicalism does not belong into the liberal, not to speak of the neo-conservative or neo-liberal tradition, which still contains much of the repressive Puritanism, with which it was once connected. Müntzer's radicalism rather belongs to the great *heretic* movements, which since the 12th and 13th centuries had become an essential element in Western Civilization: libertarian trends in Christianity, libertarian humanism, Brothers of the Free Spirit, Edomites, – and Thomas Müntzer, and their followers. While historical materialism remains irreconcilable with Christian dogma and its institutions, it finds an ally in those tendencies and groups and individuals – like Thomas Müntzer before – committed uncompromisingly against inhuman, exploitative, humiliating power. From the First World War on, these radical religious tendencies, which once appeared in Thomas Müntzer and others have come to life again in the priests and ministers and laymen who joined the struggle against fascism in all its forms, e.g. Dietrich Bonhoeffer, and those who have made common cause with the liberation movements of the Third and Fourth World, especially in Latin and Central America: e.g. the liberation theologians and the base Christian communities of El Salvador, Guatemala, Nicaragua and Chile. They are part of the global anti-authoritarian movement against the now globalizing self-perpetuating capitalist power structure, which is less and less interested in human progress. While the neo-conservatives try to continue the economic modernization, they cancel the cultural modernization: e.g. the bourgeois, Marxian and Freudian enlightenment movements. However, that anti-authoritarian movement brings to life once more the long forgotten or reduced *heretic*, socialistic and material-democratic tendencies, which were once at work in Müntzer's life, work, and martyrdom. Even the three great youth movements should be taken very seriously in the tradition of Thomas Müntzer. The student movements have expressed the fact, that the young people have lost patience with the traditional forms of opposition, which go on and on without really changing essentials in the modern paradigm: not to speak of the political culture of corruption in Washington D.C. and elsewhere. As the traditional forms of opposition go on and on, they still sustain the ghettoes in the big cities and in the countryside, and thus even help to extend poverty and misery. They still go on, while hundreds are daily tortured, burned, and killed in immoral, unjust and illegal wars. There is, indeed, a Müntzerian force in this kind of youthful opposition, with which religion and the Churches should properly come to grips, because there is a strong moral element in it that has for too long been neglected or overlooked. Already with Thomas Müntzer's theology of revolution, this moral element had started to become a social and a political force.

Truth Value

Libertarian radicalism seems to link Müntzer and his friends also with Sigmund Freud and his followers, and vice versa. If the development of religion before and after Müntzer contains the basic ambivalence, i.e. the image of domination and the image of liberation, then Freud's (1961) thesis in his book *Future of an Illusion* needs to be reevaluated. Müntzer, who stressed the image of liberation in religion and in economic, social and political life, can still help with this reevaluation. In his book, Freud stressed the role of religion in the historical deflection of energy from the real improvement of the human condition to an imaginary world of eternal salvation and bliss. Müntzer rejected such deflection and demanded justice here and now for the farmers. Freud thought that the disappearance of this so-called religious illusion of eternal salvation would greatly accelerate the material and intellectual progress of human kind. Freud praised science and scientific reason as the great liberating antagonists of religion. No other writing besides the *Future of an Illusion* shows Freud closer to the great tradition of the Enlightenment. However, no other book shows him more clearly succumbing to what the critical theorists of society have called the dialectic of enlightenment. In the present transition period between the Modern and the Post-Modern Macro-Paradigm, the progressive ideas of bourgeois, Marxian and Freudian enlighteners can be recaptured only when they are critically reformulated. With the transition to the Post-Modern Paradigm, which set in with the end of World War I, the function of science on one hand, and religion on the other, and their interrelation has changed. Within the total mobilization of man and nature that marks the globalization of antagonistic civil society in the present transition-period, science has become one of the most destructive instruments: destructive of that freedom from fear and mastering of fate that it once promised. As this promise has evaporated into an abstract utopia, science has become almost identical with denouncing the notion of an earthly Paradise and happiness, as Thomas Müntzer and his revolutionary farmers pronounced it in the 16th century. The scientific attitude has long since ceased to be the militant antagonist of religion. Since Thomas Müntzer and the victory of the feudal counter-revolution, religion also has to a large extent effectively discarded its explosive elements, which his revolutionary theology still contained, and has often accustomed man to entertain a good conscience in the face of meaninglessness, suffering and guilt. In the household of culture in the present transition period, the functions of science and religion have become complementary. Through their present usage in late capitalist society, both religion and science deny the hopes that they both once aroused, and instead in there positivistic form teach people to appreciate the facts and data in a world of alienation. They have become allies not in revolution, but in counter-revolution. They indulge in positivism as the metaphysics of what is the case. Nothing could be more distant from Müntzer's theological thinking than such secular and religious positivism, which today pervades all our universities and sometimes even our churches. In this sense, religion is no longer an "illusion" in the Marxian or the Freudian sense, and its academic promotion in Departments of Comparative Religion or even Departments of Theology falls often in line with the dominant positivistic trend. However, where religion – as once did Thomas Müntzer's theology of revolution – still preserves the uncompromised aspirations for justice, peace and happiness, its so called illusions still have a higher truth value than a positive science that works for their elimination. The repressed and transfigured content of critical religion, e.g. of Müntzer's theology of revolution, cannot possibly be liberated by surrendering it to the scientistic, positivistic or naturalism attitude.

The Not-Yet

At the end of his wonderful book on Thomas Müntzer, Ernst Bloch (1972) discovered in the last chapter of the *"Evangelium Johannis"* the pathos of the "not yet." The Greeks had two notions of nothingness: the creative *mae on* – the "not yet" – and the *ouk on*, the malignant nothingness, from which nothing comes. Bloch was always concerned with the *mae on*: creative destruction. In the last chapter of his book, Bloch also remembered once more the "honest thought of youth" of the great German idealist Friedrich W. J. Schelling, a friend of Hegel, to not to forget the producer over the produced history. Even in his later philosophy, Schelling did not come to rest at the product of history, at that which had come about so far. Not only the German enlightener Gotthold E. Lessing (2004), the author of *Nathan the Wise* and the three rings of Judaism, Christianity and Islam and their truth, touched upon the "Brothers of the Free Spirit," but also the contemplative "theogony" of Schelling could not pass them by: out of the force of circumstances – the final depth! In so far as there was with Schelling a "genealogy of time," it could not let stand the script, the word, even the world. Here Thomas Müntzer appears again and again. Müntzer was also still announced in the last things of Schelling's speculations. Admittedly, Müntzer did not relax or ease the immediate cares and worries of everyday life. As a matter of fact, Müntzer did that so little that a consideration of the Ultimum – the totally Other – stimulated and irritated the deficiency of what is the case in the world as it grounds it. The color "Red" in the *"Evangelium Johannis"* with its realm of freedom, was with Thomas Müntzer the consequential compulsion of the "Red" everywhere, and was also materialistically put on its feet, particularly in relation to the status quo, be it of the feudal or the capitalist social order, or disorder. Müntzer had the inherited revolutionary religious remembrance, the secret, latent element in socialism, which Marx overlooked and had to overlook if he finally wanted to force need, want, trouble, necessity, the social problems and contingencies of proletarian life in the liberal – capitalist world. Yet, that revolutionary religious dimension of socialism will have to be remembered in the future, after the present neo-liberal counter-revolution has run its course. Still unheard of, the underground history and tradition of revolution waits to surface. Its manifestation has already begun in the upright walk of many wonderful Christian believers before and after Thomas Müntzer and his brave farmers, a cloud of witnesses: the Valley-Brothers, the Cathari, the Waldenses, the Albigenses, the Abbot Joachim of Calabrese, the Brothers of the Good Will, the Brothers of the Common Life, the Brothers of the Full Spirit, the Brothers of the Free Sprit, Master Eckhart, the Hussites, Sebastian Franck, the Illuminates, the humanistic mystics Jean J. Rousseau and Immanuel Kant, Weitling, Franz von Baader, and Leo Tolstoy. They all may unite some day. The conscience of this enormous revolutionary tradition may someday knock and pound through against fear, antagonistic civil society, authoritarian state, unbelief, faithlessness, and universal despair, and everything else that belongs to the globalized bourgeois ruling class and establishment, in which the human being does not occur and does not come foreward.

The Revolutionary Spark

In this great history and tradition, in which Thomas Müntzer has been a leading figure, is burning the revolutionary spark. It does not stay anywhere. It conforms to the most definite demand of the Torah and the New Testament: We have no remaining place, but we are searching for the future one. With Thomas Müntzer, a new Messianic disposition, view, and conviction could arise once more and spread, which finally would be familiar with traveling and pilgrimage, and with the incorruptible and insatiable longing for home – for the totally Other. It is not the longing for blood and soil; for works, which have become rigid; for false cathedrals – which according to Bernhard of Clairveaux should never have been built; for burned out Transcendence, which does not pour, or gush forth, or swell with anything any longer. The longing could rather be directed toward the clearing and the glade of the lived moment itself; for the satisfaction of our amazement, our presentiment, our continual deepest dream of happiness, truth, and disenchantment of ourselves: our dream of secret Divinity and Glory.

During the funeral of Loretta King in February 2006, President Carter, a Baptist, confessed his hope that she and her husband Martin Luther King had met in Glory. The world never would be so dark if there would not be in store and imminent and approaching most immediately, the absolute storm and central light. However, our *over there, on the other side, beyond* has called itself already and heard itself. Only behind a thin crackling, rustling wall is hidden the innermost name: *Princess Sabbath*. She is no less superior to all gods, who left us on earth, than ever the weeping, furiously breaking-in miracle struck the *palliatives*. Once more could shine the spirit of unblocked and undisguised concrete – what Müntzer's contemporary, the Erasmian Thomas More (2002), had called the first time – "utopia," (ouk topos – no place yet), high above the ruins of World War I and II, and the Cold War, and Vietnam, and Afghanistan, and Iraq, and the so-called war on terror, and the broken cultural spheres of this globalizing late capitalist world. This utopia is certain of its pole only in the innermost Ophir, Atlantis, and

Orplid: in the house of absolute, solidary we-appearance. In this way, Bloch, Benjamin and Adorno and their disciples unite themselves in the spirit of Thomas Müntzer, for the secular reconstructed historical materialism and the Jewish and Christian and Islamic dream of the Unconditional and the totally Other in the same walk, and march, and campaign plan. They unite themselves as energy of the journey and as the end of all environments, in which humanity has been as a non-recognized, oppressed, contemptible, exploited, humiliated, crucified, and lost and missing being. They unite themselves as reconstruction and alteration of the star earth. They unite themselves as vocation, and creation, and as enforcement of the Messianic realm. Thomas Müntzer remains, with all Chiliasts, a prophetic voice on this stormy pilgrimage. In Thomas's spirit not only new life should start in the old world, but open has become every exuberance and open lies the world and eternity: the new world of warmth and of breakthrough, of the light, which roars broadly out of the innermost being of man. In Thomas's spirit, the Messianic time and light must become real now. Toward this Messianic time has been directed the radiation of man's never renouncing and never disappointed spirit. We all have certainly had enough world-history. We have had too much form, polis, and work. We have been hoodwinked enough. There has been enough blocking, closing off, and barricading through culture and "clashes of civilizations." In the spirit of Thomas, another irresistible life stirs and is moving. The all too narrow background of the stage of history, the stage of the polis, the stage of culture escapes and disappears. In Thomas's spirit, soul, depth, and extended dream – heaven, with stars from the bottom to the top – shines into the world. The true firmaments develop themselves. The "Road of Counsel" stretches and moves irresistibly up to that secret Messianic Symbol, toward which has moved the dark, searching, and troubled earth since the beginning of times.

The Real Genesis

Our Dubrovnik Circle has learned gratefully from Thomas Müntzer and Ernst Bloch and the other critical theorists of society that without the thought of an unthinkable infinite happiness, there is not even the consciousness of the earthly finite happiness, which in view of the impossibility of abolishing its impermanence and transitoriness can never be without sorrow. With the help of the critical theorists, we have learned from Thomas Müntzer and all the other Chiliasts, the perspective that in the face of the universal despair all things have to be considered as they represent themselves from the standpoint of Messianic redemption. Knowledge has no light except that, which shines from the Messianic redemption into the all too dark world. Every other knowledge exhausts itself in reconstruction of facts and data and their interconnections, and remains a piece of statistical technique. With the help of the critical theorists, we have learned from Thomas Müntzer and all the other Chiliasts, that also today – i.e. in 2007 – humanity does still live everywhere in his pre-history. That is particularly true after the victorious neo-conservative and neo-liberal counterrevolution of 1989, in which the farmers and workers of the world were once more defeated. According to Bloch, informed by Müntzer, everything was still standing before the creation of the world, as it ought to be, and as the right one. The real genesis was not in the beginning, but at the end. The real genesis would begin, when human society and existence would become radical: i.e. if they would comprehend themselves at their very root. However, the "radix" or the root of history is the speaking and remembering, and working, and loving human being, who struggles for the always broader circles of the recognition of his dignity, and his freedoms, and his rights and duties: who continually transforms and transcends what is given to him in this world. If humanity would comprehend itself and ground its being without externalization and alienation in a real, not only formal, but also material democracy, then something would arise in the world, which is calling all people into their childhood, where no one has ever been: home! May the spirit of Thomas Müntzer, the theologian of revolution, continue to guide and help us on our way home: and to fulfill our longing for light, friendship, and love and for alternative Future 3 – a reconciled society, and ultimately for the imageless and nameless totally Other as the most radical negation of that, which on earth is called injustice, human abandonment, loneliness, and alienation, shortly, our longing for the Truth.

About the Authors

REIMON BACHIKA is professor of the sociology of religion at Bukkyo University, Kyoto. He was born in Belgium in 1936, did religious studies in Louvain, Belgium (1958–62), and completed graduate studies in sociology at the University of Osaka, Japan (1966–75). He is co-author of *An Introduction into the Sociology of Religion*, (in Japanese, with M. Tsushima, 1996), editor of *Traditional Culture and Religion in a New Era* (Transaction 2002), contributed to several other books, and wrote numerous articles both in Japanese and English on the sociology of religion and related problems of culture and values.

ALEXANDRA BASA is from the University of Novi Sad, Faculty of Philosophy in the Department of Sociology. She is a member of ISORECEA (International Study of Religion in Eastern and Central Europe Association) and IARS (Independent Academic Research Studies). She has participated in international conferences regarding the scientific research of religion, and has articles published in foreign and local scientific publication. Her main interests are the sociology of religion as well as human rights and peaceful conflict solution.

JAN FENNEMA is a physicist and philosopher, who earned his degrees from the Free University in Amsterdam. He has a long history of teaching in grammar schools, professional schools and as a professor of science and philosophy at the University of Twente, Enschede, Netherlands. For thirty years, he was also a scientist/philosopher at the Foundation for Fundamental Research on Matter (in Dutch: "Stichting voor Fundamenteel Onderzoek der Materie") and the Netherlands Organization for Scientific Research (in Dutch: "Nederlandse Organisatie voor Wetenschappelijk Onderzoek"). He retired from these positions in 1994. However, he continues his international travels and participates in international seminars and courses where he continues to struggle with the antagonism between the religious and the secular, between faith and knowledge, between the natural sciences and theology and work for their reconciliation. It was this interest to reconcile the religious and the secular that led him to the international course on the Future of Religion, in which he has been a long time participant. He also has a number of publications in academic journals on the topics of science and religion and the future of humanity.

ANJA FINGER received an MA degree in Sociology and Catholic Theology from the Johann Wolfgang Goethe University at Frankfurt/Main. Her chapter on Robert Owen and religion summarises some main points of the thesis submitted for this degree course. Anja also studied the Critical Theory of Religion with Professor Rudolf Siebert at Western Michigan University and is currently working on a sociological PhD thesis critiquing religious and secular sleep disciplines. This project has included a stay at the University of Warwick and is based at the Max Weber Centre for Advanced Cultural and Social Studies at the University of Erfurt.

HELMUT FRITZSCHE was born in Torgau in Saxonia, Germany in 1929. He studied theology at the Humboldt-University in Berlin, where he received his doctorate and habilitation. He served as a pastor in the Lutheran Church for ten years and taught religious pedagogy at the University of Jena. From 1969 to 1991, he was professor of systematic theology at the University of Rostock. His main fields of interests are philosophy of religion and issues of dialogue. In 1988, he was awarded an honorary doctorate from the Reformed Academy in Debrecen/Hungary.

DENIS R. JANZ is Provost Distinguished Professor of the History of Christianity in the Religious Studies Department of Loyola University, New Orleans. He has been a regular participant in the Dubrovnik "Future of Religion" circle for some 18 years. Author or editor of five books, his current publication project is the 7 volume *People's History of Christianity*, forthcoming from Fortress Press.

HANS-HERBERT KÖGLER is an Associate Professor and Graduate Studies Coordinator, Department of Philosophy, University of North Florida, Jacksonville. He has held guest professorships at Charles University, Prague, and University of Klagenfurt, Austria. His books are: *The Power of Dialogue: Critical Hermeneutics after Gadamer and Foucault*, Cambridge, Mass.: MIT Press 1996/1999; *Michel Foucault*, Stuttgart: Metzler Verlag 1994/2004; *Empathy and Agency: The Problem of Understanding in the Human Sciences*, co-edited with Karsten Stueber, Boulder, Colorado: Westview Press 2000. He has numerous articles published on social and political theory, philosophy of the social sciences, hermeneutics, and philosophy of language.

WERNER KRIEGLSTEIN was a student with Theodore W Adorno and Max Horkheimer at the Frankfurt School and holds a doctorate from the University of Chicago. He has taught at the University of Helsinki, Finland, and Western Michigan University, Kalamazoo. He currently teaches philosophy at the College of DuPage. Krieglstein is a course director at the Interuniversity Center in Dubrovnik, Croatia, and board member of the International Society for Universal Dialogue. He is author of *The Dice-Playing God* (UPA, 1992) and *Compassion, A New Philosophy of the Other*, (Rodopi, 2002) and *Compassionate Thinking, An Introduction to Philosophy*, (Kendall/Hunt, 2006) Krieglstein's Webpage is www.perspectivism.com.

GOTTFRIED KÜENZLEN was born in 1945 and holds the degrees of Dr.rer.soc. and Dr.phil. habil. He is a University Professor and chair of Protestant theology and social ethics (University of the Federal Army, Munich). His main fields of interest in the areas of Protestant theology, sociology and philosophy are: The secular and religious culture in the Modernity, Max Weber's sociology of religion. He has numerous publications, including: *Die Religionssoziologie Max Webers* (Berlin 1980); *Der Neue Mensch. Zur säkularen Religionsgeschichte der Moderne* (München 1995; Neuauflage Frankfurt 1997); *Die Wiederkehr der Religion* (München 2003).

MISLAV KUKOČ, Ph. D., was born in Split, Croatia, 1952, and is a senior research associate at the Institute of Social Sciences "Ivo Pilar" – Center Split. He currently teaches *Social Philosophy, Philosophy of Techics*, and *History of Social Theories* at the University of Zagreb and University of Split. He is president of the *Croatian Philosophical Society* and co-director of the international course: *Future of Religion* at the Interuniversity Centre, Dubrovnik, Croatia. He conducted sub-regional UNESCO research program "Post-communism and Multiculturalism"; held lectures at the Loyola University, New Orleans, Universität der Bundeswehr, München, Sapporo University, Japan; and was a Visiting scholar at the Woodrow Wilson Center, Washington DC. He is the author of *Fate of Alienation; Enigma of Post-communism; Critique of Eschatological Reason* (in Croatian). He also is a co-author of *Inter-disciplinary Dictionary: Education for Human Rights and Democracy* (in Croatian); and co-editor of *Ukraine & Croatia: Problems of Post-communist Societies*.

AURELIA MARGARETIC received her academic education at the school of the Ursulines in Bielefeld and at the Free University of Berlin, Germany. She studied German literature with Frau Professor Dr. Bennholdt-Thomsen and Protestant Theology with Professor Helmut Gollwitzer and Professor W. F. Marquardt. Particularly from Professor Gollwitzer, she learned about a humanistic and ecumenical Christianity. After completing her Master's thesis on Karl Philipp Moritz, who where a friend of J. W. v. Goethe, she moved to the island of Sipan, nearby Dubrovnik where she met her late husband and raised her three children. During the war, her family was evacuated from the island and came later to Aurelia's parents who lived in Gütersloh, Germany. Since 2001, Aurelia has worked as a teacher for inter-religious dialogue in the Europaschute in Dortmund. Before and after the Yugoslav Civil War, Aurelia continued to participate in the international course on the Future of Religion in Dubrovnik, where she delivered most interesting and exciting lectures about themes from contemporary history, philosophy and theology. She also contributed much to our friendly social life in Dubrovnik and internationally.

MICHAEL R. OTT is an Assistant Professor of Sociology at Grand Valley State University, Allendale, Michigan. He received his Master of Divinity degree from Princeton Theological Seminary in 1975 and his Ph.D. in Sociology from Western Michigan University in 1998, where he studied with Dr. Rudolf J. Siebert. Dr. Ott is also an ordained minister of the United Church of Christ, having served the church as a full-time pastor for 25 years prior to his becoming a professor. As a minister, he developed in both theory and praxis the connection between the Frankfurt School's critical theory of society and religion and a critical, political theology of social critique and liberation toward a more reconciled future society. His book, *Max Horkheimer's Critical Theory of Religion: The Meaning of Religion in the Struggle for Human Emancipation* gives expression to this dialectical development. As a professor, he continues to research, teach and write on the liberational negative or inverse theology of the critical theory of society and religion as a critique of neo-liberal/neo-conservative globalization. His writings have been published in the United States, France, and the Ukraine. Dr. Ott is a Co-Director of the international courses "The Future of Religion" held annually at the Inter-University Centre in Dubrovnik, Croatia and of "Religion and Civil Society" held annually in Yalta, Ukraine.

DUNJA POTOČNIK was born and educated in Croatia. She obtained her degree in Sociology in 1999. In 2000 she obtained a diploma of Peace Studies in Zagreb. Currently she is a research assistant at the Institute for Social Research in Zagreb and a PhD candidate in Sociology at the Faculty of Philosophy in Zagreb. Her first professional experiences were teaching at junior high school and a counseling position at the Croatian Employment Service. Her research activities have been focused on the youth issues, particularly on education, employment, new technologies and political issues (i.e. European integration). Dunja has written seven scientific papers and seven expert reports/reviews. Her research interests also include scientific policy, professional aspirations and intergenerational mobility. She is one of the founders and the first president of the Young Scientists Network in Croatia. Dunja is EURODOC (the European Council of Doctoral Candidates and Junior Researchers) Secretary for 2006/2007.

A. JAMES REIMER is Professor of Systematic Theology at Conrad Grebel College in the University of Waterloo, and the founding director of the Toronto Mennonite Theological Centre in the Toronto School of Theology. He is the author of many articles and books among them *The Emanuel Hirsch and Paul Tillich Debate: A Study in the Political Ramification of Theology* [Edwin Mellen Press, 1989] and *The Influence of the Frankfurt School on Contemporary Theology: Critical Theory and the Future of Religion. Dubrovnik Papers in Honour of Rudolf J. Siebert* [Edwin Mellen Press, 1992]. He is currently working on a history of Christian attitudes to war.

KJARTAN SELNES was born in 1943 in Sweden. He earned his Ph.D. in Sociology at the University of Oslo, Norway, where he concentrated his studies on social anthropology, philosophy, psychology and old Norse/Icelandic philology. He has been teaching basic sociological theories and methods for several years at different universities and colleges. He has been working as a practical sociologist for some years with organizational problems and social services. Main professional interests: Philosophy and sociology of knowledge, science and religion. He has for the last fifteen years been employed as an advisor of philosophy and social science in the Norwegian Humanist Association. He is presently mostly involved in humanitarian and developmental projects in South-East Asia through the Norwegian Humanist Association.

RUDOLF J. SIEBERT was born in Frankfurt am Main, Germany, in 1927. He studied history, philology, philosophy, sociology, psychology, social work and theology at the Universities of Frankfurt am Main, Mainz and Münster, and at the Catholic University of America, Washington D.C. He is Professor of Religion and Society, Director of the Center for Humanistic Future Studies at Western Michigan University, Kalamazoo, Michigan, and, since 1975, Director of the international course on the "Future of Religion" in the Inter University Center, Dubrovnik, Croatia, and he is director of the international course on "Religion and Civil Society" in Yalta, Crimea, Ukraine. Siebert has taught and lectured at many universities in Western and Eastern Europe, the United States and Canada. His major works are: *From Critical Theory of Society to Theology of Communicative Praxis; Hegel's Philosophy of History: Theological, Humanistic and Scientific Elements; Horkheimer's Critical Sociology of Religion: The Relative and the Transcendent; Hegel's Concept of Marriage and Family: The Principle of Free Subjectivity; The Critical Theory of Religion: Frankfurt School; Recht, Macht und Liebe: Georg W. Rudolphi's Prophetische Politische Theologie; From Critical Theory to Critical Political Theology: Personal Autonomy and Universal Solidarity; Manifesto of the Critical Theory of Society and Religion: The Wholly Other, Liberation, and the Rescue of the Hopeless.* Siebert and his late wife Margaret had 8 children.

HANS K. WEITENSTEINER was born 1936 in Frankfurt a.M. He studied germanistik history, philosophy, politics, and pedagogy in Frankfurt a.M. and Freiburg i. Brsg. He earned his doctorate in 1976 with a work on the Frankfurt social politician Karl Flesch at the Johnan Wolfgang Goethe University. For more than 30 years, he was a master of grammar-schools in the Hessen region. He is the author of *Warum denn wir, immer wir...? War diese Stadt Frankfurt schuldiger als London? Katholisches Gemeindeleben im Dritten Reich und waehrend der ersten Nachkriegsjahre 1932–1950. Dokumente und Darstellung* [Haag & Herchen Verlag, 2002].

BRIAN C. WILSON is Professor and Chair of Comparative Religion at Western Michigan University, Kalamazoo, Michigan. He earned a B.S. in Medical Microbiology from Stanford University (1982), and, after four years in the Peace Corps (Honduras, Dominican Republic), went on to earn an M.A. in Hispanic Studies from the Monterey Institute of International Studies (1990) and an M.A./Ph.D. in Religious Studies from the University of California, Santa Barbara (1991/1996). Dr. Wilson joined the faculty of Comparative Religion at WMU in 1996 and became its chair in 2001. His areas of interest include religion in America, with an emphasis on religion in the Midwest, and theory and method in the academic study of religion. Among Dr. Wilson's publications are *Christianity* (Prentice Hall and Routledge, 1999) and, as co-editor, *Reappraising Durkheim For the Study and Teaching of Religion Today* (Brill, 2001) and *Religion as a Human Capacity* (Brill, 2004). Dr. Wilson is also past president of the Midwest Regional American Academy of Religion.

References

Adorno, Theodor. W. 1950. *The Authoritarian Personality*. New York, NY: W & W Norton & Company, Inc.

———. 1973. *Negative Dialectics*. New York: The Seabury Press.

———. 1974. *Minima Moralia*. New York: Schocken Books.

———. 1980. *Minima Moralia. Reflexionen aus dem beschädigten Leben*. Frankfurt a.M.: Suhrkamp Verlag.

———. 1981. "Erziehung nach Auschwitz' (1966) in *Erziehung zur Mündigkeit*. (Suhrkamp Taschenbuch Bd. 11), Frankfurt a.M.: Suhrkamp Verlag. [English translation: 2003. "Education after Auschwitz" in *Can One Life after Auschwitz? A Philosophical Reader*, edited by Rolf Tiedemann. Stanford, California: Stanford University Press].

———. 1997. *Gesammelte Schriften*. Frankfurt a.M.: Suhrkamp Verlag.

Adorno, Theodor W. and Benjamin, Walter. 1999. *The Complete Correspondence: 1928–1940*. Cambridge, MA: Harvard University Press.

Albanese, Catherine L. 1990. *Nature Religion in America: From the Algonkian Indians to the New Age*. Chicago: The University of Chicago Press.

Alberts, L. and Chikane, F. [eds.] 1991. *The Road to Rustenburg: The Church looking forward to a new South Africa*. Cape Town: Struik Christian Books.

Aleotti, L. 1975. "In fondo, l'uomo è un buon uomo. Colloquio con Erich Fromm" in *L'espresso*. Roma 21 (Feb. 2, 1975).

Analytical Bulletin. 2003. Vol. V(2), The Croatian Employment Service, Zagreb.

Anonymous, 1989. *Maravilla Americana: Variantes de la Iconografía Guadalupana, Siglos XVII y XIX* (Guadalajara, México: Patrimonio Cultural del Occidente, A.C., 1989).

Arendt, Hannah. 1958. *The Human Condition*. Chicago: University of Chicago Press.

Ash, Timothy Garton. July 17, 1997. "True Confessions" in *New York Review of Books*, 44.

———. February 19, 1998. "The Truth About Dictatorship," in *New York Review of Books*, 45.

Ashby, W. Ross. 1966. *Introduction to Cybernetics*. J. Wiley Publisher.

Audi, Robert. 2000. *Religious Commitment and Secular Reason*. Cambridge MA: Harvard University Press.

Augustine, St. 1987. *Ispovijesti* [Confessions], Kršćanska sadašnjost. Zagreb.

Bachika, Reimon. 1999. "Differentiation of Culture and Religion" in *Bukkyo daigaku Shakaigakubu ronshu*, 32: 47–64. Kyoto: Bukkyo University.

Bachofen, Johann, J. 1967. *Myth, Religion, and Mother Right: Selected Writings of J. J. Bachofen* (Bollingen series). Princeton, NJ: Princeton University Press.

Bačić, Lovorka; Ofak, Lana; Parić, Andrijana; Perasović, Benjamin; Potočnik, Dunja; Puljić, Dražen; Šelo Šabić, Senada; Tomašević, Tomislav. 2004. *Human Development Report Croatia*. The United Nations Development Program. Zagreb.

Bainton, Roland. 1979. *Christian Attitudes toward War and Peace*. Nashville, TN: Abingdon Press.

Baldwin, N. 2001. *Henry Ford and the Jews: The Mass Production of Hate*, New York: Public Affairs.

Baranović, B. 1999. "What Youth Think about Education" in *Youth in Transition in Croatia*, edited by Ilišin, V.; Radin, F. Zagreb: Institute for Social Research and State Institute for the Protection of Family, Maternity and Youth.

Baum, Gregory. 1997. "The Role of the Churches in the Polish-German Reconciliation," in *The Reconciliation of Peoples: Challenge to the Churches*, edited by G. Baum and H. Wells. Maryknoll: Orbis Press.

Bauman, Zygmunt. 1997. "Postmodern Religion?" in *Postmodernity and its Discontents*. Cambridge: Polity.

Benjamin, Walter. 1969. *Illuminations*, edited by Hannah Arendt. New York: Schocken Books.

———. 1977a. *The Origin of German Tragic Drama*, trans. by John Osborn. London, New York: Verso.

———. 1977b. *Illuminationen, Ausgewählte Schriften*. Frankfurt a.M.: Suhrkamp Verlag.

———. 1979. *Reflections: Essays, Aphorisms, Autobiographical Writings*, edited by Peter Demetz. New York and London: Harcourt Brace Jovanovich.

———. 1991. *Gesammelte Schriften*. Frankfurt a.M.: Suhrkamp Verlag, Vol. I–VII.

———. 1996. *Walter Benjamin: Selected Writings, Volume 1, 1913–1926*. Cambridge, MA: The Belknap Press of Harvard University Press.

———. 1999. *Arcades Project*, trans. by Howard Eiland and Kevin McLaughlin, edited by Rolf Tiedemann. Cambridge, Massachusetts and London, England: The Belknap Press of Harvard University Press.

Berger, Peter L. 1970. *A Rumor of Angels: Modern Society and the Rediscovery of the Supernatural*. Penguin Books.

Berliner Morganpost, November 6, 1997.

Bertalanffy, Ludwig. 1969. *General System Theory*. G. Brazille Publisher.

Blagojevic, Milos and Petkovic, Sreten. 1989. "Serbia during the period of Nemanjic dynasty, 1168–1371." Illustrated newspapers, *Vajat* edition and IRO *Belgrade*.

Blet, Pierre, SJ. 2000. *Papst Pius XII. und der zweite Weltkrieg – aus den Akten des Vatikans*, Paderborn.

Blic News, 06.02.2002.

Bloch, Ernst. 1967. *Das Prinzip Hoffnung*. Frankfurt a.M.: Suhrkamp Verlag.

———. 1970a. *Man on His Own*. New York: Herder and Herder.

———. 1970b. *A Philosophy of the Future*. New York: Herder and Herder.

———. 1971. *On Karl Marx*. New York: Herder and Herder.

———. 1972. *Thomas Müntzer*, Frankfurt a.M.: Suhrkamp Verlag.

———. 1989. *Atheismus im Christentum. Zur Religion des Exodus und des Reichs*, 2nd ed., Frankfurt a.M.: Suhrkamp.

———. 2000. *The Spirit of Utopia*, trans. by Anthony A. Nassar. Stanford, California: Stanford University Press.

Bloch, K. & Reif, A. [eds.] 1978. *Denken heisst Überschreiten. In Memoriam Ernst Bloch 1885–1977.* Köln, Frankfurt a.M.: Europäische Verlagsanstalt.

Bonfiglio, O. 2005. *Heroes of a Different Stripe. How one Town Responded to the War in Iraq.* Kalamazoo, Michigan: Fidlar Double Day.

Borowik, I. 1997. "Institutional and Private Religion in Poland 1990–1994" in *New Religious Phenomena in Central and Eastern Europe,* edited by I. Borowik and Gz. Bainski Krakow: Nomos.

——. 1999. "Integrational and Desintegrational Function of Religion" in *Transformation Process of Central and Eastern Europe. Religion and Integration,* edited by I. Grubišić and S. Zrinscak Institute for Social Sciences Ivo Pilar. Zagreb.

Brading, D. A. 1991. *The First America: The Spanish Monarchy, Creole Patriots, and the Liberal State, 1492–1867.* Cambridge, MA: Cambridge University Press.

Brandom, Robert. 1944. *Making It Explicit,* Cambridge, MA: Harvard University Press.

Brantley, Richard. 1984. *Locke, Wesley, and the Method of English Romanticism.* Gainesville: University of Florida Press.

Brecht, Bertholt. 1967. "An die Nachgeborenen" in *Gesammelte Werke.* Frankfurt a.M.: Suhrkamp Verlag.

Brinkley, A. 1982. *Voices of Protest: Huey Long, Father Coughlin and the Great Depression.* New York: Vintage Books.

Buber, Martin. 1949. *Die Erzählungen der Chassidim.* 12 Auflage. Zürich: Manesse Verlag.

Burkhardt, Louise M. 1989. *The Slippery Earth: Nahua-Christian Moral Dialogue in Sixteenth-Century Mexico.* Tucson: The University of Arizona Press.

——. 1993. "The Cult of the Virgin of Guadalupe in Mexico" in *South and Meso-American Native Spirituality: From the Cult of the Feathered Serpent to the Theology of Liberation,* edited by Gary H. Gossen in collaboration with Miguel León-Portilla. New York: Crossroad.

Bush, George W. 2001. A speech before a Joint Session of Congress, September 20.

Cahill, L. S. 1997. *Love Your Enemies: Discipleship, Pacifism, and Just War Theory,* Minneapolis, MN: Augsburg Fortress Publishers.

Carroll, James. 2001. *Constantine's Sword: The Church and the Jews.* Boston and New York: Houghton Mifflin Company.

Caspers, Bernhard. 1967. *Das dialogische Denken. Eine Untersuchung der religionsphilosophischen Bedeutung Franz Rosenzweigs, Ferdinand Ebners und Martin Bubers.* Freiburg, Basel, Wien: Herder.

Charon, Jean. 1979. *Der Geist der Materie.* Wien: Zsolsnay.

Christian Century. Dec. 10, 1997.

Claeys, Gregory [ed.] 1993. *Selected Works of Robert Owen,* 4 vols., London: William Pickering.

Clark, Elizabeth Mattern. 2005. "Owens renews call to fire Churchill: CU professor's scholarly work under scrutiny" in *The Daily Camera.* February 10, 2005. www.dailycamera.com/bdc/buffzone_news/article/0,1713,BDC_2448_3536907,00.html

Clubture. www.clubture.org

Cohen, Hans. 1961. *Martin Buber: Sein Werk und seine Zeit. Ein Beitrag zur Geistesgeschichte Mitteleuropas 1880–1930*. Köln: Melzer Verlag.

Cole, G. D. H. 1965. *The Life of Robert Owen*. New Introduction by Margaret Cole, 3rd ed., London: Frank Cass & Co.

———. 1999. "Modell nicht erfüllt. Von Kant zu Hegel. Zu Robert Brandoms Sprachpragmatik" in *Wahrheit und Rechtfertigung*, Frankfurt a.M.: Suhrkamp Verlag.

———. 2000. *Articulating Reasons*, Cambridge, MA: Harvard University Press.

Colpe, C. & Schniudt-Biggemann, W. 1993. [eds.] *Das Böse. Eine historische Phänomenologie des Unerklärlichen*, Frankfurt a.M.: Suhrkamp Verlag.

Coughlin, Ch.E. 1932. *Ch. E. Father Coughlin's Radio Discourses 1931–1932*. Royal Oak, Michigan: The Radio League of the Little Flower.

———. 1933. *Eight Discourses on the Gold Standard and Other Kindred Subjects 1932–1933*. Royal Oak, Michigan: The Radio League of the Little Flower.

Craven, Wesley Frank. 1956. *The Legend of the Founding Fathers*. New York: New York University Press.

Črpić, G., Valković, M. 2000. *Mladi u Hrvatskoj u sociologijskoj perspektivi*. Bogoslovska smotra 70 (1):1–63. Zagreb.

Dalai Lama. 2000. *The Meaning of Life*. Trans. and edited by Jeffrey Hopkins. Boston: Wisdom Publications.

Davis, M. and Stone, T. [eds.]. 1995. *Folk Psychology*. Oxford: Blackwell.

Delumeau, Jean. 1990. *Sin and Fear: The Emergence of a Western Guilt Culture, 13th–18th Centuries*, New York: St. Martin's Press.

De Quincey, Thomas. 1986. *Confessions of an English Opium Eater*, edited with an Introduction by Alethea Hayter, London: Penguin Books.

Derrida, Jacques. 1996. "Faith and Knowledge: The two Sources of Religion at the Limits of Reason Alone" in *Religion*, Jacques Derrida and Gianni Vattimo, [eds.], Stanford: Stanford University Press.

Digeser, Elizabeth DePalma. 2000. *The Making of a Christian Empire: Lactantius and Rome*. Ithaca and London: Cornell University Press.

Dostoyevsky, Fyodor. 1950. *The Brothers Karamazov*. New York: Vintage Books.

Dow, Charles Mason. 1921. *Anthology and Bibliography of Niagara Falls*, Vol. II, Albany, NY: J. B. Lyons Co.

Drake, H. A. 2000. *Constantine and the Bishops: The Politics of Intolerance*. Baltimore and London: The John Hopkins University Press.

Duffy, Stephen. 1993. *The Dynamics of Grace: Perspectives in Theological Anthropology*. Collegeville, MN: Liturgical Press.

Dupuis, Serge. 1991. *Robert Owen. Socialiste Utopique 1771–1858*. Paris: Editions du Centre National de la Recherche Scientifique.

Durkheim, Emil. 1964. *Essays on Sociology and Philosophy*, New York: Harper & Row.

Eagleton, Terry. 2000. *The Idea of Culture*. Oxford, United Kingdom: Blackwell Publishing Ltd.

Erickson, Eric H. 1942. "Hitler's Imagery and German Youth" in *Psychiatry* 5:475–493. November.

Erickson, R. P. 1985. *Theologians under Hitler. Gerhard Kittel, Paul Althaus, Emanuel Hirsch.* New Haven and London: Yale University Press.

Ferrara, Alessandro. 2002. "Öffentliche Vernunft und die Normativität des Vernünftigen" in *Deutsche Zeitschrift für Philosophie*, Berlin 50.

Flaubert, Gustave. 1979 [1926]. *Die Erziehung des Herzens. Geschichte eines jungen Mannes.* E. A. Reinhardt [Tr.]. Zürich: Diogenes Verlag AG.

Flint, James. 1816. *A Discourse Delivered at Plymouth, December 22, 1815, at the Anniversary Commemoration of the First Landing of Our Ancestors at that Place.* Boston: Lincoln and Edmunds, 1816; Evans Index S37619.

Floren, Franz Josef and Binke-Orth, Brigitte. 1994. *Politik 2. Ein Arbeitsbuch für den Politikunterricht.* Paderborn: Verlag Ferdinand Schöning.

Floyd, Chris. 2003. "God . . . Instructed Me to Strike at Saddam: Errand Boy," *Moscow Times*, June 26, http://globalresearch.ca/articles/FLO306A.html.

Frankfurter Allgemeine Zeitung, pg. 6 – January 5, 2001, #4.

——. Jan. 11, 2003.

Freud, Sigmund. 1950. *Totem and Taboo.* New York: W. W. Norton & Company, Inc.

——. 1961. *The Future of an Illusion.* New York: W. W. Norton & Company.

——. 1977. *Introductory Lectures on Psychoanalysis.* New York: W. W. Norton & Company.

——. 1992. *Das ich und das Es. Metapsychologische Schriften.* Frankfurt a.M.: Fischer Verlag.

Friedländer, Saul. 1965. *Pius XII und das Dritte Reich. Eine Dokumentation.* Reinbeck bei Hamburg: Rowolt Verlag.

Fritzhand, M. 1961. *Mysl etyczna mlodego Marksa.* [Ethical Thinking of Young Marx.] Warszawa.

Fromm, Erich. 1966a. *Dialogue with Erich Fromm* by Richard I. Evans. New York: Harper & Row, Publishers.

——. 1966b. *You Shall Be As Gods. A Radical Interpretation of the Old Testament and Its Tradition.* New York, Chicago, San Francisco: Holt, Rinehart and Winston.

——. 1973. *The Anatomy of Human Destructiveness.* Greenwich, Connecticut: Fawcett Publications, Inc.

——. 1980. *The Working Class in Weimar Germany: A Psychological & Sociological Study.* Cambridge, MA: Harvard University Press.

——. 1997. *Love, Sexuality, and Matriarchy: About Gender*, edited by Dr. Rainer Funk. New York: Fromm International Publishing Corporation.

Fukuyama, Francis. 1992. *The End of History and The Last Man*, New York: The Free Press.

Funk Kolleg. 1970. *Erziehungswissenschaft. Eine Einführung von Wolfgang Klafki.* Bd. 1. Frankfurt a.M.: Fischer Bücherei GmbH.

Fustel de Coulanges, Numa Denis. 1956/1864. *The Ancient City: A Study of the Religion, Laws, and Institutions of Greece and Rome*. Garden City, NY: Doubleday Anchor Books.

Gadamer, H. G. 1989. *Truth and Method*. New York: Crossroad Press.

Gatzen, Helmut. 1993. *Novemberprogram 1938 in Güterslow. Nachts Orgie der Gewalt, tags organisierte Vernichtung*. Gütersloh: Flöttmann Verlag GmbH.

Gay, William and Alekseeva, Tatiana. [eds.]. 2004. *Democracy and the Quest for Justice, Russian and American Perspectives*. Amsterdam: Rodopi.

Geertz, Clifford. 1973. *The Interpretation of Cultures*, New York: Basic Books.

Gellner, Ernest. 1992. *Postmodernism, Reason and Religion*, London/New York: Routledge.

Giddens, Anthony. 1992. *The Transformation of Intimacy*, Cambridge, UK: The Polity Press.

Giordana, Ralph. 1998. *Die zweite Schuld oder Von der Last Deutscher zu sein. Neuausgabe zum 75 Geburtstag des Autors*. Hamburg: Rasch und Röhring.

Glass, Matthew. 1995. "'Alexanders All': Symbols of Conquest and Resistance at Mount Rushmore" in David Chidester and Edward T. Linenthal [eds.], *American Sacred Space*. Bloomington, IN: Indiana University Press.

Goethe, Johann Wolfgang. 1961. *Goethe's Faust*, trans. by Walter Kaufmann. Garden City, NY: Doubleday & Company, Inc.

Goja, J. 2000. "Some Aspects of Religiosity of Croatian Youth in 1986 and 1999." *Political Thought* (0032–3241) 37 (2000), 1; 148–160. Zagreb.

Goldhagen, Daniel Jonah. 1996. *Hitler's Willing Executioners: Ordinary Germans and the Holocaust*. New York: Vintage Press.

Groh, R. 1998. *Arbeit an der Heilosigkeit der Welt, Zur poliotische-theolopgischen Mythologie und Anthropologie Carl Schmitts*. Frankfurt a.M.: Suhrkamp Verlag.

Gubiljic, Mischa, et al. 1999. "Nature and Second Nature in McDowell's Mind and World" in *Reason and Nature, Lecture and Colloquium in Münster*, edited by Marcus Willaschek. Münster: Lit-Verlag, [Internet].

Guthrie, Stewart. 1993. *Faces in the Clouds: A New Theory of Religion*. New York: Oxford University Press.

Haag, K. H. 1983. *Der Fortschritt in der Philosophie*. Frankfurt a.M.: Suhrkamp Verlag.

Habermas, Jürgen. 1978. *Politik, Kunst, Religion*. Stuttgart: Philipp Reclam.

——. 1981. *The Theory of Communicative Action: Reason and the Rationalization of Society*, Volume One, translated by Thomas McCarthy. Boston, MA: Beacon Press.

——. 1985. Moral i običajnost: Da li Hegelovi prigovor i Kantu pogadaju i diskursnu etiku?" [Morality and Morals (Sittlichkeit): Do Hegel's Objections to Kant Affect Discourse Ethics as Well?], *Filozofska istraživanja*. Vol. 5, No. 15, Zagreb.

——. 1987. *The Theory of Communicative Action: Lifeworld and System – A Critique of Functionalist Reason*, Volume Two, translated by Thomas McCarthy. Boston, MA: Beacon Press.

——. 1991. *Erläuterungen zur Diskursethic*. Frankfurt a.M.: Suhrkamp Verlag.

———. 1993a. "Remarks on the Development of Horkheimer's Work" in *On Max Hork-heimer: New Perspectives*, Cambridge, MA: The MIT Press.

———. 1993b. "To Seek to Salvage an Unconditional Meaning Without God Is a Futile Undertaking: Reflections on a Remark of Max Horkheimer" in *Justification and Application: Remarks on Discourse Ethics*, Cambridge, MA: The MIT Press.

———. 2001. *Glauben udn Wissen. Friedenspreis des Deutschen Buchhandels 2001*. Laidatio: Jan Philipp Reemtsma. Frankfurt a.M.: Suhrkamp Verlag.

———. 2002. *Religion and Rationality, Essays on Reason, God, and Modernity*, Eduardo Mendieta [Ed.], Cambridge, MA: The MIT Press.

———. 2003. "From Kant to Hegel: On Robert Brandom's Pragmatic Philosophy of Language" in *Truth and Justification*. Edited by Barbara Fultner. Cambridge, MA: The MIT Press.

Halbig, Christoph. 2002. "Motivierende Gründe" in *Deutsche Zeitschrift für Philosophie*. Berlin 50.

———. 2003. "Normative Gründe" in *Deutsche Zeitschrift für Philosophie*. Berlin 51.

Hänsel, Dagmar. 1987. "Handbuch Projektunterrich" in *Pädagogische Epochen: Von der Antike bis zur Gegenwart. Mit Beiträgen von Dieter Lenzen*, edited by Rainer Winkel. Düsseldorf: Schwann.

Haralambos, Michael and Holborn, Martin. 2002. *Sociologija. Teme i perspective*. Golden Marketing, Zagreb.

Harnack, Adolf. 1905. *Militia Christi. Die christliche Religion und der Soldatenstand in den ersten drei Jahrhunderten*. J. C. B. Mohr.

Harrison, J. F. C. 1969. *Robert Owen and the Owenites in Britain and America. The Quest for the New Moral World*, London: Routledge and Kegan Paul.

Hawthorne, Nathaniel. 1876. "My Visit to Niagara," in his *The Dolliver Romance and Other Pieces*. Boston: James R. Osgood and Company.

Hegel, G. W. F. 1956. *Philosophy of History*. New York: Dover Publications, Inc.

———. 1967a. *Phenomenology of Mind*. New York and Evanston: Harper & Row, Publishers.

———. 1967b. *Hegel's Philosophy of Right*, trans. by T. M. Knox. New York: Oxford University Press.

———. 1969. *Hegel's Science of Logic*, trans. by A. V. Miller. New York: Humanities Press.

———. 1975. *Phänomenologie des Geists*. Frankfurt a.M.: Suhrkamp Verlag.

———. 1984. *Hegel Lectures on the Philosophy of Religion: Volume I: Introduction and the Concept of Religion*, edited by Peter C. Hodgson. Berkley, Los Angeles, London: University of California Press.

———. 1987. *Hegel Lectures on the Philosophy of Religion: Volume II: Determinate Religion*, edited by Peter C. Hodgson. Berkley, Los Angeles, London: University of California Press.

———. 1989. *Werke*. Frankfurt a.M.: Suhrkamp Verlag.

Heibert, Helmut. 1963. *Lagebesprechungen im Führerhauptquartier Protokollfragmente aus Hitlers militärischen Konferenzen 1942–1945*. Darmstadt.

Heitmeyer, Wilhelm. 1993. *Warum handeln Menschen gegen ihre eigenen Interessen? Materialien zur Auseinandersetzung mit den Ursachen, ein >ran< Buch für Jugendliche.* 3 Auflage [Edition]. Koln: Bund Verlag.

Hervieu-Legger, Daniëlle. 1999. *Le pèlerin et le converti. La religion en movement.* Paris: Flammarion.

Herzog, Roman. 1998. "Ich gehe gern nach Bethel, um den Einsatz der dort tätigen Menschen zu würdigen." An Interview. Zeitgeschehen, Neue Westfälische, Nr. 131, Dienstag, 9 Juni.

Hitler, Adolf. 1971. *Mein Kampf.* Boston: Houghton Mifflin Company.

Hobbes, Thomas. 1968. *Leviathan,* edited by C. B. Macpherson. New York, NY: Penguin Books.

Hochhuth, Rolf. 1963. *Der Stellvertreter (The Deputy).* Reinbeck bei Hamburg: Verlag Rowohlt.

Hoffman, M. 2000. *Empathy and Moral Development. Implications for Caring and Justice.* Cambridge, MA: Cambridge University Press.

Holy Bible: New Revised Standard Version. 1990. Grand Rapids, Michigan: Zondervan.

Homann, Heinz Theo. 1997. *Das funktionale Argument. Konzepte und Kritik funktionslogischer Religionsbegründung.* Paderborn-München-Wien.

Horkheimer, Max. 1970. *Die Sehnsucht nach dem ganz Anderen: Ein Interview mit Kommentar von Helmut Gumnior.* Hamburg: Furdie-Verlag H. Rennebach KG.

——. 1972. *Critical Theory: Selected Essays.* New York: Seabury Press.

——. 1973. "Forward" in Martin Jay's *The Dialectical Imagination: A History of the Frankfurt School and the Institute of Social Research, 1923–1950.* Boston, MA: Little, Brown and Company.

——. 1974. *Eclipse of Reason.* New York: The Seabury Press.

——. 1978a. *Dawn & Decline: Notes 1926–1951 & 1950–1969.* New York: The Seabury Press.

——. 1978b. *The Essential Frankfurt School Reader,* edited by Andrew Arato & Eike Gebhardt. New York: Urizen Books.

——. 1980–1996. *Gesammelte Schriften.* Frankfurt a.M.: Fischer Verlag.

——. 1985a. "Psalm 91" in Max Horkheimer, *Gesammelte Schriften Band 7: Vorträge und Aufzeichnungen, 1949–1973.* Frankfurt a.M.: Fischer Taschenbuch Verlag.

——. 1985b. "Zur Zukunft der Kritischen Theorie: Gespräch mit Claus Grossner" in Max Horkheimer, *Gesammelte Schriften Band 7: Vorträge und Aufzeichnungen, 1949–1973.* Frankfurt a.M.: Fischer Taschenbuch Verlag.

——. 1985c. *Max Horkheimer Gesammelte Schriften, Band 7: Vorträge und Aufzeichnungen, 1949–1973.* Frankfurt a.M.: S. Fischer Verglag GmbH.

——. 1987. *Nachgelassene Schriften 1914–1931.* Frankfurt a.M.: Fischer Verlag.

——. 1988. *Schriften 1936–1941.* Frankfurt a.M.: Fischer Verlag.

——. 1989. *Critical Theory and Society: A Reader,* New York: Routledge.

———. 1993. "The Present Situation of Social Philosophy and the Tasks of an Institute for Social Research" in *Between Philosophy and Social Science Selected Early Writings*. Cambridge, MA: The MIT Press.

———. 1995a. "Theodor W. Adorno an Max Horkheimer, Hollywood, New York, 18 September 1940" in *Max Horkheimer, Gesammelte Schriften*. Band 16: Briefwechsel 1937–1940. Frankfurt a.M.: Fischer Verlag.

———. 1995b. "Max Horkheimer an Theodor W. Adorno, New York. The Montecito, 6650 Franklin Avenue. Hollywood, California. 24 September 1940" in *Max Horkheimer, Gesammelte Schriften*. Band 16: Briefwechsel 1937–1940, Frankfurt a.M.: Fischer Verlag.

———. 1996a. "Max Horkheimer an Leo Löwenthal, Port Chester, July 24, 1944" in *Max Horkheimer Gesammelte Schriften*. Band 17: Briefwechsel 1941–1948. Frankfurt a.M.: Fischer Verlag.

———. 1996b. "Leo Löwenthal an Max Horkheimer. Pacific Palisades. Port Chester, N.Y. August 4, 1944" in *Max Horkheimer Gesammelte Schriften*. Band 17: Briefwechsel 1941–1948. Frankfurt a.M.: Fischer Verlag.

———. 1996c. "Max Horkheimer an Herbert Marcuse, Washington D.C. Pacific Palisades, July 15, 1944" in *Max Horkheimer Gesammelte Schriften*. Band 17: Briefwechsel 1941–1948, Frankfurt a.M.: Fischer Verlag.

Horkheimer, Max and Adorno, Th.W. 1972. *Dialectics of Enlightenment*, New York: Herder and Herder.

Hornsby-Smith, M. P. 1997. "The Catholic Church in Central and Eastern Europe" in *New Religious Phenomena in Central and Eastern Europe*, edited by I. Borowik and Gz. Babinski. Krakow: Nomos.

Huntington, Samuel P. 1996. *The Clash of Civilizations and the Remaking of World Order*. New York: Simon & Schuster.

Huxley, Aldous. 1946. *Brave New World*. San Francisco: Harper & Row Publishers.

Ilišin, Vlasta. 1999. *Mladi na margini društva i politike*. Alinea, Zagreb.

Ilišin, Vlasta; Radin, Furio. [eds.] 2002. *Youth and Transition in Croatia*. Zagreb: Institute for Social Research and State Institute for the Protection of Family, Maternity and Youth.

James, William. 1956. "Is Life Worth Living?" in *The Will To Believe and Other Essays in Popular Philosophy*. New York: Dover Publications.

———. 1958. *The Varities of Religious Experience*. New American Library of Canada.

Jaynes, Julian. 1993. *The Origin of Consciousness in the Breakdown of the Bicameral Mind*. London: Penguin Books.

Jerusalem Bible. 1968. New York: Doubleday & Company, Inc.

Jiménez, Fray Francisco. 1926. "Vida de Fray Martín de Valencia, escrita por su compañero Fr. Francisco Jiménez," [Ed.] P. Atanasio López. *Archivo Ibero-Americano* 26.

Joas, Hans. 1996. *Die Krativität des Handelns*, Frankfurt a.M.: Suhrkamp Verlag.

Johnston, Francis. 1981. *The Wonder of Guadalupe, The Origin and Cult of the Miraculous Image of the Blessed Virgin of Mexico*. Rockford, IL: Tan Books.

Jüngel, Eberhard. 1979. "Wertlose Wahrheit." in *Tyrannei der Werte*. Edited by Sepp Schelz. Hamburg.

Juster, Susan. 1994. *Disorderly Women: Sexual Politics and Evangelicalism in Revolutionary New England*. Ithaca, NY: Cornell University Press.

Kafka, Franz. 1956. *The Trial*. New York: Alfred A. Knopf.

Kangrga, Milan. 1963. *Etički problem u djelu Karla Marxa* [Ethical Problem in the Work of Karl Marx]. Zagreb.

———. 1966. *Etika i sloboda* [Ethics and Freedom]. Zagreb.

———. 1970a. *Razmišljanja o etici* [Reflections on Ethics]. Zagreb.

———. 1970b. *Smisao povijesnoga* [The Meaning of the Historical]. Zagreb.

———. 1975. *Čovjek i svijet* [The Man and the World]. Zagreb.

———. 1983. *Etika ili revolucija* [Ethics or Revolution]. Belgrade.

Kant, Immanuel. 1929. *Critique of Pure Reason*, trans. by Norman Kemp Smith. New York: St. Martin's Press.

———. 1951. *Critique of Judgment*, trans. by J. H. Bernard. New York: Hafner Press.

———. 1956. *Critique of Practical Reason*, trans. by Lewis White Beck. Indianapolis: Bobbs-Merrill Educational Publishing.

———. 1974. *Kritika praktičnoga uma*. [Critique of Practical Reason]. Naprijed, Zagreb.

———. 1982. *Werkausgabe*. Frankfurt a.M.: Suhrkamp Verlag.

Karajić, N. 2001. *Poverty and the Underground Economy in Croatia: Qualitative Aspects*. www.ijf.hr/eng/UEposto202002/karajic.pdf.

Kauffman, Stuart A. 1995. "What is Life? Was Schrödinger right?" in *What is Life? The Next Fifty Years, Speculations on the Future of Biology*, edited by Michael Murphy and Luke A. J. O'Neill. Cambridge, MA: Cambridge University Press.

Keesing, Roger. 1971. *New Perspectives in Cultural Anthropology*. New York: Holt, Rinehart and Winston.

Kersaw, Ian. 2000. *Hitler: 1936–1945: Nemesis*. London: The Penguin Press.

Klafki, W. 1991. "Hervorhebungen bei Klafki" in *Didaktische Modelle*, edited by Werner Jank & Hilpert Meyer. 3rd Auflage. Frankfurt a.M.: Cornelsen Verlag Scriptor GmbH & Co.

Klor de Alva, J. Jorge. 1993. "Aztec Spirituality and Nahuatized Christianity," in *South and Meso-American Native Spirituality: From the Cult of the Feathered Serpent to the Theology of Liberation*, edited by Gary H. Gossen in collaboration with Miguel León-Portilla. New York: Crossroad.

Koestler, Arthur. 1978. *Janus: A Summing Up*. New York: Random House.

Kogon, Eugon. 1965. *SS-State, Das System der Deutschen Konzentrationslager*. Frankfurt a.M.: Europäische Verlagsanstalt.

———. 1967. "Revolution und Theologie – Das Neue in unserem Zeitalter/Ein Symposion," in *Frankfurter Hefte. Zeitschrift für Kultur und Politik*, 22. Jahrgang. Heft 9, September.

Kögler, H. H. 1999. *The Power of Dialogue*. Cambridge, MA: The MIT Press.

Kögler, H. H. and Stueber, K. [eds.] 2000. *Empathy and Agency*. Boulder: Westview Press.

Korczak, Janusz. 1974. *Wie man ein Kind lieben soll [How One Should Love a Child]*, edited by Elisabeth Hempel und Hans Roos. Göttingen: Vanderhoeck & Ruprecht.

———. 1996. *Sämtliche Werke. Subskriptions-angebot für den Bezug des Gesamtwerkes in 16 Bänden*, edited by Friedhlem Beiner and Erich Dauzenroth. Warszawa: Verlag Oficyna Wydawnicza Latona.

———. 1997. *Leben für andere. Gedanken und Meditationen*. Gütersloh: Kiefel/Gütersloher Verlagshaus.

Korsgaard, Christine M. 1996. *The Sources of Normativity*. Cambridge, MA: Cambridge University Press.

Krieg, R. A. 2004. *Catholic Theologians in Nazi Germany*. New York: Continuum.

Krieglstein, Werner. 2002. *Compassion, A New Philosophy of the Other*. Amsterdam: Rodopi.

Küenzlen, Gottfried. 1994. *Der neue Mensch. Eine Untersuchung zur säkularen Religions-geschichte der Moderne*. München: W. Fink

———. 1995. "Die Religionssoziologie Max Webers und Emile Durkheims: Ein bleibender Gegensatz," in *društvena istraživanja* 15/4. Zagreb.

Küng, Hans. 1994. *Das Christentum. Wesen und Geschichte*. München, Zürich: Piper Verlag.

———. 2004. *Der Islam. Geschichte. Gegenwart. Zukunft*, München, Zürich: Piper Verlag.

Lafaye, Jacques. 1987. *Quetzalcóatl and Guadalupe: The Formation of Mexican National Consciousness, 1531–1813*. Chicago: University of Chicago Press.

La Jornada, Galeano. 2005. Quoted in "Bully Goes to War – Blames God," by Saul Landau, ZNet Commentary, Jan. 05, 2004. www.zmag.org/sustainers/content/2003–12/25landau.cfm.

Lenin, Vladimir Ilyich. 1905. "Socialism and Religion", quoted from: www.marxists.org/archive/lenin/works/1905/dec/03.htm.

Lessing, Gotthold Ephraim. 2004/1779. *Nathan the Wise*. New York: Bedford/St. Martin's Press.

Liebermann – Shiber, Ella. 1997. *Am Rande des Abgrunds, übersetzt von Ulrike Harnische. [On the Edge of the Abyss.]* Frankfurt a.M.: Alibaba Verlag.

Lortz, Joseph. 1962a. *Die Reformation in Deutschland, Band I. Vorraussetzungen. Aufbruch. Erste Entscheidungen*. Freiburg, Basel, Wien: Herder Verlag.

———. 1962b. *Die Reformation in Deutschland. Band II. Ausbau der Fronten. Unionsversuche. Ergebnis*. Freiburg, Basel, Wien: Herder Verlag.

———. 1964. *Geschichte der Kirche in Ideengeschichtlicher Betrachtung*. Münster: Verlag Aschendorff.

Luckmann, Thomas. 1967. *The Invisible Religion*. New York: McMillan.

Maekawa, Michiko. 2001. "The Dilemma of 'Authentic Self' Ideology in Contemporary Japan" in *International Journal of Japanese Sociology*. 10:16–28. Tokyo: The Japan Sociological Society.

Mandarić, Valentina. 2000. *Religious Identity of Zagrebian Adolescents*. Zagreb.

Mannheim, Karl. 1949. *Ideology and Utopia. An Introduction to the Sociology of Knowledge*. With a Preface by Louis Wirth, London: Routledge and Kegan Paul.

Marcuse, Herbert. 1960. "New Preface: A Note on Dialectic" in *Reason and Revolution: Hegel and the Rise of Social Theory*. Boston: Beacon Press.

———. 1962. *Eros and Civilization. A Philosophical Inquiry into Freud*. New York: Vintage Books.

———. 1964. *One Dimensional Man*. Boston: Beacon Press.

Marin, Carlos Martinez. 1972. "Santuarios y Perigrinaciones en el México Prehispánico," in *Religion en Mesoamerica: XII Mesa Redonda*, edited by Jaime Litvak King and Noemi Castillo Tejero. México: Sociedad Mexicana de Antropología.

Marinović Jerolimov, D. 1999. "Religiosity, Non-religiosity and Some Values of Youth," in *Youth in Transition in Croatia*, edited by V. Ilišin and F. Radin. Zagreb: Institute for Social Research and State Institute for the Protection of Family, Maternity and Youth.

Marvin, Carolyn and Ingle, David W. 1999. *Blood Sacrifice and the Nation: Totem Rituals and the American Flag*. Cambridge, MA: Cambridge University Press.

Marx, Karl. 1961. *Das Kapital*, Berlin: Dietz Verlag, Vol. I & III.

———. 1964. *On Religion*. New York: Schocken Books.

———. 1976. *Capita*. Volume I. New York: Vintage Books.

———. 1979. *The Letters of Karl Marx*, trans. by Saul K. Padover. Englewood Cliffs, NJ: Prentice-Hall, Inc.

———. 2002. *Marx On Religion*, edited by John Raines. Philadelphia: Temple University Press.

McDowell, John. 1996. *Mind and World*. Cambridge, MA: Harvard University Press.

———. 1999. *Reason and Nature, Lecture and Colloquium in Münster*. Edited by Marcus Willaschek. Münster: Lit-Verlag [Internet].

———. 2000. *Mind, Value and Reality*. Cambridge, MA: Harvard University Press.

McGreevy, Patrick. 1985. "Niagara as Jerusalem," *Landscape* 28:2.

———. 1994. *Imagining Niagara: The Meaning and Making of Niagara Falls*. Amherst: University of Massachusetts Press.

McKinsey, Elizabeth. 1985a. *Niagara Falls: Icon of the American Sublime*. Cambridge, MA: Cambridge University Press.

———. 1985b. "An American Icon," in *Niagara, Two Centuries of Changing Attitudes, 1697–1901*, edited by Jeremy Elwell Adamson. Washington, D.C.: The Cocoran Gallery of Art.

Mendeš, I. and Potočnik, D. 2003. *Developing Common Approaches in Vocational Education and Training for Disadvantaged Young People in the Western Balkan Countries, European Training Foundation and Human Resource Development Centre*. Sofia.

Mendieta, Eduardo. [ed.] 2002. *Jürgen Habermas, Religion and Rationality. Essays on Reason, God, and Modernity*. Cambridge, MA: The MIT Press.

——. 2005. *The Frankfurt School on Religion. Key Writings by the Major Thinkers*, edited by Eduardo Mendieta. New York and London: Routledge.

Mendieta, Gerónimo de. 1870. *Historia eclesiástica Indiana*, edited by Joaquin García Icazbalceta. México: Antigua Libreria.

Merton, Thomas. 1960. *The Wisdom of the Desert*. Gethsemani.

Meyer, Jeffrey F. 2001. *Myths in Stone: Religious Dimensions of Washington, D.C.* Berkeley: University of California Press.

Mitscherlich, Alexander und Margarete. *Die Unfähigkeit zu trauern, Grundlagen kollektiven Verhalten*. 13 Auflage [Edition]. München: R. Piper & Co. Verlag.

Mizuno, Kogen. 1973. *Bukkyo no Kiso Chishiki* (Basic Knowledge of Buddhism). Tokyo: Shunshusha.

More, Thomas. 1965. *Utopia*, trans. by Paul Turner. New York, NY: Penguin Books.

——. 2002. *Utopia*. New York: Cambridge University Press.

Morgan, Edmund. 1998. "The Big American Crime," in *New York Review of Books*, 45.

Musil, Robert. 1996. *The Man without Qualities Vol. II: Into the Millennium, from the Posthumous Papers*. New York: Vintage International.

New Orleans Times-Picayune. Oct. 14, 1998.

Niebuhr, Richard R. 1997. "William James on Religious Experience" in *The Cambridge Companion to William James*, edited by Ruth Anna Putnam. Cambridge, MA: Harvard University Press.

Nietzsche, Friedrich. 1967. *On the Genealogy of Morals and Ecce Homo*, trans. by Walter Kaufmann and R. J. Hollingdale. New York: Vintage Books.

——. 1988a. *Morgenröthe* (Dawn). Aph. 92, Kritische Studienausgabe (Critical textbook edition), Volume 3, München: Deutscher Taschenbuch.

——. 1988b. Die fröhliche Wissenschaft (The Gay Science), Aph. 125, Kritische Studienausgabe (Critical textbook edition), Volume 3, München: Deutscher Taschenbuch.

NIN, NIN d.o.o Belgrade; number: 2753, Feb. 10, 2003.

Nishitani, K. 1982. *Was ist Religion?* Frankfurt a.M.: Insel.

Novalis. 1986. "Die Christenheit oder Europa. Ein Fragment von Novalis" (Christianity or Europe. A fragment by Novalis, 1799.) in *Die Deutschen Romantiker* (The German Romanticists), Volume 1, Salzburg.

Oehler, Klaus. 2002. "Hilary Putnams Religionsphilosophie," in *Hilary Putnam und dies Tradition des Pragmatismus*, edited by Marie-Luise Raters and Marcus Willaschek. Frankfurt a.M.: Suhrkamp stw.1567.

Oelmüller, W. [ed.] 1990. *Theodizee – Gott vor Gericht*. München: Wilhelm Fink Verlag.

Oliver, W. H. 1971. "Owen in 1817: The Millenialist Moment," in *Robert Owen. Prophet of the Poor. Essays in Honour of the Two Hundredth Anniversary of his Birth*, edited by Sidney Pollard and John Salt. London: Macmillan.

Orwell, George. 1949. *1984*. New York: Harcourt Brace Jovanovish.

Ott, Michael R. 2001. *Max Horkheimer's Critical Theory of Religion: The Meaning of Religion in the Struggle for Human Emancipation*. New York: University Press of America.

———. 2006. "Psalm 91" (A translation.) in *Marx, Critical Theory, and Religion: A Critique of Rational Choice*, edited by Warren S. Goldstein. Leiden, Boston: Brill.

Otto, Rudolf. 1997. *Das Heilige. Über das Irrationale in der Idee des Göttlichen und sein Verhälltnis zum Rationalen*. München: Beck.

Owen, Robert. 1993a. [1817]. "New View of Society. Address," in *Selected Works of Robert Owen*, vol. 1, edited by Gregory Claeys. London: William Pickering.

———. 1993b [1830]. "The New Religion," in *Selected Works of Robert Owen*, vol. 2, edited by Gregory Claeys. London: William Pickering.

———. 1993c [1842–4]. The Book of the New Moral World in *Selected Works of Robert Owen*, vol. 3, edited by Gregory Claeys. London: William Pickering.

———. 1993d [1857]. "The Life of Robert Owen, written by Himself" in *Selected Works of Robert Owen*, vol. 4, edited by Gregory Claeys. London: William Pickering.

Pals, Daniel L. 1996. *Seven Theories of Religion*. New York/Oxford: Oxford University Press.

Petrović, Gajo. 1973. *Filozofija i revolucija, Model za jednu interpretaciju Marxa*. [Philosophy and Revolution: Model for an Interpretation of Marx.] Naprijed, Zagreb.

Political encyclopedia, 1975. *Contemporary administration*. Beograd.

Pollard, Sidney and Salt, John [eds.] 1971. *Robert Owen. Prophet of the Poor. Essays in Honour of the Two-hundredth Anniversary of his Birth*. London: Macmillan.

Prigogine, Ilya. 1984. *Order Out of Chaos*. New York: Bantam Books.

Putnam, Hilary. 1991. *The Many Faces of Realism*. Illinois: Open Court LaSalle.

———. 1996. "On Negative Theology" in *Faith and Philosophy* 14, edited by William Haskers. Wilmore, Kentucky: Asbury College and Society of Christian Philosophers.

———. 1998. *Renewing Philosophy*, Cambridge, MA: Harvard University Press.

———. "God and the Philosophers" in *Midwest Studies in Philosophy* 21, edited by Peter A. French and Howard K. Wettstein. Blackwell Publishing.

Quante, Michael. 2002. "Exstentielle Verpflichtung und Toleranz" in *Hilary Putnam und dies Tradition des Pragmatismus*, edited by Marie-Luise Raters and Marcus Willaschek. Frankfurt a.M.: Suhrkamp stw.1567.

Raines, J. C. & Dean, Th. [eds.] 1970. *Marxism and Radical Religion. Essays Toward a Revolutionary Humanism*. Philadelphia: Temple University.

Rawls, John. 1971. *A Theory of Justice*. Cambridge, MA: The Belknap Press of Harvard University Press.

———. 1997. "The Domain of the Political and Overlapping Consensus" (1989) reprinted in *Contemporary Political Philosophy* edited by Robert E. Goodin and Philipp Pettit. Oxford: Blackwell Publisher.

Reimer, James [ed.] 1989. *The Emanuel Hirsch und Paul Tillich Debate. A Study in the Political Ramifications of Theology*. Lewiston/Queenston. Lampeter: The Edwin Mellen Press.

———. 1992. *The Influence of the Frankfurt School on Contemporary Theology. Critical Theory and the Future of Religion. Dubrovnik Papers in Honor of Rudolf J. Siebert*. Lewiston/Queenston/Lampeter: The Edwin Mellen Press.

———. 2001. "Trinitarian Orthodoxy, Constantinanism, and Radical Protestant Theology," in *Mennonites and Classical Theology: Dogmatic Foundations for Christian Ethics*. Pandora Press/Harold Press.

Rohrmoser, Günter. 1975. *Die metaphysische Situation der Zeit*. Stuttgart.

———. 2000. Nietzsche als Diagnostiker der Gegenwart (Nietzsche as a diagnostician of the present); Munich: M. Grimminger.

Rorty, Richard. 1986. "Freud and Moral Reflection" in *Pragmatism's Freud*, edited by Joseph H. Smith and William Kerrigan. Baltimore/London: John Hopkins University Press.

Rosenbaum, R. 1999. *Die Hitler-Debatte. Explaining Hitler. Auf der Suche nach dem Bösen*. München-Wien: Europa Verlag.

Rousso, Henry. 1991. *The Vichy Syndrome: History and Memory in France Since 1944*. Cambridge, MA: Harvard University Press.

Royle, Edward. 1998. *Robert Owen and the Commencement of the Millenium. A Study of the Harmony Community*. Manchester/New York: Manchester University Press.

Sachs, Nelly. 1961. *Die Gedichte der Nelly Sachs: Fahrt ins Staublose. In den Wohnungen des Todes. [Moving into Dust, In the House of Death.]* Frankfurt a.M.: Suhrkamp Verlag.

Šagi, B. Z. 1995. *Church Facing the Current Challenges*. Svesci (85–86):82–90, Zagreb.

Sallnow, Michael J. 1991. "Pilgrimage and Cultural Fracture in the Andes," in *Contesting the Sacred: The Anthropology of Christian Pilgrimage*, edited by John Eade and Michael J. Sallnow. New York: Routledge.

Sankta Familia Chronike – Newsletter of the Sankta Familia Parish, Frankfurt a.M.: Germany.

Scammell, Michael. December 3, 1998. "The Solzhenitsyn Archipelago," in *New York Review of Books*, 45.

Schaeffler, Richard. 1973. *Religion und kritisches Bewußtsein*. Freiburg/Br.

Scholem, Gershom. 1992. *The Correspondence of Walter Benjamin and Gershom Scholem: 1932–1940*, trans. by Gary Smith and Andre Lefevere, edited by Gershom Scholem. Cambridge, MA: Harvard University Press.

Schopenhauer, Arthur. 1989. *Sämtliche Werke*. Frankfurt a.M.: Suhrkamp Verlag.

Schrödinger, Erwin. 1967. *What is Life?* Cambridge, MA: Cambridge University Press.

Schroeder, Susan. 1989. "Chimalpahin's View of Spanish Ecclesiastics in Colonial Mexico," in *Indian-Religious Relations in Colonial Latin America*, edited by Susan E. Ramirez. Syracuse: Maxwell School of Citizenship and Public Affairs.

Schüler, Else Lasker. 1977. *Sämtliche Gedichte*, edited by Friedhelm Kemp. München: Kösel Verlag.

Schultz, Hans Jürgen. [ed.] 1990. *Es ist ein Weinen in der Welt; Hommage für deutsche Juden unseres Jahrhunderts*. Stuttgart: Quell Verlag.

Schwan, Gesine. 1997. *Politik und Schuld: Die zerstörerische Macht des Schweigens*. Fischer Taschenbuch.

Sears, John F. 1989. *Sacred Places: American Tourist Attractions in the Nineteenth Century*. New York: Oxford University Press.

Semprun, Jorge. 1994. "Dank-Worte bei der Verleihung des Friednspreises des Deutschen Buchhandels." Gehalten am 9. Oktober 1994 in der Paulskirche, Frankfurt am Main: Mit freundlicher Genehmigugn des Autors, des Suhrkamp Verlags und des Börsenveriens des Deutschen Buchhandels verteilt der Bertelsmann Club die Rede Sempurns. [Distributed with the friendly permission of the author by the publishing house of Suhrkamp and the Boersenveriens of the German book trade of the Bertelsmann club.]

Shiels, Dean. 1980. "The Great Ancestors are Watching: A Cross-Cultural Study of Superior Ancestral Religion," *Sociological Analysis* 41.

Shimazono, Susumu. 1996. *Seishin sekai no yukue* (New Spirituality Movements in the Global Culture). Tokyo: Tokyodo shuppan.

———. 2002. "The New Spirituality Movements and Culture" in *Traditional Religion & Culture in a New Era*, edited by Reimon Bachika. New Brunswick, NJ: Transaction Publishers.

Shriver Jr., Donald W. 1995. *An Ethic for Enemies: Forgiveness in Politics*. NY: Oxford.

Siebert, Rudolf J. 1965. *Michael Helding: A Catholic Humanist in the Context of the Renewal of the 16th Century (1506–1561)*. Sigmaringen.

———. 1985. *The Critical Theory of Religion: The Frankfurt School. From Universal Pragmatic to Political Theology*. Berlin, New York, Amsterdam: Mouton Publishers, Chapters I–III.

———. 1993. *Recht, Macht und Liebe. Georg W. Rudolphi's Prophetische Politische Theologie*. Frankfurt a.M.: Haag und Herchen.

———. 1994. *From Critical Theory to Critical Political Theology. Personal Autonomy and Universal Solidarity*. New York, Washington D.C./Baltimore, San Francisco, Bern, Frankfurt a.M., Berlin, Vienna, Paris: Peter Lang.

———. 2001. *The Critical Theory of Religion. The Frankfurt School*. Lanham, Maryland, and London: The Scarecrow Press.

———. 2003. *The Critical Theory of Religion*. www.wmich.edu/religion/siebert/critical_theory.html.

———. *Hitler's Religion: Faith in Providence. Case Study in Nationalism, Anti-Semitism, Anti-Communism and Anti-Democratism*. (in process).

———. *The Longing for the Entirely Other: The Rescue of the Hopeless*. (in process).

———. *A Comparative Critical Theory of Religion: Inversions*. Vol. I–IV. (in process).

Simmel, Georg. 1989. *Gesammelte Schriften zur Religionssoziologie*. Berlin: Duncker & Humblot.

Singer, Peter. 1996. "On the Nature of Bioethics," *Drustvena istrazivanja*, Vol. 5, No. 23–24.

Skrbina, David. 2003. "Panpsychism as an Underlying Theme in Western Philosophy" in *Panpsychism, Journal of Consciousness Studies* Vol. 10, No. 3.

———. 2005. *Panpsychism in the West,* Cambridge, MA: The MIT Press.

Smolin, Lee. 1997. *The Life of the Cosmos.* Oxford University Press.

Spranger, Eduard. 1928. *Types of Men.* Trans. by Paul J. W. Pigors, Halle: Niemeyer Verlag.

Stojanovic, S. 1969. *Izmedu ideala i stvarnosti.* [Between Ideals and Reality.] Belgrade.

Stone, H. W.; Cross, D. R.; Purvis K. B. and Young, M. J. 2003. "A Study of the Benefit of Social and Religious Support on Church Members During Times of Crisis," *Pastoral Psychology;* March, Vol. 51 Issue 4.

Strogatz, Steven. 2003. *Sync, The Emerging Science of Spontaneous Order.* New York: Hyperion Books.

Sweeny, Kevin M. 1993. "Meetinghouses, Town Houses, and Churches: Changing Perceptions of Sacred and Secular Space in Southern New England, 1720–1850." *Winterthur Portfolio* 28:1, Spring.

Szymborska, Wislawa. 1995. *View with a Grain of Sand: Selected Poems.* New York: Harcourt Brace.

Tadić, S. 1999. *Sociohistorical and Socioreligious Factors and the Genesis of Ecclesiastical Movements.* Ivo Pilar, Zagreb: Institut Drustvenih znanosti.

Tavuchnis, Nicholas. 1991. *Mea Culpa: A Sociology of Apology and Reconciliation.* Stanford, CA: Stanford.

Taylor, Charles. 1979/1997. "What's Wrong with Negative Liberty?" in *The Idea of Freedom,* edited by Alan Ryan. Oxford University Press, reprinted in *Contemporary Political Philosophy,* edited by Robert E. Goodin and Philipp Pettit Oxford: Blackwell Publishers.

———. 2002. *Die Formen des Religiösen in der Gegenwart.* Frankfurt a.M.: Suhrkamp Verlag.

———. 2003. *Varieties of Religion Today. William James Revisited.* Cambridge, MA: Harvard University Press.

Tenbruck, Friedrich H. 1984. *Die unbewältigten Sozialwissenschaften oder Die Abschaffung des Menschen.* Graz-Wien Köln.

———. 1986. "Einleitung." in Michael Bock's, *Soziologie als Grundlage des Wirklichkeitsverständnisses. Zur Entstehung des modernen Weltbildbildes,* Stuttgart.

———. 1996. *Perspektiven der Kultursoziologie* (Perspectives of Cultural Sociology), C. Albrecht/W. Dreyer/H. Homann, Opladen.

The Daily Vidette. 2005. "Colorado professor's comments could cost job." Illinois State University's Student Newspaper, February 14, Online Edition.

The Educational System in the Republic of Croatia. 2003. Zagreb: Hrvatska gospodarska komora.

The Lanthorn. 2003. "Teaching Empathy," Grand Valley State University Newspaper, Thursday, April 3.

Tillich, Paul. 1957. *Dynamics of Faith.* New York: Harper & Row, Publishers.

———. 1966. *On the Boundary: An Autobiographical Sketch.* New York: Scribner.

———. 1967. *Systematic Theology*, Vol. I (1951), Vol. II (1957), Vol. III (1963). Chicago, IL: The University of Chicago Press.

———. 1972. *The Courage to Be*. New Haven and London: Yale University Press.

———. 1977. *The Socialist Decision*, trans. by Franklin Sherman. New York, Hagerstown, San Francisco, London: Harper & Row, Publishers.

Timmermann, Jens. 2000. "Of Historical Monstrosities: Aristotle, McDowell, and Second Nature" in *Rationality, Realism, Revision. Proceedings of the 3rd International Congress of the Society for Analytical Philosophy September 15–18, 1997*, edited by Julian Nida-Rümelin. Berlin New York: de Gruyter.

Tolstaya, Tatyana. April 24, 1997. "The Way They Live Now," in *New York Review of Books*, 44.

Tomić-Koludrović, Inga. 1999. *The Concept of Integration in Contemporary Sociological Theories, Religion and Integration*. Ivo Pilar, Zagreb: Institute for Social Sciences.

Tsipko, Alexander. 1990. *Is Stalinism Really Dead? The Future of Perestroika as a Moral Revolution*. San Francisco: Harper.

Tugendhat, Ernst. 1981. *Selbstbewußtsein und Selbstbestimmung*. Frankfurt a.M.: Suhrkamp Verlag.

Turner, Victor and Turner, Edith. 1978. *Image and Pilgrimage in Christian Culture: Anthropological Perspectives*. New York: Columbia University Press.

UNESCO. 2002. Youth Vulnerability: Assessment of Risk Factors, Threatening the Well-Being of Youth.

USATODAY.com. 2005. "Colorado president: Words won't get professor fired." March 5, Associated Press.

Veljkovic, Vidimir. 2001. Political moral of Serbs – From Nemanjic dynasty till Milosevic. Beleg, Prosveta, Nis.

Viminitz, Paul. 2005. "A Defence of Terrorism" in the *Journal of Philosophical Research*. Bowling Green, OH: Bowling Green State University.

Vrcan, S. 1999. "New Challenges in Modern Sociology of Religion. Politicization of Religion and 'Regionalization' of Politics" in *Post-communism*. Sociological Review 30(1–2):45–64, Zagreb.

Walsh, James P. 1980. "Holy Time and Sacred Space in Puritan New England," *American Quarterly* 32.

Ward, L. B. 1933. *Father Charles E. Coughlin. An Authorized Biography*. Detroit, Michigan: Tower Publications, Incorporated.

Weaver, J. Denny. 2001. "Trinitarian Orthodoxy, Constantinianism, and Radical Protestant Theology," in A. James Reimer's *Mennonites and Classical Theology: Dogmatic Foundation for Christina Ethics*. Kitchener and Scottdale: Pandora Press/Harold Press.

Weber, Max. 1958. *The Protestant Ethic and the Spirit of Capitalism*, trans. by Talcott Parsons. New York: Charles Scribner's Sons.

Webster, Daniel. 1821. *A Discourse Delivered at Plymouth, December 22, 1820. In Commemoration of the First Settlement of New-England*. Boston: Wells and Lilly.

Weitensteiner, H.K. 2002. *Warum denn wir, immer wir...? War diese Stadt Frankfurt schuldiger als London? Katholisches Gemeidneleben im Dritten Reich und währen der ersten nachkriuegsjahre 1932–1950.* Dokumente und Darstellung, Frankfurt a.M.: Haag und Herchen.

Whitehead, Alfred North. 2001. *Religion in the Making. Lowell Lectures 1926.* New York: Fordham University Press.

Wilson, Brian C. 2001. "Altars and Chalkstones: The Anomalous Case of Puritan Sacred Space in Light of Durkheim's Theory of Ritual" in *Reappraising Durkheim for the Study and Teaching of Religion Today,* edited by Thomas A. Idinopulos and Brian C. Wilson. Leiden: Brill.

———. 2003. "What Does Jerusalem Have to do With Amecameca: A Case Study of Colonial Mexican Sacred Space," in *Religion as a Human Capacity: A Festschrift in Honor of E. Thomas Lawson,* edited by Timothy Light and Brian C. Wilson. Leiden: Brill.

Wingert, Lutz. 2000. "Genealogie der Objektivität Zu Robert B. Brandoms 'expressiver Vernunft'" in *Deutsche Zeitschrift für Philosophie* 48.

Winkel, Rainer. [ed.] 1987. *Pädagogische Epochen: Von der Antike bis zur Gegenwart. Mit Beiträgen von Dieter Lenzen.* Düsseldorf, Schwann.

Yeo, Eileen. 1971. "Robert Owen and Radical Culture" in *Robert Owen. Prophet of the Poor. Essays in Honour of the Twohundredth Anniversary of his Birth,* edited by Sidney Pollard and John Salt. London: Macmillan.

Yibu, Mari and Yasue, Kunio. 1995. *Quantum Brain Dynamics and Consciousness.* Amsterdam: Benjamin.

Yoder, John H. 1981. *Christian Attitudes Toward War, Peace, and Revolution: A Companion to Bainton.* Elkhart, IN: Co-op Bookstore.

———. 1984a. "Radical Reformation Ethics in Ecumenical Perspective" in *The Priestly Kingdom: Social Ethics as Gospel.* Notre Dame: University of Notre Dame Press.

———. 1984b. "The Constantinian Sources of Western Ethics," *The Priestly Kingdom: Social Ethics as Gospel.* Notre Dame, IN: University of Notre Dame Press.

Zimmer, Carl. 1998. "The Slime Alternative" in *Discover.* September issue. New York.

Zrinščak, S. 2001. *There is a Secret Connection. Youth Religiosity as an Indicator of Social and Religious Changes.* Zagreb: Drustvena istrazivanja (1330–0288):1–2; 19–40.

Index